Liberation Movements in Power

Reviews of *Liberation Movements in Power*

'An important comparative study ... essential reading for anyone interested in this topic.'
Chris Saunders, *Strategic Review for Southern Africa*

'Encyclopaedic in detail and scope, elegantly written and carefully analysed, and makes a convincing and nuanced argument for the degeneration of NLMs. ... [This] important volume should become essential reading to anyone hoping to unpick the failures of liberation in southern Africa.'
Leo Zeilig, *Review of African Political Economy*

'With meticulous detail and extensive documentation, Southall analyses the theoretical and political environment of Southern Africa and the growth of the liberation movements. ... Highly recommended.'
R. M. Fulton, *Choice*

'A welcome addition to the literature [which] should be viewed as required reading for anyone wanting to get to grips with the topic.'
John Warhurst, *Commonwealth & Comparative Politics*

'A theoretically rich and empirically grounded account of an important subset of African political regimes ... This highly recommended book is essential reading.'
Michael Bratton, *International Journal of African Historical Studies*

'An important achievement in particular for its synthetic vision and persuasive overall argument.'
Reinhart Kößler, *Africa Spectrum*

'A mine of information for researchers and those wanting to pick over the wide literature on the topic.'
Keith Somerville, africanarguments.org

'A sobering and unsparing account of just how limited the gains realized by the extended struggle for liberation in southern Africa have proven to be ... and of what might yet be done to redeem that struggle's original promise.'
John S. Saul, York University (Canada)

Liberation Movements in Power

Party & State
in Southern Africa

Roger Southall
Professor Emeritus in Sociology, University of the Witwatersrand

JC JAMES CURREY

University of KwaZulu-Natal Press
PIETERMARITZBURG

James Currey
is an imprint of Boydell & Brewer Ltd
PO Box 9
Woodbridge, Suffolk IP12 3DF (GB)
www.jamescurrey.com

and of

Boydell & Brewer Inc.
668 Mt Hope Avenue
Rochester, NY 14620-2731 (US)
www.boydellandbrewer.com

Published in paperback in southern Africa by
University of KwaZulu-Natal Press
Private Bag X01
Scottsville, 3209
South Africa
www.ukznpress.co.za

First published 2013
James Currey paperback with minor revisions 2016

British Library Cataloguing in Publication Data
A catalogue record is available on request from the British Library

ISBN: 9781847011343 (James Currey paperback)
ISBN: 9781869142483 (University of KwaZulu-Natal Press paperback)

Front cover photograph: The Frontline States Summit in Lusaka, Zambia, March 1985.
(*left to right*): Sam Nujoma, leader of SWAPO of Namibia, Samora Machel of Mozambique;
Kenneth Kaunda of Zambia and Robert Mugabe of Zimbabwe. (© Ernst Schade / Panos)

Typeset in 10/11pt Photina MT by Avocet Typeset, Somerton, Somerset TA11 6RT

CONTENTS

4.

5.

6.

7.

PREFACE

This book has its origins in assertions by Henning Melber, then Director of the Dag Hammarskjöld Foundation, and a colleague and friend with whom I have worked very closely over recent years, that while there are numerous surveys which address post-liberation politics in the individual countries of southern Africa, comparative reviews were few and far between, and that I should try to remedy the situation. What was needed, he suggested, was a short overview. Well, once I got down to it, I began to appreciate that the task was considerably more ambitious than either I or Henning had envisaged, and that serious analysis of any depth would require extended treatment: hence vanished the next two years. With friends like Henning, who needs enemies? The result, I fear, may cause anguish amongst country specialists while failing to satisfy those seeking further understanding of regional dynamics and the differences and similarities between the three national liberation movements upon which I have focused – the African National Congress, the South West African People's Organization and the Zimbabwe African National Union-Patriotic Front. Nonetheless, whether or not readers find the text satisfactory, I have attempted to provide a comparative evaluation across history and diverse vectors of the present, while recognizing the need to be selective in the interests of economy.

The book is overwhelmingly synthetic rather than based on my own primary research. My own writing on the region has very largely focused upon South Africa, and before launching upon this enterprise, I had largely steered clear of analysis of developments in Namibia and Zimbabwe. Writing this book has consequently involved a considerable process of learning, and I am hugely indebted to all those who have contributed to the very fine and extensive literature upon the region and the individual countries. It has been impossible to acknowledge the understanding and information I have absorbed from each and every source I have read. I can only offer a generic 'thank you' to scholars far and wide who have assisted me, whether or not I have explicitly cited their work in the text.

The debts I have accumulated are legion, but particular debts are owed first, of all, to Henning Melber for constant encouragement, provision of references and sense of fun, as well as enabling me to spend two weeks as a visiting researcher at the Dag Hammarskjöld Foundation in Uppsala at a critical point during the writing (although I am going to be a lot more wary about his inventive suggestions in the future). David Moore of the University of Johannesburg similarly provided valuable source material on Zimbabwe, as well as organizing a conference on Zimbabwean political economy in December 2010 which later resulted in a special edition of the *Journal of Contemporary African Studies*, of which I was then editor. I am also indebted to, variously, Leslie Bank, John Daniel, Paul Hoffman, Sam Kariuki and Lungisile Ntsebeza, as well as to Leah Gilbert, who relieved me of administrative duties for a period to allow me more time to write. Other colleagues within the Department of Sociology and the

Society, Work and Development Institute (SWOP) at the University of the Witwatersrand have provided a wonderful environment wherein to work, teach and learn. I also record my gratitude to the Faculty of Humanities Research Committee at Wits which provided a grant which facilitated travel to Namibia and Zimbabwe, and to the Ford Foundation, for funding a research project on ANC within SWOP. Jacqueline Mitchell and Frances Kennett at James Currey have been unfailingly helpful, the latter's editing making huge improvements to my at times tortuous attempts to write clearly in the English language. I am also immensely grateful to both Chris Saunders of the University of Cape Town and Lionel Cliffe of the University of Leeds for their (initially anonymous) reports on the initial text for the publishers, which prompted me to correct important omissions and to refine my arguments. I am also delighted that the University of KwaZulu-Natal Press agreed to co-publish in South Africa, thereby making the book more easily available to readers within the region. The eagle-eyed editors at UKZN Press were exemplary in their picking up of errors and inconsistencies in the proofs.

On the home front, I owe much – as ever – to my wife Hilary, who has had to put up with the constant obsession of 'getting the book done', which would have been impossible without her love and understanding. Finally, thanks are also due to Poppie and Jasper, who reminded me, coming up to 4 p.m. every day, that there is more to life than sitting in front of a computer, and that it's time to go for a walk.

Roger Southall,
Department of Sociology,
University of the Witwatersrand.

LIST OF ABBREVIATIONS

AAC	All Africa Convention
AAC	Anglo-American Corporation
AAG	Affirmative Action Group (Zimbabwe)
AALS	Affirmative Action Loan Scheme (Namibia)
ABZ	Anyone But Zuma (South Africa)
ACC	Anti-Corruption Commission (Namibia)
ACR	*Africa Contemporary Record*
ACR	African Consolidated Resources (UK)
ADS	African Defence Systems (South Africa)
AIPPA	Access to Information and Protection of Privacy Act (2002) (Zimbabwe)
ANC	African National Congress (South Africa)
BAE	British Aerospace
BBBEE	Broad Based Black Economic Empowerment
BC	Black Consciousness
BCEA	Basic Conditions of Employment Act 1997 (South Africa)
BEE	Black economic empowerment
BIG	Basic Income Grant
BSRs	business-state relations
BUSA	Business Unity South Africa
CAZ	Conservative Alliance of Zimbabwe
CCJP	Catholic Commission for Peace and Justice (Zimbabwe)
CCP	Chinese Communist Party
CFU	Commercial Farmers' Union (Zimbabwe)
CHH	Chancellor House Holdings (South Africa)
CIO	Central Intelligence Organization (Zimbabwe)
CLA	Caprivi Liberation Army (Namibia)
COD	Congress of Democrats (Namibia)
Congress	African National Congress (Rhodesia)
CONTRALESA	Congress of Traditional Leaders of South Africa
COPE	Congress of the People (South Africa)
COSAS	Congress of South African Students
COSATU	Congress of South African Trade Unions
CPP	Convention People's Party (Ghana)
CPSA	Communist Party of South Africa
CZI	Confederation of Zimbabwean Industries
DA	Democratic Alliance (South Africa)
Dare	Dare re Chimurenga (ZANU executive in exile)
DC	Delimitation Commission (Zimbabwe)
DRC	Democratic Republic of Congo
DTA	Democratic Turnhalle Alliance (Namibia)
ECN	Electoral Commission of Namibia

ED	Election Directorate (Zimbabwe)
EISA	Electoral Institute of Southern Africa
EPZ	Export Processing Zone
ESAP	Economic Structural Adjustment Programme (Zimbabwe)
ESC	Electoral Supervisory Commission (Zimbabwe)
ESCOM	Electricity Supply Commission (South Africa)
FAPLA	Armed Forces for the Liberation of Angola
FLS	Front Line States
FNLA	Angolan National Liberation Front
FPTP	first past the post
FRELIMO	Front for the Liberation of Mozambique
FROLIZI	Front for the Liberation of Zimbabwe
FYDP	Five Year Development Plan (Zimbabwe)
GEAR	Growth, Employment and Redistribution (South Africa)
GDP	Gross Domestic Product
GIPF	Government Institutions Pension Fund (Namibia)
GNS	General Nyanda Security Risk Advisory Services (South Africa)
GNU	Government of National Unity
IBDC	Indigenous Business Development Centre (Zimbabwe)
ICT	Imperial Crown Trading
ICU	Industrial and Commercial Workers' Union (South Africa)
IDC	Industrial Development Corporation (South Africa)
IEC	Independent Electoral Commission (Namibia and South Africa)
IFP	Inkatha Freedom Party (South Africa)
ISL	International Socialist League
IWA	Industrial Workers of Africa
IWW	Industrial Workers of the World
IZG	Independent Zimbabwe Group
JCI	Johannesburg Consolidated Investments
JOC	Joint Operations Command (Zimbabwe)
JSC	Judicial Services Commission (Namibia and South Africa)
JSE	Johannesburg Stock Exchange
KP	Kimberley Process
LOMA	Law and Order Maintenance Act (1960) (Zimbabwe)
LRA	Labour Relations Act 1995 (South Africa)
MAT	Media Appeals Tribunal (South Africa)
MDC	Movement for Democratic Change (Zimbabwe)
MDC-M	Movement for Democratic Change (Mutambara) (Zimbabwe)
MDC-T	Movement for Democratic Change (Tsvangirai) (Zimbabwe)
MEC	Member of Executive Council (South Africa)
MEC	minerals-energy complex
MK	Umkhonto we Sizwe (South Africa)
MMCZ	Minerals Marketing Corporation of Zimbabwe
MMP	Mixed Member Proportional
MP	Member of Parliament
MPL	Member of Provincial Legislature (South Africa)
MPLA	People's Movement for the Liberation of Angola

NAFCOC	National African Federated Chamber of Commerce (South Africa)
NATO	North Atlantic Treaty Organisation
NBC	Namibian Broadcasting Corporation
NCA	National Constituent Assembly (Zimbabwe)
NDF	Namibian Defence Force
NDP	National Democratic Party (Rhodesia)
NDPP	National Director of Public Prosecutions (South Africa)
NDR	national democratic revolution
NEC	National Executive Council (of the ANC)
NEDLAC	National Economic Development and Labour Council (South Africa)
NGO	non-governmental organization
NIEF	National Indigenization and Empowerment Fund (Zimbabwe)
NLM	national liberation movement
NNP	New National Party
NP	National Party
NPA	National Prosecuting Authority (South Africa)
NRP	National Resettlement Policy (Namibia)
NSHR	Namibian Society for Human Rights
NUM	National Union of Mineworkers
NUNW	National Union of Namibian Workers
NYSP	National Youth Service Programme (Zimbabwe)
OAU	Organisation of African Unity
OPC	Ovamboland People's Congress (South West Africa)
OPO	Ovamboland People's Organisation (South West Africa)
PAC	Pan-Africanist Congress (South Africa)
PF	Patriotic Front (Zimbabwe)
PLAN	People's Liberation Army of Namibia
POSA	Public Order and Security Act 2002 (Zimbabwe)
PR	Proportional Representation
PTC	Posts and Telecommunications Company (Zimbabwe)
R&E	Randgold Exploration
RBVA	Rhodesian Bantu Voters' Association
RDP	Rally for Democracy and Progress (Namibia)
RDP	Reconstruction and Development Programme (South Africa)
RENAMO	Mozambique National Resistance
RF	Rhodesian Front
RG	Registrar-General (Zimbabwe)
RMI	Renova Manganese Investments
RST	Roan Selection Trust
SABC	South African Broadcasting Corporation
SACOB	South African Chamber of Business
SACP	South African Communist Party
SACTU	South African Congress of Trade Unions
SACU	Southern African Customs Union
SADC	Southern African Development Community
SADF	South African Defence Force
SADTU	South African Democratic Teachers' Union

SAF	South Africa Foundation
SAIRR	South African Institute of Race Relations
SANDF	South African National Defence Force
SASO	South African Students' Organisation
SCOPA	Standing Committee on Public Accounts (South Africa)
SECC	Soweto Electricity Crisis Committee (South Africa)
SWANU	South West Africa National Union
SWAPA	South West African Progressive Association
SWAPO	South West African People's Organization
SWATF	South West African Territorial Force
TAC	Treatment Action Campaign (South Africa)
TRC	Truth and Reconciliation Commission (South Africa)
TTL	Tribal Trust Land (Zimbabwe)
UANC	United African National Congress (Rhodesia)
UDF	United Democratic Front (South Africa)
UDI	unilateral declaration of independence (Rhodesia)
UDM	United Democratic Movement (South Africa)
UMK	United Manganese of Kalahari
UNITA	National Union for the Total Independence of Angola
WBWS	willing buyer, willing seller
WVA	War Veterans' Association (Zimbabwe)
ZANLA	Zimbabwe National Liberation Army (ZANU)
ZANU	Zimbabwe African National Union
ZANU-PF	Zimbabwe African National Union-Patriotic Front
ZAPU	Zimbabwe African People's Union
ZBC	Zimbabwe Broadcasting Corporation
ZCTU	Zimbabwe Congress of Trade Unions
ZDI	Zimbabwe Defence Industries
ZEC	Zimbabwe Electoral Commission
ZIPRA	Zimbabwe People's Revolutionary Army (ZAPU)
ZMDC	Zimbabwe Mining Development Corporation
ZUM	Zimbabwe Unity Movement

LIST OF TABLES

Introduction.
Analysing National Liberation Movements as Governments

The struggle for liberation in southern Africa was a cause célèbre for most of the second half of the 20th century. The colonizing powers vacated the major portion of Sub-Saharan Africa, with varying degrees of grace, during the three decades following the end of the Second World War – yet the 1960s saw only the beginning of what the activist-scholar John Saul has come to term, with an ironic nod to European history, the 'thirty years war' for national liberation in the Portuguese-ruled territories of Angola and Mozambique, settler-ruled Rhodesia, and apartheid South Africa. The sacrifices incurred in the different yet closely related and inter-dependent struggles for independence are remarkable. Indeed, they probably remain underestimated by the majority of historians today. Nonetheless, the long-drawn-out process of liberation – in so far as this refers to crude racial domination – was eventually to become complete: the Portuguese beat a hasty retreat from Angola and Mozambique in 1975 following a coup (prompted by the strains imposed by running a costly and brutal war) the previous year; the settler regime in Rhodesia, after having declared unilateral independence from Britain in 1965, had to concede majority rule to 'Zimbabwe' in 1980, following, notably, a crucial withdrawal of support by neighbouring South Africa in the late 1970s; South West Africa, the United Nations' Trust Territory which had been under *de facto* South African rule since 1916 was transformed into independent Namibia in 1989 following extensive international pressure; and South Africa itself made its widely celebrated move to democracy in 1994, after an intense, troubled, compelling but ultimately inspiring period of political transition.

In so far as these liberation struggles ended in defeat for racial minority rule and victory for the principle of democracy, an historic triumph was won. Yet looking back, from the early 21st century it is a widely held view that 'national liberation movements as governments' have proved to be a disappointment not only to their many sympathizers internationally but above all, to the majority of people over whom they now rule. Whereas at one time liberation movements represented 'the answer' to southern Africa's woes, they are now increasingly seen as 'the problem'. This book sets out to examine what that 'problem' is, where its origins lie, and suggests in what direction we should look for a new set of 'answers'. It will do so by analysing the diverse experiences of Namibia, South Africa and Zimbabwe, the focus being upon their hegemonic liberation movements – the South West African People's Organization (SWAPO), the African National Congress (ANC), and the Zimbabwe African National Union-Patriotic Front (ZANU-PF) – as governments. The purpose of the exercise will be to explore both the implications of 'liberation movement' status for the character of their governance after the transition to democracy, and how their individual histories and legacies shape the nature and quality of their rule.

Liberation movements and African nationalism

'National liberation movements' (NLMs) belong to the generic set of anti-colonial movements which developed in reaction to colonialism. However, those African nationalist movements which earned the sobriquet of 'NLMs' and identified themselves as such did so in particular circumstances. In most of Sub-Saharan Africa, colonial rulers 'withdrew' as much as they were 'pushed', for calculating that the costs of hanging on to power were becoming greater than the advantages of staying. As 'dependency' theory emphasizes, the nature of the historical experience of colonialism was such that it tended to structure the political economies of colonies so that they remained heavily 'dependent' upon their former colonial powers even after they had handed over political management to successor nationalist governments. Nonetheless, in some countries and regions, notably in those where sizeable minorities of white 'settlers' had made Africa their home, African nationalist movements were confronted by a refusal of incumbent regimes to concede power. Of course, the roots of African nationalism go deep into colonial history, planted in the soil of original African resistance to the very imposition of colonialism, and subsequently moving through formative stages of respectful lobbying for rights before, generally, flowering into a phase – or phases – of mass protest and action. In the large majority of countries in Sub-Saharan Africa, post-Second World War colonial calculations of the costs of long-term repression of such resistance led to a reasonably dignified withdrawal. Yet in settler territories, where nationalist movements met concerted resistance, they found themselves having to resort to armed struggle – from Algeria in the far north, through Kenya in the east, down to the countries in the south.

Armed struggle required the transformation of nationalist movements into what have become widely known as NLMs, (unless, as in Kenya, armed struggle was militarily defeated by the colonial power preparatory to its making political concessions to a more conservative nationalism). Belonging to the same anti-colonial family, nationalist movements and NLMs share many traits. Up to a certain point, they had tended to follow a similar trajectory. Indeed, southern African nationalist movements had widely assumed that their various lobbying and mass mobilizations of protest would, as in other African territories, lead ineluctably to majority rule. Yet once it had dawned upon them that more than good manners would be required for majority rule to be achieved, their subsequent resort to arms forced a realization that vastly different organizational forms, strategies, and tactics of struggle would become necessary. Above all, such a transformation would require the formation of an armed wing of the nationalist movement and the articulation of political and military struggles (implying the need for military hierarchy, discipline, and security, thereby raising problems around the potential subordination of political openness and accountability to such influences). This might incur a legal banning of the organization by the oppressor regime; and it would require a particular form of heroism from activist individuals (who would be expected to evince willingness to lose life and limb, risk incarceration, leave home, abandon families, and become full-time revolutionaries). Furthermore, liberation struggle would require a higher level of both

2

popular participation and accompanying class consciousness of diverse social strata (peasants, workers, and progressive bourgeoisie) recording their dedication to a radical agenda and 'class struggle', normally suggesting the supersession of the struggle for self-rule by a more far-reaching struggle for 'socialism'. Thus NLMs were widely projected as being more organizationally and theoretically advanced than the first wave of nationalist movements which achieved office during the initial phase of post-1945 decolonization. Whether or not they were more advanced in practice is a moot point. However, what is important is that legitimacy came to be conferred upon them by the Organization of African Unity (OAU) which formally recognized only those organizations which engaged in armed struggle as liberation movements.

There were two further dimensions which related particularly to the three countries which are of prime interest here, both relating to the ambiguous heritage of 'settler colonialism'. First, there was an ambiguity around 'race' and citizenship. It was easy enough to depict 'white settlers' as the principal beneficiaries of 'white domination'. Yet what constituted a 'settler'? Was it someone who themselves had just recently 'settled' upon Africa as their home? If so, what about those whites whose forbears had 'settled' in their countries of residence two, three or even more generations ago, and who had known no other 'home' but Africa? Why was a third- or fourth-generation white resident of Zimbabwe, Namibia or South Africa any more a 'settler' than an African who had recently migrated to one of these countries, or who sprung from ancestors who had moved from other parts of the continent in earlier times? Why weren't all Africans (save those defined controversially or otherwise as 'indigenous inhabitants') also 'settlers'? Suffice it to say here that NLMs found themselves awkwardly situated with regard to the status of whites who viewed themselves as living at 'home' while at the same time they identified 'white settlers', whose power was embodied in racially exclusionary regimes, as manifestly 'the enemy' of political liberation. Not surprisingly, this awkward circumstance led to debate, confusion, and division. The dilemmas it presented could only be resolved by commitment to the notion of a conception of citizenship which was open to all, regardless of 'race', and which was founded upon notions of individual racial equality and democracy. 'White settler regimes' therefore referred to those governments which were founded upon the racial exclusion of Africans from power and opportunity by restriction of the franchise to whites, and therefore became a definition founded upon political rather than racial criteria. Even so, questions around whether 'white citizens' could also claim to be authentically 'African' were to linger on well into post-liberation era and were to retain political volatility.

The second ambiguity revolved around the developmental potentialities which settler colonialism had brought. White settlers had tended to migrate towards territories which seemed to offer a temperate climate along with wealth and opportunity in terms of mineral resources and/or apparent availability of fertile and productive land, and where they were granted advantageous access to such opportunity by colonial or already established settler governments. White settler benefits were then backed up by manifold structures of political and economic oppression, the overthrow of which became central to the mission of 'national liberation'. Yet alongside this goal came an uncomfortable recognition that settler capitalism had facilitated much higher levels of capi-

3

talist development and industrialization than in non-settler territories in Africa. On the one hand, this was recognized as having promoted advanced levels of both class- and racial-consciousness amongst the oppressed, thereby supposedly granting a high level of vitality and historical potential to NLMs.[1] On the other, the economic legacy of settler colonialism also heightened expectations of the rewards of national liberation, not only amongst the adherents of NLMs but also in the wider network of international solidarity support which developed around them.

International solidarity was to prove crucial to all anti-colonial struggles but reached its apogee in the support given to the liberation struggles in southern Africa. Broadly, we can identify three overlapping streams. First, there was straightforward Anti-Colonialist support, drawn principally from countries which themselves had experienced colonialism, and which found its expression in Third Worldist or Pan-Africanist sentiment in bodies such as the United Nations and the OAU. Second, there was Moralistic support, whose origins lay in religious and liberal sentiment (dating back to the Anti-Slavery Movement) and which was intellectually and politically founded upon rejection of racism and acceptance of democracy and human rights. Third, there was support from socialist and specifically working-class organizations, although this was to be substantially compromised by differences between Social Democrats and Communists which went back to the great divide of 1917, and which were deeply complicated by the global polarizations of the Cold War.

All these streams of support carried their own aspirations for the nature of the societies which would develop with the overthrow of racial domination. Nonetheless, they all shared fulsome hopes for the governments which would follow national liberation in the countries of southern Africa. It was not only that by the last two decades of the 20th century there was already widespread disillusionment with the performances in power of 'ordinary' African post-nationalist regimes, and that the economic potential of former settler colonies was substantially greater than the run of impoverished postcolonial territories, or that their former racist governments were peculiarly nasty. It was rather that southern African NLMs were widely deemed to have special qualities, whether these related to ideological sophistication, representativeness of advanced class formation or simply commitment to high-minded principle. This found its apogee in the global idolatory which was to be accorded to the ANC and its iconic leader, Nelson Mandela, around South Africa's transition to democracy in 1994.

Perhaps the hopes vested in the southern African NLMs were always unrealistically extravagant; perhaps a degree of disillusion with their post-liberation performance as governments was inevitable, especially given their difficult economic inheritance (for the developmental potential of settler capitalism was always highly problematic). However, today the reality of NLMs as governments has given rise to widespread feelings of disappointment. This arises not only from their failure to live up to expectations; rather it is that NLMs as governments have come to be widely perceived as embodying alarming post-liberation pathologies. They have become authoritarian, intolerant, careless if not actively abusive of human rights, and ironically, often racist. Worse, they are also seen

---

[1] Kenneth Good (1976), 'Settler colonialism: Economic development and class formation', *Journal of Modern African Studies*, 14: 4, 597–620.

as having become corrupt, consumptionist, classist and anti-developmental. While the Mugabe regime in Zimbabwe has become a parody of all that is bad about postcolonial governments, SWAPO and the ANC are too often for comfort depicted as embodying ZANU-PF-like tendencies.[2]

So what has gone so wrong? Broadly we can identify three explanations, rooted in overlapping perspectives on NLMs as governments. The first is the 'Exclusivist Nationalism' approach, which focuses upon how NLMs use their struggle heritage to claim the right to rule; the second approach identifies post-liberation pathology as expressed via 'party dominance'; and the third, following Frantz Fanon, depicts the post-liberation NLM as an instrument of an avaricious post-nationalist bourgeoisie.

All three approaches provide important insights. However, the argument here is that the reality is more complex than any one of these approaches allows, and consequently we need to supplement them by returning to an earlier literature upon political parties in postcolonial Africa. But first, let us outline the three approaches to NLMs which presently predominate.

Exclusive nationalism

Writers from different intellectual traditions stress the monopolistic tendencies within national liberation thought which challenge democratic ideals and the legitimacy of political difference. From this perspective, the liberation struggle was conceived by NLMs as revolving principally around 'self-determination' (or in the South African case, the overthrow of apartheid) more than it was about achieving democracy. This was far from illogical, for there was no democracy under colonialism. However, the problem was that for the NLMs, 'self-determination' and 'democracy' became conflated, whereas they were neither identical nor necessarily congruent.[3] In other words, struggle for self-determination was more about equality of *peoples* as 'nations' than it was about equality for *people* as individuals.[4] This conflation allowed for NLMs to adopt a perspective which was not dissimilar to that propounded by Francis Fukuyama in relation to a propounded global ideological triumph of liberal democracy over communism at the end of the Cold War, as 'the end of history'. In the NLMs' case, however, the implication was that once the liberation movement had vanquished colonialism, history would dictate that it should (or would) stay in power for ever. R.W. Johnson has expressed this well when he writes of NLMs as sharing a 'common theology' which dictates that:

> National liberation is both the just and historically necessary conclusion of the struggle between the people and the forces of racism and colonialism. This has two implications. First, the NLMs – whatever venial sins they commit – are the righteous.

[2] James Hamill and John Hoffman (2011), 'The African National Congress and the Zanuification debate', in John Daniel, Prishani Naidoo, Devan Pillay and Roger Southall (eds), *New South African Review 2: New Paths, Old Compromises?* Johannesburg: Wits University Press, 50–67.

[3] Henning Melber (2003), 'Limits to liberation: An introduction to Namibia's postcolonial political culture', in Henning Melber (ed.), *Re-examining Liberation in Namibia: Political Culture since Independence*, Uppsala: Nordic Africa Institute, 9–24.

[4] Roger Southall (2003), 'Democracy in southern Africa: Moving beyond a difficult legacy', *Review of African Political Economy*, 30: 96, 255–72.

They do not merely represent the masses but in a sense they are the masses, and as such they cannot really be wrong. Secondly, according to the theology, their coming to power represents the end of a process. No further group can succeed them for that would mean that the masses, the forces of righteousness, had been overthrown. That, in turn, could only mean that the forces of racism and colonialism, after sulking in defeat and biding their time, had regrouped and launched a counter-attack.[5]

This essentially totalitarian mindset had a number of consequences. First, it demanded a conception of the colonially oppressed 'people' or 'nation' as one. In the context of anti-colonial struggle, in which NLMs were trying to forge national consciousness against a background of colonial divide and rule of diverse ethnic groupings, it made sense for NLMs to stress the 'oneness' of the 'oppressed nation'. Yet this supposed that the NLMs indubitably represented the will of the people, or in Rousseauian terms, 'the general will' – whereas in practice it meant that diversity amongst the oppressed along lines of ethnicity, gender or historical development was denied or suppressed. A second outcome was that, because NLMs could claim the authority of history, they and their leaders were imbued with a particular legitimacy, and challenges to their rule were therefore morally and politically illegitimate. Dissent was translated into disloyalty to the nation, as internal democracy transmogrified into obeisance to an authoritarian leader. Then again, a third outcome was what Terence Ranger has called the construction of 'patriotic history'.[6] Christopher Saunders describes this approach as:

> Not really history at all, but myth and propaganda. It does not tell the truth about the past, but emphasizes selected aspects of the past to present a picture of a glorious, continuous revolutionary tradition. It rejects academic history writing as an attempt to complicate the story of the past, and, instead, attempts to impose a hegemonic view of the liberation struggle. This writing...is not concerned with the liberation struggle versus the colonial oppressors as one of right against wrong, for the right-fulness of the independence struggle against white minority rule is taken for granted. It stresses, instead, another divide, between those who led the fight and won and those who compromised and should therefore be denounced as unpatriotic and sell-outs.[7]

Where such a theology has guided NLMs once they are in power, then scholars have depicted 'liberation' as working *against* democracy.[8] Indeed, in so far as national liberation has been based upon the gaining of national independence (or racial equality in South Africa) without having been linked to a project of fundamental social and economic transformation, it is seen as having 'exhausted' its progressive historical potential.[9] Worse still, such a constrained

[5] R.W. Johnson (2001), 'The final struggle is to stay in power', *Focus*, 25. Johannesburg: Helen Suzman Foundation.

[6] Terence Ranger (2003), 'Nationalist historiography, patriotic history, and the history of the nation: The struggle over the past in Zimbabwe', *Journal of Southern African Studies*, 30: 2, 215–34.

[7] Christopher Saunders (2003), 'History and the armed struggle: From anti-colonial propaganda to "patriotic history"?' in Melber (ed.), op. cit., 13–28.

[8] John Saul (1997), 'Liberal democracy vs. popular democracy in sub-Saharan Africa', *Review of African Political Economy*, 24: 73, 339–52.

[9] Samir Amin (1990), 'The social movements in the periphery: An end to liberation?' in Samir Amin, Giovanni Arrighi, Andre Gunder Frank and Immanuel Wallerstein (eds), *Transforming the Revolution: Social Movements and the World System*, New York: Monthly Review Press, 96–138.

version of national liberation is depicted as positively reactionary, for as Abrahamsen has pointed out, a transformation of the structures of domination of the predecessor colonial state 'requires a parallel and profound change of their epistemological and psychological underpinnings and effects'.[10]

The Exclusive Nationalism approach clearly has much going for it, for it offers an essentially dialectical understanding of how and why victorious liberation movements can turn into regimes which are as oppressive as those they have replaced. Yet it is ultimately static, for while offering valuable critique of the political culture of NLMs, it tends to overlook processes of change which take place within them as time progresses – whether this be through death or ageing of the 'struggle generation' and the rise through the ranks of younger cadres, or through challenge to existing power-holders. In this, it shares failings akin to the second perspective, that of 'party dominance'.

The dominant party approach

The dominant party approach has been developed theoretically largely in relation to the ANC, although as we shall see, much of its thrust has been pursued in analysis of the political dominance of SWAPO, if rather less so in the case of ZANU-PF. But let us start with its South African foundation, which lies in the ANC's overwhelming electoral majority and its apparent invincibility at the polls.

By far the strongest argument for what some construe as the ANC's presently unassailable electoral dominance has been made by Susan Booysen, who demonstrates how the ANC-in-government uses its liberationist electoral appeal in combination with other 'repertoires of engagement' to regenerate its 'hegemonic power'.[11] Although she sees the ANC as faced by accumulating challenges, she projects a vision in which it will retain its hold on power for the foreseeable future. However, because she eschews explicit use of the 'party dominance' framework it is more informative to turn to the analyses of Hermann Giliomee and Charles Simkins, together with various associates.

Giliomee and Simkins define dominant parties as those which establish electoral dominance for a prolonged period and enjoy domination in the formation of governments and in determining the public agenda.[12] They argue that there is an inherent tension between dominant party rule and democracy, for whereas party dominance can lead to competitive democracy (as in, say Sweden), it can also lead to facade democracy and authoritarianism (as in Nazi Germany). However, in contrast to the Scandinavian precedent, they assert that dominant parties in semi-industrialised countries are far more likely to abuse their power, for their control over the state is more fragile and they have difficulty in establishing autonomy from capitalist interests. This leads to the following assertions about ANC-dominant party rule:

[10] Rita Abrahamsen (2003), 'African studies and the postcolonial challenge', *African Affairs*, 102: 407, 189–210.

[11] Susan Booysen (2011), *The African National Congress and the Regeneration of Political Power*, Johannesburg: Wits University Press, xvi.

[12] Hermann Giliomee and Charles Simkins (eds), (1999), *The Awkward Embrace: One Party Domination and Democracy*, Cape Town: Tafelberg.

First, elections take on the character of a 'racial census', with the over-whelming black majority of the electorate regularly pledging their support to the ANC.

Second, although the transitional 1994 constitution provided for a distri-bution of power between the national state and nine provinces, the ANC has pursued a goal of greater centralization.

Third, whereas both the 1994 and 1996 constitutions (the latter drawn up by the first democratically elected parliament acting as a Constituent Assembly) insist upon the neutrality of public service, the ANC has subverted the inde-pendence of the state machinery, notably through the practice of the 'deploy-ment' of party loyalists to public positions. This blurring of party and state has undermined the separation of powers and has marginalized parliament.

Fourth, the ANC has delegitimized opposition by asserting a crude majori-tarianism which results in the alienation of minorities. This often takes an explicitly racial character, with opponents of the party accused of promoting white interests.

Finally, the ANC has adopted the principles of democratic centralism (borrowed from the Communist Party of the Soviet Union) and has utilized this to curb internal dissent.[13]

The thrust of the dominant party thesis is thus that the ANC has rendered itself largely unaccountable, and despite its regular return to power following free elections, constitutes a threat to the democracy. Prolonged concentration of power leads to abuse, and only the presence of opposition parties as viable alternative governments will ensure the success of democracy.

Undoubtedly, the dominant party thesis has proved a powerful tool for analyzing the ANC in power. Nonetheless, the thesis has lent itself to gross exag-geration, notably in its suggestion of the ANC's quasi-totalitarianism and its capacity to exert its authority over state and society (where it faces limits ranging from decisions of the Constitutional Court through to protests by its own constituency over 'failures of delivery'). In contrast, critics of the domi-nant party thesis have stressed that it was the ANC which was the harbinger of democracy in South Africa; it was the force which primarily responsible for the human rights-based nature of the constitution; and it continues to secure its electoral dominance because it retains the organizational capacity to mobilize popular support at election time. Thus, whilst a 'weak' notion of the ANC as a dominant party can be useful (for the fact of the ANC's electoral dominance and its domination of most state arenas is indisputable),[14] application of a tidy thesis tends to run up against the messiness of South African reality.

Not least of the limitations of the dominant party thesis is its inability to address the issue of change. Its assumption of the ANC's quasi-totalitarianism, notably in the form of its 'democratic centralism', implies a party which is unambiguously controlled from above by an elite. Yet manifestly this does not describe the ANC of today. This was demonstrated dramatically by the defeat of Thabo Mbeki when he ran for a third term as President of the ANC at the

13 Hermann Giliomee, John Myburgh and Lawrence Schlemmer (2001), 'Dominant party rule, opposition politics and minorities in South Africa', in Roger Southall (ed.), *Opposition and Democ-racy in South Africa*, London: Frank Cass, 161–82.
14 Roger Southall (2001), 'Conclusion: Emergent perspectives on opposition in South Africa', in Southall (ed.), op. cit., 275–84.

latter's 52nd National Conference at Polokwane in December 2007, and his subsequent ousting from the state presidency in September 2008. There are a variety of interpretations of the 'meaning' of Polokwane.[15] However, what is clear is that the incumbent elites within the party proved unable to meet the challenge posed by a candidate who was significantly supported by popular forces 'from below'. So much, we might say, for the salience of 'democratic centralism'!

Yet a further problem is that, while the ANC continues to claim genuine popular majorities at successive elections, its electoral dominance is increasingly under threat, as the loyalty of its mass constituency begins to crumble and as voters become rather more pragmatic.[16] Indeed, it is apposite to note that Raymond Suttner, a long-time activist within the liberation struggle, today sees danger to constitutional democracy in the erosion of ANC dominance, with its post-Mbeki internal divisions encouraging a resort to political intolerance and what he terms the 'formulaic thinking' of an anti-pluralist, authoritarian, and centralist 'NLM model'.[17]

There are many aspects of the Namibian situation which lend themselves to analysis through the lenses of 'party dominance', for SWAPO combines popular support, registered at regular elections, with a marked shift towards authoritarianism.[18] However, the limits to the utility of the 'dominant party' approach are illustrated by the Zimbabwean case. Zimbabwe has experienced successive multi-party elections since independence, yet these have been subject to wide-ranging manipulation by the regime to produce victories for ZANU-PF, which all too graphically indicate that it does not consider its hold on power as ultimately subject to popular choice. At root, the notion of 'party dominance' rests upon an acceptance of 'democracy'. In other words, for all that popularly elected political parties may seek to strengthen their hold on power through institutional and other means, they ultimately concede the validity of results at the ballot box, and if they lose their popular hegemony as recorded by elections, they stand down from office.

In short, the 'dominant party' thesis may well illuminate important dimensions of both the ANC and SWAPO as ruling parties, but its basis in electoral performance limits its utility. Indeed, precisely because it points to how dominant parties may resort to electoral abuse in order to reproduce successive electoral powers, it points to possession and use of state power as the major factor requiring analysis – not least in the case of NLMs whose theology prescribes their historic right to rule. This leads us to examine the approach of those following in the footsteps of Frantz Fanon, who focus upon how the colonial experience has distorted the paths pursued by nationalist movements which have succeeded to power.

[15] Roger Southall (2009), 'Understanding the "Zuma tsunami"', *Review of African Political Economy*, 121: 317–33.
[16] Anthony Butler (2009), Considerations on the erosion of one-party dominance', *Representation: Journal of Representative Democracy*, 45: 2, 159–72.
[17] Raymond Suttner (2009), 'The challenges to African National Congress dominance', *Representation: Journal of Representative Democracy*, 45: 2, 173–92.
[18] Henning Melber (2011), 'SWAPO is the nation, and the nation is SWAPO: Government and opposition in a dominant party state – the case of Namibia', in Katharina Hulterström, Amin Kamete and Henning Melber, *Political Opposition in African Countries: The Cases of Kenya, Namibia, Zambia and Zimbabwe*, Uppsala: Nordic Africa Institute, 61–83.

Fanon in southern Africa

'The Revolution Betrayed' is almost as old an idea as that of social revolution itself, for human history offers a litany of examples of frustrated revolutionary hopes. In southern Africa, the liberation struggles invoked particularly high levels of popular participation. Notions of 'people's war', founded upon liberation movements' claimed or genuine politicization of the masses, peasantry and proletariat, promoted widespread revolutionary hopes, and regularly conflated the struggles against white supremacy, colonialism, and apartheid into struggles for socialism.[19] Subsequently, too, the legacy of massive popular resistance to oppression encouraged hopes that bonds between the liberation movements and 'the people' would remain strong and provide a foundation for the construction of 'popular democracy' rather than mere liberal democracy. Generally, however, such hopes have been disappointed, for in one liberated country after another, rather than socialism, capitalism continues to reign, embraced by liberation movements whose political character is often disturbingly authoritarian. In such circumstances, it is scarcely surprising that disillusion abounds. Nor is it surprising that those disappointed with liberation struggle outcomes should turn to Frantz Fanon for explanation.

According to Fanon, the national bourgeoisie that takes power at the end of colonialism is an underdeveloped class, small in number, lacking economic power and primarily located in service rather than directly productive occupations. Lacking intellectual resources, it seeks little more than to step into the shoes of departing colonials, seeking to transfer into its own hands their resources through strategies of nationalization and Africanization. Once in control of key posts, it will insist that all big foreign companies should deal with it directly, whether they simply want to keep their connections with the country or to open it up. Thus 'the national middle class discovers its historic mission: that of intermediary'.[20] Although often prepared to resort to a (defensive) racism against a cynical Western bourgeoisie, the national bourgeoisie nonetheless seeks to emulate the latter's lifestyle and ultimately, to identify with it. It engages in 'scandalous enrichment' and 'immoderate money making', and plunges into 'the mire of corruption and pleasure'.[21] In such circumstances, 'the economic channels of the young state sink back inevitably into neo-colonialist lines', dependent upon external capital and handouts.[22]

It is scarcely surprising that Fanon's characterization of the postcolonial situation should spread to post-liberation southern Africa. An illustration is the analysis provided by John Saul in a bitterly unhappy essay where he takes as his cue the statement offered by George Dangerfield,[23] concerning the fate of the

[19] For an overview of the envisaged socialist promise, see John Saul (1994), 'The Southern African revolution', in John Saul (ed.), *Recolonization and Resistance: Southern Africa in the 1990s*, Trenton: Africa World Press, 1–34.
[20] Frantz Fanon (1974), *The Wretched of the Earth*, London: Penguin, 122.
[21] Ibid., 134–35.
[22] Ibid., 134.
[23] George Dangerfield (1997), *The Strange Death of Liberal England*, Stanford CA: Stanford University Press.

British Liberals following their triumph at the polls at the end of the First World War: they emerged from the fray 'flushed with one of the greatest victories of all time, yet from that victory they never recovered'. Something similar, Saul suggests, can be said of FRELIMO in Mozambique,[24] the MPLA in Angola,[25] SWAPO, ZANU-PF, and the ANC. Although all still in power, they have come to preside over the death of the promise that they were once thought to epitomize. The importance of their victories (over colonialism, racism, and apartheid) should never be minimized, yet the socialist hopes that they embodied have succumbed to political degeneration. In Mozambique, corruption and the pursuit of individual profit have undermined the legitimacy of FRELIMO party leaders, while the election of Guebeza – 'holder of an expansive business network'[26] – as President in 2002 signalled commitment to a neo-liberal agenda. Much the same has happened in Angola where the liberation struggle descended into a bloody war between the MPLA and UNITA,[27] which was little more than a raw struggle between rival elites for oil and diamonds. It is the same story in both Namibia, where the party elite lives in luxury disregarding the abject poverty of the majority, and Zimbabwe, where Mugabe's ZANU-PF has engaged in vicious repression of the opposition Movement for Democratic Change (MDC). However, it is South Africa which provides the most disappointing case of 'false decolonization', for by enthusiastically embracing capitalism, the ANC has 'squandered an opportunity of world historic proportions'.[28] Yet why, asks Saul, has this happened to NLMs which had promised so much?

Saul acknowledges that NLMs have been pressured by the World Bank, IMF, and Western governments to join the global capitalist game. But the implication is that regional leaders have too easily accepted the apparent inevitability of capitalism as being the only strategy capable of providing for development. Thus the ANC government may have opted for a reformist version of capitalism hoping that it would provide sufficient surplus to allow social policies capable of alleviating social inequality. However, while this option might to a limited extent be possible in South Africa, it is much less plausible in neighbouring countries which are located even more at the periphery of global capitalism. In these circumstances, it is scarcely to be wondered if NLMs have opted for self-enrichment. Thus, Saul ends up with an explicitly Fanonesque explanation involving the selling out of the revolution by new elites, their comfortable adjustment to neo-colonialism, the diversion of a revolutionary class consciousness amongst the majority into racial consciousness, and the adoption of market values and consumerism. In so doing he is by no means alone. Take, for instance, the views of Henning Melber with regard to Namibia:

> More than forty years ago Frantz Fanon had already expressed in his revolutionary manifesto, *The Wretched of the Earth*, disgust for the emerging new elites he witnessed in independent (West) African countries...he demonstrated that the

---

24 Front for the Liberation of Mozambique.
25 People's Movement for the Liberation of Angola.
26 John Saul (2008), *Decolonization and Empire: Contesting the Rhetoric and Reality of Resubordination in Southern Africa and Beyond*, Johannesburg: Wits University Press, 156.
27 National Union for the Total Independence of Angola.
28 Saul (2008), op. cit., 164.

psuedo-revolutionary rhetoric of the representatives of new state power was a misleading façade. His scathing attacks on a new hegemonic nationalist elite project, with its particular blend of populist nation-building, questioned the extent of meaningful social change for the majority of the previously underprivileged colonized population in the wake of decolonization. In contrast to the settler colonialism endured for so many decades under the apartheid regime, the sovereign Republic of Namibia in its present state has, despite many short-comings, much to offer most of its people. But it also fails to meet some of the more substantive and essential original ideals, ambitions and aims that were once articulated by the same social forces and their leaders who now exercise political power.[29]

All this can be illuminating, and importantly, it locates the one-time liberationist bourgeoisie within a context of global capitalism, imperialism, and dependence. However, ultimately Fanonism tends to substitute 'class' for 'party', proposing that the liberation movements have become nothing more than the instruments of the postcolonial bourgeoisie for political domination and economic accumulation. Further, the uniformity of Fanonism's portrayal of the NLMs in power minimizes important realities: the existence within them of continuing factionalism, of debates between nationalist and socialist tendencies, between populists and political progressives, and contested as well as collaborative relationships with foreign and domestic capital.

Is there a mode of explanation which allows for all this, while simultaneously acknowledging that characteristics of NLMs may change over time? It is suggested here that there is, located in the idea of 'the party machine'.

NLMs as party machines

In 1996, Artur Carlos Maurício Pestana (under his nom de guerre, Pepetela) published a novel based on his experiences in 1971 in the guerrilla war waged by the MPLA in the rainforests of Angola's Cabinda province. The book displays a remarkable insight into the complexity of social transformation subsequent to armed resistance to colonial occupation. In a revealing dialogue, the commander of the guerrilla unit, 'Fearless', proclaims his fears and ideals to the unit's political commissar, 'New World', for whom he ultimately sacrifices his life in battle:

> We don't share the same ideals...You are the machine type, one of those who are going to set up the unique, all-powerful Party in Angola. I am the type who could never belong to the machine...One day, in Angola, there will no longer be any need for rigid machines, and that is my aim...what I want you to understand, is that the revolution we are making is half the revolution I want. But it is the possible. I know my limits and the country's limits. My role is to contribute to this half-revolution...I am, in your terminology, adventurist. I should like the discipline of war to be established in terms of man and not the political objective. My guerrillas are not a group of men deployed to destroy the enemy, but a gathering of different, individual beings, each with his subjective reasons to struggle and who, moreover, behave as such...I am happy when I see a young man decide to build himself a personality, even if politically that signifies individualism...I

---

[29] Melber (2003), op. cit., 9–25.

cannot manipulate men, I respect them too much as individuals. For that reason, I cannot belong to a machine.[30]

Fearless clearly had enough of the early Marx in him to recognize the dangers inherent in revolutionaries changing themselves into apparatchiks, dreary hacks who would sacrifice their ideals to every whim of an all-powerful party in pursuit of safety, personal advantage, and a career. For Pestana, reality was dialectical: the NLM as the vehicle of collective freedom would turn into a 'machine' whose inherent characteristic was to subordinate individualism and individual freedoms.

Pestana was not alone in foreseeing the dangers represented by the NLMs' transformation into political machines. Even before any of the regional NLMs took power, Rick Turner, the activist academic (eventually assassinated by apartheid security forces) was bold enough to discuss the potential threat to democracy their victory might represent:

> The political party as mediator between the individual and government tends to take on the characteristics of the system itself, the 'party machine' dominates the membership and the rank and file become increasingly divorced from policy making...The political arena becomes polarised between an atomised mass and a number of small groups trying to manipulate the mass in order to get political jobs. The result of this is to move the source of power in society out of the political arena and into the control of functional power groups.[31]

The analyses of Pestana and Turner were deeply rooted in Marxist theorizing, yet ironically conventional political science had already most clearly depicted the rise of the party machine in postcolonial Africa, as notably examined in Aristide Zolberg's classic study of the trajectories of the victorious nationalist parties in Ghana, Senegal, Mali, and Ivory Coast.[32]

In all four states which Zolberg examined, the handover of power to nationalists saw the emergence of parties to which he ascribes the label 'dominant'. He describes how it was widely assumed that this outcome was the result of the victorious parties' greater political capacities relative to their rivals. Hence contrasts were drawn between 'mass' and 'cadre' parties, and more tendentiously, 'revolutionary centralizing' and 'pragmatic pluralist' parties, with the former categories generally being described as more vital, dynamic, and inclusive. Yet, such a contrast was to prove misleading, for in practice both types of parties tended to take upon themselves the supposed qualities of the other. Even where successful (usually 'mass') nationalist parties went on to establish themselves as single parties, it was regularly found that their resemblance to parties of the European left (upon which many had modelled themselves) was no more than superficial.

Zolberg's thrust proceeded as follows. The victorious nationalist parties triumphed following an initial spurt of mobilization which captured the spirit of post-Second World War popular aspiration. Although winning pre-

---

[30] Pepetela (1996), *Mayombe*, London: Heinemann, 197. I am grateful to Henning Melber for this reference.

[31] Richard Turner (1971), 'The relevance of contemporary radical thought', in Peter Randall (ed.), *Directions of Change in South African Politics*, Johannesburg: Spro-Cas, 81.

[32] Aristide Zolberg (1966), *Creating Political Order: The Party-States of West Africa*, Chicago: Rand McNally Publishing Company.

independence elections, the popular support such parties received was limited, for rates of electoral registration were often quite low, and minority parties often took a substantial slice of the vote. Subsequently, after assuming office, nationalist parties benefited from gaining access to well-paid jobs, state resources and control over national budgets, all of which allowed them to determine who would obtain benefits and where they should be located. Thereafter, popular participation expanded via enlargement of electorates, while at the same time, the authority of parliaments and African executives was increased. As a result, nationalist parties faced two contrary trends: on the one hand, they benefited from a bandwagon effect, as numerous individuals identified with them as winners; on the other, they encountered the risk of fragmentation, for competition for control of the new institutions intensified as new political entrepreneurs entered the game. Very often, political entrepreneurship entailed an appeal to primordial loyalties, usually in the form of ethnic affinities. This in turn posed the threat that the nationalist movements would suffer from a 'reverse bandwagon' effect and relapse into ethnicity or regionalism. In response, the parties sought to increase control from the centre, often accompanied by their ideological radicalization. Furthermore, because their organizational capacity was indeed superior to that of their rivals, they were enabled to consolidate their political dominance, in some cases installing themselves as single parties with a revolutionary ideology: to proclaim the necessity of national unity under the aegis of the ruling party itself. This was succinctly put in Nkrumah's famous slogan: 'The CPP is Ghana and Ghana is the CPP.'[33] 'National unity' was then obtained by suppression of the opposition and electoral manipulation.

Such a process described so-called 'revolutionary mobilizing' regimes. Although such parties aspired to mobilize the entire nation, their capacity to do so rarely extended beyond occasional electioneering; participant members were relatively few; support had both regional and ethnic dimensions; 'they had a large head in the capital but fairly rudimentary limbs'; and although speaking the language of democratic centralism, internal structures of accountability and control only functioned intermittently. Indeed, Zolberg cites David Apter, one of the earliest observers of the CPP in Ghana, as referring to it as 'a Tammany type machine with a nationalist ideology',[34] a reference to the Democratic Party political machine that controlled Manhattan from 1854 to 1932 through strong-arm tactics, patronage, and corruption.

Single-partyism led on to the 'party state', the merger of government and party. Nationalist leaders had two principal instruments of rule: the party and the state bureaucracy. The former, supposedly, was mass based, united and disciplined, yet was often little more than 'a loose movement which naturally incorporated the characteristics of the society in which it grew'.[35] The government, in contrast, was alien, and until recently run by Europeans according to strange bureaucratic norms. Nonetheless, it was the most concrete expression of central authority available. Given a huge shortage of educated personnel within the party, many of the most capable loyalists were appointed to govern-

---

[33] The Convention People's Party.
[34] Zolberg, op. cit., 22, citing David Apter (1955) *The Gold Coast in Transition*, Princeton: Princeton University Press, 202.
[35] Ibid., 123.

ment, depriving the party itself of their skills. Meanwhile, a deep-seated suspicion of government bureaucrats led to attempts to incorporate civil servants into the party. The outcome was predictable: the coherence of the party machinery declined, matched by the decline in efficiency of the civil service. Simultaneously, an accompanying trend towards centralization of authority in the hands of the President led to his reliance upon lieutenants, some of whom owed their position to the party and others of whom had risen through the bureaucracy, but all of whom, ultimately, owed their loyalty and legitimacy to their 'chief'. Because this hybrid pattern extended downwards throughout the party-government complex, the lines of authority became confused. The outcome was contestation between party and state; the centre and the periphery; in-groups and out-groups; and indeed between the President and his lieutenants, with the awkward mix becoming dependent upon personal and political loyalties.

The study of political parties in Africa has by now moved well beyond Zolberg's schema. Nonetheless, there is still considerable value to be drawn from his analysis.

First, the analysis of the party-state, with its implications of simultaneous strength (resting upon institutional foundations) and fragility (its incorporation of the cleavages inherent in 'underdeveloped' societies), is suggestive of strong parallels in southern Africa, notably the shift from liberation movements to institutionalized hegemony, albeit with such dominance rendered incomplete by the ruling party's own heterogeneity, internal contestations, and intermittent internal democracy.

Second, a return to Zolberg (and other students of the early nationalist parties) has the virtue of taking political parties seriously. As any perusal of those writings demonstrates, the nationalist parties were faced by a multiplicity of challenges, the meeting of which involved them in a diversity of roles: what Tordoff (amongst others) refers to as their integrative, legitimizing, policy, mobilization, reconciliation, patronage, and political communication functions.[36] Doubtless a great deal of such analysis underplayed the emergence of new class structures, the transformation of ruling parties into agencies of class rule, and the contradictions involved in countries where radical parties, themselves subject to such tendencies, were simultaneously committed to socialist transformation. Nonetheless, at the time, experiments in one-party democracy and African socialism were taken seriously by radical analysts, most notably those concerned with the attempt to promote socialism in Tanzania.[37] While in a later era Saul and others are correct in emphasizing the formidable battery of means which Western capitalism utilized to discipline African countries, that does not justify a dismissive approach to former NLMs which, like it or not, are performing (with varying success) the political roles of their predecessors. The question should rather be: how are they performing, why, and in whose interest?

Third, there is much to be said in returning to Zolberg's notion of the nationalist (or liberation) movement as transforming into a party machine. This, we suggest, allows for:

[36] William Tordoff (2010), *Government and Politics in Africa*, London: Palgrave Macmillan.

[37] Lionel Cliffe and John Saul (eds), (1972), *Socialism in Tanzania: An Interdisciplinary Reader. Vol. 1. Politics*, Nairobi: East African Publishing House.

(i)   Examination of the capacities of NLMs for undertaking those various *functions of the political party*. In particular, it invites analysis of the functioning of the NLMs' structures in terms of control from above; participation from below; and 'official' versus 'unofficial' lines of authority. It also requires an understanding of how capacities to mobilize are underpinned by the raising and allocation of resources (the issue of party funding).
(ii) Analysis of *the role of the party in providing avenues of recruitment, advancement, and social class formation*. This allows for the possibility that the nature of the party may change over time, perhaps from being a vehicle of liberation to one which is an instrument of political control and economic accumulation by an elite.
(iii) A focus upon the party as a *machine for the allocation of positions, privileges, resources, and contracts*. Perhaps this does signify something of a return to the earlier doctrines of US political science, of notions of politics as the allocation of values, of who gets what, why and when, yet it also interlocks with Fanonist notions of the party as an instrument of class domination. Critically, because the party is operating within a context of resource scarcity, it demands analysis of party relations with the state and with capital, for it is they which constitute the primary founts of resources.
(iv) Finally, *resource scarcity implies intra-party competition between 'ins' and 'outs'; between different components of the coalition which a ruling party represents; and between different segments of the political elite*. This points to the necessity of the identification of groups linked together by bonds of interest (not exclusive of ideology) and their location within the party-state across level, class, and ethnicity.

By focusing upon the NLMs of Namibia, South Africa, and Zimbabwe as 'party machines' it is possible to appropriate the utilities of all existing approaches to liberation movement rule. In particular, the intention here will be to examine the *differences* between the liberation movements as they have developed, as much as the *similarities* between them, given the diversity of their colonial heritages and postcolonial global locations. But as Pestana and Turner suggest, once the purpose of the machine translates into the objective of aggrandizement, it is likely to launch upon a process of political, social, and ideological decline. The argument of this book is that this is the challenge facing the NLMs in southern Africa. However, before that can be pursued, it is necessary to examine their origins and development in their struggles against settler colonialism.

1.

Settler Colonialism in Southern Africa

Ken Good noted some years ago that settler colonialism in Africa had received little systematic consideration. In a review of the trajectories of the settler colonies of Algeria, Kenya, Rhodesia, and South Africa, he argued that while each of these territories had their own distinct histories they were driven by similar dynamics of development and class. Above all, settler societies represented an exception to the general colonial rule, in that they had shown a marked 'capacity for independent capitalist development', and because of that had evolved 'relatively advanced class formations'.[1]

Furthermore, because the settler states had developed a strong taste for political autonomy, they had assumed an ambivalent position in relation to imperialism and had proved resistant to decolonization. The dominated (African/ black) social classes in settler societies were therefore forced towards growth and militant action, ultimately rendering settler colonialism dangerous to imperialism, and eventually breaking the external supports that were vital to the *colon* state. In the years that followed Good's analysis, the tempo of armed and popular struggle against the settler regimes of Rhodesia, South West Africa, and South Africa culminated in the political triumph of the NLMs and the respective transitions to independence and/or democracy.[2]

The migration of whites from Europe to far-flung countries was one of the defining aspects of the historical expansion of Empire, its impact upon indigenous peoples brutal where not genocidal. Africa was originally viewed by European powers as climatically hostile and was not regarded as a potential world area for European settlement. Yet as imperial expansion proceeded, conjunctures of history and economics were to see white settlement take place in a handful of countries identified as both habitable and useful to the imperial enterprise. The resultant phenomenon of 'settler colonialism' was to have dynamics which distinguished it from other forms of colonialism found elsewhere in Africa – and to give rise to 'armed struggle'. Hence 'settler colonialism' constitutes the starting point for any historical understanding of the liberation movements today.

The abiding characteristic of settler colonialism was the privileging of whites on grounds of 'race' – a socially constructed marker of identification of 'white settlers' and subordinated racial groupings. In our particular context, it has provided for a nationalist discourse which argues that the intransigent nature of settler-dominated societies forced oppressed peoples into taking up armed struggle, leading to their eventual triumph against oppression. In turn, this discourse leads to the tendency of NLMs to claim historical primacy as the

---

[1]   Kenneth Good (1976), 'Settler colonialism: Economic development and class formation', *Journal of Modern African Studies*, 14: 4, 597.

[2]   Where appropriate, as in this chapter where I am dealing principally with settler colonial forms, I refer to Namibia and Zimbabwe by their colonial names.

authentic representatives of the oppressed, an approach whose suggestion is that 'race' and 'nation' are primordial social fractures that have excluded compromise. However, compromise with settler regimes did eventually come about, this indicating that any approach to 'settler colonialism' which presumes unity within 'races' and unrelenting opposition between them is lacking substantially in explanatory power, and if it is to be utilized, it needs considerably greater traction.

Generally, the solution has been to turn to 'class', not least because of the massive influence which Marxist thinking has had upon African struggles for freedom. Broadly, rather than discounting the social realities of either race or nation, these have come to be seen to exist in some complex articulation with class (pioneered, notably, by Jack and Ray Simons's classic account, *Class and Colour in South Africa*).[3] Within the NLMs themselves, this approach has come to be embodied in the adoption of the notion of the 'National Democratic Revolution', which is seen as being propelled forward by alliances of classes amongst the racially or nationally dominated. Ultimately, recognition of differences within racial and national groupings along lines of class and interest provides the basis for theories of transition which illuminate the dynamics underlying the transfer of power to nationalists from settler rule.

Settler occupation

Settler colonialism in southern Africa was born out of an accident in that the origins of white settlement at the tip of the continent were the product of the ambition of Dutch and British merchant capital to expand their trade with India, and their need for a supply depot at the Cape. The early history, the development of a slave society, the establishment of British rule at the Cape, the formal abolition of slavery, and expansion of the frontier by Dutch settlers moving north to escape British domination, need not delay us. Suffice it to say that, in the imperial mind, what became South Africa was never envisaged as a settler colony in the same sense that Britain came to regard Canada, Australia, and New Zealand. To be sure, in 1819, Britain encouraged the emigration of around 5,000 Britons to the Cape to relieve the domestic economy of 'surplus labour' following the end of the Napoleonic war while simultaneously securing the Cape frontier against hostile African societies. Nonetheless, southern Africa was not regarded as a source of likely wealth, and its chief value was seen in providing the Royal Navy with a base in the defence of India and the Empire.

All this was to change from the 1860s with the discovery of diamonds and then of gold in 1886 in the Transvaal, to the north of the Cape. The sudden prospect that southern Africa could become the new Eldorado was to culminate in the South African (Anglo-Boer) War of 1900–02 in which Britain engaged in an ultimately victorious, but hugely costly struggle with the two Boer republics of Transvaal and Free State – many say at the behest of British mining capital. The outcome was fateful. The year 1910 saw the birth of South Africa,

[3] Jack Simons and Ray Simons (1969), *Class and Colour in South Africa*, Harmondsworth: Penguin.

which brought together the former Boer republics with the British colonies of the Cape and Natal under a Union government in Pretoria whose institutions were modelled on Westminster. Post-war compromise between Boer and British was initially embedded in the South African Party, led first by former Boer General Louis Botha, and subsequently by General Jan Smuts.

Many contemporary observers regarded the settlement as generous, for the new formation was granted effective political autonomy from Britain and the Boers granted equal political rights with the British population. But the peace between whites had been forged on the basis of a compromise which sacrificed black political rights and entrenched settler domination. The blacks' worst fears were soon to be realized. Within the space of three years the new parliament had passed a land act which sought to achieve the twin goals of providing land for settler agriculture and cheap black labour for the mines by forcing Africans off the land, and corralling them into 'native reserves' which were to be restricted initially to no more than 7 per cent (increased to 13.7 per cent after 1936) of the total land area of South Africa. Although, notably from the mid-1920s, there were to be significant attempts by emergent Afrikaner nationalism to assert autonomy from Empire and British capital, these were not to come to fruition until after a National Party (NP) which had been divided by the Depression had reunited to secure a narrow victory over Smut's United Party in the election of 1948.[4] Yet even after that, differences which arose over apartheid and decolonization between London and Pretoria were to be subordinated to shared economic interests and the pursuit of anti-Soviet Cold War goals.

The discovery of gold and diamonds on the Witwatersrand had seriously exacerbated tensions between rival European powers. Hitherto, advanced capitalist nations had been reluctant to impose direct rule upon African peoples, for following the suppression of slavery, 'legitimate commerce' whereby metropolitan merchant interests traded with African communities had provided for profitable exchange without the political, military, and financial costs of direct colonial rule. However, as the European powers became increasingly driven by the expectation that Africa could prove a treasure trove of valuable raw materials, they became drawn into a scramble for control of the continent.

A rapidly industrializing Germany, feeling excluded by the informal 'spheres of influence' claimed by Britain, France, Portugal, and Belgium, convened a conference in Berlin in 1884–85 whose outcome was a doctrine which laid down that European governments would only recognize a claim to any part of Africa by another European power if it was backed by effective occupation. Within days, the 'scramble for Africa' was unleashed by Bismarck's proclamation of German protectorates over the relatively few significant areas of Africa where other powers did not predominate. On the basis of a strong presence established since the 1840s by the Rhenish Missionary Society and the prior arrival of increasing numbers of German traders, settlers, and businessmen, Bismarck laid claim by Germany to South West Africa. This was backed by the despatch of German troops in 1888 to enforce a 'protection treaty' which had allocated land for European settlement, signed three years earlier by Herero

---

4   Smuts's South African Party had 'fused' with Prime Minister J.B. Hertzog's National Party to form the United Party in 1933 to confront the Depression, only for D.F. Malan to break away with his followers to form the Gesuiwerde Nasionale Party (or Purified National Party).

Chief Maharero but which he had now rejected. It was to take over two decades to secure German occupation and the imposition of a settler economy on the basis of wholesale dispossession of Africans after their defeat in the Herero-German and Nama-German wars (1904–08), this involving a deliberate strategy of genocide of indigenous inhabitants.[5] Even then the Germans never really controlled the more populous, northern part of the territory beyond the so-called 'Red Line', south of which was the 'Police Zone'. It was only after the Germans were defeated in 1915 by South African forces, acting at the request of the British, that the north was finally subjected to the full panoply of colonial power, albeit largely under a system of indirect rule. This was accomplished after the First World War, when South Africa, acting on behalf of Britain, was charged with administering South West Africa under a League of Nations' mandate.

The British interest in southern Africa had been further secured by the establishment of colonial hegemony over a large swathe of central Africa. In 1888, Cecil Rhodes, who had already cornered the Kimberley diamond fields, had obtained mineral rights through treaties with the most powerful traditional leaders in the area to the north of British-controlled Bechuanaland and the Transvaal. The British government then granted Rhodes' British South Africa Company the right to administer territory stretching from the Limpopo River to Lake Tanganyika under charter as a protectorate. Rhodes used this to justify dispatching a Pioneer Column of settlers under the well-armed British South African Police into Matabeleland and into Shona territory to establish a fort and capital named after the then British Prime Minister, Lord Salisbury. After emerging victorious over uprisings by the Ndebele and Mashona in 1896, the Company extended control via treaty over territory to the north of the Zambezi which became the British protectorate of Northern Rhodesia in 1911. White settlers remained politically predominant in what, after 1901, was known as Southern Rhodesia. Although after the First World War opinion in London and Pretoria favoured this becoming part of South Africa, the settlers – asserting 'Rhodesia's essential Britishness' against the spectre of Afrikaner domination[6] – opted for Responsible Government in a 1922 referendum (amongst the whites). Effective self-government was granted to them from 1923, with Britain retaining no more than nominal control. Fatefully, when Britain attempted to force the pace of majority rule in the early 1960s, the territory's settler population again asserted their demands for political autonomy by backing Ian Smith's 1965 unilateral declaration of independence (UDI).

Rhodes's ambition had been to extend British control from the Cape to Cairo, an idea dismissed by London as impractical. Yet the promotion of a settler colony in Rhodesia was viewed as a means of protecting British interests against a strategically located Portuguese empire (which controlled Angola and Mozambique), the assertive Boer republics, and Germany. Indeed, Rhodes's plan to take over the Transvaal in 1896 by dispatching a small party of armed men from Bechuanaland, with the idea of their provoking an uprising by *uitlanders*,

---

[5]   Jeremy Sarkin (2011), *Germany's Genocide of the Herero: Kaiser Wilhelm II, His General, His Settlers, His Soldiers*, Woodbridge, Suffolk: James Currey.

[6]   A.J. Chennels (1989), 'White Rhodesian nationalism: The mistaken years', in Canaan Banana (ed.), *Turmoil and Tenacity: Zimbabwe 1890–1990*, Harare: The College Press, 26–27.

had been secretly backed by London. The *uitlanders* (immigrants attracted by the sparkle of diamonds and the glitter of gold) had been denied citizenship. However, when the Jameson raid collapsed in a humiliating defeat, the British government declined all responsibility and Rhodes's political career ended in ignominy. Nonetheless, British determination to smash the Boer republics remained as strong as ever, culminating in the Anglo-Boer War. With British victory, the political conditions required for British control over the major source of the world's gold supply had been secured.

Colonial capitalism and economic development

Settler colonialism provided for a relatively autonomous process of capitalist development which was more advanced than was to be found in African countries directly subject to metropolitan rule. This was partly because settlers had been attracted to territories which seemingly offered prospects of good living on the basis of exploitation of munificent resources, land, and minerals, away from what many regarded as the oppressive restrictions of their home countries. Equally, the metropolitan powers themselves recognized the necessity of providing attractive conditions for settlers if a territory was to be developed. While the Boer farming community had much in common with African peasantries, later waves of settlers from Britain, Germany, and elsewhere arrived with the expectations and capacities forged by industrializing societies. The settler, wrote Brett in regard to Kenya, 'came out as a fully developed capitalist man'.[7] This does not mean that all settlers were capitalists; manifestly, they were not, for South Africa and Zimbabwe in particular acquired a significant white working class. However, it is to say that the state in settler colonies needed to respond to demands by whites for services, such as schools, hospitals, roads, railways, and leisure facilities in a competitive situation where, for the British at least, they could head off to Australia, New Zealand or Canada if local conditions were not to their liking. Provision of these facilities 'required the establishment of a relatively highly evolved export-oriented economy, an economy which, given the conditions of the times, could only take fully evolved capitalist forms'.[8]

Development necessitated an 'active and interventionist state', notably with regard to the provision of supplies of land and labour.[9] In South Africa, the demand of the mines and settler agriculture for African labour was voracious. The Union has been portrayed as an alliance of 'gold and maize', which rapidly transformed South Africa from a peripheral mercantile economy based upon the export of agricultural produce to Europe to the world's foremost supplier of gold.[10] It was gold and maize together, albeit primarily the former, which imposed a constellation of coercive measures upon African society in order to secure cheap labour through the creation of an extensive system of labour

[7]   E. A. Brett (1973), *Colonialism and Underdevelopment in East Africa: The Politics of Economic Change 1919–1939*, London: Heinemann, 168.
[8]   Ibid.
[9]   Good, op. cit., 605.
[10] Stanley Trapido (1971), 'South Africa as a comparative study of industrialisation', *Journal of Development Studies*, 7: 3, 309–20.

migrancy. Labour was thus 'cheap,' induced at a price far lower than would have been available in a 'free market'. White employers' reliance upon 'extra-economic' coercion had long predated Union, while the mines in their early days had imported semi-slave labour from territories outside South Africa. But it was after Union that coercion was to be elaborated via three main elements.[11]

The first was white land seizure and the driving of Africans into 'Native Reserves' which functioned as reservoirs of labour. Territorial segregation was officially defined by the Natives Land Act of 1913, which set aside 'reserve' land for exclusive African occupation and prohibited them from owning land outside scheduled territories. Thereafter, African occupation of land on white farms was on sufferance, tolerated in return for the provision of labour or crops. These measures smashed the potential for an African peasantry to provide commercial competition to white agriculture, while also undermining the capacity of African society to resist pressures designed to extrude black labour power on to the market. The Reserves were expected to provide for the immediate needs of migrants' families, enabling the mines to pay labourers as single men. However, the increasing burden of population upon limited supplies of land ensured a crisis of productivity which, by the post-1945 period, meant that the 'home-lands' (as the Reserves were to become under NP rule) were to become synonymous with chronic rural poverty.

The second element was the restriction of the rights of black workers, regulating the formation, duration, and termination of their contracts. The essential feature of these contracts was that their breach constituted a criminal offence, making offenders liable to imprisonment. Restrictions upon the length of their contracts (usually between nine months and two years) ensured that workers were forced to return to their rural homes, and were designed to block the emergence of an urbanized black working class. In 1911, the Native Labour Regulation Act extended criminal sanctions to workers on the mines, who were expressly denied the right to strike. The same Act made mineworkers subject to the Pass Laws which denied black workers the freedom to move their place of residence or to take up alternative employment elsewhere without first obtaining a pass. Meanwhile, the mines formed employment agencies to procure adequate flows of labour while eliminating wage competition between them.

The third element consisted of measures to control African lives in urban areas. Despite official attempts to limit African settlement in towns, the growth of secondary industries around the needs of the mines and the white population led to requirements for a stabilized black labour force. Imposition of racial segregation saw such Africans living in separated 'locations' while in white employment. Thus in 1923 parliament ratified the Natives Urban Areas Act which was based upon the philosophy of a commission which, reporting in 1921, had declared that any African in urban areas was only temporarily resident and 'should only be able to enter urban areas, which are essentially the white man's creation, when he is willing to enter and to minister to the needs of the white man and should depart therefrom when he ceases so to minister'. The thrust of this law was that Africans who were unemployed, sick, 'idle' or surplus to

---

[11] Roger Southall (1983), *South Africa's Transkei: The Political Economy of an 'Independent' Bantustan*, London: Heinemann, 24–25.

requirements could be dispatched to the reserves until they were needed again by the white economy.

The land and labour regime which arose in South Africa was replicated in its essence throughout the region. In Namibia, however, the German administration was the author of its own misfortunes, for the period between 1903 and 1907 was one of state-driven genocide which eliminated up to 60 per cent of the African population, this having a markedly adverse impact upon the labour market. The response was yet more oppression, with the passage of measures to restrict African grazing of cattle in order to undermine the last shreds of African economic independence, with a decree of 1898 having already outlined the establishment of Native Reserves and outlawed African rights to landholding. Subsequent legislation further proscribed both landholding and cattle-raising by Africans, who from the age of seven were now required to carry a pass. Yet Namibia's fragile, dry ecology rendered the country problematic for large-scale settler agriculture, so that while this required the administration to embark upon a comprehensive programme of assistance to farmers, there was simply not enough labour available to provide for their needs. Ironically, this led to some caution in efforts to recruit workers from outside the 'Police Zone'. In Ovamboland, where German rule was still only tentatively imposed, it was recognized that military offensives would adversely affect the procurement of labour, although by 1910 some 10,000 Ovambo contract workers were already coming south to work on the mines and railways.[12] However, after 1915, when the British and South African forces conquered the north, labour was drafted to the south through legislative and other measures. Even so, the shortage of labour was to remain acute. As late as 1957, when settler farms employed nearly 26,000 Africans (some 16,000 from outside the Police Zone), it was reckoned that demand exceeded supply by as much as nearly 11,000 men. Farmers were forced to recruit from other areas, while South African contractors, who were mostly engaged in large public works, were required to import their own labour.[13]

In Rhodesia, Africans initially retained reasonable access to land. The early expansion of mining and government services had taken place without any comparable development of capitalist agriculture. White farming was slow to develop, and although African agriculture was not officially encouraged, it was permitted to expand, not least because the mines wanted a supply of food at affordable prices. However, as white farming got going, so did efforts to restrict African competition. Under the Charter, Reserves (known as Tribal Trust Lands, or TTLs) had already been designated for African occupation, albeit generally situated in less fertile areas away from markets and railway lines. Poll taxes were imposed to encourage Africans to work on the mines and white farms, while Africans occupying hitherto unalienated land were charged rent. As European farming developed, so did pressures upon Africans to move out of white areas. By 1924 some two-thirds of the African population was living in Reserves which, as in South Africa, were to be launched into a history of overstocking,

---

[12] Peter Katjavivi (1988), *A History of Resistance in Namibia*, London: James Currey.

[13] Tsudao Gurirab (1988), 'Preliminary notes on the process of land theft and the genesis of capitalist relations of production in Namibia's agriculture (1884–1960)', in Brian Wood (ed.), *Namibia 1884–1984: Readings on Namibia's History and Society*, London and Lusaka: Namibia Support Committee and United Nations Institute for Namibia, 314–23.

soil erosion and declining productivity. Subsequently, the Land Apportionment Act of 1930 and its successor, the Land Tenure Act of 1970, reserved roughly half the land for whites, even though the latter at this time were hugely outnumbered by Africans.[14] By 1970, some 98 per cent of land suitable for afforestation, fruit growing, and intensive beef production lay in white areas, as did 82 per cent of the land suitable for intensive farming.[15] State coercion was instrumental in providing the labour necessary for capitalist agriculture, and market mechanisms only came to play a significant role following the development of a secondary industrial sector which was eager to promote a stabilized African labour force in urban areas.[16]

State support for mining, farming, and industrialization provided for relatively self-propelling economies. In South Africa, the state provided extensive subsidies to white agriculture; branch line construction by state-owned railways was geared to white farmers' needs; and a nationalized Land Bank was established to provide credit before farmers were guaranteed prices secured by producer-controlled marketing boards. Yet although the Union had been created to safeguard the mining industry, and although industrialization was constructed around the 'minerals-energy complex' (MEC),[17] it was surplus generated by the mining industry which was appropriated by the state to finance the costs incurred by the promotion of capitalist agriculture. It is not surprising that from the 1920s the rate of new foreign capital slackened, while leading mining companies looked for new investment fields outside South Africa. Indeed, mining came increasingly under local control. In 1920 the government created a Reserve Bank which took from mine owners the right to sell gold, and which gradually established control over monetary policy. By the 1930s, local share ownership of the mines had increased from 15 to 40 per cent. Symptomatic was the creation of the Anglo-American Corporation (AAC) by the magnate, Sir Ernest Oppenheimer, whose 'catalytic' capital was largely American rather than British. During the 1920s, Anglo acquired control of the diamond industry before opening new gold mines in the Free State and on the Witwatersrand.[18]

The demands of the mining industry had stimulated the local production of construction materials, explosives, and the construction of engineering works. Increasingly, mining capital began to diversify into the food, drink, and tobacco sectors. Agricultural raw materials, processing, and import-substitution manufacturing began to pick up, notably after the introduction of protective tariffs in 1925. Further impetus was provided by the establishment of ESCOM in 1923 to generate state electricity, the further development of railways, ports, and harbours, and the establishment of Iscor, a state-owned iron and steel producer which went on to acquire control of major subsidiaries in metals and engi-

---

[14] Roger Riddell (1978), *The Land Question in Rhodesia*, Gwelo: Mambo Press.

[15] Martin Loney (1975), *Rhodesia: White Racism and Imperial Response*, Harmondsworth: Penguin, 55.

[16] Giovanni Arrighi (1973), 'Labour supplies in historical perspective: A study of the proletarianization of the African peasantry in Rhodesia', in Giovanni Arrighi and John Saul, *Essays on the Political Economy of Africa*, New York and London: Monthly Review Press, 180–234.

[17] Ben Fine and Zavareh Rustomjee (1996), *The Political Economy of South Africa: From Minerals Energy Complex to Industrialisation*, London: Hurst.

[18] Martin Legassick (1974), 'South Africa: Capital accumulation and violence', *Economy and Society*, 3: 3, 253–91.

neering.[19] Major foreign firms were forced to establish a local presence if they wished to avoid protective tariffs, supply the mines, take advantage of the developing steel industry or to undertake construction work. By 1939, therefore, South Africa already boasted a significant industrial base. However, it was global conflict that provided the major stimulus for further development by boosting military production and increasing manufacturing to replace imports.

The Industrial Development Corporation (IDC), established in 1940, played a key role in directing finance to sectors regarded as crucial, and together with other state corporations such as Foskor (producing concentrates for the fertilizer industry), Sasol (oil from coal) and Iscor (iron and steel mining) promoted collaboration between foreign and domestic capital across an array of sectors. This led to a significant increase of foreign investment in the 1950s and 1960s, drawn by the prospect of low labour costs and some of the highest levels of profit in the world.[20] Although over a thousand British firms had assets in South Africa in the 1970s, Britain's share of foreign capital invested in South Africa declined from around a quarter of the total in the 1950s to about 18 per cent in the 1970s, as investments flowed in, notably from the US, Canada, and Western Europe. British firms' investments in South Africa represented more than half of their investments in the whole of the rest of Africa, US direct investment representing some 40 per cent of its African total.[21] While foreign investment was broad based, much of it flowed into high-growth, capital-intensive sectors such as electronics, chemicals, computers, advanced engineering, and oil, with the most dramatic development being that of the local car industry, stimulated by a tariff-enforced local content programme.[22] Increased foreign investment was accompanied by the rapid advance of local industry, its key feature being the entry of agricultural capital, largely Afrikaner, into industry, mining, and finance. This presaged a growing interpenetration of Afrikaner and 'English' capital from the 1960s, assisted by the short-lived slump in foreign investment after Sharpeville, and subsequently by the more significant withdrawal of foreign capital in the 1980s as the apartheid regime became more politically exposed. However much the economy remained inhibited by the low purchasing power of the black population, it had long become the most industrialized on the continent.

After 1915 South West Africa's economy was to become little more than an extension of that of its more powerful neighbour. Its development was founded upon the exploitation of raw materials, notably minerals (including uranium, diamonds, copper, lead, and zinc) but also its coastal fisheries and agriculture (for production of beef and Karakul pelts). Subsequently, it never advanced much beyond the exploitation of natural resources, 90 per cent of domestic production going for export as late as the 1980s. This export dependence saw the closure of a large part of the mining industry during the Depression of the 1930s, before renewed demand for minerals after 1945 saw an inflow of British and foreign capital (although diamond mining remained dominated by Consol-

---

[19] Fine and Rustomjee, op. cit., 137.
[20] Ann Seidman and Neva Seidman Makgetla (1980), *Outposts of Monopoly Capitalism: Southern Africa in the Changing Global Economy*, Westport CT: Lawrence Hill & Company; London: Zed Press, 69.
[21] Ibid., 80.
[22] Legassick, op. cit., 272.

idated Diamond Mining, a major member of the De Beers/Anglo-American group). A South African stranglehold was maintained via an alliance of South African and transnational corporations, with little attention paid to local industry, except for a secondary service for the mining industry which expanded after 1945 and also in the processing of fish and meat for export. Virtually all South West Africa's import and export trade went through South Africa, which viewed the territory as a valuable addition to its regional market. Overall, this configuration of South African and foreign capital interests gave the Namibian economy 'a distortion extreme even by the standards of 20th century colonialism'.[23]

The Rhodesian economy developed a considerably higher level of autonomy. Although Rhodes's gold bonanza never materialized, gold mining contributed significantly to the economy. Furthermore, large coal deposits were found at Wankie, and deposits of lead, chrome, tungsten, and asbestos were also discovered, making mining the largest stimulus to the economy and providing the large proportion of exports. As late as 1943, some 50 per cent of national income was provided directly or indirectly by gold.[24] Yet, significantly, as Arrighi notes, colonial Zimbabwe was characterized by a white rural bourgeoisie consisting of owners of small- and medium-sized mines as well as farmers who were committed to the country's development. 'This national character of the white rural bourgeoisie, even at that time, distinguished Southern Rhodesia from practically all other African territories north of the Limpopo and south of the Sahara, where exploitation of resources was carried out by large-scale international capitalism.'[25] International capitalism was represented mainly by the British South Africa Company which, apart from its control over the railways and the bulk of gold production, and coal mining, also owned extensive land for the production of cattle, maize, and other crops.

Initially, the secondary sector was centred around agricultural processing, construction, and the railways. Subsequently, manufacturing was stimulated by five main factors. First, while the 1930s Depression encouraged diversification, the Second World War made import-substitution imperative. Second, the demand for minerals and the location of a major British Air Force base created a boom. Subsequently, third, post-war immigration from Britain increased the size of the internal market, making local manufacturing more profitable. Fourth, the associated increase in the size and earning power of the African population similarly increased the local market for manufacturers, especially in the textile sector, a welcome break given the continuing strong preference amongst white consumers for high-quality imported goods. Finally, the creation of the Central African Federation which linked Southern to Northern Rhodesia (Zambia) and Nyasaland (Malawi) in 1953 gave local manufacturing preferential access to a larger market while simultaneously allowing for the diversion of revenues from the Northern Rhodesian Copperbelt to improve economic infrastructure. In addition, after 1948, Rhodesia featured as an alternative outlet for foreign, notably British, capital frightened by the prospect of extremist

[23] Richard Moorsom (1980), 'Namibia in the frontline: The political economy of decolonization in South Africa's colony', *Review of African Political Economy*, 17: 72.
[24] Loney, op. cit., 68.
[25] Arrighi, op. cit., 337.

nationalist policies in South Africa.[26] Overall, the post-war period saw impressive growth in agriculture, featuring notably the remarkable expansion of tobacco production, which tripled between 1945 and 1958, and which overtook gold as the country's major export. By 1957 the gross value of capitalist agriculture stood at £41.8 million, compared to the mining output of £25.8 million and manufacturing output of £105.1 million.[27]

Rhodesian development was fostered by a coalition of the national capitalist class, a white petty bourgeoisie, and white workers who were employed in services and mining. Settlers' political power had been strengthened by 'Responsible Government', even though the state was forced to balance the interests of national and international capital. As in South Africa, state intervention played an important role in expanding overhead capital and strengthening the bargaining power of national capital. Public works, notably road building, were carried out on a large scale; various state enterprises, notably the Electricity Supply Commission power stations, the Iron and Steel Commission foundries, and the Cotton Industry Board mills, were established in the 1930s and 1940s, while raw materials processing plants and marketing organizations were also set up. In 1936, a Tobacco Marketing Act sought to strengthen the hands of local tobacco growers relative to the powerful United Tobacco Company, although the government continued to complain that the tobacco price was manipulated by powerful external interests.[28] Nonetheless, relations between national and international capital changed after 1945 as foreign investors became more influential. The AAC, through its various subsidiaries, dominated coal and iron pyrites mining, the ferro-chrome and cement industries, and, together with Roan Selection Trust (RST), came to control iron and steel production, while having fingers in numerous other industrial pies. Other giant companies, such as Lonrho, developed major interests in areas of primary production apart from mining (cattle, gold, and ownership of the major oil pipeline), while the UK's Turner and Newell held a near monopoly over the asbestos industry. By 1960, two-thirds of total recorded net operating profits were earned by companies not domestically controlled.

The increased weight of international capital had political consequences. Although international firms involved in manufacturing shared some interests with national capital, those engaged in primary production had little to do with the country's wider industrialization. Indeed, their particular concern was to block nationalist policies which might interfere with their local operations, and predisposed them to reformist capitalist policies which might accommodate emerging African nationalism. But this did not sit well with the majority of the white electorate, who in 1962 rallied to the flag of the Rhodesian Front (RF). The declaration of UDI in 1965 indicated a rejection of the preference of the British government and international capital for a neo-colonial solution in favour of continued rule by the settlers themselves.[29] Indeed, the relatively advanced level of economic development provided the settler community with the confidence to launch out on its own.

[26] Ibid., 351.
[27] Loney, op. cit., 68–69
[28] Arrighi, op. cit., 344–45.
[29] Ibid., 367.

Political rigidity and nationalist response

For Good, the key political problem for settler society was the containment of the new African classes brought forth by economic development, a situation made more acute by that fact that settlers constituted a marked minority. When Namibia was rocked by a general strike by black workers in 1971, whites were outnumbered by blacks (Africans and Coloureds) by more than 7 to 1. In Zimbabwe, in 1975, when the regime was fighting a guerrilla war, whites were outnumbered more than 20 to 1. In 1951, blacks outnumbered whites in South Africa by 3.8 to 1; by 1976, when schoolchildren pushed Soweto to the front of resistance, the ratio had increased to nearly 5 to 1. Stanley Uys, a leading journalist, wrote of 'self-doubt spreading among the 4 million whites', but as he also noted, the tragedy was that the majority of them had resolved to 'dig in'.[30] As observed by John Day in relation to Rhodesia, the fact that whites and blacks lived in segregated worlds meant that they created myths about each other that blocked mutual accommodation.[31]

Settler communities believed that the greater their independence, the more easily their control over land and labour would be maintained.[32] Their aim was to resist liberalizing concessions to black majorities. In South Africa, the minimal political rights of representation in parliament that had been conceded to the different black communities under Union were steadily eroded from 1936, culminating in post-1948 moves towards their total relegation to representation in racially and ethnically defined, subordinate legislative institutions. During the 1950s, South Africa's opposition to the status of South West Africa as a UN mandate was driven by concern to brook all international opposition to its determination to absorb it as a fifth province. In Rhodesia, the settler regime opted for UDI rather than concede moderate advances in the constitutional status of Africans as advocated by Britain.

Settlers' domination resulted in a nationalist response which asserted the demand for racial equality and political freedom. In his discussion of the 'thirty years war' Saul takes note of the distinct 'histories' which determined the course of struggles in the different countries of southern Africa, yet refers to them as sharing a simultaneous chronology, shaped by regional and global dynamics.[33] The broader point is that their historical trajectories were profoundly influenced by developments in South Africa, the most advanced formation in the region. We see this in the formation of resistance movements in Rhodesia and South West Africa which tended to follow developments in South Africa (while reflecting the specificities of local conditions). Equally, while the apartheid regime's brutal responses to popular resistance were ruthlessly extended to South West Africa, they also gave strong encouragement to similar moves taken by governments in Rhodesia.

---

[30] Cited in *Africa Contemporary Record (ACR) 1976–77*, B799.
[31] John Day (1975), 'The creation of political myths: African nationalism in Southern Rhodesia', *Journal of Southern African Studies*, 2: 1, 52–65.
[32] Good, op. cit., 610.
[33] John Saul (1994), 'The Southern African revolution', in John Saul (ed.), *Recolonization and Resistance: Southern Africa in the 1990s*, Trenton NJ: Africa World Press, 1–34.

2.
The Evolution of the Liberation Movements

Nationalist historiography portrays the struggle for liberation as an inexorable unfolding of an heroic past by the nation in process of creation, resulting in ultimate triumph over the forces of oppression. Indeed, the making of a new nation as was required by transitions from colonialism or minority rule entailed the deliberate construction of an historical memory of how the nation had been forged and how it was to imagine itself. Yet while the rigidity of settler colonialism invoked its contradiction in the form of militant nationalist movements, the processes whereby the latter developed were often messy, incoherent, partial, and far from complete: they divided as much as they united. Even so, it is possible to identify the steady evolution of nationalist sentiment and organization across the decades.

Early currents of protest

Save for the completion of white conquest in northern South West Africa following the defeat of German forces during 1914–15, the 'primary resistance' of African societies to white conquest and their desire to establish Union in South Africa met with failure. The swift formation of the ANC (initially known as the South African Native National Congress) in 1912 by a mission-educated elite represented the first attempt to organize resistance along genuinely national lines, to overcome inter-ethnic divisions, and to secure the support of the chiefly aristocracy.[1] Guided by Christian and liberal precepts, its protestations were made on moral and constitutional grounds. While these actions were to prove 'conspicuously ineffective' in reversing the provisions of the 1913 Land Act and Union,[2] the early ANC managed to position itself as a broad-based organization and as the leading voice of African opinion, even though what was a rather conservative elite was to have difficulty connecting with both an emergent urbanized working class and the large mass of Africans residing on communal land in the Reserves or working on white farms. In Rhodesia, in contrast, the formation of the Rhodesian Bantu Voters' Association (RBVA) in 1923 was overwhelmingly concerned with the problems of the small, emerging African elite. Yet when the efforts of the RBVA and other elitist organizations, such as the Gwelo Native Welfare Association and the Rhodesian Native Association, failed to stop the passage of the Land Apportionment Act of 1931, which like the South African Land Act, instituted a division of land between whites and blacks which overwhelmingly favoured the former, they soon gave

---

[1] Andre Odendaal (1984), *Vukani Bantu! The Beginnings of Black Protest Politics in South Africa to 1912*, Claremont: David Philip.
[2] Saul Dubow (2000), *The African National Congress*, Johannesburg: Jonathan Ball Publishers, 8.

way to the Southern Rhodesian African National Congress,[3] formed in 1934. However, although the Southern Rhodesian ANC was to emerge as the major vehicle of mass nationalism in the 1950s, this transition had to await other developments.[4]

African urbanization was an inevitable accompaniment of secondary industrialization. The percentage of Africans living in towns in South Africa increased from 12.6 in 1911 to 17.3 in 1936 and 23.7 in 1946.[5] Nonetheless, urbanization amongst Africans remained obstructed by the migrant labour system and segregationist legislation. Even so, by the 1940s, the Natives Law (Fagan) Commission was declaring the idea of 'total segregation...utterly impracticable', asserting the reality of a permanently settled African urban population and that the migrant labour system could not be maintained in the long run, save on a limited scale.[6]

The expansion of industry set in train a process of African proletarianization and protests against the impositions of settler colonialism. The elitist ANC remained steadfastly aloof from these developments. However, in 1918, the Transvaal ANC was involved alongside the revolutionary syndicalist Industrial Workers of Africa (IWA) and International Socialist League (ISL) in a general strike across the Witwatersrand and in the following year played a key role in pushing the ANC into an anti-pass law campaign. Later that year, IWA/ISL members, linked to the Cape Native Congress, joined the Industrial and Commercial Workers' Union (ICU) in waging a bruising dockers' strike. Subsequently, members of the IWA/ISL failed to gain the support of the ANC for a programme of mass actions, but they were instrumental to the calling of a black trade union conference in Bloemfontein. At this event the IWA and other groupings merged under the ICU banner into 'one great union of skilled and unskilled workers of South Africa, south of the Zambesi'.[7]

The ICU, led by a Malawian, Clements Kadalie, promoted a militant message that reverberated around the country, spanning urban and rural areas. Drawing from anarcho-syndicalist ideas, it invoked the vision of 'abolishing the capitalist class' through one big strike. Although too eclectic to be called truly syndicalist as it was subject to other influences such as Garveyism, 'syndicalism was certainly part of its heady ideological mix'.[8] Nonetheless, for a period the ICU thoroughly eclipsed the ANC with a membership exceeding 100,000. Furthermore, its influence spread to neighbouring countries: to South West Africa, where a branch was formed in Luderitz in the early 1920s, and to Zimbabwe, where the Rhodesian ICU was initiated by Robert Sambo in

---

[3]   Henceforth 'Congress'.

[4]   Martin Loney (1975), *Rhodesia: White Racism and Imperial Response*, Harmondsworth: Penguin, 96.

[5]   David Welsh (1975), 'The growth of towns', in Monica Wilson and Leonard Thompson (eds), *The Oxford History of South Africa: Volume Two, South Africa 1870–1966*, Oxford: Clarendon Press, 172–243.

[6]   Ibid., 190.

[7]   Lucien van der Walt (2011), 'Black syndicalists and the radicalisation of the SA Native National Congress (SANNC), 1917–1920: The industrial workers of Africa, the International Socialist League and the left wing of Congress', presented to the conference, 'One Hundred Years of the ANC: Debating Liberation Histories and Democracy Today', Universities of Johannesburg and the Witwatersrand, 20–24 September.

[8]   Ibid., 28.

1927.[9] The latter never achieved the importance of its mother organization, although in its appeal to class interest, it left an important legacy which outlasted its subsequent disappearance, owing to official hostility, in the mid-thirties.[10]

The ANC: from elite to mass nationalism

The ANC played a secondary role during the social ferment of the 1920s when it was outpaced by more popular movements.[11] Often, in a countryside stalked by rural poverty, these were inspired by Africanist dreams (some stimulated by early Pan-African influences imported by Afro-American missionaries) which resulted in millenarian imaginations of an existence free from white influence. In urban areas, the Communist Party of South Africa (CPSA), formed in 1921, had embarked upon a contentious debate about the relationship between the national question and socialist revolution.

The CPSA's initial programme called for the overthrow of South African capitalism, with white workers as the shock troops of the class struggle. In this vision, questions of racism and national oppression would be resolved under the dictatorship of the proletariat. Emergent national movements such as the ANC were viewed as bourgeois and reformist.

In 1922, white workers, led by the CPSA took part in the Rand Revolt, an armed uprising against the state which called for 'Workers of the World to fight and unite for a White South Africa'. The revolt was bloodily crushed by the government of General Smuts, but at the cost of the defeat of his South African Party at the following election in 1924, when the white working class pledged its allegiance to a coalition of the National and Labour parties. This provoked a bitter struggle within the CPSA over the national question, forcing the Communist International to intervene. At its sixth Congress in 1927, held in Moscow, attended by James la Guma on behalf of the CPSA, it was resolved (in line with a shift in Communist policy regarding how to respond to colonialism internationally) that the national question was the 'foundation of the revolution', whose moving force was the black peasantry allied with but led by the working class. As a result, the CPSA declared its struggle would now be for an 'independent Native Republic', and committed to working with the ANC in order to transform it into a 'fighting nationalist revolutionary organization against the white bourgeoisie and British imperialists'.

La Guma had been accompanied to Moscow by Josiah Gumede, the newly elected President of the ANC, who had been strongly influenced by the ideas of Marcus Garvey, the Jamaican prophet of the gospel of 'Africa for the Africans'. Here began the relationship between the two organizations, which, while undergoing various tribulations, was to endure. The Native Republic policy provided the basis for an alliance between nationalist and socialist forces. Nonetheless, it was strongly opposed by elements within the CPSA. It must be remembered that at the time, although the ANC may have passed as the premier vehicle of

[9] Van der Walt, op. cit.
[10] Loney, op. cit., 93–96.
[11] I draw liberally upon various existing accounts of the rise of the ANC and the Congress Alliance.

African nationalism, its membership was tiny (rarely exceeding more than a few hundred) and was largely restricted to the small elite and members of the chieftaincy. It was not surprising, therefore, that militants within the CPSA argued that the new line diluted the class struggle. As a result, the CPSA was to be riven by factionalism, with many leading figures being purged. Its membership shrank from 1,750 in 1928 to just 150 in 1935. For some years it ceased to exist as an effective force, not least because of the expulsion of many of those who had played a key role in organizing an early wave of independent trade unions established by former members of the ICU and other activists.

The CPSA's influence had been further diminished by the election of Pixley Seme to the presidency of the ANC in 1930 in place of Gumede, whose association with the Communists had alarmed the movement's establishment. Seme's election was only secured amid bitter debates, with more radical elements accusing the leadership of undue timidity in the face of new segregationist measures proposed by Prime Minister J.B. Hertzog. Over the next few years, the ANC was weakened by divisions along factional, regional, and ethnic lines, allowing itself to be eclipsed in its opposition to Hertzog's 'Native Bills' in 1936 by a specially constituted All Africa Convention (AAC). Ironically, this worked to the ANC's good fortune, for although the ANC cooperated closely with the AAC, the Convention was to become identified with a much reviled compromise it made with Hertzog which involved the sacrifice of the principle of the African franchise. Nonetheless, although the ANC was spared the major force of criticism, the failure of the politics of negotiation to prevent the passage of the Native Bills opened the way to intellectual and political renewal.

Phil Bonner argues that the key to the survival of the ANC lies in its attempts throughout its history to mobilize and unite often conflicting constituencies – traditional leaders, the Christianised elite, the urban masses, and the rural population, alongside the diverse ethnic groups distributed amongst the four provinces. Nonetheless, during its early decades, its successes were uneven: in the Reserves, the ANC was viewed as largely irrelevant (until the election of Albert Luthuli, a chief, as President of the organization in 1952), and the urban masses were largely excluded from at least the early part of its history. Indeed, the ANC survived largely because it was galvanized into action by government attempts, as in 1936, to further restrict the rights of Africans.[12] Nonetheless, during the 1940s, the ANC began its transition from an organization of the African elite to one engaged in a mass-based politics.

Under the leadership of A.B. Xuma, who became President in 1940, membership increased to 4,000. Even so, the ANC remained aloof from numerous expressions of social unrest, such as bus boycotts and the formation of squatters' movements. These were the signs of a surge in working class activity and reflected multiple impulses. One was increased levels of urbanization, but this also signified a 'silent revolution' whereby the growing presence of African women in townships led to their becoming a major force within an increasingly urbanized ANC. Indeed, the 1940s was the decade when township Africans demanded to be regarded as urban.[13] Furthermore, African workers

---

[12] Phil Bonner (2011), Plenary presentation to the conference 'One Hundred Years of the ANC: Debating Liberation Histories and Democracy Today', 20–24 September.
[13] Ibid.

were not shy in exercising their new economic muscle, acquired during the Second World War. Whereas 171,088 African man-hours had been lost to industry in the period 1930–39, some 1,684,915 were lost in the following decade, reflecting the rapid growth of militant African trade unions and the recovery of the CPSA, which (after the ignominy of supporting the Soviet-Nazi pact) looked to build a united front against fascism. This included its cooperation with the ANC on various issues, notably the formation of an African mineworkers' union and an anti-pass law campaign in 1943–44. Leading members of the CPSA were elected to the ANC's National Executive. Collaboration was strengthened by the massive strike by 100,000 African mineworkers in 1946 which, although defeated, constituted a significant moment in the ANC's turn to mass politics.

Even so, the ANC's top leadership remained suspicious of militant action. This was to change with the establishment of the Youth League in the early 1940s, when young radicals (key individuals amongst whom, such as Nelson Mandela and Walter Sisulu, had been politicized at Fort Hare University College, the sole such institution for African students) challenged the movement's conservative establishment, eventually toppling Xuma and replacing him with Dr James Moroka. In 1949 the Youth League secured adoption by the ANC as a whole of its Programme of Action, which committed it to the achievement of 'national freedom' and mass action. Yet relations between the Youth League and the CPSA were far from easy. In 1947 a pact between Xuma and Drs Naidoo and Naicker of the newly radicalized Natal Indian Congress had signified growing awareness of the need for all oppressed groups to unite, yet the Youth League remained suspicious of communist and non-African influence. However, the coming to power in 1948 of the NP, dedicated to a re-invigoration of white supremacy, concentrated minds and encouraged the ANC to strike up broad alliances. This set the scene for the mass-based protests of the 1950s and the formation of the Congress Alliance.

The government embarked upon its own programme to curtail black political activity. A flurry of legislation, including passage of the Suppression of Communism Act of 1950 which outlawed the CPSA, defined virtually any form of protest as communist and gave the state sweeping powers to suppress opposition. These measures brought forth a counter-movement: the emergence of stay-aways from work and boycotts as major forms of protest.

The most notable campaign was the 1952 Defiance Campaign against Unjust Laws, whereby the ANC sought to implement its Programme of Action through passive resistance. Although broken by state repression, it generated massive support for the ANC whose membership shot up from just 7,000 to nearly 100,000 over a few months. Significantly, too, it increased coordination between the ANC and the Indian Congress, the (Coloured) African People's Organization, and the Council of Non-European Trade Unions. In addition, following the CPSA's enforced dissolution in 1950, many African communists joined the ANC, many devoted themselves to the trade union movement, and white communists formed the Congress of Democrats, while the party itself cautiously re-established itself underground as the South African Communist Party (SACP) in 1953. Also important was the formation in 1955 of the South African Congress of Trade Unions (SACTU) which brought together a complicated mix of racially divided unions. Much influenced by communist theorizing, it adopted a strategy which argued that struggles for economic rights could not be distinct from those for political rights.

Via the Defiance Campaign, the evolving Congress Alliance sought to test the limits of mass civil disobedience, its aim being to clog the jails with protestors and to bring the administration of unjust laws to a halt. Acts of defiance took place in many towns and cities and provoked direct confrontation with the authorities. However, while this created a powerful political legacy, the state itself responded to mass action by elaborating its repertoire of repression. This included a series of banning orders and arrests which decimated the Congress Alliance leadership. Not one unjust law was repealed, and the government's heavy-handed response enabled it to increase its majority in the election of 1953.

All this compelled the ANC and its allies to rethink their strategy, culminating in the convening of the Congress of the People in June 1955 at which some 3,000 delegates adopted the Freedom Charter. This called for all people to be equal before the law and for 'the people to govern'. Controversially, it called for the common ownership of the country's mineral wealth, banks, and monopolies. It was this provision which (after the police had broken up the Congress on its second day) encouraged the state to use the Freedom Charter as the basis for a charge of treason against 156 leaders of the Congress Alliance. Although the five-year Treason Trial was to end ignominiously for the state with the acquittal of the accused, it had the important effect of taking the large body of the leadership of the mass movement out of political circulation during a period when mass action was developing.

Although the Congress Alliance provided a framework for collaboration between different political tendencies, mutual suspicion remained. A key outcome was the split from the ANC in 1958 of an Africanist faction. Led by Robert Sobukwe, the Africanists proclaimed that the ANC had abandoned the African nationalism of the 1949 Programme of Action, and had become the tool of whites and communists. In 1959, they formed the Pan-Africanist Congress (PAC), which repudiated the Freedom Charter alongside any idea of cooperation with any member organizations of the Congress Alliance. Influenced by Ghana's attaining independence in 1957 under Nkrumah, the PAC's commitment to Pan-Africanism appealed to wider African support during the early era of African independence, while its anti-communism positioned it to lure Western support as the Cold War intensified.

The ANC and PAC were drawn into outright competition. In March 1960, the PAC staged a protest against the pass laws a week in advance of a similarly planned action by the ANC. When a crowd of protestors converged on a police station at Sharpeville, in the industrial area of Vereeniging south of Johannesburg, police shot and killed 69 people and injured another 180. A wave of protest reverberated around the country. The scene was now set for a denouement. The regime clamped down heavily upon all mass-based political parties, banned both the ANC and PAC, and proclaimed a State of Emergency. However, it suffered a humiliating setback the following year with the acquittal of all those accused in the Treason Trial. But this convinced key actors within the ANC, notably Nelson Mandela, that the regime was impervious to all forms of legal and non-violent protest. Indeed, for many political activists, the banning of the ANC in 1960 signified the failure of non-violent resistance as a strategy for undermining state power and for persuading sufficient whites to abandon apartheid.

The violent crackdown upon the mass movements finally turned the tide. Thus was born, in 1961, Umkhonto we Sizwe (MK), with Mandela as its Commander-in-Chief, as the military wing of the ANC. Its early actions, experimental and amateurish, were directed at sabotage of state installations, designed to signal that the ANC was still active, and a last despairing appeal to whites to turn away from intransigence. The state responded with yet more draconian action, culminating in the arrest of the ANC's underground high command at a farm in Rivonia outside Johannesburg in 1963. The conviction of these leaders, in 1964, to long terms of imprisonment signified the government's determination to smash opposition and left the mass movement leaderless and dispirited. It also cleared the ground for the regime to implement its plan for dividing Africans along ethnic lines via the creation of homelands, the first of which, the Transkei, acceded to 'self-government' in 1963 before proceeding to 'independence' in 1976.

Popular struggle and divided nationalism in Zimbabwe

The developments in South Africa reverberated throughout the region. In Rhodesia, African urbanization during and after the Second World War had laid the basis for a wave of labour militancy. The Rhodesian Railways African Employees' Association was formed in Bulawayo in 1944. The following year, some 2,400 African railway workers went on strike, the action rapidly spreading to other railway centres in both Rhodesias and lasting for two weeks before being called off by a government promise to investigate grievances. Then, in 1948, a general strike broke out, starting amongst municipal workers in Bulawayo before spreading to every urban and mining centre in the country. The strike attracted the support of other organizations, notably the Congress, which played a role in the negotiations with government that brought it to an end.[14]

African workers were subject to severe controls. In 1934, under pressure from white workers, the government had passed an Industrial Conciliation Act which excluded Africans from being defined as 'employees', and barred them from engaging in collective bargaining. However, the 1945 railway strike resulted two years later in the passage of a Native Labour Boards Act. This prescribed conditions of employment for Africans in all industries except agriculture and domestic service, although Africans were still denied the right to negotiate directly with their employers. However, the continuing growth of African trade unionism during the 1950s forced the government to reconsider. In 1959 a revised Industrial Conciliation Act was passed which now referred to all workers, save (again) African workers in agriculture and domestic service, alongside public servants, and employees of the railways, who were separately catered for in terms of a Railways Act. Although this opened up union-management negotiations for a limited number of skilled workers, the conditions of African workers continued to be largely regulated by industrial boards.

---

[14] Loney, op. cit., 99–100.

Unions were allowed to represent workers only in single industries and were precluded from affiliation to any political party.[15]

A key change was foreshadowed in 1958 with the report of an Urban Affairs Commission which stressed the importance of stabilizing industrial labour. This was endorsed by the government, which pronounced that it would encourage permanent settlement by African families in urban areas. Thereafter, the government restructured labour legislation to allow Africans to participate directly in institutionalized wage negotiations, opened up apprenticeships to Africans, and allowed Africans access to previously reserved positions in the civil service. Yet, just as the Fagan Commission had preceded the defeat of Smuts in 1948, so this new commitment to labour stabilization in Zimbabwe was to be reversed, for with the election of the RF in 1962, government lay in the hands of a party which believed in the perpetuation of migrant labour and rural dependency. This had the significant effect of slowing the growth in black industrial workers' wages, which had increased significantly between 1945 and 1962.[16]

Growing worker militancy was matched by a radicalization of African politics which now reached into the countryside. A catalyst was the passage of the Native Land Husbandry Act of 1951 which forced rural families to reduce their cattle herds and change their land tenure practices. Benjamin Burombo, leader of the British African Voice Association, was the most active figure in opposing this hated legislation, and influenced many who were soon to emerge as nationalist leaders. Amongst the latter were James Chikerema, George Nyandoro, and Edson Sithole who together formed the City Youth League in Salisbury in August 1955, later changing its name to the African National Youth League. This represented a challenge to those amongst the African elite who were prepared to work with the imperial scheme to create the Central African Federation (of the two Rhodesias and Nyasaland), which would inevitably have been dominated by the white regime centred in Salisbury. The Federation, created in 1953, supposedly inaugurated a politics of 'partnership', but was bitterly opposed by the majority of Africans in all three territories. Amongst those active in opposing the Federation was Joshua Nkomo. Educated in Rhodesia and trained at tertiary level in South Africa, he had returned home in 1947 to work for the Rhodesian Railways Employees' Association. He went on to revive Congress, which had become largely moribund, and participated in the All Africa Convention that campaigned against the Federation. He went on to stand for election to the Federal parliament in 1953, but was rejected by the overwhelmingly white electorate.[17]

As in South Africa, the Youth League galvanized African politics through strategies of mass action, its most notable triumph being its organization of an effective three-day boycott protesting against a rise in bus fares in August 1956. In 1957, the Youth League merged with the Bulawayo ANC to launch a revitalized national ANC with Nkomo as its President. When Garfield Todd, who had emerged as Prime Minister of Southern Rhodesia with the creation of the

[15] David Martin and Phyllis Johnson (1984), *The Struggle for Zimbabwe: The Chimurenga War*, London and Boston: Faber & Faber, 59–60.
[16] Peter Harris (1975), 'Industrial workers in Rhodesia, 1946–1972', *Journal of Southern African Studies*, 1: 2, 139–61.
[17] Richard Gibson (1972), *African Liberation Movements: Contemporary Struggles against White Minority Rule*, London: Oxford University Press, 158.

Federation, was removed by a cabinet revolt in 1958 because of his relatively liberal politics, a number of Africans who had worked with his United Federal Party (UFP) now joined Congress.

Any illusion of 'partnership' was finally shattered when large-scale protests in Northern Rhodesia and Nyasaland led to proclamation of a State of Emergency throughout the Federation. Then, in February 1959, Congress in Southern Rhodesia was banned, 500 members arrested, and 300 detained. Nkomo, however, was out of the country, having travelled to Accra in December 1958 to represent the ANC at the First All-African People's Conference before proceeding to Cairo, where he learnt of the imposition of the Emergency. For the next year he remained abroad, seeking to rally support while giving assurances to the British government of his reasonableness. Yet although the British were in the throes of transferring power to appropriately moderate governments elsewhere in Africa, they were not prepared to intervene forcefully in Zimbabwe, where the settlers remained in firm control.

Nkomo had assumed the presidency of the National Democratic Party (NDP), which replaced the banned Congress, in October 1960. His influence was its zenith, and he led his party into constitutional talks in Salisbury in early 1961. The NDP had agreed to insist on parity between African and European seats in a reformed Legislative Assembly. Instead, Nkomo agreed to proposals which would have left Africans with just 15 seats to 50 for Europeans, with the races voting on separate electoral rolls. The NDP executive was outraged and decided to boycott a constitutional referendum which was won handsomely by Sir Edgar Whitehead, who had succeeded Todd as Prime Minister. Under pressure from London, Whitehead announced proposals to reform the Land Apportionment Act, to get more Africans on to the voting roll. But he also banned the NDP for refusing to recognize the new constitution – only for the NDP to reappear as the Zimbabwe African People's Union (ZAPU) with Nkomo as its president once more. ZAPU proceeded to boycott the 1962 elections, at which 14 of the UFP's 35 seats were won by Africans. But by now the RF had been formed to contest 'forced integration', and it swept to power.

Although ZAPU looked to Britain to force the settlers to give way, it recognized the likelihood of its being banned. Indeed, some within ZAPU now argued the necessity of turning to armed struggle, and a first group of young recruits was sent abroad to begin military training in Algeria, China, Czechoslovakia, and Ghana. On their return to Zimbabwe they were to form the first cadres of the Zimbabwe Liberation Army, and initiated various forms of low-scale violence, although publicly, ZAPU was forced to deny any connection with them. It was to be four years before guerrilla warfare was launched, but when it came, it was the newly formed Zimbabwe African National Union (ZANU) which led the way.[18]

The ban on ZAPU came in September 1962. Again, Nkomo was out of the country (lobbying for support from the newly formed OAU whilst his fellow leaders were placed under restriction). In April 1963 he persuaded his colleagues to attend a meeting in Dar es Salaam to discuss establishing a government in exile, but Tanzanian President Julius Nyerere advised him to return home. This acted as catalyst to those who wanted a stronger resistance

[18] Ibid., 161.

to settler power, and who viewed Nkomo's leadership as obsessed with international diplomacy rather than organizing resistance. The upshot was the formation of ZANU in August 1963, with Ndabaningi Sithole as its first President and Robert Mugabe as its Secretary-General.

Mugabe, born and educated at a Roman Catholic mission at Kutama in the Zvimba district, west of Salisbury (Harare), had won a scholarship to Fort Hare, where he studied for three years from 1949, and was much influenced by ANC Youth Leaguers and the Africanist ideology of Anton Lembede while also having his first encounters with Marxism via contacts with members of the CPSA. Thereafter, he returned to Rhodesia where he continued his studies, picking up a second degree from the University of South Africa by correspondence. Then he moved to Northern Rhodesia (Zambia), where he taught at a teacher training college in Lusaka (acquiring yet another degree, this time from the University of London). From 1958–60, he taught in Ghana just after it had achieved its independence. He then returned to Rhodesia in 1960 and threw himself into nationalist politics, swiftly becoming the NDP's publicity secretary before joining with Sithole in forming ZANU. When he was jailed by Smith in 1964, he used the long years that followed to acquire no less than a further three degrees.[19] Meanwhile, he was deeply affected by the death from malaria of his only child in 1966. The refusal of Prime Minister Ian Smith to allow him to attend the funeral is judged by historian Alex Callinicos as having consolidated 'the radical nationalism' which he came to embody after his release in 1974.[20]

Nkomo responded to the launch of ZANU with the formation of the People's Caretaker Council (PCC) as a front for ZAPU. The split 'was over methods, rather than objectives and reflected the greater militancy of the ZANU leaders', for both were strongly committed to the creation of an independent Zimbabwe, both subordinated class to nationalist struggle, and both drew their leadership from a black petite bourgeoisie of teachers and small businessmen, although the labour movement provided ZAPU in particular with a number of its leading figures and a significant urban base amongst workers.[21] However, from the beginning, particular intellectuals such as Sithole, Mugabe, and Herbert Chitepo were to be predominant within ZANU.

A disastrous interlude followed the split as supporters of the rival organizations clashed violently. Undoubtedly, the conflicts embodied a significant ethnic dimension, underpinned by complicated historical suspicions between Shona and Ndebele which were never subsequently absent from relations between ZANU and ZAPU, and later, between ZANU-PF and the MDC.

The response of the government, now led by Ian Smith, was to ban both the PCC and ZANU in August 1964. Nkomo, Sithole, Mugabe, and numerous of their supporters now began more than a decade in detention, leaving behind them those they had sent outside the country to launch the armed struggle, declaring it an 'inevitable development'.[22] Inside the country, despite ZAPU's

---

[19] Martin Meredith (2002), *Robert Mugabe: Power, Plunder and Tyranny in Zimbabwe*, Johannesburg and Cape Town: Jonathan Ball Publishers, 19–24.

[20] Alex Callinicos (1981), *Southern Africa after Zimbabwe*, London: Pluto Press, 32.

[21] Ibid., 28.

[22] ZANU (1973), 'Zimbabwe: From confrontation to armed liberation struggle', in Olav Stokke and Carl Widstrand (eds), *Southern Africa: The UN-OAU Conference, Oslo, 9–14 April 1973, Papers and Documents*, Uppsala: Scandinavian Institute of African Studies.

hopes to the contrary, Africans failed to greet Smith's proclamation of UDI in November 1965 with violence. Meanwhile, attempts by independent African states were made to get ZANU and ZAPU to re-unite. When these failed, the OAU reluctantly resolved to recognize both as liberation movements. An enduring era of rivalry had begun.[23]

The origins of Namibian nationalism and the launch of SWAPO

Opposition to South African rule after 1945 was initially led by Chief Kutako and the Herero Chiefs' Council, a small group of nationalists active in student bodies and in the South West African Progressive Association (SWAPA). During the years since South Africa had administered the mandate, 'the flame of resistance had been kept alive by the tribal chiefs and their councils', pressing land claims and pointing to long-violated treaties made with Europeans. But nothing was achieved, save the chiefs' talking had 'kept alive their peoples' feelings of the injustice done to them'.[24] But matters had begun to change with the formation of the UN in 1948 and its assumption that South West Africa had automatically become a trust territory under its Charter. Accordingly, when in 1950 the South African government announced that it was choosing to ignore the decision of the International Court of Justice that South West Africa was indeed a territory held under international mandate, various Africans managed to testify to the UN's Fourth Committee, joining in with the lobbying already being made on behalf of Namibians by the Reverend Michael Scott, a turbulent Anglican priest who worked hard to remain a constant thorn in Pretoria's side. In 1957, Jariretundu Kozonguizi was sent by the Herero Chiefs' Council to speak before the UN, which was now in regular receipt of petitions from the people of South West Africa.

The educational situation for blacks in South West Africa was dismal, and it was only in 1948 that the first black student finished secondary school and matriculation.[25] However, a few Namibians had been able to attend schools in South Africa, and a select number of those, like Kozonguizi, gained entry to Fort Hare, where they were able to mix with politically active South Africans, and were to be caught up in the upsurge of the Youth League which revitalized the ANC. Upon returning to South West Africa, they established educational and cultural associations which had goals such as improving educational facilities for blacks, reforming the apartheid curriculum, and establishing independent schools. By the mid-1950s, these had crystallized in SWAPA, reconstituted from a South West African Student Body formed in South Africa in 1952. SWAPA hoped to seek the formation of a truly national body out of a congerie of existing political groupings, all of which were tribally based.

After various abortive attempts at unity,[26] SWAPA came together with these groups (except for one representative of Coloureds, which was under the

---

[23] Gibson, op. cit., 160–64; Martin and Johnson, op. cit., 63–73.
[24] Gibson, op. cit., 119.
[25] Donald Sparks and December Green (1992), *Namibia: The Nation after Independence*, Boulder CO: Westview Press, 24.
[26] Notable in this respect was the formation of the National Unity Democratic Organization, which failed because it was an extension of the Herero Chiefs' Council.

complete control of the South African government) to form the South West Africa National Union (SWANU). However, whereas the Chiefs' Council aimed to graft a mass movement onto its own system of authority, SWAPA aimed for a new movement transcending traditional loyalties. Friction developed between the two currents, as while the SWANU president, Jariretundu Kozonguizi, sought to distance the organization from tribal politics, the Council felt threatened by the younger, intellectually inclined and more assertive nationalist leaders. Tensions culminated in the withdrawal of Kutako's councillors from SWANU's executive in April 1960.

Contemporary with these developments, a group of some 200 Namibian migrant workers based in Cape Town, many active within the ANC and South African unions, had formed the Ovamboland People's Congress (OPC), whose aim was to improve the conditions of contract workers from Ovamboland. Out of this grew the Ovamboland People's Organisation (OPO) formed in Windhoek in April 1959 under the leadership of Sam Nujoma, who had been fired from the railways for seeking to form a union. Its organizational difficulties were immense. Strikes by the (South African) African Food and Canning Workers' Union in the early 1950s had met with violent repression, and only occasional strikes happened thereafter. Trade union leaders met with constant harassment, and many were imprisoned. Toivo ya Toivo was dispatched to Robben Island for nearly thirty years. Nonetheless, the OPO had persevered, and it succeeded where other ventures failed because, while it primarily focused upon the welfare of workers from Ovambo, it included amongst its aims commitments to wider change and political independence. This was to prove crucial in its transformation into a party drawing on a multi-ethnic membership.[27]

The three currents of resistance represented by the Chiefs' Council, SWANU and the OPO built upon a movement of wider protest which during the early 1950s had launched a defiance campaign in tandem with equal action in South Africa. But what brought matters to a head was a campaign of resistance to forced removals from the Old Location outside Windhoek. The South African administration planned to relocate the residents of the Location in a new settlement called Katatura ('the place where no one lives') more distant from Windhoek, imposing severe financial burdens upon residents in the form of increased travel and rent costs, as well as separating them into ethnic groups. Faced by resistance, the police responded with violence: on 10 December 1959, they killed eleven people and injured many more. Anticipating Sharpeville, the Windhoek Shootings were to earn widespread international condemnation, embarking South Africa on the road to international ignominy and isolation.

After the Shootings, Nujoma had been deported from Windhoek to Ovamboland, from where he left for exile. In Monrovia, Liberia, he met with Kozonguizi, where they signed a letter calling for the merger of their two organizations at home. Nothing came of this, and the two organizations continued on their separate courses, sometimes friendly and cooperative, but increasingly divided by ideological and tribal conflicts (many SWANU leaders being Herero, although wanting to rise above ethnicity and to form a national organization

---

[27] Gibson, op. cit., 130–34; Peter Katjavivi (1988), *A History of Resistance in Namibia*, London: James Currey, 17–23.

with a broad base of support). Both groups continued to operate in quasi-legality at home, as well as establishing rudimentary organizations in exile.[28]

In September 1959, Nujoma and other OPO members had participated in SWANU's conference, and he and Louis Nelengani had been elected to its national executive, with the hope that it would become a united nationalist party. However, continuing divisions made unity difficult. Then, in June 1960, the OPO transformed itself into a broader movement, reconstituting itself as SWAPO with Nujoma at its head. Significantly, the formation of SWAPO had the blessing of the Herero Chiefs' Council which feared that the radical young men in SWANU were opposed to the principle of chieftaincy. Meanwhile, although SWAPO sought to incorporate all tribal groups, it retained its strong ethnic base in Ovamboland, a factor which was to prove vital when the movement in exile decided to launch armed struggle.[29]

Initially, both SWANU and SWAPO were recognized by the OAU. However, outside South West Africa, SWANU had become increasingly identified with the personality of Kozonguizi, who aroused conservative anxieties by building close ties with China and becoming a member of the militant Afro-Asian Peoples' Solidarity Organisation. Yet what proved most damaging was Kozonguizi's negative assessment of the prospects for armed struggle and his vocal criticism of those liberation movements which espoused it. Thus when the OAU had been founded, SWANU welcomed its creation, but declined to create a military force under the sponsorship of its liberation committee. SWAPO had no such inhibitions, and by mid-1965 had emerged as the only nationalist organization the OAU would support. SWANU remained active internationally, but was to become increasingly divided by the ramifications of the Soviet-Chinese conflict. Indeed, whereas the Congress Alliance in South Africa had originally pinned its hopes on SWANU, its alignment with the Chinese was to alarm the staunchly pro-Soviet SACP and to provide the basis for alliance between the ANC and SWAPO (despite the latter having considerable sympathy for the Africanist position of the PAC). SWANU's fate was now to decline into international irrelevance. Meanwhile, SWAPO's readiness to commit itself to armed struggle was matched by the importance it gave to representation in Dar es Salaam and other African centres by full-time activists.[30]

In 1959, African foreign ministers had referred the legal status of South West Africa to the International Court of Justice (ICJ) in The Hague. The case was put by Ethiopia and Liberia as founding members of the League of Nations. However, reflective of the vacillation of the UN around the issue of South Africa at this time, in July 1966 the ICJ handed down a judgement which refused to address the substance of the case, declaring that Ethiopia and Liberia had no special right to bring it. South Africa was triumphant, but in October 1966, African states secured a vote in the General Assembly which terminated the mandate, declared South African occupation illegal, and established a UN Council for South West Africa to administer the territory until independence. For SWAPO, this provided the international legitimation it needed for its turn to

---

[28] Gibson, op. cit., 122.
[29] Ibid., 132.
[30] Ibid., 134. Gibson discusses how Kozonguizi's pro-Chinese position led to divisions within SWANU, eventually leading to his resignation. However, Nujoma remained on friendly terms with him, and even offered him a position with SWAPO, an offer which Kozonguizi declined.

41

armed struggle.[31] To avoid weakening its international position, the administration left SWAPO unbanned, although hemming it in with oppressive restrictions which helped swing the balance of authority within the organization towards the leadership in exile.

The stamp of history

Settler colonialism imposed similar patterns of white domination on South Africa, Namibia, and Zimbabwe, yet did so in a manner that was highly asymmetrical. Unsurprisingly, it evoked nationalist responses which, whilst feeding into each other, were also uneven and differed in form.

The formation of the ANC in South Africa was a deliberate effort by the early African elite and chiefs to construct an African nation across the boundaries of ethnicity. Nonetheless, up to the 1950s, the ANC was scarcely a national movement. It was dominated by an African elite deeply concerned to maintain respectability; it was largely cut off from the urban masses; and its tenuous links to the rural population in the reserves were filtered through the chiefs. Even so, it displayed staying power, and for all its limitations, it established itself as the premier vehicle for the voicing of African political aspirations.

After the Second World War, the ANC was to be transformed by an internal upheaval generated by the growth of towns and the development of industry which, on the back of heightened levels of working class protest and organization, allowed an urban-based and impatient younger generation to steer it towards mass action. This generation was led by key individuals who had come to political activism through education at mission schools and universities, where they had absorbed heady notions of democracy and African freedom. Vitally, although there were always those within the organization who were wary of, if not opposed to, joint actions with – variously, whites, Indians, Coloureds, and Communists – the ANC forged a tradition which was self-consciously inclusive of other groupings, including trade unions, and individuals committed to the struggle against apartheid. Of course, it proved unable to contain all internal differences – its failure to prevent the split with the Africanists who formed the PAC being the most obvious example. Indeed, even after the breach, there was always a strong Africanist current within the ANC which was deeply suspicious of influences it construed as subversive of African leadership. Nonetheless, while always taxed by the issue of how to work with bodies representative of other races, the ANC proved able to project itself as the principal vehicle of a multi-class, multi-racial alliance, and worked its way towards an imagination of nation which envisaged citizenship for all those who lived in South Africa. In so doing, it offered the prospect that if a democratic society could be established, the distinction between 'settlers' and 'indigenes' could be overcome.

Developments in South Africa were always to have a profound effect upon neighbouring territories, yet the interactions which took place between the ANC and the nationalist movements in Zimbabwe and Namibia were overwhelmingly those of the personal experiences of migrants or activists rather than

---

[31] Katjavivi, op. cit., 41–58.

direct organizational linkages. While the project of overthrowing white minority rule was shared, ZANU and SWAPO were less subject to the variety of impulses to which the ANC had continuously to respond. The ANC emerged from struggles within a far more advanced, more complicated, more urbanized, and more diverse society, and its predisposition to embrace difference was a vital outcome. In contrast, while the nationalist elites who formed the core of the liberation movement in Zimbabwe found a significant early base amongst the emergent working class in the major towns, ZANU in particular came to emit a deep suspicion of trade unions and was to root itself more self-consciously amongst the rural population. Further, neither ZAPU nor ZANU proved able to surmount the challenges posed by rivalries which were to revolve as much around ethnic fears and cabals as strategy, and which eventually were to lead to bitter hostility between them. In Namibia, SWAPO was launched to overcome the limitations of ethnicity, but never lost its Ovambo centre of gravity. While heavily based upon the representation of migrant worker grievances, SWAPO's breach with SWANU was to cut it off from nascent traditions of intellectualized militant radicalism. Although the struggles for liberation were closely linked, it was always likely that they would have outcomes which would be as marked by their differences as their similarities.

3.
The War for Southern Africa

The intransigence of the settler states propelled the liberation movements in Zimbabwe, Namibia, and South Africa into following a revolutionary path. However, armed struggle dictated a tortuous and long-term route, demanding not only the political and military training of guerrilla armies and the securing of military and logistical support from international allies, but also massively intensifying foreign involvement throughout the region. On the one hand, the liberation movements were required to balance the need for engagement with relevant Western powers against ideological and military support from the Soviet Union and China; on the other, as the settler regimes were forced to confront the rising costs of containing popular power and armed struggle. Britain and the US came to reassess their regional interests, ultimately leading them to force through an accommodation between settlers and nationalists constructed around the twin objectives of containing communism and maintaining a capitalist economy.

The struggle for Zimbabwe

Britain proceeded with the dismantling of the Central African Federation and the granting of independence to its non-settler colonies from the 1960s. But more threatening to settler states was the spread of insurgency. Earliest developments occurred in Angola and Mozambique, forcing Portugal to respond with extensive counter-insurgency, while opening its territories to increased international investment to build up the Western stake in its victory. Ironically, this strengthened those in Portugal who were seeking to re-orient Portuguese capitalism towards the European Economic Community, while as the costs of occupation rose higher, the Portuguese monopolies became less committed to Africa. Ultimately, Portuguese fascism proved unable to hold the line, and in 1974 the Armed Forces Movement, itself sympathetic to the liberation movements, seized power. Mozambique was granted independence under FRELIMO in 1975, although in Angola, the West was determined to prevent the Marxist MPLA acceding to power, and lent support to the Angolan National Liberation Front (FNLA) and UNITA, which also drew support from South Africa and US, both of which were eager to cut off support to SWAPO armed bases in Angola. The MPLA, which proclaimed independence in 1975, was saved; first, by the decision of the US at this point against becoming more embroiled in the Angolan war; and second, by the intervention of Cuban troops, which drove the Angolan forces of FNLA/UNITA beyond the borders, South Africa having previously withdrawn its troops.

Although Britain was broadly disposed to finding accommodation with anti-communist African nationalism, it was simultaneously deeply embedded in the economics of settler power and had no appetite for military involvement. All calls for Britain to end the white rebellion in Rhodesia were brusquely dismissed in London, where strategic doubts about the viability of armed intervention were supplemented by warnings that South Africa would fight, and references to the morality of seeking a non-violent solution.[1] Successive negotiations between the British and the Smith regime did nothing to shift the latter's resolve, and an Anglo-Rhodesian agreement reached between them in 1969 guaranteed the continuation of white rule with only very slow concessions to majority rule. When tested by the Pearce Commission, set up in 1972 to assess their acceptability within Rhodesia, they were soundly rejected by the African population, significantly mobilized by the African National Council which was led by Abel Muzorewa, a Bishop of the United Methodist Church and the Reverend Canaan Banana, but dominated by ZAPU and ZANU veterans. By this time, the liberation war was beginning to make an impact.

Guerrilla raids had been made by both ZAPU and ZANU from Zambia across the Zambezi River in 1966, but the Rhodesian regime had initially proved capable of holding that front. A joint raid made in 1967 by guerrillas from ZAPU and the ANC announced an alliance between their two movements, but provided an excuse for Pretoria to trumpet the dispatch of South African military assistance to Rhodesia (although South African forces had actually been in the country before the attack). When the guerrilla foray ended in disaster in the Wankie Game Reserve, it was nonetheless pronounced a symbolic triumph by ZAPU and the ANC. However, it occasioned considerable dissent within both organizations and elicited strong criticism from ZANU and the PAC, which argued that it illustrated a lack of preparation for the successful waging of guerrilla warfare. Guerrilla infiltrations continued across the Zambezi from Zambia, yet 'not a single white person died as a result of guerrilla action' between 1967 and 1972.[2]

The situation changed from 1968 when FRELIMO moved into Tete province in Mozambique and provided a base for ZANU to launch armed struggle amongst peasants in eastern Zimbabwe in earnest. ZANU's Zimbabwe National Liberation Army (ZANLA) established a presence among peasants and engaged in guerrilla operations in the northern districts of the country, attacking a white farm in the north-eastern Centenary district on 21 December 1972. Meanwhile, ZAPU's Zimbabwe People's Revolutionary Army (ZIPRA), was regrouping in Zambia after a political split within ZAPU in March 1971 when frustrated guerrillas had sought to overthrow incumbent leaders. For a period, this split had given life to a new grouping, the Front for the Liberation of Zimbabwe (FROLIZI) which, formed under Zambian pressure, was announced as uniting the two liberation movements. It proved to have a short life when it failed to do so.[3]

---

[1]   George Thomson, the Labour Minister responsible for the Rhodesian question, in a meeting with ZANU in November 1968. Cited by Richard Gibson (1972), *African Liberation Movements: Contemporary Struggles against White Minority Rule*, London: Oxford University Press, 180.

[2]   David Caute (1983), *Under the Skin: The Death of White Rhodesia*, Evanston, IL: Northwestern University Press; London, Allen Lane, 40.

[3]   Joseph Mtisi, Munyaradzi Nyakudye and Teresa Barnes (2009), 'War in Rhodesia, 1965–1980', in Brian Raftopoulos and Alois Mlambo (eds), *Becoming Zimbabwe: A History from the Pre-Colonial Period to 2008*, Harare: Weaver Press, 141–66.

The Portuguese collapse fundamentally shifted regional dynamics, as Pretoria was now faced by hostile regimes in Angola and Mozambique which had close relations with the Soviet Union and Cuba. It also meant that the Rhodesian regime lost an ally, and had to confront the long border with Mozambique which was now opened up to guerrilla incursions. It also meant the redirection of Rhodesian trade through South Africa, increasing costs and congestion on the railways and at the ports, as well as making Smith increasingly dependent upon the will of the South African Prime Minister, B.J. Vorster. Ultimately, independence for Angola and Mozambique forced South Africa to reassess its priorities, Vorster coming to the conclusion that an early settlement of the Rhodesian imbroglio was vital for the survival of apartheid. Hence he now sought to establish better relations with black-ruled southern African states, finding a willing partner in President Kenneth Kaunda of Zambia, who was similarly disposed to see an end to the crisis in response to his own country's pressing domestic problems. Thus followed the 'détente' period, beginning in late 1974, that saw protracted efforts by Kaunda and Vorster to negotiate a solution between Smith and his African opponents.[4] Fundamentally, their agreement centred around Pretoria's determination to push Smith into a constitutional conference under British chairmanship in exchange for concession by the leaders of the Front Line States (FLS) that their territories would not be used as bases for insurgency against South Africa.

The situation was rendered more difficult by continuing divisions within and between the nationalist groupings. Divisions were founded upon lines of ideological, personal, and not least, ethnic tensions. ZAPU was severely weakened by infighting from 1970–71, and was shaken by assassinations of two major party figures, Jason Moyo in early 1977, and Alfred Mangena in mid-1978, very probably killed by party insiders. But the long-term implications of strife within ZANU were far more profound.

In November 1974, Ndabaningi Sithole was challenged by a group of detainees who appointed Mugabe as the new leader of ZANU. Ironically, in the spirit of détente, Pretoria now instructed Ian Smith to release some imprisoned nationalist leaders, including Mugabe, who proceeded immediately to lead a delegation to Lusaka. There he was met with the refusal of leaders of the FLS to recognize the coup and their demand that Sithole be reinstated. However, the situation was then transformed by the assassination in a bomb blast on 18 March 1975 of Herbert Chitepo, national chairman and leader of ZANU's external supreme council.

The background to the assassination lay in the 1973 election to the ZANU executive in exile, Dare re Chimurenga (Dare), when older and more conservative leaders were replaced by younger radicals, notably Josiah Tongogora. The change reflected the rapid expansion of ZANLA, with large numbers of young men who had flocked to join the war wanting a leadership which was more responsive to them.[5] It was also widely claimed that there was something of a tribal element between Shona sub-groups, and at the time many in Zambia ascribed responsibility for Chitepo's death to a group of Karanga guerrilla commanders led by Tongagara, who were said to have resented the Manyika's

4   Ibid., 144–48.
5   Alex Callinicos (1981), *Southern Africa after Zimbabwe*, London: Pluto Press, 29–30.

alleged domination of the civilian leadership (although this has been strongly contested).[6] Whatever the cause, in November–December 1974, a group of guerrillas led by Thomas Nhari (possibly abetted by Rhodesian security forces) had hit back against the new high command, accusing Tongagara of indifference to the fate of those under him while living the high life in Lusaka.

To clear his name, Kaunda had established an international commission to investigate the death of Chitepo, who had accused him of undermining the liberation struggle. When the commission reported in March 1976, it claimed that the ZANU high command under Tongagara's chairmanship had authorized Chitepo's murder two days before he was killed. As a result, all members of the ZANU leadership in Zambia were detained and their guerrilla camps closed down, but Mugabe was quick enough to make his escape to Mozambique. Before fleeing, he accused Kaunda of complicity in Chitepo's murder because he was an obstacle to détente, a line subsequently maintained by ZANU-PF.[7] In turn, there were those who accused Mugabe of having orchestrated Chitepo's death. Whatever the truth of the matter, Mugabe benefited from the death of a powerful rival who had refused to accept his coup.[8]

Central to the task of propelling Smith into a settlement was a further attempt by the FLS to forge a united front between ZAPU, ZANU, FROLIZI, and Muzorewa's Council. However, this foundered on the refusal of ZANU and ZAPU to recognize Muzorewa, and by an associated struggle between Muzorewa and Nkomo for the leadership of any new umbrella organization. Subsequently, in November 1975, in face of threats by Zambia to expel guerrillas, a group of young, Marxist-inspired guerrillas from Tanzania formed the Zimbabwe People's Army (ZIPA). Its declared purpose was to unite ZANLA and ZIPRA. Apparently prompted by Tongogara and the ZANU executive which was still in detention in Zambia, ZIPA backed Mugabe as the leader of a united nationalist movement. Mozambican President Samora Machel, who had originally detained Mugabe when he arrived in Mozambique (on the grounds that leaders of an armed struggle should emerge from guerrilla ranks) then invited guerrilla leaders based in Mozambique to choose a new political head to balance ZAPU leadership within ZIPA. When they chose Mugabe, the FLS leaders conceded, agreeing in October 1976 to release ZANU executive members from detention in exchange for Mugabe joining Nkomo in a loose alliance (the Patriotic Front, PF) to negotiate with Smith at forthcoming conference in Geneva.[9]

For his part, Ian Smith remained obdurate, combining preparations for negotiations with promises to his electorate that he would make no concessions to terrorists. The most he would concede was 'responsible majority rule', by which he meant the slow integration of Africans into a white-dominated, multi-racial state. A lack of willingness to compromise on either side led to the failure of negotiations at Victoria Falls in August 1975. In any event the Rhodesian government had been pushed into them by the US and South Africa. Subsequently, aware of his narrowing options, Smith, with Kaunda's assistance,

---

6   For instance, by David Martin and Phyllis Johnson (1984), *The Struggle for Zimbabwe: The Chimurenga War*, London and Boston: Faber & Faber, 183–90.

7   Ibid. Tongagara always resolutely denied any responsibility for Chitepo's death.

8   Daniel Compagnon (2010), *A Predictable Tragedy: Robert Mugabe and the Collapse of Zimbabwe*, Philadelphia: University of Pennsylvania Press, 10–12.

9   Ibid., 12–14; Mtisi et al., op. cit., 146–49.

negotiated secretly with Nkomo in Lusaka, regarding him as both acceptably moderate and likely to be acceptable to majority African opinion. However, this initiative collapsed around their inability to agree when majority rule would be attained. Nonetheless, for the first time, Smith had conceded the principle of majority rule, a breakthrough which US Secretary of State Henry Kissinger seized upon in the lead-up to a further conference in Geneva in late 1976. But this too failed to make progress, as the four nationalist delegations led by Muzorewa, Mugabe, Nkomo, and Sithole (still at the head of a ZANU rump) were agreed on the necessity of transferring power to a black majority government, but on nothing else.

The struggle now entered its darkest hour. Mugabe returned to Mozambique from Geneva with enhanced authority. At a party congress in Chimoio, he was formally elected ZANU President. Then, in order to tighten his grip on ZANU, he persuaded Machel to neutralize Chinese-trained guerrillas led by Wilfred Mahanda, a former ZANLA commander and now highly placed in the ZIPA command. ZIPA had opposed the Geneva conference and had accused Mugabe of selling out to the imperialists. This was merely a prelude to the elimination of the ideologically oriented cadres who had spearheaded ZIPA and who were distrusted by the older, authoritarian leaderships of both ZANU and ZAPU. Thereafter several hundred guerrillas (some in Tanzania) were arrested or murdered. A group of cadres, including two party central committee members, were detained following criticism of Mugabe in the camps over the destruction of the main ZANU base in Chimoi by Rhodesian forces in November 1977. On both occasions, Tongogara and Rex Nhongo (Solomon Mujuru) used brutal force to establish Mugabe's supremacy.[10]

Meanwhile, in 1978, with the cost of war mounting on both sides in materials, morale and men, Smith opted for an internal settlement with the politically conservative United African National Congress (UANC) of Bishop Abel Muzorewa, allowing the latter to become Prime Minister of 'Rhodesia-Zimbabwe' in 1979 in a coalition government which included Sithole and a government stooge, Chief Chirau. But Muzorewa lacked any strategy for confronting settler power. Neither Muzorewa nor Sithole had armies (although they were soon to be equipped by Smith with militias), and the initiative passed completely to the liberation movements, notably ZANU. From 1978 the war entered its most intensive phase, with both ZANLA and ZIPRA now using increasingly sophisticated weapons and establishing their authority over extensive areas of the country where Rhodesian security forces only ever ventured during the day.[11] At the August 1979 Commonwealth Heads of Government meeting in Lusaka, Britain was put under enormous pressure to resolve the crisis.[12]

Thus it was that Smith and Muzorewa conceded to pressure from the US and the UK that they meet again with the liberation movements with a view to a

---

[10] Compagnon, op. cit., 12–14.

[11] In the former Portuguese territories, the limited settler presence had enabled the liberation movements to establish fully 'liberated areas'. In Zimbabwe, liberation forces had to work amongst peasant populations based in African reserves interspersed among white areas through which passed the major arteries of communication. Rhodesian security forces largely maintained control of these routes.

[12] Mtsi et al., op. cit., 164–66.

pre-independence election. South Africa, hoping for a Muzorewa victory, acquiesced and ZANU and ZAPU, under pressure from the FLS, agreed to enter negotiations as the PF. These culminated in the Lancaster House agreement which provided for progression to independence under majority rule, albeit with protections for the white minority embedded in the constitution for a period of ten years. In the ensuing election, the unrealistic hopes placed by whites in Muzorewa's UANC were dashed by ZANU-PF which, campaigning separately from ZAPU, secured a handsome victory.

SWAPO's war in Namibia

South Africa's initial backing of UDI was founded upon the perceived necessity of maintaining a *cordon sanitaire* of white-run regimes around apartheid's own borders, but within a few short years the regime was compelled to reassess. In South West Africa, where SWAPO maintained a perilous legal presence, the regime was faced by a wave of resistance, at the centre of which was the SWAPO Youth League. The latter confronted school authorities, mounted public rallies, and helped in organizing the general strike in 1971, as well as thereafter contributing to challenges to largely government-appointed chiefs in Ovamboland. In South Africa, a wave of strikes hit Durban from 1973 before spreading to other parts of the country and thereafter inspiring the growth of independent black trade unions. Further, after the collapse of Portuguese rule, Pretoria was faced by the enormous upheaval of the 1976 Soweto uprising, which internationally was taken as signalling the beginning of the end of its capacity to contain the drive to majority rule. In the wake of Zimbabwean independence, which brought the prospect of ANC guerrillas edging closer to South African borders, the long-term survival of apartheid was placed in constant doubt. The South African government responded by identifying its fight with a global struggle for Western values against an international communist onslaught.

By 1968, SWAPO's armed wing, the People's Liberation Army of Namibia (PLAN) had embarked upon an extensive guerrilla offensive. South West Africa offered a landscape which was overwhelmingly open, flat, and unsuitable for guerrilla warfare, and fighters were highly vulnerable to air raids. Yet PLAN could depend upon the support of the majority of the population, notably in Ovamboland and throughout the north, although it was soon operating in many other areas, aided by civilians who regularly moved weapons. But PLAN was small, and could only undertake sabotage on facilities such as electrical installations and police stations, with occasional small-scale clashes with security forces. However, SWAPO capacities were to be hugely improved by the opening up of the border with Angola as a result of the Portuguese coup, for this facilitated a mass exodus of young Namibians (perhaps as many as 10 per cent of the African population) who left the country to join SWAPO in exile during the 1970s. Many joined PLAN and were sent for training in Africa, China, Russia, and North Korea, others for training as medical personnel or teachers in refugee camps established in Angola and Zambia. By the late 1970s, SWAPO was far better prepared for carrying the war to the enemy. PLAN had acquired increasingly sophisticated weaponry, its fighters had moved boldly south (occasionally even to Windhoek and Swakopmund), and a dramatic escalation of the conflict occurred: from fewer than 500 clashes with security forces in 1978, the number increased to over 900 a year later. The South Africans received a further shock when one of their planes was shot down by anti-aircraft guns over Angola in 1980. The war continued at a similar pace throughout the following decade.[13]

Two complementary projects to contain 'communism' presented themselves to Pretoria. The first was to defeat the MPLA in Angola and install a friendly government as a buffer against the guerrillas, thereby denying SWAPO space to operate. The second was to outpace SWAPO by forging a neo-colonial accommodation with 'moderate' forces. However, as already noted, by 1978 the first option had been closed down with the US decision to withdraw from the Angolan imbroglio and the determined entry of Cuba. Although South Africa maintained a massive build-up of forces in South West Africa and continued to make aggressive raids into Angola, the buffer state strategy proved increasingly costly. Harsh security was imposed throughout the war zone (virtually the whole of the north of South West Africa), and as its war in Angola escalated (South African forces clashing with Cubans for the first time in 1975), Soviet military assistance to Angola increased. Meanwhile, South Africa's Angolan adventures ramped up international pressure (notably at the UN) to transfer power to Namibians. Thus South Africa was forced to rely on the second strategy via the Turnhalle talks of 1975 to which it invited representatives of all ethnic groups.

The Turnhalle Declaration stated that by end of 1978 South West Africa would move to independence as a single state with participation of all ethnic groups via a confederation of three tiers of government. In essence, this formula left the status quo unchanged, leaving an ethnic sub-states system in place. Even so, the proposals split the settler community: the South West African NP retained the majority of its supporters, but Pretoria backed a minority following the lead of Dirk Mudge into a new Republican Party.[14]

The Turnhalle constitutional talks were dissolved in 1977, following the initiative of five Western members of the Security Council (the Contact group) aimed at securing an internationally acceptable solution for Namibian independence. This involved free elections under UN supervision for the election of a Constituent Assembly (Resolution 435). South Africa accepted the proposal in early 1978. However it combined this acceptance with cracking down heavily on SWAPO internally and despatching the SADF (South African Defence Force) to raid SWAPO camps, notably Kassinga, in Angola. Even so, SWAPO accepted the proposals, and 20,000 SWAPO supporters met Martti Ahtisaari, the UN Special Representative for Namibia, when he arrived in Windhoek to make a preliminary assessment. His report provided for a UN peacekeeping force and transitional civilian team, with independence elections to be held seven months after UN acceptance of his proposals. However, progression to independence was then disrupted by two developments.

---

[13] Donald Sparks and December Green (1992), *Namibia: The Nation after Independence*, Boulder CO: Westview Press, 30–32.

[14] Reginald Green and Kimmo Kiljunen (1981), 'Unto what end? The crisis of colonialism in Namibia', in Reginald Green, Marija-Liisa Kiljunen and Kimmo Kiljunen, (eds), *Namibia: The Last Colony*, Essex: Longman, 1–22.

First, South Africa rejected the UN proposal, and declared it would unilaterally call an election without delay. General elections were held in December 1978, with the Democratic Turnhalle Alliance (DTA), a South African-backed coalition of ethnic parties led by the Republican Party, sweeping to victory. However, the contest had been boycotted by SWAPO and widely condemned by civil society, including the churches. SWAPO now intensified the armed struggle, South Africa responding with intensified military operations and political repression. Pretoria, however, played a double game by continuing to parlay with the Contact group while seeking to strengthen its hold domestically.

The second development was an effective reversal in strategy by the US with the 1980 election of the Reagan government. As expressed by Chester Crocker, Secretary of State, rather than the Soviet and Cuban presence in Angola being justified by South African aggression, the South African role was justified as shoring up anti-communist forces seeking to liberate their country from the imperialism of Moscow. Thus the West should back UNITA until such time as MPLA was prepared to negotiate and expel communist forces. In this context, Namibian independence was a minor issue, 'linked' to the Cuban withdrawal from Angola. In short, South Africa was not given merely more breathing space but incorporated into an aggressive US-driven, internationalized war in Angola. There, PLAN was now working ever more closely with FAPLA (the MPLA's armed wing)[15] and with the Cubans, both of which were backed by Soviet strategic and logistical support. The years of war which followed saw PLAN's campaigns in northern Namibia severely constrained by South African counter-insurgency, as southern Angola became the principal locus of fighting, and as guerrilla struggle transformed into conventional warfare and a proxy confrontation between the superpowers.[16]

A series of battles in 1987–88 culminated in a clash at the town of Cuito Cuanevale in March 1988, when a joint UNITA-South African attack was driven back by the MPLA backed by the Cubans. The South African commanders could have launched an attack on the town months earlier, but had been constrained by the South African government (which was by now under pressure to reach an accord with SWAPO linked to the gradual withdrawal of Cuban troops). Hence the MPLA was allowed to claim the outcome as a major victory, which in turn made it possible for the Cubans to persuade them to take part in negotiations with the US and South Africa. By this stage, South Africa was confronting a massive domestic upheaval, disinvestment and a downwardly spiralling economy as well as the huge costs of running what was being recognized as an unwinnable war. For its part, the Gorbachev regime in Moscow was presiding over the collapse of the Soviet system, while Cuba – with 50,000 troops in Angola – was bleeding men and money. Meanwhile, the US feared it was being drawn into a Vietnam-style confrontation alongside a government in South Africa whose international profile was increasingly indefensible. The outcome was an agreement drawn up in New York in July 1988 whereby Cuba and South Africa agreed to leave Angola and SWAPO and South

[15] Armed Forces for the Liberation of Angola.
[16] Two detailed and insightful analyses of the long struggle for Namibia are provided by Colin Leys and John Saul (eds), (1995), *Namibia's Liberation Struggle: The Two-Edged Sword*, London: James Currey, and Lauren Dobell (1998), *Swapo's Struggle for Namibia, 1960–1991: War by Other Means*, Basel: Basel Africa Bibliographien.

Africa agreed a ceasefire, clearing the way for the implementation of UN Resolution 435 providing for UN-supervised elections in Namibia. These duly took place in 1989, leading to a SWAPO victory and Namibia's subsequent independence.

War and stalemate in the battle for South Africa

South African aggression in Angola had been part of a wider counter-insurgency strategy to cope with a mounting popular resistance at home and increasing dangers from across the country's borders. 'Total strategy', justified as the regime's response to a 'total onslaught' by global communism, constituted a mix of repression and reform domestically combined with destabilization of regimes providing support for the armed struggle of the ANC and SACP.

The political quiescence which settled upon South Africa after the suppression of the ANC, PAC, and their allies was shattered by the revival of black trade unionism from the early 1970s and the Soweto revolt of 1976. Together, their intertwined effects were to provide a foundation for mass insurrection in the 1980s which not only placed the state on the defensive, but raised major questions about the capacity of white minority rule to survive.

Since the suppression of SACTU in the 1960s, African trade unionism had been effectively crippled, and by 1969 only a handful African unions remained as passive appendages of registered white trade unions. However, the coercive industrial peace was shattered by a massive, spontaneous strike wave in 1973, which began in Durban and spread to other industrial centres to involve some 98,000 black workers, before meeting with heavy state repression. Nonetheless, for all that the government continued to propagate the myth that African township dwellers were indissolubly linked to their rural homelands, and for all that the mining and agricultural sectors continued to depend heavily upon migrant labour, manufacturing, commerce, construction, and transport and so on increasingly drew their workforce from amongst an African population which was permanently urbanized and significantly composed of younger generations which were wholly urban bred and born. Further, employers found themselves facing a growing scarcity of white labour (which was upwardly mobile) and hence increasingly dependent upon African labour in skilled and semi-skilled as well as unskilled positions.

The shift away from primary towards secondary industrialization and associated changes in the composition of the workforce provided a fertile soil for the revival of black trade unionism, despite an endemically high rate of unemployment. Emerging in the wake of the Durban strike wave from diverse origins (notably worker educational organizations), black trade unions slowly but steadily established themselves, securing important concessions as the result of factory-based struggles. Soon the state became deeply concerned about the growth of an African trade union movement which, because of existent legislation, was forced to operate outside the formal industrial relations system. Consequently, in 1977, the government established a commission under Professor Nic Wiehahn to inquire how labour laws might be reformed to take account of the growing industrial muscle of African workers. When it reported, in 1979, it recommended the opening up of the hitherto racially exclusive industrial relations system to African trade unions, which at present had no legal status, by allowing them to become officially registered. Suffice it to say here that, for all that the Wiehahn reforms were widely perceived as an initiative for extending state control, it was also recognized within the emergent union movement that acquiring the rights that would be granted by registration offered major opportunities and legal protections. Whether to register or not triggered an acrimonious debate within the union movement, with those against registration arguing that to register would be tantamount to collaboration with the regime. However, the view in favour of registration prevailed, and from the early 1980s, Wiehahn provided the basis for a significant expansion of the emergent trade unions, from a claimed membership of around 120,000 in 1979 to around 450,000 in 1985. In turn, their growing strength propelled them towards greater unity which was significantly influenced by SACTU's tradition of political unionism. This was to culminate in the formation in 1985 of COSATU (the Congress of South African Trade Unions), which from the beginning established itself as South Africa's largest and most formidable union federation.

COSATU represented a confluence of 'workerist' and 'Charterist' strategic positions. The former, principally located in the hitherto largest independent trade union formation, the Federation of South African Trade Unions, emphasized working class struggle centred around shop-floor strength, worker democracy, and independence from political formations. The latter, principally located in various general unions (some of which had a significant base in peripheral industrial areas, such as East London), argued the indissoluble link between industrial struggle and that for political liberation. As the 1980s progressed, and as the struggle for liberation reached its zenith, COSATU was to find itself increasingly drawn into the orbit of the ANC, even while the tradition of internal democracy within the unions remained strong.

The trade union movement had developed on the basis of economic factors, including not merely the increasing significance of black workers in key industrial sectors but a declining growth rate, increased inflation, black impoverishment, and low wages. In contrast, the revolt of the youth which began in Soweto in June 1976 was stimulated by factors which were primarily social and political, not least of which was a growing contempt amongst the younger generation for what they regarded as the political acquiescence of their parents' generation in their own oppression. For many, the ANC and PAC were ancient history.

Youthful disaffection found its initial focus within the black student movement and the development of Black Consciousness (BC). The number of Africans at universities had quadrupled since the early 1960s, the large majority grouped in segregated black campuses. In the late 1960s, black student activists threw off the leadership of the white-dominated National Union of South African Students, and formed the South African Students' Organisation (SASO). From its foundation, SASO saw itself as an agent of 'conscientization', stressing the need for the mobilization of black resistance to white oppression. In this they demonstrated continuity with Africanism, yet differed significantly from the earlier streams of Africanism by their recognition that there were divisions amongst blacks (notably of class) and secondly, by their stress that blackness included Indians and Coloureds as well as Africans.

53

Lodge stresses that the growing influence of BC was located in a context of a changing social composition of the African population in the major urban centres. The corollary of the economy's expansion was the growth of an African clerical workforce, while the expansion of primary and secondary education, albeit under the auspices of the much-hated Bantu Education policy, had led to increasing literacy. Fed by the development of a mass tabloid press, this population was receptive to relatively complex political ideas. In particular, BC encouraged a growing political assertiveness amongst an urban black intelligentsia revolving around notions of black identity. BC, Lodge continues, reflected 'the coming of age, despite the institutions of apartheid, of a new African petty bourgeoisie'. However, against the background of both these developments, the spark for communal insurrection was provided by police over-reaction on 16 June 1976 to a street procession of secondary school students protesting against the recent insistence by educational authorities that arithmetic and social studies be taught in Afrikaans. A violent response by the police saw the students retreating, and carrying the flames of revolt across the entire township. The revolt spread rapidly across the Rand and other parts of the country, and over succeeding months, the students were to draw in worker and parental support. By the end of 1976, the only African communities to remain relatively unaffected were those in Natal, and the revolt had left in its wake at least 575 dead and 2,389 wounded.[17]

For the moment, the regime proved capable of containing the revolt. As Lodge notes, Soweto was neither an 'organised mass struggle' nor indicative of a widespread 'revolutionary consciousness'. At no stage was it conceivable that the revolt could lead to the overthrow of the regime. Nonetheless, 'the effects of the uprising were to stimulate a generalization of resistance movements among Africans in South Africa', evidenced by the spread of resistance across classes and local communities which, in 1983, was to culminate in the formation of the United Democratic Front (UDF).[18]

Total Strategy had sought to combine reform with repression, pursuing strategies of divide and rule. On the one hand, the regime implemented various proposals which, interlocking with the Wiehahn reforms, sought to privilege an urbanized African working class, separating it from migrants and the unemployed, while also favouring the development of an urban black middle class, which was envisaged as being drawn into *de facto* collaboration with the regime by the grant of increased authority to African municipalities. On the other, the government clamped down hard on organizations which evinced radical political aspirations whilst continuing to implement the Bantustan strategy under which African rights to participate in the central polity would be extinguished in favour of citizenships of 'independent' ethnic states. Yet by far the most comprehensive reform which the regime introduced was a new constitution of 1982, whereby 'white' rule was supposedly dissolved by the introduction of separate houses of parliament for Coloureds and Indians to complement the 'white' National Assembly. Needless to say, the reworking of political institutions, which also saw the introduction of an executive presidency, was struc-

---

[17] Tom Lodge (1983), *Black Politics in South Africa since 1945*, Johannesburg: Ravan Press, 328–30.
[18] Ibid., 336.

tured to guarantee ultimate white control whilst devolving various responsibilities for 'own affairs' to the Coloured and Indian communities. As such, the 'tricameral' constitution was vigorously rejected by progressive opinion across all racial groups, and provided the immediate stimulus for a campaign of rejection. Although the campaign to block the new constitution failed, its significant outcome was the establishment of the UDF, formed from a composite of popular organizations, largely urban based, but also reaching out to rural areas and, to some extent, the homelands. While largely led by middle-class elements, the UDF had strong roots in local communities, and within a short space of time was to be drawn into effective alliance with COSATU which provided it with major organizational weight which it would otherwise have lacked. Deeply informed by Charterist sentiments, the UDF swiftly became an effective surrogate for the ANC, whose influence increased rapidly in the wake of Soweto. As such, the UDF faced successive waves of repression, implemented under States of Emergency from June 1986, yet continued alongside COSATU to provide the major focus of internal opposition to apartheid.[19]

Meanwhile, newly independent Zimbabwe was the victim of major destabilization activity, as South Africa bombed ANC houses and ZANU headquarters in 1981, before disrupting rail, road, and oil-pipeline connections to the coast, and launching a hugely damaging raid upon the Zimbabwean Air Force base at Gwelo in 1982. South Africa may also have been involved in arms caching by ZAPU after independence, which in turn helped justify a ZANU military crackdown on Matabeleland, eventually forcing ZAPU to accede to a Unity Accord in which it merged itself into the ruling party in 1987. A year previously, South Africa had engineered a coup in Lesotho, replacing the pro-ANC Jonathan government with a military proxy, after years of support for an opposition Lesotho Liberation Army and damaging raids upon ANC quarters in Maseru in 1982 and 1985.

Following Zimbabwean independence, South Africa had taken up support of RENAMO (Mozambique National Resistance), a counterforce to FRELIMO originally created by the Rhodesians which had wreaked havoc throughout the central areas of Mozambique, destroying roads, schools, hospitals, and other infrastructure, while leaving a trail of indiscriminate killing. Eventually, Mozambique was bludgeoned into signing the Nkomati Accord in March 1984 which bound FRELIMO to stop helping the ANC in exchange for South Africa withdrawing support to RENAMO. The upshot was MK being forced to leave Mozambique, with the ANC being allowed to retain only a diplomatic presence in Maputo. However, intelligence and military factions within the apartheid regime continued to actively support RENAMO. Then, in October 1986, President Samora Machel was killed in an air crash. It remains unclear whether elements within the South African military were responsible, yet the crash took place at a moment when RENAMO was making its strongest-ever push to set up a corridor of occupied territory from Malawi to the coast. Yet whatever the cause, the crash drew Pretoria's enemies together, leading to the dispatch of Zimbabwean, Malawian, and Tanzanian troops to Mozambique, both to stem the rot in Mozambique and to protect their own interests.

[19] Jeremy Seekings (2001), *The UDF: A History of the United Democratic Front in South Africa 1983–1991*, Claremont: David Philip.

South African support for RENAMO had been designed in part to place pressure upon Zambia, and more particularly, Zimbabwe, from where the ANC was able to infiltrate its cadres across the border. ANC operations had been constrained by historically poor relations with ZANU consequent upon its closeness to ZAPU. However, ZAPU's enforced merger into ZANU-PF in late 1987 provided for improved relations with the ANC. This was to prove a boon, for the agreement which had been negotiated to secure independence for Namibia had, ironically, constituted a major setback for the ANC, for as part of the New York settlement, it had been forced to close down all its Angolan bases and to move out of the country where it had concentrated most of its forces from the late 1970s. By this time, the ANC had as many as 10,000 cadres located in its Angolan camps, trained and ready to fight, yet with little opportunity to engage the South African army. Immense frustrations within the camps were to be compounded by MK's being drawn into the struggle for Angola, thrown into the fray against UNITA as the enemy of the MPLA and SWAPO. Worse was to follow when, from November 1988, in accordance with the agreement providing for the withdrawal of Cuban and South African troops from Angola to facilitate implementation of Resolution 435, the ANC was forced to move its guerrillas in Angola to camps in Zambia, Tanzania, and Uganda. Many of these guerrillas were part of the Soweto generation which had left South Africa to wage armed struggle, but now they were further away from South Africa than ever.[20]

Despite South Africa's relative success, a government now increasingly subordinated to security imperatives was beginning to unravel. While the ANC military threat could be contained, there was a need for a political solution if long-term stability was to be achieved. Despite severe differences between the security establishment and NP politicians, it now seemed increasingly likely that the government was going to have to negotiate seriously with representatives of its black majority. The international situation was critical. The Cuban withdrawal from Angola signified that the communist threat could no longer be justified to maintain aggressive military action, while the Soviet Union's escalating internal difficulties led to the rapid withdrawal of its support for armed struggle. Western backers, weary of an unpopular ally in Pretoria, declined accordingly. The apartheid regime not only found itself locked into an apparently unwinnable confrontation, but was itself draining support from within the white community, as large-scale investors increasingly urged a deal with the ANC. The culmination was the surprise announcement on 2 February 1990 by President de Klerk of the unbanning of the ANC and the SACP, and the launch of the era of negotiations.

The politics of exile

To rehearse the pre-independence histories of the NLMs is to point to legacies which bear on the present. War is violent, and the use of violence in politics

---

[20]   See, *inter alia*, Steven Ellis and Tsepo Sechaba (1992), *Comrades against Apartheid: The ANC and the South African Communist Party in Exile*, London: James Currey; Joseph Hanlon (1986), *Beggar Your Neighbours: Apartheid Power in Southern Africa*, London: James Currey.

comes at the expense of the gentler virtues which make for a good society. So the decision of the liberation movements to take up armed struggle, even though morally just, was one which was likely to have some undesirable consequences. Here it is apposite to highlight two aspects.

First, armed struggle reinforced hierarchy within the NLMs at the expense of internal democracy. This was a reversal of what was meant to happen according to influential theories of guerrilla warfare in which political mobilization is given priority over military strategy, guerrilla armies inspiring a following amongst oppressed populations by virtue of their democratic practices. Yet such theories, often bowdlerized amongst the solidarity groupings, tended to give rise to suggestions that the NLMs were more democratic than the predecessor nationalist movements which had taken power in Africa. However, as observed by Reinhardt Kossler, with the benefit of hindsight, armed struggle loses much of the appeal of the 'salubrious radicalism or Fanon-style overcoming of internalized violence'. Instead, the militarization of anti-colonial nationalism may be a reason for the closing down of political alternatives and for the establishment of political monopolies by exiled leaderships.[21] Nonetheless, it may well be that we may find clues to different styles and content of post-liberation politics in Zimbabwe, Namibia, and South Africa in the somewhat different modes of their struggles for liberation.

It has already been shown how Mugabe and those who backed him dealt ruthlessly with ZANU internal opponents. Going beyond such observations, Norma Kriger has argued persuasively that ZANU's mobilization efforts in the countryside relied far more on coercion than they did on eliciting peasant support.[22] She advances her argument in explicit debate with Terence Ranger, whose work proposes that peasant radical nationalist consciousness, fused with Shona cultural beliefs, 'was highly conducive to mobilization for guerrilla war', and allowed for a 'direct input by the peasantry into the ideology and programme of the war'.[23] Thus spirit mediums, who served as a bridge between the present generation and their ancestors, promoted the guerrillas, while for their part, the guerrillas stressed the continuities between their struggle and the First Chimurenga of 1896–97. In turn, while guerrillas would seek to politicize the peasants, the latter offered their support in expectation that a ZANU government would return settler-expropriated lands and no longer interfere in peasant production, contenting itself with 'ensuring high prices, good marketing facilities, supplies of cheap fertilizer and so on'.[24] Thus at its highest stage, a 'fusion of Shona cultural nationalism and peasant radicalism proved potent enough to allow the spread of ZANLA's guerrilla action'.[25] In contrast, while Kriger allows that guerrilla mobilization *was* effective and produced ZANU-PF support committees that were responsible for providing logistical support for the guerrillas (food, clothing, money and information), their 'mobilisation was achieved

---

[21] Reinhardt Kossler (2010), 'Images of history and the nation: Namibia and Zimbabwe compared', *South African Historical Journal*, 62: 1, 38.

[22] Norma Kriger (1992), *Zimbabwe's Guerrilla War: Peasant Voices*, Cambridge: Cambridge University Press.

[23] Terence Ranger (1985), *Peasant Consciousness and Guerrilla War in Zimbabwe: A Comparative Study*, London: James Currey, 14.

[24] Ibid., 180.

[25] Ibid., 137.

through guerrilla coercion rather than guerrilla ideology'.[26] Thus, if people chose not to elect support committees, guerrillas would appoint them, and those that resisted would pay the penalty of those identified as not supporting the war. Similarly, Alex Callinicos tells of attending a ZANLA meeting in the TTLs where the ZANU activists gave out a radical message, a choice between imperialism (Smith and Muzorewa) or socialism (ZANU-PF). However, the role of the peasants was clearly meant to be a passive one, that of giving material and moral support to the party.[27] To be fair, a recent, informed review of the war by Paul Moorcroft claims that the record of ZANLA guerrillas was much more mixed, that the manner in which they mobilized and maintained support was a model of the people's war, and that generally the population in the TTLs was largely sympathetic to them.[28] Nonetheless, he admits that 'selective terrorism' was used by the guerrillas, for their methodology was to be ruthlessly re-applied against Mugabe's opponents after independence. Lloyd Sachikonye concurs, arguing that ZANU-PF's entrenchment of a 'pervasive culture' of violence during the war was to find expression in the systematized deployment of state-organized violence against opponents after 1980.[29]

The SWAPO leadership was no less ruthless in cracking down heavily on three rounds of dissent within its exiled ranks. On the first occasion, in 1968, a group of returnees from training in China who were located at SWAPO's Kongwa camp in central Tanzania had protested about a perceived lack of understanding of military strategy amongst the leadership, which they also accused of corruption. They were handed over to the Tanzanian army and thrown into jail. Subsequently, in 1976, the leadership reacted sharply to a challenge to its authority posed by dissidents, who had flocked to join SWAPO, following the inflow of young people on the opening up of the border with Angola. This involved complaints made by soldiers in PLAN, including some commanders, about abuses of authority, and demands for accountability made by a group of new cadres, many of whom had been active in the SWAPO Youth League during the early 1970s, in a wave of internal resistance. The latter group spearheaded a call for a democratic congress which was forcefully taken up by the soldiers. However, rather than responding positively, the leadership invoked Zambian assistance to round up the dissidents. Key leaders were shipped off to Tanzania where they were kept in detention until 1978, while the majority (about 1,600) were illegally detained in Zambia.[30] Finally, the military reverses which occurred following the massive South African counter-insurgency operation in Angola in the early 1980s led not only to declining morale, but also to widespread doubts

[26] Norma Kriger (1988), 'The Zimbabwean war of liberation: Struggles within the struggle', *Journal of Southern African Studies*, 14: 2, 312.
[27] Callinicos, op. cit., 38.
[28] Paul Moorcroft (2012), *Mugabe's War Machine*, Johannesburg and Cape Town: Jonathan Ball Publishers, 71–82.
[29] Lloyd Sachikonye (2011), *When a State Turns on its Citizens: Institutionalised Violence and Political Culture*, Johannesburg: Jacana Media.
[30] It was one of the contradictions of 'socialism' in Tanzania that the country did not have a law allowing for habeas corpus, which enabled President Nyerere to oblige liberation movements by detaining their internal dissidents quite legally. There was such a law in Zambia, but its provisions – as in this case – were not always applied. In this case, the fate of the detainees (at a camp in Mboroma) was unknown to the world until 1977, at which point the Zambian authorities felt constrained to secure their release.

about the competence of the military command, as well as to rivalries between generational and ethnic groups. It is reported that the response by the leadership was the institutionalization of a 'system of organized terror', with almost a thousand South Africans, alleged to be spies within the organization, being subjected to beatings and torture in detention centres in Lubango until they 'confessed'.[31] Henning Melber is by no means alone in relating SWAPO's history of intolerance during the war to the evolution of its post-liberation culture which, while formally democratic, is deeply authoritarian.[32]

The ANC likewise went through its own convulsions. As early as 1968, when five dissidents fled camps in Tanzania for Nairobi, there were indications that there was widespread dissatisfaction within MK. By the mid-1970s, complaints were rife about authoritarian, corrupt and politically unaccountable leadership. Then, following earlier rumblings, in early 1984, a crisis erupted at Kagandale, some 80 kilometres south of MK's major training camp at Caculama. MK combatants refused orders to join counter-insurgency operations against UNITA. The soldiers' demands were for an immediate end to the war against UNITA and the transfer of men to the main theatre of war in South Africa (where the government was by now confronting major popular uprisings); an immediate suspension of the ANC security apparatus; and an investigation of events at the movement's Quatro prison camp where alleged spies within MK had been tortured and some executed. Informed that they would meet with the ANC leadership, the dissidents agreed to move to Viana, an ANC transit camp outside Luanda, where they declined to lay down their arms and instead disarmed the ANC's security personnel. Joined by members from other ANC bodies in and around Luanda, the dissidents elected a Committee of Ten to represent them. They then repeated their calls for the suspension of the security apparatus and for an investigation of Quatro, alongside a call for the convening of a fully representative conference to review the course of the struggle and to elect a new NEC (National Executive Council). They also received support from MK cadres and officers who had remained at Caculama. At this point, according to one account by former dissidents, the mutiny acquired a 90 per cent majority among the whole trained forces of MK in Angola, which was then the only country where the ANC still had guerrilla camps.

These demands proved totally unacceptable to the leadership, which proceeded to quell the rebellion with the assistance of the Angolan army. Negotiations led to the rebels laying down their arms on the promise of the appointment of an investigatory commission, to be headed by James Stuart (nom de guerre for Hermanus Loots, a veteran trade unionist). However, a group of about thirty rebels were arrested and transferred to two camps north of Luanda, Qibaxe and Pango, where they were imprisoned. After making submissions to the Stuart Commission, they were subjected to brutal interrogations by ANC security and some were transferred to Luanda prison.

In May 1984, a further rebellion broke out in the Pango camp, leading to an armed battle between dissidents and loyalists, before being suppressed by ANC

---

[31]   John Saul and Colin Leys (1995), 'The politics of exile', in Leys and Saul (eds), op. cit., 40–62.
[32]   Henning Melber (2002), 'From liberation movements to governments: On political culture in Southern Africa', *African Sociological Review*, 6: 1, 161–72.

crack troops. Seven of the rebels were executed. Subsequently, the ANC NEC did convene a National Consultative Conference at Kabwe and released some of the imprisoned guerrillas. However, the more dangerous amongst them were transferred to Quatro, before being moved on to the party's Development Centre in Dakawa in Tanzania in November 1988, when the ANC moved out of Angola. There they were formally reintegrated into the ANC and allowed to participate in its structures. However, when some among them were elected to the ANC's local and regional committees, ANC security intervened, an action subsequently backed up by the NEC which banned many of these men from taking office in ANC structures.[33]

The standard justification for the detention of dissidents was the need for security in the face of the threat posed by the capacity of the Rhodesian and South African security forces to infiltrate the ranks of the liberation movements. As Saul and Leys observe, the world of the southern African liberation movements was 'honeycombed' with intelligence operatives from many countries, and the South Africans, particularly, became adept at penetrating their ranks. Nonetheless, the security threat was systematically misused by party leaderships to reinforce their authority. Paul Trewhela, former member of MK and the SACP and subsequently a trenchant critic, insists that 'the ANC security apparatus rule[d] with all the arrogance of a totalitarian power'.[34] Such authoritarianism had a logic of its own which was highly destructive of impulses for democracy, and fostered an atmosphere in which fear and subservience to the command structure supplanted ideals with loyalty.

A second outcome of the politics of exile was its reinforcement of the NLMs' conviction of their historical legitimacy to the exclusion of competing forces in the struggle for freedom. Such a belief was backed up by Marxist-Leninist theory, which emphasized the leading role in struggle to be played by the revolutionary party. Whether in Maoist or Soviet variants, emphasis was laid upon the party merging with the people, yet it was never expected that 'the people' would supersede the party. Ultimately, NLM theorization was one of what critics of the Marxist tradition have often referred to as 'guided democracy'. The reality of internal democracy was that it was top down, subject to the constraints of party ideology, instruction and discipline. This meant that the revolutionary party was constantly deemed to be ahead of the people, knowing their best interests, and that those who disagreed with it were misguided, disloyal or malevolently intentioned. This in turn implied that the exiled revolutionary movement had authority over popular forces, such as trade unions, civics, and oppositional political parties at home.

In the wake of Soweto, the ANC absorbed several thousands of recruits who left the country to join the armed struggle. However, although MK proved able to respond to the student uprising with a concerted sabotage campaign which drew in local activists (some 2,500 people allegedly involved with guerrilla

---

[33] Bandile Ketelo, Amos Maxongo, Zamxola Tshona, Ronnie Masango and Luvo Mbengo (2009), 'A miscarriage of democracy: The ANC security department in the 1984 mutiny in Umkhonto weSizwe', in Paul Trewhela (ed.), *Inside Quatro: Uncovering the Exile History of the ANC and Swapo*, Johannesburg: Jacana Media, 8–45. A treatment far more sympathetic to the ANC hierarchy is provided by Janet Smith and Beauregard Tromp (2009), *Hani: A Life Too Short*, Johannesburg and Cape Town: Jonathan Ball Publishers.

[34] Trewhela (ed.), op. cit., 4.

attacks were brought to court by the police), it remained unable to engage in meaningful military action. Even so, the relatively small number of guerrillas it was able to infiltrate into South Africa played an important symbolic role in proclaiming the increased presence of MK and the ANC. Then, following a visit of the MK and ANC leadership to Vietnam 1978 to learn from the legendary General Võ Nguyên Giáp, MK adopted a three-year plan which made military tactics part of a wider political strategy. Given that MK was in no position to base its guerrillas permanently in South Africa and to launch sustained attacks, its immediate aim was to be the pursuit of 'armed propaganda' which would help inspire and mobilize the population in preparation for a later phase of 'people's war'.

Although the overwhelming body of its forces remained in Angola, the ANC managed to infiltrate South Africa with increased numbers of guerrillas. After an initial phase of 'armed propaganda', it shifted to 'people's war' from the end of 1981, centred on the formation of local defence units and street committees which would be the nerve centres of the popular uprising.[35] Nonetheless, the extent to which the popular uprising which took place in the early 1980s was directly organized or indirectly influenced by the ANC remains a matter of debate. What is less in dispute is that, as popular struggle gained in intensity, the ANC/SACP alliance successfully imposed its political hegemony upon the UDF and COSATU. The eventual outcome was to be the decision after its return from exile in 1990 that the UDF should be dissolved, and the absorption of COSATU into the ANC-led Tripartite Alliance with the SACP. However, it needs to be said that both UDF and COSATU imported participatory democratic traditions into the ANC which continue to vie with an official emphasis on a top-down 'democratic centralism'.

These tendencies within the politics of exile reinforced the 'exclusive nationalism' approach to the liberation struggle which suggested that, ultimately, the oppressed colonial peoples would triumph over settler colonialism. Notable has been the determination of both SWAPO to block and the ANC to circumscribe investigation of the extensive abuses of dissidents during the years of exile.

Stories began circulating inside Namibia after independence about SWAPO's maltreatment of detainees. These proved difficult to ignore after some 153 detainees returned home, under UN auspices, in mid-1989, especially when their harrowing stories gave rise to later allegations that some 700 detainees had been murdered. A document by a 'Parent's Committee', formed in 1986 by the families of detainees held in Lubango, offered *A Report to the Namibian People: Historical Account of the SWAPO Spy Drama*. However, during the subsequent election campaign, SWAPO rejected the allegations made in the report. In debates which followed in the new parliament, SWAPO offered assurances that it was investigating the cases of people who had died or gone missing in its care, while polishing an official line that any independent investigation would run contrary to the interests of national reconciliation. However, thereafter, with SWAPO obtaining a two-thirds majority in the 1994 election, attempts to raise the issue had to move outside parliament, the key event being the publication of a book by a German pastor, the Reverend Siegfried Groth, seeking to breach

[35] See Ellis and Sechaba, op. cit.

61

SWAPO's 'wall of silence'.[36] This time round, while repeating the now-standard line that investigation would threaten reconciliation, those demanding an inquiry were abused. One SWAPO MP called for the banning and burning of the book; SWAPO Secretary-General Moses Garoeb issued dark threats against the 'forces of evil'; and President Sam Nujoma launched a blistering attack upon Groth and also Christo Lombard, a Professor of Theology at the University of Namibia, who was supporting him. Attempts by a committee comprising former detainees and supporters to 'Break the Wall of Silence' were met by an equally negative response.[37] It remains the case that SWAPO has never officially admitted any wrongdoing.[38] This is deeply ironic, given its umbrage at Germany's continuing refusal to formally apologize for the colonial genocide (presumably, because Berlin fears this will morally reinforce demands for reparations).

In contrast to SWAPO, the ANC was to admit, to a degree, that abuses had taken place in its own camps. As noted, a first commission had been established under James Stuart in 1984 to investigate alleged abuses in the camps in Angola. Subsequently, a second was appointed under Advocate Thembile Louis Skweyiya, in 1992; and when the report of this commission was widely deemed inadequate, a third was appointed under Sam Motsuenyane, a director of ICI (South Africa) and chairman of the National African Federated Chamber of Commerce, in 1994. The latter two commissions followed relentless exposures of abuses in the camps by *Searchlight South Africa*, a journal produced by leftist historians of the struggle, notably Paul Trewhela and the late Baruch Hirson, (author of one of the first major studies of the Soweto revolt) who had long engaged in a critique of what they regarded as the ANC's Stalinist tendencies. Thereafter, testimony on human rights abuses in the camps was also given to the Truth and Reconciliation Commission (TRC), established in 1995.

The Skweyiya Commission reported that there had been 'a situation of extraordinary abuse of power and lack of accountability', and of 'staggering' brutality by the ANC Security Department, findings which were more than backed up by the report of the Motsuenyane Commission. However, the general thrust of the findings of both commissions was that while the ANC was guilty of torture and abuses, these had been the work of specific individuals. The ANC accepted these findings but stated that it was inappropriate to take action when the NP had no such policy in place with regard to its own members. Subsequently, when the TRC sent advanced proofs of its report in 1995 to the ANC indicating that the liberation movement as well as the apartheid government had been guilty of gross violations, Thabo Mbeki (by now ANC President although not yet State President) initially sought to prevent their publication, denouncing the Commission's 'scurrilous attempts to criminalise the heroic struggles of the people of South Africa', and objecting that it was seeking to uphold a position of 'moral equivalence' between those who had implemented and those who had fought apartheid. This resulted in a strong disagreement with Mandela, who wanted to accept the report, which subsequently was

[36] Siegfried Groth (1995), *Namibia: The Wall of Silence*, Wuppertal: Peter Hammer Verlag.
[37] John Saul and Colin Leys (2003), 'Lubango and after: "Forgotten history" as politics in contemporary Namibia', *Journal of Southern African Studies*, 29: 2, 333–53.
[38] Lauren Dobell (1997), 'Silence in context: Truth and/or reconciliation in Namibia', *Journal of Southern African Studies*, 23: 2, 372–73.

published, over the head of the ANC's objections. Mbeki, argues Mark Gevisser, was 'driven by the imperatives of transformation rather than reconciliation'.[39] However, the more fundamental issue was that the Stuart, Skweyiya and Motsuenyane Commissions sought to negate any suggestion that the abuses had either occurred with the knowledge of, or been instigated or endorsed by the senior leadership of the ANC in exile, notably Oliver Tambo, Joe Modise, and the SACP's Chris Hani.[40]

In a subsequent twist to the story, stories appeared in the press that Jacob Zuma, head of ANC counter-intelligence from 1987, was linked to the deaths of various ANC members in exile, including that of a particular cadre, Thami Zulu, who had been poisoned in Lusaka following seventeen months of interrogation by the ANC. In response to the party's National Working Committee deploring the reports on 31 March 2009, Trewhela published an extensive list of queries about Zuma's possible involvement, claiming that it was 'morally unacceptable' for him to become President of South Africa without answering them.[41]

The politics of exile appears to bear a heavy responsibility for the liberation movements' ambiguous attitudes to democratic accountability.

From liberation struggle to democracy

Van Zyl Slabbert presented a cogent argument that the negotiated settlement in South African case was *sui generis* in southern Africa. He viewed the transitions in Zimbabwe and Namibia as externally imposed, via the UK-conducted Lancaster House negotiations and the implementation of Resolution 435 guided by the UN respectively. In contrast, because South Africa had long been a sovereign state, it did not have the option of colonial transition to solve its problem of white minority rule. It therefore had to find its own strategies to rid itself of racial domination and in face of the ANC's commitment to revolutionary transition.[42]

Central to this 'transitions' approach is an emphasis upon constructive political agency by actors on both sides of the divide who wish to reach agreement, even while they may disagree upon what basis such agreement can be reached. Van Zyl Slabbert saw De Klerk as having embarked upon a bold step on 2 February 1990; in announcing the unbanning of the ANC and SACP, he split

---

[39] Mark Gevisser (2007), *The Dream Deferred: Thabo Mbeki*, Cape Town and Johannesburg: Jonathan Ball Publishers, 711–12.

[40] Hani appeared before the Skweyiya Commission to 'express his revulsion' at the oppressive practices within the ANC, but was not subject to cross-examination. A report by a Durban advocate, Robert Douglas, commissioned by the Washington-based International Freedom Foundation received 60 depositions from former inmates of the camps, and likewise raised issues of Tambo's possible responsibility, noting that as President of the ANC he was also Commander-in-Chief of MK. Trewhela's judgement (op. cit., 75–84) is that 'Tambo has a powerful case to answer.' Luli Callinicos responds that having delegated responsibility for the camps to trusted lieutenants, Tambo was not in receipt of information about what was occurring within them. Nonetheless he took 'ultimate responsibility'. See Luli Callinicos (2004), *Oliver Tambo: Beyond the Engeli Mountains*, Claremont: David Philip, 466.

[41] Paul Trewhela (2009), 'The ANC NWC on Thami Zulu', *Politicsweb*, 1 April.

[42] Frederick Van Zyl Slabbert (1992), *The Quest for Democracy: South Africa in Transition*, London: Penguin.

the NP's constituency between those who favoured a negotiated transition and those who did not, and irreversibly launched himself upon the search for new allies via pacts and alliances. Critically, he had managed to sideline the military and security establishment, which was itself highly divided about the desirability and tempo of transition. Furthermore, he had not precipitated the transition because the government was on the point of collapse but because he appreciated a need to move away from a politics of repression. However, whilst his pre-emptive strike constituted a bid to seize the advantage, his agreeing to talk to the ANC meant that he had to surrender unilateral control of the negotiations process.

By opting for negotiations towards a non-racial state, De Klerk forced the ANC into a profound, strategic re-evaluation which allowed the bubbling to the surface of the political divisions and ideological contradictions which had been transcended by the revolutionary struggle, while making it vulnerable to being outflanked by more radical, militant, predominantly black organizations. This meant that, just as De Klerk had had to abandon his right wing, so the leadership of the ANC/SACP also had to outflank its own radicals, some of whom remain committed to the notion of overthrow of the state. The mutual process of marginalizing their 'hardliners' meant that the 'softliners' within the NP and ANC/SACP were disposed to seek a mutual accommodation while they similarly shared an interest in shutting down the options to potential 'spoilers', notably the Inkatha movement of Chief Mangosuthu Buthelezi. The eventual outcome was agreement upon a liberal-democratic constitution whose legitimacy lay as much in the inclusiveness of the process of its adoption as of its content.

The transitions approach throws a bright light upon the end-game in the region as a whole. For all that Van Zyl Slabbert argues that the Zimbabwean and Namibian settlements were externally imposed, their negotiation processes similarly required the reining in of 'hardliners' and 'militants' by those in favour of agreement. For all the differences in the journey, the formal destination was much the same as in South Africa: liberal democracy. However, transition theory needs supplementation by a focus upon the changing relations between the liberation movements and large-scale capital, for these formed a counterpoint to the political negotiations process and paved the way not merely for 'elite transitions'[43] in all three countries, but ones which provided for an overtly capitalist basis for the economy. Suffice to say for the moment that the uneasy mix of liberation perspectives with liberal democracy and capitalist economy was to have profound consequences.

---

[43] Patrick Bond (2000), *Elite Transition: From Apartheid to Neoliberalism in South Africa*, Pietermaritzburg: University of Natal Press.

4.
Contradictions of Victory

The settlements in Zimbabwe, Namibia, and South Africa were constructed around a mutual acceptance by the major contending forces of a mix of liberal democracy and capitalist economics. Settler populations lost political power in exchange for guarantees of rights of minorities and property; liberation movements were promised control of the state in exchange for an accommodation with domestic and international capital. However, there were fundamental contradictions at the heart of all this. On the one hand, the liberation movements prioritized exclusive nationalisms over democracy. This meant that while they viewed democracy (via transitional elections) as a legitimizing route to gaining power, their principal concern then became to consolidate their control over the state. The thrust thereafter was that democracy was acceptable, as long as they won. On the other hand, reaching an accommodation with capital was vital if the economy was to generate sufficient surplus to fuel the party and its various constituencies, but if it failed to do so, then the liberation movements' already ambiguous commitments to democracy were placed under considerable threat.

This chapter will seek to provide an overview of the transitional settlements and the contexts in which they were located. In so doing, it will provide a reference point for subsequent chapters which explore selected dimensions of the record of NLMs in power.

The political settlements

The foundations which underpinned Zimbabwe's new constitution were to prove substantially less sound than those upon which the political architecture of the other two states was to rest. Laid in Lancaster House, where so many other constitutions for Britain's postcolonial brood had been conceived, the political settlement formally provided for a constitutional state, where parliament was subject to the constitution. In practice, however, Zimbabwe inherited what was fundamentally a Westminster-style political order built upon the pre-existing institutions of the settler state, while (fatefully as it turned out) providing for reserved seats for whites within the new parliament.[1]

The internal settlement, whereby in 1978 the Smith government had sought to cut a constitutional deal with Bishop Abel Muzorewa, had been implemented via a first election which granted Africans the vote. The new legislature was to be composed of a House of Assembly and a Senate. The Assembly was to consist

---

[1]   Greg Linington (2012), 'Reflections on the significance of constitutions and constitutionalism for Zimbabwe', in Eldred Masunungure and Jabusile Shumba (eds), *Zimbabwe: Mired in Transition*, Harare: Weaver Press, 63–98.

of 100 members, 72 to be elected by voters on a common roll, 20 by whites on a separate roll, and an additional 8 whites to be elected by the House of Assembly. All citizens were eligible to register on the common roll, but in effect the latter was for blacks. For the first parliament, common roll representatives were to be elected on a party-list system, rather than a constituency system, which was retained for the white roll. The Senate was to consist of 30 members (10 elected by the 72 common roll representatives, 10 by the white, and 10 by the Council of Chiefs). The ceremonial President was to be elected by parliament acting as an electoral college. A further provision was that each party gaining five seats or more would be represented proportionately in the cabinet (guaranteeing white representation).

Conducted over 17–21 April 1979, the election resulted in a sweeping victory for the UANC with 67 per cent of the common roll vote, enabling Muzorewa to become the country's first African Prime Minister, presiding over a government in which Smith's RF continued to play a major role. However, with the PF boycotting the election, the armed struggle continued, forcing the new government into renewed negotiations for a constitutional settlement via the Lancaster House Conference. The resulting agreement between the contending parties provided for transitional elections, which took place on 27–29 February 1980 and which were to provide ZANU-PF on its own with an outright majority.

The Lancaster House agreement retained key features of the internal settlement, notably a bicameral parliament made up of a 100-member Assembly elected by common roll and white roll voters, an indirectly elected Senate and ceremonial presidency. Eighty rather than seventy-two representatives were to be elected by African voters on the common roll, using a system of Proportional Representation (PR) for the transitional election, before a registration of voters and demarcation of constituencies would allow for a move to British-style, first-past-the-post elections (FPTP) in succeeding contests.[2] Twenty seats, to be elected on a separate roll, were reserved for whites (who comprised less than 3 per cent of the population), with white fears further catered for by various safeguards, notably regarding the rights of property (particularly land), and agreement that these arrangements could not be changed for seven years and only then by a two-thirds majority in parliament. Meanwhile, unlike the internal settlement, there was no enforced provision for a government of national unity, the selection of the cabinet to be the prerogative of the Prime Minister serving under a ceremonial President. Subsequently, in 1987, the post of Prime Minister was abolished and Mugabe was elevated to an executive presidency and was subsequently to have original law-making powers conferred upon him by parliament, a move of dubious constitutionality. In short, Zimbabwe was born with a constitution which, in all its essentials, Britain had handed down to its former colonies from Ghana in 1957 on and which, in one country after another, had failed to stem the tide of African dictatorship.

Shorn of the centuries' long conventions which underlay Britain's own democracy, the new constitutional order prescribed a system which offered

---

[2] Ironically, unlike in 1979, the common roll was open only to African voters, rendering these elections under British supervision more comprehensively racially segregated. For purposes of voting, 'Asians' were classified as white. See Colin Baker (1982), 'Conducting the elections in Zimbabwe 1980', *Public Administration and Development*, 2, 45–58.

minimal protections for minority parties from a Prime Minister capable of mustering a majority in parliament. Parliament, albeit subject to special majorities (70 per cent in the House of Assembly, two-thirds of the members in the Senate) would be able to amend any provisions of the constitution (although abolition of the separate representation of whites for seven years could only be approved by total unanimity in the lower House), while in essence, the senior judiciary was to be appointed by the President on the advice of the Prime Minister.[3]

Clearly, the key to power was winning the transitional elections. Win those, and effectively, 'majority rule' could translate into 'winner takes all', as ZANU was quick to appreciate. Mugabe broke with ZAPU, and ZANU-PF campaigned separately in the common roll elections, determined to secure a unilateral majority whether by fair means or foul. Its securing of 57 seats provided the absolute majority it wanted. Thereafter, inclusion of other parties in government was on sufferance, and over the years, the constitution was to fall easy victim to the manipulations of Mugabe and ZANU-PF. The culmination was eventually to be Mugabe's refusal to stand down as President following his and ZANU-PF's defeat in parliamentary and first-round presidential elections by the MDC in March 2008, and the backing given to him by the military. By this time, a long-standing crisis of governance had come to a head, but ruling party intransigence forced regional backing for the formation of a coalition government whereby a prime ministership and key economic ministries were conceded to Morgan Tsvangirai and his MDC, but in which Mugabe retained the presidency and ZANU-PF retained control, notably, of the security and other major portfolios.

The extent to which the Zimbabwean example was a direct influence upon the constitution-making process in Namibia and South Africa is not clear. Certainly, both SWAPO and the ANC recognized the sheer importance of securing victories in the transitional elections (although, with good reason, they were far more confident of gaining substantial majorities in free and fairly conducted elections than was ZANU-PF). Nonetheless, the transitional settlements in these latter countries differed constructively in two major ways.

First, and fundamentally, the new political institutions were founded far more firmly upon principles of constitutional rather than parliamentary supremacy. In both countries, post-transitional Constituent Assemblies made provisions for directly elected lower houses (the National Assemblies) and indirectly elected upper houses (the National Council in Namibia, the Senate in South Africa).[4] The National Assemblies, in turn, would elect their respective Presidents who would convene cabinets drawn from parliament. However, although the imprint of the Westminster model (upon which Union had been constructed in 1910) remained strong, important safeguards of democracy

---

[3]   A Judicial Service Commission was established to advise the Prime Minister, but neither he nor the President was to be bound by their advice. Further, although judges of the High Court were not formally removable before reaching retiring age, the constitution gave considerable leeway to the President to appoint tribunals to advise whether they should be removed from office.

[4]   In Namibia, the first democratic elections were for a Constituent Assembly which proceeded to adopt a constitution in January 1990, with members of the Assembly being accepted as members of the new National Assembly. In South Africa, the first democratic parliament became a Constituent Assembly which negotiated a new constitution to replace the interim constitution under which it had been elected.

were built into the Namibian and South African constitutions which were much weaker in the Lancaster House settlement. The latter did include a Declaration of Rights, but broadly, in the Westminster tradition, the courts were there to enforce laws made by parliament and to secure redress for those whose rights under the Declaration of Rights had been infringed rather than to strike down legislation if this was deemed to be unconstitutional. When, on a few occasions, actions were deemed to be unconstitutional, they were to be largely ignored by an executive upon which there were few effective controls. In contrast, Bills of Rights were backed up in Namibia, by a Supreme Court, and in South Africa, by a Constitutional Court, with full authority to give final judgements on disputes about the constitutionality of law. Overall, the formal authority accorded to the executive (as represented by the Prime Minister) in Zimbabwe was considerably more than was accorded to the presidents in either Namibia or South Africa. Subsequently, Namibia's constitution was to be amended, to provide for direct presidential elections from 1994, and in South Africa, parliament, sitting as an elected Constituent Assembly, renegotiated the constitution during 1994–96 (*inter alia* replacing the Senate with a National Council of Provinces). In both countries, the constitutional changes worked to substantively strengthen the powers of the ruling party and executive. Nonetheless, the fundamental principles of constitutional supremacy were not broached, ensuring greater levels of protection for the rights embedded in the two constitutions against executive or ruling party encroachment. In contrast, it is not insignificant that, whereas Mugabe was to succeed in enforcing unity with ZANU-PF by brute force upon ZAPU in 1987, his campaign for a one-party state faltered upon the rocks of *internal party*, rather than *parliamentary*, opposition.[5]

Second, whereas for all practical purposes the Lancaster House constitution entrenched Westminster-style parliamentary majoritarianism (albeit temporarily constrained by separate white representation), the Namibian and South African constitutions entrenched provisions for minority representation. Furthermore, the interim South African constitution required formation of a Government of National Unity (GNU), composed of ministers drawn proportionately from parties winning more than 10 per cent of seats in the first election. However, whereas there was always the intention for the PR system used in the common roll elections in 1980 in Zimbabwe to give way to a plurality (FPTP) system by the time of the first general election after independence (i.e., 1985), negotiators in both Namibia and South Africa came to agreement about abandonment of FPTP (used hitherto under white rule) in favour of list PR. This had two important outcomes. First, given provisions in both constitutions that constitutional amendments could only be ratified by the securing of two-thirds majorities in parliament, it offered significant constitutional protections to parliamentary minorities. Second, it provided the guarantee not only that minorities would be proportionately represented in the new parliaments, but that they would be represented as *politically* rather than *racially* defined minorities. Indeed, the very logic of the PR system adopted was that if political parties wanted to maximize their vote, they would need to look beyond racial and ethnic boundaries.[6]

---

[5] For Mugabe's drive for a one-party state, see Chapter 5.
[6] Daniel Horowitz (1991), *A Democratic South Africa? Constitutional Engineering in a Divided Society*, Berkeley CA: University of California Press.

Such provisions did not make either constitution immune from the incursions of ruling party dominance. Nonetheless, constitutionalism not only imposed boundaries on ruling party power which were not lightly overcome, but at times gave impetus to internal party democracy. Thus Nujoma was able to cajole SWAPO into amending the constitution to provide him with a third term in office as President in 1998, but was constrained to stand down by the party in favour of Hifikepunye Pohamba in 2004. Likewise, Thabo Mbeki attempted to subvert the spirit of the two-term limit imposed upon state Presidents by the South African constitution by running for a third term as ANC President, with the apparent motivation of retaining power by the back door, yet he was to fall foul of an internal party rebellion. In both cases, constitutional propriety was formally maintained even though it is evident that it was employed instrumentally by internal party factions wanting change at the top.

Liberation culture and democracy

John Saul argues that the struggles in southern Africa were simultaneous struggles for liberation from gender, ethnic, and economic oppressions as well as from the racial oppressions of the settler state.[7] He is undoubtedly correct if we read off the best aspirations of the struggle from the beliefs of such inspirational leaders as Samora Machel, Nelson Mandela, Oliver Tambo, and Chris Hani, and take these as reflecting wider hopes within the liberation movements. Certainly, as noted in the introduction, much international solidarity support was given to the liberation movements because their supporters chose to perceive them as harbingers of futures for a democratic southern Africa which would go far beyond the boundaries of mere formal political equality. Nonetheless, we need to be cautious about the extent to which an expansive definition of liberation guided the liberation struggles on two counts.

First, as Norma Kriger has reminded us in her book on *Zimbabwe's Guerrilla War* (significantly subtitled *Peasant Voices*), it is far wiser to ask people what they want rather than imposing theories about what they should want upon them. In other words, we need to question how deeply aspirations for an expansive liberation were shared, especially among overwhelmingly male leaderships subject to militarist influences.[8]

Second, there is a strong case for arguing that the struggle for liberation was more one for majority rule than it was for political democracy. Whereas political democracy envisages the principle of majority decision-making as being constrained by respect for numerous rights of individuals and minorities,

[7]   John Saul, in many writings, but see, for instance, (2011), 'The success and failure of the "thirty years war for southern African liberation" in South Africa and beyond', Conference on One Hundred Years of the ANC: Debating Liberation Histories and Democracy Today, Universities of Johannesburg and the Witwatersrand, 20–24 September.

[8]   See notably, Raymond Suttner (2009), *The ANC Underground in South Africa, 1950–1976*, Boulder CO: First Forum Press, which problematizes the manner in which the ideological beliefs of the ANC and SACP interfaced with 'traditional' belief systems. He notes in particular how the ANC was infused with gendered notions of the personal, heroism, masculinities and femininities, as well as the potential and actual experience of abuse as it arose within underground activity.

there was (and is) a tendency embedded in national liberation thought which crudely equates majoritarianism with democracy. This does not mean that the NLMs were crudely regardless of individual rights. In all three states, their members had been the victims of arbitrary killings, violence, torture, and other gross offences of human rights, and there was a widely shared determination that such things should not happen again. Notably, the ANC was insistent upon writing a host of individual rights into the constitution (including some, such as rights for gays and lesbians, which undoubtedly went beyond the wishes of the majority of its own constituency). This stance had been presaged by its important policy document, *Ready to Govern*, issued in 1992, which stressed the need for the separation of powers and for a Bill of Rights to be upheld by the courts. At the same time, however, advanced democratic thinking was at considerable odds with significant dimensions of national liberation theorizing.

The tendency to equate majority rule with democracy was to be demonstrated by the manner in which the NLMs consolidated their hold on power following the transitional elections. Suffice it to say here that ZANU-PF enforced its hegemony by brutally subjugating ZAPU, blatantly manipulating electoral procedures, and flouting the constitution when it was faced by major challenges by the MDC from the election of 2000 onwards. In contrast, neither SWAPO nor the ANC were ever endangered electorally (although this is not to say that they were consistently tolerant of political opposition from either within or outside their own ranks). Nonetheless, from the moment of taking power they used their domination of the political arena in a manner which belied commitment to constitutional democracy and which significantly shifted the balance of powers in favour of the executive, justifying their actions by reference to their possession of majorities in parliament (see Chapter 5).

The ambiguity towards democracy can be seen as rooted in liberation political culture and thinking. Three aspects need to be highlighted. First, the use and reinvention of history to confirm the identification of the liberation movement with 'the people', and 'the people' with the liberation movement, with particular emphasis upon the 'armed struggle' as providing historical legitimacy; second, the forging of international solidarity links between the liberation movements themselves to shore up their legitimacy in the face of proclaimed internal and external threats; and third, the blending of the theology of liberation with the post-1927 Comintern theorizing which gave rise to the theory of the NDR (national democratic revolution). All three sources of liberation thinking clash with constitutionalism.

Reinventions of history

There is now an extensive literature on the uses and construction of 'patriotic history' and the associated tendency to officialize liberation movement interpretations of the past in public memorials. To be sure, as Kossler has observed, the relative lack of historiographical material on the liberation struggle in Namibia compared with Zimbabwe (we could add, South Africa) has rendered the construction of a credible image identifying SWAPO as the embodiment of a nation-forged liberation struggle more difficult. Nonetheless, the thrust of much official discourse in both Zimbabwe and Namibia is manifestly to promote 'the military image of the liberation struggle, the focus of the victorious and now ruling party and its claim to perpetuity'.[9]

In Zimbabwe, Mugabe was to designate his post-2000 land reforms as the 'Third Chimurenga', claiming historical continuities with the wars of primary resistance against colonialism in the 1890s (the First Chimurenga), and the war for liberation of the 1960s and 1970s as the 'Second'. This interpretation served two purposes. First, by identifying the 1987 merger of ZAPU into ZANU-PF as the consummation of national unity, it projected ZANU-PF as the ultimate embodiment of the nation.[10] It followed that when the newly formed MDC came to challenge the ruling party, it could be reviled as illegitimate, treacherous, and as outside the nation. Second, the presentation of politics (notably land reform) as war enabled those opposed to ZANU-PF's initiatives to be depicted as enemies rather than opponents, thus implicitly – and often explicitly – justifying violence against them.

In Namibia, however, although valiant attempts have been made by SWAPO-inclined historians (including Sam Nujoma himself)[11] to link primary resistance to the liberation struggle, they have encountered the particular difficulty that the wars of subjugation waged by the Germans affected peoples inhabiting the central and southern areas of the Police Zone and left the Ovambo in the north largely untouched. Thus whereas in the years leading up to independence in 1990 the Herero genocide by the Germans was successfully appropriated by the nationalist forces allied to SWAPO, immediately after independence it became the preserve of Herero elites (some with connections to SWANU) opposed to the new government. Whereas the latter began seeking a formal apology and reparations from Germany, the SWAPO government (dominated by people who knew their support base was largely to be found in the Ovambo north) sought to ensure that their demands would remain muted or couched within the nation-state they controlled.[12] Meanwhile, alongside a host of public activities which tend to place greater emphasis upon the armed struggle than upon internal resistance and the diplomatic initiatives taken in the international arena to secure independence, public holiday celebrations are largely monopolized by SWAPO, and the glorification of sacrifices on the battlefield are articulated in memorials such as Heroes Acre, built in Stalinist-heroic style by the North Koreans outside Windhoek.[13]

In South Africa, the complicated historical terrain, along with an official discourse which celebrates a unity in diversity of racial and ethnic groups (famously conceptualized by Archbishop Desmond Tutu as the 'rainbow

---

9   Reinhardt Kossler (2010), 'Images of history and the nation: Namibia and Zimbabwe compared', *South African Historical Journal*, 62: 1, 41.

10   Robert Mugabe (1989), 'The Unity Accord: Its promise for the future', in Canaan Banana (ed.), *Turmoil and Tenacity: Zimbabwe 1890–1990*, Harare: The College Press, 336–59.

11   See Sam Nujoma (2001), *Where Others Wavered: The Autobiography of Sam Nujoma*, London: Panaf, which is valuably critiqued by Chris Saunders' (2003) 'Liberation and democracy: A critical reading of Sam Nujoma's "Autobiography"', in Henning Melber (ed.), *Re-examining Liberation in Namibia: Political Cultures since Independence*, Uppsala: Nordic Africa Institute, 87–98.

12   Jan-Bart Gewald (2003), 'Herero genocide in the twentieth century: Politics and memory', in Jon Abbink, Mirjam de Bruijn and Klaas van Walraven (eds), *Rethinking Resistance: Revolt and Violence in African History*, Leiden and Boston: Brill, 279–304.

13   Henning Melber (2003), 'Namibia, land of the brave: Selective memories on war and violence within nation-building', in Abbink et al. (eds), op. cit., 305–27.

nation') has placed significant limits on attempts to project the ANC as the sole embodiment of the struggle against apartheid. Against what Bonner has termed 'the smoothing down' of patriotic history,[14] academic historians combine with past participants and present partisans to assess the contributions made by individuals and groupings guided by liberalism, Black Consciousness, Trotskyism or whatever. Nonetheless, a developing heritage-trail centred around monuments which celebrate the heroism and sufferings of 'struggle heroes', such as the Apartheid Museum, Robben Island, the prison at Constitutional Hill in Johannesburg, the Rivonia Farm museum, and the new Liberation Park outside Pretoria all contribute to a framing of history which stresses the centrality of the ANC. Similarly, although formally acknowledging the often-independent bases of the internal struggles during the 1970s and 1980s, ANC-inclined historians often reproduce the ANC/SACP interpretations of those years which attempted to claim them for the external liberation movement.[15] Butler notes the ANC's tendency to recast the 1980s insurrections of ordinary communities as the creations of MK, and to remilitarize the political imaginations of the 'born frees' (those born after 1994).[16]

Liberation movement solidarity

Construction of patriotic histories interweaves with a regional syndrome of solidarity among the former liberation movements to reinforce their belief in their inherent legitimacy. Thus ZANU-PF national chairperson, Simon Khaya Moyo, declared to a meeting of the party's National Conference in December 2010:

> No liberation movement will ever be replaced by people coming from nowhere. This applies to ZANU-PF in Zimbabwe, ANC in South Africa, FRELIMO in Mozambique, SWAPO in Namibia, MPLA in Angola and Chama Cha Mapinduzi in Tanzania. We are not just neighbours with South Africa. We share a common liberation history, culture and values. Any of us who are not part of this revolutionary journey should think again...[17]

Such expressions are not just rhetoric, for the former liberation movements meet together as parties in regional meetings where the memories of the past are rehearsed to reinforce mutual identities that the NLMs are a breed apart. There is need to do so, for such sentiments brush over much that is inconvenient in the past, inventing unities in struggle which were often totally absent in practice. Interrelations between different liberation movements were infused with rivalries, mutual suspicions, and ideological disputes, even apart from the impact of the Sino-Soviet split which aligned them with different international patrons. ZANU-PF, for instance, was closer to the PAC than it was to the ANC, and deeply

---

[14] Phil Bonner (2011), Plenary presentation to the Conference 'One Hundred Years of the ANC: Debating Liberation Histories and Democracy Today', 20–24 September.
[15] For discussion of SACTU's attempts to delegitimize independent trade unions which were well beyond its influence in the 1970s, see Roger Southall (1995), *Imperialism or Solidarity? International Labour and South African Trade Unions*, Cape Town: University of Cape Town Press, Ch.9.
[16] Anthony Butler (2011), 'Born frees set to repeat patterns of prejudice', *Business Day*, 14 October.
[17] Cited in Sabelo Ndlovu-Gatsheni (2011), *Reconstructing the Implications of Liberation Struggle History on SADC Mediation in Zimbabwe*, Johannesburg: South African Institute of International Relations.

resentful of movements, such as the MPLA and ANC that had close ties with
ZAPU. Relations between ZANU-PF and the ANC were peculiarly difficult, the
latter rejecting overtures which were made for military collaboration in 1977
on the grounds of its relationship with ZAPU, with many within the ANC fully
expecting the latter to win the transitional elections in Zimbabwe in 1980.
Bonds of struggle between MK and ZIPRA cadres were particularly strong
because of their joint military tradition of having undergone training in
Moscow, and there being linguistic affinities between the largely Ndebele-
speaking ZIPRA and the largely Zulu- and Xhosa-speaking MK cadres. MK
cadres were arrested, imprisoned, and tortured alongside former ZIPRA
commanders during the crackdown on ZAPU in the early 1980s, and ANC military infrastructure within Zimbabwe was destroyed. ZANU-PF subsequently
moved to improve its relations with the ANC, offering it a comprehensive deal
to support the armed struggle, although much of its motivation was to claim the
title for being the sole authentic liberation movement in Zimbabwe and to isolate
ZAPU.[18]

Against this background, there has been a need for a conscious reinvention
of history to stress commonalities rather than differences. Since 2000, ZANU-
PF has been particularly active in efforts to cultivate stronger links with movements such as the MPLA, with which it had had weak ties prior to 1980.
Similarly, whereas links between ZANU-PF and SWAPO during the latter's exile
years were virtually non-existent, signified by Mugabe's failure to attend the
independence celebrations in Windhoek, a close relationship between Mugabe
and Nujoma developed during the mid-1990s as a result of a perceived threat
to struggle hierarchies represented by the global celebration of the leadership of
Mandela and the admission of South Africa into SADC.[19]

Inter-NLM solidarities build upon the continued resonance in nationalist
discourses of anti-colonialism and anti-imperialism. These have been used to
particular effect by Mugabe to shore up wider African support for his land
reforms, and more generally to blunt regional criticism of ZANU-PF's dictatorship. The reluctance of an ANC government to deal harshly with a regime
which has crudely trashed human rights and presided over a regionally
damaging political-economic meltdown is widely said to have compromised the
independence of SADC-backed efforts by Thabo Mbeki to mediate a resolution
of the post-2008 crisis in Zimbabwe. Brian Raftopoulos, for example, sees
Mbeki's strategy as centred around the hope that Mugabe could be constrained
to stand down as President and for government to be assumed by a reformed
ZANU-PF rather than by a democratically endorsed MDC.[20] Yet even though
the subsequently more robust efforts of the Zuma administration to discipline
Mugabe's worst excesses have been acknowledged, and even though there are
increasing tensions between the ANC and ZANU-PF,[21] there is a tendency for

---

[18] Ibid., 11.

[19] Ibid., 1.

[20] Brian Raftopoulos (2010), 'The global political agreement as a "passive revolution": Notes on
contemporary politics in Zimbabwe', *The Round Table*, 99: 411, 705–18.

[21] In September 2011, ZANU-PF youth leaders complained publicly about the ANC leadership's
decision to press charges against ANC Youth League President Julius Malema, describing them
as 'persecution'. In 2010, Malema had endorsed ZANU-PF revolutionary credentials and called
for Zimbabwe-style land reforms in South Africa. See *Business Day*, 26 September 2011.

liberation movements to close ranks in the face of the challenges presented by opposition parties.

There is particular hostility to critiques of their party dominance. Any suggestions that democracy requires the eventual replacement of NLMs as governments are brusquely dismissed as counter-revolutionary. Thus a communiqué issued after a meeting between Zuma as leader of the ANC with President Hifikepunye Pohamba and former President Nujoma in December 2008 denounced the 'recurring reactionary debate around the need to reduce the former libration [*sic*] movements on the continent'.[22] On his return to South Africa, Zuma went on to muse:

> Political analysts and all who claim to know Africans better than they know themselves tell us that it is good for Africa and democracy if the majority of former liberation movements was reduced. How do we as former liberation movements ensure that we do not steer away from our mandate of serving the poor and all our people, in the current climate of counter-revolution?[23]

As Ndlovu-Gatsheni has perceptively observed, the MDC has fallen victim to such 'liberation war conservatism'. With the passing away of liberation war veterans, the myth-making of solidarity and the common front may have less effect on a younger generation. However, it is difficult to believe that it will disappear from a region that is 'still saturated with anti-colonial and anti-imperialist memories'.[24]

Theorising the NDR

ZANU-PF, SWAPO, and the ANC all propounded the view that the transfer of political power to liberation movements would prove meaningless unless they were to embark upon a fundamental restructuring of their respective economies. For true liberation, declared SWAPO in one of its few systematic analyses of Namibian colonial subjugation, 'the attainment of state power is only the beginning'.[25] Once achieved, it would be the responsibility of liberation movement governments to press ahead with the further building of the nation, the continued democratization of society, and the achievement of such goals as economic development, social justice, non-sexism, and the overthrow of imperialist domination.

Such goals were formalized in the theory of the NDR, although here an important qualifier is required. Successive versions of the ANC's Strategy and Tactics documents, updated according to circumstances, are presented in turgid quasi-Marxist-Leninist terminology, with the notion of the NDR at the heart of them, implying that the party's actions are guided by theory. In practice, the theory of the NDR is used selectively, employed only to guide particular policies and practices. One reason is that as a broad church, the ANC includes groupings of different ideologies, and that various precepts of liberalism (although, for

---

22. Joint Communiqué between the Swapo Party and the African National Congress, 9 December 2008, http://www.anc.org.za/show.php?doc=ancdocs/pr/2008/pr1209.html
23. Jacob Zuma (2008), 'Letter from the President: A common history and a shared future', *ANC Today*, 8: 49, 8 December.
24. Ndlovu-Gatsheni, op. cit., 16.
25. SWAPO (1981), *To Be Born a Nation: The Liberation Struggle for Namibia*, London: Zed Press, 293.

peculiarly South African reasons, that term is not used) are embedded in the history of a party drawing considerable inspiration from Christianity.[26] However, what the ANC's employment of the NDR does do is simultaneously hark back to the revolutionary spirit of the party in exile and cement its long-standing relationship with the SACP, for which justification of actions in Marxian terms is *de rigeur* to convince itself and others that it is on the path to revolution. In contrast, whereas ZANU-PF in its earlier years made occasional references to its pursuit of the NDR, and some Zimbabwean Marxist academics have chosen to analyse the struggle and post-independence developments from within its frameworks,[27] it meant very little in practice to either Mugabe or the party. One reason may have been that the theory's Soviet provenance rendered it somewhat embarrassing once ZANU-PF had moved into the Chinese orbit (which early on, led the party to issue at least one statement dividing the world into a retrogressive capitalist or imperialist camp and a progressive socialist camp, and placing the Soviet Union in the former).[28] SWAPO likewise has not only had little time for the theory of the NDR, but for any theory in any shape or form. One reason is that from the early days of its final break with SWANU, SWAPO largely divorced itself from Namibia's small, educated intelligentsia, not least because the leadership was threatened by them. Subsequently, the challenge to the incumbent leaders of both SWAPO and PLAN represented by the influx of more educated youngsters (many from the South) contributed to what Saul and Leys identify as a cult of 'anti-intellectualism' and a 'contempt for individuals'.[29] Nonetheless, for all these reservations, the logic of the NDR is embedded in ZANU-PF and SWAPO perspectives.

The theory of the NDR has built upon ideas developed after 1927 in the Soviet Union about the strategies to be pursued by revolutionary parties in colonial conditions. Because imperialism had blocked the local flowering of capitalism, nascent anti-colonial, national bourgeoisies were deemed to have a progressive role to play in alliance with other nationally subordinated classes. However, while providing analytical justification for class alliances in the struggle for independence, the theory of the NDR was to leave much room for debate about the actual content of 'national democracy' and the class dynamics it would encourage.

The thrust of the theory is that because capitalism has left the colony in a state of backwardness, the forces of production must be developed under capi-

---

[26] Liberalism has a long, if chequered history in South Africa, yet its association with white parliamentary oppositional politics under apartheid has rendered it identical to white interests for that strand of thought which wishes to declare all above-ground opposition to the regime which took place after the ANC went into exile as illegitimate. Beware the individual who is dismissed as a 'white liberal'!

[27] Exemplified, for instance, by Ibbo Mandaza (1986), 'The state and politics in the post-settler situation', in Ibbo Mandaza (ed.), *Zimbabwe: The Political Economy of Transition 1980–1986*, Dakar: Codesria; Harare: Jongwe Press, 21–74, who argues strongly of the need for a 'patriotic bourgeoisie'.

[28] See the radical policy statement, known as Mwenge II, issued in 2010, in Ndlovu-Gatsheni, op. cit., 8–9.

[29] John Saul and Colin Leys (1995), 'The politics of exile' in Colin Leys and John Saul (eds), *Namibia's Liberation Struggle: The Two-Edged Sword*, London: James Currey, 54. But SWAPO's deep suspicion of intellectuals has not stood in the way of Sam Nujoma collecting honorary degrees from Ahmadu Bello University in Nigeria, Lincoln University in the US, and inevitably, the University of Namibia (of which he was the first Chancellor).

talist auspices before a progression to socialism becomes possible for the post-colony. During the struggle for national liberation, the small native bourgeoise, inhibited by colonial restrictions, throws in its lot with the working class and peasantry, guided by the revolutionary party. Once liberation is achieved and the national democratic phase commences, this native bourgeoisie must be encouraged to spearhead a process of national capitalist development, that is, to become a 'patriotic bourgeoisie' (its patriotism contrasted with the metro-politan affiliations of imperialist capital). The danger is obvious, however, for even a native capitalist class is likely to put profit before patriotism. Conse-quently, the historic task falls to the party to seize control of the state in order to ensure that the patriotic bourgeoisie remains loyal to the project of the revo-lution. In short, capitalism can be encouraged so long as it is under the control of the party.

Suffice it to say that the theory of the NDR, whether or not it is embraced explicitly by the individual NLMs, describes their approach to the project of liber-ation as a phased procession to socialism or some similarly described utopia. Not least of the advantages of such an approach is that it is sufficiently elastic to justify a wide variety of policies by self-proclaimed revolutionary parties in power. Just as the accommodations with large-scale capital made by the ANC and SWAPO can be described as necessary compromises in order to develop the productive forces of the economy, so the 'revolutionary land programme' imple-mented by ZANU-PF can be transcribed as the seizure of productive resources from unpatriotic settler farmers in the cause of empowering a patriotic bour-geoisie.[30] Yet what also lies at the heart of the theory of the NDR is the notion that its pursuit demands an extension by the liberation movement of its control of over state and society.

As expressed by the ANC in 1998, 'transformation of the state entails, first and foremost, extending the power of the NLM over all levers of power: the army, the police, the bureaucracy, intelligence structures, the judiciary, the parastatals, and agencies such as regulatory bodies, the public broadcaster, the central bank and so on'.[31] In essence, the NDR prescribes a project of the revo-lutionary party exercising a political monopoly, justifying this in quasi-scien-tific terms. It is a prescription which, as indicated in the introduction, has allowed some analysts to go overboard and to describe the ANC as virtually totalitarian, although as this book will demonstrate, the party's capacity in practice for imposing its will on society at large is severely compromised (by, *inter alia*, the power of large-scale capital, dissident popular forces, and not least, the constitution). Nonetheless, notionally the ANC's strategy of extending the power over all 'levers of power' is revolutionary, and deeply at odds with the notion of the separation of powers and of constitutional supremacy embedded in the constitution.

They may not explicitly subscribe to the theory of the NDR, but both ZANU-PF and SWAPO embrace the values and practice of 'transformation' and the

---

[30] On Zimbabwe, for instance, see Sam Moyo and P. Yeros (2005), 'Land occupations and land reform in Zimbabwe: Towards the national democratic revolution', in Sam Moyo and P. Yeros (eds), *The Resurgence of Rural Movements in Africa, Asia and Latin America*, London: Zed Press, 44–77.

[31] ANC (1998), 'The state, property relations and social transformation', *Umrabulo*, 5: 3, for which see http://amandlandawonye.wikispaces.com/1998.ANC

theory of state power which accompanies it, at considerable cost to democratic values.[32] As we shall see, the gospel of 'transformation' has increasingly lost all social content except that of extending party power alongside race-based policies of transferring jobs, opportunities, and privileges from whites to blacks – but without tackling the social relations of capitalist production. Transformation may not challenge capitalism, but it does represent a challenge to democracy.

The retreat from socialism: political transitions and macro-economic policy

It is often argued that the post-liberation adjustments to capitalism represent a 'betrayal' of the revolution. SWAPO's 1976 Programme was described as 'unabashedly Marxist',[33] ZANU-PF proclaimed itself as committed to 'scientific, Marxist-Leninist, socialism',[34] and alongside the SACP, the ANC was committed to radical social transformation. Certainly, hopes that the NLMs would pursue socialist strategies were widespread amongst many supporters internationally as well as amongst radicalized constituencies on the ground, yet retrospectively it is also clear that the parties were themselves consistently ambiguous. Some time ago, Ibbo Mandaza lamented the impact of 'revolutionary romanticism', complaining that the 'logic of protracted struggle' had resulted in the 'mechanistic' view that the armed struggle 'would develop *logically* [emphasis in original] a revolutionary capacity for national liberation and therefore advance almost immediately towards socialism'. This provided the platform for early disappointment. 'Thus Machel, who in 1975 was viewed as a revolutionary leader of a socialist state, in 1984 became a sell-out leader of a country going capitalist!'[35] Yet, argues Mandaza, liberation movement strategies were always more ambiguously calibrated than the romantics allowed. Hence it is difficult to disagree with Andre Astrow's critique of the theory of the NDR as prioritizing the struggle for national democracy (a capitalist phase) while actually postponing the struggle against capitalism until some unspecified time in the future.[36] Whether such a formulation was a cynical device employed by 'petit-bourgeois nationalist leaders' to retain the support of the masses (as Astrow implies) or whether, as Ben Turok argues in relation to the ANC/SACP alliance, differences in interpretation of the relationships between the two phases allowed for the two wings of the liberation movement to retain overall unity,[37] need not detain us here. But what if, at the time they came to assume power, the libera-

---

[32] For a discussion of the lack of concern for democratic principles of Marxist scholars aligned to ZANU-PF, see Brian Raftopoulos (2006) 'The Zimbabwean crisis and the challenges of the left', *Journal of Southern African Studies*, 32: 2, 203–19.

[33] Economist Intelligence Unit (1991), *Namibia Country Profile: Annual Survey of Political and Economic Background 1989–92*, London: EIU.

[34] Rob Davies (1988), 'The transition to socialism in Zimbabwe: Some areas for debate', in Colin Stoneman (ed.), *Zimbabwe's Prospects: Issues of Race, Class, State and Capital in Southern Africa*, Basingstoke: Macmillan, 18–31.

[35] Ibbo Mandaza (1986), 'Introduction: The political economy of transition', in Mandaza (ed.), op. cit., 5 and 6.

[36] Andre Astrow (1983), *Zimbabwe: A Revolution That Lost Its Way?* London: Zed Press, 141–44.

[37] Ben Turok (2009), *From the Freedom Charter to Polokwane: The Evolution of ANC Economic Policy*, Cape Town: New Agenda, 26–29.

tion movements came to accept 'the reality' that the possibilities for an assault upon the ramparts of capitalism were remote? Did this mean that, in the words of the famous ANC promise of a 'better life for all', their progressive commitments were wholly vacuous? Or did it mean that despite the difficulties of inheriting capitalist legacies, they committed to using state power to shift capitalism in a socialist direction? Let us seek to answer such questions by following the advice of Mandaza to seek to explain 'why things are what they are'.

A first path to tread is to look at the transitional contexts in which the NLMs found themselves when coming to office. In all three cases, their forging of transitional political agreements with outgoing regimes was founded upon acceptance of the principles of market economy. Take for instance the key issue of nationalization. A UN report commissioned by the PF in 1978 raised the possibility of nationalizing the banking system and of extending greater state control over mining and other private industry, but by September 1980 the new government's philosophy was expressed as one of 'co-existence of State and private industry', as long as, added Mugabe, private enterprise made itself open to local and, 'in certain cases', government participation.[38] By 1989, the economic policy statement of the formerly 'Marxist' SWAPO made no mention of socialism and its central plank was to achieve a measure of national control over the country's resources and to bring about a balance between just economic returns to the Namibian people and reasonable profits for foreign and local investors.[39] From the mid-1980s, the mobilization of popular forces against apartheid had propelled elements of South African large-scale capital into developing a counter-revolutionary strategy to shape a socio-economic transition that would parallel the political one and dissociate capitalist exploitation from racial oppression. Contacts, covert and otherwise, with senior members of the ANC were seen as a way of securing a transition which would safeguard the essentials of the established economic system.[40] Famously, Mandela released a statement a month before his release from prison which, citing the Freedom Charter, declared that 'the nationalization of the mines, banks and monopoly industry' was the policy of the ANC and that any change of views in this regard was 'inconceivable'.[41] Nonetheless, by February 1992, he had declared that the inconceivable was necessary, having been persuaded by delegates from China and Vietnam at the World Economic Forum in Davos, Switzerland how they had come to accept the interdependence of national economies and consented to private enterprise after the collapse of the Soviet Union. 'Chaps', Mandela was to recall later of his subsequent conversations with the ANC, 'we either keep nationalization and get no investment, or we modify our attitude and get investment.'[42] Not all the chaps came round to his

[38] *ACR 1980–81*, B938–39.
[39] Ibid., *1990–92*, B629.
[40] John Saul (2005), 'The post-apartheid denouement', in John Saul, *The Next Liberation Struggle*, Pietermaritzburg, University of KwaZulu-Natal Press, 203.
[41] Note incidentally Mandela's own position that the Freedom Charter was not a blueprint for socialism but for 'African-style capitalism', and that nationalization was an instrument for African empowerment just as the NP had used it for Afrikaner empowerment. Nelson Mandela (1994), *Long Walk to Freedom*, Boston PA: Little, Brown and Co., 527.
[42] Anthony Sampson (1999), *Mandela: The Authorised Biography*, Cape Town; Jonathan Ball Publishers, 434–35.

new way of thinking, but those who were in charge of economic policy – if they had not done so already – did.

The shift in thinking about nationalization was just one outcome, albeit a key one, of the pressure of external forces. In Zimbabwe's case, combined pressures from Britain, the Rhodesian army, and the FLS forced a dubious ZANU-PF to sign the Lancaster House compromise which preserved the structures of the settler state, committed the future government to guaranteeing pensions of civil servants, and provided a ten-year guarantee on the inviolability of private property. The liberation struggle had been hugely motivated by the 'land question', yet the cost of buying even the estimated 40–60 per cent of settler land not being fully utilized would have been totally beyond the financial capacity of a new government. The latter's vulnerability was made only too clear by the promise of aid from Britain and the US which was linked to the PF's acceptance of the Lancaster House terms.[43]

Over the next two decades, the global context changed radically. By the late 1980s African economies elsewhere were seriously struggling and even revolutionary movements were questioning the efficacy of state ownership. Then, of course, the revolutions in Eastern Europe caused a major rethink. By the 1990s, global shocks and crises had prompted a wave of corporate takeovers, resulting in a closely interlocked system of global trade and investment oiled by unregulated capital movements which severely constrained the freedom of action of capital-short countries, notably those in the South. In turn, the system was policed by financial disciplines imposed upon debtor states by the IMF and World Bank, which demanded fiscal regimes constructed around freedoms of trade, investment, and capital movement. The Washington Consensus, declared the ANC, looking back in 2005, was constructed around the needs of developed rather than developing countries, and insisted upon 'tax reforms, liberalizing interest rate, abolishing exchange-rate control, trade and capital market liberalization, privatization, deregulation and the entrenchment of property rights...',[44] linked to homilies about 'good governance' and human rights. 'Whether we like it or not', declared Thabo Mbeki to a party conference in 2000, '...it would neither be possible nor desirable to cut ourselves off from the world economy.'[45] The strategy of engagement was to be pursued by all three liberation movements on assuming state power, but on different terms and outcomes, with Zimbabwe, as in other spheres, being the outlier, and effectively (albeit disastrously) shifting to disengagement before negotiating something of a return to the global fold under the coalition government after 2008. The outlines of the macro-economic policies pursued are well known, and need only a brief outline before we highlight the extent to which these have blocked or facilitated the aspirations with which the liberation movements came to power.

[43] Astrow, op. cit., 155.
[44] ANC National General Council (2005), 'Development and underdevelopment', NGC discussion document, 26.
[45] Cited by Turok, op. cit., 67.

From market to meltdown: economic policy in Zimbabwe

Moeletsi Mbeki has described Zimbabwe in 1980 as 'a promising, almost pros-
perous African economy, well-endowed with an array of minerals and a diversified agriculture'. Despite years of sanctions imposed after UDI, there
remained a fairly sophisticated manufacturing sector and a competent financial services sector run by British banks and insurance companies.[46] Yet 'everything that could possibly go wrong has done so', and Zimbabwe has become
not only a failed state, but a failed economy. Even so, he adds, 'the collapse of
the economy is not due solely to mismanagement by Robert Mugabe's ZANU-
PF'.[47] The government made interventions which allowed for the introduction
of new export products such as platinum, beef, and cut flowers as well as the
expansion of sugar, maize, clothing, and textiles as well as iron and steel products, while at the same time, engaging in a painstaking process of introducing
cotton as a cash crop amongst peasants. Independence also brought with it
foreign aid, and even a 'trickle of foreign direct investment'.[48] Against this,
there was a failure to bridge a growing gap between imports and exports (not
least because of a significant fall in important export prices, notably of
asbestos, gold, and tobacco); a consequent rise in foreign debt and a resulting
inability to modernize industrial machinery, this rendering manufacturing
increasingly uncompetitive at exactly the time that South African exports were
expanding into Africa; a shortage of capital to fund investment in agriculture;
and on top of this, demands imposed by the IMF that sought to address the
deteriorating balance of payments situation by slashing domestic expenditure
while opening up the economy to international competition. The resulting
collapse in value of the currency, sky-rocketing inflation, out-migration of
skilled workers, growing unemployment, and decimation of the education and
health sectors were to push the government into desperate measures, notably
its land seizure policies, which were then to plunge the economy into yet deeper
crisis.[49]

Mbeki's review points to three factors accounting for the trajectory of the
economy: the structural difficulties which the government faced in seeking to
transform the previously settler-dominated economy; the damaging consequences of interventions by the IMF; and the erosion of the capacity of the
government to manage the economy, with the resultant fall in its popular
support and its subsequent resort to a strategy of plunder in order to divert
declining resources to its narrowing constituency.

In 1980, the government set out to balance an accommodation with capital
with a redirection of economic benefits to the African majority. Its initial
macro-economic policy, expressed in the Transitional National Development
Plan (for 1982–85) and the first Five Year Development Plan (FYDP) adopted
in 1986, was constructed around achieving the twin objectives of growth and

---

[46] Moeletsi Mbeki (2009), *Architects of Policy: Why African Capitalism Needs Changing*, Johannes-
      burg: Picador Africa, 102.
[47] Ibid., 101.
[48] Ibid., 104.
[49] Ibid., 101–14.

equity.[50] Inequalities were even more extreme than in South Africa, with average earnings for whites (4 per cent of the population) more than ten times those for blacks in formal employment (just 15 per cent). Further, while the industrial sector was 'fairly sophisticated and diversified', it had been badly affected by sanctions, and it was largely oriented to providing consumer goods for the white minority. The well-being of the economy was therefore heavily dependent upon the export of a 'well-diversified' basket of primary products, half a dozen metals, and key agricultural products (notably tobacco). Short-term strengths of the economy thus contained the source of longer-run weaknesses: industry was not only biased towards serving white consumer needs, but heavily dependent upon white skills.[51]

If significant redistribution was to be achieved, there was therefore need for both growth and forging of an appropriate agreement with the interlocked interests of the white minority and foreign capital. The latter had increased its presence despite sanctions. Foreign investment had grown by about Z$1 billion under UDI, and by independence, Z$3.3 billion (or 70 per cent) of the total capital stock of the country was under foreign control (mostly owned by some 130 British and 43 South African companies), with foreign-owned mining operations accounting for more than 90 per cent of mining production.[52] Yet constraints upon structural change in the economy were imposed by the constitution, the central provisions of which revolved around maintenance of property rights. Thus whites and foreign investors would continue owning half or more of the economy unless they were willing to dispose of their assets (farms, mines, manufacturing firms, and other businesses) on a 'willing buyer, willing seller' basis. Commercial agriculture accounted for 75 per cent of gross agricultural output, 95 per cent of marketed surplus, and nearly 100 per cent of agricultural earnings, and was dominated by a 'pampered, powerful yet hostile white agrarian bourgeoisie which had to be handled with extreme caution'.[53] Compensation in the case of compulsory purchase had to be paid immediately in foreign exchange, which ruled this out, unless there was to be a boom in exports or massive amounts of foreign aid designated for the purpose. It was not surprising that the political decision was taken not to contest the Lancaster House agreement, notwithstanding the government's continuing declared commitment to the establishment of an egalitarian society.[54] ZANU-PF initially opted for collaborative relations with capital, as the latter responded with the appointments of politically connected individuals to the boards of many companies. This provided for what Bond and Manyana describe as a 'bureaucratic-financial *comprador* elite',[55] although as will be discussed in Chapter 8, this was not to prove sufficient to protect the interests of white business when its economic utility to ZANU-PF declined.

[50] Xavier Kadhani (1986), 'The economy: Issues, problems and prospects', in Mandaza (ed.), op. cit., 99–122.

[51] Colin Stoneman (1988), 'The economy: Recognizing the reality', in Stoneman (ed.), op. cit., 43–62.

[52] Duncan Clarke (1980), *Foreign Companies and International Investment in Zimbabwe*, Gweru: Mambo Press.

[53] Clever Mumbengegwi (1986), 'Continuity and change in agricultural policy', in Mandaza (ed.), op. cit. 210.

[54] Stoneman, op. cit., 45.

[55] Patrick Bond and Masimba Manyana (2003), *Zimbabwe's Plunge: Exhausted Nationalism, Neo-liberalism and the Search for Social Justice*, Pietermaritzburg: University of KwaZulu-Natal Press.

Buoyed by the end of the war and sanctions, stimulation of internal demand by large wage increases, a corresponding increase in capacity utilization by manufacturing, access to foreign aid, high crop prices, and good rains, the first two years of independence saw remarkable growth at 12 per cent per annum, based significantly upon a 27 per cent increase in exports in 1980 with 7 per cent more in 1981. But thereafter crop (notably maize) and commodity prices fell, and although there were years of recovery during the 1980s, the decade was largely one of foreign-exchange shortages, contracting internal demand, drought, weakening terms of trade, high interest rates and oil prices, and wage gains being eroded by inflation. GDP growth rates averaged only 1.3 per cent per annum during 1982–90, outstripped by a population growth of 3.3 per cent. Similarly, only 10, 000 new jobs were created per annum during the first decade of independence, a figure which fell far short of the annual number of school-leavers (approximately 100,000 per year).[56]

Nonetheless, the independence decade was not without its advances. External financing (mostly foreign loans or aid, principally from the World Bank, the USA, the UK, and the European Economic Community) contributed to the government's ability to tackle infrastructure development (roads, schools, clinics, boreholes, and sanitation facilities), resettlement, and notably education and health. Between 1980 and 1990, the number of schools rose by a remarkable 80 per cent from 3,358 to 6,042, and by 1988, some 84 per cent of the population had access to safe drinking water. Additionally, a minimum wage was introduced, and workers' muscle was improved through the intro-duction of collective bargaining.[57] Against this, while foreign aid was heavily oriented towards developing rural areas, there was little interest amongst donors in funding a redistribution of land.

By as early as late 1982, the government had been forced to turn to the IMF for assistance to bridge the deficit on its current account, and a subsequent loan was granted only on condition of cuts in what the IMF regarded as excessive public expenditure (a first outcome being a freeze on civil service employ-ment).[58] Subsequently, popular resistance to cuts, official reluctance to curb health and educational expenditure, and continuing balance of payments deficits led the government in 1984 to freeze external remittances of dividends and profit, this prompting an immediate suspension of the IMF programme. However, despite a significant devaluation of the currency, the public debt mounted, not least because of the government's understandable commitment to increased defence expenditure, notably by deployment of 15,000 troops to defend its oil pipeline in Mozambique against South African aggression. By 1990 Zimbabwe had been forced back into the hands of the IMF.

In 1991, at the behest of the IMF, the government introduced its Economic Structural Adjustment Programme (ESAP) for 1991–95 which promised a 25 per cent cut in the civil service, along with the demise of labour restrictions, price controls, exchange controls, interest rate controls, investment regulations, import restrictions, and many subsidies, as well as reform (privatization) of a

[56] James Muzondidye (2009), 'From buoyancy to crisis', in Brian Raftopoulos and Alois Mlambo (eds), *Becoming Zimbabwe: A History from the Pre-Colonial Period to 2008*, Harare: Weaver Press, 167–200.
[57] Ibid., 168.
[58] Theresa Chimombe (1986), 'Foreign capital', in Mandaza (ed.), op. cit., 123–40.

parastatal sector which had, 'increasingly changed from production and marketing mechanisms into sites of political patronage as the State appointed boards based less on technical competence than on clientilism'.[59]

Meanwhile, user fees were introduced for children attending urban schools (an estimated 500,000 out of 2.3 million primary school pupils were expected to drop out) and for health services. The benefits were hailed as being a rise in annual growth rates to 5 per cent per annum, easier repayment of government debt, increased private investment, a growth in exports, and a reduction in inflation (from 20 per cent in 1991 to 10 per cent by 1994). But ESAP was introduced without any popular participation, and not surprisingly received a hostile response as, in practice, it 'failed miserably', with GDP growth averaging just 1.2 per cent during 1991–95, inflation averaging 30 per cent, and the budget deficit remaining at 10 per cent rather than reaching the targeted figure of 5 per cent by the end of the period. Adversely affected by droughts in 1992 and 1995, ESAP oversaw an increase in imports whilst exports decreased. Subsequent extension of the ESAP through to 1997 did little to assist. De-industrialization saw manufacturing's contribution to GDP decline from 22.8 per cent in 1990 to 17.1 per cent in 1998; employment levels plunged, the private sector shedding more than 50,000 jobs and the public sector nearly 25,000; and many of the gains made during the first independence decade in the education and health sectors were wiped out. Rural poverty intensified as spending on rural infrastructure and agricultural extension programmes was also cut back, increasing pressure on rural families and reducing peasant earnings. The severely deteriorating state of the economy resulted in extensive worker protest as the Zimbabwe Congress of Trade Unions (ZCTU) steadily distanced itself from government, providing the backdrop to the formation of the MDC.[60]

The crisis came to a head on 14 November 1997, following a crash of the Zimbabwe Stock Exchange in August, when the Zimbabwe dollar plunged, losing 40 per cent of its value in just four hours. Clearly the collapse was rooted in 'the 1970s crisis, 1980s stagnation and 1990s austerity',[61] but the proximate causes lay in the political interests of ZANU-PF. First was the government's decision made earlier in the year to become involved in the war in the Democratic Republic of Congo (DRC), and second, Mugabe's capitulation to demands made by 50,000-odd 'war veterans', led by Chenjerai Hunzvi, to grant a handout of Z$50,000 each, plus a Z$2,000 per month pension. These profligate developments were to be followed by the government's further decision to breach its hitherto broadly cooperative relationship with white agriculture by transferring some 15,000 white-owned farms into black hands, with compensation only for buildings and infrastructure, Mugabe's view being that purchase costs for land should be paid by the British government. Relations with the IMF, already tense, deteriorated further.[62] In September 1999, the IMF suspended a US$193 million loan designated as balance of payments support, citing the government's refusal to reveal its expenditure on the war in the DRC and its

[59] Martin Dawson and Tim Kelsall (2012), 'Anti-developmental patrimonialism in Zimbabwe', *Journal of Contemporary African Studies*, 30: 1, 49–66.
[60] Peter Gibbon (ed.), (1995), *Structural Adjustment and the Working Poor in Zimbabwe*, Uppsala: Nordic Africa Institute.
[61] Bond and Manyana, op. cit., 38.
[62] Ibid., 30–44.

failure to meet progress in implementing the latest ESAP. The government was forced to default on some of its foreign commitments, its debt standing at some US$7.5 billion (or around a quarter of GDP). By this time, Zimbabwe's foreign debt had become unpayable, with some 38 per cent of export earnings being spent on servicing foreign loans.[63] The situation was thereafter worsened by the postponement of the latest stabilization plan, adopted in late 1999, until after the 2000 election.[64]

Thus it was that the Zimbabwean economy was to be thrust into a 'world record decline'. As the government ramped up both its commitment to fast track land reform and its expenditure on defence, relations with the IMF verged on total breakdown. The IMF closed its office in Harare in 2004 and threatened Zimbabwe's expulsion from the organization. By 2006, GDP per capita was 47 per cent lower than in 1980, and 53 per cent below its 1991 peak; two years later, the rate of decline of real GDP had accelerated to minus 12.6 per cent. The government's ability to pay its way fell calamitously, expenditure financed by successive currency devaluations and its resort to printing money. External debt had risen to US$5.3 billion by 2008, while domestic debt had risen to an astounding Z$791 quadrillion. By this time, inflation had rocketed, and by July 2008 had reached an official level of 231 million per cent.[65]

Zimbabwe was bankrupt. Formal employment had shrunk from 1.4 million in 1998 to 998,000 in 2004. The share of wages in GDP had decreased from an average of 49 per cent between 1985 and 1990 to 29 per cent between 1997 and 2003. The education and health sectors became paralysed, drained of staff, equipment, and funding; food security for millions was imperilled; hundreds of thousands of Zimbabweans fled the country; electricity and water supplies dried up; and poverty increased dramatically. Meanwhile, inequality worsened, for those with the ability to borrow or access foreign currency (notably those with political clout) were enabled to reduce their debt burden by waiting for hyperinflation to wipe it out. Paradoxically, as the crisis deepened, the proportion of profits relative to GDP increased from 50 per cent during 1985–90 to 73 per cent during 1997–2003 while the poor became increasingly dependent upon the receipt of external remittances. The economic meltdown, latterly sustained by political repression, provided the backdrop to the bitterly contested 2008 election.

Only with the establishment of the coalition government, and the MDC's assuming responsibility for key areas in economic policy (although constantly frustrated by Mugabe's incumbent, Gideon Gono, at the Reserve Bank alongside militarized plundering of newly opened diamond fields) did the economy begin making a hesitant recovery.

[63] Ibid., 45.
[64] *ACR 1998–2000*, B855.
[65] Brian Raftopoulos (2009), 'The crisis in Zimbabwe', in Raftopoulos and Mlambo (eds), op. cit., 201–32; Amin Kamete (2004), 'Zimbabwe', in Andreas Mehler, Henning Melber and Klaas van Walraven (eds), *Africa Yearbook 2004*, Leiden: Brill, 480–92; and Amin Kamete (2008), 'Zimbabwe', in Mehler et al. (eds), *Africa Yearbook 2008*, 505–16.

Life at the margins: macro-economic policy in Namibia

Namibia's was often described in liberation circles as 'a branch plant economy', an extension of the apartheid order with extensive South African ownership of resources in all the advanced sectors of the economy.[66] GDP in 1989 amounted to R4.3 billion with a per capita income of R3,300 for a population of around 1.3 million, but this masked a huge disparity between the white population, a tiny black middle class, and the mass of the population, who were overwhelmingly subsistence-level peasants. Mining contributed 29.1 per cent of GDP; government 19.8 per cent; trade, hotels and catering 12.3 per cent; agriculture and fisheries 11.3 per cent, with manufacturing coming in at just 4.9 per cent. However, mining accounted for 70 per cent of the country's exports.[67] Meanwhile, up to 70 per cent of Namibians were involved in agriculture, primarily in the subsistence sector. In the formal sector, government and social services accounted for 40 per cent of employees; agriculture and fisheries 20 per cent; and mining and manufacturing just over 5 per cent each, with unemployment being about 30 per cent.[68]

Clearly, Namibia's options were massively circumscribed. At best, it seemed that the country might be able to increase mineral exports and broaden minerals refining and agricultural production and processing, but prospects for expansion of manufacturing were inherently limited by the small population. Further difficulties were presented by the forthcoming loss of direct South African budgetary support and, ironically, by the South African military withdrawal, which for decades had pumped massive expenditure into Namibia. Most of this money had been raised commercially in South Africa at high interest rates, increasing the debt to at one time nearly a third of GDP, although determined efforts had been made to reduce this (so that by independence it had fallen to about one quarter). One reason was the anxiety of the South African financial community that a SWAPO government would renege on the debt.[69] However, the prospects for that were limited, for Namibia was in dire need of securing its international credit rating. Namibia, stated Louis Pienaar, the last Administrator-General, needed external support, as it simply could not pay its way – a strong hint that South Africa's withdrawal would come with a considerable financial cost. SWAPO, in short, had little choice but to dilute its previously socialist image, to accept that it would have to continue to trade with its apartheid neighbour, and to submit to pressure from influential sources to adopt pro-market policies. While SWAPO looked forward to developing Namibia's infrastructural and trade links with SADC countries, growth would depend heavily upon attracting external public assis-

---

[66] See for instance, Douglas Anglin (1991), 'Namibian relations with South Africa: Post-independence prospects', in Larry Swatuk and Timothy Shaw (eds), *Prospects for Peace and Development in Southern Africa in the 1990s: Canadian and Comparative Perspectives*, Lanham NY: University of America Press, 93–114.

[67] Economist Intelligence Unit, op. cit., 10–13.

[68] *ACR 1989–90*, B575–79.

[69] Anglin, op. cit., 101.

tance from international agencies as well as increased levels of private sector investment.

With such minimal room for manoeuvre, SWAPO was to opt for a strategy whereby the small political elite was absorbed into the capitalist structure of the economy (via political office, the parastatals or black economic empowerment), while only limited gains were passed on to workers and only a small proportion of economic surplus was diverted to the party's broader constituency. Officially, however, the early years of independence saw the government identifying four major official objectives: a growth rate of 5 per cent per annum; increased employment; a reduction of inequalities in income distribution; and the designing of programmes to alleviate poverty. A National Planning Commission was established in 1992 and was to produce a Transitional National Development Plan in 1993. This in turn was to prove a precursor to successive Five Year Plans. However, although plan formulation involved consultation with both business and labour, SWAPO macro-economics were aggressively pro-market, with little impact made by 'planning'.[70]

Major emphasis was laid upon attracting foreign investment, but this was to prove insufficient to effect significant structural change. During the 1990s, whilst diamond mining was maintained, the production of most other minerals declined, with mechanization and mine closures leading to reduced employment (down to 7,700 in 1998 compared to 20,000 in the early 1980s). Subsequently, diamond mining fluctuated wildly, although slack in the sector was taken up by the rapid increase in uranium production as Namibia became the fourth main global supplier after Canada, Kazakhstan, and Australia. Overall, although the contribution of mining to GDP had fallen to around 13 per cent by the late 2000s, dependence upon mineral exports had remained critical (25–28 per cent of merchandise exports). Similarly, the fishing industry had experienced contrasting fortunes. While the sector had continued to be of high interest to investors (who were generally expected to go into partnership with Namibians), and while fishing output was by the early 2000s three times as great as it had been in the early 1990s, efforts to encourage growth of a domestic market had failed dismally (97 per cent of production being regularly exported). Furthermore, the industry confronted severe limits, faced with the threat of over-fishing and the need for sustainable exploitation. Meanwhile, although tourism had increased markedly, it met with severe competition from neighbouring countries and was highly sensitive to global conditions. Agriculture had remained dominated by white-owned commercial farms and devoted largely to livestock production, while continuously subject to the constraints of drought and the country's fragile ecology.[71]

Hopes were placed in an expansion of manufacturing, yet the sector's performance proved disappointing. Its contribution to job creation decreased after independence, despite various tax and other concessions granted to attract foreign investment.[72] One of the most significant initiatives was the establishment of Export Processing Zones (EPZs) in 1995 to encourage export-oriented industry. Within a few years, it attracted investments from Chinese, German,

---

[70] *ACR 1992–94*, B637–59; *1996–98*, B682–96.
[71] *Inter alia*, Robin Sherbourne (2010), *Guide to the Namibian Economy 2010*, Windhoek: Institute for Public Policy Research.
[72] Ibid., 203.

Italian, Lebanese, British, Taiwanese, and Malaysian companies. By 2001, 31 companies with EPZ status (meaning that they received tax advantages and ducked established labour market regulations) had been established, and had created some 2,500 jobs. Apart from that made by a Malaysian textile company Ramatex, which probably accounted for about 1,000 of those jobs, the major investments were made in the minerals' beneficiation sector by (what is now) Namibia Custom Smelters in a copper smelting plant and by Namzinc (an Anglo-American subsidiary) in zinc refining, while there was also some growth in the area of cutting and polishing diamonds.[73] Even so, notably after Ramatex opted to pull out of the country after conflicts with labour (see Chapter 7), manufacturing continued to centre around food processing (meat and fish), and the production of beer, soft drinks, dairy, and other items. Overall, manufacturing output had climbed to nearly 19 per cent of GDP by the late 2000s, yet the EPZ strategy brought dubious gains, while the textile industry in particular had aroused major environmental concerns regarding the pollution of Namibia's scarce water resources.[74] Subsequent to the Ramatex saga, the EPZ concept has fallen out of political favour.[75]

By the early 2000s, the one other area which had consistently grown was government spending, national debt having risen to around 30 per cent of GDP. Much of this was occasioned by expansion of public employment. This was necessary to benefit SWAPO's constituency – although the Finance Minister of the day referred to the civil service as 'bloated'– along with rising defence expenditures, occasioned in part to integrate PLAN fighters into the established army. Alarmingly, for a country with no apparent external threat, the latter had reached the 10 per cent of the budget spent on health and social services. In 2004, the government dropped a previous refusal to deal with international financial institutions, and took a loan of some US$1.7 million from the World Bank. By 2006, it was working with the IMF to reduce the public debt through such strategies as 'fiscal consolidation' and privatization of certain government assets.[76]

Bringing about structural reform of the economy was never going to be easy. By the mid-2000s, the government was facing the further challenge of South Africa's determination to restructure the Southern African Customs Union (SACU) and to introduce new free trade arrangements which were expected to significantly reduce revenue flows to Botswana, Lesotho, and Swaziland as well as to Namibia. To be sure, the first two decades of Namibia's independence realized certain gains for the mass of the population. In particular, the number of people living in absolute poverty decreased from 58 per cent of individuals in 1993–94 to 38 per cent in 2003–04, while over the two decades of independence, an average growth in the population of 2.6 per cent per annum was surpassed by an average growth rate of 3.6 per cent a year, implying that 'the average Namibian' had become 'better off'.[77] Yet against this, according to strict

---

[73] Ibid., 203–06.
[74] *ACR 2000–2002*, B807–24.
[75] Sherbourne, op. cit., 211.
[76] Henning Melber (2004), 'Namibia', in Mehler et al. (eds), op. cit., 443–50; Henning Melber (2006) 'Namibia', in Mehler et al. (eds) *Africa Yearbook 2006*, Leiden: Brill, 458–67.
[77] Sherbourne, op. cit., 6. According to the National Planning Commission, poor households are those that spend more than 60 per cent of their income on food (ibid., 73).

definitions, the unemployment rate had increased from around 19 per cent in the early 1990s to nearly 30 per cent in 2008, whilst the absolute numbers of people employed had remained static at around 380,000. Meanwhile, there had been a significant drop in the number of people dependent upon communal farming (down from nearly 138,000 in 1991 to just over 30,000 in 2008).[78] This implied an increasing dependence upon informal sector income rather than social grants, for official figures suggest that the proportion of people who drew the principal source of their income from old age pensions or remittances and grants had actually declined (from 15.6 per cent in 1993–94 to 12 per cent in 2003–04).[79] While the government has added allowances for war veterans to its welfare coverage and made more generous child maintenance grants available, it has vigorously resisted calls for implementation of a Basic Income Grant (BIG).[80] Thus, although they have declined somewhat since independence, Namibia has retained apartheid patterns of inequality. In 2004, it was calculated by the Central Bureau of Statistics that the wealthiest 10 per cent of the population (no longer exclusively white) had consumption levels some 50 times higher than the poorest 10 per cent, and that the Gini co-efficient stood at 0.63. As the Bureau confessed, 'in addition to being among the most unequal societies in the world, Namibia is among the most polarized'.[81]

In June 2004, the government introduced Vision 2030. This aims to place the quality of life of all Namibians on a par with people in the developed world by 2030. It assumes that Namibia will have a population of around 3 million people and an unemployment rate of less than 5 per cent of the workforce. Given past performance, this seems pie in the sky. Two decades into independence, Namibia remains an extension of the South African economy, and remains yoked to the constraints of its development pattern.

Realism and neo-liberalism: macro-economic policy in South Africa

Two visions of ANC economic management regularly present themselves. From the right, the post-1990 ANC is seen as having adapted to global 'realities' by implementing responsibly pro-market strategies and returning the economy to levels of growth which, although modest, have exceeded those attained during the last two decades of NP rule. Nonetheless, this perspective simultaneously argues that growth would occur even faster if current restrictions on the economy (retained because of pressures imposed upon ANC economic managers by the party's organized left) were dropped, and both the labour and capital markets were made more 'flexible'. From the left, the ANC is subject to a critique that upon assuming power, it rapidly abandoned the collectivist-oriented Reconstruction and Development Programme (RDP) in favour of the 'neo-liberal' Growth, Employment and Redistribution (GEAR) strategy and

---

[78] There have been significant increases in employment in fishing, wholesale and retail, and hotels and restaurants, while employment in mining has halved and remained relatively constant in manufacturing. Sherbourne, op. cit., 63–72.
[79] Ibid., 70
[80] Ibid., 32–33.
[81] Mehler et al. (eds) (2004), op. cit., 443–50.

enthusiastically embraced free-market capitalism. Regularly dubbed the '1996 class project', this perspective sees ANC policy as having been hijacked by a coterie of devils – not only large-scale capital, but an aspirant class of black capitalists championed by, above all, Thabo Mbeki and Trevor Manuel. The outcome has been that the mantra of 'growth' has replaced the idea of 'development' and the possibilities of South Africa embarking upon a progressive path productive of a 'better life for all' have been seriously curtailed. However, as Hein Marais has argued, while both of these opposed visions incorporate partial truths, they do as much to obscure as to illuminate South Africa's economic dilemmas.[82] Neither unfettered engagement with, nor frontal disengagement from, the global economy constituted a sensible strategy. Rather, a carefully calculated mix was needed. South Africa could have pursued a development path that 'combined carefully selected orthodox adjustments with traditional Keynesian measures and some radical innovations', thereby providing 'enough leeway and manoeuvring space for the achievements of national development priorities while realizing the rights and entitlements of citizens'.[83] Instead, the path that the ANC chose was one which embraced a futile attempt to 'catch up' with the industrialized world, despite South Africa's location in a world capitalist system in which 'the weaker zones of the world' are adjusted to the 'requirements of global accumulation'.[84] While this path was not without gains, it also came at considerable costs – and propelled South Africa along a trajectory which faces inevitable and worrying limits.

As outlined above, the accumulation strategy pursued by the South African economy historically was constructed upon the MEC. Economic development revolved around the mining and minerals sector, and the state and the mining industry prompted growth of manufacturing and parastatal sectors with strong links to the MEC.[85] In contrast, manufacturing sectors that had weaker connections to the MEC (with the exception of a few sectors, like the car industry) received limited support from the state. Manufacturing therefore remained dominated by sectors with strong links to the MEC, and these, with the exception of engineering and capital equipment, were capital- and energy-intensive process industries, such as electricity generation, minerals beneficiation (notably iron and steel, and aluminium) and the Sasol oil-from-coal process and its chemical byproducts.[86]

It is true that this provided for the most advanced level of industrialization on the continent and allowed South Africa to dominate the region economically. However, the industrialization process was far from linear. While during the 1960s manufacturing grew at almost 12 per cent annually, the economy was becoming increasingly capital-intensive. Further, the manufacturing sector failed to diversify sufficiently into capital and intermediate goods production,

[82] Hein Marais (2010), *South Africa Pushed to the Limit: The Political Economy of Change*, Cape Town: University of Cape Town Press.

[83] Ibid., 93.

[84] Samir Amin (1997), 'For a progressive and democratic new world order', conference paper, Afro-Asian Solidarity Conference, Cairo, April, cited by Marais, op. cit., 93.

[85] Ben Fine and Zavareh Rustomjee (1996), *The Political Economy of South Africa: From Minerals Energy Complex to Industrialisation*, London: Hurst.

[86] Seeraj Mohamed (2010), 'The state of the South African economy', in John Daniel, Prishani Naidoo, Devan Pillay and Roger Southall, (eds), *New South African Review 2010: Development or Decline?* Johannesburg: Wits University Press, 39–64.

and remained overwhelmingly committed to satisfying the MEC and domestic consumer needs, this in turn meaning that the bulk of technologies, machines, and equipment had to be imported. Thus although manufacturing's contribution to GDP came to exceed that of both mining and agriculture by far, export earnings remained overwhelmingly dependent upon mineral exports (70–85 per cent in most years). This meant that the foreign exchange needed to pay for much-needed capital and intermediate goods imports had to be provided not only by minerals export (notably of gold) but by foreign capital inflows. As long as minerals prices (notably of gold) and access to foreign exchange held up, the model could be sustained; at the same time, the terms of South Africa's insertion into the international economy rendered it structurally vulnerable. Ultimately, this was to prove critical to apartheid's downfall.[87]

By the end of the 1970s, the economy was looking increasingly battered. The 1973 oil crisis had plunged the global economy into recession; manufacturing's growing capital intensity rendered it increasingly dependent upon semi-skilled, skilled, and technical rather than migrant labour, a factor which underpinned the growth of the emerging black trade union movement; and the post-Soweto, post-1976 growth in black political resistance led to a massive outflow of foreign capital. Foreign confidence, further dented by international solidarity campaigns against foreign investment, thereafter remained peculiarly fragile, as was to be dramatically demonstrated when, in 1985, to the despair of Western governments, and after raising expectations of internal political reform, President P.W. Botha refused to 'cross the Rubicon' and triggered a massive debt crisis.

The withdrawal of foreign capital intensified a massive concentration and consolidation of domestic capital. During the 1950s and 1960s, the major mining houses had diversified into finance and manufacturing, and 'English' and 'Afrikaner' capital steadily merged their interests with each other and foreign capital. A further development was the greater interpenetration of private capital and the parastatals.[88] By 1981, over 70 per cent of the total assets of the top 138 South African companies were controlled by state corporations and 8 private conglomerates spanning mining, manufacturing, construction, transport, agriculture, and finance.[89] Manufacturing (along with public sector projects) had been heavily dependent upon foreign investment.[90] Meanwhile, South African investors faced severe official restrictions on their capacity to invest outside the immediate region. When foreign capital dried up in response to the mounting political crisis, foreign companies sold their assets locally to the conglomerates who faced limited options for investing their surplus capital. By 1990, just three conglomerates – Anglo-American, Sanlam and Old Mutual – controlled a massive 75 per cent (R425 billion) of the total capitalization (R567 billion) of the Johannesburg Stock Exchange (JSE).[91] However,

[87] Marais, op. cit., 28.
[88] Hermann Giliomee (1979), 'The Afrikaner economic advance', in Heribert Adam and Hermann Giliomee, *The Rise and Crisis of Afrikaner Power*, Cape Town: David Philip, 145–76.
[89] Robert Davies, Dan O'Meara and Sipho Dlamini (1984), *The Struggle for South Africa: A Reference Guide to Movements, Organisations and Institutions*, London: Zed Books, 58.
[90] Jill Nattrass (1981), *The South African Economy: Its Growth and Change*, Cape Town: Oxford University Press, 86–87.
[91] Andrew McGregor, Robert Rose and Steven Cranston (2009), 'Power-shift', *Financial Mail*, 23 January.

this increasing concentration of capital was not underpinned by a coherent industrial strategy capable of providing direction and synergy linking state and private enterprise, and the potential advantages of economies of scale were never realized. In short, the pattern of accumulation was becoming increasingly dysfunctional, and by the late 1980s, South African capital was urgently seeking a resolution to the political crisis which was seen as holding the economy back. A transition to democracy became a condition for the realization of further value – as long as the more radical aspirations of the ANC could be contained.[92]

The IMF and World Bank had ceased to lend money to South Africa in 1967, but by the early 1990s were eager to return, pending not only progress towards democracy but agreement on a feasible structural adjustment programme for an economy in crisis. However, although the ANC was equally eager to convince international investors that a new South Africa would be open to business, it was extremely cautious about becoming financially indebted to multilateral institutions. For all that Mbeki, Manuel and others rapidly became converts to fiscal austerity and market-friendly policies, there was equally serious concern about losing control over the direction of the economy to foreign creditors.[93]

On the one hand, the ANC was subject to massive lobbying by large-scale capital.[94] At the same time the government was aware of the urgent need to address the desperate legacy of apartheid: mass poverty, distorted production patterns, gross social inequalities,[95] enormous spatial disparities, and a misdirected public sector. The outcome of the resulting pressures – from the international financial institutions, capital, COSATU, the SACP, and civil society – were various 'social contract' scenarios that culminated in the ANC's adoption of the RDP. This was intended to lay the foundations for meeting mass expectations. It 'linked growth to development and highlighted the need to democratize both state and society', and was built around the four themes of meeting basic needs, developing human resources, building the economy, and democratizing society,[96] and became the ANC's manifesto for the 1994 election. Subsequently adopted in a somewhat watered down version by the GNU, the RDP became the key instrument of a proposed social contract.[97]

The RDP attracted support from large-scale capital as it came to appreciate the value of the new government seeking to kick-start a stagnant economy. But by as early as June 1996, the RDP was replaced by GEAR. This featured the familiar neo-liberal menu of reducing the deficit and countering inflation by cutting government expenditure, adopting a strict monetary policy, committing to a competitive exchange rate, removing obstacles to the free flow of capital, liberalizing the trade regime, promoting exports, privatizing 'non-essential' state enterprises, commercializing the others, seeking wage restraint, and

---

[92] Marais, op. cit., 29–34.
[93] Ibid., 57–58.
[94] Patrick Bond (2000), *Elite Transition: From Apartheid to Neoliberalism in South Africa*, Pietermaritzburg: University of Natal Press, 53–85.
[95] Citing *Business Day*, 6 January 1994, Turok, op. cit., 81 records that just 5 per cent of all South Africans owned 88 per cent of the country's wealth in 1993, while twenty families held shares worth R14.4 billion plus other undisclosed personal assets.
[96] Turok, op. cit., 89.
[97] Ibid., 88–90.

introducing 'regulated flexibility' into the labour market. GEAR promised creation of some 400,000 jobs annually, an annual growth rate of 6 per cent by 2000, an increase of exports by an average of 8.4 per cent per annum, and a radical improvement in social infrastructure.[98]

The adoption of GEAR is regularly depicted as the original sin of the ANC in government. Certainly, it was to cause major tensions within the Tripartite Alliance, and ultimately, COSATU and the SACP were to wreak vengeance upon the '1996 class project' when they combined with other forces to defeat Thabo Mbeki, the principal driver of GEAR, when he sought a third term as ANC President at Polokwane in December 2009. Further, the manner of GEAR's introduction caused deep bitterness within the party, for it was drawn up in secretive conditions before being peremptorily presented to the ANC in parliament (and then only to a small group of finance committee members) before it was tabled in the National Assembly, with Finance Minister Trevor Manuel declaring the plan 'non-negotiable'. Yet although GEAR was seriously at odds with the ANC's proclaimed vision regarding poverty, employment, and inequality, the left should not perhaps have been so surprised at the policy shift. It was not merely that the world had changed with the fall of the Berlin Wall and the collapse in confidence of social democracy globally; nor was it merely that the ANC was subject to enormous pressures from conservative forces internationally and domestically, nor indeed that there was, in truth, a serious need to tackle the serious debt inherited from the apartheid regime. It was also that the ANC's economic policies were highly schematic: plans drawn up by progressive economists to develop new macro-economic strategies which preceded adoption of the RDP had been hampered by infighting within the movement;[99] and above all, there was a significant class element within the ANC which was distinctly pro-capitalist. After all, as was clearly articulated by the theory of the NDR, the ANC was committed to the promotion of a 'patriotic bourgeoisie'. GEAR therefore fed a hope for 'mutually beneficial accommodation with domestic and international capital, in which drastic and conservative economic adjustments could be reconciled with the goal of quickly engineering a black capitalist class and achieving social upliftment'.[100] Certainly, Mbeki and Manuel were forthright in declaring GEAR the necessary means for implementing the RDP!

According to Alan Hirsch, Chief Director of Economic Policy in the Presidency, GEAR was less a lurch towards neo-liberalism than a necessary response to market uncertainties and provided the foundation for a bid to transform an inward-looking and protectionist economy into a more competitive global player, and one that was more caring of its poorer citizens.[101] Whatever, GEAR set the ANC's South Africa upon an economic path from which, although adjustments have been made, it has never fundamentally deviated.

The controversies which have swirled around the ANC's economic management reveal a record which is decidedly mixed. Certainly, GEAR failed to realize its promised objectives in terms of a 6 per cent growth rate, employment

---

[98] Marais, op. cit., 113.

[99] On the demise, particularly, of the left-leaning Macro-Economic Research Group in 1992, see Bond, op. cit., 77–78; and Marais, op. cit., 107–08.

[100] Marais, op. cit., 109.

[101] Alan Hirsch (2004), *Season of Hope: Economic Reform under Mandela and Mbeki*, Pietermaritzburg: University of KwaZulu-Natal Press.

creation, export promotion, and diversification. Nonetheless, there were considerable achievements. Real GDP grew at an average rate of 3 per cent between 1995 and 2003, considerably less than hoped for, but nonetheless double the growth rate recorded between 1980 and 1994; and by 2009, GDP per head had climbed to R35,909 (at constant 2005 prices), although it had not been until 2006 that this indicator had climbed above the previous high of R33,841 recorded as far back as 1981.[102] Above all, the ANC deserves credit for its substantial transfer of resources to the old, disabled, unemployed, and for child support, and so on, via an expansion of welfare payments which recorded a massive leap in the number of beneficiaries of social grants from 3.4 million in 2001 to fully 12.4 million in 2008.[103] This occurred alongside a decline in the proportion of people living in absolute poverty from 4.2 per cent of the population in 1996 to 1.4 per cent in 2008.[104] Such gains have led to the government becoming globally regarded as far more competent, in macro-economic terms, than its NP predecessor. Equally, however, there is a strong case that its achievements were not only dangerously short term, but failed to achieve a fundamental transformation of the economy.

To risk a brief summary of key features of an immense body of work:

First, fiscal deregulation has led to an extensive internationalization of the economy which, rather than attracting hoped-for inflows of foreign investment capital, have rendered South Africa grossly dependent upon international currency flows. Heightened global exposure has made government policy increasingly responsive to the short-term demands of what Trevor Manuel once termed the 'amorphous market',[105] rather than being able to pursue long-term strategies of development.

Second, while deregulation has enabled Johannesburg to become the African continent's primary financial centre, it has also provided for a major outflow of investment capital as, from the early 1990s, major conglomerates unbundled, with key entities – notably Billiton, South African Breweries, Anglo-American, Old Mutual, and Liberty Life – moving their primary listings to London. While foreign investors have moved in to purchase assets from this unbundling, most such investment has been made by institutional investors guided by fund managers, who have notoriously short-term financial objectives. By the end of 2007, foreign shareholders held 45 per cent of the JSE's issued shares.

Third, increased dependence upon short-term capital inflows has been accompanied by an alarming de-industrialization of the economy. The opening of the economy has exposed the manufacturing sector to international competition from low-wage producers, notably from China and the East. Inflows of short-term capital led to increased private sector credit but this was associated with increased debt-driven consumption by households and speculation in real estate and financial asset markets. The largest beneficiaries of capital stock growth after government services during 2000–06 were finance and insurance services, while almost all manufacturing sectors (save motor vehicles, the one

[102] South African Institute of Race Relations (SAIRR), *South Africa Survey, 2009–10*, 95–96.
[103] Ibid., 526.
[104] SAIRR, *South Africa Survey 2008–09*, 302. The definition of poverty is not made explicit, but is borrowed from the World Bank.
[105] *Business Times*, 15 March 1998.

sector for which government had a coherent industrial policy) experienced low or negative growth in capital stock.[106]

Fourth, partnered by COSATU, the ANC government implemented such measures as the Labour Relations Act of 1995, the Basic Conditions of Employment Act of 1997, the Skills Development Act of 1998, and the Employment Equity Act of 1998 which together provide extensive rights for labour, inclusive of protections versus arbitrary dismissal and implementation of a minimum wage for formal employment. These embodied the trade unions' advocacy of a progressive labour regime, inclusive of extensive tripartite engagement between labour, business, and capital, rejecting notions that global competitiveness could be enhanced by lowering wages and increasing labour flexibility. Yet while labour 'may have won the battle for progressive legislation', it 'lost the war for progressive economic policies'.[107] The government has consistently argued that the loss of old jobs has been more than replaced by new ones (albeit with more jobs having been created in the informal sector). Nonetheless, unemployment has remained consistently high at an official level of around 25 per cent (or 40 per cent by less restrictive measurements). According to one study, even if 'official' unemployment were to be halved to 13 per cent by 2014, 35 per cent of the population would continue to live below a poverty line of R2,500 a month unless they were to be rescued by receipt of social grants.[108] However, the government worries that continued growth in the number of grant recipients may render its version of the 'welfare state' increasingly unaffordable.[109]

Fifth, the impact of high unemployment is made worse by the continuing high level of social inequality. In 2008, while the richest 10 per cent of the population received 53.1 per cent and the richest 20 per cent received 70 per cent of national income, the poorest 20 per cent got 1.6 per cent, while the very poorest 10 per cent received just 0.57 per cent. These proportions have not changed significantly since the early 1990s, despite some modest shift of the overall proportion of national income to blacks. Annual disposable income for whites (9 per cent of the population) dropped from 44.3 per cent of the total in 1998 to 40.3 per cent in 2008.[110] Whites, as a category, have prospered financially under the ANC. In 2009, whites accounted for 61.8 per cent of 'affluent individuals', defined as those with incomes in excess of R600,000 per annum, compared with an equivalent proportion of 26.9 per cent for Africans.[111] Political strains, notably in the form of one of the world's highest strike rates, are incurred by corporate and parastatal CEOs and senior managers (now black as well as white) receiving remuneration at globally competitive levels, resulting in obscene disparities with workers on the shop floor.

[106] Mohamed, op. cit., 55–59.
[107] Ibid.
[108] Cited in Roger Southall (2010), 'South Africa 2010: From short-term success to long-term decline?' in Daniel et al. (eds), op. cit., 9.
[109] The number of grant recipients is expected to rise to 16 million by 2013, but there is concern that this will not be matched by an appropriate increase in the relatively small base of direct personal taxpayers (*Business Report*, 22 February 2010).
[110] Republic of South Africa (2009), 'Development indicators', http://www.info.gov.za/other-docs 2009/developmentindicators2009
[111] SAIRR, *South Africa Survey 2009–10*, 248.

Sixth, while manufacturing has stagnated and the financial and service sectors have grown substantially, the economy continues to bear the heavy imprint of the MEC. In 1990, mining accounted for just 15.3 per cent of exports and just 1.64 per cent of imports. However, by 2008, it accounted for 37.9 per cent of exports and 20.3 per cent of imports. Globalization would seem to have enhanced dependence upon the MEC rather than having encouraged a wider diversification of the economy. Not surprisingly, commentators are becoming concerned that the present development model is reaching its limits politically, economically, socially, and – increasingly – ecologically.[112] True, the government now seeks to overcome such limits by rendering South Africa a 'developmental state' through more strategic use of parastatals as public investment vehicles both domestically and throughout the African continent.[113] However, its ability to do so remains drastically constrained by the limited capacity of state-owned enterprises whose efficiencies have become severely compromised by their designation as sites of political patronage. South Africa's entry into BRICS,[114] the intercontinental club of leading 'emerging economies', may well open up increased possibilities for inward investment, notably in mining, yet at potential costs of the reinforcement of the MEC and the contradictory impulses of 'a new scramble for Africa'.[115]

Against this background, there are major concerns for the country's social coherence. ANC policy has fostered a small if growing black bourgeoisie in both the state and private sectors via black economic empowerment (see Chapter 8). This has remained overwhelmingly dependent upon political backing, and many regard it as more parasitic than patriotic because of its extensive involvement in rent-seeking. An associated black (lower) middle class has developed within, notably, the state but also in the professions and private business. However, their prospects are clouded by a failure of the educational system to provide the supply of highly skilled young people that the economy needs. COSATU continues to represent one of the ANC's core constituencies, and one the government is reluctant if not unable to ignore, even though union battles are often fought by workers within a public sector, vast swathes of which are noted for their incompetence and lethargy. This only increases the growing gap between unionized workers in the formal sector and the larger majority of non-unionized working poor struggling in the informal and rural sectors, a contradiction which the ANC seeks to contain through its growing infrastructure of social grants. As a broad church, the ANC seeks to hold its diverse constituencies together, and hitherto it has done so with reasonable success. However, the global crisis which has unleashed its impact on South Africa since 2008, accelerating job losses and squeezing the limited amount of fiscal surplus available, threatens to dissolve the economic glue which is so important in holding the ANC together.

[112] Marais, op. cit., passim; Devan Pillay (2010), 'South Africa and the eco-logic of the global capitalist crisis', in Daniel et al. (eds), op. cit., 24–38.
[113] For a recent statement, see Kgalema Motlanthe (2011), 'A new world is possible!' *ANC Today*, 7–13 October.
[114] Composed of Brazil, Russia, India, China, and – from 2010 – South Africa (not in the same league, but required as a representative of Africa).
[115] Roger Southall and Henning Melber (eds), (2008), *A New Scramble for Africa? Imperialism, Investment and Development*, Pietermaritzburg: University of KwaZulu-Natal Press.

Constraints and contradictions

This chapter has outlined the difficult path which had to be trodden by the NLMs on their assumption of power in highly constrained circumstances. For the liberal democracies which their transitional settlements prescribed to function successfully, commitments by the new ruling parties to democratic norms and practices were required alongside the capacity and willingness to operate a capitalist economy. However, the political cultures of the liberation movements severely compromised their democratic orientations, with their espousal of a vanguard role inclining them to a commandist politics which aspired to a totalizing control of the state and society. Such perspectives proved peculiarly pernicious in the case of ZANU-PF, strongly inclined SWAPO to notions of political monopoly and, alongside the ANC, to embark on a comprehensive blurring of the party and the state. Meanwhile, the running of relatively advanced capitalist economies required economic strategies which could combine cooperative relations with capital while securing strategic concessions from capital to bring about some degree of structural economic reform in favour of greater equity. As will be explored later, the manner in which the three liberation movements set about this task varied considerably, the principal distinction being the blatant manner in which the political class as represented by ZANU-PF embarked upon a crude project of rent-seeking and primitive accumulation, destroying the conditions for capitalist profit upon which, contradictorily, it depended. The result was Zimbabwe's plunge into an orgy of decline and dictatorship from which it will take decades to recover. In contrast, SWAPO engaged in a functional accommodation with capital which allowed for the incorporation of its small elite and kept the economy afloat, but did little else. The ANC, faced by a far more complex economy, forged a bargain with large-scale capital which provided for a combination of reasonable growth, incorporation of an emergent black bourgeoisie, and the allocation of reasonable levels of surplus to core sectors of its constituency, not excluding the poor. Hitherto this has proved sufficient to sustain its political dominance in successive democratic elections. However, the dilemma that the ANC now faces is whether the deal it has constructed with capital is sufficient to sustain its rule against a backdrop of still-brutal social inequality, massive unemployment, and growing social protest. Democracy will demand that it opts to maintain its rule through the ballot rather than, like ZANU-PF, the bullet.

5.
Liberation Movements and Elections

The political settlements in Zimbabwe, Namibia, and South Africa cast victory in democratic elections as the principal *rite de passage* before power was to be transferred from the old regimes to the new. The rules of the game differed in all three cases. However, the thrust of the arrangements was that transitional elections were required not merely to elect new governments but to confirm popular acceptance of the new constitutional orders. Furthermore, whilst enabling newly elected governments to secure access to office, these elections would provide the opportunity for winning parties to make a political accommodation with both key constituencies of the old regime and other political competitors. Yet in the age of post-Cold War, 'third wave' democracy, it was necessary to do more than win one just election. Rather, it was necessary for NLMs, if they were to retain power with legitimacy, to perpetually renew their mandates via repeat victories in successive democratic elections.

This requirement was a potential paradox, for while liberation movements might lay claim to embodying 'the nation', post-transitional elections opened the possibility to demonstrations that, in electoral terms, they did not; in turn, loss of elections should, in constitutional terms, mean loss of power. Yet if for NLMs the logic of history dictated that they represented the nation, then electoral defeat would constitute a reversal of history, even while democratic experience worldwide demonstrates that it is quite customary for even highly popular governments to lose support over time. After all, the whole thrust of liberal democracy is to provide for competitive elections and peaceful alternations in power.

There was also another factor, for incumbent governments regularly embody sectional or class interests even while claiming to represent the general will. The implication was that NLMs might transform into instruments of class or sectional rather than popular rule. In short, the different NLMs were to face the perpetual challenge of proving that they embodied both the national and popular wills simultaneously. To the extent that they failed to achieve this, the prospect was that the state would be thrust into crisis if nationalism chose to trump democracy.

This chapter will proceed by examining the basis for the victories in transitional elections obtained by ZANU-PF, SWAPO, and the ANC. While the latter pair have managed to establish their 'dominance' by demonstrating the continuing support of the voting electorate, ZANU-PF has not, and to retain power has had to resort to systematic electoral fraud and political violence. This would seem to suggest a fundamental difference between ZANU-PF and its fellow NLMs; yet if, as argued in this book, NLMs are members of the same family, do apparently very different electoral outcomes obscure important similarities? To answer this question, this chapter will compare how electoral systems have been managed; how resources for electoral purposes have been allocated; the extent to which the different NLMs have been prepared to resort to political and/or military coercion to secure desired results; and how the need to secure control over the state has transformed the liberation movements into electoral machines.

Winning transitional elections

Whether or not they were effectively imposed by external actors or forged by political adversaries themselves, the electoral arrangements adopted were all fundamental components of the political transitions. It is now history that all three NLMs secured sufficiently generous victories to establish their right to rule, ZANU-PF securing 63 per cent of the popular vote in Zimbabwe in 1980, SWAPO obtaining 57.3 per cent in Namibia in 1989, and the ANC triumphing with nearly 63 per cent in South Africa in 1994.

The victories secured by the three parties were all obtained in conditions which were proclaimed by the electoral authorities and electoral monitoring bodies to have been, in the given circumstances, 'free and fair'. While all three liberation movements secured substantial majorities, all three transitional elections recorded substantial votes for minority parties, whether rival nationalist or formerly white ruling ones. Thus whilst all three election victories were impressive, none were sufficiently comprehensive to endorse any claim that the NLM concerned represented the 'nation' if the 'people' and the 'nation' were truly one.

Initially, however, the focus of all three NLMs was to consolidate their hold on power by increasing their majorities in (and between) subsequent elections, and in so doing, to establish their political hegemony. As with any governments, this depended in considerable part upon increasing their appeal to voters through their performance in power. Yet, notably in Zimbabwe, it was also to be facilitated by changes made to the electoral and political systems, sometimes through blatant manipulation of the constitution.

At this point it is helpful to begin by examining the experiences of Namibia and South Africa before turning to the more turbulent developments in Zimbabwe.

SWAPO: establishing electoral dominance in Namibia

The negotiations process which preceded Namibia's transition to independence was largely conducted without the involvement of Namibians themselves. Its principal actors were the US, which was intent on securing withdrawal of Cuban troops from Angola; Cuba, whose enthusiasm for remaining in southern Africa was eroded by the loss of interest in the region by its sponsor, the Soviet Union; and South Africa, Namibia's *de facto* colonial power.

By mid-1988, agreement had been reached regarding the essential principles for peace in the region, including the implementation of the UN Security Council Resolution 435 of 1978 which would set Namibia's independence process in motion. The first day of April 1989 was confirmed as the date for implementation of Resolution 435 whereby South Africa would withdraw all but 1,500 of its military forces from Namibia; the UN would guarantee the independence process and oversee free elections; and Cuba would begin a withdrawal from Angola. From mid-1988, powers were progressively handed over to the UN, whose activities were supervised by its special envoy, Martti Ahhtisari, with day-to-day administration taken over by a Transitional Government which was largely representative of the DTA and various ethnic parties. In May 1988 the Transitional Government had invited Sam Nujoma to participate in the drafting of a constitution acceptable to all, but the SWAPO leader turned this down as it would have run contrary to the procedure outlined in UN 435 which dictated prior election of a Constituent Assembly, and thereafter elections for a government. Subsequently, once a final agreement had been signed between Angola, Cuba, and South Africa on 22 December 1988, the authority of the Transitional Agreement was gradually reduced until it dissolved itself on 28 February 1989. Although South Africa retained an active presence, authority passed steadily over to the UN.[1]

About 4,560 troops, nearly 1,000 police, 760 administrative staff and 650 electoral personnel drawn from some 90 countries were deployed by the United Nations Transition Assistance Group (UNTAG), enjoying wide powers and responsibilities. These included overseeing the withdrawal of South African troops and the demobilization of the South West African Territorial Force. These tasks were not accomplished without difficulty. For instance, there were credible complaints that South African forces actively encouraged anti-SWAPO propaganda in the Ovambo-dominated north and were intimidating war-weary villagers. However, the most controversy was caused by the UN's backing of a South African military repulse of the crossing over the Angolan border into Namibia of some 1,500 SWAPO guerrillas, the UN claiming its own troops were not in place to undertake this role themselves and were engaged for peacekeeping rather than combat operations. Motives for the incursion were not clear, but may have included a determination to claim that, following years of warfare, SWAPO had managed to establish a base in Namibia. Suffice it to say, the foray was widely deemed adventurist, leading to the massacre of some hundreds of its combatants before SWAPO was induced to withdraw its troops back across the border. Thereafter, while SWAPO began to rally support in Africa against an alleged unholy alliance between the UN and South Africa, the UN found that, broadly, South Africa adhered to the demands of the transitional programme, although it was rumoured that Pretoria would be prepared to confront SWAPO militarily if the latter, failing to obtain a majority, opted to return to armed struggle.[2]

SWAPO had wanted to retain the FPTP electoral system which hitherto had been in use in South West Africa for ethnic and national elections, probably calculating that this would amplify the size of its expected majority. However, the 'liberation' election, when it came in November 1989, was conducted under a national list PR system, without a minimum threshold of votes required to obtain a seat. This system had been proposed by South Africa as far back as 1982 and was accepted by the UN as providing for the widest possible representation. As far as Pretoria was concerned, the danger was that SWAPO would

[1]   *ACR 1988–89*, B625–35.
[2]   *ACR 1989–90*, B560–68.

obtain a two-thirds majority, which according to the agreement reached would enable it to impose a constitution upon the Assembly (a dangerous precedent for potential developments in South Africa itself). In the event, the election produced what many regarded as an optimal result, with SWAPO winning 41 seats out of 80, enabling it to establish its legitimacy as a majority party yet not winning enough seats (48) to write a new constitution on its own. The opposition, headed by the DTA, while regarded as tainted by their ethnic past nonetheless secured enough seats to sit as a convincing opposition and to serve as a serious counterbalance in the constitution-making process.[3]

Following its victory, SWAPO readily accepted the need to work with minority parties, notably the DTA, in drawing up a constitution and became 'remarkably compliant with the insistence on democratic procedures'.[4] Against prior expectation it accepted constitutional principles adopted by the UN in 1982 which provided for a unitary and democratic state, an independent judiciary, a bill of fundamental rights, universal elections, and the separation of powers of the three branches of government. After a first meeting on 21 November 1989, the Constituent Assembly completed its work on 9 February 1990, its final draft being passed unanimously and earning plaudits for being one of the most enlightened constitutions to be found anywhere in the world. This set the stage for the withdrawal of the last remaining South African troops and Namibia's proceeding to independence on 21 March 1990 under Sam Nujoma who had been elected by the Assembly as President. Following the election the Constituent Assembly transformed itself into the National Assembly.[5]

During the decades that have followed SWAPO has substantially increased its parliamentary majority and can be said to have established itself as a dominant party. This is recorded by the results of the three post-transitional elections for both the National Assembly and for the President, an elective presidency (limited to two terms from 1994) having been introduced under the constitution. The results of the four elections hitherto for the National Assembly have been as shown in Table 5.1 on page 101.

Nujoma secured election as President with 74.46 per cent of the votes in 1994 and 76.84 per cent in 1999, while Hifikepunye Pohamba, his successor as SWAPO's presidential candidate, obtained 76.45 per cent in 2004 and 75.25 per cent in 2009. In turn, this electoral dominance has been reinforced, first by the right of the President, from 1994 to nominate six persons to the National Assembly; second, from 1992, by successive SWAPO victories in elections for some 13 Regional Councils and over 40 local authorities – the first elected every six years using FPTP, the latter according to party list PR; and third, by the election by the Regional Councils of two of their members to a National Council, the upper chamber of parliament, which although having very limited powers of review, has served as a handy sphere of patronage for the ruling party.

Namibian elections have been regarded as reflecting the will of the Namibian electorate, with diverse (African, regional and other) election observer missions reporting that the election processes have been largely free and fair. However, in recent times there has been increasing criticism regarding, for instance, the

---

[3] ACE Electoral Knowledge Network, undated, 'Namibia: National list in southern Africa', http://aceproject.org/ace-en/topics/es/esy/esy_na
[4] *ACR 1988–89*, B574.
[5] *ACR 1989–90*, B560–68.

Table 5.1 Namibian National Assembly Elections 1989–2009[6]

Party	Valid Votes	% Valid Votes	Elected Seats
		1989 Election	
SWAPO	384,567	57.32	41
DTA	191,532	28.55	21
UDF	37,874	5.64	4
Other	56,857	8.5	6
Total	670,830		72
		1994 Election	
SWAPO	361,809	72.72	53
DTA	101,748	20.45	15
UDF	13,309	2.68	2
Other	12,779	2.57	1
Total	489,645		72
		1999 Election	
SWAPO	408,174	76.15	55
DTA	50,824	9.48	7
COD	53,289	10.05	7
UDF	15,685	2.93	2
Other	8,064	1.5	1
Total	536,036		72
		2004 Election	
SWAPO	620,609	75.83	55
COD	59,464	7.23	5
DTA	42,070	5.14	4
NUDO	34,814	4.25	3
UDF	30,355	3.71	3
Other	31,127	3.81	72
Total	818,439		
		2009 Election	
SWAPO	602,580	74.29	54
RDP	90,556	11.16	8
DTA	25,393	3.13	2
NUDO	24,422	3.01	2
Other	57,616	7.11	6
Total	800,567		72

strong bias of the state broadcaster, the Namibian Broadcasting Corporation (NBC) in favour of SWAPO. Furthermore, opposition parties and civil society organizations have regularly filed complaints about various procedural irregularities and the performance of the Electoral Commission for Namibia (ECN). Indeed, following the formation of the Congress of Democrats (COD), estab-

[6] *ACR 1989–90*, B573; Graham Hopwood (2007), *Guide to Namibian Politics*, Windhoek: Namibia Institute for Democracy; Directorate of Elections for 2009, http://www.ecn.na/Pages/home.aspx

lished by Ben Ulenga, a former senior figure within SWAPO, who objected to plans to amend the constitution to enable Nujoma to serve a third term as President, the climate surrounding the elections in 1999 was grim, and numerous instances of intimidation of opposition parties by SWAPO were reported. Additionally, inconsistencies in the electoral procedures, discrepancies in the voters' list, and the casting and counting of votes, as well as an undue delay in announcing the results, provoked a legal intervention questioning the result of the parliamentary vote. The High Court ordered a recount, resulting in only minor differences from the original results and leaving the distribution of parliamentary seats unchanged. There was no appeal in court, but a judgement by electoral observers that there was considerable room for improvement in the way elections were regulated, managed, observed, and monitored.[7] Subsequently, in 2009, there were again court interventions regarding alleged irregularities, but more particularly complaints were made about denial of the right to campaign freely, notably by the Rally for Democracy and Progress (RDP). This new party had been founded by two former members of cabinet, both political heavyweights from the first-struggle generation in exile, who had lost out in a SWAPO internal power struggle over the succession of Sam Nujoma as head of state. Given the new party's affinity to parts of SWAPO's regional stronghold in the north, the RDP was considered to be a serious challenger to SWAPO's dominance, resulting in an aggressive response from both higher party levels as well as from local activists, contributing to an atmosphere of repression hitherto unknown and raising worries about the tolerance of any idea of defeat by the ruling party.[8]

For all such concerns, SWAPO's electoral dominance remains founded upon the broad consent of the majority of Namibian voters. Nonetheless, there are numerous criticisms that the ruling party has used state power to consolidate a cycle of party dominance which is deeply inimical to any party daring to challenge its political hegemony. Part of the responsibility lies with opposition parties themselves, which have remained divided along a host of lines, and have hitherto offered no ideological alternative to the ruling party.[9] However, the reluctance of civil society to speak upon on matters 'appertaining to maintenance and preservation of moral, ethical and social values and standards' has also contributed (see Chapter 7).[10]

The ANC: establishing electoral dominance in South Africa

President De Klerk's lifting of the bans on the ANC, SACP, PAC, and other parties and movements on 2 February 1990 led to a remarkable process of negotia-

[7] Phanuel Kaapama (2005), 'Pre-conditions for free and fair elections: A Namibian country study', in Jeanette Minnie (ed.), *Outside the Ballot Box: Preconditions for Elections in Southern Africa 2004/05*, Windhoek: Media Institute for Southern Africa.

[8] On the events of 1999, see Oda van Cranenburgh (2006), 'Namibia: Consensus institutions and majoritarian politics', *Democratization*, 13: 4, 584–604.

[9] Justine Hunter (ed.) (2005), *Spot the Difference: Namibia's Political Parties Compared*, Windhoek: Namibia Institute for Democracy.

[10] Harold Pupkewitz (1996), 'Perceptions and performance of government and opposition in Namibia', in *Building Democracy: Perceptions and Performance of Government and Opposition in Namibia*, Windhoek: Namibia Institute for Democracy and Konrad Adenauer Stiftung.

tion between contending parties culminating in the democratic elections of 28–29 April 1994. The adoption of an 'interim constitution' in late 1993 (which embodied key principles which would have to provide the basis for a final constitution to be adopted by a post-transition election parliament acting as a Constituent Assembly) reflected a broad consensus around liberal democratic principles (free elections, a Bill of Rights, the independence of the judiciary, and so on). This was a product of the defensive powers retained by the government (control of the state, military, and policing apparatus plus significant support among demographic minorities, notably whites) in contrast to the offensive powers enjoyed by the ANC (ability to contest state control in both township and rural areas based upon majority support among the mass of the population).

Electorally, the outcome was similar to that which occurred in Namibia. Adoption of a national list PR system (rather than FPTP which the ANC had originally preferred, as had SWAPO) provided for maximum representation of all shades of opinion, although unlike in Namibia, the transitional election also involved elections (via list PR) for the nine new provinces. Again, as in Namibia, the outcome of the election was regarded by substantial minorities in South Africa as peculiarly beneficent, for while the ANC secured an indisputable majority, it fell short of the two-thirds majority which, in terms of the interim constitution, would have enabled it to drive the finalization of the constitution-making process without the support of other political parties. However, whereas in Namibia SWAPO has been able to amplify the level of its political support significantly amongst voters during the course of successive post-transitional elections, the ANC has proved less able to make substantial further inroads into the electorate and has faced consistently higher levels of opposition, both nationally and regionally, even though the opposition parties have remained very fragmented, with potential for their unity constrained by race, ethnicity, style, ideology, regional affiliation, and party leaderships' ambition (see Table 5.2 on page 104).

As in Namibia, there have been various allegations regarding the supposed partiality of the Independent Electoral Commission (IEC) for the ANC, yet no substantial complaints have been upheld. Overall, the body is regarded as having maintained a commendable level of independence which it has combined with notable efficiency,[11] in spite of some serious problems in 1994. Notably, there is strong reason to believe that the KwaZulu-Natal provincial election result was manipulated to provide a narrow margin of victory for the IFP (Inkatha Freedom Party) to secure its participation in a settlement to which it had stridently objected. In spite of various irregularities elsewhere at other times, elections have been declared by international and domestic electoral observers and media as free and fair, and there is no reason to believe that the different results distort the views of 'the people'.

Unlike in Namibia since 1994, the South African President is elected by parliament rather than directly by the people. Perhaps because this has been no bar to a considerable centralization of power under the presidency (notably during the era of Thabo Mbeki), there has been no concerted move by the ANC

---

[11]   Judith February (2009), 'The electoral system and electoral administration', in Roger Southall and John Daniel (eds), *Zunami! The 2009 South African Elections*, Johannesburg: Jacana Media, 47–64.

Table 5.2 South African National Assembly Elections 1994–2009[12]

Party	Valid Votes	% Valid Votes	Elected Seats
1994 Election			
ANC	12,237,655	62.65	252
NP	3,983,690	20.39	82
IFP	2,058,294	10.54	43
DP	338,426	1.73	7
Other	915,433	4.68	16
Total	19,533,498		400
1999 Election			
ANC	10,601,330	66.35	266
DA	1,527,337	9.56	38
IFP	1,088,664	8.58	34
NNP	1,098,215	6.87	28
Others	1,378,783	8.62	34
Total	15,977,142		400
2004 Election			
ANC	10,880,915	69.69	279
DA	1,931,201	12.37	50
IFP	1,088,664	6.97	28
NNP	257,824	1.65	7
Others	1,454,067	9.3	36
Total	15,612,671		400
2009 Election			
ANC	11,650,748	65.90	264
DA	2,945,829	16.66	67
COPE	1,311,027	7.42	30
IFP	804,260	4.55	18
Others	968,865	5.49	21
Total	17,680,729		400

to change the system. Meanwhile, ANC dominance has been largely replicated in the upper chamber of parliament (initially a Senate, subsequently the National Chamber of Provinces, both elected by provincial legislative assemblies) and rather more by its continuous hold over seven or more provinces. The principal outliers have been the Western Cape (where whites, Coloureds, and Indians taken together outnumber Africans) and KwaZulu-Natal, where the ANC has had to confront the predominantly Zulu ethnically based IFP of Chief Mangosuthu Buthelezi.

In the Western Cape, although the ANC was enabled to take control of the province in coalition with the renamed *New* NP in 2002 (following a controversial process of floor-crossing by members of political parties) and to confirm this via a coalition victory in 2004, rampant divisions within the provincial

---

[12] John Daniel and Roger Southall (2009), 'The national and provincial electoral outcome: Continuity with change', in Southall and Daniel (eds), op. cit., 215–31.

ANC along largely African versus Coloured lines led to its loss of the province to an invigorated DA (Democratic Alliance) in 2009.[13]

In KwaZulu-Natal the IFP was enabled to assume leadership of the provincial government from 1994 (when, officially, it obtained a bare 50.5 per cent popular majority) through to 2004. However, the level of support for the ANC (32 per cent in 1994, improving to 39 per cent in 1999) was such that it was forced to rule in uneasy coalition with the ANC, until in 2004, the ANC became the leading party with 48 per cent of the vote, with that of the IFP down to 37 per cent. Subsequently, the IFP's remaining grip on the province was shattered by a 63 per cent victory by the ANC in 2009, this generally ascribed to the elevation of Jacob Zuma, a Zulu, to the leadership. The party was now enabled to indulge in its own particular brand of ethnic mobilization and its erosion of the IFP's traditional base in rural areas.[14] Meanwhile, although facing varying levels of opposition, the ANC has established virtually unchallengeable dominance in every other province. This has been reflected at the local government level where the ANC has been predominant since the first democratic local elections in 2001 (conducted according to a mixed system of party lists elected by PR and wards elected by FPTP). In contrast to trends in other provinces, the party lost control of the Cape Town City Council in 2006.

ANC dominance was initially contained by the requirement of the interim constitution that the post-transitional government should be one of national unity (replicated at provincial level) wherein parties gaining 10 per cent or more of the vote could choose to be represented. This resulted initially in a GNU which united the formerly ruling NP and IFP under Nelson Mandela's leadership and was symbolized by former President De Klerk serving as a co-Deputy President alongside Thabo Mbeki. However, since the withdrawal of the NNP from the coalition following the promulgation of the new constitution in 1996 (and De Klerk's objections to what he deemed the ANC's marginalization of the NNP in cabinet),[15] the ANC has enjoyed total control of the government. However, it has continued to include of a handful of ministers from minority parties, notably the IFP, until the latter withdrew after the 2009 election.

As in Namibia, the ANC has found national list PR much to its liking. Not only does it translate its support into proportional majorities, but it has also facilitated the manipulation of party lists so as to ensure that the party's legislative representation include members of demographic and political minorities thus formally expressing its commitment to non-racialism and gender equality. While this is praiseworthy, critics have complained that the elimination of constituencies (used before 1994), has embodied the loss of accountability of MPs and Members of Provincial Legislatures (MPLs). Rather than being responsible to local voters, they are responsible to their party superiors, not least because under the constitution, parties are able to move ('redeploy') their representatives in and out of legislatures at will. Thus, despite survey evidence that a substantial majority of voters would prefer to move to a Mixed Member

[13] Zwelethu Jolobe (2009), 'The Democratic Alliance: Consolidating the official opposition', in Southall and Daniel (eds), op. cit., 131–46.

[14] Anthony Butler (2009), 'The ANC's national campaign of 2009: *Siyanqoba!*' in Southall and Daniel (eds), op. cit. 85–113.

[15] F.W. de Klerk (1998), *The Last Trek: A New Beginning*, London and Basingstoke: Macmillan, Ch.33.

Proportional electoral system (MMP) whereby MPs would be elected from regionally demarcated multiple member constituencies, the ANC has consistently chosen to override the majority recommendation of an Electoral Task Team, established in terms of the constitution in 2002, to review the electoral system. The team favoured a move to MMP, but the ANC argued that the national list system provided for maximum representativeness of a diverse society.[16]

In contrast, the ANC proved rather less concerned with the ideal of representativeness when, in 2002, the government opportunistically passed legislation to allow for crossing the floor in national and provincial legislatures, a practice hitherto barred by the constitution. The move had its origins in a crisis in the ranks of the opposition. The NNP, having moved out of the government of national unity, had sought to arrest its very evident decline by merging with the DP (Democratic Party) to form the DA, only for its leading elements to become uncomfortable in opposition. Offered a lifeline in the form of a return to collaboration with the ANC, the NNP under its new leader Marthinus van Schalkwyk took the bait and returned to coalition with the ANC in the Western Cape, enabling an ANC-NNP coalition to wrest control of both the provincial and Cape Town municipal governments from the DA.[17] Subsequently, floor-crossing – albeit allowed only during two annual windows – worked overwhelmingly in favour of the ANC, as members of small parties sought to feather their nest by ensconcing themselves in the ruling party. Indeed, so blatant was the process, and 'cross-stitutes' so cynically regarded by the public, that the legislative provision was reversed in 2007 (the NNP having folded itself completely into the ANC in 2005).[18]

By this time, the ANC may have reckoned that it was wise to restore barriers to the consolidation of the opposition under the leadership of the DA, which had steadily improved its standing via its able performance in parliament. ANC dominance has been considerably enhanced by the fragmentation of the opposition: after 1999 there have been never less than thirteen parties represented in parliament. However, there has been a consistent trend towards the strengthening of the DA as major force in parliament for holding the ANC accountable (up from the DP's 7 seats in 1994 to 67 in 2009). Even so, it is a much repeated point that the racial profile of the DA (overwhelmingly white, albeit incorporating increasing black support) inhibits its potential for growth and rules it out as a serious contender for power at the national level. Furthermore, as is frequently stated, the principal threat to ANC hegemony comes from within the Tripartite Alliance. As it happened, internal rebellion (in the form of the Congress of the People [COPE], based on supporters alienated by Mbeki's displacement as President) failed signally to deliver on its promise as a non-racial alternative to the ruling party in the 2009 election.[19] However, many

[16] Robert Mattes and Roger Southall (2004), 'Popular attitudes towards the South African electoral system', *Democratization*, 11: 1, 51–76.
[17] Roger Southall (2004), 'The state of party politics: Struggles within the Tripartite Alliance and the decline of the opposition', in John Daniel, Adam Habib and Roger Southall (eds), *State of the Nation: South Africa 2003–2004*, Cape Town: HSRC Press, 53–77.
[18] February, op. cit.
[19] Susan Booysen (2011), *The African National Congress and the Regeneration of Political Power*, Johannesburg: Wits University Press, Ch. 9.

consider that the possibility of COSATU (or key segments of it) coalescing with forces of civil society to form a party of the left constitutes the major potential threat to continuing ANC electoral dominance (see Chapter 7).

ZANU-PF: claiming hegemony, imposing domination

The ANC and SWAPO enjoy 'hegemony' obtained through popular consent, even if there are worrying signs that the latter party, in particular, is becoming increasingly intolerant. In contrast, while initially enjoying the support of the majority of voters, ZANU-PF has since 2000 experienced a series of defeats which, despite its deployment of massive intimidation to induce people to vote for it, unambiguously indicate that, if electoral processes had been free, fair, and honoured, it would now be out of power. Thus although ZANU-PF has perpetually claimed hegemony, in the sense of embodying the 'true interest' of the Zimbabwean people, it has never enjoyed 'party dominance' in the sense that it has relied upon coercion rather than consent to secure 're-election'. In Zimbabwe, 'dominance' has been imposed.

The consolidation of power

Between 1980 and 2009, Zimbabwe experienced seven elections for the National Assembly, two for the Senate, two for the presidency (inclusive of a run-off in the second instance) and a constitutional referendum in 2000. These are usefully analysed according to the pre- and post-constitutional referendum periods.

The transitional election was to be administered by the same National Election Directorate which had been created for the internal settlement election in 1979, albeit under ultimate British supervision. Furthermore, because of insufficiency of time to prepare, given the return of guerrillas (to assembly points) and the large number of displaced persons as a result of the war, there was no electoral register. The right to vote was awarded to those who were eighteen or over and who were citizens or permanent residents. Finally, another decision saw the retention of the party list system for the common roll election for practical reasons, with the 80 common roll seats being proportionally allocated to the eight electoral districts used in the previous election according to the 1979 voting patterns, this eliminating the need for demarcation and reducing electoral bureaucracy.[20]

Following Lancaster House, ZANU-PF had chosen to break from ZAPU and to contest the elections separately. With Smith's RF capturing all twenty white seats, the common roll result was as shown in Table 5.3 on page 108.

Mugabe became Prime Minister, and during this early period, earned much favourable credit by actively seeking reconciliation with whites, and by appointing Nkomo and other members of ZAPU to his cabinet.

Several factors explain the victory for ZANU-PF. First, ZANLA guerrillas had a presence throughout two-thirds of the country, and whether the inhabitants of those areas were ZANU-PF enthusiasts or not, voters were tired of the war

[20] Colin Baker (1982), 'Conducting the elections in Zimbabwe 1980', *Public Administration and Development*, 2, 45–58.

Table 5.3 Zimbabwe National Assembly Election 1980[21]

Party	Valid Votes	% Valid Votes	Seats
ZANU-PF	1,668,992	62.99	57
PF-ZAPU	638,879	24.11	20
UANC	219,307	8.28	3
Others	123,351	4.62	0
Total	2,649,529		80

and believed that only Mugabe could bring peace.[22] Guerrillas were meant to be kept within seventeen assembly points for the elections, but Mugabe substituted large numbers of untrained young men in their stead, keeping his superior troops outside the camps to prepare for emergencies. Some were held back in Mozambique, but many others were infiltrated into the TTLs to 'encourage' voters.[23] Second, Mugabe earned kudos by appearing to be the most unpopular of all the competing leaders with Ian Smith, South Africa, and the West. Third, Muzorewa (and Ndabaningi Sithole, whose rump ZANU had taken only 2 per cent of the vote) had been discredited by the internal settlement. Fourth, once ethnicity had become a political issue in the 1970s nationalist movement, ZAPU had become a minority party, overwhelmingly rooted in Matabeleland, while ZANU-PF carried the majority Shona-speaking areas. Finally, although there were numerous allegations about the use of intimidation by all the contestants, it was particularly difficult for other parties to campaign in former ZANLA areas.[24] While the British Governor, Lord Soames, had insisted that no party would be able to repudiate the result on the grounds that he had taken inadequate steps to curb intimidation, Mugabe had threatened to resume the war if ZANU-PF failed to win the election.[25] This instrumental attitude towards elections was to become a feature of ZANU-PF's approach to democracy henceforward.

---

[21] Masipula Sithole (1986), 'The general elections: 1979–1985', in Ibbo Mandaza (ed.), *Zimbabwe: The Political Economy of Transition 1980–1985*, Dakar: Codesria; Harare: Jongwe Press, 75–98.

[22] It is important here to refer again to Norma Kriger's critique of analyses of the relationship between peasants and ZANU-PF from scholars such as Andre Astrow, Lionel Cliffe and Terence Ranger, arguing for the radicalization of the peasants due to the oppressions of settler colonialism and discounting ZANU-PF's use of coercion during the election campaign. Kriger, in contrast, argues that peasants were 'reluctant supporters of the guerrillas', only turning to them during the war under duress, but voted for ZANU-PF because they hoped that if they did so, 'it would compensate them for the sacrifices – the loss of resources, labour time, and lives – forced upon them by the ZANU guerrillas...peasants in Shona areas where ZANU guerrillas had operated, had no such claim against other parties. In Ndebele-areas exposed to ZANU guerrillas, the guerrillas' insensitive efforts to impose Shona cultural nationalism were an early signal to expect nothing from ZANU.' Norma Kriger (1992), *Zimbabwe's Guerrilla War: Peasant Voices*, Cambridge: Cambridge University Press, 165.

[23] Paul Moorcroft (2012), *Mugabe's War Machine*, Johannesburg and Cape Town: Jonathan Ball Publishers, 85.

[24] Sithole, op. cit., 86.

[25] Baker, op. cit., 55.

The following three elections for the National Assembly, matched by that for the presidency, were used to consolidate ZANU-PF's supremacy. As required by the independence constitution, the common roll elections were from 1985 to be conducted upon a constituency-based plurality basis (i.e., FPTP). Whilst the delimitation and registration exercises encountered numerous practical difficulties in the lead-up to the 1985 elections, their conduct was generally regarded as 'beyond reproach'.[26] The independence constitution provided for the appointment of an Electoral Supervisory Commission (ESC), comprising five notables, whose function was to overview the registration of voters, the election of MPs, the drafting of electoral legislation, and to make reports as appropriate to the President. The actual running of elections was to be conducted by an Election Directorate (ED, with a Chairman appointed by the President), the Registrar-General and other members appointed by the Ministries of Justice, Legal and Parliamentary Affairs. However, by 1990, concerns were already being raised regarding the neutrality of the electoral authorities. Jonathan Moyo, whose entry into politics on ZANU-PF's behalf in a later era was to become highly controversial, was at this time one of the country's leading political scientists, and his thorough study of the elections of that year noted, *inter alia*, that the independence of the ESC appeared to have been worn down by the 'seeming omnipotence of ZANU-PF rule'.[27] The ED was composed, amongst others, of permanent secretaries of relevant ministries, who served at the pleasure of the President. Further, following an increase in the number of representatives to parliament from 100 to 120, there were complaints that constituency boundaries were manipulated to favour ZANU-PF.[28] Yet the key political factors that shaped the outcome of these elections were beyond the immediate electoral arena.

The first development was the crackdown by the army upon ZAPU militants in Matabeleland following the discovery of arms caches in Nkomo strongholds in 1982. The army was itself undergoing a difficult process of integration between former Rhodesian troops and ZANLA and ZIPRA guerrillas. Although denying that ZAPU was working in league with South African intelligence (deemed responsible for the destruction of much of the air force at its Gwelo base earlier in 1982), Nkomo and three other members of ZAPU were dismissed from the cabinet. The violence wreaked upon Matabeleland by the military (headed by the Fifth Brigade who were trained by North Korean advisers) was to account for around 20,000 deaths and instil an atmosphere of fear amongst ZAPU supporters in Matabeleland. The Gukurahundi ('the rain that sweeps away the chaff') thereby intensified political regionalism:

> In the eyes of the Ndebele public, what was portrayed as a mission to stamp out dissidents became an anti-Ndebele campaign that deliberately identified Joshua Nkomo, PF-ZAPU, ex-ZIPRA combatants and every Ndebele-speaking person with the political rebels. The Fifth Brigade unit was almost entirely Shona, and justified its violence in political and ethnic terms. For many, this represented a Shona political crusade against the Ndbele.[29]

26 Sithole, op. cit., 89.
27 Jonathan Moyo (1992), *Voting for Democracy: Electoral Politics in Zimbabwe*, Harare: University of Zimbabwe Press, 52.
28 Ibid., 48–49.
29 James Muzondidye (2009), 'From buoyancy to crisis', in Brian Raftopoulos and Alois Mlambo (eds), *Becoming Zimbabwe: A History from the Pre-Colonial Period to 2008*, Harare: Weaver Press, 185.

Inevitably, it provided reinforcement of the popular basis for later expressions of Ndebele ethnic opposition to ZANU-PF domination. However, its most immediate outcome was a reduced vote for ZAPU and a larger majority for ZANU-PF amongst the common roll seats in the 1985 election.

Meanwhile, the retention of reserved seats for whites in parliament aggravated ZANU-PF antipathy. In large part, this could be ascribed to Ian Smith and the RF. In deference to the new era, the RF had changed its name to the Conservative Alliance of Zimbabwe (CAZ). Skilled in parliamentary procedure and highly knowledgeable about the economy, the RF/CAZ constantly embarrassed the government, prompting Mugabe to issue dire warnings about the dangerous consequences of white opposition to black rule. While this prompted a breakaway in early 1982 by a number of RF MPs and resulted in the formation of a more conciliatory alternative, namely the Independent Zimbabwe Group (IZG), the outcome of the 1985 white roll election saw a strong recovery of Smith's position, resulting in the CAZ winning fifteen seats. Mugabe took this as a willful rejection of the friendship which the government had extended to them. With ZANU-PF having won 64 out of the 80 seats, Mugabe moved swiftly to abolish the reserved seats, securing the support of sufficient opposition MPs to obtain the two-thirds majority required under the constitution to pass a constitutional amendment.

The crackdown on ZAPU dissidence had been accompanied by Mugabe stepping up a campaign for a one-party state which was associated with a drive for Marxist-Leninist socialism. Despite post-independence assurances concerning acceptance of diversity, Mugabe became increasingly critical of multi-party democracy, claiming that the Lancaster House agreement fettered the rights of the majority.[30] However, one-partyism remained controversial even within ZANU-PF, and he was unable to avoid a promise made to parliament in August 1981 that it would never be imposed by force and would require a referendum. For his part, Nkomo strongly opposed suggestions for a merger of the two major parties. However, the Matabeleland crisis presented the government with the opportunity to crush its only viable opponent militarily and to reap the rewards politically. This resulted in Nkomo's reluctant accession to a Unity Accord between ZANU-PF and ZAPU in late 1987, the former's domination indicated by retention of its own name for the united party. Although talks were facilitated by the release of ZAPU detainees, the room for manoeuvre available to Nkomo had been severely restricted by widespread bans on ZAPU meetings, raids on ZAPU offices, and the party's eventual banning altogether in September 1987. The signing of the Unity Accord increased ZANU-PF's majority in parliament to 99 out of 100. It was only then that the atrocities in Matebeleland were brought to an end.[31]

Further constitutional amendments prior to the March 1990 general elections created an executive presidency, to be popularly elected, and the abolition of the Senate, creating a unicameral legislature which, expanded to 150, was to include 30 members effectively appointed by the President (8 provincial governors, 12 chiefs, and 12 to represent special interest groups).

---

[30] Ibid., 181. See also Ibbo Mandaza and Lloyd Sachikonye (eds) (1991), *The One Party State and Democracy: The Zimbabwe Debate*, Harare: SAPES Trust, for different perspectives.
[31] Muzondidye, op. cit., 179–80.

Ironically, although the use of violence and ZANU's discourse of unity had been used to subordinate ZAPU, the merger of the two parties undermined the ruling party's claim to political hegemony. The government had already used its powers to curb protest from civil society and trade unions, yet this proved insufficient to quell growing disquiet about various government policies and increasing evidence of corruption. Furthermore, the effective imposition of a one-party state by removing an external enemy turned ZANU-PF in upon itself, providing space for expression of internal dissidence. It was not merely that the ZANU-PF hierarchy had difficulty in asserting its authority at lower levels of the party, nor that ex-ZAPU figures openly contested Marxism-Leninism, but that key figures, such as Edgar Tekere, the party's Secretary-General, voiced a wider concern about corruption and about violations of a Leadership Code which had been introduced in 1987. This led to his expulsion and to his subsequent formation of the Zimbabwe Unity Movement (ZUM). The new party failed dismally in the general election that followed (obtaining only two seats), but its campaigning – along with that of a dozen former ruling party members who had stood as independents after having been denied nomination as ZANU-PF election candidates – served to block the agenda for a one-party state.[32] Overall, in 1990 ZANU-PF massively increased its majority over its opponents and attained a sweeping victory (117 out of the 120 elective seats) in the National Assembly election, with Mugabe overwhelming Tekere in the concurrent presidential election:

Table 5.4 Zimbabwe National Assembly Elections 1985 and 1990[33]

Party/Contestant	Valid Votes	% Valid Votes	Elected Seats
1985 Elections			
ZANU-PF	2,233,320	77.19	64
PF-ZAPU	558,771	19.31	15
Others	101,194	3.5	1
Total	2,893,285		80
1990 Assembly Elections			
ZANU-PF	1,690,071	80.55	117
ZUM	369,031	17.59	2
Others	29,115	1.85	2
Total	2,088,217		120
1990 Presidential Election			
Robert Mugabe (ZANU-PF)	2,026,976	83.04	
Edgar Tekere (ZUM)	413,840	16.95	
Total	2,440,816		

---

[32] Ibid., 181.
[33] Tom Lodge, Denis Kadima and David Pottie (eds) (2002), *Compendium of Elections in Southern Africa*, Johannesburg: Electoral Institute of Southern Africa, 429–70.

Despite ZANU-PF's overwhelming victory, the low turnout – notably in urban constituencies – pointed to growing disaffection from the ruling party and popular concern with its management of the economy, which after 1991 became subject to the constraints of the IMF-directed ESAP. This provided the background to mounting protest, spearheaded by ZCTU and the decision by eight opposition parties, including ZUM, to boycott the 1995 election in which ZANU-PF won all but 2 of the 120 elective seats. In the presidential election, Mugabe similarly trounced his challengers, securing 92.7 per cent of the vote against Muzorewa's 4.2 per cent and Ndabaningi Sithole's 2.4 per cent. ZANU-PF was thus in total control of the machinery of state – but its hold over society was slipping.

The 2000 referendum and its aftermath: ZANU-PF's negation of electoral democracy

Zimbabwe had seen significant gains during its first decade of independence, yet many of these were to prove unsustainable. Little had been done to alter the colonial economy; much-needed land reform had been constrained by limited donor funding and lack of government application; there was a low rate of foreign investment; and successive structural adjustment programmes had resulted in cutbacks in social services, low growth rates, and a failure to make inroads into poverty. Combined with recurrent droughts, all this contributed to the government's growing unpopularity. Strikes became more frequent and revelations of corruption eroded its standing, which was further undermined by Zimbabwe's involvement in war in the DRC.

The ZCTU's increasingly critical stance of government policy had led to debate within the trade union movement about whether it should explicitly enter the political arena. Its awareness of the commonality of the struggles of workers with those of wider social communities led to its centrality in the formation of a constitutional reform movement, the National Constituent Assembly (NCA), on 31 January 1998.[34] Alongside growing disillusionment with the constitution, the NCA was tapping into concern about multiple amendments which had strengthened the grip of ZANU-PF on the state and concentrated power in the hands of the President.[35]

The NCA provoked a national discussion about citizenship, government accountability, and democracy which culminated in the calling of a National Working People's Convention in February 1999 at which the decision was taken to form a political party. This resulted in the launch of the MDC the following September. Morgan Tsvangirai, hitherto General Secretary of the ZCTU, became President of the new party, with other senior posts assumed by labour leaders and figures from civil society, including a few from the shrinking white community who favoured involvement in issues around economic liberalization, constitutionalism, and democracy. Thereafter, the campaign for constitutional reform merged with idea of a change in government.

---

[34] Brian Raftopoulos (2009), 'The crisis in Zimbabwe', in Raftopoulos and Mlambo (eds), op. cit., 208–09.

[35] Lovemore Matombo and Lloyd Sachikonye (2010), 'The labour movement and democratization in Zimbabwe', in Bjorn Beckman, Sakhela Buhlungu and Lloyd Sachikonye (eds), *Trade Unions and Party Politics: Labour Movements in Africa*, Cape Town: HSRC Press, 109–30.

The government responded to the NCA by establishing its own Constitutional Commission. This undertook countrywide consultations, but its draft constitution, while providing for the acquisition of land without compensation unless this came from the UK, ignored widespread public sentiment in favour of Mugabe's retiring and the introduction of a limit to the number of terms which could be served by a President. This draft was put to a constitutional referendum in February 2000. Given its well-funded campaign and the strong backing of the media, state administration, and ZANU-PF, the government was confident of winning. However, to its consternation, the coalition of interests embodied in the NCA and MDC led to the proposed constitution being rejected by a 54 per cent majority of the 1.3 million (mainly urban) Zimbabweans who voted. The government had little alternative but to accept the result, but ZANU-PF ascribed the rejection of the proposed constitution to a conspiracy between the black urban middle class, white farmers, and the government's external enemies, and saw an opportunity to fight the forthcoming elections as if they were a re-run of the war for liberation.[36]

The referendum defeat signalled to ZANU-PF that it could lose the general elections of 2000 and the presidential election of 2002. This became a motivating factor in the government's launch of its fast track land reform. This constituted both a potentially revolutionary rupture and a major shift in power relations within the ruling party, as Mugabe consolidated his personal control. Critical was his forging an alliance with the War Veterans' Association (WVA).[37] Formed in the early 1990s in response to the slow pace of demobilization and land resettlement, the WVA – probably with support from elements in the army – had in 1997 invaded State House and forced Mugabe to concede pensions to war veterans that the government could not afford and to promise speedier land reform. Despite the massively deleterious impact upon public finances, the government now gave concerted support to a wave of land invasions which were spearheaded by the WVA but also backed by ZANU-PF youth and popular elements drawn from both communal and urban areas. Henceforth, the government used the land issue to drum up political support, justifying forced seizure of white farms and using the allocation of seized lands as a means of patronage and a tool of retribution against white farmers deemed to be supporters of the opposition. Henceforth, ZANU-PF resorted to war rhetoric to maintain power, depicting land seizures as the 'third Chimurenga'.[38]

The MDC emerged as the major force of opposition. The election for the National Assembly held on 24–25 June 2000 constituted a major turning point in Zimbabwe's postcolonial history. For the first time, a generation born immediately after independence was able to vote, and ZANU-PF was faced by a viable, nationwide alternative. Confronted by the prospect of defeat, the government launched a campaign of systematic violence, intimidation and even murder against its opponents, spearheaded by the WVA and ZANU-PF youth.[39] In the cautiously chosen words of the Commonwealth Observer team, this 'impaired

---

[36] Raftopoulos, op. cit., 207–10; Matombo and Sachikonye, op. cit., 114–16.
[37] Raftopoulos, op. cit., 211.
[38] David Moore (2001), 'Is the land the economy and the economy the land? Primitive accumulation in Zimbabwe', *Journal of Contemporary African Studies*, 19: 2, 253–66.
[39] Amnesty International (2000), *Zimbabwe: Terror Tactics in the Run up to Parliamentary Elections, June 2000*, London: Amnesty International.

the freedom of choice of the electorate'.[40] Even so, the MDC delivered a major shock to the ruling party, securing 57 seats to ZANU-PF's 62 in an increased vote (Table 5.5 below).

The MDC's sudden rise sounded a loud warning that Mugabe himself confronted possible defeat in the presidential elections to be held in 2002. The government's response was ruthless, systematic exploitation of its control over the state, the electoral machinery, and the means of violence to fundamentally disadvantage the opposition and to intimidate its supporters. Yet even in these highly dangerous circumstances, Tsvangirai performed remarkably well, taking 42.1 per cent of the vote compared with 56.06 per cent for Mugabe. However, government repression exacted its toll over the longer term so that in the 2005 National Assembly elections, the MDC's haul of seats (41) was significantly reduced.

Table 5.5 Zimbabwe National Assembly Elections 2000 and 2005[41]

Party/Contestant	Valid Votes	% Valid Votes	Seats
2000 Assembly Elections			
ZANU-PF	1,205,844	48.10	62
MDC	1,171,167	46.72	57
Others	129,962	5.18	1
Total	2,506,973		120
2002 Presidential Elections			
Robert Mugabe	1,681,212	56.06	
Morgan Tsvangirai	1,262,403	42.10	
Others	55,145	1.85	
Total	2,998,760		
2005 Assembly Elections			
ZANU-PF	1,569,867	59.59	78
MDC	1,041,292	39.52	41
Others	23,486	0.89	1
Total	2,634,645		120

ZANU-PF's winning of 78 seats, together with some 30 presidential nominees, chiefs, and provincial governors, handed it the two-thirds majority which enabled it to amend the constitution, a power it immediately utilized to reintroduce the Senate, which it had abolished in 1989. Out of a total of 66 Senators, 50 were to be directly elected, 5 from each province, to sit alongside 6 nominated by the President and 10 held by traditional chiefs.

The first Senate elections were held on 26 November 2005, but not surprisingly, the voter turnout (19.48 per cent) was the lowest in the country's post-independence history, and MDC took just 21.18 per cent of the vote in a contest in which no real power was at stake. However, the wider significance of the

---

[40] Commonwealth Secretariat (2002), *Zimbabwe Presidential Election 9–11 March 2002: Report of the Commonwealth Observer Group*, London: Commonwealth Secretariat, 32.

[41] Susan Booysen and Lucient Toulou (2009), 'Zimbabwe', in Denis Kadima and Susan Booysen (eds), *Compendium of Elections in Southern Africa 1989–2009: 20 Years of Multiparty Democracy*, Johannesburg: Electoral Institute of Southern Africa, 629–58.

election was that it caused a split within the MDC, the larger element under Tsvangirai having called for a boycott, the smaller dissident faction, led by Arthur Mutambara, favouring participation. Differences between the two factions relating to issues of strategy and internal democracy resulted in the split becoming entrenched, with the party divided into factions known as MDC-T and MDC-M.

ZANU-PF served as both the architect and beneficiary of these years of electoral authoritarianism even while the country plunged into a desperate crisis. Land seizures and calamitous drops in both agricultural and manufacturing production resulted in widespread hunger and mass exodus of Zimbabweans to neighbouring countries, notably South Africa. Furthermore, as the crisis deepened, the government resorted to printing money, resulting in a spectacular hyperinflation which destroyed the value of savings and pensions and led to a thriving black market, gains on which provided for a good living for those members of the elite with access to state-controlled foreign currency.

Nonetheless, although ZANU-PF now presided over a ruined economy and its resort to violence was an affront to democracy, regional leaders were reluctant to denounce the various elections as fraudulent, for key figures amongst them, notably Nujoma, remained strongly supportive of the Zimbabwean President as a champion of anti-imperialism and liberation.[42] However, most were eager to find a resolution to a wide-ranging crisis which affected the region negatively.

A SADC summit at the end of March 2007 mandated South African President Mbeki to facilitate negotiations aimed at resolving the crisis in Zimbabwe, the objective being to establish conditions for the holding of free and fair elections in 2008. Later in the year, agreement appeared to have been reached regarding the drawing up a new constitution and key changes to laws governing security, the media, and elections in exchange for the MDC conceding a constitutional amendment which provided for harmonized presidential, senatorial, House of Assembly, and local elections. Apart from reducing the tenure of the President from six to five years, the resulting amendment saw the House of Assembly expanded from 120 to 210 elective seats and the Senate from 66 to 93 seats, 60 of which would be elective. A principal motivation, apparently, was to dilute the MDC's standing in both houses (notably by increasing the number of seats in rural areas traditionally controlled by ZANU-PF). However, ZANU-PF's unwillingness to relax political conditions contributed to a deadlock in the negotiations over the time frame and means for implementing reforms, the manner and enactment of a new constitution, and the date for the next election.[43]

The MDC had been hoping for Mbeki to persuade ZANU-PF to agree to an amended constitution before announcing an election. However, Mugabe unilaterally proclaimed 29 March 2008 as the date of the harmonized elections, arguing that a new constitution could only be introduced via a referendum.

[42] Nujoma obtained the nickname 'Mugabe-lite' to characterize his rhetoric within regional politics in defence of his ally. See Henning Melber (2006), '"Presidential indispensibility" in Namibia', in Roger Southall and Henning Melber (eds), *Legacies of Power: Leadership Change and Former Presidents in African Politics*, Cape Town: HSRC Press; Uppsala: Nordic Africa Institute, 112–13 (note 8).

[43] Raftopoulos, op. cit., 227–31.

The elections were therefore held under terms prescribed by the existing constitution, although concessions made to SADC meant that they took place under conditions where, unlike in previous elections, freedoms of assembly, association, and speech could be generally exercised 'without undue hindrance', albeit against the background of violence meted out to the MDC in 2007. In contrast, however, 'the electoral process was severely wanting in respect of fairness, as most of the critical aspects of the process lacked transparency'.[44] Indeed, delay by the Zimbabwe Electoral Commission (ZEC) in releasing the results, alongside a lack of transparency in the counting process, fuelled widespread rumours of vote rigging and military intervention. Furthermore, there was explicit backing to ZANU-PF given by the security forces, with statements made by high-ranking officers to the effect that they would not accept a pro-MDC election result.

ZANU-PF proceeded to lose its majority in the National Assembly, with the MDC-T taking some 99 seats to ZANU-PF's 97, and the MDC-M taking a further 10. (As can be seen from Table 5.6 on page 117, the results announced by the ZEC were proclaimed as manipulated in favour of ZANU-PF by civil society election monitors who provided their own version of the parliamentary vote. This was calculated according to results announced at polling station level which were sent to a counting centre in South Africa by mobile phone). Even more dramatic was Tsvangirai's triumph in the presidential poll, taking an announced 47.9 per cent of the votes cast compared to Mugabe's 43.2 per cent (there being strong grounds for believing that he was denied a majority only by political intervention in the counting process).

Whilst this was a convincing win for Tsvangirai, it did not take him beyond the 50 per cent-plus threshold required to prevent a run-off with Mugabe.

This was subsequently scheduled for 27 June 2008. However, the period following the March elections saw ZANU-PF unleash a massive campaign of violence, war rhetoric, and hate speech against the opposition. This resulted in so many murders and injuries to his supporters, along with extensive displacement of people and destruction of homes, that Tsvangirai, who was arrested a number of times during the campaign, eventually opted to pull out, claiming that a free and fair election was impossible in a climate of state-sponsored violence. However, the ZEC announced on 25 June that his withdrawal had occurred too late, and that the contest would continue. With MDC supporters cowed, Mugabe won some 90.22 per cent of the votes cast, his engorged victory ascribed to the extreme violence which deprived voters of the freedom to abstain. Indeed, the MDC advised its supporters to vote if this would help save their lives.[45] Three by-elections for House of Assembly seats not held in March owing to the deaths of candidates were also held, narrowing the gap between ZAANU-PF and MDC to just one seat.

The overall outcome of the 2008 elections was that ZANU-PF had bludgeoned an effective draw. The MDC-T had gained a small edge over ZANU-PF in the Assembly, yet could only secure a majority along party lines in alliance with the Mutambara faction and ultimately, Mugabe had retained the presidency. Meanwhile, although the MDC-T (24) and MDC-M (6) tied with ZANU-PF (30)

---

[44] Electoral Institute of Southern Africa (EISA) (2008), *Zimbabwe: The Harmonised Elections of 29 March 2008*, EISA Election Observer Mission Report No. 28, Johannesburg: EISA, 9.

[45] Ibid., 78.

Table 5.6 Zimbabwe National Assembly and Presidential Elections 2008[46]

Party/Contestant	Votes	% Votes	Seats
MDC-T	1,021,370*	45.2	99 (+1)**
	1,038,617***	2.8	
ZANU-PF	1,057,841*	46.8	97 (+2)*
	1,111,625***	45.8	
MDC-M	152,705*	6.8	10
	206,868***	8.5	
Others	27,955*	1.2	1
	67,698***	2.8	
Total	2,259,871*		207(210)
Presidential Election First Round			
Morgan Tsvangirai	1,195,562	47.87	
Robert Mugabe	1,079,730	43.24	
2 Others	221,973	8.89	
Total	2,497,265		
Presidential Election Run Off			
Robert Mugabe	2,150,269	90.22	
Morgan Tsvangirai	233,000	9.78	
Total	2,383,269		

* Totals as calculated by civil society formations
** Including seats won in 3 by-elections contested after 29 March 2008
*** ZEC official results, widely regarded as manipulated in favour of ZANU-PF. Zimbabwe Election 2008, www.Sokwanele.com/election2008

in the elections for the Senate, the President's prerogative of appointments to that body gave ZANU-PF control over the upper house. It was in this context that Mbeki was enabled to mediate the power-sharing agreement of September 2009 whereby Mugabe and ZANU-PF conceded to share power with the MDC. Tsvangirai became Prime Minister and his party took control of key finance portfolios which rapidly yielded significant gains for the economy. By abolishing the Zimbabwean dollar in favour of foreign currencies, the MDC abolished the cause of the hyperinflation. Fatefully, however, Mugabe retained presidential power and ZANU-PF control of the military, police, and means of coercion.

NLMs as electoral machines

Political party organizations in modern democracies have been largely constructed around the need to win elections. The extension of the franchise to incorporate all men and women of voting age forced political parties to transform from elite to mass organizations capable of contesting elections. Thus even conservative parties, largely dedicated to the interests of land and property, found they needed to expand their social base to incorporate the middle and working classes if they were to compete with socialist movements. The nature

---

[46] Booysen and Toulou, op. cit., 652.

of the party, wrote Robert Michels, is to 'organize the masses upon the vastest scale imaginable':

> 'Party organization' signifies the aspiration for the greatest number of members. 'Parliamentarism' signifies the aspiration for the greatest number of votes. The principal fields of party activity are electoral agitation and direct agitation to secure new members. What, in fact, is the modern political party? It is the methodical organization of the electoral masses.[47]

When confronted by the need to move from the battlefield to the arena of electoral politics, NLMs have had to take on key characteristics of the classical political party. Without electoral organization during their transitional elections, they would have been unable to secure control of the state; without electoral organization, they would be unable to maintain it.

Elections in southern Africa are supposedly governed by SADC principles whereby an election will only be deemed free and fair if there is: full participation of citizens in the political process; freedom of association and political tolerance; elections are held at regular intervals as provided by national constitutions; equal opportunity for all political parties to access the media, and equal opportunity for individuals to vote and be voted for. Further, the judiciary and electoral management institutions are to be neutral between parties; and there must be acceptance of and respect for election results, alongside a right to challenge them according to agreed procedures. It would follow from what has been set out above that while elections in Namibia and South Africa appear to have broadly conformed to these principles, those in Zimbabwe have not. So a number of questions follow. Why is it that SWAPO and the ANC have been able to become 'dominant parties' while ZANU-PF has not? How do they compare as 'electoral machines' and how have their capacities been augmented by their possession of state power? Finally, how do their common characteristics as liberation movements affect their electoral behaviour and what are the implications for democracy?

Level playing fields? NLMs and electoral institutions

These political transitions dictated that the bodies administering the transitional elections were placed beyond the control of any political parties. In both Namibia and Zimbabwe, the transitional elections were, in essence, run by the existing electoral authorities established by the former minority regimes, yet under close supervision: by the UN in the case of Namibia, by the British in Zimbabwe. Inevitably this led to suspicions on the part of the liberation movements that the electoral processes worked against them, but while there were instances where neutrality was infringed, there was no convincing evidence of serious bias and resultant impact upon the outcome. Indeed, an attempt by General Peter Walls, the Rhodesian army commander, to have the transitional election in Zimbabwe nullified on the grounds of alleged intimidation of voters by ZANU-PF was dismissed out of hand by the British authorities.[48] For all that

---

[47] Robert Michels (1912), *Political Parties*, New York: Dover Books, 2nd edn. 1959, 367.
[48] According to Moorcroft (op. cit., 86), Governor Soames responded to General Walls's request to ban ZANU-PF activity in certain areas because of the large presence of ZANLA guerrillas with

both Britain and South Africa hoped for conservative outcomes in the Zimbabwean and Namibian elections respectively, their first priority was to nail down
international recognition of the political settlements and get out. In South
Africa, in contrast, the interim constitution provided for the establishment of a
completely new body, the IEC, to run the first democratic election. Composed
of five commissioners, none of whom could hold high political office and one of
whom had to be a judge, and shielded from arbitrary dismissal, the IEC was
responsible for supervising a Chief Executive Officer who headed the actual electoral administration. To be sure, it is now accepted that numerous administrative mistakes were made by the electoral authorities in 1994, and that the
KwaZulu-Natal provincial election result was 'negotiated' to secure an IFP
victory and political stability. Nonetheless, given that the political climate in the
run-up to the election was scarcely propitious for running a free and fair election (with high levels of political violence and IFP recalcitrance), the IEC's
achievement was remarkable, and there were no major complaints about its
neutrality.[49]

The temptation to structure electoral institutions to facilitate successive
ruling party victories was obvious. However, the nature of the settlements in
Namibia and South Africa was such as to ensure that the neutrality of electoral
institutions was maintained.

The Electoral Commission of Namibia was established in 1992 to supervise
elections at all the different levels (national, regional, and local). From 1992
until 2000, the ECN was administered as part of the Prime Minister's office, but
after criticism that this might affect its independence, it was established in its
own right and given its own budget. Furthermore, reforms in the late 1990s
rendered the selection of Electoral Commissioners more transparent. They were
no longer to be appointed directly by the President but were to respond to open
advertisements, prior to appearing before a selection committee consisting of a
member of the Supreme or High Court appointed by the Chief Justice, a lawyer
nominated by the Law Society, and staff member of the Office of the
Ombudsman. In turn, this committee would put forward eight candidates to
the President, who would then select five. Similarly, the Director of Elections,
the Chief Executive of the Commission, was to be appointed after the Commissioners had interviewed five candidates and recommended two to the President,
to make the final choice.[50]

The body which ran the 1994 election in South Africa was temporary, and
was subsequently replaced by a permanent organization of the same name. The
Electoral Act of 1996 established the new IEC with the responsibilities of
strengthening constitutional democracy and promoting democratic electoral
processes. Apart from administering elections, it was to compile a voters' roll,
demarcate wards for local government (for which elections were to be conducted

the following reflection: 'You must remember this is Africa. It isn't Puddleton-on-the-Marsh,
and they behave differently here. They think nothing of sticking poles up each other's whatnot,
and doing filthy beastly things to each other. It does happen, I'm afraid. It's a very wild thing an
(African) election.'

49 Claude Kabemba (2005), 'Electoral administration: Achievements and continuing challenges',
    in Jessica Piombo and Lia Nijzink (eds), *Electoral Politics in South Africa: Assessing the First Demo-
    cratic Decade*, Cape Town: HSRC Press, 87–105.
50 Hopwood, op. cit., 36.

on a mixed member basis), review electoral legislation, and conduct voter education. There were again to be five commissioners, one of whom was to be a judge. The commissioners were to be nominated by an all-party committee of the National Assembly charged with considering eight candidates, none of whom should have a high political profile, chosen by a panel of the President of the Constitutional Court, and composed of nominees of the Human Rights and Gender Commissions, and the office of the Public Protector. Their recommendations were to be assessed and approved by the National Assembly, and appointees were to serve for up to seven years. In practice, the IEC was to operate through a permanent staff (originally around 250, latterly 300 plus), and appoint temporary staff (as many as 160,000 for the 1999 election) to assist with elections. The majority of these have tended to be teachers and municipal employees. From the 2004 elections on, municipal electoral officers have also recruited volunteers to provide assistance at the nearly 17,000 voting stations across the country.[51]

The careful arrangements put in place have shielded the electoral institutions in both Namibia and South Africa from major controversy. To be sure, the large majorities which both ruling parties enjoy in their respective Assemblies have offered a guarantee that those appointed to head the Commissions will be to their liking, yet there has been no substantial suggestion that the electoral institutions have been politically subverted. There have been regular critiques of their competence regarding their capacity for registering voters timeously and efficiently, yet there has been no substantive suggestion that they have systematically disadvantaged the registration of particular categories of voters. Inevitably, there have been complaints of bias by IEC and ECN staff made by opposition parties at election times,[52] and it is not unlikely, given the authority of municipal electoral officers in South Africa to appoint local staff, that selection will reflect local political preferences. However, given the PR national list system, it is unlikely that local biases will accumulate to a high enough level to affect election outcomes significantly, although this may happen at ward level in local elections. Perhaps this is one reason why the South African IEC has consistently aligned itself with ANC rejections of any call to move from PR to a mixed electoral system for national elections, for there is widespread evidence that in African countries whose elections use a constituency-based system, numerous results end up being referred by unsuccessful candidates for adjudication by the courts.

In contrast to the carefully protected neutrality of the electoral institutions in Namibia and South Africa, those in Zimbabwe have become not merely progressively politicized, but militarized as well. Reference has already been made to how the electoral institutions were becoming subject to ZANU-PF influence by as early as the 1990 election. This has become far more explicit since from the time of ZANU-PF's defeat in the constitutional referendum.

Before 2004, electoral management in Zimbabwe was conducted by four bodies: the Electoral Supervisory Commission (ESC); the Registrar-General (RG);

[51] Susan Booysen and Grant Masterson (2009), 'South Africa', in Kadima and Booysen (eds), op. cit., 387–460.

[52] EISA (2009), *Namibia: Presidential and National Assembly Elections 27 and 28 November 2009*, Election Observer Mission Report No. 34. Johannesburg: EISA, 56 (note 12).

the Election Directorate (ED); and the Delimitation Commission (DC). Members of all four organizations were presidential or government appointees, and as such lacked independence from the state.

Even in the most propitious circumstances, the ambiguity of roles allotted to these bodies would have been a recipe for confusion; in the hands of ZANU-PF, it contributed directly to a lack of transparency. The two most important structures were the ESC and the RG. The former's ascribed role was to supervise registration, overview the elections themselves and consider proposed changes to electoral legislation, yet to do this, it needed to be able to access reports on registration and other electoral matters from the RG. Equally, in terms of the law, the office of the RG – the *de facto* body actually running the electoral process – was not obliged to pass any information to the ESC and on key occasions chose not to do so. Thus in the 2002 Assembly election, the RG refused to provide information to the ESC on the number of ballot books printed, claiming the information was classified. Furthermore, during the presidential election of that year, the RG not only failed to provide the ESC with the election calendar, but again, refused to pass on the number of ballot papers printed, failed to inform the ESC of the number of eligible voters by constituency and province until polling day, and also of the number of the people on the supplementary voters' roll. In short, it would have been very difficult for the ESC to do its job properly even if it had wanted to. Even so, for all its squabbles with the office of the RG, the Commission, which was supposedly non-partisan, was widely regarded as having little autonomy from the ruling party. Not least of its problems in this regard was that its funding was provided by the Ministry of Justice which had the further right of deciding how its funds might be used.

A decision was taken in 2000 to weaken the ESC in favour of the RG.[53] The latter had not only been in that position for decades but, allegedly, had an 'uncompromising' faith in the ruling party. His office was assisted by the Election Directorate, which supposedly was nothing more than a support structure to ensure that resources and logistics were in place to conduct elections, as the RG did not have the power to command them. Inevitably, this led to a growth in the role of the ED, which from 2000 was empowered to accredit election observers on the recommendation of the Ministry of Foreign Affairs. Finally, apart from the dubious role played by the DC (discussed below), enormous powers regarding the electoral process were vested in the executive in terms of Section 158(2)(b) of the Election Act which empowered the President and the Minister of Justice to issue statutory regulations regarding the conduct of elections, and in terms of the Presidential Powers (Temporary Measures) Act of 1986, also gave the President powers to affect electoral competition and participation.

The near loss of the 2000 Assembly and 2002 presidential elections prompted the government to reform the electoral institutions in such a way as to enable it to stage 'credible, but heavily manipulated' parliamentary elections in 2005.[54] At the opening of parliament in July 2004, Mugabe announced elec-

---

[53] Claude Kabemba (2004), 'An assessment of Zimbabwe's electoral administration', in Wole Olaleye (ed.), *Negotiating the Impasse: Challenges and Prospects for Democratization in Zimbabwe*, Johannesburg: EISA Research Report No. 9, 9–27.

[54] Peter Kagwanja (2005), *When the Locusts Ate: Zimbabwe's March 2005 Elections*, Electoral Institute for Southern Africa Occasional Paper No. 32, 2.

toral reforms and later endorsed electoral principles adopted by SADC at their Mauritius summit in August of that year. The public debate that followed argued for a reform of political conditions which constrained free and fair elections (such as a host of repressive laws which undermined fundamental freedoms), but the government restricted its reforms to much narrower electoral concerns. On 17 January 2005, Mugabe signed into law the Zimbabwe Election Commission Bill and the Electoral Bill.

The first of these appointed a Zimbabwe Electoral Commission as the sole electoral management body and abolished the ED, DC, and ESC, although the RG continued to be responsible for registration, supposedly under the ZEC's supervision. The latter Act introduced polling day changes, such as requiring polling to take place on a single day, the counting of votes at polling stations, and introducing translucent polling boxes, whilst also introducing an Electoral Court to hear election petitions. However, for all that these changes received glowing praise from SADC, they contributed to ZANU-PF's ability to control the 2005 election. On the one hand, the Electoral Act, whilst introducing changes allowing for a 'clean' election day, failed to address issues of the wider political environment which impinged on the fairness of voting before polling. On the other, whereas in practice the ZEC lacked the capacity to supervise the RG, its composition was such as to shore up rather than contain Mugabe's system of patronage. After consultation with the Judicial Service Commission, on 21 January 2005 he appointed Justice George Chiweshe, a High Court judge, as chairperson, but by this time, the judiciary had already become packed with ZANU-PF sympathizers. Furthermore, although the other four commissioners were appointed from a list of seven names submitted to the President by a bipartisan parliamentary committee, a provision of the Act provided for state employees (inclusive of the defence, police, and prison forces) to be seconded to the Commission during elections.[55]

The electoral institutions had already become progressively militarized. Chiweshe himself was a former judge advocate responsible for military tribunals in the army, and a veteran of the liberation war, who had been appointed to head the Delimitations Commission charged with drawing up new constituencies for the 2005 elections. From 2000 to 2003, the chairperson of the ESC was Mr Sobusa Gula-Ndebele, a lawyer and also a retired army colonel. During his tenure, the Chief Executive of the Commission was Brigadier Douglas Nyikayaramba, who after his stint at the body returned to command the 2nd Infantry Brigade.[56]

There are, in addition, a whole set of other provisions of the law, often buried in small print, which have systematically skewed elections in favour of ZANU-PF.[57] However, two final aspects stand out. The first is the disenfranchisement of voters assumed to be MDC supporters; the second is the distortion of the delimitation process to favour ZANU-PF.

---

[55] Ibid., 5.
[56] Crisis in Zimbabwe Coalition (2005), *Things Fall Apart: The 2005 Parliamentary Election: Prospects of True Democracy in Zimbabwe*, Harare: Crisis in Zimbabwe Coalition.
[57] See notably the detailed chapters on 'The Subversion of the electoral process' in Derek Matyszak (2010), *Law, Politics and Zimbabwe's 'Unity' Government*, Harare: Konrad Adenauer Stiftung in association with the Research and Advocacy Unit.

The registration of voters, undertaken by the office of the RG, has long been mired in controversy. Supposedly, registration of voters is done on a continuous basis, meaning that voters' rolls are updated provided that people register as voters, register deaths of deceased relatives, or moves. In practice, this scarcely works for urban residents, let alone rural ones. There are also registration campaigns, during which people are supposed to produce required documentation, such as their national identity card or passport to register.[58] But prior to the 2002 presidential election, the RG declined to reveal how many people had registered, and there were complaints from opposition parties that they were not allowed to inspect the voters' roll. Furthermore, there were a series of measures that curtailed the right to vote.

High up on the list was the Citizenship of Zimbabwe Amendment Act of 2001 which outlawed dual citizenship and compelled millions of naturalized Zimbabweans to reapply for citizenship or lose it. Children born in Zimbabwe of foreign parents were also affected and needed to renounce their parents' citizenship to qualify as citizens of Zimbabwe. However, the most affected category were families of migrants from Malawi, Mozambique, and Zambia, many of whom had been resident in Zimbabwe for years. The same applied to remaining whites, many of whom were seen as opposition supporters.[59] Similarly, the Electoral Act (Modification) Notice 2002, introduced by Mugabe, restricted the right to vote only to those granted permanent residence after 31 December 1985 – another measure directed at whites and migrants deemed to favour the MDC. Critically, too, the Notice restricted postal voting to three categories of people: those belonging to a disciplined force (the defence, police, and prison services) and election officials who could not be in their constituencies on polling day; Zimbabwean government officials outside the country; and spouses of the people in these two groupings.[60] The failure of a challenge to this provision by the Diaspora Vote Action Group in court meant an effective block from voting on the estimated 3.5 million Zimbabwean exiles – the overwhelming majority of whom were reckoned to be MDC supporters.[61]

Further stringent requirements introduced in 2005, such as the provision of certain documents, led to the disenfranchisement of thousands of people in poor urban areas, while those residing in rural areas (ZANU-PF's principal stronghold) needed only to have their village head or farm employer vouch for them. Thus although the number of registered voters increased from just over 5 million in 2000 to 5.9 million in 2008, since then there has been a very low rate of registration of youth who have turned eighteen from 2000 onwards. The electoral roll has been shown to have numerous anomalies, not least the inclusion of the names of those who have died.[62] Although widely flawed, the election rolls are used by the DC to determine constituency boundaries and the number of polling stations. There have been constant complaints that the

---

[58] Kabemba (2004), op. cit., 21.
[59] Amongst them was democracy activist Judith Todd, daughter of Sir Garfield Todd, the liberal Prime Minister between 1953–57 whose overthrow prepared the way for a right-wing shift in white politics and the triumph of the RF in 1962.
[60] Commonwealth Secretariat, op. cit.
[61] Kagwanja, op. cit., 6.
[62] Apocryphal, yet symbolic, is the rumour that Ian Smith, who died in 2007, remains on the voting roll.

former have favoured ZANU-PF, but the situation certainly worsened after 2002. In 2004, the DC reduced the number of constituencies in urban areas (mostly known for their support for the opposition) whilst increasing the number in rural areas traditionally supporting ZANU-PF. Likewise, for the 2008 parliamentary elections, when the number of constituencies was increased from 120 to 210, areas supportive of ZANU-PF appear to have been disproportionately favoured in the allocation of constituencies. Such bias has been compounded by manipulation of the number of polling stations. In 2002, their number in urban areas was reduced by some 30–40 per cent, while an equivalent increase took place in rural areas. While the ESC justified this as decreasing the distance that rural voters would have to walk, it decreased the opportunity for urban voters to vote.[63]

If in Namibia and South Africa, the independence of electoral institutions has been largely maintained, in Zimbabwe they have increasingly become subordinated to ZANU-PF. We turn now to how this difference has played in the behaviour of NLMs as electoral machines.

SWAPO and the ANC as electoral machines

There are various ways for parties to win elections. First and foremost, they can mobilize support through their election campaigns, rounding these off by seeking to ensure that their supporters vote. These objectives are the essence of electoral contests, although the extent to which parties confront level playing fields varies immensely according to the rules which govern the conduct of electoral campaigns. For instance, there are major differences even amongst established liberal democracies regarding the rules governing campaign funding, broadcasting, and advertising. Yet a second way in which parties can seek to win elections is by systematically disadvantaging the opposition, perhaps even preventing opposition supporters from being able or willing to vote. This latter aspect can go well beyond the structuring of electoral institutions and regulations, as already discussed, to characterize many other aspects of electoral campaigning.

The most striking aspect of their first decades in power has been how SWAPO and the ANC have utilized their status as dominant parties to consolidate their political power. SWAPO, in particular, has continuously emphasised its role as the party of liberation with the slogan of 'SWAPO is the nation and the nation is SWAPO', this translating into vigorous assaults upon the legitimacy and patriotism of the opposition parties it has had to face, especially those formed by its own former members.[64] During the 1999 campaign, the newly formed COD was met with smear campaigns and character assassinations, whilst the appearance of the RDP for the 2009 elections elicited an even more aggressive response, its leaders denounced as agents of imperialism seeking 'regime change'. On occasions this led to the denial of the rights of RDP activists to campaign, with SWAPO effectively declaring its claimed territory as no-go areas

[63] Kabemba (2004), op. cit., 23–25.
[64] Henning Melber (2003), 'Limits to liberation: An introduction to Namibia's post-colonial political culture', in Henning Melber (ed.), *Re-examining Liberation in Namibia: Political Culture since Independence*, Uppsala: Nordic Africa Institute, 9–25.

for the opposition. There were violent clashes between members of both parties, and for the first time, an election campaign in Namibia turned visibly ugly. Worryingly, this occurred against a background of survey data conducted notably by Afrobarometer, which demonstrated a relatively low level of support for democracy (around 60 per cent across three surveys between 1999 and 2006), with commitment to elections as the best way of selecting leaders declining by nearly 30 per cent between 2002 and 2008.[65]

The ANC's campaigning has generally been far more sophisticated than that of SWAPO, and the party has elaborated a highly efficient electoral machine capable of mobilizing mass support and delivering the vote. It has been strongly guided by research conducted by polling companies which, with the advice of professional public relations firms, has burnished its image and emphasized issues likely to appeal to its supporters, such as job creation, poverty reduction, and the battles against crime and HIV-AIDS. Its strategies and tactics have been tailored to particular situations. In 2004, the party largely eschewed attacks on its competitors, refusing to assign them the status of serious rivals, and contrasting their impotence with its own strength; this was much to the frustration of the DA, which wanted to establish its status as the principal party of opposition. Yet with the formation of COPE following the displacement of Mbeki by Zuma as leader in 2009, the ANC came out with guns blazing, determined to strangle at birth the attraction of COPE for its own less committed supporters, particularly in its homeland of the Eastern Cape.[66]

The ANC has learned fast and well about how to win, and has evolved an impressive electoral organization. Thus for the 2009 campaign, the ANC established a national campaign team at party headquarters, Luthuli House, with parallel teams set up at provincial and regional level. Luthuli House also had a 'mobilization team' designed to put out local fires quickly. It was deployed to the Western Cape, where local ANC elites were engaged in debilitating infighting, and to the North West where the COPE breakaway had created paranoia about infiltrators and spies. The campaign was backed up by the human and organizational resources of its alliance partners, COSATU and the SACP, with the former seconding numerous officials to the parties as full-time organizers. Alongside activists drawn from the ANC Youth League and networks of MK veterans, many were active in organizing the door-to-door canvassing carried out by volunteers, this backed up by a profusion of community hall meetings and mass rallies which ensured that the party's message was carried to virtually every township, suburb, and village in the country. Finally, the methods that ANC campaigners deployed were closely tailored to specific electoral constituencies and target groups, whether these were particular provinces, religious communities, racial minorities, professionals, traditional leaders, black business groups, among others. The ANC was projected as the party for Everyman (and woman).[67]

There have certainly been occasions when opposition parties have been blocked from campaigning freely in so-called ANC areas. The first democratic

[65] Henning Melber (2010), 'Namibia's National Assembly and presidential elections 2009: Did democracy win?' *Journal of Contemporary African Studies*, 28: 2, 203–14.
[66] Tom Lodge (2005), 'The African National Congress: There is no party like it; Ayikho Efana Nayo', in Piombo and Nijzink (eds), op. cit., 109–28; see also Butler, op. cit.
[67] Butler, op. cit.

election, conducted amidst a virtual civil war in KwaZulu-Natal and right-wing violence on the Witwatersrand, was tense as well as being ultimately triumphant, with as many as 300 people killed in each of the six months leading up to the April 1994 poll. Thousands more were injured or forced from their homes as both the ANC and IFP engaged in 'cleansing' their turf of opposition supporters. Again, in 1999, nearly 300 people died in election-related violence in the five months prior to the poll, most of it again occurring in KwaZulu-Natal. Yet, overall, violence levels have markedly declined, with much-reduced levels of killing and intimidation characterizing both the 2004 and 2009 campaigns, pointing to a lowering of levels of political enmity and hopefully a shift for the better in the nation's political culture.[68]

In both Namibia and South Africa, the ruling parties' campaigns have been assisted by ample funding and use of the media. A detailed examination of party funding will follow in Chapter 10. Suffice it to say here that in both countries there is a system of public financial support which allocates parties state funding proportional to their representation in parliament. This works to the huge advantage of both SWAPO and the ANC. In 2007, for example, the former received 11 times as much state funding as any other party represented in parliament and 3.2 times as much as all the other opposition parties put together.[69] Yet equally important is that in both, there are few restrictions on the right of parties to receive private funding, whether from home or from abroad. In Namibia, parties are legally required to declare their foreign funding, yet few do, whilst in South Africa there is no such regulation at all. The overall effect is that in elections in both countries there is a huge mismatch in funding, with the ruling parties massively ahead of their competitors. Thus Butler estimates that the ANC campaign in 2009 cost between R400 and R500 million, with major sums coming from foreign political parties ranging from the Indian National Congress and the Chinese Communist Party through to the ruling parties of Libya, Angola, and Equatorial Guinea.[70] No such estimates are available for opposition parties, but they were quite unable to compete. Meanwhile, they are also assisted by considerable blurring of state with party funding, with numerous instances of government officials using their official time and access to resources, such as vehicles, to back the ruling party.

Funding is vital to parties for getting their message across, but the campaigns of both SWAPO and the ANC have been assisted by their being parties of government. Notwithstanding rules which ensure free air-time for opposition parties, SWAPO and the ANC have both benefited immensely from arrangements that advantage the larger parties. In 2009, the NBC was explicitly criticized by the SADC Observer team for its pro-SWAPO bias.[71] Similar criticisms have been regularly aimed at the SABC in South Africa by opposition parties, although they have not been reliably sustained by academic analysis of election coverage.[72]

---

[68] Daniel and Southall, op. cit.
[69] EISA, op. cit.
[70] Butler, op. cit., 74.
[71] *The Namibian*, 2 December 2009.
[72] Gavin Davis (2005), 'Media coverage in Election 2004: Were some parties more equal than others?' in Piombo and Nijzink (eds), op. cit., 231–49.

Meanwhile, in both countries, the state media is balanced by the privately owned media, this providing for relatively independent coverage of campaigns. However, this does not necessarily translate into support for the opposition: as reported regarding South Africa in 2009, various covert pressures upon media freedom may well have served to inhibit the privately owned media's willingness to call explicitly for an opposition vote.[73] Things have been very different in Zimbabwe.

ZANU-PF as an electoral machine

The fundamental difference between SWAPO and the ANC, as dominant parties, and ZANU-PF as a party which has enforced its domination, has been the latter's uninhibited resort to state power and violence to reverse its loss of majority support. This at one level reflects the substantially different popular bases of the various movements. Although its origins and core support lie amidst the Ovambo, SWAPO has survived as a pan-ethnic movement. Likewise, although Xhosa and Zulu elements have been predominant historically, the ANC has consistently sought to unite all Africans and during latter decades has stressed its non-racial nature. Faced by an ideology which sought to divide blacks along racial and ethnic lines, both SWAPO and ANC have placed great ideological emphasis on their representing the entire nation. In contrast, for all that ZANU-PF claims to embody the nation, its history is one of division, symbolized since 1980 by its breaking the PF to contest the transitional elections independently; its initial treatment of ZAPU as a junior partner in government; its campaign of terror against its rival in Matabeleland and Midlands provinces in the early 1980s; and its enforced incorporation of ZAPU in 1987. For all that it was able to maintain majority support in the 1980s, its hold on power and popular affection had a considerable ethnic dimension, built on historical tensions between Ndebele and Shona. From the late 1990s, the relative fragility of its electoral foundations was to be exposed by its loss of popular support even amongst its traditional base.

Apart from tightening its grip on the electoral institutions, ZANU-PF has maintained itself in power through, first, erecting a panoply of restrictive laws to inhibit opposition; second, clamping down on media freedom; third, appropriating state and other resources whilst restricting them to forces of opposition; fourth, unleashing massive violence upon its adversaries; and fifth, not least, declining to accept adverse outcomes in elections. These various devices have been widely documented in numerous reports on elections and political crisis in Zimbabwe in recent years. What follows is merely a summary.

Restrictive laws

Important democratic gains were made during the first two decades of independence but after ZANU-PF's hold on power was threatened in 2000, these have been steadily been rolled back. Political freedom and civil rights are enshrined in the constitution but the rule of law is only very imperfectly

---

[73] Jane Duncan (2009), 'Desperately seeking depth: The media and the 2009 elections', in Southall and Daniel (eds), op. cit., 215–31.

observed. Human rights abuses have become systematic. The press is tightly controlled and the private media constantly harassed. Indeed, by 2003 ZANU-PF had overseen the 'promotion of the political culture of fear and the negation of the democratic ethic'.[74] Illustrating this, in 2008 the Electoral Institute of Southern Africa produced a long list of legislative enactments and constitutional amendments which had shaped an increasingly repressive electoral environment since the early 2000s. These included the Access to Information and Protection of Privacy Act of 2002 (AIPPA) which, *inter alia*, required the accreditation of journalists, criminalizing those practising without a licence; the Public Order and Security Act of 2002 (POSA), passed in the run-up to the 2002 presidential election, which gave extensive powers to the executive to ban public meetings and marches; the Electoral Amendment Act of 2002, which gave the RG the power to alter the voters' roll at any time without directly informing the voters concerned or giving them the right to appeal; and the General Laws Amendment Act of 2002 which was intended to amend the Electoral Act relating to powers of the RG to amend the voters' roll, the eligibility of electoral observers and monitors, and the provision of voter education. When the Supreme Court ruled on 22 February 2002 that this Act was illegal, its key provisions were simply enacted by the promulgation by the Minister of Justice in a statutory instrument on 1 March. In addition, amongst a cumulatively impacting series of other laws, the government put forward a Non-Governmental Organizations Bill which threatened to impose severe controls upon NGOs, already suffering under threats of repression and lack of funding. Workers for foreign NGOs were regularly denied entry and work permits.[75]

Following SADC mediation in 2007, amendments were made to AIPPA which removed the criminalization of journalists operating without a licence, and to POSA, which meant that appeals against the banning of a march were no longer to be decided by the executive authority but by the magistrate's court. For all that these changes somewhat improved the situation, none of them were in place for the harmonized elections of 2008. The continued existence of a battery of heavily restrictive laws severely inhibits not only the opposition but Zimbabwe's already marginalized civil society.

Restrictions on the media

Additional to numerous measures inhibiting freedom of association and organization, there have many others restricting media freedom. Historically, media coverage has systematically favoured ZANU-PF. Jonathan Moyo reported that during the 1990 election, although the ESC was charged with ensuring that all contestants had fair access to the media, ZANU-PF not only used the state broadcaster, the Zimbabwe Broadcasting Corporation (ZBC) to dominate the airwaves, but was in violation of all ethical standards regarding advertising, using slogans that equated voting for ZUM as equivalent to dying: 'Don't commit suicide, vote ZANU-PF'.[76]

At the time alternative media outlets were thin on the ground, with a few

---

[74] John Makumbe (2003), *Zimbabwe's Turmoil: Problems and Prospects*, Pretoria: Institute for Security Studies.
[75] EISA (2008), op. cit., 16.
[76] Moyo, op. cit., 74–75.

monthly and weekly magazines of limited circulation. However, during the late 1990s, a more vigorous independent media emerged with major financial assistance from foreign sources and international NGOs. A key development was the appearance of the first-ever viable opposition paper, the *Daily News*. With backing from Australian, British, and South African interests, this was produced under the auspices of a large newspaper group, Associated Newspapers of Zimbabwe, which also published five community newspapers.[77] Mugabe's response was twofold.

The first was violence and intimidation, the bombing of first the offices and then the printing press of the *Daily News* (although, inevitably, the government blamed this on the MDC), as well as the persecution and torture of leading journalists. The *Daily News* folded in 2003, followed by the closure of *The Tribune* in 2003 and *The Weekly Times* in 2004.[78]

The second was a swift resort to legislative provisions aimed at gagging the media, borrowed from the Smith-era Law and Order Maintenance Act. When these were deemed insufficient, the regime replaced the Law and Order Act with POSA (Public Order and Security Act), which included stronger measures for controlling the media. New restrictions on the media were also conjured up via the passage of AIPPA (Access to Information and Protection of Privacy Act). However, for all that the usually supine Supreme Court had ruled unconstitutional a clause in AIPPA that imposed criminal sanctions on any journalist convicted of publishing false information, the restrictions on and intimidation of the opposition media were particularly heavy during the 2002 presidential election campaign.

The architect of the new measures was the same Jonathan Moyo (by this time Minister of Information) who had criticized the clampdown on the media during the 1990 election. His subsequent falling out with Mugabe gave hope for a more relaxed atmosphere, and in the run-up to the 2005 elections, the government published a set of regulations to be followed by all parties regarding access to the electronic media. However, the state-controlled media continued to overwhelmingly favour ZANU-PF, and the intimidation of journalists and the harassment of opposition newspapers continued unabated.[79]

The SADC negotiations which preceded the harmonized elections of 2008 had led to an agreement that independent broadcasters would be able to operate in a more relaxed environment, and that the media were compelled to give equal coverage to all political parties. However, although there was less overt intimidation of the independent media, the state-controlled media remained unashamedly pro-ZANU-PF, providing little or no coverage of the MDC campaign. What it did feature was negative.[80] In short, the media remained 'in chains'.[81]

---

[77] Shumbana Karume (2004), 'An assessment of the impact of democratic assistance', in Olaleye (ed.), op. cit., 28–45.

[78] Catholic Commission for Justice and Peace in Zimbabwe (CCJP) (2000), *Crisis of Governance: A Report on Political Violence in Zimbabwe, Volume 2*, Harare: CCJP, 96–98; EISA (2008), op. cit., 37–40.

[79] Kagwanja, op. cit., 9.

[80] EISA (2008), op. cit., 37–40.

[81] Kagwanja, op. cit., 9.

Control of state and other resources

ZANU-PF has claimed the state as its own and has absorbed its powers into its electoral machine. A feature of all campaigns from at least 1990 onwards has been the use of state resources (e. g., buses, army trucks, and other government vehicles) to ferry supporters to mass rallies. In the elections of 2000 and 2002, Mugabe used the land issue to buy support and to invoke memories of liberation struggle. The thrust of ZANU-PF's campaign in both elections was upon land: the promise and actual redistribution of land featured strongly. More sinister was the use of food as an electoral weapon.[82] The land invasions from 2000 were at the base of the serious food shortages which afflicted numerous parts of the country, but they were particularly acute in the opposition strongholds of Masvingo, Midlands, and Bulawayo during the 2005 elections. There were numerous reports of the government punishing MDC supporters by refusing them food aid – much of it provided by international agencies – whilst rewarding ZANU-PF supporters in the same areas with the meagre resources available. Meanwhile, restrictions had been imposed upon food distribution by NGOs, even whilst many of the latter's capacities had been severely undermined by restrictions on their operations. 'Thus food distribution remained in the hands of partisan chiefs in rural areas with all the credible risks of the politicization of food security.'[83]

The EISA (Electoral Institute of Southern Africa) Report on the 2008 elections captured the essence of the ZANU-PF's use of state resources which probably holds good for previous contests. Mugabe himself made multiple donations of buses, motor vehicles, generators, television sets, food aid, and agricultural equipment to communities and organizations across the country, funded, apparently, by the Reserve Bank of Zimbabwe. The handouts took place mostly at high-profile and lavish government occasions, with the participation of cabinet ministers and extensive state media coverage. Police and military staff were continually deployed to bolster images of presidential power.[84]

Deployment of political violence

If there is one feature for which Zimbawean elections since 2000 have become internationally notorious it is the high levels of political violence perpetrated by the government and ruling party upon its opponents. Intimidation and violence has become so central to ZANU-PF campaigning that, for many Zimbabweans, elections have become equated with civil war.

In its review of developments prior to the 2000 parliamentary election, Amnesty International declared:

> There is evidence that the Government of Zimbabwe is either instigating or acquiescing in serious violations of human rights including extra-judicial executions, torture and other cruel, inhuman or degrading treatment or punishment. There

---

[82] Ibid., 26.
[83] Ibid., 9.
[84] EISA (2008), op. cit., 40.

appears to be a deliberate and well-thought out plan of systematic human rights violations with a clear strategy, constituting state-sponsored terror...[85]

It also noted that there was a total lack of accountability for those responsible for violence. This, it proposed, needed to be located against, first, the background of serious violations of human rights which had taken place during the liberation war by both sides but which were covered up by a blanket amnesty; and second, the terror and violence that was inflicted upon Matabeleland by the 5th Brigade in the early 1980s, these atrocities themselves amnestied in 1988. Official violation of key court rulings and threats against the independence of the judiciary had also compounded the problem of impunity.

There were already disturbing instances of violence in the elections preceding those of the early 2000s. Intimidation and violence directed at candidates and supporters of ZUM in 1990 represented a foretaste of what the MDC was to encounter later on.[86] Against the background of the violent seizure of farms by ZANU-PF activists and war veterans, the 2000 parliamentary and 2002 presidential elections were preceded by systematic attacks upon those suspected of sympathizing with the MDC. Numerous civil servants, teachers, local government workers, and police officers viewed as opposing the land invasions or viewed as supporting the MDC were variously threatened, dismissed, beaten, raped or tortured; similar treatment was handed out to many MDC candidates and supporters. Often, attacks were made by large groups of ZANU-PF youths, the so-called 'green bombers', in total disregard of international observer groups, who called for official interventions to stop the violence and to ensure conditions for a free vote with no effect.[87] Although such groups noted that MDC supporters sometimes retaliated, the 'overwhelming preponderance of political violence was perpetrated by ZANU-PF youths and supporters against known or suspected supporters of the MDC'.[88]

The level of violence prior to the 2005 election was considerably less than during the 2000 and 2002 campaigns, this borne out by analyses made by not only the MDC itself but other groups such as the Zimbabwe Human Rights NGO Forum, the Zimbabwe Peace Project, and the Zimbabwe Election Support Network. According to the last mentioned, there was a 'surprising level of political tolerance', a major contributing factor being early and consistent calls for zero tolerance of violence made by the President, party leaders, police chiefs, and security chiefs.[89] Even so, detailed analysis demonstrated, first, that there were still a large number of serious violations (3,783 recorded by the Zimbabwe Peace Project for the period November 2004–March 2005); second, that there was a trend towards more subtle forms of violation replacing overt violence, particularly towards interference with basic freedoms, inclusive of unlawful arrest and detention under POSA; and third, there was a steady rise in viola-

[85] Amnesty International, op. cit., 1.
[86] Moyo, op. cit., 77–78.
[87] Commonwealth Secretariat (2000), *The Parliamentary Elections in Zimbabwe 24–25 June 2000: The Report of the Commonwealth Observer Group*, London: Commonwealth Secretariat; Commonwealth Secretariat (2002), op. cit.
[88] Commonwealth Secretariat (2000), 29.
[89] Tony Reeler and Kuda Chitsike (2005), *Trick or Treat? The Effects of the Pre-Election Climate on the Poll in the 2005 Zimbabwe Parliamentary Elections*, Cape Town: Institute for Democracy in Southern Africa, 27.

tions as the election approached. Such evidence led Kagwanja to conclude that having for the moment contained the MDC's challenge to Mugabe's incumbency, the decline of violence was 'a political decision by ZANU-PF'.[90] Improved, yet far from violence-free conditions, characterized the 2008 elections, prior to which Mugabe had been forced into negotiations by SADC.

Non-compliance with electoral outcomes

If all else fails, governments that lose elections yet retain the backing of the security forces can stay in power. Significantly, this had been demonstrated prior to Zimbabwe's 2008 elections by events in Kenya, when the results of the peculiarly violent December 2007 election in that country should have seen the exodus of President Kibaki and the replacement of his Party of National Unity by Raila Odinga's Orange Democratic Movement. Instead, Kibaki clung to power, disputed the result, and with the backing of various international players who feared Kenya would collapse into civil war, forced a power-sharing agreement in which he retained the presidency whilst Odinga became Prime Minister. It would be an insult to Mugabe's cunning to suggest that he needed such an example to stage a similar show of imperviousness to electoral defeat in the harmonized elections of 2008, but the precedent was certainly helpful in providing a veneer of legitimacy to the power-sharing agreement eventually negotiated under SADC and other pressures following the elections.[91] Yet there had been clear previous indications of the regime's likely reactions well before the results came in (and were delayed and manipulated). There had been numerous statements by senior figures in the security forces that they would not accept an MDC victory and Tsvangirai as President, while Mugabe himself stated on numerous occasions before the election that power would never be yielded to the opposition.[92] On the day before the elections, he declared that in the event of the MDC winning he would take his war veterans back into the bush.[93] ZANU-PF's disbelief in the connection between the national interest and electoral outcomes had never been made so clear: elections were simply for Zimbabweans to express 'fealty and obeisance to power'.[94]

Dominance, hegemony, and democracy

NLMs' access to state power has depended upon their winning elections and evolving into electoral machines to maintain themselves in office. In Namibia and South Africa, SWAPO and the ANC have secured repeated victories which have confirmed their status as 'dominant parties'. Securing initial victories in the turbulent contexts of transitional elections, their successive triumphs have been achieved in electoral conditions which, although not without flaws, have with justification been regarded as broadly 'free and fair'. Certainly there are

[90] Kagwanja, op. cit., 7
[91] Nic Cheeseman and Tendi Blessing-Miles (2010), 'Power-sharing in comparative perspective: The dynamics of unity government in Kenya and Zimbabwe', *Journal of Modern African Studies*, 48: 2, 203–30.
[92] EISA (2008), op. cit., 41.
[93] Ibid., 42.
[94] Matyszak, op. cit., 46.

concerns that their dominance has, in one way or another, begun to shape their respective electoral environments to their advantage; and likewise, at times their political activists have resorted to violence and intimidation against electoral opponents. Yet hitherto they have not yet confronted the ultimate test of how they would behave if they were to lose an election and as a consequence be required under their nations' constitutions to stand down from power. Certainly, the ANC has conceded power at the provincial level, notably in the Western Cape following the elections of 2009, but losing power nationally could be another story. Only time will tell what will happen when SWAPO and the ANC are so challenged, and it will be a theme of later chapters that there is an important role for parties of opposition and civil society to keep both of these parties honest. Not surprisingly, there are some observers who fear that, if push comes to shove, there will be many among the ranks of both SWAPO and the ANC who will wish to emulate the example of ZANU-PF by blatantly rigging elections, using concerted state violence, and refusing to accede to the expressed wishes of the people.

Embedded in this latter perspective is the suggestion that the NLMs share the same genes. Parties of dominance, it is implied, are happy enough with democracy whilst they are winning, but will abruptly cast it aside for an enforced hegemony if, as is one day is likely, they lose power. To some considerable extent, SWAPO and the ANC are both partially responsible for such thinking through the extensive support, covert and overt, that they have provided to ZANU-PF since the year 2000, which seems to say that, come what may, the NLMs should stick together.

6.
Liberation Movements and the State

The ANC's Strategy and Tactics documents remain the most explicit statements of the different liberation movements' goals of 'capturing' and 'transforming' the state. Central to the strategy is the policy of 'deployment' of party personnel to all key institutions of the state to enable the liberation movement to control the 'levers of power'. 'We place a high premium on the involvement of our cadres in all centres of power', stated Jacob Zuma in his speech on the occasion of the ANC's 99th anniversary on 8 January 2011, involving their deployment 'in key strategic positions in the state as well as the private sector'.

According to its proponents, political deployment takes place in virtually all political systems, democratic and despotic alike. In democracies, capture of the state through winning elections enables parties to appoint their own nominees to all major state positions. In South Africa deployment was particularly neces-sary, for the state inherited from apartheid was totally unfit to serve the needs of all South Africans. If no changes to personnel had been made, the civil service would have had the potential to undermine the elected government. The reform of the state therefore demanded 'a value-driven constitutional approach to deployment' which 'included deploying historically disadvantaged groups and the employment of professional political experts'. Not all those from disad-vantaged backgrounds who were to be employed in senior management levels were necessarily political deployees, yet 'political deployment of professionals' was a necessary phenomenon in the managing of the state.[1]

The counter-argument to deployment is based upon Weberian notions of a bureaucracy which delivers loyal service, according to established rules and constitutional law, to any government in power. This prescribes distinct spheres of responsibility for politicians and civil servants, and sets limits upon the powers of the former, whereas the ANC's deployment strategy blurs the distinc-tion between party and state and subordinates the latter to the former. ANC deployees, argue the critics, have a conflict of interests. Whereas they may be appointed to positions of state which constitutionally require them to be polit-ically impartial, they are on the other hand bound to follow their instructions from the ANC. According to one commentator, therefore, 'Cadre deployment is unique to political parties (like the ANC) steeped in the Leninist tradition of democratic centralism. This principle commits every cadre to defending and implementing the will of the party leadership...even if it means acting outside the Constitution and the Law.'[2] Fundamentally, therefore, deployment consti-tutes an assault upon the constitutional state established in 1994. In contrast,

---

[1]   Daniel Plaatjies (2010), 'Deployment of loyalists is crucial for the survival of ruling parties', *Sunday Independent*, 21 March.
[2]   Gavin Davis (2010), 'An independent cadre is a contradiction in terms amid party loyalty', *Mail & Guardian*, 19–25 November.

although civil servants in mature democracies may well have their own polit-ical sympathies, they perform their jobs impartially. The outcome of deploy-ment has been: subordination of supposedly constitutionally independent institutions to the ANC; preference for political disposition over competence regarding appointments to a wide range of bodies, ranging from parastatals to hospitals to local government, resulting in inefficiency and failures in 'service delivery'; a turnover of top positions in the public service and parastatals, leading to perpetual crises of leadership; and not least, the penetration of ANC factionalism into the state resulting, for instance, in the ejection of Mbeki appointees by Zuma loyalists at national, provincial, and local government levels following Polokwane in 2010.[3] Even Nyami Booi, a veteran ANC MP, complained in 2010 that deployment had drained parliament of experienced MPs in favour of government.[4] Deployment, concludes the DA, adds up to cronyism and corruption. According to the *Mail & Guardian*, the ANC's 'myste-rious deployment policy' is about the provision of jobs, with little thought going into what the job might entail and whether those selected are suitable.[5]

Booysen has tracked the development of the ANC's deployment policy, stressing how its formalization after the movement's 50th Conference at Mafikeng in 1997 followed up on its earlier practices in exile. A National Deploy-ment Committee was established in late 1998, with provincial and local deploy-ment committees to come. Thereafter the history of the deployment process is very much one of successive internal complaints against, suspensions of, re-appointments of, and messy battles around deployment committees at all levels of the party, the intensity of struggles suggesting that deployment committees wield very real powers of appointment of personnel. Although the rationale for deployment in party documents has remained that of the need for the placing of revolutionary cadres in strategic positions, even the ANC's own reflections, embodied in its documentation, lament the extent to which deployment has become an instrument for patronage, material accumulation, and upward mobility. Yet the principal remedy for the misuse which the party regularly comes up with is an increase in the powers of the National Deployment Committee, which presumes its capacity and willingness to impose discipline upon deployment committees at lower levels, ambitions which seem equally regularly to be thwarted. Thus although the government responded to a major deterioration in the capacity of numerous local governments to perform even their most basic functions by passing a Municipal Systems Amendment Act in 2010 which prohibits municipalities from employing local party officials, there is no serious indication that its provisions are yet being implemented.[6]

Fiona Forde has recently suggested that the ANC is aspiring to run South Africa on the model of the corporatist state which the Chinese Communist Party (CCP) operates in contemporary China, yet points to major differences. First, whereas the ANC accepts virtually anyone as a member, membership of the CCP is often only by invitation only, and as a structure, the CCP is secretive.

[3]   George Devenish (2010), 'Constitution vs "national democratic constitution"', *Mail & Guardian*, 14–20 May.
[4]   Cited in *Sunday Times*, 12 September 2010.
[5]   Editorial, *Mail & Guardian*, 16–22 October 2010.
[6]   Susan Booysen (2011), *The African National Congress and the Regeneration of Political Power*, Johannesburg: Wits University Press, 373–78.

Second, although a small elite (only about 5 per cent of the population), the CCP's influence is immense,

> due largely to the deployment of cadres in all walks of life who entrench the ideology and identity of the party...A party representative sits on the board of every company and they are also found within government departments and ministries, in addition to the appointed public servants. They oversee the judiciary, are active in media houses, prominent in trade unions, and generally present across all sectors. Although the ANC does likewise, China's deployed cadres are not only loyal members but highly skilled and educated men and women fit for the task at hand.

CCP deployees who perform inefficiently not only lose their jobs but their party membership. In contrast, ANC members who fail in one position often get redeployed to another. Third, the CCP has a Central Party School which grooms future leaders and provides a think tank for party decision-making. Fourth, all this is made possible by a very strong state underpinned by a very strong party. In contrast, the ANC is weak and fractured, and rather than dropping non-performers, it tends to 'redeploy' them to positions where, presumably, it is thought that they can do less damage. Furthermore, the ANC has an aversion to alienating potentially powerful party players and their followers by blocking them off from access to state positions and resources.[7]

The problem with all this is that while deployment excites so much debate, there is a lack of systematic data regarding its workings. Because deployment committees operate behind closed doors, we have no clear indication as to whether deployment is conducted according to whatever criteria the party has prescribed, or whether it has degenerated into little more than an instrument whereby elites appoint those close to them in personal or political terms to key positions. What is clear is that some notion and practice of deployment is at the heart of any party-driven strategy of state transformation, as much in Namibia and Zimbabwe as in South Africa. However, given the problems in identifying how deployment actually operates, the only way to study it is through indirect means, by asking related questions: How do we assess the developing relationships between the party and particular state institutions? Can we identify particular instances and general trends where party loyalties would seem to have trumped professionalism in the making of appointments? What is the connection between deployment and the pursuit of the NDR and/or a more generic goal of 'transformation'? Let us start by exploring the relationship between deployment and postcolonial affirmative action strategies.

Liberation movements and the post-liberation state

The settlements in Namibia, Zimbabwe, and South Africa shared the same fundamental characteristics. In all three countries the political economies remained white dominated; the subordinated racial populations lacked the skills to run them; and if 'socialist democracy' was to be attained, it would be through

---

[7]   Fiona Forde (2011), *An Inconvenient Youth: Julius Malema and the 'New' ANC*, Johannesburg: Picador Africa, 217–20.

the course of further 'struggle'. Simultaneously, the transitions involved the adoption of formally liberal-democratic constitutions which outlined a separation of powers between the government and parliament, and which recognized the independence of the judiciary and other major institutions of state. Yet even in established democracies, the separation of powers is relative, while in white-ruled southern Africa there had been a long history of parliamentary subordination to the executive, along with extension of ruling party influence over appointments to the civil service, judiciary, military, parastatals, and so on. This was most dramatically illustrated in South Africa in the 1950s when the NP resorted to manipulation of the senior judiciary and the expansion of the Senate in order to secure the passage through parliament of the Separate Representation of Voters Act which removed Coloured and Indian men in the Cape and Natal from the common voters' roll.[8] Even so, ruling party dominance of the political, military, and judicial spheres during the era of white rule was never absolute, for the Westminster imprint allowed for parliamentary oppositions and courageous individual MPs like Helen Suzman to criticize governments, demand information, and embarrass the executive, and likewise for the judiciary – whilst largely politically reliable – to sometimes pass down judgements which ran contrary to government desires (a key case in point being the dismissal of the Treason Trialists in South Africa in 1960). It was precisely because they had a sound knowledge of their own highly compromised constitutional histories that white parties in Namibia and South Africa were so insistent on abandoning the Westminster system for one under which the legislature and executive would both be subject to a constitution.

For their part, the NLMs were ambivalent about liberal democracy. Having been subject to numerous dictatorial suppressions, there was a significant commitment to guaranteeing individual and political freedoms. On the other hand, commitment to 'transformation' implied the need for a revolutionary state capable of overcoming all obstacles. Thus radical critics within the NLMs regarded the transitional settlements as having been designed to safeguard the capitalist mode of production and to forge the necessary class alliances between petty bourgeois nationalists within the incoming regime and the established white dominant bloc.[9]

Against such a background, it is scarcely surprising that NLMs regarded the state as requiring not merely Africanization (Zimbabwe) or 'affirmative action' to ensure 'representivity' (Namibia and South Africa), but its becoming the key instrument of 'transformation'.

Race and transformation: the civil service in Zimbabwe, Namibia, and South Africa

For the majority of whites, the liberation movements were communist and terrorist, and represented a threat to Western civilization. President P.W. Botha

[8] David Welsh (2009), *The Rise and Fall of Apartheid*, Jeppestown: Jonathan Ball Publishers, 52–54.
[9] For instance, Arnold Sibanda (1988), 'The political situation', in Colin Stoneman (ed.), *Zimbabwe's Prospects: Issues of Race, Class, State and Capital in Southern Africa*, Basingstoke: Macmillan, 257–83.

captured such sentiments when he called for 'total strategy' to combat the 'Soviet-backed' ANC's 'total onslaught'. Correspondingly, there were many forebodings that southern Africa's 'racial conflicts' would end up in a 'bloodbath'. In such circumstances, the transitional settlements which brought about compromise endings to the different wars were widely hailed as remarkable. In each case, too, policies of racial reconciliation pursued by the incoming regimes were often portrayed as indicating an unexpected depth of generosity upon the part of the victors. To a considerable extent, this generosity was associated with the three leaders as they went out of their way to placate former enemies whilst simultaneously advocating an inclusive nationalism. 'There are no losers in the elections', declared Nujoma, after SWAPO's victory in 1989: all would be able to enjoy the fruits of freedom, and the new government would go out of its way to work with all sectors of society.[10] Mugabe stressed that there should be no reprisals but forgiveness. Whites were 'still on top economically', but black Zimbabweans would not make them suffer.[11] Yet Mandela was the individual leader who was to become most highly associated with the spirit of reconciliation, not merely because apartheid had elevated white superiority to new heights, but also because of the commitment with which he pursued his vision of racial inclusiveness. It was this strategy that was to account for his status as a secular saint.[12]

The role of political leadership was clearly of critical importance in stabilizing these post-conflict situations. However, there was much more to racial reconciliation than a spirit of generosity. It was rather dictated not only by the terms of the different settlements, but also by recognition of the incoming regimes that they would continue to rely heavily upon white skills until the state and political economy had been 'transformed'.

Herbst has depicted the Mugabe government's relationship with remaining whites as a 'racial bargain'.[13] This bargain – never discussed openly but generally understood – laid down that while older whites in the public sector could expect to be moved on, those in the private sector could continue to operate their businesses and farms and lead their colonial lifestyle (servants, large houses, swimming pools, and tennis courts) whilst retaining an 'exit option' in the form of a foreign passport. However, younger whites were discouraged from staying by the foreclosure of economic opportunities: *de facto* blocked access to public employment, government lines of credit, or success in tendering for government business, while only foreign-owned companies which sold their assets in Zimbabwe to black Zimbabweans would be able to remit their funds to foreign destinations. The racial bargain therefore implied that Zimbabwe would not have to Africanize the economy by force because the size and significance of the white population would dwindle within a generation (not least because with the emigration of younger whites during the war, the white population was disproportionately old). Furthermore, because whites occupied most highly

---

[10]   *ACR 1990–92*, B624.

[11]   Sibanda, op. cit., 260.

[12]   John Daniel (2006), 'Soldiering on: The post-presidential years of Nelson Mandela', in Roger Southall and Henning Melber (eds), *Legacies of Power: Leadership Change and Former Presidents in African Politics*, Cape Town: HSRC Press, 26–50.

[13]   Jeffrey Herbst (1990), *State Politics in Zimbabwe*, Harare: University of Zimbabwe Publications, 221–27.

skilled positions, they were not in direct competition with the vast majority blacks, most whites in low-skilled positions having emigrated by independence.

Herbst regards the racial bargain in Zimbabwe as having limited relevance to South Africa (and by implication, Namibia) because of the very different demographic situation. There were proportionately more whites in South Africa, a majority of them were Afrikaners lacking easy possibilities of emigration, the white population would continue to reproduce itself, and many more whites were in lower-skilled positions and hence in potential direct competition with blacks. Forging a racial bargain would therefore prove more difficult.

Contrary to Herbst's expectations, whereas the racial bargain in Zimbabwe broke down fairly rapidly, those in Namibia and South Africa have been far better maintained hitherto. It is therefore pertinent to explore the reasons.

The Lancaster House constitution served as an important precedent for the subsequent settlements in Namibia and South Africa. Muzorewa's Rhodesia-Zimbabwe government and the nationalist forces were compelled to seek a negotiated settlement by the potential consequences of a continuation of the war. Even though Smith could and would not publically admit it, it was clear by 1977 that his government was losing the war, and this was a major factor in his attempting to undercut support for the guerrillas by constructing the internal settlement. For their part, ZANU and ZAPU recognized that although over the next few years a military victory was ultimately obtainable, it would come at massive cost to the country's economy. The war was also hurting the nationalists' allies in neighbouring countries badly, while South Africa had by now come to regard Rhodesia as dispensable. The outcome was agreement around a constitution whereby in return for various safeguards, the whites agreed to a black government on the Westminster model.

White Rhodesians had liked to contrast the efficiency of their own civil service with what they viewed as the administrative chaos obtaining elsewhere in Africa. However, by the late 1970s, this projection had been placed under considerable strain by inter-departmental tensions related to the deteriorating security situation and the enormous pressures which the war imposed upon white civil servants (who were themselves subject to military call-ups). As Hancock and Godwin observe, a small white society which had deliberately limited possible assistance from the black majority to lower levels of the civil service lacked the human resources to maintain a wartime and a peacetime administration simultaneously.[14] Nonetheless, an emphasis upon continuity in senior positions and maintenance of high quality in appointments and promotions meant not only that the civil service presided over the 1980 election with 'considerable integrity and maximum bureaucratic effort',[15] but that at independence there was no prospect of collapse.

At independence there were some 40,000 public servants, of whom 29,000 were black, these being overwhelmingly teachers or clerks. Of the 10,570 'Established Officers' some 3,368 were black, but no blacks held posts above the 'senior administrator' level. The problem that was posed to the incoming government was that while it had little option but to initially rely on the existing

---

[14] Peter Godwin and Ian Hancock (1993), *Rhodesians Never Die: The Impact of War and Political Change on White Rhodesia, c1970–1980*, London: Macmillan, 304.

[15] Ibid., 244.

incumbents, their commitment to the new regime was dubious. The strategy taken was therefore initially cautious and not to force whites out, in part because of the policy of racial reconciliation, in part because it wanted to take advantage of their experience. The government therefore adopted the tactic of expanding the civil service to allow more blacks in while waiting for the whites to retire or resign. Thus the public service was rapidly expanded to 80,000 (the majority of the new recruits being teachers) even whilst top positions continued to be largely occupied by the old guard. Nonetheless, in May 1980 a presidential directive came into effect requiring Africanization of senior government posts. As a result of this and retirements, whereas in 1981 whites constituted 57 per cent of the total number of permanent secretaries, by 1984 they constituted only 14 per cent, and blacks 86 per cent. Likewise, whites filled 53 per cent of posts at under-secretary and above in 1981, but by 1984 they accounted for only 22 per cent and blacks 78 per cent.[16] If whites were to have a future, it was manifestly to be elsewhere.

As noted previously, during these early years, the white electorate largely shunned more conciliatory political alternatives in favour of the CAZ, the renamed RF which continued to be led by Ian Smith and which gave the new government a testing time in parliament. Yet most whites were 'decent ordinary folk who, as a whole, never dreamed beyond their immediate security and happiness', and were curiously apolitical. During the years of war, they had constantly deluded themselves about the continued viability of their racially privileged way of life, so once the props for this fell away, the majority looked to leave the country. A white population of 232,000 in mid-1979 had fallen to around 80,000 by 1990, and thereafter declined rapidly in response to the invasions of white farms and subsequently, an increased tempo of measures requiring 'indigenization' of businesses.[17] By 2010, the white population had fallen to as few as 13–14,000.

The 'racial bargain' therefore made no lasting impact. Much is made of Mugabe's particular annoyance at whites' continued support for Smith in the 1985 election. This led to the sacking of all but one white from ministerial positions, and in particular, the ejection of Denis Norman from the key post of Ministry of Agriculture. It also led very directly to Mugabe's using ZANU-PF's newly strengthened position in parliament to secure the abolition of the reserved seats in 1987 even while for the moment he remained steadfast in his determination to stick to the property clause laid down in the constitution. Thus although whites were initially agreeably surprised by the policy of racial reconciliation and life returned to some kind of peacetime normality, their commitment to staying in the country was steadily eroded. Three reasons for leaving were regularly cited: fears for individual safety, concern about maintenance of the standard of living, and for some, an objection to 'Marxist rule'. Yet a basic concern was the rate of Africanization which affected the career prospects of younger whites and threatened the joys of grandparenting for older ones.[18]

It is highly doubtful whether, as Sibanda argued, that an institutionalism of racism in the form of the reservation of twenty seats for whites in parliament

[16] Sibanda, op. cit., 276; Herbst, op. cit., 30–31.
[17] Godwin and Hancock, op. cit., 315.
[18] Ibid., 314–15.

'was a fundamental requirement for the reproduction of imperialist-dominated capitalism in independence Zimbabwe'.[19] By 1979, Smith and Muzorewa were in no position to argue if the British, South Africans, and the nationalists had between them insisted upon a wholly non-racial constitution. Nonetheless, they had come away from Lancaster House with the concession to the whites of reserved seats. In retrospect, however, this appears to have been unwise short-termism. Whilst it gave comfort to whites that they would be disproportionately overrepresented in parliament for as much as ten years, it did nothing to encourage them to look forward politically. Rather, it thrust them back into the lap of 'Good old Smithy' who was totally unrepentant about UDI and resisting 'terrorism'. Little thought was given to how whites who chose to remain would best be able to survive as a tiny minority over the longer term.

The 'racial bargains' crafted in Namibia and South Africa were laid on firmer foundations. The reasons why are fairly straightforward. In Namibia as well as South Africa, whites constituted larger demographic minorities than in Zimbabwe. Furthermore, whereas the majority of whites in Zimbabwe had arrived only after 1945, white settlement in South Africa went back over three hundred years. The Afrikaner community was solidly rooted in the country, and unlike many English speakers (and other immigrants of European origin) had no alternative 'home'. In addition, Afrikaners had a long political history involving not only the establishment of the independent republics of Transvaal and Orange Free State in the 19th century, but their own brand of vigorous resistance to British imperialism, and, during the 20th century, their domination of the post-1910 state. Thus their emotional and political commitments to South Africa were far higher than those of the majority of whites to Rhodesia. Similarly, German speakers in Namibia had demonstrated their permanence by surviving as a distinct community despite South Africa's involvement in the two world wars on the side of Britain. Third, whites owned and ran the highly complex South African economy, and their skills and management were, for the foreseeable future, irreplaceable. Finally, the greater political weight of whites in both Namibia and South Africa was strongly backed up by Western powers. Rhodesia had become viewed by the West by the late 1970s as both destabilizing and dispensable. In contrast, a settlement broadly acceptable to whites was regarded as necessary in Namibia because it constituted a stepping stone to the more important goal of a settlement in South Africa.

There was no formal requirement in the Namibian constitution for a SWAPO government to share power, but it nonetheless included two white Namibians in key positions (Otto Herrigel, identified with the German community, as Minister of Finance, and Gerhard Hanekom, an Afrikaner, as Minister of Agriculture, Fisheries, Water, and Rural Development), while the Chief Justice was confirmed in his position and former white South African policemen appointed to top positions in the new police force.[20] In South Africa, the interim constitution dictated that in the wake of the 1994 election, the ANC share power with the NP and IFP. However, there was no such provision in the final constitution adopted in 1996, and Mandela was unconcerned when the NP made its exit from the government. Thereafter, the ANC was set upon a course whereby the

[19]   Sibanda, op. cit., 262.
[20]   *ACR 1990–92*, B625.

large majority of appointments to cabinet and high state positions would be made from its own membership, although significant efforts were made to include senior members of the IFP as members of cabinet, such appointments lapsing only under President Zuma after any political threat to the ANC from the IFP in KwaZulu-Natal had been extinguished. In both countries, whites were retained in key senior positions in the judiciary, civil service, and military in the interests of 'reconciliation', representativeness, stability, and continuity, although as the years passed by, there was a marked tendency towards the replacement of whites with blacks.

Key to the progression of the South African transition had been the 'sunset' clause negotiated by Joe Slovo, leader of the SACP, whereby old-order civil servants were guaranteed their jobs for five years and their pensions. Yet it was not just a matter of the ANC (as with ZANU-PF in Zimbabwe) waiting for whites to retire or resign, for the situation in the public sector in both Namibia and South Africa was initially complicated by the need to forge unified services out of racially distinct antecedent institutions: SWAPO/ANC, the white-dominated government services, and those of the different ethnic homelands. Indeed, the process was rendered even more complex by the need to forge new regional councils and provinces with associated administrations in Namibia and South Africa respectively, and to refashion the system of local government. These would have been daunting tasks for the most experienced of governments, but they were immense for liberation movements moving into power that lacked significant cohorts of highly trained personnel and were faced by absorbing into their administrations large numbers of individuals (black as well as white) whose loyalty could not be counted upon. Thus in South Africa there were, in 1993, some 38 central government departments, 76 in the four 'independent' homelands, and 62 in 'self-governing' homelands, these ending up as some 22 departments at central level and 90 departments in the nine new provinces within a short space of time.[21] That there were numerous tensions during the years of integration is scarcely surprising, nor is it to be wondered at that in both countries the resultant public services have faced severe challenges of capacity and efficiency.

'Transformation' is a term in South Africa which, although deliberately left ill-defined, refers primarily to racial complexion: thus institutions in which white personnel remain predominant at senior levels are said to be 'untrans-formed'. The implication is that the composition of personnel in all institutions in the public sector (and in private companies) should reflect the demographics of the country. To this end, legislation has been enacted which requires institutions to report the demographic make-up of their personnel to government using the old apartheid categories. In turn, it has raised a host of controversies. Can the ANC's commitment to 'non-racialism' be logically pursued through neo-apartheid categories? Who counts as black, and who is to measure 'blackness' (in a country, despite apartheid, of historical inter-racial mixing) and by what criteria? Are some blacks (Africans) more equal than others (Indians and Coloureds)? Should the transformation of institutions follow national or

[21] Vino Naidoo (2008), 'Assessing racial redress in the public service', in Kristina Bentley and Adam Habib (eds), *Racial Redress and Citizenship in South Africa*, Cape Town: HSRC Press, 99–128.

regional demographics? If the former, Africans should predominate over Coloureds in the Western Cape provincial administration, but if the latter, the reverse should be the case.[22] Furthermore, what weighting should be given to colour-coding relative to the capacity to do a particular job? Suffice it to say that the ANC has steered clear of attempting to resolve these and other dilemmas, while maintaining a firm commitment to a broad strategy of 'transformation', leaving it to the courts to pick their way through the legal morass in the surprisingly few cases where the entire project has been challenged.[23]

The first major policy pronouncement signalling changes in the racial profile of the public service was expressed in the RDP (Section 5.2) which subsequently became the 1994 White Paper on the Reconstruction and Development Programme. This made specific mention of the need to promote 'affirmative action', while a later White Paper on the Transformation of the Public Service in 1995 identified the goal of creating a 'genuinely' representative public administration reflecting South African demography. In turn, the 1996 constitution recognized a public service that was broadly representative of the population as one of the values which should underpin public administration. Yet another White Paper on Affirmative Action in the Public Service in 1998 pulled these various threads together, in the same year that passage of the Employment Equity Act gave them legal substance, its twofold purpose being to promote equity in the workplace by eliminating 'unfair discrimination' and to redress racial imbalances by 'affirmative action', this entailing promoting the employment of black people. The outcome was to be a significant change in the composition of the public service.

Africans actually constituted the largest racial segment of public servants prior to 1994. According to Naidoo, in 1989, they contributed 50.2 per cent of the total composition (915,545) of the total employment of central government, the then four provinces and the 'self-governing' states, whilst whites accounted for 33 per cent, Coloureds 13.1 per cent, and Indians 3.4 per cent.[24] But Africans (and other blacks) inevitably staffed lower-level occupations, whilst senior occupational categories were overwhelmingly staffed by whites, the latter accounting for between 89 per cent and 94 per cent of management according to the calculations used.[25] Initially, demographic targets of 50 per cent black people and 30 per cent women in management by 1999 were set, and certainly, the first target was reached on time, subsequent to which the target figure for black managers was raised to 75 per cent by 2005. Women fared far less well, having started from a low base of only 7.9 per cent of public service managers, and overall, gender imbalances were not reduced at the same pace as racial imbalances. Nonetheless, representation of women at middle management level had climbed to above 30 per cent by 2004.

22 In early 2011 Jimmy Manyi, simultaneously Jacob Zuma's spokesperson and President of the Black Management Forum, caused a furore when the DA publicized an earlier speech he had made in which he had stated that there was a 'surplus' of Coloureds in the Western Cape and that they should spread out across the country. This earned him an open letter from Trevor Manuel, Minister of Planning, in which Manyi was labelled a racist, and the launch of an investigation into what he had said by the Human Rights Commission.
23 Roger Southall (2007), 'Does South Africa have a racial bargain? A comparative perspective', *Transformation*, 64, 66–90.
24 Calculated from Naidoo, op. cit., Table 4.2.
25 Ibid., 103.

These changing profiles need to be located within broader changes occurring within the public service. Between 1995 and 2001 there was a rise in the number of white as well as black managers from around 24,000 in 1995 to over 70,000 by 2001, even while the total employment figure for the public service declined between 1994 and 2001 by as much as 124,959 persons (this reflective of the implementation of GEAR). Overall, by 2006, whites (9.6 per cent of the population) constituted just over 13 per cent of the aggregate composition of the public service, compared to African representation which stood at just under 73 per cent – although African representation remained highest at the lower-skilled levels while decreasing towards the upper end.[26] This was within the context of an increase in the number of public servants from 1,025,137 in 2001 to 1,166,753 in 2006. Within a workforce composed of 78.3 per cent Africans, 9.9 per cent Coloureds, and 2 per cent Indians in 2007, the composition of the public service in 2008 was 78.3 per cent, 9.9 per cent, and 2.8 per cent respectively, rendering it very near to a representative bureaucracy in terms of race.[27]

Similar changes have occurred in Namibia where at independence all central government management positions were occupied by white men (with the exception of one white woman). The transitional settlement (via Article 141 of the constitution) guaranteed all existing civil servants their jobs. However, the constitution (Article 23) also allowed the government to implement affirmative action policies, this culminating in the passage of the Affirmative Action Act of 1998. Meanwhile, the Public Service Commission had been given the task of making the civil service more representative of the population, and introduced a policy of giving black Namibians (including Coloureds) and women preference in appointments, promotions and transfers, relaxing requirements of work experience in so doing. By 1996, about 70 per cent of management posts were held by people from disadvantaged groups, most of them black men (52 per cent) with only 13 per cent women.[28]

There were sound reasons for both SWAPO and the ANC implementing affirmative action. Ndletyana argues that the official rationale for affirmative action in South Africa was both normative (seeking racial redress) and instrumental (bestowing legitimacy on the public service).[29]

For all that whites remain slightly over-represented in public service there is little doubt that the broad trend has been defined by the overwhelming majority of whites, and especially younger whites, as indicating that the public service has become black territory. This is implied by the high levels of vacancy which now characterize the public service, where in 2005–06 the vacancy rate at senior management levels was over 25 per cent and 31 per cent at middle management level.[30] This would indicate more than just an inadequate supply of qualified black applicants, for given that they continue to dominate

---

[26] Ibid.

[27] C. Milne (2009), 'Affirmative action in South Africa: From targets to empowerment', *Journal of Public Administration,* 44: 4.1, 969–90.

[28] Herbert Jauch (1999), 'Human resource development and affirmative action in Namibia: A trade union perspective', Windhoek: Labour Resource and Research Institute (LaRRI).

[29] Mcebesi Ndletyana (2008), 'Affirmative action in the public service', in Bentley and Habib (eds), op. cit., 77–98.

[30] Naidoo, op. cit., 122.

the ranks of the better qualified, it would seem that whites are either rejected as candidates or, far more likely, that they do not apply, no longer seeing the public service as offering an attractive career. Their future they are likely to see as lying in the professions, certain public institutions (like universities) and, of course, the private sector, to whose role in the 'racial bargain' we will return later. For the moment, let us consider further the accession of NLMs to state power.

The erosion of the autonomy of parliaments

The classic role of parliaments is threefold: to provide recruits for high political office; to debate, pass, amend or reject proposed legislation; and to hold the executive accountable. The growth of strong party systems has ensured that even in established liberal democracies, the influence of the executive over the legislature has in most systems become predominant. Having gained election to parliament on the back of their party, most MPs are reluctant to exhibit a level of independence which would see them lose their party's backing at the next election. The result is that parliaments today exercise only spasmodic control (usually in conditions where governments' majorities are non-existent, small or unsure) although, nonetheless, exerting considerable pressures for accountability (via debate, questions, adroit use of publicity, and so on). In southern Africa, the pressures upon MPs to follow party discipline are yet more intense (and indeed, in Namibia and South Africa, MPs who resign from or are expelled from their parties automatically lose their seat in parliament). Most MPs deployed to parliament are reluctant to offer any hint of disloyalty for fear of losing the patronage of their ruling party hierarchy. As a result, given that liberation movements have customarily enjoyed substantial majorities, they have used these to strengthen the powers of the executive and have very deliberately sought to bring parliaments to heel.

The recruitment role of parliament has remained largely uncontroversial, as the different National Assemblies have continued to provide the overwhelming majority of cabinet ministers from amongst the ranks of ruling party MPs (inclusive of Mugabe's appointing former members of ZAPU as ministers following the enforced unity in 1987, but with the obvious exception of ministers being appointed from all three parties in parliament following the Global Political Agreement of 2008). However, it is worthy of particular note that in Namibia, the large size of the political executive relative to parliament has provided an inherent barrier to parliamentary oversight. Taken together, the number of ministers and deputy ministers has consistently exceeded 40, overwhelmingly drawn from a National Assembly of just 72 elected members and up to 6 additional non-voting members appointed by the President for their special status or expertise. Thus the combined vote of the government outnumbers that of all other MPs, thoroughly undermining any potential for accountability, let alone the occasional function enjoyed by parliaments of 'throwing the rascals out'. In contrast, if Thabo Mbeki had declined to follow the 'invitation' of the ANC to resign as President in September 2008, he would presumably have been subject to a vote of no confidence in parliament which would have required him to stand down.

In 1987, in Zimbabwe, successive constitutional amendments abolished the twenty reserved seats for whites and established an Executive Presidency, to the considerable detriment of parliament. While the first President would be elected by the existing parliament, subsequently he would be directly elected by the voters. Once elected, he would become Commander-in-Chief of the armed forces, and appoint all judges, ambassadors, defence force commanders, the Attorney-General, Comptroller, and the Auditor-General, while retaining the right to appoint the cabinet. Although not having a vote, he would be able to attend and speak in parliament. In addition, he would be able to veto parliamentary bills and could only be overridden by a two-thirds majority in the National Assembly, a similar majority being required to dismiss him. Yet much of the thrust of the amendment was in the small print. Byron Hove, a well-known lawyer who had briefly served in Muzorewa's government, pointed out (ultimately to no avail) that the President would be able to declare martial law or a state of war on merely the 'advice' of his cabinet, without any resort to parliamentary approval – in the event, clearing the way for Mugabe to authorize intervention in the war in the DRC in 1998. A journalist commented that outside parliament there were widespread feelings that the change was inimical to democratic principles, and warned that it would 'elevate the incumbent President to the status of being an elected Monarch'.[31]

In Namibia in 1998, SWAPO used its two-thirds majority in parliament to change the constitution, which barred Presidents from serving for more than two terms in office, in order to allow Sam Nujoma, as the founding President, to serve for a third. SWAPO was fully enabled to pass the measure without offending any legal principles, yet in so doing it pronounced the clear malleability of the constitution to party rather than national considerations. Significantly, when a few years later Nujoma was angling for a fourth term, it was internal party rather than parliamentary opposition which made him give way and hand-pick Hifikepunye Pohamba as his successor.[32] In South Africa, Thabo Mbeki was to find his election by parliament no block to his erecting a highly centralized and very powerful presidency which was largely immune to restraint by the National Assembly.[33]

In all three countries, there have been systematic efforts to undermine parliamentary opposition. In Zimbabwe, although Mugabe's drive for a one-party state met unexpected opposition from within ZANU-PF's own ranks, the enforcement of unity upon ZAPU and the farce of the 1995 elections reduced parliament to little more than rubber stamping the decisions of the party's central committee. In South Africa, the ANC sought to take advantage of divisions within the newly formed DA by pursuing a constitutionally dubious course of passing legislation to allow floor-crossing in 2000. This enabled it to induce the bulk of the NNP to cross back into government, and for an ANC-NNP coalition to replace the DA as the government of the Western Cape. Indeed, the very

---

[31] *ACR 1987–1988*, B840.
[32] Henning Melber (2006), '"Presidential indispensability" in Namibia: Moving out of office but staying in power', in Southall and Melber (eds), op. cit., 98–119.
[33] Roger Southall (1998), 'The centralization and fragmentation of South Africa's dominant party system', *African Affairs*, 97, 443–69.

rules adopted to govern floor-crossing – demanding that floor-crossers constitute at least one-tenth of the party they were leaving – enabled easy passage for individuals out of the smaller parties into the ranks of the ANC, while making it difficult for disaffected MPs to exit the ruling party itself. In all three countries, there has been a marked tendency for the ruling party to equate opposition with disloyalty, one critic accusing SWAPO of having nurtured a 'psychosis of fear',[34] while in Zimbabwe, the MDC is routinely accused by ZANU-PF as being a front for Western imperialism. In South Africa, the opposition DP/DA has regularly been attacked by members of the ANC as reactionary and racist, seeking to reinstall white domination by the back door.[35] Furthermore, Thabo Mbeki invested his relations with the DA leader, Tony Leon, with a vitriol that aggravated the latter's confrontational style and terminated the courtesy meetings between President and leader of the opposition which had been regular occurrences under Mandela.[36]

More alarmingly, government majorities and control of parliamentary procedure have been used to clamp down on the independent investigative powers of parliamentary committees, the most notorious example being the clipping of the wings of the Standing Committee on Public Accounts (SCOPA) when, amongst others, ANC MP Andrew Feinstein was leading the charge to investigate corruption involved in the 1998 arms deal (see below). A disinclination on the part of some ministers to provide answers to questions asked by the DA has been matched by the refusal of others to impart information on the grounds of security: in 2010, this even extended to refusal to give retrospective details of flights taken in the presidential jet by President Zuma.

Party loyalty is paramount. In 2012, the abstention from the parliamentary vote on the notorious 'Secrecy Bill' (see below) saw the 85-year-old Ben Turok being rebuked by a party disciplinary committee. This invited general ridicule because not only was he one of the party's few outstanding MPs, but also because he was a life-long loyalist who before spending over two decades in exile had been a signatory to the Freedom Charter in 1956. In all three countries, a lacklustre performance by parliament is strongly related to the heavy reliance upon their salaries of the majority of ruling party MPs in conditions in which opportunities for well-paid employment for people of their limited educational backgrounds are scarce beyond the sphere of politics.

Nonetheless, parliament in all three countries remains a space where on occasion governments can be held to account. In Zimbabwe, in 1997 a group of parliamentarians backed independent MP Margaret Dongo when she called for the Auditor-General to probe the Z$450 million War Victims Compensation Fund, refused to endorse the raising of loans for construction of the Harare airport terminal, and objected to the raising of levies to meet the costs of gratu-

34 Joseph Diescho (1996),'Government and opposition in post-independence Namibia: Perceptions and performance', in *Building Democracy: Perceptions and Performance of Government and Opposition in Namibia*, Windhoek: Namibia Institute for Democracy and Konrad Adenauer Stiftung, 4–25.

35 Ivor Sarakinsky (2001), 'Reflections on the politics of minorities, race and opposition in contemporary South Africa', in Roger Southall (ed.), *Opposition and Democracy in South Africa*, London, Portland: Frank Cass, 149–60.

36 Mark Gevisser (2007), *The Dream Deferred: Thabo Mbeki*, Cape Town and Johannesburg: Jonathan Ball Publishers, 429; Tony Leon (2008), *On the Contrary: Leading the Opposition in a Democratic South Africa*, Jeppestown: Jonathan Ball Publishers, 523–28.

ities for war veterans. Even so, the inspiration for the formation of the National Constitutional Assembly, which resulted in the formation of the MDC, came from outside rather than inside parliament. Subsequently, the power-sharing agreement implemented in 2008, and the balance of power within parliament between ZANU-PF and the MDC led to occasions when MPs from both parties used committees to work cooperatively and productively, even while they remained confrontational in the body of the House. Yet overall, the potential for parliaments to rein in the executive remains limited, not only by the lack of traditions of 'loyal opposition' but also by governments' determination to clamp down on external scrutiny of their actions.

Assaults upon judicial independence: Zimbabwe

Given the role of many judges in shoring up white supremacy in the past, there was an understandable desire on the part of NLMs to transform justice systems to make them appropriately responsive to newly installed democratic systems. At the same time, the independence of the judiciary and of legal institutions was constitutionally enshrined, with formal recognition being given to their principal tasks as not only to administer justice but to protect the constitutions and defend human and individual rights. The management of these tensions was always going to be challenging, with the potential that attempts to transform the judiciaries might undermine their independence and open up the way to arbitrary rule.

The most extensive assault upon judicial independence has taken place in Zimbabwe.[37] By the end of the 1990s, the Zimbabwe Supreme Court had established an international reputation for upholding the constitution and human rights. However, the adoption of the fast track land reform policy and the challenge presented to ZANU-PF by the MDC in the 2000 National Assembly elections precipitated a judicial crisis, which resulted in the government purging incumbent judges and replacing them with individuals known to have allegiance to the ruling party. The reconstituted judiciary thereafter failed conspicuously to protect fundamental rights against government incursions, while the allocation of farms expropriated from white farmers to several judges has made them beholden to the executive.

A first case contesting the expropriations was heard by two black judges in the High Court who declared that the land reform programme was being conducted in an illegal manner. When this was ignored, dispossessed farmers sought legal protection from the Supreme Court, which similarly declared the farm invasions illegal and prohibited the government from continuing with the acquisition of further farms and implementing its resettlement plans until a proper plan was in place and the rule of law restored. Even so, while judging the reform process unconstitutional, the Supreme Court gave the government the latitude of remedying the illegality by suspending the ban for six months.[38]

---

[37] Karla Saller (2004), *The Judicial Institution in Zimbabwe*, Cape Town: University of Cape Town Press.

[38] Gugulethu Moyo (2007), 'Corrupt judges and land rights in Zimbabwe', in Transparency International, *Global Corruption Report 2007*, Cambridge: Transparency International and Cambridge University Press, 35–39.

Meanwhile, the MDC had decided to challenge the results of the June 2000 National Assembly elections in 39 constituencies, alleging that they were marred by violence and intimidation in violation of Zimbabwe's electoral law. This followed the issue of a presidential amnesty in October 2000 which pardoned all politically motivated crimes, except those involving rape and murder, thus ensuring that perpetrators of such crimes would never be brought to court.[39]

The government's response to these developments was vicious. First, it portrayed the Supreme Court judgement as a racist attempt to protect white farmers, and launched public attacks on white judges. Mugabe and several ministers, amongst them Justice Minister Patrick Chinamasa, condemned the judges as relics of Rhodesia, while on one occasion, war veterans invaded the Supreme Court and threatened to kill opponents of land reform.[40]

Second, the government resolved to replace independent judges with those loyal to ZANU-PF. 'The judiciary found itself besieged.'[41] On 21 December 2000, Chief Justice Anthony Gubbay, acting on behalf of a unanimous Supreme Court, issued a stinging indictment of the government's growing lawlessness. On 30 January 2001, he ruled that an attempt by Mugabe to invalidate the MDC's electoral challenges was unconstitutional.

Three days later, Gubbay was visited by the Justice Minister and forced into retirement. Chinamasa then met with other justices of the Supreme Court and recommended that they also resign, indicating that he did not want them to come to any harm. In this at least he was non-racial, as amongst those whom he addressed were a number of vigorously independent black judges. Over the ensuing three years, three of the four remaining Supreme Court justices and nine of the eighteen High Court judges either resigned, were suspended or otherwise left the bench.[42] At lower levels, judges who had sufficient integrity to resist undue influence from the government and ZANU-PF were likewise subject to intimidation. In one case, Walter Chikwanha, magistrate for Chipinge, was dragged from his courtroom in August 2002 and assaulted after he dismissed an application for the state to remand five MDC officials held in custody. In December 2003, Judge President Michael Majuru of the Administrative Court resigned and fled the country after an altercation with the Minister of Justice over a controversial case involving a government agency and Associated Newspapers of Zimbabwe, publishers of the *Daily News*.[43] Gubbay was replaced by Justice Godfrey Chidyausika, who was soon alleging that his predecessor and the Supreme Court had prejudged in favour of white commercial farmers in all the cases they had brought before the court.

The results of such pressures were, for ZANU-PF, suitably gratifying. When a fresh land case was brought before the Supreme Court in September 2001, the new Chief Justice denied an application by the Commercial Farmers' Union

[39] Solidarity Peace Trust (2005), *The Role of the Judiciary in Denying the Will of the Zimbabwean Electorate since 2000*, Port Shepstone: Solidarity Peace Trust.
[40] Moyo, op. cit.
[41] *ACR 2001–02*, B885.
[42] Solidarity Peace Trust, op. cit., 13.
[43] Moyo, op. cit.

(CFU) that he should recuse himself because of his close association with ZANU-PF and his public statements endorsing the land reform. His reconstituted Supreme Court thereupon determined that the government had fully complied with the order to put in place a lawful programme, despite clear evidence from the CFU that the rule of law had not been restored. Its reward was that Chidyausika and all the new appointments to the Court were soon allotted farms, while two judges, Benjamin Hlatshwayo and Tendai Chinembiri Bhunu, invaded and took over farms personally.[44] Meanwhile, of the 39 applications regarding the 2000 election, only 16 were eventually heard by the High Court, the remainder having been withdrawn for varied reasons, including intimidation and violence against the MDC applicants. Of the sixteen heard, seven were ruled in favour of the MDC, nine in favour of ZANU-PF. Thirteen of these rulings were then appealed in the Supreme Court. Of these appeals only three had been heard by the time of the next election – yet even so, judgements were never handed down. Thus although in seven cases the High Court had decided that the elections were null and void, ZANU-PF MPs had continued to sit in parliament.[45] Subsequently, after the 2002 presidential election, when Morgan Tsvangirai challenged the outcome, the case was heard by Judge Ben Hlatshwayo. Prior to this, Chief Justice Chidyausika had changed the system from one whereby cases would come before individual judges according to a roster to one whereby he allocated judges to cases himself. It was thus not surprising that he should allocate this major case to a judge who had never ruled against ZANU-PF and who had been a direct beneficiary of the party's largesse; nor that Hlatshwayo should disregard the evidence regarding massive breaches of the Electoral Act in favour of agreeing with the defence which had based its case on the historical justice of the need for land reform. Hlatshwayo provided merely a one-page dismissal of Tsvangirai's petition, and subsequently has never spelled out his reasons for doing so.[46]

Although there remain a number of judges who have courageously swum against the stream, ZANU-PF has systematically compromised the independence and impartiality of Zimbabwe's judiciary while simultaneously transforming the police into an unaccountable arm of the party. Together they have contributed to a disastrous human rights situation, so that for instance, after the March 2008 general elections, there were at least 163 politically motivated extra-judicial killings, almost entirely of MDC supporters, yet the police managed only two arrests. The power-sharing agreement of September 2008 has done little to address the situation. Chinamasa and Chidyausika have remained in their jobs, and human rights observers have continued to report the routine and arbitrary arrest and harassment of MDC activists.[47] The lack of reform bodes ill for the prospect of legal checks being placed upon ZANU-PF for any forthcoming elections.

---

44 Ibid.
45 Solidarity Peace Trust, op. cit., 6–10.
46 Ibid., 17, 33, 36.
47 Sokwanele (2008), '"Our hands are tied": Erosion of the rule of law in Zimbabwe', http://www.sokwanele.com/node/757

The autocratic temptation? Judicial independence in Namibia

SWAPO has sought to erode judicial independence through what the Namibian Society for Human Rights (NSHR) has termed a triangular strategy of attacks upon the judiciary; the passage of incursive legislation; and the maintenance of an acting judicial officer system.[48]

At independence, Namibia was enabled to formally disengage its legal system from that of South Africa, yet its judiciary and legal system remained overwhelmingly white and sustained by those who had served under apartheid. However, the constitution provided for judicial independence. Appointment of judges was to be made by the President but only upon the recommendation of a Judicial Services Commission (JSC) which was to consist of the Chief Justice, a judge nominated by the President, and two representatives of the legal profession. Overall, the view of respected observer bodies is that judicial independence has survived. Nonetheless, as argued by the NSHR and others, this has been in spite of rather than because of the actions of government and SWAPO.

There were a number of verbal attacks upon senior judges by high-ranking members of government and SWAPO officials in the early 1990s, but the most notable ones followed rulings regarding the rights of imprisoned members of the Caprivi Liberation Army (CLA). The Caprivi strip, located in the north east of the country bordering Zimbabwe, Zambia, and Botswana, has had a highly contested history, and its population had long been disenchanted with SWAPO rule. In August 1999, the CLA had launched a rebellion which was swiftly crushed by the Namibian security forces. Subsequently, some 130-odd accused were imprisoned, charged with high treason, and denied legal aid, although this was a constitutionally enshrined right. In June 2002, the High Court, sitting under Chief Justice Johan Strydom, ruled that the accused were entitled to adequate legal representation at the expense of the state. When at last the treason trial made its way to court, Judge Elton Hoff ruled that thirteen of the defendants, who had been illegally captured from beyond Namibia's borders, should be released. However, both rulings elicited unprecedented levels of abuse from leading SWAPO officials including demands that Strydom's salary should be sequestered to pay for the defence of those accused as well as statements in 2004 that Hoff was 'disloyal and unpatriotic' and the 'wrong judge'. Such judges did not rule according to the 'expectations of the majority of the population' and should 'pack and go'. They were paid by the government to defend its interests, yet 'they hate SWAPO' and were counter-revolutionaries seeking to reverse 'our gains in this country'. Nujoma himself stated that the judiciary 'cannot be independent while the national security of our country is threatened'.[49] The outcome is that the trial of the secessionists has dragged on for well over a decade, been subject to perpetual delays, refusal of bail and, regardless of

---

[48] Namibian Society for Human Rights (2004), 'Concern over judicial independence and integrity', http://www.nshr.org.na/index.php?module=News&func=display&sid=319
[49] *The Namibian*, 26 February 2004.

the death of a number of the accused, and has attracted continuous international criticism. The reasons for this injustice would appear to pertain to SWAPO's self-identity as the sole authentic representative of the nation, but the attacks upon the judiciary more worryingly reflect a drift towards a political culture of 'growing intolerance and totalitarian tendencies'.[50]

More insidious than the frontal attacks upon the judiciary have been various attempts to increase the authority of the executive to intervene in legal affairs. One such saw the Attorney-General (a political appointee) claiming to exercise ultimate authority over the Prosecutor-General, but this was defeated by the Supreme Court when it ruled that only the latter official had the right to decide whether or not to prosecute. Even so, in November 2002, the country's first Prosecutor-General opted to stand down following a long-running campaign by the Attorney-General to pressure him into early retirement. This precipitated a change in the Legal Practitioners' Act of 1995 to enable his subordinate, who was favoured by the government but who did not qualify for the position, to succeed him. There have also been attempts by the executive to influence the composition of the JSC, which on occasion has made appointments of judges whom critics allege have been unduly close to government. Finally, despite a constitutional provision that the Supreme Court shall consist of the Chief Justice and other judges appointed on a permanent basis, it has never had more than three permanent judges amongst its number, with various acting judges appointed from countries which, critics claim, have lacked a tradition of judicial integrity. According to one analysis, foreign judges have tended to pass more judgements in favour of the government than local ones.[51]

In general, albeit with the major exception of the Caprivi issue, judicial independence and the rule of law in Namibia have been maintained. However, the government's various attempts to acquire greater weight in the legal process suggest that continuous vigilance by civil society is needed to prevent its succumbing to 'the autocratic temptation'.[52]

Politics and the judiciary under the ANC

It was understandable that the ANC should want to render the judiciary suitably responsive to the newly democratic era. Equally, NP and liberal opinion were eager to entrench constitutional supremacy and the independence of the judiciary. At the heart of these conflicting approaches was the recognition that the role of judges is inherently political. Richard Calland observes that democracy requires arbiters of power to both uphold the law and to protect individuals against the executive.[53] Judges perform this role, and this cannot avoid having political implications, even though they are more distant from 'politics' than either the executive or parliament. In South Africa, other than its required duties

---

[50] Henning Melber (2009), 'One Namibia, one nation? The Caprivi as contested territory', *Journal of Contemporary African Studies*, 27: 4, 463–82.

[51] P. van Doepp (2006), 'Politics and judicial decision making in Namibia: Separated or connected realms?' IPPR Briefing Paper 39, October.

[52] Christopher Tapscott (1993), 'The autocratic temptation: Politics in Namibia now', *Southern Africa Report*, 12: 3, 3.

[53] Richard Calland (2006), *Anatomy of South Africa: Who Holds the Power?* Cape Town: Zebra Press.

(to which the state will usually be party), the Constitutional Court also creates jurisprudence by setting precedents and establishing new legal principles.

Further, South Africa's constitution (Section 165) lays down that the courts are 'independent and subject only to the Constitution and law'. Further, in an important case in 2002, *Van Rooyen v The State*, the Constitutional Court stressed that judicial independence requires individual objectivity to matters before them (i. e., rather than judges allowing political affiliation or undue defer- ence to the executive to influence them), while to preserve institutional inter- ference there should be 'structures to protect courts and judicial officers against external interference'.[54] At the same time, the constitution stated the need for the composition of the judiciary to broadly reflect the racial and gender compo- sition of the population. How were the new government and the judiciary itself to manage these challenges, and how were they to balance the need for 'trans- formation' against the importance of the 'rule of law'? According to Theunis Roux,

> From 1995–1996, [the interest of the ANC] was bound up with the Court's role in stabilizing the transition, and particularly its role in stabilizing the 1996 Constitution. For the transfer of political power to South Africa's black majority to be properly consolidated, and for the certification process to be seen to be legitimate, the ANC needed an independent constitutional court. After the adoption of the 1996 Consti- tution, however, this rationale fell away, and the ANC's interest in the Court's inde- pendence shifted to its role in overseeing the party's social transformation project...the ANC's respect for the Court's independence became more volatile, contingent as it was on changes to the presidency, factional shifts within the party, and the perceived advantages to be had from association with the negotiated settle- ment.[55]

What Roux implies is not that the Court has lost its independence, but that the political context in which it has operated since 1994 has changed considerably, undoubtedly for the worse.

R.W. Johnson has argued that, from the start, the ANC had done its best to 'pack the court' and that its eleven-member composition was sufficient to gener- ally guarantee 'a safe pro-government majority'.[56] However, even a commen- tator as hostile to the ANC as Anthea Jeffrey allows that the extent to which the Court has proved to be 'executive-minded is difficult to gauge'.[57] Jeffrey, along with the commentators more favourably disposed to the ANC, such as Calland,[58] as well as leading constitutional lawyers, cite major cases where the Court has made judgements which have gone against the government, notably the Grootboom case in 2001 and the Treatment Action Campaign case in rela- tion to the provision of nevirapine for AIDS patients/treatment in 2002. The former held that the state had failed to make proper provision for people in

---

[54] Cited in Anthea Jeffrey (2010), *Chasing the Rainbow: South Africa's Move from Mandela to Zuma*, Johannesburg: SAIRR, 40.

[55] Theunis Roux (2012), *The Politics of Principle: The First South African Constitutional Court*, Cambridge: Cambridge University Press, Ch. 4. I am grateful to Professor Roux for allowing me access prior to publication.

[56] R.W. Johnson (2009), *South Africa's Brave New World: The Beloved Country since the End of Apartheid*, London: Allen Lane,153.

[57] Jeffrey, op. cit., 48.

[58] Calland, op. cit., 223.

desperate need of shelter and had violated its constitutional obligations to take reasonable measures within its available resources to provide access to adequate housing. The latter required the government to extend the roll-out of anti-retro-viral medication to all state hospitals with the necessary capacity to administer the drug in order to prevent the transmission of HIV-AIDS from mother to child (this in the era of Mbeki's AIDS-denialism). Yet for all that the Court has carved out an important role for itself in many of its interpretations (such as in its decision to rule against the constitutionality of the death penalty in 1995 which the new government itself had been reluctant to legislate against, given a popular majority favouring the death penalty amongst voters), its decisions in key cases relating to the immediate political fortunes of the ANC have tended to favour the government.

The first, in 1996, saw the Court approve the final draft of the new constitution which approved the new principle of 'cooperative governance'. This eroded the already limited degree of provincial autonomy granted by the interim constitution;and allowed for the inclusion of socio-economic rights in the Bill of Rights (against prior agreement regarding their exclusion during the negotiations process). Most controversially, it also allowed for the Bill of Rights to have horizontal application (that is, that it should be binding upon private persons as well as the state) as well as vertical application – argued for by the ANC unsuccessfully hitherto – although the Court itself had previously warned that this principle would erode both the justiciability of rights and separation of powers.[59]

The second, during the run-up to the 1999 election concerned the right to vote of South Africans without bar-coded identification books (IDs). In 1994, anyone with an ID (including non-citizen permanent residents) had been allowed to vote. In 1999, the government's determination was to restrict the vote to South Africans with bar-coded IDs (in order, it said, to increase security and speed up voting). However, according to opposition parties, this would have the effect of excluding up to 2.5 million potential voters with older, non-barcoded IDs. This was despite the fact that the older IDs were not illegal, that the right to vote was entrenched in the constitution, and that the Department of Home Affairs did not have the capacity to renew IDs before the election. One motive was that those affected would mostly be whites, Coloureds, and Indians who were less likely than Africans to vote for the ANC, so it was probable that the opposition parties would be disproportionately affected. Judge Kriegler, Chair of the IEC, led a delegation to meet then Deputy President Mbeki (who was driving the issue) and resigned when the rest of the IEC Commissioners gave way. When the issue came to the same Constitutional Court that had ruled, weeks earlier, that prisoners should be allowed to vote, it now concluded by a majority of ten to one that the government's position was reasonable.[60]

During the constitutional negotiations, the ANC had favoured a prohibition on floor-crossing in parliament, and the Constitutional Court had explicitly backed this position. In endorsing the final constitution, it ruled that floor-crossing would negate the will of the electorate and would provide incentives to larger parties to encourage members of smaller parties to defect. However, as

---

[59] Johnson, op. cit., 151–56; Jeffrey, op. cit., 49.
[60] Johnson, op. cit. 157–59; Jeffrey, op. cit.

noted above, in 2002 the ANC opted to seize political advantage of divisions within the partnership between the DP and NNP and passed legislation which allowed for floor-crossing, its immediate objective being to align itself with the bulk of the NNP, consolidate its shaky hold over the Western Cape and gain control of the Cape Town City Council. When the United Democratic Movement (UDM), a minor party led by Bantu Holomisa, who had been expelled from the ANC during the first parliament, took the validity of the legislation to the Constitutional Court, the Court reversed its opinion and ruled that it was neither undemocratic nor incompatible with the electoral system. The outcome was predictable. The ANC used its powers of patronage to attract the overwhelming majority of those who crossed the floor, only to reverse the legislation some years later when it was clear that it had become hugely unpopular amongst voters and amongst its own membership. The latter saw recruits from other parties accessing positions and opportunities they hankered after for themselves.[61]

These pro-ANC rulings do not demonstrate that the Court itself was inherently biased. But they do suggest that the Court was hugely reluctant to engage in outright confrontation with the ruling party where its particular political interests were at stake. This reflects perhaps its fears of what the government might do to undermine its independence if it acted in contrary fashion.

However, something the ANC was in a position to do was to change the composition of the Constitutional Court with a view to making it more malleable. Constitutional Court judges may serve for no more than 12 years or until they reach the age of 70. They are appointed through a process of open hearings conducted by the Judicial Service Commission (JSC), chaired by the Chief Justice, and otherwise composed of a further 22 persons composed of a mix of political and legal representatives. In effect, the ANC as the ruling party enjoys a plurality, with the power to appoint six representatives from parliament, to sit alongside the Minister of Justice and four other persons appointed by the President (who also appoints two practising attorneys and two practising advocates). Critics claim that as a result the JSC is ANC dominated. Calland, himself a lawyer, argues that this is not necessarily inappropriate, and that its open proceedings have introduced an important element of accountability to the appointment of judges. Yet he also implies that the first generation of outstanding judges has given way to a degree of mediocrity. It is too easy to go along uncritically with those who would ascribe this to the Court's becoming increasingly black, but interestingly, Calland suggests that various recent black appointments are likely to shift the Court in a more conservative direction regarding social issues than if white appointments had been made. Such appointees would usually come from the ranks of the liberal minded.[62]

Its special status has ensured that the ANC has been unable to 'deploy' its personnel to the judiciary, or at least, to do so openly. Instead, emphasis has been laid upon the need for the bench to become demographically representa-

[61] Calland, op. cit., 226–29.
[62] An indicator of this may be an incident when during a judicial appointment process in 2009 in the Eastern Cape, one outstanding advocate – who had retired from the Anglican clergy because he had lost his faith – was subjected to intense questioning about the fact that he did not believe in God. He was refused elevation to the bench.

tive. In 1994, 161 (or 97 per cent) of judges were white males.[63] By 2008, 71 (36 per cent) of the 199 judges of the superior courts were African, 15 (7.5 per cent) were Coloured, 17 (8.5 per cent) were Indian, and just 96 (48 per cent) were white. Of the magistracy, 38 per cent were African, 7.0 per cent were Coloured, 8 per cent were Indian, and 47 per cent were white. Overall, 69 per cent of all judges and magistrates were male and 31 per cent female.[64] Whether or not the majority of black appointments to the judiciary are ANC in their political sympathies, and whether they have allowed such sympathies to influence their judgements, cannot be determined, although what can be said is that opposition politicians, such as Tony Leon,[65] have claimed that 'ANC-inclined' judges have been appointed to the Constitutional Court, while in 2008 Judge Carole Lewis of the Supreme Court caused a storm by stating that a perception had arisen that 'political fealty' was a more assured path to appointment as a judge than professional ability.[66] By 2012, the JSC was finding difficulty in making appointments to high judicial positions, including replacements to the Constitutional Court, due to the lack of sufficiently qualified applications. This was widely taken as indicating that the legal profession increasingly viewed the JSC as shaping its recommendations to accord with the ANC's preferences.[67]

The sense that the ANC was bent on a general bid to undermine the independence of the judiciary followed the highly controversial appointment of a new Chief Justice in 2011.[68] Initially, President Zuma sought to extend the expiring term of Chief Justice Sandile Ngcobo, but was faced with indications that if he chose to do so, he would face legal challenges as to his actions' constitutionality. Ngcobo wisely evaded the President's dilemma by announcing that he would decline any such extension. At this point, the ball was back in Zuma's court: now it was his constitutional responsibility to nominate candidates after consulting with the JSC and political leaders.[69]

Many jurists were of the strong opinion that the outstanding candidate for the position was the Deputy President of the Constitutional Court, Judge Dikgang Moseneke. Once a protégé of the PAC, Moseneke's political activities had led to his imprisonment on Robben Island. After his release he had become a lawyer, eventually being elevated to the Constitutional Court, where on his appointment he indicated openly that his duty was to the constitution rather than the ANC. However, Zuma bypassed Moseneke, eventually appointing Constitutional Court Judge Mogoeng Mogoeng to the post of Chief Justice.

His choice has proved immensely controversial, first, on the personal grounds that Mogoeng's judicial record was said to be less than inspiring. None of his past judgements had broken new ground, but in addition he had been the sole Constitutional Court judge dissenting in a case in March 2011 in which a man brought an action against others for depicting him as a homosexual. The

---

[63] Leon, op. cit., 413.
[64] SAIRR (2010), *South Africa Survey 2009/10*, 686.
[65] Leon, op. cit., 415.
[66] *Mail & Guardian*, 26 April–3 May 2012.
[67] *Sunday Times*, 18 March 2012.
[68] *Mail & Guardian*, 17–23 February 2012.
[69] Section 174 (3) of the Constitution reads: 'The president as head of the national executive, after consulting the Judicial Service Commission (JSC) and the leaders of the parties represented in the National Assembly, appoints the Chief Justice.'

plaintiff argued that this was defamatory, only for the majority of the judges to dismiss the claim on the grounds that it could not be defamatory to describe someone as being a member of a constitutionally protected group. Mogoeng himself had failed to give reasons (despite his being required to do so by the Code for Judicial Conduct). It was generally thought that his commitment as an ordained pastor in an evangelical Christian sect was the cause: the Winners Chapel SA is the local branch of a chain of Nigerian ministries which holds that homosexuality is a perversion. Other of Mogoeng's judgements in cases concerning rape have also suggested that he holds a highly conservative attitude towards the role of women. Second, it was argued that Zuma had failed to consult sufficiently widely (and certainly not with opposition political leaders) and further, by nominating only one candidate for consideration by the JSC, he was subverting the spirit (if not the letter) of the constitution. In the event, Mogoeng was subsequently subjected to a contentious grilling process by the JSC (during which he assured the members that he had been chosen by God) before the ANC-inclined majority ensured his approval. Overall, against the background of recent comments that had been made by ANC Secretary-General Gwede Mantashe that the Constitutional Court tended to act as if it were the political opposition, and that judges tended to be 'counter-revolutionary', the deeply controversial appointment of Mogoeng seemed to signal the President's wish to appoint a Chief Justice who would favour the executive.[70] Zuma did little to assuage judicial fears when, in welcoming Mogoeng, he asserted that 'the powers conferred on the courts cannot be regarded as superior to the powers resulting from a mandate given by the people in a popular vote'.[71]

The 'transformation' of the judiciary has undoubtedly led to major stresses and strains amongst its ranks. There have been complaints of racism within the judiciary made by black judges against white, and complaints about inadequate training and experience among black judges made by white judges. A particularly unpleasant spat occurred in November 2004 involving Judge John Hlophe, Judge President of the Western Cape. He had previously been accused of receiving some R470,000 from a company called Oasis Group Holdings in defiance of the prohibition which forbids judges from holding positions of profit without the consent of the Justice Minister. On this occasion he filed a complaint about racism within the Cape High Court. In the event, the rumpus was smoothed over. Individual judges were cleared of racism but it was agreed that racism on the part of judges constituted improper conduct. However, the issue of transformation remains highly sensitive.[72] One indication was the hostile reception given to the government's Constitution Fourteenth Amendment Bill of 2006 which proposed to give greater authority to the Minister of Justice over the administration of the courts (a function traditionally exercised by senior

---

[70] See *inter alia*, Makhuda Sefara (2011), 'The rise of unreason', *Sunday Independent*, 21 August; Hugh Corder (2011), 'Constitution reigns whether Zuma likes it or not', *Business Day*, 31 August.

[71] Address by President Zuma to a Special Joint Session of Parliament, 1 November 2011, text issued by The Presidency of the Republic of South Africa.

[72] Judge Hlophe was also to find himself at the centre of a major controversy when in 2008, Constitutional Court Judges Bess Nkabinde and Chris Jafta complained that he had attempted to influence them in favour of Jacob Zuma in arms deal cases involving Zuma and the French arms company, Thint (see next section). Hlophe denied the charges, initiating a long legal process which is set to end in a decision of the Constitutional Court whether Hlophe should be impeached. At time of writing, the matter continues.

court officials) as well as allowing the Minister to appoint acting judges to the Constitutional Court without the concurrence of the Chief Justice (as required hitherto). While the government insisted that the Bill was essential for transformation, senior judges countered that it would seriously erode the independence of the judiciary. In the event, the government withdrew the Bill, but at its December 2007 National Conference, the ANC nonetheless resolved to extend the authority of the Minister of the Justice to administer the courts. However, Polokwane also constituted a culmination of a titanic struggle within the ANC which had severely threatened the administration of justice through its importation of party factional struggles into key institutions.

The arms deal and the ANC: factional politics and government agencies

The arms deal has been described as the poisoned well of South African politics which corrupted key members of the ANC. R.W. Johnson poses questions around its making which the ANC is unlikely to address.[73] His thesis is that while the assassination on 10 April 1993 of Chris Hani, the charismatic deputy leader of the SACP and Chief of Staff of MK, was the independent work of right-wing extremists, the plan was known about by both apartheid security forces and ANC intelligence agencies under the control of Joe Modise, the head of MK. Both had a common interest in seeing Hani eliminated. Modise's concern was to head off an inquiry into his responsibility for human rights atrocities committed by MK against ANC dissidents in camps in Angola, as well as his own dubious connections with apartheid security forces. Meanwhile, Thabo Mbeki, who at the ANC's 1992 Conference had emerged as the likely successor to Mandela, had reason to fear that Hani would emerge as a serious rival and shift post-apartheid politics in a dangerously anti-capitalist direction. Thus 'the resulting alliance between Mbeki and Modise' became the 'pivot on which ANC politics turned'.[74] This meant that when Modise, as the ANC's first Minister of Defence became central to the making of the arms deal (this despite the objections of Trevor Manuel, the Minister of Finance) he received Mbeki's protection.

The deal had been justified by the need to modernize the country's security forces, mainly the Navy and Air Force. It involved purchases of corvettes, submarines, fighter aircraft, and helicopters from German, French, British, Swedish, Italian, and South African consortia and firms. Mbeki announced the cost at R29.9 billion, with promised 'offset benefits' (i.e., investments) in South Africa of R104 billion and the creation of 65,000 jobs.

The cost was to rise to R43.09 billion by 2008, with a further R4.3 billion to be spent by 2011, with little to show in terms of offsets and job creation. However, the cost to the political fabric was huge. Various inquiries, court hearings, and media revelations have pointed to a dense web of corruption involving senior figures within the ANC. The objections of Air Force commanders were overruled in preference for fighters which the politicians deemed more appro-

[73] Johnson, op. cit., 33–35.
[74] Ibid., 32.

priate, and which were considerably cheaper than the Hawks sold by British Aerospace (BAE). Furthermore, there are indications that Mbeki himself assisted the bid of Thomson-CSF, the French firm involved in the supply of the corvettes, and also helped push through the deal which opted for BAE participation over a more economical Italian alternative. Most of all, there is hard evidence concerning the 'commissions' paid to key figures within the ANC. In 2007, probes by the British Serious Fraud Squad, conducted in collaboration with the Directorate of Special Operations (the South African elite police unit popularly known as the Scorpions) revealed that R1 billion in commissions had been paid to eight people to secure the decision in favour of BAE. Much of this pay-off probably went to Modise himself and to Fana Hlongwane, his special adviser and former member of MK. Daimler Aerospace (party to the German consortium supplying the corvettes/submarines) has also admitted to paying bribes including the provision of luxury vehicles to 30 South Africans, including Tony Yengeni, then Chair of the Parliamentary Portfolio Committee on Defence. ThyssenKrupp has similarly confessed to paying bribes to secure the contract to supply frigate and submarine parts.[75]

The deal helped to establish a pattern whereby foreign firms earned favourable consideration by forging alliances with companies closely linked to senior ANC personnel. One such was Conlog, selected as an offset partner by BAE, featuring individuals close to Modise (including his own daughter) and apartheid-era players from Denel and Armscor (state arms companies) on its board, which was also joined by Modise himself after he retired as Minister of Defence in 1999. Another company, Nkobi Holdings, was the vehicle of the Shaik brothers, scions of a Muslim 'struggle family' from Durban, which had long been very close to Zuma. One of the brothers, Mo Shaik, had worked under Zuma in MK intelligence; the other, Schabir Shaik, according to Johnson, had served as the exiled ANC's banker, clandestinely importing huge sums money into the country. In 1996, Nkobi signed an agreement with Thomson-CSF making it the joint venture partner in all of Thomson's South African dealings.[76]

The arms deal excited suspicions from the start. In November 1998, the Auditor-General, Shauket Fakie, instituted a first investigation. Soon afterwards, PAC MP Patricia de Lille announced to parliament she possessed a document naming certain individuals (including Chippy Shaik, the third brother, and Tony Yengeni) as possibly involved in corrupt activity, although she did not reveal their identities. Although her report was brushed aside, the government allowed the Auditor-General's investigation to go ahead, although it used apartheid-era legislation to restrict its inquiries to 'primary' deals (i.e., not secondary deals involving offsets). The eventual report, delivered in August 2000, implied that the award of the Hawks deal to BAE, using a 'non-costed' option, had flouted the rules of government procurement and that the secondary contracts required investigation.

By this time, there were also other agencies on the trail. The Special Investigations Unit, an anti-corruption unit with wide-ranging powers headed by

[75] See Terry Crawford-Browne (2004), 'The arms deal scandal', *Review of African Political Economy*, 100, 329–42, and Paul Holden (2008), *The Arms Deal in Your Pocket*, Jeppestown: Jonathan Ball Publishers.
[76] Johnson, op. cit., 45–46.

Judge Willem Heath, had started its own investigation. In February 2000, the Scorpions likewise admitted they were starting a preliminary inquiry, as did the Public Protector's Office, headed by Selby Baqwa. Subsequently, in October 2000, SCOPA, headed by IFP MP Gavin Woods, conducted its first public hearing in which Chippy Shaik was forced to admit that the offsets were unlikely to come to fruition and that the cost of the deal had risen dramatically. Chippy Shaik also had to defend himself against accusations that in not recusing himself from meetings concerning the selection of the management information system for the corvettes, he might have influenced the decision in favour of African Defence Systems (ADS), whose representative at those meetings was his brother, Schabir. Such admissions resulted in SCOPA urging the government in November 2000 to form an overarching team to examine the arms deal, recommending explicitly that this should include Judge Heath.

The government's response was swift and hostile. It declared that it would not allow itself to be diverted into 'fishing expeditions', and barred Heath – regarded as an unguided missile – from participating in any further investigation. More importantly, it clamped down on SCOPA. ANC MPs were subjected to an internal tirade; the Speaker of Parliament, ANC MP Frene Ginwala, ruled that a recommendation from parliament (re Heath's inclusion) to the executive was not an instruction that had to be obeyed; and Woods received a letter from Zuma (probably written by Mbeki) alleging that SCOPA was biased against the government. The ANC members of SCOPA cracked and Andrew Feinstein, a key ANC member of SCOPA pushing for a full investigation was swept aside.[77]

With SCOPA and Heath excluded, the National Prosecuting Authority (NPA), under Bulelani Ngcuka, the Public Protector's Office, and the Auditor-General undertook their overarching review, presenting their report to parliament in November 2001. It took swipes at Chippy Shaik for failing to recuse himself from the award of the contract to ADS and at Joe Modise for omitting the cost factor regarding the selection of BAE's Hawks, yet still somehow found the decision to purchase acceptable. When the speaker refused Woods' request for the report to be discussed with SCOPA, he resigned. Soon after the report was published, media revelations demonstrated that it had been substantially edited by government, leaving many questions unanswered.[78]

By now the arms deal saga was thoroughly embroiled in ANC factional politics. By late 1999, the relationship between Mbeki and Zuma as his Deputy President was beginning to fall apart. This made the latter available as a standard-bearer for the hopes of the left, COSATU and the SACP having been alienated by GEAR. Having resolved to secure the election of a candidate to eventually succeed Mbeki as leader of the ANC, their choice fell upon Zuma. However, in November, it was revealed that Zuma was being investigated by the Scorpions in connection with corruption charges related to Thales (the new name for Thomson-CSF) and Schabir Shaik, it being alleged that he had solicited a R500,000 per annum payment from the company to secure its participation in the arms deal. Those now backing Zuma claimed that the investigation was

---

[77] Andrew Feinstein (2007), *After the Party: A Personal and Political Journey inside the ANC*, Johannesburg and Cape Town: Jonathan Ball Publishers, 208–36.

[78] Holden, op. cit., 295–300.

being conducted to discredit him ahead of the ANC National Conference to be held in December 2003 (although, in the event, he was to be unanimously re-elected as party Deputy President). The emerging Zuma faction also struck back via Mo Shaik's claims that a 1989 ANC intelligence report had labelled Bulelani Ngcuka an apartheid spy.

On 25 August 2003, Ngcuka announced that the NPA was about to charge Schabir Shaik with arms deal-related corruption. However, in an aside to the media, Ngcuka reported that although the agency had a *prima facie* case of corruption against Zuma, it was not going to charge him. The same day, Mac Maharaj, formerly Transport Minister under Mandela who himself had fallen out with Mbeki (and who had also been identified as a possible recipient of a bribe from Schabir Shaik), presented the ANC intelligence report to the President. Mbeki responded by establishing an investigative commission under Judge Hefer whose eventual report found that Shaik's evidence was flawed, and cleared Ngcuka's name. Nonetheless, Hefer criticized the NPA for its steady drip of information to the media about its various investigations. Ngcuka was soon to be further criticized by Public Protector Lawrence Mushwana (a recent appointment to that post, labelled by critics an ANC 'deployee'),[79] who stated to parliament that Ngcuka's statement about the NPA having a *prima facie* case against Zuma was 'unfair and improper'. Although not required to do so, Ngcuka resigned in July 2004.[80]

In May 2005, following a six-month trial, Schabir Shaik was convicted in the High Court. Critically, the court proceedings had revealed that Zuma – even while Deputy President – was heavily dependent financially upon Shaik, who had used the connection to secure advantage for Nkobi Holdings. Shaik was found guilty of soliciting the bribe of R500,000 per annum for Zuma and was sentenced to fifteen years in prison.

The political fall-out was dramatic. Within days, Mbeki 'relieved' Zuma of his responsibilities as Deputy President, while the NPA launched a prosecution against him. Yet Zuma's own supporters rallied, and Mbeki was censured by the party's National Working Committee which dictated that Zuma should retain the deputy presidency of the party until proven guilty in the courts. The decision was crucial, for not only did it give expression to the view that Zuma was a victim of a political conspiracy headed by Mbeki, but it left him with his power-base from which to campaign for the party presidency in the lead up to the ANC's 52nd National Conference to be held in Polokwane in December 2007.

That position was wide open: if Zuma were to win the party presidency, he would succeed Mbeki as state President following the April 2009 election. Mbeki, enjoying his second term as President, was barred by the constitution from standing for a third. However, there was a lack of congruence between this prohibition and the ANC's own constitution, which imposed no such obstacle. Fatefully, Mbeki opted to stand for a third term as party leader, the implication being that he was determined to block Zuma in favour of his own

---

[79] Catherine Musuva (2009), *Promoting the Effectiveness of Democracy Protection Institutions in South Africa: South Africa's Public Protector and Human Rights Commission*, Johannesburg: EISA Research Report 41, 20.
[80] Holden, op. cit., 301–04.

preferred candidate. As indicated previously, the mobilization of popular forces behind Zuma culminated in his victory at Polokwane, his personal triumph matched by that of his supporters who won control of the party machinery. However, with the Zuma faction determined that Mbeki should now relinquish the remaining months of his state presidency to the control of the party, the battle between the two factions continued.

The struggle continued against the background of the NPA's continuing pursuit of Zuma through the courts. This was countered by his lawyers who adopted a 'Stalingrad' strategy to challenge every legal move made by the state. Matters came to a head on 12 September 2008 when, in their latest appeal to the High Court, Zuma's defence counsel secured backing for their claim that his prosecution was politically motivated. In a ruling that the prosecution of Zuma was invalid, Judge Chris Nicholson asserted that there had been executive interference with the independence of the NPA, and that Mbeki's bid for a third term as ANC President lay at the heart of the NPA's decision to charge Zuma. This provided the opportunity which many of Zuma's backers had been looking for. The outcome was a decision in September 2008 of the ANC's NEC to 'recall' Mbeki from the presidency.[81]

Mbeki could have challenged the ANC to secure his removal through passage of a two-thirds majority in parliament. However, he opted for a dignified resignation. He was replaced by Kgalema Motlanthe, the ANC's Deputy President, Zuma having taken the position that he would not assume office until after the return of the ANC in forthcoming election. Yet the threat remained that he could still find himself prosecuted for corruption, for the Scorpions were still pursuing the case against him.

The NPA had appealed to the Supreme Court against the Nicholson ruling and received its reward. In January 2009, the Court overturned various legal reasons adduced by Nicholson, and ruled that he had erred in making findings about political interference in Zuma's prosecution. The effect of the judgement was to reinstate the charges of corruption against Zuma, just four months before he was to become President.

Enormous political pressure now built up within the ANC for the charges against Zuma to be withdrawn. That the resolve of the NPA to prosecute him was now weakened was due to yet another instance of 'executive interference'. In December 2008, Motlanthe – now President – took the controversial decision to sack Vusi Pikoli, the Director of Public Prosecutions. Pikoli had earlier been suspended by Mbeki on the dubious grounds of the 'irretrievable breakdown' of his relationship with the Minister of Justice. However, this was a cover for Mbeki's protection of Jackie Selebi, Chief Commissioner of Police and his close ally. Pikoli had been investigating Selebi for his links with Glen Agliotti, a well-known drug lord, who was suspected of involvement in the death (apparently an assisted suicide) of Brett Kebble, a mining magnate and ANC backer (who in turn was suspected of criminal involvements). Mbeki, via the Minister of Justice, had instructed Pikoli not to proceed with his prosecution of Selebi until he was sure that he had 'sufficient' evidence against him. When Pikoli responded that both the Minister and the President had been kept fully informed of the

---

[81] Roger Southall (2009), 'Understanding the "Zuma tsunami"', *Review of African Political Economy*, 121, 317–33.

evidence, he had been asked – but had refused – to resign, at which point Mbeki proceeded to suspend him from office.[82]

Mbeki had been unable to dismiss Pikoli because he was bound by the National Prosecuting Authority Act, which required an investigation into his fitness to hold office. Even were he to be found to be unfit, the President would not be able to remove him unless parliament agreed. Mbeki accordingly appointed Frene Ginwala, the former Speaker of Parliament, to head an inquiry. Her eventual report – released in December 2008 – indicated that the government had failed to demonstrate that Pikoli was not a fit and proper person to hold office as the National Director of Public Prosecutions (NDPP) and that he should be restored to office. However, Ginwala also noted that Pikoli had observed that he 'might' have 'defied' the President if the latter had insisted on a delay in prosecuting Selebi, and that this might possibly have undermined national security.

By December 2008, the triumphant wing of the ANC was desperate to prevent the NPA from proceeding with its prosecution of Zuma. This culminated in the decision of Motlanthe, as President, to dismiss Pikoli, using Ginwala's hint that he was insensitive to the needs of national security (despite neither the constitution nor the National Prosecuting Authority Act listing this as grounds for dismissal). Under the Act, Motlanthe's decision had to be confirmed by parliament within 30 days, so it was summoned from its summer recess, and an *ad hoc* committee appointed to consider the matter. This swiftly found against Pikoli, and the ANC used its huge majority to ram its endorsement of the dismissal through parliament in February 2009.

The way was now clear for the ANC to exert pressure upon Moketedi Mpshe (who had been appointed acting NPDD whilst Pikoli had been suspended), to drop the charges against Zuma. Mpshe had displayed some independence of mind when, in defiance of pressure from Mbeki, he had proceeded to charge Selebi with having accepted R1.2 million from Agliotti in return for giving him protection (Selebi was eventually to be found guilty of corruption and sentenced to fifteen years in jail). However, in April, just a few weeks before the 2009 election, Mpshe announced that although the case against Zuma remained strong, the NPA was withdrawing all charges against him. He had no choice to act otherwise, he declared, because Zuma's legal team had provided him with secret intelligence tapes recording conversations between Bulelani Ngcuka and the head of the Scorpions in which, allegedly, they had agreed that charges should not be laid against Zuma in the run-up to Polokwane as this might generate sympathy for him and disadvantage Mbeki at the conference.[83]

Mpshe's decision ignored whether the taped conversations had been monitored legally and whether the Zuma defence team had acquired them by lawful means. Yet the ANC declared – contrary to the overturning of the Nicholson judgement – that the tapes vindicated the view that the prosecution of Zuma had been politically motivated. Zuma himself praised the various judges who had ruled in his favour and issued strident criticisms of the Supreme and Constitutional Courts, contesting the suitability of judges who acted 'like God in a democracy'. Subsequently, his administration moved swiftly to implement the

[82] Jeffrey, op. cit., 72–74.
[83] Ibid., 406–07.

resolution of the Polokwane conference that the Scorpions be closed down – despite their major successes in investigating cases of corruption and organized crime, and their immense popularity amongst the public. Some three years later, following a determined challenge through the courts by an individual businessman who was outraged by the decision, the Constitutional Court ruled by a majority verdict that the Directorate for Priority Crime Investigation (the 'Hawks'), which had replaced the Scorpions, was not independent as required by the constitution, and gave parliament eighteen months to rectify the matter. Opposition politician Bantu Holomisa expressed the view of many critics when he alleged that the sole aim of the decision to disband the Scorpions had been to prevent 'certain leaders from facing corruption charges'.[84]

The arms deal saga indicates the preparedness of the ANC to undermine the independence of state investigatory and prosecutorial agencies when key figures are under pressure. Mbeki may not have been directly guilty of driving the NPA's prosecution of Zuma, yet there is little doubt that he used executive powers to block investigation of the arms deal and to protect Selebi. For his part, Zuma's own behaviour with regard to the rule of law was highly instrumental, using his ascendancy within the ANC, and every legal means at his disposal to block having to stand trial. Finally, the Mbeki/Zuma conflict demonstrates the dangers to state institutions not only of their becoming captured by the ANC, but in that event, of their being used by one element within the party to wage war against another. In South Africa, as in Zimbabwe and Namibia, there are severe costs when the party seeks to trump the state.

Liberation movements and the military

ZANU-PF, SWAPO, and the ANC all faced the problem of having to forge integrated defence and intelligence services out of armies and agencies that had previously been at war with one another. The Namibian Defence Force (NDF) was created in 1990 by combining troops of PLAN (the People's Liberation Army of Namibia) and the South West African Territorial Force (SWATF). Nujoma was technically Commander-in-Chief of the NDF, but effective command lay with Major General Solomon 'Jesus' Hawala. Because he was known as the 'Butcher of Lubango' for his notoriety in the oversight of SWAPO dissidents in exile (a considerable number of whom had died or been murdered), his appointment was greeted with considerable apprehension by many Namibians. Even so, he managed the development of an integrated force highly effectively. By 1998, the NDF included one presidential guard battalion, four infantry battalions, and one combat support brigade with an active strength of 6,000.[85]

Both the NDF and the police recruited from previously opposed forces. However, over time, former SWAPO cadres have come to dominate ranks, while major new drives to recruit ex-combatants into the police, especially the Special Field Force (created in 1998) have almost exclusively drawn on former exiles.[86]

---

[84] *Business Day*, 18 March 2011.
[85] *ACR 1992–1994*, B644.
[86] Rosemary Preston (1997), 'Integrating fighters after war: Reflections on the Namibian experience, 1989–1993', *Journal of Southern African Studies*, 23: 3, 453–72.

Likewise a Development Brigade Corporation, a 1990s training programme for ex-combatants, initially for fighters from both sides, drew almost from the first from former members of PLAN. It was subsequently extended to former SWATF fighters after they had adopted protest tactics modelled on demands made by out-of-work PLAN ex-combatants.[87]

The bias in favour of former members of PLAN (who had engaged in large-scale demonstrations in the 1990s) is explained by SWAPO's determination to hang on to the loyalty of a key constituency and to neutralize the possibility of their disclosing contentious events regarding the suppression of dissidents in exile. Yet it was also the consequence of a narrative which distinguishes between patriotic Namibians who struggled for independence and those who 'collaborated' with apartheid. In this discourse, former SWATF fighters can be portrayed as traitors and mercenaries, having fought on the 'wrong' side. It is a mutual hostility which continues to characterize contemporary politics, detract from national reconciliation, and define lines of political inclusion and exclusion.[88]

Similar integration processes have taken place in South Africa. The challenge of integrating the old SADF (60,000 plus citizen force and commando units of around 40,000), MK (around 13,000), the PAC's (small) Azanian People's Liberation Army, and the militaries of the four 'independent' homelands of Transkei, Bophuthatswana, Venda, and Ciskei (7,000) was managed in a remarkably uncontentious manner, initially under the command of Lieutenant-General George Meiring before he was replaced by MK's General Siphiwe Nyanda. Over the course of subsequent years, the size of the force was gradually reduced (to around 70,000 in the early 2000s) through a process of demobilization and pensioning off. As elsewhere in the state, military demography changed. By 2003, whites constituted only 24.7 per cent of the SANDF (South African National Defence Force), a proportion that was destined to reduce further. To be sure, there were to be many absurdities. The political pressures of integration meant that by the early 2000s, the average age of the defence force was 40 and of combat troops 32, and by this time, the SANDF had as many as 207 generals, a ratio of 1: 338 soldiers compared to 1: 4,000 in the US army.[89] This undoubtedly presented acute challenges to the SANDF as it was increasingly required to undertake peace-keeping operations in Africa. Yet the key achievement was the institutionalization of civilian oversight of the military through the Ministry of Defence and the holding of many parliamentary defence force committee hearings in public, even though during the Zuma era latterly, Defence Minister Lindiwe Sisulu was to use reasons of 'national security' as justification for denying apparently basic information to the opposition.

The militaries in both Namibia and South Africa are undoubtedly commanded by senior figures loyal to the ruling parties. In both armies, too, the political loyalties of the majority of the rank and file lie almost certainly lie

---

[87] Guy Lamb (2007), 'Militarising politics and development: The case of post-independence Namibia', in Lars Buur, Steffen Jensen and Finn Stepputat (eds), *The Security-Development Nexus: Expressions of Sovereignty and Securitization in Southern Africa*, Uppsala: Nordic Africa Institute; and Lalli Metsola (2007), 'Out of order? The margins of Namibian ex-combatant "reintegration"', in Henning Melber (ed.), *Transitions in Namibia: Which Changes for Whom?* Uppsala: Nordic Africa Institute, 130–52.

[88] Metsola, op. cit., 137.

[89] Johnson, op. cit., 336.

with the ruling parties (although this does not mean that civilian-military relations are without their strains, as demonstrated in 2010 by the determination evinced by Sisulu to abolish the right of soldiers to unionize). Fundamentally, however, the military draws on two complementary traditions – the SADF's recognition that it was subject to civilian control under apartheid, and PLAN's and MK's subjection to political control by the SWAPO and ANC during exile. Hence, in neither country does the army feature as a significant political player. Indeed, a report of South Africa's parliamentary Defence Review Committee in 2012 made it starkly clear how the influence of the Defence Force has declined, for by this time the once powerful apartheid war machine has been reduced to a shell. Ironically, the arms deal – justified as the means for modernizing the armed forces – had diverted massive resources away from where they were needed. The Air Force has by now acquired its Gripen fighter jets, but has too few pilots to fly them and a newly acquired submarine has already been decommissioned. Meanwhile, the army has too few trained soldiers, discipline is questionable, and most infantry combat vehicles are between 30 and 50 years old, many of them obsolete. In short, the Defence Force seems alarmingly incapable of undertaking the diverse roles required of it, these ranging from peacekeeping operations and border patrols through to combating rhino poaching and piracy in the Mozambique channel. It is fortunate, commented a wit, that Lesotho has no intention to invade.[90]

The situation is very different in Zimbabwe, where politics has become effectively militarized, and the lines between ZANU-PF and the military thoroughly blurred. The initial process of integrating some 35,000 ZANLA and ZIPRA guerrillas into the former Rhodesian army was successfully completed in May 1981 when the last 12,000 bush combatants handed in their arms. At that time, the armed forces numbered around 65,000, and a second phase of military reorganization began later in the year with the demobilization of about 20,000 soldiers. The new Zimbabwe Defence Force was originally headed by Lieutenant-General Peter Walls, who had headed the Rhodesian Army and who had reluctantly agreed to oversee the integration process, only to be dismissed within a few months for ill-judged remarks, while on a trip to South Africa, about Zimbabwe's continuing instability. He was replaced by Lieutenant-General Sandy Maclean, another former Rhodesian military commander, who headed the Joint High Command which included Lieutenant-Generals Solomon Mujuru (Rex Nhongo), the former ZANLA Commander, and Lookout Masuku, the former ZIPRA Commander. Integration was supervised by a British Military Advisory Training Team, which continued its training once integration was complete.[91] However, the initial compromise of balanced integration was rapidly undone by events.

Apart from the need to guard the eastern border areas against South African-assisted attacks by RENAMO, the new government was rocked in July 1982 by the blowing up of a large part of the air force – thirteen planes – at Thornhill airbase, near Gwelo. This led to the arrest of eleven white air force officers, including the top brass. All denied the charges brought against them in court a year later, but the prosecution claimed that they had worked in league with South African intelligence.

---

[90] *Mail & Guardian*, 4–10 May 2012.
[91] *ACR 1981–82*, B882–83.

Even more challenging were the discoveries of vast arms caches, supplied by the Soviet Union to ZAPU, on farms owned by senior party officials, including Joshua Nkomo. According to prior agreement between ZANU-PF and ZAPU, the arms and equipment that their military wings had accumulated were to have been inventoried before being imported into Zimbabwe and placed under the control of the new army during 1980. However, huge consignments of weapons brought in by train from Zambia had been diverted by ZAPU to Gwaii River Assembly Point, where there were some 6,000 ZAPU guerrillas formally awaiting integration. Initially, Mugabe chose to avoid confrontation with ZAPU over the arms issue. However, outbreaks of fighting between ZANLA and ZIPRA guerrillas at Entumbane, near Bulawayo, in November 1980 and February 1981 led him to use the still largely white-officered army to crush the ZIPRA guerrillas. It was at this point that ZIPRA units, on the orders of senior ZAPU officials, began to move arms out of Gwaii to cache them on properties which, according to the government some time later, had been purchased at strategic points throughout the country. ZAPU, however, claimed that these were merely farms purchased by former guerrillas who had pooled their demobilization grants. Furthermore, officials soon discovered that many of the 14,000 personnel whom ZAPU had committed for integration into the army had obviously no prior military training, the implication being that ZIPRA guerrillas were being retained for a new round of warfare. In the event, the ZIPRA elements at Gwaii were coaxed out of the assembly point and dissidents among them passed on information about the arms caches, many of them located on the 33 farms that Nkomo had purchased after independence. Nkomo himself denied knowledge of the buried arms, and denied accusations that he had been working covertly with South African intelligence to destabilize Zimbabwe. However, claiming that the only way to destroy a snake is to 'strike and destroy its head', Mugabe dismissed Nkomo and three other ZAPU members from his cabinet, backing this up with a final crackdown on ZIPRA. The Gukurahundi campaign, 'sweeping away the chaff', had begun. The two former ZIPRA commanders, Dumiso Dabengwa and Lookout Masuku, were subsequently tried for treason and illegal possession of arms. Although acquitted, they were immediately re-detained.[92]

Mugabe had been preparing for the showdown with ZAPU/ZIPRA for some time. A secret agreement had been signed with North Korea in October 1980 for the training of a new army brigade to deal with internal dissidents, but some 100 North Korean military advisers did not arrive until October 1981. Their presence immediately fuelled ZAPU suspicions. Nkomo claimed that the new brigade was intended to become ZANU-PF's private army; he was not far wrong. Confident that the army had completed its integration exercise, Mugabe chose to announce the 'discovery' of the ZAPU arms caches in February 1982 (although their existence had been known well before this, and indeed, Nkomo and Dabengwa had been sitting alongside Mugabe on a committee to decide how to deal with the problem). Thereafter, the position of former ZIPRA guerrillas in the national army became increasingly perilous; many were beaten, and hundreds fled to Matabeleland. Subsequently, South Africa recruited a number of them to join with black soldiers from the former Rhodesian army,

---

[92] Ibid., B867–68; *1982–83*, B876–82.

trained them at a base in the Northern Transvaal, and then infiltrated about 100 men into Matebeleland to stir up trouble. The brutal crackdown on Matabeleland followed, even though there were probably never more than about 400 armed dissidents involved. Nonetheless, their activities were used to justify Gukurahundi during the years 1982–84 as the brutal accompaniment of Mugabe's drive for a one-party state.[93]

All this took place against a background of distrust between ZANLA and ZIPRA. It was also a reflection of Mugabe's own triumph in 1978 in his internal battles against those within ZANU who had favoured closer relations with ZAPU and ZIPRA, and the assertion of his greater supremacy over ZANU with the firm backing of its military commanders.[94] In turn, Gukurahundi made it plain that ZANU's political domination was actively backed by military power, and cleared the way for the military to assume a veto power on political developments which it has yet to relinquish.

The militarization of Zimbabwean politics was to become increasingly explicit with the rising influence of the war veterans. The War Veterans' Association was initially led by ZANU-PF politburo member Chenjerai 'Hitler' Hunzvi (who died in 2001). As well as spearheading the land invasions, war veterans were to play a crucial political role. Not all the 30,000 members of the WVA were involved in the electoral mobilization and intimidation of opposition supporters, nor had all those who claimed to be war vets actually fought. Yet the war vets morphed into the ZANU-PF youth militia and from 2002, the National Youth Service Programme (NYSP), whose establishment coincided with the run-up to the presidential elections. The NYSP established camps at government expense which recruited unemployed school leavers, concentrating on their military-style physical training and their political education, the latter stressing ZANU-PF's liberation credentials and illegitimacy of any other political parties. Becoming known and feared as the 'green bombers', the ZANU-PF youth and NYSP products, along with war veterans, sometimes donned police uniforms or were incorporated as military reserves. Throughout successive elections, the war vets and party militia were deployed by ZANU-PF as its assault force to intimidate the opposition, customarily without any restraint being exerted by the police. On different occasions, in 2002, for instance, war veterans targeted civil servants and teachers deemed to be MDC; invaded businesses said to be pro-MDC and force-marched managers to ZANU-PF headquarters where they were compelled to reinstate workers they had dismissed or to pay allegedly exorbitant amounts of compensation for jobs lost; and raided the offices of the German Friedrich Ebert Foundation, which they accused of funding the opposition party.[95]

A further factor drawing the military into politics was Mugabe's dispatch of troops (initially 3,000, later increasing to 12,000) to the DRC in August 2008, to prop up the tottering regime of Laurent Kabila, who was facing overthrow by rebels backed by Rwanda and Uganda. The intervention took place amidst a worsening economic crisis domestically at an estimated cost of US$1 million a

---

[93] Martin Meredith (2002), *Robert Mugabe: Power, Plunder and Tyranny in Zimbabwe*, Johannesburg and Cape Town: Jonathan Ball Publishers, 59–76.

[94] Andre Astrow (1983), *Zimbabwe: A Revolution That Lost Its Way*, London: Zed Press, 127–30.

[95] *ACR 2001–02*, B881; Crisis in Zimbabwe Coalition (2005), *Things Fall Apart: The 2005 Parliamentary Election: Prospects of True Democracy in Zimbabwe*, Harare: Crisis in Zimbabwe Coalition.

day. Mugabe's justification was that he was coming to the defence of Congolese sovereignty. In return for this support, Kabila handed out mineral and timber concessions and offered preferential trade deals in cobalt, diamonds, and other minerals. Supposedly this was to enable Zimbabwe to recoup its expenses, but the major benefits flowed to a small group of senior military, defence officials, and politically connected businessmen, with Mugabe's own family and his wife themselves being heavily involved. Emmerson Mnangagwa, entrusted by Mugabe to manage the commercial involvements in the DRC, was at the centre of the network, constructing deals with DRC through such shadowy figures as John Bredenkamp, a former Rhodesian sanctions-buster. Benefits trickled down to the army in the form of special allowances, but ordinary soldiers were also encouraged to undertake their own business deals in fields such as transport and consumer goods, whilst the smuggling of diamonds was reportedly rife. However, Zimbabwean troops came under increasing pressure from rebels and suffered major setbacks in December 2000, when they were forced to flee their stronghold in eastern DRC, reportedly suffering significant fatalities (unofficially estimated as 600). Meanwhile, there were indications that the military was in serious disarray, with rumours of senior officers having refused to obey orders.[96]

Discord within the military had already led to the arrest of 23 officers and soldiers in December 2008 for allegedly plotting a coup. According to the independent Sunday newspaper, *The Standard*, the plotters believed that their commanders were more interested in pursuing business deals than in the welfare of their soldiers.[97] The government's response was to arrest and torture the newspaper's editor and the reporter who had written the offending article. Rumours of a coup were also rife before the 2000 election, one theory being that it would be staged by middle-ranking officers who had lost out in the scramble for Congolese wealth.[98] Even so, the loyalty of the army to ZANU-PF was never really in doubt, as was to be demonstrated by its explicit support during successive elections. Thus the army commander, Lieutenant-General Constantine Chigwenga urged soldiers to vote for Mugabe in the presidential 2002 election. In January of that year, the head of the Defence Force, General Vitalis Zvinavashe, called a press conference at which, flanked by the chief of police and commanders of the CIO (Central Intelligence Organization), army, air force, and prison services, he declared that the State President had to 'observe the objectives of the liberation struggle' and that the Defence Force would not accept anyone with another agenda. Augustine Chihuri and Chigwenga later added that they would never salute Tsvangirai, whilst Chigwenga again declared in 2008 that the army would refuse to support and salute 'sell-outs and agents of the west'.[99] These and numerous other statements were all indications that the security forces would not tolerate any electoral outcome that was unfavourable to ZANU-PF. The crunch came in 2008.

It was not merely that during the elections of that year, the security forces deployed massive violence against supporters of the MDC, causing so much mayhem that Tsvangirai felt constrained to pull out of the run-off presiden-

[96]   *ACR, 1998–2000*, B852.
[97]   Meredith, op. cit., 149.
[98]   *ACR, 1998–2000*, B852.
[99]   *ACR, 2001–2002*, B884.

tial election. It was also that by this time it was becoming increasingly difficult to distinguish between the senior ranks of the party and the militariat,
that is, former soldiers having been deployed to numerous positions within
the state. In particular, the Chairman of the Electoral Supervisory Commission, George Chiweshe, was a former Colonel, and was to play a key role in
rejecting the MDC's submissions that Tsvangirai had won an absolute
majority in the presidential vote at the first attempt. Subsequently, there were
suggestions that Mugabe himself had been prepared to accept such a result
and to stand down, but that a powerful cadre of generals had insisted that he
stay on to contest a second round, fearing that an MDC victory would leave
them vulnerable to prosecution for abuses of human rights. There were
strong indications that real power now lay with the Joint Operations
Command (JOC), as proposed by independent newspaper owner, Trevor
Ncube. This followed Operation Murambatsvina in 2005, when armed police,
soldiers, and ZANU-PF militants joined hands to raze thousands of homes
and businesses in informal settlements that were deemed to be MDC strongholds.[100] Tsvangirai himself was later to declare that Zimbabwe was run by
a military junta. Even though there 'were no tanks on people's lawns', there
had been a 'military coup by stealth'.[101] For well-placed observers, these
developments signified the rise of a 'military-security' complex which had
assumed control of the state and its policy-making processes, with civilian
structures (notably the cabinet) doing their bidding.[102]

When MDC entered the power-sharing agreement with ZANU-PF in
September 2008, Mugabe, as President, remained the Commander of the
Defence Force and maintained his party's firm grip over security portfolios. He
likewise appointed ZANU-PF loyalists to all ten provincial governorships (in
contravention of the agreement), his appointments leaving the MDC with what
he described as 'the crumbs'. In effect, the provisions within the September
agreement for the overhauling of legislation to depoliticize the security forces
were nullified. However, there were subsequently suggestions that Tsvangirai's
decision – before the final collapse of the Zimbabwe dollar – to pay the security
forces in foreign currency would win over the rank and file of the army to the
MDC, undercutting the sway of the JOC.[103]

Although Tsvangirai as Prime Minister sought to establish détente with the
military, and finally earned a salute from the generals on Defence Forces Day in
August 2009, his attempts to establish a working relationship with them was
to be tested by MDC proposals which would, effectively, seek to cut the army's
link with ZANU-PF by promoting their independence. Under the proposals, the
Defence Forces' Commission, which oversees appointments to senior military
positions, would be overhauled so that a new board with independent members
would sit in consultation with commanders of the army and air force. Yet military enthusiasm for such reforms was simultaneously diminished by the MDC's
naming of senior army and government figures as perpetrators of the murder

---

[100] Ambrose Musiyiwa (2005), 'Military dictatorship in Zimbabwe', http://www.worldpress.org/
Africa/2200.cfm
[101] *Time Magazine*, 11 June 2008.
[102] Zimbabwe Institute (2008), *The Security-Military Business Complex and the Transition in
Zimbabwe*, Cape Town: Zimbabwe Institute.
[103] *Financial Mail*, 20 February 2009.

of some 200 of its supporters during the recent elections.[104] However, it was to be the opening up of the Marange diamond fields and the access they gave the military to enormous wealth which was to guarantee that the alliance between the army and ZANU-PF would remain firm during the run-up to further elections. Thus, Mugabe, continuing to control the major levers of power, was increasingly confident he could win any forthcoming contest.

The party-state in southern Africa

In demanding transformation of postcolonial political economies, the liberation perspective necessarily required a theory of transition. This was to become formalized in the notion of the NDR. The assumption of such thinking was that it would be possible for a socialist party to seize state power in a capitalist society and to use it to evolve towards socialism. Yet the reality was that a transition towards socialism could not be assumed to be a linear process, for the very notion of 'transition' indicated that capitalist contradictions had not been resolved. The transitional period would therefore remain a period of class struggle in all arenas, notably with regard to the state, but also within the NLM itself, for as a *national* liberation movement, it was a conjunctural alliance of diverse classes whose interests – once they were free of racial oppression – would likely diverge. The major characteristic of any transitional period therefore would be one of ambiguity. Much would rest upon the nature of the ruling party: would it use state power to intervene in the class struggle on the side of the oppressed? The liberation movement itself would become a crucial area of struggle in which socialist tendencies would need to battle with capitalist and nationalist elements whilst attempting to transform capitalist economy.[105] In contrast, conservative writers have tended to portray the liberation movements as quasi-totalitarian, with the strategy of the ANC, for instance, pointing to its ambition to assume the character of a vanguard party along the lines of the Communist Party in the Soviet Union, ultimately extinguishing any notion of state autonomy. [106]

This analysis indicates the limitations of any analogy between the NLMs and the history of communist parties in power. The transitional situations in Zimbabwe, Namibia, and South Africa have all proved far too ambiguous to be described as totalitarian. The liberation movements may have aspired to take over their different state machineries, but the outcomes have been starkly different.

In Zimbabwe, ZANU-PF has indeed captured the key institutions of power within the state, presenting the formidable challenge to the MDC of trying to unscramble the omelette from a position of weakness within the unity government. Even so, ZANU-PF's capture of the state, although expressed in anti-imperialist rhetoric, has proved to be far more nationalist than socialist, and as much ethnic as nationalist, but above all it is geared to Mugabe's need for survival.

---

[104] *Mail & Guardian*, 14–20 February 2009.
[105] Rob Davies (1988), 'The transition to socialism in Zimbabwe: Some areas for debate', in Stoneman (ed.), op. cit., 20–22.
[106] Hermann Giliomee, James Myburgh and Lawrence Schlemmer (2001), 'Dominant party rule, opposition parties and minorities in South Africa', in Southall (ed.), op. cit., 161–82.

Thus in deploying personnel to party and state positions, Mugabe has played on party factionalism, and manipulated regional and ethnic identities to buttress his authority. Much has been made of his attempts to build up the power of those from his own ethnic background, the Zezurus (in Mashonaland West), yet Mugabe has equally consistently sought to split power amongst rival groups of Zezurus. Thus Compagnon asserts that personal loyalty to Mugabe has always been more important than tribal solidarity.[107]

In contrast, in both Namibia and South Africa, the liberation movements may have established positions of dominance, but their various attempts to extend their control over key institutions have been subject to much contestation (from opposition parties, the media, and civil society). Critically, however, SWAPO and the ANC have found themselves constrained by the constitution. While they may have reduced the clout of their parliaments relative to the executive, their judiciaries have displayed more vigorous tendencies towards independence. This was illustrated in dramatic fashion in late 2011 when, following an application by activist Terry Crawford-Browne to the Constitutional Court asking it to instruct Zuma to appoint a commission of inquiry into the arms deal, Zuma pre-empted its ruling by announcing that he would indeed appoint such a body. This went against all previous attempts by the ruling party under both Mbeki and Zuma to block investigation, but it appeared that Zuma had come to the conclusion that the majority of members of the Constitutional Court would rule in favour of the application. He calculated that he could limit any political damage by deciding the terms of reference for such a commission rather than having them laid down for him by the Court. According to one report by an anonymous high-ranking member of the ANC, during Zuma's announcement of the decision to the party's NEC:

> He spent a lot of time complaining about the attitude of the Constitutional Court judges to justify his decision. He said the ANC and his government were under attack from some reactionaries who go to court on everything. He told us that even in the arms deal case we had no way out. He said there was no way we could win it...He said if there was any other choice, he would not have taken the route of appointment of a Commission of Inquiry.[108]

However, there is concern that if the commission bares its teeth, it could add fuel to the ANC government's increasing impatience with judicial constraints.

Greater influence over the judiciary would be in line with an accompanying tendency towards the securitization of the state. The battles over the arms deal demonstrated how profoundly the ANC's factional battles had penetrated the various legal institutions, investigatory bodies, and intelligence agencies established under the constitution. Subsequently, as President, Zuma was to make a series of key appointments of former close associates from Operation Vula to key positions in the security apparatus. These included Siphiwe Nyanda, previously Chief of the SANDF as Head the Ministry of Communications (a post from which he eventually had to be fired after revelations of corruption); Mo Shaik, as Director of the Secret Services; and Solly Shoke, a former Field Commander in MK, as Commander of the SANDF in 2011. These and other such appoint-

---

[107] Daniel Compagnon (2010), *A Predictable Tradegy: Robert Mugabe and the Collapse of Zimbabwe*, Philadelphia: University of Pennsylvania Press, 17–22
[108] *Mail & Guardian*, 23–29 September 2011.

ments confirmed that Zuma was determined to secure his control over the country's security apparatus in order to fight his internal party battles. When combined with his strong backing for a Protection of Information Bill (see Chapter 7) which, if passed, would massively extend the state's ability to hide matters declared to be vital to national security from public view, the politicization of the security services lent credence to those who warned about the deliberate construction of a shadow state. Dominated by a powerful clique of politicians, intelligence officials, military figures, and businessmen, it was increasingly beyond the reach of accountability to the courts and the constitution.[109]

From this perspective, Zolberg's notion of the party-state, in which constitutionality is assailed but power fluctuates between competing elites, offers a more productive approach than one which posits that come what may, the party dominates the state. Rather, as we shall see in the next chapter, the notion of the party-state should provide for a marked variety of outcomes.

[109] Paul Holden and Hennie van Vuuren (2011), *The Devil in the Detail: How the Arms Deal Changed Everything*, Jeppestown: Jonathan Ball Publishers.

7.
Liberation Movements and Society

During the struggle for liberation, NLMs presented themselves as embodiments of the oppressed nation. This meant that where there was more than one such movement claiming to represent the nation, contestation between rivals was bitter. Although ZANU and ZAPU patched up an alliance during final negotiations with the colonial regime, ZANU thereafter claimed hegemony and was subsequently to enforce ZAPU's merger into ZANU-PF. Yet alongside rival parties, there were also always other organizations – trade unions, civics, churches, and so on – representing sectoral interests. Most such bodies would see themselves as contributing to the struggle, and would explicitly or implicitly subject themselves to the ultimate leadership of the liberation movement. For instance, although there was fierce debate amongst civics regarding political orientation in South Africa in the 1980s, the UDF came to acknowledge its subordinate status to the ANC and dissolved itself into the latter after the movement had returned from exile. However, whereas during the struggle there were strong reasons for asserting unity, the triumph of the NLM was always likely to see a reassertion of diversity as, in turn, different groups would put forward claims which would compete with the new government's agendas. Further, once a liberation movement assumed power, it had to make policy choices which at times dismayed or even alienated components of the societal alliance which had fallen in behind it. Once they had assumed state power, liberation movements were likely to come under challenge from below. This presented them with different strategic choices: to incorporate, to partner, to repress, to accept diversity or to straddle these alternatives. This chapter will now examine how ZANU-PF, SWAPO, and the ANC have dealt with trade unions, civil society, rural populations, and the media.

Liberation movements and trade unions

The literature on union-party relations in postcolonial Africa indicates that nationalist leaders have believed trade unions should give priority to their contribution to national development over representing the interests of their members, based on the assertion that they represent only a relatively privileged minority of the total workforce. Trade union movements were often regarded by governments as dangerous, for they often constituted the most highly organized formations in society. In many countries, trade unions have been subject to combinations of incorporation and repression by the ruling party – only to assert their independence when conditions have combined to challenge the latter's hold on power, contributing for instance to the defeat of Kenneth Kaunda's government in 1990.

At independence in 1980, the trade union movement in Zimbabwe was weak and divided into five federations, none of which had close links to ZAPU or ZANU (although unions belonging to the National African Trade Union Council had splintered in 1976 according to their leaders' allegiance to Nkomo, Muzorewa, and Ndabaningi Sithole). Despite its early support amongst workers, ZAPU had joined ZANU in de-emphasizing the role of workers in the liberation struggle, favouring guerrilla struggle. The unions were thus regarded with suspicion by the ZANU-PF government which had little hesitation in repressing a wave of strikes which followed independence. Furthermore, the government bulldozed the creation of the Zimbabwe Congress of Trade Unions (ZCTU) as the sole coordinating centre under the slogan of 'One country, one federation'. Its intended subjection to ZANU-PF was indicated by the appointment of Albert Mugabe, the Prime Minister's brother, to be its first Secretary-General, with other ZANU-PF loyalists being deployed to key senior posts. However, over its first four years, the ZCTU was plagued by corruption, nepotism, and authoritarianism, leading eventually to the ousting of its senior office bearers.[1]

Under a new executive, the ZCTU exhibited greater independence, yet proved unable to slough off corruption. This led to the election of yet another executive in 1988 which was more sensitive to the mood of the rank and file, and now emerged as 'the most articulate organized critic of the government',[2] so much so that in October 1989 the Secretary-General was detained in a general clampdown on opposition.

Conflict between the ZCTU and the government intensified as the latter accelerated the implementation of ESAP. By the early 1990s, inflation was rising and worker incomes eroding. Food riots broke out in 1993 and 1995 alongside rapid de-industrialization.[3] Notwithstanding weak union organizing under ZANU-PF hegemony, shop-floor protests increased, outpacing the ability of bureaucratic union leaderships to direct them.[4] Conflict with government also resulted from a 1992 Labour Relations Amendment Act which while dropping the policy that recognized just one union per sector, limited the right to strike, gave the Minister of Labour the right to intervene in union affairs, and signalled the intention of the state to withdraw from wage-setting machinery established in the 1980s. Thereafter, in 1994, significant industrial action was taken by workers in both the private sector (bank employees and construction workers) and public sector (posts and telecommunications, Air Zimbabwe workers, and hospital doctors). Subsequently, a major test of strength was offered by a strike by some 160,000 civil servants which carried on for nearly two weeks in mid-1996, attracting the support of the ZCTU (which hitherto had failed in its attempts to incorporate the civil servants' own organization) and forcing the government to concede on wage demands.

---

[1] Sakhela Buhlungu, Roger Southall, and Edward Webster (2006), 'Conclusion: COSATU and the democratic transformation of South Africa', in Sakhela Buhlungu (ed.), *Trade Unions and Democracy: COSATU Workers' Political Attitudes in South Africa*, Cape Town: HSRC Press, 199–218.

[2] Albert Musarurwa (1990), 'A. Trade unionism and the state', conference on 'Zimbabwe's first decade of political independence: Lessons for Namibia and South Africa', Harare, 30 August – 2 September.

[3] Patrick Bond and Masimba Manyanya (2003), *Zimbabwe's Plunge: Exhausted Nationalism, Neoliberalism and the Search for Social Justice*, Pietermaritzburg: University of KwaZulu-Natal Press, 35.

[4] Ibid., 87.

A year later, it was the turn of private employers to admit defeat when they were themselves confronted by a wave of strikes involving as many as 100,000 workers, before they and the government were rocked by yet further strike actions which received near-universal worker support in December 1997. In March and November 1998, these actions were backed by extensive protests and riots in township communities affected by increases in the cost of food and petrol.[5]

Morgan Tsvangirai, then Secretary-General of the ZCTU, had diagnosed ESAP as forcing the government to quell popular protests on behalf of the IMF. Speaking in 1991, he declared: 'The only way to defend against international capital marginalizing further the indigenous businessman, the worker, the peasant' was to bring all these groups together.[6] He and the ZCTU leadership had been attracted by the corporatist model of labour relations adopted in South Africa in 1994 whereby government, business and labour negotiated together in NEDLAC (the National Economic Development and Labour Council). However, confronted by ZANU-PF's authoritarianism, Tsvangirai moved towards building a popular front to dislodge the ruling party. When the government responded by calling a National Economic Consultative Forum in January 1999, Tsvangirai led a walk-out by the ZCTU. A few weeks later he organized a National Working People's Convention, which resolved to mobilize in favour of a 'working people's' economic agenda and to 'implement a vigorous and democratic political movement for change'. Subsequently, he chaired the National Constitutional Assembly process, before in mid-1999 the ZCTU allied with civil society organizations to form the MDC, the 'first political organization in the post-independence period founded on a working class base'.[7] Tsvangirai, who now assumed the presidency of the MDC, was soon to declare the MDC 'post-nationalist'. According to ZANU-PF, he declared, everyone in Zimbabwe owed the nationalist movement its freedom. In contrast, the MDC would be pragmatically driven by issues, by working-class interests placed alongside those of civil society, and business.

The close relations between the ZCTU and the MDC allowed ZANU-PF to contend that workers were being betrayed. One response, abandoning the 'One country, one federation' approach, was to form a rival Zimbabwe Federation of Trade Unions (ZFTU), which although possessing negligible membership received widespread state support. Another was to use draconian legislation to block meetings convened by the ZCTU or its affiliates, while in 2001 using ZFTU to stage 'factory invasions' to extort concessions from employers. Yet the assumption that ZCTU and the MDC were one and the same was misguided, for the former retained 'its own institutional personality and autonomy'.[8] Indeed,

---

[5] Edward Webster and Dinga Sikwebu (2010), 'Tripartism and economic reforms in South Africa and Zimbabwe', in Lydia Fraile (ed.), *Blunting Neoliberalism: Tripartism and Economic Reforms in the Developing World*, London: Palgrave Macmillan, 177–222.

[6] Ibid.

[7] Lloyd Sachikonye (2002), 'The state and the union movement in Zimbabwe: Cooptation, conflict and accommodation', in Bjorn Beckman and Lloyd Sachikonye (eds), *Labour Regimes and Liberalization: The Restructuring of State-Society Relations in Africa*, Harare: University of Zimbabwe Publications.

[8] Lovemore Matombo and Lloyd Sachikonye (2010), 'The labour movement and democratization in Zimbabwe', in Bjorn Beckman, Sakhela Buhlungu and Lloyd Sachikonye (eds), *Trade Unions and Party Politics: Labour Movements in Africa*, Cape Town: HSRC Press, 109–30.

there were major debates within the ZCTU regarding the appropriateness of allying with the MDC. Some argued that close alliance would endanger the unions. Others criticized MDC as not guided by workers' interests. Yet others, led by Tsvangirai, argued for a strategic alliance with the MDC, with the ZCTU retaining its right to withdraw its support if the party reneged on its commitments to the working class.[9]

The MDC's evolution into a political movement drawing support from across a wide spectrum of society – the middle class, business, professionals, the informal sector, youths, and civil society as well as workers – was reflected in its adoption of programmes which were ambiguous in class terms and which did not offer a clear alternative to those put forward by ZANU-PF. For instance, while railing against cronyism in the distribution of appropriated farms, the MDC had little choice but to claim that the broad thrust of the land reform programme was irreversible. Such developments led to a critique within ZCTU that the MDC was drifting ideologically from left to right, encouraged by the increasing domination of its leadership by middle-class elements. Thus of the 57 parliamentarians elected in 2000, only 12 were trade unionists, the rest being largely composed of academics, lawyers, professionals, businessmen, and farmers.[10] Clearly, whether organized labour was to remain influential within the party was uncertain, as was the value and potential for strategic alliance – not least given the internal split within the MDC which resulted in the formation of MDC-M.

The problems for the ZCTU were manifold. Its major strategy revolved around the idea of a social contract. This had been facilitated by the formation of the Tripartite Negotiating Forum between labour, business, and government in 1998, and found fruit in the Kadoma Declaration of Intent in 2003 whose thrust was to promote social partnership. However, the forum was bedevilled by 'high levels of mistrust'.[11] Whereas the ZCTU sought to take this project forward (although simultaneously reluctant to grant the government legitimacy), the government largely ignored it and pursued actions such as the imposition of a wage freeze in 2007 without consulting the labour movement. Meanwhile, the status of the ZCTU was severely undermined by the shrinking of formal employment, hyperinflation, escalating layoffs from factories, and the increasing adoption by workers of individualist survival strategies. Such difficulties encouraged factionalism within the ZCTU, which was severely shaken by divisions amongst its leadership in 2006 which were actively encouraged by state assistance to individual renegade unions and its continued backing for the ZFTU. The immediate challenge for the ZCTU was to maintain its pre-eminent position within the labour movement. In the longer term, however, because no possibility of economic recovery was possible under ZANU-PF's authoritarian rule, the ZCTU had no option but to throw its (diminishing) weight behind a *de facto* strategic alliance with the MDC.[12] Nonetheless, by early 2012, the political effectiveness of organized labour was severely compromised by the descent of the ZCTU into majority and minority factions, divided by competing accusa-

[9]   Peter Alexander (2000), 'Zimbabwean workers, the MDC and the 2000 election', *Review of African Political Economy*, 85, 385–406.
[10] Ibid.
[11] Webster and Sikwebu, op. cit., 210.
[12] Matombo and Sachikonye, op. cit., 109–30.

tions of mismanagement of resources, inflation of union memberships, and appeals to the courts to resolve issues of legitimacy.[13]

Organized labour has fared better in both Namibia and South Africa than in Zimbabwe. Whereas ZANU-PF has actively sought to disorganize the trade union movement, the relationships between SWAPO and the National Union of Namibian Workers (NUNW) and between the ANC and COSATU have been founded upon alliance and collaboration. Even so, the relationships have been contested, plagued by differential perceptions of the extent to which projected social partnership between unions and parties represents equality or subordination.

The emergence of democratic trade unions in South Africa (from the early 1970s) and in Namibia (from the mid-1980s) culminating in the formations of COSATU in 1985 and NUNW in 1988 ensured that organized labour played a key role in mass mobilization of workers against apartheid. Both NUNW and COSATU unions linked the struggle at the workplace with the broader struggle for democracy and formed strong links with other organizations in civil society, subscribing to a 'social movement unionism' which developed organic links to the liberation movements. Nonetheless, there were early signs that NUNW was more disposed to subjecting itself to SWAPO's political authority than COSATU was to accepting the unquestioned leadership of the ANC. This was a reflection of a different historical relationship, for whereas SWAPO had itself formed NUNW (in exile) in 1970 (to represent Namibian workers internationally), the ANC as a nationalist organization had forged alliances over time with both the CPSA/SACP and SACTU through the Congress Alliance of the 1950s and thereafter in exile. Thus whereas the trade unions which emerged within Namibia in the 1980s chose to constitute themselves as an internal wing of SWAPO, unions within COSATU were to conduct a vigorous debate about the pros and cons of allying with the ANC and SACP. Furthermore, the decision to ally with the ANC, when it was made, was to a considerable extent on COSATU's terms, symbolized by the dissolution of SACTU (whose relationship to the emergent unions had been ambivalent) into the domestic federation. Thereafter, while the relationship between the ANC, SACP and COSATU was formalized into the Tripartite Alliance, it was left fluidly undefined.[14]

Both NUNW and COSATU were to prove themselves critical to the various election campaigns conducted by SWAPO and the ANC respectively. The unions both enjoyed widespread support beyond their immediate membership, and possessed an organizational capacity which effectively transformed them into the shock-troops of SWAPO and the ANC at election times, with both playing a highly active role in electoral mobilization of workers and communities. Within COSATU, certainly, the political commitment of individual union members to the ANC in electoral terms has remained remarkably high (around 75 per cent) and consistent over time (principal variation occurring amongst Coloured workers in the Western Cape). In the 1994 and

[13] Nunurayi Mutyanda and Taurai Mereki (2012), 'ZCTU congress aftermath: cracks deepen', *South African Labour Bulletin*, 36: 1, 54–57.

[14] Herbert Jauch (2010), 'Serving workers or serving the party? Trade unions and politics in Namibia', in Beckman, Buhlungu and Sachikonye (eds), op. cit., 167–90; Sakhela Buhlungu (2010), *A Paradox of Victory: COSATU and the Democratic Transformation in South Africa*, Pietermaritzburg: University of KwaZulu-Natal Press, Ch. 8.

later elections COSATU released a number of leading trade unionists so that they could stand as candidates for the ANC at both national and provincial levels.[15] However, whether SWAPO and the ANC have provided a fair return to the workers' organizations for their electoral support has occasioned huge debate.

The post-apartheid governments honoured debts by reforming the labour relations system, via the Labour Act of 1992 in Namibia and the Labour Relations Act of 1995 in South Africa. These established new frameworks for collective bargaining based upon an entrenchment of basic workers' and trade union rights and providing protections against unfair labour practices. Both Acts were drawn up via consultative processes which appeared to promise a social corporatism reminiscent of post-war Sweden and Germany and seemingly opened up a path to 'co-determination' and a break with the adversarial culture which had hitherto characterized employer-worker relations.[16] However, while the new labour dispensations brought about a significant improvement for formal sector workers compared with the past, the overall gains to workers of their federations' close associations with the respective ruling parties was to prove ambiguous. Above all, the adoption by SWAPO and the ANC of conservative economic policies challenged the sustainability of the gains made by labour.

SWAPO's 1976 political programme declared its aspiration to become 'a vanguard party capable of safeguarding national independence and of building a classless, non-exploitative society based on the ideals and principles of scientific socialism'. However, the deepening crisis within the Soviet Union in the 1980s and the refusal of South Africa to implement UN Resolution 435 encouraged SWAPO to seek Western support by embracing market-oriented policies. Thus the socialist rhetoric of the 1970s was replaced by the 'pragmatism' of accepting a non-racial capitalist order as, with the securing of independence, SWAPO dropped all notions of revolutionary working-class politics in favour of NUNW buying into 'social partnership'.[17] A similar process took place in South Africa. GEAR indicated that large-scale capital and the financial markets were going to remain far more influential than organized labour in economic policy-making, and confirmed the subordination of COSATU within the Alliance. Thereafter, COSATU was to complain vociferously about its marginalization, and strains between the federation and the ANC became explicit. In the run-up to the ANC's national conference in 2002, complaints by the SACP and COSATU that the government's turn to neo-liberalism was leading to greater poverty and unemployment were countered by Mbeki with statements that the Alliance was being subverted by a shadowy 'ultra-left' in defiance of agreed policies. Although these and other differences were usually patched up (and smothered at election times) differences between the SACP and COSATU and the ANC hierarchy were never really resolved. They were to translate from 2005 into the organized left's vocal (although never unanimous) support for Jacob Zuma in his undeclared but viciously fought battle to

---

[15] Buhlungu (ed.), op. cit.
[16] Edward Webster (2001), 'The Alliance under stress: Governing in a globalizing world', in Roger Southall (ed.), *Opposition and Democracy in South Africa*, London: Frank Cass, 255–74.
[17] Jauch, op. cit.

replace Mbeki as ANC President at the party's National Congress at Polokwane in December 2007.[18]

Whereas ZANU-PF has sought to smash trade union opposition, SWAPO and the ANC have sought to incorporate it. In Namibia, trade unions outside NUNW have consistently argued that the federation's alliance with SWAPO compromises its independence and inhibits its capacity to act for the working class. In contrast, the dominant forces within NUNW have argued that affiliation to SWAPO provides the federation with a positive influence upon government decision-making. Thus the leadership claims it was successful in influencing the drafting of the National Development Plan and the setting up of a Labour Advisory Council in 1992.[19] Similarly, NUNW claims credit for nudging the government into adopting an amendment to the Export Processing Act of 1995. When originally passed, this Act had empowered the government to declare the non-application of the Labour Act of 1992 within an EPZ. The government had argued that the exclusion of EPZs from the Labour Act would allay foreign investors' fears about the costs of labour and industrial unrest. It was a 'delicate compromise', declared Nujoma, 'necessary to achieve the larger goal of job creation'.[20] In response, NUNW had objected that such a compromise would violate international labour standards and the Namibian constitution, and instructed lawyers to challenge the Act in court. This led to a tripartite meeting between the government, SWAPO, and NUNW and the reaching of an agreement whereby the Act would apply within the EPZ but strikes and lock-outs would be outlawed for some five years. However, for all that NUNW greeted this as a victory the substance of the government's concession was minimal.

When Ramatex, a Malaysian clothing and textile company started operations in Namibia as an EPZ company, receiving all sorts of benefits such as tax holidays, duty-free imports, and exports, it received vigorous support from the government, even though it embarked upon some of the most ruthless employment conditions yet seen in Namibia. When workers fought back, they were accused of betraying the national interest despite the fact that Ramatex had by this time imported some 1,500 migrant workers from China, Bangladesh, and the Philippines to work alongside some 5,500 Namibians. By 2005, some 500 workers had been retrenched as it appeared that the company was planning to shift production to Asia. Then in October 2006, workers went on strike, forcing the company into concessions which led to improvements in wages and working conditions, although Ramatex mixed these with the threat – backed by the government and trade union leaders – that further strike actions would lead to the closure of the factory. Eventually, in March 2008, workers arrived at the factory to find that it had been closed without prior notice, and it took government action to force the company to pay the legally prescribed minimum retrenchment packages. Overall, the Ramatex episode demonstrated not only

---

[18] Roger Southall and Edward Webster (2010), 'Unions and parties in South Africa: Cosatu and the ANC in the wake of Polokwane', in Beckman, Buhlungu and Sachikonye (eds), op. cit., 131–66.

[19] Martin Sycholt and Gilton Klerck (1997), 'The state and labour relations: Walking the tightrope between corporatism and neo-liberalism', in Gilton Klerck, Andrew Murray and Martin Sycholt (eds), *Continuity and Change: Labour Relations in Independent Namibia*, Windhoek: Gamsberg Macmillan, 79–115.

[20] Cited in Jauch, op. cit., 172.

that the government was more eager to create an enabling environment for business than to promote worker interests, but that when conflicted by loyalty to the government versus the demands of their own members, trade union leaders were likely to side with the former. As argued by Jauch, 'the notion of social partnership in Namibia is more of an ideological construct than a reflection of the country's social and economic balance of power', which is unambiguously tilted in favour of business.[21]

A major reason why NUNW remains affiliated to SWAPO is that the alliance provides a path of upward mobility for trade union leaders, significant numbers of whom have moved into government or into the private sector. In turn, this has meant that divisions within SWAPO have penetrated the trade union movement. The most striking example of this occurred from 2004 concerning the rivalry between the supporters of Sam Nujoma – when he reluctantly bowed to pressure to retire from the state presidency at the expiry of his third term in office but who wished to stand again for the SWAPO presidency – and the supporters of Hidipo Hamutenya – aspiring to replace him. In the run-up to NUNW's congress in 2006, trade union leaders mobilized intensively for their favoured candidate, only for the Nujoma faction to gain the upper hand. NUNW dismissed its Secretary-General for the critical stance he had earlier taken towards Nujoma, and delegates from the teachers' and mining unions walked out in protest against a clampdown on the expression of dissent. Leading, independent-minded union leaderships were thereafter replaced by Nujoma leaderships.[22] The inevitable upshot was that concerns around the succession process within SWAPO predominated within NUNW at the expense of economic and social concerns raised by workers.

The growing gap between the trade union leadership and ordinary trade unionists has led to a closing down of democratic space within NUNW and a decline in leaders' accountability. This is not uncontested. At NUNW's Congress in 2010, delegates instructed their national executive's decision to rejoin the BIG Coalition of unions, churches, and NGOs after it had previously withdrawn from the coalition over the government's opposition to BIG. Delegates also insisted, to the embarrassment of various union leaders, that all those involved in a scandal surrounding the Government Institutions Pensions Fund (GIPF) should be brought to book. The scandal had involved the writing off of over N\$600 million of public servants' pension monies following ill-advised investments, amid revelations of recklessness and corruption: hitherto, key unions that operated in the public sector had failed to take any action. (Indeed the Secretary-General of the Namibia Public Sector Workers' Union had served as a director of companies which had received loans from the GIPF which had been written off.) With delegates also making other demands which ran contrary to government policy, there were indications that workers were increasingly prepared to challenge the cosy relationship between NUNW and SWAPO.[23]

In contrast to NUNW's subordination to SWAPO, COSATU's relationship to

21 Ibid., 183.
22 Henning Melber (2007), 'Namibia', in Andreas Mehler, Henning Melber and Klaas van Walraven (eds), *Africa Yearbook: Politics, Economy and Society South of the Sahara in 2006*, Leiden; Boston: Brill, 459–68.
23 Herbert Jauch (2010), 'Workers take back control: Congress of National Union of Namibian Workers', *South African Labour Bulletin*, 34: 5, 25–26.

the ANC remains more fractious. Although major differences between the government and the labour federation over economic policy have never been fully breached, the latter has continued to argue the virtues of its remaining within the Tripartite Alliance. COSATU has suffered all the blows that have been inflicted upon NUNW: loss of membership amongst private sector workers when they lost jobs, a shift to increased public sector worker membership resulting from increased union organization within government, a growing bureaucratization of union leadership, and a constant drain of its more highly educated and skilled elements through upward mobility into government and the private sector.[24] Nonetheless, COSATU has retained a level of militancy and capacity which provides it with a degree of influence which the NUNW has never attained. Most notably, this was displayed by the key role it took in securing the election of Jacob Zuma to the leadership of the ANC. Resentment at its marginalization within the Alliance under Mbeki had led COSATU to join with the SACP in devising a 'left strategy' designed to capture the ANC from within and thereby to shift government strategy in a pro-poor and pro-working class direction. Basically this meant using COSATU mobilizational capacity to ensure election of sufficient pro-Zuma candidates from branch level upwards within the ANC in the lead-up to Polokwane, in order to bring about Mbeki's replacement. Although there were various other forces at play which were significant in bringing about Zuma's victory, the 'organized left' provided the muscle which made it possible. Even so, COSATU's role in backing Zuma's rise to the presidency has translated into only ambiguous influence on government policy.

Zuma himself was always a dubious standard-bearer for the left, not least because he had been party to the implementation of GEAR as a senior member of the government. In addition, he had always been a highly skilful political operator, so that any suggestions that he would automatically repay his political backers with policy gains (in this instance, a sharp turn to the left in government policy) was always founded upon dangerous assumptions. The outcome was that while he made some personnel changes in government which acknowledged the left (notably the shifting of Trevor Manuel from Finance to a new Ministry of Planning and the appointments of trade unionist Ebrahim Patel to a new Ministry of Economic Affairs and of SACP Secretary-General Blade Nzimande as Minister of Higher Education), there was to be little substantial change in the government's economic direction. To be sure, Zuma promised a new emphasis upon job creation and, in 2010, backed Patel's introduction of a New Economic Growth Path which the government hailed as laying the basis for a more vigorous 'development state'. However, while the SACP (now closer to government) welcomed it as providing for a 'new paradigm', COSATU criticized it for failing to break with the legacy of GEAR. In short, while the formation of COSATU in 1985 constituted a 'strategic compromise' between the nationalist and shop-floor traditions of trade unionism, it was one which was far more geared to mobilizing for the final overthrow of apartheid (and we might add, securing the election and constant re-election of the ANC) than it was for determining relations between unions and the ANC following the latter's move into government.[25] COSATU retains a level of influ-

[24] Buhlungu, op. cit., passim.
[25] Southall and Webster, op. cit.,151.

ence within the ANC which the party hierarchy cannot ignore but can and will override if it deems that other interests are paramount.

Liberation movements and civil society

Taking civil society to be 'the organized expression of various interests and values operating in the triangular space between the family, state and the market',[26] we may identify state-civil society relations in Zimbabwe, Namibia, and South Africa as having traversed different stages of development.

First, in settler colonial societies, civil society had been racially bifurcated and subjected to differential conditions. Within the dominant white group, the right to free association was broadly acknowledged, allowing for economic interest groups (of business and agriculture) to lobby government and for churches to espouse (diverse) moral values, their concerns overlapping with NGOs of various hues which promoted incremental social and political changes while often undertaking worthy social projects amongst the disadvantaged segments of society. Very often, 'white civil society' would champion strong critiques of government policy, invoking reason, evidence, and often the law itself to challenge the irrationality, injustice, and inhumanity of racialized state policy. Where, however, liberal advocacy translated into radical political activity, it was likely to be banned. Heribert Adam characterized this state of affairs in South Africa as constituting a 'democratic police state' wherein a 'semblance of democratic legitimacy' was counterbalanced by a battery of repressive legislation to secure black subjugation. Thus, for all her courage in embarrassing the government, Helen Suzman served as a valuable 'democratic ornamentation for an undemocratically elected parliament'.[27] Under such circumstances, the legal opposition, the English-speaking press, bodies such as the SAIRR (South African Institute of Race Relations), the Black Sash, and some churches, promoted alternative ideas and on occasion sobered the more extreme race laws and ameliorated their implementation. Yet overall, even whites were so intimidated that only a small core of dedicated liberals and radicals kept anti-government organizations alive.

What went for South Africa went also for South West Africa and Rhodesia. Rhodesia was muscularly Christian, but its faith was used to justify a secular world which was 'anti-communist, democratic, and civilized (that is, white ruled)'. Whereas the churches themselves represented large African congregations and harboured priests who openly identified with them, they tended to avoid the big issues of race and politics. When in 1969 they sought to confront the state over the Land Tenure Act (which assigned 45 million acres each to the majority African and minority white populations), their initially firm stand was swiftly beaten back, and radical priests, for example Donal Lamont, the Catholic Bishop of Umtali, were disowned by the bulk of the white Catholic

---

[26] Adam Habib (2004), 'State-civil society relations in post-apartheid South Africa', in John Daniel, Adam Habib and Roger Southall (eds), *South Africa: State of the Nation 2003–2004*, Cape Town: HSRC Press, 227–41.

[27] Heribert Adam (1972), *Modernizing Racial Domination: The Dynamics of South African Politics*, Berkeley CA: University of California Press, 48.

laity and clergy. Subsequently, the churches professed their political neutrality and concentrated on saving souls and dealing with 'morality'.[28]

Civil society amongst the dominated black populations was not merely less coherent and more fragmented but subject to massive political restrictions. In Rhodesia, UDI trampled upon black civil society and frustrated its development by confining blacks to a tribal existence.[29] Similarly, South Africa's homeland policy sought to divert African political activity to the ethnic rather than the national arena, yet ultimately fell foul of a host of contradictions, notably the growth of African populations in urban areas and, by the 1970s, a corresponding rise in African political consciousness. When this was met by violence and repression, many popular organizations – where they developed – traversed rapidly from protest to revolution and came to accept the authority of the liberation movements. Thus, some 600-odd student, community, and activist organizations came together as the UDF in 1983, and within a relatively short space of time, this became the domestic surrogate for the ANC.

A second stage in the development of civil society was to follow after the moment of independence and/or democratization when, with political liberation deemed as 'achieved', oppositional activity gave way variously to negotiation, cooperation with, affiliation to or even dissolution into the liberation movement. Many groups of established white society sought to reposition themselves to assert their interests anew, with business associations and organized agriculture making rapid adjustments to the new order, and (as the next chapter will explore) enjoying considerable success in so doing, while policy groups sought influence through social analysis and representation. In contrast, groups within the formerly politically oppressed sector were not only weakened by a loss of key members to government but also had to prove their credentials.

In Zimbabwe, ZANU-PF went about destroying the independence of civil society associations in the name of revolution.[30] All were challenged to join the ruling party to demonstrate their patriotic commitment. 'The ruling party sought to consolidate the coalition of social forces that had supported it during the liberation war, and to expand its coalition to incorporate groups that had remained outside...on its own terms.'[31] At the University of Zimbabwe in Harare, the African-dominated Student Representative Council perceived an initial mutuality of purpose with ZANU-PF in government. It adopted ZANU-PF's language of liberation war to intimidate students, white and black, who did not share the ruling party's vision. However, the honeymoon did not last, and student hooliganism gave the government the excuse in 1990 to introduce two Bills (the University of Zimbabwe Amendment Bill and the National Council for Higher Education Bill) which massively increased its ability to control the University Council, to appoint the Vice-Chancellor, and to decide who should be admitted and what might be taught. These were immediately denounced by both staff and students. Following staff demonstrations and

[28] Peter Godwin and Ian Hancock (1993), *Rhodesians Never Die: The Impact of War and Political Change on White Rhodesia, c1970–1980*, London: Macmillan, 42–45.
[29] Jason Moyo (1993), 'Civil society in Zimbabwe', *Zambezia*, 20: 1, 1–14.
[30] Ibid.
[31] Sarah Dorman (2003), 'NGOs and the constitutional debate in Zimbabwe: From inclusion to exclusion', *Journal of Southern African Studies*, 29: 4, 846.

student boycotts of lectures, the government pushed the two Bills through parliament. Confrontations between the students and the government turned violent, legitimizing a crackdown by the latter, with the former eventually returning to the campus thoroughly chastened. Their campaigns were weakened by further violence, assaults on female students, and an intolerance of dissent which mimicked the authoritarianism of the ruling party.[32] In this arena, as in others, those resisting ZANU-PF's vision of 'one state, one society, one nation, one leader' were branded as enemies and sell-outs. The overall effect – combined with ZAPU's dissolution into ZANU-PF – was to silence the black community. Introduction of a Private Voluntary Organisations' Act to regulate NGOs went largely unprotested as the NGOs were reluctant to challenge the regime.[33]

In Namibia, a guide to civil society published in 2009 lists just 150 principal organizations for the whole country, these catering to the interests of agriculture, the arts, the disabled, democratic and human rights activists, as well as groups dealing with HIV-AIDS, education, and gender. The role of most of these is self-consciously developmental and actively supporting strategies for long-term development as contained in (SWAPO's) vision 2030 and the achievement of Millennium Development Goals.[34] Most are constrained by a lack of funds, dependent upon international donors, and need to maintain a good working relationship with government. Only a few have seriously confronted the authorities. Significantly, this has occurred mainly in the sphere of human rights. Thus, the Legal Assistance Centre (LAC), supported the Ovahimba people's objection to the government's construction of the Epupa hydroelectric power plant on the Kunene River on the grounds that it would submerge their ancestors' graves.[35] Similarly, organizations such as the National Society for Human Rights and the research bodies, the Namibian Economic Policy Research Unit, the Institute for Public Policy, LAC, and the Namibia Institute for Democracy have engaged in the promotion of social justice and human rights-oriented culture. Yet often such groups have been denounced by SWAPO as unpatriotic. As a result, a culture of silence has become 'a constitutive part of Namibia's political realities' in which SWAPO vilifies all those who deviate from its declared policies, and dissenting behaviour is marginalized.[36] Few NGOs have become actively involved in political lobbying and not many are prepared to set explicitly political agendas. Even the churches, which played a leading role in denouncing human rights violations under apartheid, have retreated from the public political sphere and have redefined the gospel as a bounded religious affair. When organizations do engage in criticism, their barbs may easily be neutralized by governmental incorporation. Thus a farmers' leader, Gabes

---

[32] Andrea Cheater (1991), 'The University of Zimbabwe: University, national university, state university or party university?' *African Affairs*, XC, 189–205.

[33] Dorman, op. cit., 847.

[34] Namibia Institute of Democracy (2009), *Guide to Civil Society in Namibia*, Windhoek: Namibia Institute of Democracy.

[35] Victor Tonchi (2002), 'Civil society and democracy in Namibia', Development Policy Management Forum, Policy Brief Series 6, Addis Ababa.

[36] Henning Melber (2009), 'Governance, political culture and civil society under a civil liberation movement in power: The case of Namibia', in Nuno Vidal and Patrick Chabal (eds), *Southern Africa: Civil Society, Politics and Donor Strategies. Angola and Its Neighbours*, Luanda and Lisbon: Media XXI & Firmamento, 199–212.

Shihepo, led a Namibia National Farmers' Union march in opposition to government land policies in 1999, but within weeks found himself appointed an MP and Deputy Minister.[37]

In South Africa, the ANC moved swiftly to transform the adversarial relationship between state and much of civil society by creating a more enabling environment. First, repressive legislation was repealed and a political climate permitting public scrutiny and protest activity was established. Second, the political environment was reorganized in order to establish reciprocity between NGOs and government. Thus a Non-Profit Act was passed that created a system of voluntary registration for its constituents and provided benefits and allowances in exchange for NGOs and community-based organizations undertaking proper accounting and providing audited statements to government. A Directorate for Non-Profit Organisations was established in the Department of Social Welfare to coordinate these processes and to facilitate the state's partnership with NGOs in the policy development and service delivery arenas. Third, actions were taken to enable the financial sustainability of civil society organizations which found themselves confronted by a fiscal crisis occasioned by foreign donors redirecting their aid funding away from NGOs towards the state. Thus the Fundraising Act of 1978 which had limited NGOs' and trade unions' capacity to raise funds was repealed, and institutions like the National Development Agency and the Lottery Commission established to fund legitimate non-profit activity. Tax regulations were also promulgated in 2009–10 to grant registered civil society organizations tax exemptions status. All this was highly beneficial for democracy and governance, and founded upon a recognition by most activists, politicians, and government officials of the diversity of civil society, even if at times this was more rhetorical than real.[38]

The third stage in the development of state-civil society relations was to see a reactivation of oppositional activity as civil society organizations responded critically to variant combinations of neo-liberal economic restructuring, political authoritarianism, corruption, and unresponsive and poor governance. Amongst especially (but not exclusively) the poorer segments of society, this gave rise to new 'social movements', that is 'politically and/or socially directed collectives, often involving multiple organizations and networks, focused on changing one or more elements of the social, political and economic system within which they are located'.[39] The extent to which this brought them into direct confrontation with the government, and the extent to which the latter has been able to reimpose or refigure its hegemony has differed according to the willingness of the state to use coercion and its adherence to the values of democracy.

Influential analyses suggest that civil society in Namibia has not yet achieved this third stage of development, and continues to be constrained by SWAPO's intolerance. This finds considerable resonance amongst the attitudes of many

---

[37] Graham Hopwood (2007), *Guide to Namibian Politics*, Windhoek: Namibia Institute for Democracy, 99.

[38] Habib, op. cit.

[39] Richard Ballard, Adam Habib and Elke Zuern (2006), 'Introduction: From anti-apartheid to post-apartheid social movements', in Richard Ballard, Adam Habib and Imraan Valodia (eds), *Voices of Protest: Social Movements in Post-Apartheid South Africa*, Pietermaritzburg: University of KwaZulu-Natal Press, 3.

Namibians themselves.[40] An Afrobarometer Network compendium of public opinion based on three surveys across African countries conducted between 1999 and 2006 concluded that among the eighteen countries surveyed, Namibians appeared to be the most deferential to their elected leaders.[41] Overall, the failure of political parties of opposition to take root has been matched by the relative compliance of NGOs and, hitherto, an absence of social movements.

The contrast with both South Africa and Zimbabwe is marked. As South Africa has opened up to globalization, civil society has become more diverse, exhibiting markedly varying relationships of cooperation and conflict with the state. In Zimbabwe, civil society has become more consistently oppositional in response to the state's increasing authoritarianism, although divided to the extent that it should engage with post-2008 efforts by the coalition government to resolve the political crisis through reform. However, whereas civil society in South Africa is increasingly 'thick' (that is, highly diverse and embodied in multiple organizations of numerous persuasions, causes, and interests), that in Zimbabwe is distressingly 'thin', (that is, overwhelmingly absorbed with the political crisis and embodied in relatively few organizations).

In South Africa, a broad distinction between established liberal and conservative groups (ranging from the SAIRR through to business lobbies) and left-inclined and radical organizations has remained, divided as much by their diversity as united by their constant engagement with and criticism of the government. Yet following the post-apartheid hiatus when previously anti-apartheid groups were seeking to reorient themselves, South Africa has seen the emergence of a large number of social movements.

Social movements are not a new phenomenon. The linkages forged between the external liberation movements and the UDF, NGOs, and churches which were central to bringing about the transition to democracy fall under that broad category. Nonetheless, the appearance since the late 1990s of a wide diversity of social struggles and groupings, overwhelmingly centred around the basic needs, demands, and campaigns of poor and marginalized communities and directed against perceived failures or wrongs of government and/or private capital constitutes one the most remarkable developments of the post-apartheid period.

Social movements have emerged in reaction to neo-liberal policies; in response to attempts by government and parastatal agencies to cut off services such as water or electricity because of non-payment (e.g., the Soweto Electricity Crisis Committee, SECC); against attempts, for one reason or another, by authorities to evict residents from housing (the Anti-Eviction Campaign); against homelessness (the Homeless People's Alliance); against the slow pace of land reform (the Landless People's Movement); and against abuses of the environment (the Environmental Justice Movement). Further, the Treatment Action Campaign (TAC) was forged around attempts to force changes in government policy regarding HIV-AIDS (notably under the presidency of Mbeki, whose AIDS-denialism constituted a significant obstacle to attempts to counter the epidemic) and to raise popular awareness about HIV-

---

[40]   Andre du Pisani (2003), 'Liberation and tolerance', in Henning Melber (ed.), *Re-examining Liberation in Namibia: Political Culture since Independence*, Uppsala: Nordic Africa Institute, 129–36.

[41]   Carolyn Logan, Telsuya Fujiwara and Virginia Parish (2006), *Citizens and the State in Africa: New Results from Afrobarometer Round 3*, Afrobarometer Working Paper 61, Cape Town: IDASA, 16.

AIDS treatment and prevention. Some of these groupings (such as SECC) are unrepentantly oppositional, arguing that the ANC has sold out to neo-liberalism and international capital, and they engage largely in grassroots mobilization; others seek to straddle criticism of the ANC whilst continuing to partner it; while others, notably the TAC, have developed a flexible strategy of simultaneously criticizing, opposing, and engaging the government whilst mobilizing in local communities, working both 'inside and beyond the institutions of the state', and using the media to develop wider support with considerable skill.[42]

The ANC's response has been highly ambiguous. Its liberation ethos attunes it to regarding social actors as either for or against it, as friend or foe, with the outcome that many social movements are regarded as hostile or irresponsibly 'ultra-left'. On the other hand, it has become aware that social movements are rooted amongst the poor, and that to alienate them may distance the party from its own supporters. The contradiction between these two responses has been particularly pronounced at local level where the machinery of ANC branches has become variously merged into local government, factionalized, inactive between elections, and unresponsive to the needs of the local communities amongst which they are based. The result has been an upsurge of local protests, which observers date from 2004–05 (when there were some 6,000-odd such events that have continued at a similar rate).[43] These have been inchoate and sparked by disparate demands, as well as often engaging in the sort of collective action (marches, tyre-burnings, destruction of public property, attacks against local councillors) which leads to direct confrontation with the police and which recalls the anti-apartheid struggles of the 1970s and 1980s. At the same time, social movement protestors perform a *pas de deux* with the ANC, returning to vote for the party at election times, with their leaderships often being reabsorbed into the party after the protests have been made. Nonetheless, for all the ambiguity of their relations with the ANC, social movements have begun to grope towards some broad unity, coming together first in a major meeting of civil society convened in October 2010 and attended by COSATU in December 2009 (to the considerable anguish of the ANC), and second at a Conference of the Democratic Left in January 2011, out of which came a Democratic Left Front which was broadly reminiscent of the UDF. Such developments served as a prompt to Moeletsi Mbeki, the former President's brother (yet a constant critic of ANC rule), to predict a 'Tunisia moment' (a reference to the popular uprisings which swept North Africa in early 2011) for the ANC in 2020, a moment he argued when the Chinese appetite for global minerals would have peaked, forcing the South African government to cut back on social grants for its impoverished supporters in response to a decline in exports and accompanying economic growth.[44]

The upsurge in social protests (and an often violent police response) points to a weakening of the bonds between the ANC and its historic community of support (a confirmation that the party will have to work increasingly hard to

---

[42] Hein Marais (2010), *South Africa Pushed to the Limit: The Political Economy of Change*, Cape Town: University of Cape Town Press, 451–57.

[43] Ibid., 457–59.

[44] *Business Day*, 10 February 2011.

retain the loyalty of its constituency in elections).[45] Nonetheless, predictions that unity amongst highly diverse social movements will be achieved easily and that it will result in a socially revolutionary movement or a party of the left capable of displacing the ANC are likely to prove illusory. It is not only that the dilemma of COSATU (and the SACP) whether to continue to partner the ANC will remain; nor is it merely that the xenophobic riots of 2008 (when 'foreigners' and ethnic outsiders were subject to violent attack in numerous impoverished communities) indicate that popular action will not automatically be socially progressive. It is rather that while the ANC's social coalition of support may fracture and thus undermine ANC dominance electorally, the party-in-government is as likely to respond to popular protest through a rene-gotiation of its alliances as it is to resort to systematic state coercion to suppress concerted opposition. In short, the political system is likely to remain relatively flexible, and rather than a Tunisia moment (which saw the overthrow of Pres-ident Ben Ali and his cronies) it might equally follow the trajectory of the Indian National Congress, which after three decades in power (and after having become increasingly authoritarian) stepped down on losing an election in 1976. The Indian Congress has, however, remained a significant electoral and political force.

The contrast with Zimbabwe could scarcely be more marked, for whilst there too, civil society has become increasingly oppositional, it has been confronted by systematic state brutality and oppression. It is appropriate to recall how the MDC was formed in response to popular demands for constitutional reform. Undermined by ZANU-PF hostility and the erosion of its structural base by the declining economy, the ZCTU had played a key role in the establishment of the NCA in 1997 and brought with it vital experience acquired since 1980 in working with other civil society organizations formed around issues of struc-tural adjustment, poverty, housing, and human rights. Its ability to combine a national capacity for organization with extended civic alliances proved decisive in the emergence of an alternative democratic voice.[46]

Strongly backed by the Zimbabwe Council of Churches, with its membership comprising 'religious organizations, trade unions, professional associations, grassroots structures, media bodies, academic institutions and business, women's, students' and human rights organizations', the NCA contributed a 'seismic shift in the development of oppositional politics after 1997'.[47] The objectives of the NCA were to identify shortcomings in the existing constitu-tion, promote popular participation in constitutional debate, and come up with proposals for constitutional reform. Yet it was to be confronted by immediate state hostility, with government actions to deny it access to the official media and to hamper its various operations. Nonetheless, backed by the ZCTU's orga-nizational structure and experience, alongside the churches' extensive influ-ence and membership, the NCA proved remarkably successful in forging

[45] Colleeen Schulz-Herzenberg (2009), 'Trends in party support and voter behaviour, 1994–2009', in Roger Southall and John Daniel (eds), *Zunami! The 2009 South African Elections*, Johan-nesburg: Jacana, 23–46.

[46] Brian Raftopoulos (2009), 'The crisis in Zimbabwe', in Brian Raftopoulos and Alois Mlambo (eds), *Becoming Zimbabwe: A History from the Pre-Colonial Period to 2008*, Harare: Weaver Press, 201–32.

[47] Ibid., 206.

national networks across civil society and in promoting national debate over constitutional reform.

In March 1999, the government responded to the NCA by establishing its own well-funded Constitutional Commission (which some within ZANU-PF saw as a potential device for bringing about a change of leadership and effecting internal party reform). This was an attempt by ZANU-PF to control constitutional reform: recognized as such by the NCA it declined to participate in the official process because of the skewed composition of the Commission and it subsequently rejected the draft constitution, which persisted with a concentration of power in the hands of the presidency.[48] Thereafter, notably after the formation of the MDC, the NCA's mobilization around constitutional reform was 'linked, in the thinking of both the ruling party and key players in the civic constitutional reform movement, to a change of government'.[49] The correctness of this perception was to be confirmed by the government's total shock when it lost the referendum on its proposed constitution in February 2000 and failed in its subsequent campaigns of violence against the MDC in the ensuing parliamentary and presidential elections.

Civil society was thereafter subjected to pressures from above and below. On the one hand, ZANU-PF responded to its loss of popular legitimacy by embarking on an authoritarian reconfiguration of the bases of its power: unilateral constitutional amendment (the reintroduction of the Senate), electoral manipulation, terrorization of the population, and the increasing militarization of the state, as well as creating pseudo-civil society organizations in its own image. On the other hand, the mounting economic crisis severely eroded the structural underpinnings of the labour movement and opposition mobilization. Trade unions were decimated by job losses and the survivalist individualism pervasive in the more precarious conditions of an increasingly informalized economy. Civil society organizations, while often courageous in face of official violence, were relatively few in number, primarily representative of urban, educated, and professional opinion, and anyway severely undermined by the migration of millions of actual or potential supporters to South Africa and further afield. Simultaneously, whilst the discourse of human rights was used very effectively to critique governmental repression and to expand the debate about democratic participation, its association with Western powers' notions of 'good governance' and donor networks enabled ZANU-PF to portray the pro-democracy movement as a puppet of imperialism.[50] Meanwhile, although ostensibly 'democratic', civil groups are regularly and 'sadly undemocratic'[51] with an ethnography of urban-based civic NGOs (notably human rights organizations) showing that their internal processes are often characterized by unconstitutional (and uncivil) procedures.[52]

---

[48] For a critique of the Constitutional Commission, see Dorman, op. cit.

[49] Raftopoulos, op. cit., 210.

[50] Brian Raftopoulos (2010), 'The global political agreement as a "passive revolution": Notes on contemporary politics in Zimbabwe', *The Round Table*, 99: 411, 705–18.

[51] John Makumbe (1998), 'Is there a civil society in Africa?' *International Affairs*, 74: 2, 311.

[52] Sarah Rich-Dorman (2001), 'Inclusion and exclusion: NGOs and politics in Zimbabwe', Ph.D. thesis, University of Oxford; Booker Magure (2009), 'Civil society's quest for democracy in Zimbabwe: Origins, barriers and prospects, 1900–2008', Ph.D. thesis, Rhodes University.

The limitations imposed upon civil society and political opposition by the perennial state of economic crisis and unrelenting political repression have been demonstrated by the highly compromised constitutional reform process which was undertaken under the auspices of the GPA (Global Political Agreement) of September 2008. During the SADC mediation process which had commenced under Thabo Mbeki on 29 March 2007, the (by now divided) MDC had set out their conditions for a free and fair election, stressing that these could only be free and fair if they were preceded by the negotiation and promulgation of a new constitution. For the MDC, human rights and constitutional matters were at the heart of the country's continuing crisis. For his part, Mbeki, eager to cajole both sides into an early election, made exaggerated claims to SADC about the extent of political agreement he had brought about between them, and claimed that the only outstanding matter related to the procedure to be followed in enacting a new constitution. A joint statement was thereafter issued by both wings of the MDC which protested bitterly to SADC that the timing and process of enactment of a new constitution were issues of fundamental substance. Its effect was undermined by Mugabe's unilateral setting of the 29 March 2008 date for the harmonized elections and thereafter ZANU-PF's brutal assault upon the opposition during the lead-up to the second-round presidential election.

The resumption of mediation by SADC following the elections resulted in the signing of the GPA and the formation of the coalition government. However, while the MDC-M regarded its acceptance of this compromise as potentially providing for an opening up of democratic space, this was negated by Mugabe's retention of a strong grip over the security forces. Thus although the implementation of the GPA saw the establishment of new Electoral, Human Rights, and Media Commissions (processes which inevitably proved contentious and appointments to which had ultimately to be approved by Mugabe as President), progress was much more problematic in the arena of constitutional reform.

In September 2007, the MDC formations had secretly agreed with ZANU-PF to the 'Kariba draft' which provided the basis for a constitutional amendment which passed through parliament later in the month. This was an uneasy compromise document which, *inter alia*, allowed parliament to nominate a successor President in the event of the death of the incumbent, enlarged the Senate, and increased the size of the Assembly from 150 to 200 – all changes which critics were later to charge would allow ZANU-PF to extend its grip on power. Yet the constitutional amendment also reduced the presidential term from six years to five and provided for harmonized elections. It was on this basis that the MDC had agreed to proceed to elections, although remaining insistent that the date had to be jointly agreed, that there should be an end to political repression, and that the millions of exiles should be allowed to vote.

Bullied by SADC and placed on the back foot by Mugabe's unbridled use of violence to retain the presidency, the MDC formations had entered into the GPA even though it severely compromised on their previous demands for popular participation in the drawing up of a new constitution. Thus clause 6.1 of the GPA laid down that constitutional reform was to be pursued under the auspices of a Select Committee of Parliament, a device which was more manipulable from above and which placed control over the process in the hands of politicians and the political parties at the expense of civil society. Subsequently, on

12 April 2008 the coalition government appointed a 25-member parliamentary committee, the Constitutional Parliamentary Committee (COPAC), to spearhead the drafting of a new constitution within eighteen months. The constitution was to be completed by February 2010 and to be followed by a national referendum five months later, this providing the basis for progression towards free and fair elections. Suffice it to say that the entire process swiftly ran into trouble.[53]

Two MPs, one from ZANU-PF (Paul Mangwana) and one from MDC-T (Douglas Mwanora) were appointed to co-chair COPAC. The Committee set about the task by engaging in a process of constitutional outreach whereby it would tour the entire country to hear the views of ordinary people.[54] The procedure elicited very mixed responses. Critics to the left of the MDC denounced it as fundamentally flawed. According to the chairman of the NCA, Lovemore Madhuku, the process was 'completely useless'. He insisted that a constitutional process should be led by an independent commission rather than by politicians. As it stood, therefore, COPAC was almost certainly likely to come up with a draft constitution which would be unacceptable to the large majority of the population. In contrast to the NCA, however, there were important elements within civil society which argued that while the process was less than perfect, it was the best obtainable and should therefore be utilized to wrest concessions from ZANU-PF. Thus organizations such as the Crisis in Zimbabwe Coalition and Zimbabwe Election Support Network argued for participation and the exertion of maximum popular influence upon politicians through the outreach programme.

As time wore on, the MDC-T was increasingly torn between concerns that the potential of the outreach programme was being undermined by civil society critics such as the NCA as well as being deliberately hampered by ZANU-PF intimidation. The evidence of the latter was very real. According to ground rules agreed in early July 2010 between COPAC and civil society organizations, the latter were to be free to deploy nominated and accredited observers to monitor the outreach programme. In practice, however, monitors were regularly subject to attack and beatings by ZANU-PF thugs and war veterans; the MDC-T complained of chiefs using their influence to transform outreach meetings into ZANU-PF rallies; and in some rural areas inhabitants were either intimidated by security forces and/or ZANU-PF youths into staying away from meetings whilst in others they were cowed by the presence of security forces into reading from ZANU-PF lines. ZANU-PF, inevitably, denied the reality of the violence which accompanied COPAC while at the same time blaming civil society organizations for fomenting trouble, inducing fear amongst the population to secure a rejection of the final outcome, peddling lies, and having 'ulterior motives'. Furthermore, while trying to block calls for political devolution emanating from Matabeleland, ZANU-PF sought to block change by pursuing a nationalist and socially conservative agenda. On the one hand, Mugabe warned that the constitution-making process should not be used to legalize foreign imports such as homosexual rights which were alien to 'our culture'; on the other, it should be used to pursue ZANU-PF's ideals. Thus, addressing the party's central

[53]   Ibid.
[54]   The following account is composed from multiple issues of the Sokwanele newsletter's 'Constitution outreach: News roundup' series, http://www.sokwanele.com/join.html

committee, Mugabe warned foreigners to 'back off' from the process and declared:

> We cannot swop our birthright for the donor's dollar...We have positions to defend, principles and policies and on these there shall be no compromise. We must ensure the product carries and consolidates our ideals as nationalist revolutionary party. We fought for the Independence and untrammelled sovereignty of this nation. That coveted status must remain solid, secure and unshaken for all time.[55]

The constitutional process, averred Mugabe, should result in a constitution that was 'truly Zimbabwean': code words for the ideas of ZANU-PF.

Despite its troubled path, the outreach programme was reasonably comprehensive. By mid-July 2008, it had held nearly a thousand meetings involving 153,000 people, and during those, amidst the violence and intimidation, it had heard popular calls for a devolution of power, major limitations upon presidential power, the accountability of politicians, and guarantees for human rights. Simultaneously, however, it was caught in the same dilemma that faced the MDC within the government of unity. On the one hand, COPAC's credibility was weakened by its being funded by donors (which allowed ZANU-PF to depict the MDC-T and civil society as pursuing a foreign agenda); on the other, while the GPA provided for COPAC to give feedback on what should be its content, the actual writing of a new constitution would remain in the hands of parliament and politicians. Furthermore, although the GPA provided for the resulting draft for a new constitution to be subject to a popular referendum, ZANU-PF officials made it explicit that the party would block any constitutional reform that deviated far from the Kariba draft. 'If the outcome does not faithfully reflect what the people have said', stated ZANU-PF Deputy Legal Affairs Secretary Patrick Chinamasa, 'you can be sure that ZANU-PF will say no'.[56]

Ultimately, neither MDC nor civil society had the leverage to carry through a significant process of constitutional reform. MDC might complain that the GPA laid down that new elections would only follow the passage of a new constitution, yet by early 2011 Mugabe and ZANU-PF were gunning to collapse the coalition and to hold an early election that they were determined to control. By early 2012, the constitutional drafting process had become bogged down over the introduction of a clause which would disqualify a person from being elected as President if he or she had already held power for ten years. ZANU-PF rejected this out of hand, leading figures in the party and the military calling upon Mugabe to dissolve parliament with or without a new constitution. In the event, Mugabe was constrained from going for early elections unilaterally by fear that riding roughshod over the conditions laid down by the GPA would consolidate SADC support behind South Africa and Botswana, whose governments were the most insistent that the political crisis could only be resolved through accordance with the conditions agreed upon 2008.

By mid-2012 the outlines of a new constitution had been achieved. Certainly, the agreed draft recorded some concessions by ZANU-PF. The next President would be restricted to serving two five-year terms (but this would not be retroactive, so Mugabe could theoretically serve another ten years); the pres-

---

[55] Sokwanele 'Constitution outreach', 12 July 2010, http://www.sokwanele.com/join.html
[56] Ibid., 18 July 2010.

idency would be less powerful; and there would be a degree of devolution (with a measure of executive control devolved to provincial executives composed of local MPs); dual citizens would be allowed to vote, but only inside the country; and MDC's call for a gender balance would lead to the election of some 70 women MPs by PR, to sit alongside the existing 210 constituency MPs (resulting in a bloated National Assembly). Against these less than startling changes, there was minimal security sector reform on offer, although securocrats coming to the end of their contracts would not be able to secure reappointment.[57] In short, although the MDC trumpeted that ZANU-PF had moved further than was imaginable three years previously, the draft did not suggest that it had serious potential for transforming the political landscape, not least because of ZANU-PF's continuing control of the security forces. Meanwhile, as civil society critics of the reform process had feared, the proposed outcome arguably catered far more to the interests of politicians than it did to those of ordinary citizens.

Formally, the new constitution would have to be approved by a referendum before the country proceeded to a further election (probably to be held in 2013). Meanwhile, a civil society structurally weakened by social crisis and unable to effectively confront ZANU-PF's militarized raw power remained ambivalent about its relationship to the MDC.

Liberation movements and rural governance

Under settler colonialism, the countryside was largely divided into white areas and African reserves wherein the majority of the African population was to fall under the ultimate authority of white officials and, closer to the ground, that of traditional leaders. The latter had mobilized resistance to the original colonial onslaught, and their participation in the establishment of new organizational forms for the expression of African opinion was viewed as essential. However, as settler government became more firmly established, traditional leaders came to be incorporated into the machinery of settler rule, being granted devolved authority over rural populations in the reserve areas. Mamdani has termed this system 'Decentralised Despotism', and observes that although Lord Lugard theorized the British 'indirect rule' system on the basis of his experiences in Nigeria, 'the creation of a separate but subordinate state structure for natives first developed in the southern African colonies and not in West Africa'.[58]

Given the immense variety of indigenous patterns of authority, and the uneven pace at which colonial control was established, the process of incorporation was uneven. However, central to the thrust of legislation was that the white administration was granted executive power over 'native authorities', who were deemed as presiding over 'tribes' according to customary law. In South Africa, the powers conferred on the Governor-General, under the Native Administration Act of 1927 were 'despotic to the extreme'.[59] The reserves were placed under the authority of Native Commissioners, but traditional leaders continued to arbitrate over civil cases under customary law and to allocate land

[57] *Sunday Independent*, 15 July 2012.
[58] Mahmood Mamdani (1996), *Citizen and Subject: Contemporary Africa and the Legacy of Late Colonialism*, London: James Currey, 62.
[59] Ibid., 71.

under systems of communal tenure. However, from the time of the passage of the Bantu Authorities Act of 1951, which put in place the foundations of the Bantustan system by provision for the establishment of Territorial, Regional, and Tribal Authorities, significantly greater powers were to be devolved to chiefs, giving them a vested interest in 'separate development'. Although the subsequent creation of ethnic 'homelands' involved the erection of recognizably 'modern' governmental machineries, the regime was always careful to ensure that potentially democratic elements within the system, such as elections for ethnic parliaments, were countervailed by the political weight of traditional leaders. The Bantustan system, as it developed in both South Africa and South West Africa, was essentially founded upon a consolidation and extension of chiefly power. In Rhodesia, similarly, although the regime (reluctantly) opted for the incorporation of Africans into the central parliament rather than any mode of separate development, traditional leaders remained central to the maintenance of settler rule within the TTLs.

The minority regimes legitimized traditional authority as embodiments of indigenous rule, and indeed, to function, it required significant elements of local trust, as expressed by the notion 'a chief is a chief by the people'. Yet overall the transmogrification of traditional leadership under settler rule established local systems that were oppressive and unaccountable, and in South Africa led to outbreaks of rural revolt against chiefly power, initially in reaction to the creation of Bantustans during the 1950s and 1960s, latterly in consort with popular uprisings against apartheid during the 1980s. While there were individual leaders who sought to rely upon popular rather than regime legitimacy (an example being Paramount Chief Sabata Dalindyebo of Thembuland in Transkei who fled the vindictive rule of Kaiser Matanzima to join the ANC in Lusaka in 1980), the alignment of chiefs with minority rule structures generally predisposed them to hostility towards the NLMs and the democratic aspirations they represented. These feelings were largely reciprocated, even though the liberation movements were pragmatic enough to distinguish between leaders who had become fully incorporated into the systems of oppression, and those who might be disposed towards alliance with progressive forces. SWAPO, for instance, dismissed traditional leaders in the north of Namibia as having 'sold out', whilst it recognized a more complex situation in the south where some were 'partially responsive to their people's aspiration for freedom' but felt threatened by modern political parties; other leaders who had opted to join Turnhalle to preserve their ethnic power base; others who had stayed out of Turnhalle but who had refused to join SWAPO; and some who had chosen to identify with the nationalist cause.[60] Similarly, especially during the latter years when apartheid rule began to crumble, the ANC proved sufficiently flexible to strike up links with 'progressive' chiefs and even with the few homeland regimes which were covertly or otherwise prepared to allow MK to operate within their territory.

The transitions to democracy provided the incoming regimes with significant dilemmas. Many traditional leaders – if not the majority – were viewed as having been collaborators with the minority regimes, with the situation

---

[60] SWAPO (1981), *To Be Born a Nation: The Liberation Struggle for Namibia*, London: Zed Press, 274–76.

complicated by some (or their forbears) having been installed by the white authorities after uncooperative predecessors had been dethroned. On the other hand, chiefs were seen as continuing to play a significant role in the lives of rural African populations as custodians of customary law. Furthermore, as the political winds had begun to change, significant numbers of chiefs had started to look to the future by inclining towards explicit alignment with the incoming liberation movements, the most notable expression this being the formation of the Congress of Traditional Leaders of South Africa (CONTRALESA) in 1987. Its constitution dedicated itself to the eradication of Bantustans, winning back land 'stolen' under colonialism, and the creation of democracy. Liberation movement governments consequently had to decide how and whether to implement systems of local democracy, and how these might be combined with established systems of rural governance. Broadly, the answer was to erect a system of dual authority, whereby popularly elected local governments were granted responsibilities for delivery of services, while traditional leaders retained significant authority over the allocation of communal lands, administration of customary law and officiating over community functions. Within this context, it is possible to identify a significant drift towards a *de facto* if not *de jure* restoration of authority to the chiefs, both to compensate for failures of service delivery and to shore up the writ of liberation government rule in rural areas.

Colonial administration in Rhodesia had resulted in the imposition of order over imagined African chaos through the identification of 'tribes'. This often entailed 'working through a mishmash of ethnic affiliations to create "purer" and clearer tribal identities as the basis for tribal authorities'.[61] Prior to the British conquest, notes Mamdani, the Ndebele were not an ethnic group but a conglomeration of peoples under the Ndebele state. When the local Native Commissioner came to the realization that the Ndebele did not behave in the manner that they were supposed to, he borrowed from the Natal Native Code of 1891 to impose a tribal hierarchy. From the earliest days, therefore, the government assumed the authority to appoint traditional chiefs, and if need be, to remove them from office. Today, these powers of appointment and dismissal have been transferred to the President under section 111 of the Constitution of Zimbabwe and section 3 of the Chiefs and Headmen Act of 1992. Chiefs are incorporated into governmental structures through provincial Councils of Chiefs which, in turn, elect representatives to a national Council of Chiefs which provides a forum for interaction between traditional leaders and the Ministry of Local Government. The principal functions of the national Council is to make representations to the Ministry on behalf of people who live on communal land and to elect some eighteen chiefs to the Senate. However, neither provincial nor national councils have minimal policy impact upon either local or national governance, with even their traditional power to allocate land having been formally transferred to Rural District Councils, upon which chiefs' representatives are far outnumbered by elected councillors.[62]

---

[61] Mamdani, op. cit., 81.
[62] John Makumbe (2010), 'Local authorities and traditional leadership', in Jaap de Visser, Nico Steytler and Naison Machingauta (eds), *Local Government Reform in Zimbabwe*, Cape Town: Community Law Centre, University of the Western Cape, 87–100.

These formal limitations upon chiefly power are a reflection of ZANU-PF's perspective of the traditional leaders as having worked in close collaboration with the settler regime. Nonetheless, having seen their influence diminish in the immediate aftermath of independence, the chiefs have made a significant political comeback.

Makumbe dates this occurring in Zimbabwe from the early 1990s, when government began to lose popular support. Sensing defeat in the 2000 parliamentary elections, ZANU-PF 'suddenly remembered the chiefs'. Chiefs were already paid a salary by government, but now allowances were increased and electricity installed in their homes. Grateful for this unwonted generosity, chiefs helped make many rural areas no-go propositions for the opposition during the election campaign. Subsequently, traditional leaders have received numerous increases in their allowances, along with other favours such as their being provided with vehicles, concessionary rates on toll routes, diplomatic passports, and in some cases firearms for their protection. More recently, chiefs have called to be cut in on deals as representatives of their communities, notably regarding investment in mining.[63] Meanwhile, annual conferences of chiefs have become opportunities for ZANU-PF to lavish attention upon them in luxury hotels, in return for which the government has demanded appropriate enthusiasm. ZANU-PF has not been disappointed. During successive elections, the large majority of traditional leaders have worked closely alongside the party and security forces in pressuring local populations to vote for ZANU-PF, not least by denying food aid to villagers said to favour the opposition.[64] Despite provisions for their political neutrality in the GPA of 2008, annual meetings of chiefs have continued to declare their open support for ZANU-PF and for Mugabe as the party's candidate for President. Meanwhile, Mugabe has clung to the constitutional right to appoint and dismiss chiefs, and ZANU-PF has retained control over the Ministry of Local Government within the inclusive government.[65]

Not dissimilar if less extreme developments have occurred in Namibia. The independence constitution more or less ignored traditional authority. While providing for the establishment of a Council of Traditional Leaders, it acknowledged customary law but placed it under the constitution rather than under chiefs directly. The limited role envisaged for traditional leaders was a reflection of SWAPO's generally negative view about their role under apartheid and their identification with ethnic political structures. Indeed, SWAPO was reluctant to envisage any devolution of power, arguing the virtues of delivery of services directly by central government. However, under Western and opposition pressure, SWAPO conceded a process of limited decentralization, and in 1991 a Delimitation Commission announced that Namibia would be divided into thirteen regions, with borders demarcated according to geography and economy, thereby erasing the institutional architecture of the former homelands. In 1992, a Local Authorities Act led to the establishment of popularly elected Regional Councils (RCs) and local authorities, although these have remained overwhelmingly dependent upon central government financing and are closely supervised by the Ministry of Regional and Local Government. Little recognition

---

[63] *The Herald*, 25 February 2012.
[64] *ZimOnline*, 31 January 2007.
[65] Makumbe (2010), op. cit., 88–94.

was granted to the status of traditional leaders, whose powers (for instance, of detention) had been radically curtailed with the abolition of the homelands. However, matters were destined to change following the report of a presidential commission on traditional leaders which was established in 1991. When this reported later in the year, its conclusion was that 'the traditional system [was] not only necessary but also viable.' Subsequently, the passage of a Traditional Authorities Act in 1995 provided for the recognition of traditional leaders, although barring them from the simultaneous holding of traditional and state office. Thereafter, the government embarked upon a process of granting recognition to chiefs, with the large majority of those being recognized having held such positions before independence.[66]

The powers granted to traditional authorities were minimal and they were destined to operate under the shadow of RCs. Nonetheless, the scope of their influence has steadily increased. A further Act led to the establishment of the constitutionally required Council of Traditional Leaders in 1997, its major role being to advise the President regarding the utilization of communal land. A strong argument had been made by civil society groups at a National Land Conference in 1991 that the state should become owner of communal land, and that land boards should replace traditional leaders and their power to allocate customary land rights. However, strong resistance by traditional leaders led to the decision being postponed, before they largely won their case at another such conference held in 1996. Their authority to administer and allocate communal lands was thereafter confirmed by a Communal Land Reform Act of 2002, although newly created Land Boards would assume the right to allocate grants of land for commercial purposes. Allocations of land by traditional leaders, it is true, were to be ratified by Land Boards established by the Act, but the only grounds whereby ratification could be refused were of a technical nature. A year later, although a Community Courts Act set out a host of provisions to regulate traditional courts (inclusive of the rights of individuals to legal representation), it similarly confirmed the role of traditional leaders in the administration of customary law.[67]

Traditional leaders remain more constrained than their counterparts in Zimbabwe, not least because some of their number have lent support to various opposition parties which have accused SWAPO of discriminating against their regions (mostly in the south) and favouring Ovambo. In some areas, such as Ohangwena Region, party-chief relations remain tense, with local leaders of SWAPO accusing traditional leaders of having betrayed the liberation struggle by backing the RDP and labelling them 'traitors'.[68] In turn, there have been regular complaints made by Herero leaders that only 4 out of some 40 of them have been recognized by the government, with only those chiefs who had declared support for the ruling party gaining the nod of approval.[69] Nonetheless, the majority of chiefs have swung strongly behind the ruling party, lending

[66] Manfred Hinz (2008), 'Traditional governance and African customary law: Comparative observations from a Namibian perspective', http://www.kas.de/upload/auslandshomepage/namibia/..../hinz.pdf

[67] Eduard Gargallo (2010), 'Land, restitution and traditional authorities in Namibia's agrarian reform', 7th Congress of African Studies, Lisbon.

[68] *Namibian*, 4 June 2008.

[69] *Namrights*, 16 June 2003; *Namibian*, 18 January 2007.

their support during elections and generally working closely with government structures. As in Zimbabwe, this has seen them receiving enhanced material rewards in terms of allowances and gifts, which strengthens their commitment to the new status quo.[70]

Matters have been more complicated in South Africa, where many rural areas in the former homelands have become sites of conflict between elected local councillors and traditional leaders. During the run-up to the democratic transition, contestations between traditional leaders and groups in civil society, especially those mobilized by the South African National Civics Organization, had become intense, most often revolving around the control of land. However, little immediate guidance for resolving these issues was given by the Constitution. Chapter 12 recognized 'traditional leadership, according to customary law', yet guaranteed it no more than a ceremonial role, and laid down that cultural rights and customary law would be subject to the Bill of Rights. However, although under the constitution a wall-to-wall system of democratic local government was to be extended across all areas of the country, including areas falling under the jurisdiction of traditional authorities, newly elected councillors were to be taken aback when it turned out that their new transitional rural councils did not have the power to allocate land. The constitution had laid down that existing laws should remain in place until repealed, the outcome being that powers to allocate land continued to lie with the old tribal authorities, even while the responsibility for providing such services as electricity and water lay with the elected councils. Suffice it to say that while the government busied itself with the devising a major reorganization of local government (which by 2000 had seen the number of municipalities drastically reduced from 834 to 284), conflicts between traditional leaders and elected councillors continued to bedevil official plans for implementing an Integrated Sustainable Rural Development Strategy which largely omitted any role for the former, except as stakeholders alongside representatives of women and farm workers. However, the pendulum began to swing back in favour of traditional leaders, this initially signalled by a White Paper on Local Government of March 1998 which made bold assertions that traditional leadership should play a major role in development in local communities – this in contradiction to the RDP which had been emphatic in its insistence that this should be the task of democratically elected structures.[71]

The reasons for the shift backwards seemed to lie with government appreciation of the mayhem that could be caused in rural areas by truculent chiefs alongside a growing recognition of their potential political utility. It should be recalled that during the late 1980s and early 1990s, the UDF and ANC had engaged in violent turf battles with Inkatha-aligned chiefs. Given the emphasis upon reconciliation and the need to maintain the IFP-led coalition with the ANC in KwaZulu-Natal, it made sense to offer concessions to traditional leaders, especially in the context of their wider resistance to the democratization of rural local governance. This had already taken the form of a tactical alliance between

[70] Anna Nakambale (2009), 'Govt rolls out cars for traditional leaders', http://www.swapoparty. org/cars_for_traditional_leaders.html

[71] Lungisile Ntsebeza (2006), 'Rural development in South Africa: Tensions between democracy and traditional authority', in Vishnu Padayachee (ed.), *The Development Decade: Economic and Social Change in South Africa, 1994–2004*, Cape Town: HSRC Press, 444–60.

the ANC-aligned CONTRALESA and the IFP in the lead-up to the 1994 elections. Subsequently, too, the ANC had faced a significant challenge in the Eastern Cape from the UDM. This had been formed in 1997 by Bantu Holomisa, the popular former military leader of Transkei who, after taking a junior post in the new government in 1994, had been expelled from the ANC for a supposed breach of discipline. During the 1999 election campaign, the UDM threatened to drive a wedge between ANC and significant segments of the Eastern Cape chieftaincy. However, the UDM was easily outrun by Mandela's personal intervention into the provincial campaign and his assurances that chiefs had a major role to play in development. The ANC's persuasive powers were capped by announcements of major pay rises for the province's 6 paramounts, 221 chiefs, and the Transkei's 997 headmen.[72]

By now, the government was backtracking fast on its previous commitments to democratic local government in favour of what it described as 'cooperative governance'. This culminated in the passage of the Traditional Leadership and Governance Framework Act (TGLFA) and the Communal Land Rights Act in 2003. The former provided for the establishment of traditional councils for areas recognized as traditional communities, even while it recognized elected local councils as the primary form of local government in rural areas. These traditional councils would be composed of traditional authorities and their appointees, along with some 25 per cent of members who would be democratically elected. This figure was later increased to 40 per cent in face of civil society protests; even so, this still left chiefs enjoying a majority. The latter Act granted these largely unelected structures 'enormous and unprecedented' powers regarding the administration of communal land. While it received the strong backing of traditional leaders, it drew strident criticism from gender and land rights activists (including some ANC MPs) who argued that the Act was restoring an apartheid-era institution. Further, its implications were deeply discriminatory against women, for under customary law women were dependent on men and vulnerable to land loss on the death of or divorce by their husbands.[73]

The formal reconstitution of traditional authorities proceeded fast. By 2007, most traditional authorities in the Eastern Cape had already registered their traditional councils as required by the TGLFA, motivated by the prospect of getting their hands on a larger share of the development action in their areas. However, 'cooperative governance' seemed to go by the board, as in most cases, the supposedly elected councillors were simply nominated to traditional councils by chiefs, and if female representatives were included at all, they were often related to traditional leaders.

Struggles between traditional authorities and elected councils continued, contributing to alarming levels of dysfunction among both types of governance institutions in rural areas. In Eastern Cape, this meant that land in communal areas continued to be allocated, not by traditional councils, but by traditional leaders working through their headmen, as had been the case under apartheid. This did not prove wholly unpopular, for in contrast to the democratically elected institutions, which very often had become undermined by factionalism

---

[72] Roger Southall (1999), 'The struggle for a place called home: The ANC versus the UDM in the Eastern Cape', *Politikon*, 26: 2, 155–66.

[73] Ntsebeza, op. cit., 457.

and corruption, it was a practice that was familiar, predictable, and actually worked, notwithstanding the *de facto* entrenchment of chiefly power and the institutional disadvantages this carried for women.

Against this background, the government suffered a reverse when, responding to the arguments of democracy activists, the Constitutional Court declared on 10 May 2010 that the Communal Land Rights Act was unconstitutional and could no longer by implemented in its present form. The reasons it gave for its decision were that there had been inadequate consultation with local communities, the Act did not address the issue of tenure of security among rural residents, and furthermore, the notion of 'community' that the Act employed reproduced apartheid-style tribal authorities and placed too much control over land in the hands of traditional leaders. In response, the Minister of Land Affairs, Gugile Nkwinti, indicated that the government would reassess.[74] Nonetheless, despite this major setback, the government continued to pilot a Traditional Courts Bill through parliament.

The Traditional Courts Bill, if passed, would allow traditional leaders to constitute traditional courts, each presided over by the officially recognized senior chief or his delegate in each defined tribal area. Although it would dispense justice in terms of customary law, it would grant effective power to traditional leaders to decide what the law is on any particular issue, and would enable them, *inter alia*, to sentence offenders to forced labour, cancel their land rights, expel them from the community, impose tribal levies, settle disputes and decide on civil claims. The writ of the traditional court would extend to civil or criminal matters arising within the tribal area, whether those concerned were residents or not; there was to be no right to legal representation; and no recourse to appeal save on procedural grounds (thereby in effect creating separate legal systems for South Africans according to geographical area). Further, the Bill would entrench the subordination of rural women, for while they constitute the majority in communal areas, it would offer no mechanism for individuals to opt out of the purview of customary law.

The Traditional Courts Bill raised a storm of protest within civil society, condemned above all for its attempt to restore chiefly despotic power, to entrench the status of 'tribal areas' as quasi-Bantustans, and for strengthening patriarchy under the guise of tradition. Further, if passed, the Bill would seem to circumvent the quashing of the Communal Land Rights Act by the Constitutional Court by empowering the ministers of land affairs or justice to delegate powers to chiefs without enacting new laws.[75] As such, even if eventually amended, it was more than likely that a resultant Act would soon find its way before the Constitutional Court facing the strong possibility of being overturned as unconstitutional.

Why then would an ANC government formally committed to democracy and gender equality risk effectively re-enacting apartheid in rural areas in face of major political and legal challenges?

---

[74] Leslie Bank (2011), 'Bring back Kaiser Matanzima? Communal land, traditional leaders and the politics of nostalgia', in John Daniel, Prishani Naidoo, Devan Pillay and Roger Southall (eds), *New South Africa Review 2: New Paths, Old Compromises?* Johannesburg: Wits University Press, 132.

[75] *Mail & Guardian*, 3–9 February 2012; Noziwe Madlala-Routledge (2012), 'Scrap the "Bantustan" Traditional Courts Bill', Wolpe Dialogue, University of the Witwatersrand, 17 May.

The most convincing suggestion is that the ANC has moved beyond its suspicion of traditional leaders to embrace them as allies in consolidating its political control over the rural areas (scenes of widespread popular disaffection in the 1980s). The process of alliance-formation has been deliberate. At one level, the government has sought to restore the legitimacy of chiefs through a bureaucratic-historical process of weeding out claimants to traditional authority whose forbears were appointed by the apartheid regime in place of 'authentic' traditional leaders who had proved uncooperative. A Commission on Traditional Leadership Disputes and Claims, appointed under Justice Nhlapo in 2004 which reported in 2008, proceeded to recognize seven legitimate kingships or queenships, and another six whose status would come to an end at the death of the current incumbent.[76] Although the Commission (and its second initiative to probe lower layers of traditional leadership) has opened up a can of worms, those leaders whose status it has confirmed will, in effect, draw their legitimacy from government as much as from 'tradition', much as they did under apartheid. At another level, as noted, the ANC has complemented its raft of chief-friendly legislation by incorporating traditional leaders into government by granting them substantial salaries and other allowances. A chieftaincy whose loyalty can be assured will be one which can be relied upon to secure the obedience of a rural population rendered largely rightless by customary law, and whose security of livelihood is dictated by their access to social grants, and in whose award or withdrawal local chiefs can expect to play a crucial (if informal) role. Indeed, it has already become the pattern that during election campaigns, the ANC and the chiefs have taken to informing the residents of tribal areas that opposition parties are intent on taking their social grants away.[77] In Mamdani's terms, such rural dwellers have become 'subjects', their rights to citizenship under the constitution eroded by a mix of law, politics, and dependence upon government grants for survival.

In each case, of Zimbabwe, Namibia, and South Africa, the liberation governments have turned away (to a greater or lesser degree) from the promise of democracy for rural African populations in favour of a restoration of 'decentralised despotism'. Extending direct rule over rural areas has proved problematic, and governments have looked to the machinery of 'indirect rule' to secure political acquiescence. Rural populations have become reduced to voting fodder, with traditional leaders viewed as holding the keys to vote banks.

Liberation movements and the media: public broadcasting

The NLMs formally subscribed to the ideals of media freedom which were to be embedded in the democratic constitutions, yet they arrived in power much influenced by struggle notions that the media were either friends or foes, and were to prove deeply suspicious of media criticism.

Under colonialism and apartheid, the national broadcasters – the Rhodesian

---

[76] 'Statement by President J.G. Zuma on the findings and recommendations of the Commission on Traditional Leadership Disputes and Claims, Union Buildings, Pretoria', 29 July 2010.
[77] Bank, op. cit., 131–32.

Broadcasting Corporation and SABC – which had both enjoyed broadcasting monopolies, had been subject to heavy state control and had been used to convey their masters' voices against 'terrorism' and 'communism'. Consequently, democratic transitions provided the opportunity for opening the official airwaves to free political debate, while also allowing for privately owned satellite television and the internet to join in (and also to provide all sorts of entertainment which under prudish minority governments had been regarded as risqué). The attainment of democracy therefore promised a flowering of media diversity. However, the extent to which this has been realized has been severely compromised.

The temptation to maintain control over state media has been particularly great because it is radio and television, especially channels broadcasting in local languages, which have continued to provide the principal sources of information for the majority of the population in all three countries. The ZBC has remained by law the sole national radio and television broadcaster (although satellite TV and radio are accessed from South Africa by the small minority of individuals and hotels and bars which can afford them). The ZBC is formally required to provide reliable information and trustworthy news, but has consistently promoted the views of government and systematically favoured ZANU-PF, especially during election campaigns. Court orders to provide unbiased reportage have been ignored. ZBC, according to one source is 'practically propaganda' and 'eulogizes Mugabe'.[78] No surprise there, then. Yet even in Namibia, where SWAPO political domination is less oppressive, 'the NBC clearly sees one of its main functions as promoting government and to a lesser extent the ruling party. News broadcasts appear to use protocol as an overriding news value – with items being ordered according to whether they feature the President, the Prime Minister, ministers and so on.'[79] In contrast, the fate of the SABC has been more complicated.

Of the SABC's importance, there can be no doubt. By 2010, of the nearly 29 million radio listeners in South Africa, 20 million regularly tuned into one of the SABC's eighteen radio stations, while the SABC's three television channels were attracting more than 17 million adult viewers each day. Importantly, too, there has been long-standing debate about the appropriate role of a public broadcaster, and considerable support within the ANC and within civil society for quality reportage, free of major interests whether commercial or government, and the pursuit of an agenda aimed at empowering citizenship and deepening democracy. However, following the adoption of GEAR, the SABC was forced to cut back heavily upon its public mandate as the government slashed public funding and pushed it towards reliance on advertising and commercial sustainability. This led to a fight back waged by concerned elements of civil society for greater reliance on public funding and a move away from commercialization. However, this was to be countered by the government attempting to link increased public funding to greater official control over governance and content, even to the extent that – according to a Broadcasting Amendment Bill put forward in 2002 – the Minister of Communications would have the responsibility of approving all editorial policies of the SABC. Although this Bill was rebuffed in parliament and withdrawn, and although the ANC Polokwane

---

[78] 'BBC country profile: Zimbabwe media', BBC News, 20 November 2008.
[79] Hopwood op. cit., 100.

Conference in 2007 called for an increase in public funding, the role of the SABC remains heavily contested.[80]

The shift to commercialization may have had an extremely negative impact upon the quality of its programming, yet the SABC has nonetheless avoided the fate of the ZBC and NBC whose public broadcasting role has been reduced to relaying the thoughts and doings of government and ruling party, despite serial claims that the ANC has sought to place ANC loyalists on the SABC board, that its news broadcasts have been skewed towards promoting government objectives, and that during election campaigns, it has favoured the ANC.

Even so, the SABC has been far from immune from political interference between elections. Indeed, in recent years its board has become a battleground between different factions and interests, and has had major conflicts with top management. Much of this controversy has centred around 'transformation' (of personnel and programming) along with a dismal lack of financial controls and transparency. But in June 2006, events took a more sinister turn when, amidst the Mbeki-Zuma contestation, it was alleged in the *Sowetan* newspaper that the then Head of News, Snuki Zikalala, had blacklisted political commentators (all of them black) critical of the Mbeki government. This was then confirmed on air by the SABC's prime talkshow host, John Perlman. Chief Executive Officer Dali Mpofu responded by appointing a commission of inquiry chaired by his predecessor, Zwelakhe Sisulu, and promised that the final report would be released in full. However, when faced by a final report that was damning, Mpofu got cold feet.

The report stated that contrary to the Broadcasting Act and the SABC's editorial policies, there was clear evidence of blacklisting, while noting further that Zikalala's authoritarian leadership style had a chilling effect on journalist initiative.[81] With the backing of his board, Mpofu released only sanitized sections of the report, but the full report made its way to the *Mail & Guardian's* website. In the end, Perlman was disciplined and left the SABC, Zikalala continued as Head of News, and the SABC never officially released the report and never implemented its recommendations. Rather than moving towards a vision of 'citizenship empowerment', the public broadcaster was enmeshed in a culture of secrecy and lack of accountability. Although yet another Public Service Broadcasting Bill which had provided for a host of new powers over public broadcasting for the Minister of Communications was withdrawn in response to a further public outcry, the SABC remains permeable to internal struggles within the ANC and to government pressure to conform.

Liberation movements and the independent media

During the struggle for democracy the NLMs looked to the alternative media outlets that emerged to outwit regime media restrictions as their allies. As ANC

[80] Kate Skinner (2011), 'The South African Broadcasting Corporation: The creation and loss of a citizenship vision and the possibilities for building a new one', in Daniel et al. (eds), op. cit. 369–86.

[81] South African Broadcasting Corporation (2006), 'Commission of enquiry into blacklisting and related matters', 14 October, http:// www.mg.co.za

media official Victor Moche proclaimed in 1987: 'A sycophantic press is the most fertile breeding ground for tyranny.'[82]

Liberation was meant to bring political accountability alongside democracy: government was meant to be open to media scrutiny. The new mood found its fullest expression in South Africa, where the constitution gave extensive guarantees of individual and media freedom. For its part, the ANC was initially concerned to promote 'transformation' of the media, by which it meant primarily deracialization of its ownership, rather than imposing restrictions on what it might have to say. But once in power, the ANC soon discovered what all democratic governments find: that the media can become a scourge of incompetence and abuse of power.

As revelations of corruption and mismanagement increased from a trickle to a torrent, the impatience of the ANC with independent reporting began to grow, especially when divisions began to open up within the party prior to Polokwane (when the competing factions were feeding the press with titbits detrimental to their rivals). It had been easy enough for the Mbeki government to deploy loyalists to the SABC's senior management and to blacklist commentators hostile to the ANC. However, it was far, far more difficult to contain the constant flow of information embarrassing to the ANC which was to become the staple of the independent media, this ranging from detailed exposure of the sexual antics of Jacob Zuma through financial excesses by ministers to at times mind-numbing exposures of corruption. A united political elite confident of itself and its mission would have been able to rebuff and debate criticism, but an increasingly divided and insecure one came instead to regard the independent media as an unruly enemy: the media, ANC Youth League President Julius Malema declared, had become 'dangerous to the revolution'.[83]

ANC thinking was embodied in resolutions at Polokwane concerning 'the battle for ideas'. These railed against 'the slow pace of transformation' (i.e., change in ownership patterns) and declared that the party was faced with a 'major ideological offensive...whose key objective is the promotion of market fundamentalism, control of the media and the images it creates of a new democratic dispensation in order to retain old apartheid economic and social relations'. Further, the media often 'conducts itself to the detriment of the constitutional rights of others'. The conference therefore recommended that establishment of a Media Appeals Tribunal (MAT) should be considered with a view to balancing the right to freedom of expression against the rights to 'equality, privacy and human dignity for all'.[84] This proposal was subsequently (July 2010) taken up in a document on 'Media Transformation, Ownership and Diversity'. Declaring that the existing system of media self-regulation via a Press Ombudsman was not merely inadequate but self-interested, the document called for establishment of a MAT, 'supported by public funds and accountable to the people through parliament'. Parliament should also investigate the ownership of the print media to enable equitable participation in the media environment.

---

[82]   Cited in Mono Badela and David Niddrie (1989), 'Restrictions on the media', http://www. sahistory.org.za/archive/restrictions-media
[83]   *Sunday Times*, 8 August 2010.
[84]   ANC 52nd National Conference 2007 Resolutions: paras 88, 126–31.

The ANC's concerns about the lack of 'transformation' of the media were to some extent justified. Although newsrooms have become increasingly demographically representative, ownership of the South African newspaper market is dangerously concentrated, and is dominated by just four companies: Independent Newspapers, Avusa Ltd, Media 24 (owned largely by a multi-national, Naspers), and Caxton. The top three media organizations, Caxton, Media 24, and Independent Newspapers, own 47.1 per cent of the titles in circulation, with other newspapers owned either by regional groups or individuals. The only national newspapers that are not owned by the four big groups are the *Mail & Guardian* and the *New Age*. The former began life as the independent *Weekly Mail* newspaper, but struggled to survive before being taken over by the Guardian group in 1995. Subsequently, ownership of the majority of its shares was sold to Zimbabwean businessman Trevor Ncube (a strong critic of ZANU-PF) in 2002. The *New Age*, a recent product launched in 2010, with the ANC's strong blessing, promised a more balanced coverage of news and views than provided by the mainstream press, but has faced criticism that its purpose is to sing the praises of the ANC. Yet for all the legitimate concerns about ownership, and related fears that this was resulting in editorial content promoting 'common-sense' worldviews which prioritize the interests of those with power and money, it has been the press which has excelled at investigative journalism, breaking far more major stories about corruption, official incompetence, and struggles within the ANC than the electronic media. It was therefore ironic that most of the ire of the ANC was directed primarily at those newspaper groups that were, in black empowerment terms, fairly well transformed, namely Avusa and the *Mail & Guardian*.[85]

The government had on various occasions suggested that it might use its substantial adspend to influence content. This started with the threat of withdrawal of advertising after the *Sunday Times'* highly critical reporting on the Minister of Health, Manto Tshabalala-Msimang, in 2007, and subsequently, there was speculation that it would use its buying power to shift advertising to 'patriotic' media outlets like the SABC and *New Age*.[86] However, after Polokwane, the ANC opted for a much more frontal assault upon media freedom.

A first run at imposing 'responsibility' upon the media was made in 2008 with publication of a Protection of Information Bill, but this was reluctantly withdrawn following stinging criticism from civil society for being too vague and giving too much power to the executive. However, subsequently, alongside a proposal for a Media Tribunal, came a new Bill which, rather than being an improvement was regarded by many as worse, and as constituting a fundamental threat to democracy. Indeed, it evinced a marked similarity with the highly restrictive law passed by the Mugabe government when it was presented with the formation of the MDC in 1999.

The Mugabe government had never embraced media freedom in the initial fashion of its South African counterpart. True, it had abolished a law which had made it illegal for the media to report debates in Parliament, but it had

---

[85] Jane Duncan (2011), 'The print media transformation dilemma', in Daniel et al. (eds), op. cit., 345–68.
[86] *Mail & Guardian*, 29 October 2010.

retained the Law and Order Maintenance Act (LOMA) of the Smith government which had imposed heavy sanctions upon those publishing information deemed prejudicial to state security. Furthermore, although it adopted a media policy whose declared purpose was secure a shift from a minority-controlled media to one whose ownership was more reflective of Zimbabwean society and which would be non-partisan, its strategy rapidly degenerated into one of attempted control, symbolized by official domination of the ZBC. Thus, for instance, official restrictions worked to minimize reportage upon the Gukurahundi massacres. Yet thereafter, the government found itself confronted by an increasingly vigorous independent media, as the ZBC and the party's mouthpiece, *The Herald*, once the country's foremost newspaper, increasingly lost credibility.

The independent media had played a key role in opposing the government's unsuccessful campaign to impose single-party rule during the mid-80s. Thereafter, the appearance of a series of new titles, such as the *Daily News*, *Financial Gazette*, and *The Standard* fed the public with exposures of scandals, corruption, looting of state finances, and government abuses of human rights. The outcome, during the lead-up to the 2002 general election, when the government felt severely threatened, was the passage of the Access to Information and Protection of Privacy Act. This replaced LOMA in law, but mimicked Ian Smith in spirit, gagging the independent media. First, access to any information relating to cabinet or local government could only be granted by the head of a public body. Second, under the rubrics of 'Abuse of Freedom of Expression' and 'Abuse of Journalistic Privilege', any journalist publishing, or any person responsible for publication of, any statement 'threatening the interests of defence, public safety, public order, the economic interests of the state, public morality or public health' would be liable to a heavy fine or up to two to three years in jail respectively. In addition, alongside a host of other restrictions, the Act established a Media and Information Commission which would register the mass media, consider applications for accreditation as journalists, and conduct investigations to ensure compliance with the Act.[87]

It was not long before the government closed down various news outlets, including the *Daily News*, and imposed bans upon the BBC, CNN, Sky, and a host of other Western broadcasting stations. As official repression of the media grew, many Zimbabwean journalists fled to neighbouring countries where they established online news sites such as Sokwanele, which could be accessed from within Zimbabwe because of the government's limited ability to control the internet. While these provided detailed coverage of the emerging opposition and a diet of items highly critical of the government, they remained of limited influence, as only a small minority of the population had access to them. According to Reporters without Borders, the media was subject to extensive 'surveillance, threats, imprisonment, censorship, blackmail, abuse of power and denial of justice'.[88]

The need for a facade of media freedom led to some relaxation of restrictions during the 2008 elections (even though government-controlled media remained terribly skewed). Furthermore, the formation of the inclusive govern-

[87] Republic of Zimbabwe, Access to Information and Protection of Privacy Act, 2002. Esp. paras. 14, 38, 64, and 80.
[88] Reporters without Borders, Press Freedom Index, 2009.

ment saw the return of certain foreign broadcasters, a reappearance of previously banned titles, and the formation of Zimbabwe Journalists for Human Rights to defend media freedom. Reporters without Borders now recorded a 'slight improvement' in media freedoms, and increased its ranking of Zimbabwe to 136th out of 175 states in terms of media freedom in 2009, compared to 151st in 2010. Even so, a host of *de facto* restrictions remained, while the ZBC and other ZANU-PF-dominated outlets remain little more than sources of pro-Mugabe propaganda. Critically, ZANU-PF secured the appointment of Tafataona Mahoso, dubbed in opposition circles the 'media hangman' for his role in closing down opposition newspapers when he was chairperson of the Media Information Commission, to lead a newly created Zimbabwe Media Commission, which had the responsibility of accrediting foreign journalists.[89]

Even allowing for known sympathies within certain top echelons of the ANC for ZANU-PF, it was somewhat surprising that the proposed Freedom of Information Bill appeared to follow the discredited example of Zimbabwe. Nonetheless, for all the ANC's formal commitments, it did just that. Consider the facts.

First, the second run of the Bill signalled the intent to pass a law whose impact would be to impose comprehensive restrictions upon the independent media. The government implied that the law's most alarming threats would be kept in reserve, only to be hauled out in the interests of 'national security'. Yet, as was demonstrated under apartheid, the mainstream media has an enormous capacity for self-censorship if its survival and profits are at stake.

Second, the Bill introduced many features of its Zimbabwean counterpart. These included the introduction of an extensive system of classification of official information by heads of 'organs of state' (national and provincial ministries, local government, and parastatals, perhaps even universities, etc) whose effect would be to restrict the right to access information in the name of the national interest, this sweepingly defined as all matters related to 'the advancement of the public good' and to 'the protection and preservation of all things owned or maintained for the public by the state'.[90] Any person unlawfully communicating such information would be liable to imprisonment for periods between three to twenty-five years, according to the seriousness of the offence.

Third, the publication of the draft Bill was prefaced by the arrest of Mzilikazi wa Afrika, a journalist who had recently written an exposé of the approval by Police Commissioner Bheki Cele of a R500 million deal to rent the Sanlam Centre in the middle of Pretoria from a property company owned by a prominent businessman, Roux Shabangu , for a new police headquarters. This action was in violation of Treasury regulations that all contracts over R500,000 must go out to tender. Wa Afrika was charged with fraud and forgery alongside Victor Mlimi, a local councillor in Mombela, Mpumalanga province, relating to the publication of a fake letter of resignation by David Mabuza, the Mpumalanga premier. Mabuza presided over a province wracked by alleged corruption, and was under media suspicion of involvement in a number of killings. Indeed, at least one provincial journalist was under round-the-clock protection for inconvenient probing. Yet following wa Afrika's arrest it came to light that Mabuza

---

[89] *The Zimbabwean*, 24 May 2010.
[90] Republic of South Africa, Protection of Information Bill 2010, Ch.5, para 11.

himself had lodged criminal charges of fraud and defeating the ends of justice against wa Afrika and Mlimi, apparently prompting the arrest, and that his own staff had played a key role in tipping off journalists about the existence of this fake letter.[91] The conclusion drawn by the press was that wa Afrika's arrest formed part of a pattern of intimidation against crusading journalists.

Fourth, the proposed MAT looked uncannily like the Zimbabwean Media Commission. As with the Protection of Information Bill, its justification was made in Orwellian terms, with duplicitous words put forward by the ANC promising protection of freedom yet threatening the reverse.

The ANC's proposals met with widespread outrage, internationally as well as domestically. Editors of all the leading newspapers launched a campaign against any attempt to curtail freedom of expression and the free flow of information. Critics labelled the Bill 'draconian', the death of investigative journalism and a frontal assault upon democracy. Analysts argued that the proposals were being pushed by politicians determined to stem the flow of stories about corruption, by a party frightened that its support base was eroding, and by a government that wanted to muddy the waters by bemoaning the state of 'media transformation'. Spokespersons for the South African National Editors' Forum Media Freedom Committee insisted that the prevailing system whereby the media regulated itself had proved robust, and that the number of complaints that had been referred by those offended by what the press had published to the Public Protector had been far less than in comparable countries. Dramatically, too, public criticisms of the proposals were made from within the ANC, notably by those icons of the struggle, Kader Asmal and Ronnie Kasrils (although, as by now both were former ministers largely associated with the Mbeki era, their influence was waning). Equally significant was the formation of a Right2Know campaign, backed by 400 civil society organizations and social movements. Furthermore, thousands of individuals signed a petition protesting against the 'Secrecy Bill', mobilized public demonstrations, inclusive of a candlelight vigil outside the Constitutional Court.[92] Across the road from parliament, a church displayed a large notice: 'The Truth will set you free. Say "No" to the Secrecy Bill!'

Shaken by the criticism and by widespread speculation that any Act based on the draft Bill would be thrown out by the Constitutional Court, the ANC returned the proposals to parliament. This saved it from immediate embarrassment, for in September 2011 South Africa was due to sign an Open Government Declaration in New York with whose provisions the Bill was in conflict.[93] Subsequently, after a High Court ruled that an investigative journalist was not required to reveal his sources, the ANC appeared to step back from its more draconian proposals for controlling the print (and digital) media. It extended a cautious welcome to the industry's own proposals for a press council composed of both public and industry representatives which would have power to impose fines upon those deemed to have offended press freedoms.[94] Nonetheless, by this time the government had announced its intentions to proceed with a Bill which

[91] *Sunday Times*, 1 August 2010.
[92] *Mail & Guardian*, 5–11 August 2010.
[93] *Star*, 20 September 2011.
[94] *Business Day*, 2 May 2012.

would disallow a 'public interest' defence for the disclosure of public information, virtually ensuring that whatever version of the Bill was eventually passed
it would end up being challenged in the Constitutional Court.[95] When during
2011 and early 2012, parliament held public hearings on the Bill, ANC MPs
proved deeply hostile to those opposing the Bill, some accusing the NGOs
concerned of being agents of imperialism, with others denying them the right
to speak.[96]

At the time of writing, the battle around the Protection of Information Bill
remains unresolved. Disturbingly, it indicated that the ANC was determined to
use as expansive a definition of national security as it could get away with in
order to narrow the scope for exposure of corruption and incompetence in
government.[97] Were the ANC to succeed in its drive to muzzle media freedom,
it would set an example which SWAPO might want to follow. Equally, however,
the episode demonstrates the potential for opposition across class and racial
lines from civil society around single issues of immense importance to the democratic freedoms for which the struggle against apartheid was fought; and it may
yet further illustrate the importance of the Constitutional Court in the defence
of democracy.

NLMs in power: machines against society?

In Zimbabwe, Namibia, and South Africa, the liberation movements have
sought to consolidate their political power not merely through dominance of
the electoral arena but by extending control over trade unions, civil society,
rural populations, and the media. The means by which they have done so have
varied according to the degree of diversity of the societies they have faced, as
well as by the extent to which constitutional rule and important freedoms have
been upheld by independent forces within those societies. Where, as in
Zimbabwe, the political machinery of the ruling party has to all intents and
purposes become merged with the military, the assault that has followed upon
oppositional groups and civil society has been overwhelmingly coercive, an
outcome which the MDC within the transitional government is having huge
difficulty in reversing. Where, as in Namibia and South Africa, the ruling parties
have sought to extend their hegemony through largely political means of domination, internal struggles within the parties (especially within the ANC) have
played a significant role in containing governmental power alongside the more
obviously oppositional roles played by civil society. A suggestion that follows is
that containment of the liberation movement's political machines rests significantly upon the linkages which opposition political parties have been able to
forge with key elements of civil society. Without backing by the ZCTU and civil
society organizations, the MDC would never have been able to pose the chal-

---

[95] *Star,* 2 September 2011; *Business Day,* 20 September 2011.
[96] *Star,* 2 April 2012.
[97] By August 2011, the ANC had made the 'concession' that only the intelligence, security, and
police services would have the power to classify state information. However, the Right2Know
campaign complained that the concession was nullified by a provision in the revised Bill whereby
other state organs could be granted permission by the State Security Minister to declare information secret if they provided 'good cause'. *Business Day,* 30 August 2011.

lenge to ZANU-PF that it has. Effectively incorporated within SWAPO, the trade union movement has left civil society relatively powerless. Allied to the ANC yet locked into a highly ambiguous relationship with it, COSATU, for the moment, leaves major confrontations with the ruling party to social movements and to a political opposition from which the latter are divorced.

8.
Liberation Movements and Economic Transformation

Liberation movements in power have been faced by the challenge of seeking to 'transform' the economies over which they preside, that is, to render them more productive, to 'deracialize' them, and to make them more equal in terms of distribution of ownership, employment, opportunity, and reward. Sadly, there is wide agreement that these goals have not been met. Even aside from the economic disaster that has overtaken Zimbabwe, there are major concerns about limited rates of growth in South Africa and Namibia, alongside the persistence of horrifyingly high levels of unemployment, poverty, and inequality. Nonetheless, while it is vital to stress the limits to economic liberation, it is equally important to ask why South Africa and Namibia have fared so considerably better than Zimbabwe. In this regard, this chapter will focus upon how the NLMs have tackled three defining themes: (i) business-state relations; (ii) black economic empowerment; and (iii) land reform and how their policies have impacted on the potential for 'transformation'.

Business-state relations under liberation movement governments

Business-state relations (BSRs) are critical to development prospects in an interconnected, global, capitalist economy. With states competing against each other for wealth, they seek to parlay their resources and labour for the capital, technology, expertise, and access to global markets that are available from transnational companies.[1] Productive BSRs therefore require negotiations, with key issues being how firms perceive states, how states perceive firms, what is bargained for and the relative strength of either party.[2] Governments at the global periphery which seek to pursue redistributional strategies have little choice but to seek class compromise: concessions from capital to enable distribution of economic surplus to coalitions of middle class, workers, peasants, and the wider poor, and concessions from those coalitions to provide adequate conditions of profitability for business. However, social contracts tend to be fragile. Although state elites usually believe that unrestricted free markets breed inequality, they need to maintain business confidence, for if they do not, they face capital flight and falling revenue. Further, the power of the global financial institutions and of transnational corporations has ensured that redistributive governments

---

[1] John Stopford and Susan Strange (1991), *Rival States, Rival Firms: Competition for World Market Shares*, Cambridge: Cambridge University Press.
[2] Susan Strange (1992), 'States, firms and diplomacy', *International Affairs*, 68: 1, 1–16.

'are tightly constrained in pursuing their goals insofar as class compromises must reassure capital by establishing strict limits to reform'.[3]

Scott Taylor argues for the virtues of 'reform coalitions', whereby alliances of public and private sector interests take joint action to exploit mutual interest. They are best organized in forums which bring business and state together, and are sites of negotiation in which public and private partners may be of highly unequal strength (although roughly equal power relationships are likely to be beneficial). Where they work, they require give and take, for just as the state is not necessarily capable of taking wise decisions about the economy, business is likely to be more concerned with its immediate interests than the general welfare of society. By contrast, BSRs that privilege a bureaucratic state bourgeoisie and/or particular corporate elites at the expense of growth-producing policies fall outside the definition of a 'reform coalition'.[4] To be sure, reform coalitions are not necessarily a prerequisite for growth, as demonstrated by contemporary high rates of resource-driven expansion of numerous African economies; nor are they magic bullets for development, especially where reform includes strong doses of neo-liberal orthodoxy (such as drastic cutbacks in public spending and safety nets for the poor). Nonetheless, they can be vital components of late development, and the extent to which they have proved operational provides valuable clues in southern Africa where the incoming NLMs all faced strong business sectors which had enjoyed strong relationships with white minority governments.[5]

Collaborative BSRs in South Africa and Namibia

Taylor views the ANC and big business as initially forging a highly functional reform coalition. The political transition was complemented by a deal in which business built alliances with elements of the incoming ANC, while the latter committed itself to market economics and abandoned plans for nationalization. However, it was not just that the ANC abandoned the RDP for GEAR. It was also that the ANC negotiated the development of institutional frameworks for dialogue, including NEDLAC, as well as the establishment of less formal networks, all of which reinforced business power. These were embedded in pre-existing business associations, notably the South African Chamber of Business (SACOB), die Afrikaanse Handelsinstituut (AHI), the National African Feder-ated Chamber of Commerce (NAFCOC), Business Unity South Africa (BUSA), and the South Africa Foundation (SAF), with key conglomerates backing such institutions by acting as important intermediaries with the state.

Overall, the ANC proved very willing to accommodate to business and capi-talism, notwithstanding its alliance with COSATU and the SACP. Not least of the reasons was its lack of experience in dealing with business actors, although more important was the conversion of key elites to orthodox capitalist economics via interactions with big business and the international financial institutions.[6]

---

[3] Richard Sandbrook, Marc Edelman, Patrick Heller and Judith Teichman (2007), *Social Democ-racy in the Global Periphery: Origins, Challenges, Prospects*, Cambridge: Cambridge University Press, 23.

[4] Scott Taylor (2007), *Business and the State in Southern Africa: The Politics of Economic Reform*, Boulder, London: Lynne Rienner Publishers.

[5] Ibid., 220.

[6] Ibid., 166; Antoinette Handley (2005), 'Business, government and economic policy-making in the new South Africa, 1990–2000', *Journal of Modern African Studies*, 43: 2, 211–39.

NEDLAC (launched in February 1995) played a vital role in bringing together labour, business, and the state and facilitating economic reform whilst linking it to goals of employment creation, equity, and participation by all sectors in the envisaged reconstruction process. In particular, it played a key role in formulating landmark labour laws – the LRA of 1995, the BCEA (1997), and the Employment Equity Act (1998) – which gave COSATU a major stake in the overall transitional programme. Yet NEDLAC's importance declined following the government's adoption of GEAR, as large-scale business acquired greater influence, exercised through associations such as the Big Business Working Group, Black Business Working Group, and Commercial Agriculture Working Group, all established in 1999. This occurred notwithstanding divisions which emerged between large-scale and smaller business interests, and more particularly between financial and mining capital as opposed to manufacturing capital, as the latter became increasingly exposed to international competition. Such divisions seriously undermined collective action by overarching business associations and played to a greater centrality of the state's relationship with the conglomerates, with smaller firms and business associations still having their voice heard, but nonetheless enjoying only an outer orbit of access. However, overall, GEAR deepened the government's dependence on large-scale capital while enfeebling NEDLAC, while at the same time, paradoxically, the government's confidence in its economic abilities increased. To be sure, there remained tensions between business and the state, not least because smaller businesses and import-sensitive sectors in manufacturing suffered adverse consequences from tight monetary policy and tariff reductions. Nonetheless, despite strains, the most powerful business actors continued to evince high levels of confidence in the ANC's economic policies as a whole. Even if the levels of growth were limited, they remained relatively constant, and provided a reasonable surplus for the government to redistribute social transfers to core elements of its constituency.[7]

However, business confidence was sapped by a distancing of relationships between business and government which became increasingly evident under Jacob Zuma. In considerable part, large-scale business was itself to blame, on several counts: for a widespread failure to take 'transformation' seriously so that by as late as 2010, senior management was still predominantly white (64 per cent versus 17.6 per cent for Africans); a widespread complacency (if not arrogance) regarding the pro-business macro-economic policy and a blatant disregard for the lot of the unemployed and the poor; for continuous collusion in oligopolistic behaviour and pricing in sectors ranging from the production and sale of bread through to construction; and not least, the marked tendency to lionize massive remuneration and retention packages for senior executives whilst deploring trade union demands for increased wages for workers.[8] Unsurprisingly, a 2012 survey indicated a slump in the decline of public perceptions of business leaders as good 'corporate citizens', this seen as weakening 'a critical pillar of stability in South Africa'.[9]

---

[7] Taylor, op. cit., 174–89.
[8] Ann Crotty and Renee Bonorchis (2006), *Executive Pay in South Africa: Who Gets What and Why?* Cape Town: Double Storey.
[9] *Business Report*, 10 May 2012.

During his early years in office, Zuma largely ignored business, which felt increasingly sidelined, and the early promise of corporatist institutions such as NEDLAC had long descended into mutual acrimony between business and unions, as social dialogue gave way to zero-sum negotiations.[10] It was in this context that, after his ascension to the ANC Youth League leadership in 2008, Julius Malema was to mobilize populist pressures for nationalization of the mines and other national assets, alongside calling for radical redistribution of the land. It may well be that his ultimate objective was 'control of the ANC',[11] but in the process his direction of virulent complaints at the still overwhelmingly white business establishment rocked business confidence and frightened foreign investors. While Michael Spicer, CEO of BUSA, could complain that there was no such thing as government – only 'a bunch of factions with different agendas' – and that business should fight its corner more effectively,[12] government and the business community were propelled by the siren calls from trade unionists about intensifying class war and their demands for urgent discussions about a return to social dialogue.[13] Relations remained systematically antagonistic, with business lamenting government regulation and 'inflexible labour laws' as disincentives to investment. Nonetheless, when the chips were down, for all its talk of the need for transformation, the government stood committed to courting corporate capital. An ANC study group headed off the debate about nationalization by warning of the massive financial costs (while asserting the need for a 'resource tax' and a state mining company) while the government's major economic decisions – notably its approval of the construction of six nuclear power stations and its backing for hydraulic fracturing ('fracking') to extract shale gas from the ecologically fragile Karoo – signified its continuing dedication to a strategy which reinforced the fundamentals of the MEC.

The incoming SWAPO government was destined in many ways to await transitional developments in South Africa and thereafter to follow in the ANC's slipstream, even while anticipating the LRA in South Africa with the passage of its own equivalent, embodying highly progressive provisions, in 1992.[14] By this time, it had declared independence from the Johannesburg Stock Exchange by assisting in the creation of a Namibian counterpart to encourage foreign investment (allowing dual listing), while steadily reducing the general corporate tax rate from 42 per cent in 1990 to 35 per cent by 1995, before undertaking successive revisions of the tax regime.[15]

Central to the tenor of BSRs was the new government's negotiations with the mining companies. The mining industry concentrated on the production of copper by the Tsumeb Corporation, uranium by Rossing Uranium, and diamonds by Consolidated Diamond Mines (CDM). Together these firms

[10] *Business Day*, 4 August 2011.
[11] Fiona Forde (2011), *An Inconvenient Youth: Julius Malema and the 'New' ANC*, Johannesburg: Picador Africa, 209.
[12] *Sunday Times*, 21 August 2011.
[13] *Business Report*, 23 September 2011.
[14] Martin Sycholt and Gilton Klerck (1997), 'The state and labour relations: Walking the tightrope between corporatism and neo-liberalism', in Gilton Klerck, Andrew Murray and Martin Sycholt (eds), *Continuity and Change: Labour Relations in Independent Namibia*, Windhoek: Gambsberg Macmillan, 79–115.
[15] Robin Sherbourne (2010), *Guide to the Namibian Economy 2010*, Windhoek: Institute for Public Policy Research, 139–40.

accounted for nearly 95 per cent of mineral production and held the rights to around 85 per cent of mineral assets. The largest of these was CDM, owned by De Beers, which as well as being a major shareholder in Tsumeb, mined 30 per cent of the world's diamonds, and headed the Central Selling Organization (CSO), the cartel which was responsible for the sale of between 75 and 80 per cent of the world's diamonds. SWAPO's dealings with De Beers were therefore going to be central to its relations with business.[16]

SWAPO's 1989 election manifesto proposed a minerals policy which would allow for partnership with foreign mining corporations in exchange for fair returns for the Namibian people. However, in 1990, the passage of the Namibian Foreign Investment Act offered protection against state expropriation but reserved to the state the right to acquire an interest in any venture for which it granted a licence or otherwise authorized foreign investors to exploit natural resources. Thereafter, the government created a Ministry of Mines and Energy which set out to restructure the legal environment for mining. One outcome was the Minerals (Mining and Exploration) Act of 1992, which allowed the state to seek a minority equity stake in all new projects. Another was the opening of negotiations with De Beers to enable the state to claim a degree of control over CDM.[17]

The result was a November 1994 agreement to the establishment the Namdeb Diamond Corporation Pty Ltd, whose ownership was divided 50-50 between the state and De Beers. This was proclaimed the successor to CDM and sole controller of the latter's diamond assets. For De Beers, the creation of Namdeb was advantageous in that it secured a long-term right to market Namibia's diamonds and ensured that it retained managerial control of operations. At the same time, the state would be required to pay half of all Namdeb's future investments in diamond mining and production. For the government, the deal secured the state 50 per cent ownership of the country's most profitable enterprise without a significant outlay of capital (ownership was to be paid for by future profits), while simultaneously signalling to SWAPO's supporters the party's commitment to state ownership. While the results proved to be mixed (the state received assured revenues but was unable to slow the decline of Namdeb's labour force from an original 6,500 to under 3,000 in 2008), the arrangement provided the framework for the shift from depleting land-based and inshore diamond operations to offshore diamond production, for which De Beers technology and capital remain a fundamental requirement.[18] It also led to the establishment, in 1998, of a diamond-cutting and polishing firm, NamGem, and in 2007, of the Namibia Diamond Trading Company, again owned jointly by the state and De Beers. Overall, argues Sherbourne, Namdeb has proved itself as a 'reliable and innovative mining company critical to the economy', even though from September 2008, it was hit hard by the global crisis.[19] Further, the engagement with De Beers demonstrated a marked increase in the state's ability to deal with business,[20]

---

[16] Donald Kempton and Roni du Preez (1997), 'Namibian-De Beers state-firm relations: Cooperation and conflict', *Journal of Southern African Studies*, 23: 4, 585–613.
[17] Ibid., 599–600.
[18] Sherbourne, op. cit., 145–50.
[19] Ibid., 149.
[20] Kempton and Du Preez, op. cit., 613.

although as in South Africa, this masked a tendency to favour corporations involved in minerals and energy over interests promising greater diversification.[21]

While Taylor is correct in arguing that cooperative BSRs are essential for the successful functioning of a capitalist economy, his emphasis underplays the extent to which in the contemporary era such cooperation is constructed upon measures taken to render economies more 'open' and globally competitive. By 2009–10, South Africa was ranked 45th and Namibia 74th out of 134 countries rated according to the World Economic Forum's Global Competitive Index for that year, with the former listed as the highest ranked in Africa. Despite incessant complaints by business about growing government requirements (and for small business, especially, 'red tape'), the contrast with Zimbabwe is as remarkable as it is notorious.

From cooperation to conflict: BSRs in Zimbabwe

Before and during UDI, business associations in mining, commercial agriculture, and manufacturing had made substantial input into state policy-making and had received selective incentives from the state. However, independence inaugurated a period of uncertainty. Although the new constitution enshrined property rights, business actors were prone to fears about economic redistribution and saw themselves as potentially vulnerable to an emergent political class. Ironically, however, 'the constraints on the state were regarded as inviolable by the ZANU regime'.[22] The latter was unwilling to put its socialist rhetoric into practice, cognizant that it was heavily dependent upon the knowledge and capital of white business. In effect, ZANU-PF forged a 'strategic alliance with white capital that preserved and promoted privilege, setting the stage for an elite cooption process' (while preserving the bogey of racial politics to be played at a later stage).[23] However, the strength of the state relative to business was to increase over time as the government pursued the strategy of economic liberalization which, ironically, key business groupings were influential in shaping.

The problems that confronted Zimbabwe by the late 1980s adversely affected business: the overvalued currency hit exports, foreign exchange shortages made the financing of outdated UDI infrastructure difficult, government spending fuelled inflation while imposing price controls, and so on. The Confederation of Zimbabwean Industries (CZI), the Chamber of Mines and the Commercial Farmers' Union (CFU) began to press for economic reform (albeit having different objectives and certain fears about the outcome). Crucially, they found an ally in Bernard Chidzero, Minister of Finance from 1982 to 1995, who served as the major conduit for selling liberalization to his ZANU-PF colleagues, among them Robert Mugabe, who while sceptical, acknowledged his government's lack of economic expertise. However, even as ZANU-PF moved towards neo-liberal reform, the state became increasingly reliant upon white business

---

[21] The government seems inclined to favour a R12 billion proposal to mine phosphates from the sea (to save money spent on importing chemicals for the uranium-mining industry) despite prospective damage to the tourism and fishing industries, *Mail & Guardian*, 28 October–3 November 2011.

[22] Taylor, op. cit., 107.

[23] Martin Dawson and Tim Kelsall (2012), 'Anti-developmental patrimonialism in Zimbabwe', *Journal of Contemporary African Studies*, 30: 1, 49–66.

associations, with bodies such as CZI, Zimbabwe National Chambers of Commerce (ZNCC), and CFU all making policy contributions on how structural adjustment should be best implemented. Taylor views the period between 1987, when farmers and manufacturers had started lobbying in favour of liberalization, and early 1991, when the government launched ESAP, as the apex of BSRs in Zimbabwe. Even so, the 'reform coalition' was less institutionalized and more pluralist than in South Africa, for while the Zimbabwe Association of Business Organizations (ZABO) sought to provide an overarching voice, business associations actually preferred to make representations to government along sectoral lines. This was to undermine their collective strength and work to the advantage of a government whose state power became increasingly ascendant following the adoption of ESAP.[24]

Major problems were incurred by the implementation of ESAP more rapidly than the IMF's programme required. The legacy of protectionism and subsidization inherited from UDI rendered manufacturing peculiarly uncompetitive. CZI officials had believed that trade liberalization would allow free access to import industrial inputs and boost exports, but Zimbabwean firms proved woefully unprepared. Import quotas had been dropped and foreign exchange controls had been virtually dismantled by mid-1994, leaving the UDI-era tariff regime as the only means of protection for domestic industries. While business leaders supported the government's move to reduce average tariffs to 30 per cent by 1995, they advocated a differentiated tariff structure in which imported goods would be classified as finished, partial or raw materials. When tariffs were dropped without this rationalization, domestic industries were damagingly exposed to external competition. However, when business leaders appealed to government to reclassify tariffs, they were met with indifference. Not least of the reasons was that government surcharges on imports provided significant revenues. Equally importantly, there was a growing appetite among ZANU-PF politicians for imported luxury goods, even while this impacted severely upon local industry. Although government eventually altered tariff structures in March 1997, it was too late for as many as 40 textile companies which been forced to close their doors. As ESAP adversely affected firms in especially textiles, clothing, footwear, and the metals industry, so CZI lost members and institutional strength, and along with it the capacity to access government.[25] In any case, by this time, ZANU-PF was far more concerned with preying on business for 'rents' than ensuring the productivity of the capitalist sector, rendering it more profitable to trade than to produce.[26]

Significantly, too, the impact of ESAP was to make the Ministry of Finance the site of economic and industrial policy at the expense of the Ministry of Industry and Commerce (with which the CZI had traditionally engaged). Further, with the retirement of Chidzero in 1995, the economic liberalizers within government lost their champion amidst declining enthusiasm within ZANU-PF for a programme which was failing to deliver promised results. Meanwhile, the ruling party was facing increasing political difficulties as economic woes were mounting – and in any case, ESAP severely threatened ZANU-PF hegemony by targeting state spending and the bureaucracy. Political power

[24] Taylor, op. cit., 111–12.
[25] Ibid., 112–15.
[26] Dawson and Kelsall, op. cit.

came to trump development concerns, while fragmentation within the business community diffused its collective strength.[27]

The exception to this trend was the retention of the influence, for the moment, of the white farmers. The CFU had embraced market liberalization and its members seized the opportunities it provided to increase exports: whereas agriculture provided 36.4 per cent of exports in 1990, this rose to 52 per cent in 2002 (whereas manufacturing exports had collapsed from 31.2 per cent to 18.6 per cent over the same period). ESAP therefore reinforced the CFU's position, not least because while the state overall held back on the privatization of state-owned enterprises, those that it did privatize it sold – despite objections by African commercial farmers' associations – to CFU-related agricultural bodies which were the only domestic private-sector organizations with the capacity, resources, and expertise to invest in former agricultural parastatals such as marketing boards. Paradoxically, therefore, despite a growing rhetoric about race and agriculture, the government's actions actually strengthened the position of the white farming community. The relationship was useful to ZANU-PF: economically, because of white agriculture's contribution to exports and downstream manufacturing (such as food processing), as well as its employment of some 350,000 labourers; politically, because the fewer than 4,000 farmers represented by the CFU were not perceived as a threat to ZANU-PF political domination. Already, too, some leading members of ZANU-PF were acquiring large-scale farms, although because the CFU was overwhelmingly a white organization, Taylor discounts the notion of an emergent interest along class lines. Yet by 2004, the 'reform coalition' between the state and the CFU had been destroyed.

Again it was exogeneous factors that were largely responsible. ZANU-PFs political problems had led to use of incendiary rhetoric about the land issue during the 1995 parliamentary and the 1996 presidential elections, as Mugabe sought to distract popular attention from ZANU-PF's failings. Yet threats of land seizures swiftly died down until, from August 1997, the war veterans mobilized, sending shock waves throughout the ruling party. Mugabe's concession of pensions to the war veterans had major consequences, as noted in Chapter 4. Determined to head off threats to ZANU-PF's claim to be the party of liberation, Mugabe revived earlier pledges to implement land reform through the seizure and subdivision of white farms. In early November 1997, he announced plans for the appropriation of 1,500 farms, threatening the abolition of constitutional safeguards for property, and ignoring international and market reaction (which led to the swift collapse of the Zimbabwean dollar).

The CFU issued dire warnings, yet sought as far as possible to maintain a non-confrontational strategy. Hitherto, aware of its political vulnerability, the CFU had sought to avoid attacks on government, and even now, it adhered to this strategy. Previous threats against the farmers issued by ZANU-PF had come to nothing, and indeed, in the wake of the pronouncements made in 1997, no farms were forcibly acquired. In any case, the CFU deemed that ultimately it had the law on its side and that it could resort to the courts. However, this was to reckon without the rapidly changing political situation.

By 1999, ZANU-PF was confronting growing opposition from the ZCTU,

---

[27] Ibid.,116–19.

civil society, and even some within the normally politically quiescent business community, resulting in the formation of the MDC. Meanwhile, although the war veterans had been contained within ZANU-PF, they remained politically restive. At a time when ZANU-PF's commitment to liberalization had weakened, any remaining commitment to maintaining a collaborative relationship with the CFU had high political costs. With the outbreak of farm seizures by war veterans from February 2000, and the government's adoption of its fast track land reform programme, the die was cast, and the CFU – fatally split between those who wanted a more confrontational approach to government and those who favoured appeasement – increasingly lost members, clout, and influence. By 2004, there were only around 300 members of the CFU who were still actively farming, and it was but a shadow of its former self.[28]

In Zimbabwe, neo-liberalism had originally facilitated the construction of a reform coalition by steering the state towards a more open, export-oriented economy, yet ironically its pursuit undermined a white, multi-national business-state coalition which was always vulnerable and whose political utility to ZANU-PF steadily declined. In South Africa, the ANC's continuing heavy reliance upon large-scale capital has preserved the continuing viability of the reform coalition, even while this is coming under populist threat. In Namibia, SWAPO's acute dependence upon large-scale mining ensures the continuance of cooperative BSRs, while in any case the economy's 'branch plant' status severely constricts its potential for deviance from the macro-economic policy pursued in South Africa. However, the durability of any 'reform coalition' in southern Africa will also depend upon the extent to which business manages to forge alliances across racial lines.

Black economic empowerment (BEE)

The stark racial inequalities of settler colonialism made inevitable demands for racial redress. However, it was to be South Africa, the latecomer to democratization, which was to elaborate the most comprehensive strategy for BEE. It was adopted as a template in both Namibia and Zimbabwe to legitimate certain past actions and also to formalize policy changes regarding 'empowerment'.

South Africa leads, Namibia follows

Moeletsi Mbeki claims that BEE was the invention of South Africa's white economic oligarchs 'who control the commanding heights of the country's economy, that is, mining and its associated chemical and engineering industries and finance'.[29] He illustrates this by reference to the creation of New Africa Investments Limited (NAIL) in 1992 by Sanlam (South Africa's second-largest insurance company). Shares in NAIL, funded by the IDC, were handed out to certain leaders of the ANC and other prominent members of the incoming black

---

[28] Ibid., 120–28.
[29] Moeletsi Mbeki (2009), *Architects of Poverty: Why African Capitalism Needs Changing*, Johannesburg: Picador Africa, 66.

elite.[30] Verhoef likewise stresses the proactive role played by Afrikaner capital.[31] Similarly, Anglo-American transferred a range of industrial assets into black hands. The logic of such initiatives, argues Mbeki, was to wean the ANC away from radical economic ambitions; provide the oligarchs with influence in ANC policy-formulation; secure their companies' first bite at ANC government contracts; and to protect them from foreign competition.[32]

Mbeki is both right and wrong: he is right in his analysis of the motivations of large-scale capital. After all, claims Michael Spicer (then a highly placed member of the Anglo oligarchy), 'what else were we to do?' There had to be artificial intervention in a situation where there was no black capital if the interests of capitalism were to be protected and promoted.[33] Yet, apart from overlooking late NP initiatives which had encouraged (within racially defined parameters) black entrepreneurs, Mbeki is wrong in claiming that the ANC was a latecomer to the idea of BEE, for BEE was written into its genes.

Dale McKinley has reminded us that, from its early days, the aspirations of the ANC's black elite embraced a nationalist politics that envisaged a class of blacks joining (and perhaps eventually replacing) white capitalists as the precursor to wider-scale 'empowerment' of the masses. 'It is of less importance to us whether capitalism is smashed or not', he cites Dr A.B. Xuma (ANC Secretary-General) as declaring in 1945: 'It is of greater importance to us that while capitalism exists, we must fight and struggle to get our full share and benefit from the system.' This conception of 'black empowerment' then became embedded in the ANC's theory of the NDR.[34] This, in turn, was to dictate the logic followed after 1994.[35]

Given white domination of the economy, the ANC had to first capture and then use state power to assert greater black ownership and control. Precisely because aspirant black capitalists lacked capital, it was vital for the ANC to use its inheritance of apartheid's extensive parastatal sector (some 300-odd state-owned enterprises employing 300,000 people) to appoint black directors and management as a means of extending black control of the economy, expanding the black middle class, and promoting BEE through privatization and procurement. In turn, the acquisition of management experience offered by employment within the state-owned enterprises provided a platform for aspirant black capitalists to move into the private sector as shareholders, directors, and executives. Simultaneously, the necessity for large-scale capital to forge alliances with the ANC, and the latter's determination to promote black control of the 'commanding heights of the economy', saw major deals constructed around the transfer of assets, particularly across the minerals, energy, and financial

30 Although Mbeki omits to mention that when it listed, the financial manoeuvrings resulted in 11,000 first-time black shareholders and drew the first-ever direct investment from the trade union movement.

31 G. Verhoef (2003), '"The invisible hand": The roots of BEE, Sankorp and societal change in South Africa 1995–2000', *Journal for Contemporary African History*, 28: 1, 22–47.

32 Mbeki, op. cit., 66–74.

33 Spicer is cited in Jenny Cargill (2010), *Trick or Treat: Rethinking Black Economic Empowerment*, Johannesburg: Jacana, 8.

34 Dale McKinley (2011), 'The real history and contemporary character of "black economic empowerment" (Part 1)', http://www.sacsis.org.za/site/article/600.1

35 Roger Southall (2006), 'Ten propositions about black economic empowerment in South Africa', *Review of African Political Economy*, 34: 111, 67–84.

sectors to party notables. (Amongst these Cyril Ramaphosa, Tokyo Sexwale, Saki Macozoma, and Patrice Motsepe – the 'fab four' – were the most promi-nent). However, because apartheid had stunted the development of a black capi-talist class, it was too under-financed to develop on its own. As 'capitalists without capital', aspirants required advantaged access to finance. Consequently, whilst many of the empowerment deals were immensely convoluted, they revolved around the tenet that the only way to get significant capital into black hands was through loans or gifts to blacks who had a track record within busi-ness and/or valuable political connections. Black empowerment financing was thus overwhelmingly provided by large banks and finance houses, or by state institutions. Both routes were supplemented by government procurement poli-cies favouring recognized empowerment ventures.

The complexity of the course of BEE defies easy summary. Reference will be made here only to three phases of BEE, followed by brief discussion of BEE's outcomes.[36]

The first phase of BEE, initiated in the 1980s but which took off during the political transition was brought to a halt by the 'Asian crisis' of 1997–98. During this period, the IDC and other state institutions (such as Khula, a government small-business-promotion agency) provided substantial funding for black ventures across the telecommunications, mining, finance, manufac-turing, retail, and wholesale sectors. Nonetheless, the funding provided was considerably less than that provided by banks and private financial institutions. This initial burst of empowerment saw black business capturing up to 10 per cent of shares on the JSE between 1994 and 1997, but when the JSE crashed in 1997, many of these early deals came unstuck. By the end of the decade, the number of directly black-owned shares on the JSE had collapsed to between 1 and 4 per cent. However, characteristic of this period was that black business was involved primarily in financial investment rather than entrepreneurship. Black investor groups typically took up less than 20 per cent of equity offered to them, and did not acquire executive control. Many were not really motivated to add value to their investments as they had acquired them on highly advan-tageous terms and felt that they had little to lose.

The shock of the Asian crisis, alongside discontent among elements of black business sidelined by those with ANC connections, led to demands that the state take a more prominent role in promoting black empowerment, thus initiating a second phase in BEE. This took shape in the report of the Black Economic Empowerment Council, chaired by Cyril Ramaphosa, which had been estab-lished in May 1998 by the Black Business Council, an umbrella body of eleven business organizations. When delivered to President Mbeki in April 2001, the report recommended adoption of a wide-ranging, state-driven programme which would set guidelines and regulations, fix targets, and establish obliga-tions for the private sector, public sector, and civil service over a ten-year period. (Significantly, when questioned about whether such measures were necessary to avoid 'another Zimbabwe', Ramaphosa responded in the affirmative). The

---

[36] Roger Southall (2004), 'The ANC and black capitalism in South Africa', *Review of African Political Economy*, 31: 100, 313–28; and (2007), 'The ANC, black economic empowerment and state-owned enterprises: A recycling of history?' in John Daniel, Sakhela Buhlungu, Roger Southall and Jessica Lutchman (eds), *State of the Nation: South Africa 2007*, Cape Town: HSRC Press, 201–25.

government acted swiftly. President Mbeki announced the drawing up of a 'transformation charter' that would set BEE benchmarks, time frames and procedures, and the government followed up with a flurry of legislation. (Most notable was the Mineral and Petroleum Resources Act of 2002 which vested all mineral rights in future in the state and laid down BEE targets which eventuated in the industry drawing up a mining charter.) The government also announced it would draw up a global empowerment charter to serve as a model for BEE charters in different sectors of industry. These initiatives forced the pace of change, as companies scrambled to set in place increased black ownership, recruitment and other targets. However, the progress of BEE was hampered by the slow pace of the stock market recovery. Yet the factor which attracted most public attention was that the principal BEE deals of the period regularly favoured a small, politically connected, empowerment elite, with the Department of Trade and Industry (DTI) reporting that 72 per cent of the total BEE deal value in 2003 involved at least one of six BEE heavyweights.

Extensive criticism of 'elite empowerment' inaugurated a third phase which was initiated by the passage of the Broad Based Black Economic Empowerment (BBBEE) Act of 2003. This sought to consolidate BEE through the issue of ten codes of good practice (to which sectoral codes would have to conform). A first round of codes related to the measurement of ownership (generally to be 25 per cent of equity), management, and control; and a second round, introduced in December 2005, covered employment equity, skills development, preferential procurement, enterprise development, residual matters, and the measurement of qualifying small enterprises. Together, the codes would provide the basis for a 'generic scorecard' against which firms' empowerment credentials would be measured when they competed for government contracts. Industry-wide charters developed by particular sectors would have to prove that their drawing up had been sufficiently consultative and embodied the broad objectives of BBBEE.

Fears abounded within business that it was about to get caught up in a web of red tape. However, despite much hype, the commitment of business to the charter process was questionable, with the government systematically appeasing large-scale capital by making major concessions over BEE targets and compliance.[37] Indeed, whereas almost 30 per cent of all major deals in the pre-codes era transferred control to black investors, this figure was just 10 per cent for the post-codes period up to 2008. Nonetheless, whereas the value of disclosed transactions between 1996 and 2003 was some R90 billion, this figure escalated to around R350 billion between 2004 and 2008. Yet according to one estimate, if the 25 per cent ownership milestone was to be achieved, then between another R450 to R700 billion (according to whether black-owned indirect funding such as retirement funds was counted) would need to be transferred to BEE entities.[38] Meanwhile, progress in other areas was also uneven, although the presidency could report in 2009 that the number of black senior managers in private industry had increased from 18.5 per cent in 2000 to 32.5 per cent in 2008.[39] However, at the time of writing, it is uncertain quite how

[37] Roger Tangri and Roger Southall (2008), 'The politics of black economic empowerment in South Africa', *Journal of Southern African Studies*, 34: 3, 699–716.

[38] Cargill, op. cit., 54–59.

[39] Republic of South Africa, 'Development indicators 2009', http://ww.info.gov.za/other-docs 2009/developmentindicators2009

BEE transactions have fared since the stock market crash of 2008, although it would seem that BEE has been affected badly.

Cargill estimates that, in the foreseeable future, black shareholding will level out at between 15 and 20 per cent, or between 25 and 40 per cent if third-party managed black funds are included.[40] While these record progress since 1994, such statistics continue to leave corporate capital dangerously exposed, as illustrated by the withdrawal of the Black Management Forum (set up in 2008 to represent all sectors of business) from Business Unity South Africa in July 2011, alleging the continuing sidelining of black business. Hence the outcome of BEE has been highly problematic. Three principal issues present themselves.

First, BEE is accused of having created an empowerment elite whose inordinate wealth has been derived far more from their political connections than their entrepreneurial abilities. Early commentary focused heavily upon the inclusion of one or more of the 'fab four' in all the major deals constructed, although there were of course other beneficiaries. Latterly, the public gaze has focused upon the rise of 'tenderpreneurs': politically connected individuals who secure contracts through opaque means from government departments and entities. Certainly, the overall effect has been to somewhat change the complexion of the South African 'power elite', for by as early as 2003, the *Financial Mail* was naming nine black men (all closely aligned to the ANC) as among the country's top twenty business people.[41] However, the fundamental critique is that far from creating the NDR's beloved 'patriotic bourgeoisie', BEE has shifted South Africa towards 'crony capitalism'. The emergent black capitalist class is merely a local version of the state-dependent and kleptocratic bourgeoisies which have sprung up throughout much of the rest of Africa. Yet while this argument has power, it is important to be wary of assumptions that 'normal capitalism' operates upon a basis of rational and legal Weberian-style behaviour by business elites. Rather, in contemporary capitalism, 'the mandarins of capitalist politics and business have perfected the art of creating a sustained symbiosis between the private and the public interest'.[42] For 'normal' capitalist development to take place, the test must rather be whether the outcome is systematically parasitical and predatory, or whether the politically connected gains are directed into productive investment, or whether they provide the conditions for such investment. Presently there is no agreed measure of outcomes, although the thrust of most opinion is that BEE is overwhelmingly parasitic.

Second, BEE within the public service has become increasingly difficult to distinguish from corruption, as the allocation of tenders by public servants is skewed towards family and friends as well as those enjoying political connections to ANC elites at national, provincial, and/or local levels. Further, while the parastatals, alongside the public service, have provided opportunity for the growth and upward mobility of the black middle class, there is substantial evidence that they have become heavily politicized. Many who obtain senior positions guide the allocation of tenders to favoured business interests, this in

---

[40] Cargill, op. cit., 73.
[41] 19 December 2003. Meanwhile, the only woman in the top twenty was Maria Ramos, consort of Finance Minister Trevor Manuel, who was CEO of the major parastatal, Transnet.
[42] Dale McKinley (2010), 'The age of polipreneurship', http://www.sacsis.org.za/site/article/592.1

turn importing ANC factionalism into their organizations. Following Zuma's ascendancy to the presidency, for instance, there were major battles regarding appointments to Transnet, SAA, ESCOM, Armscor, and Denel, which were all being led by acting CEOs. Consequently, the authority of a new Minister of Public Enterprises, Barbara Hogan was undermined by ANC infighting. Such political contestation inevitably intruded on long-term strategic planning, and contributed to the image of a public sector which was simultaneously expensive and inefficient.[43]

Thirdly, as stressed by Lindsay, BEE has developed a multifaceted character that is not appreciated by the leadership of government, business or civil society. BEE, in short, has come to mean different things to different departments within government; to trade unions and civil society; and to the media, with all these groupings having diverse interests. This profound lack of consensus is represented in the plethora of conflicting laws, policies and programmes that seek to address different aspects of BEE. This makes any discussion of BEE and its place in contemporary South Africa increasingly problematic.[44]

Outcomes have been similar in Namibia where there is still no comprehensive framework set in place to achieve BEE. Instead, there have been piecemeal measures relating to affirmative action, land reform, the fishing sector, and loan schemes falling under the Agricultural Bank of Namibia. It is only in retrospect that the government has claimed that these add up to a concerted approach to 'socio-economic transformation', although the private sector (including mining, finance, and tourism) has followed its counterpart next door by voluntarily formulating charters, as well as introducing a preferential procurement framework (although none of these are binding). As late as 2007, officials from the Reserve Bank conceded that little was known about the status of BEE, partly because of political sensitivity, partly because there was no proper definition of what constituted empowerment. Even so, they pointed (without detail) to considerable strides in the Namibianization of the fishing industry, the introduction of an agricultural loan scheme to empower communal farmers and assist black Namibians to move into commercial farming, and a considerable increase of local ownership in the banking sector. 'This was specifically evident for First National Bank Namibia which increased local ownership from 22 per cent to 45 per cent and Bank Windhoek which increased from 65.6 per cent to 100 per cent, between 2001 and 2005 respectively.'[45]

As in South Africa, most analysis coming from outside government is excoriating. Melber accuses the liberation elite of having becoming a class of rent-seekers who divert state resources into politically connected private hands. Affirmative action in both the public and private sectors has seen some modification of the class structure, so that senior management has become less white. However, senior managers in parastatals and other state organs, from the Development Bank of Namibia through to municipalities, draw excessive salaries and

[43] The explosion of corruption under the ANC is dealt with in the following chapter.

[44] Don Lindsay (2011), 'BEE reform: The case for an institutional perspective', in John Daniel, Prishani Naidoo, Devan Pillay and Roger Southall (eds), *New South African Review 2: New Paths, Old Compromises?* Johannesburg: Wits University Press, 236–55.

[45] Floris Fleermuys, Florette Nakusera, Fenni Shangula and John Steytler (2007), 'Overview of broad-based empowerment in Namibia', in *Broad Based Economic Empowerment: Experience from Other Developing Countries*, Bank of Namibia Annual Symposium, Windhoek.

often huge bonuses. From this perspective, BEE has become far less a vehicle of legitimate redress than a morally dubious tool for serving the class interests of a bureaucratic elite.[46]

There are several prominent examples of skewed activities within BEE, such as the investments made by the GIPF in dubious black empowerment projects in the early 2000s, resulting in losses of up to N$650 million (officials claiming it was 'only' N$350 million). Another was the transfer by senior officials of the Social Security Commission of some N$30 million to a private financial institution (Avid) whose political connections were far stronger than its ability to repay the money. But the return of money owing is not the style of BEE: when the cabinet resolved in early 2007 to liquidate the massively loss-making National Development Corporation (formerly part of the South African Bantu Investment Corporation), it was able to secure repayment of only N$3 million of the N$24 million it had extended to black businessmen.[47] For its part, having received some 94 loan applications during 2005, the Development Bank granted just 7, the 2 largest to companies with strong political connections, one (Namibia Poultry Industries) involving a former Deputy Minister of Foreign Affairs, while another, to a firm which was on the verge of liquidation before it was bought up by a foreign company, Ongopolo Mining and Processing, involved the Director-General of the National Planning Commission.[48] Finally, reference may be made to the saga of 'big fish' for 'fat cats', that is, how BEE has been pursued within the fishing industry, for this has effectively translated into the privatization of natural resources and the siphoning off of profits by allocating quotas to party comrades. From 2000, the established, mostly foreign-owned companies that dominated the industry were required to team up with Namibians if they wished to continue to receive exploitation rights. However, rather than 'empowerment', the outcome has been to generate income by transferring the utilization of quotas to companies that have managed to link up with politically well-connected Namibians but which are in fact internationally owned and managed.[49]

The cross-over between BEE and corruption has caused massive unease within the ranks of the ANC and SWAPO themselves. The GIPF pension funds scandal, declared Namibia's then Prime Minister, was just 'asset-stripping' which, by widening the gulf between rich and poor could lead to 'class war'.[50] In contrast, ZANU-PF has been far less concerned with such niceties, for, with the decline of state resources, it has increasingly utilized 'indigenization' to favour the interests of its elites.

---

[46]   Henning Melber (2007), 'Poverty, politics, power and privilege: Namibia's black economic elite formation', in Henning Melber, (ed.), *Transitions in Namibia: Which Changes for Whom?* Uppsala: Nordic Africa Institute, 120–29.

[47]   Ibid., 117–21.

[48]   *Insight Corruption Tracker*, 15 August 2005.

[49]   Henning Melber (2003), 'Of big fish and small fry: The fishing industry in Namibia', *Review of African Political Economy*, 30: 95, 142–49. One of the fat cats was the Minister of Fisheries, who established a committee to collect funding for his forthcoming wedding, with the major contributions being made by fishing companies. President Nujoma pre-empted an inquiry into his conduct by exonerating the Minister from all allegations.

[50]   *The Namibian*, 7 September 2005.

Indigenization in Zimbabwe

During the 1980s, ZANU-PF favoured accommodation with white and multi-national capital rather than with a nascent black business class which had been deliberately stunted under settler rule. Indeed, the government initially took extraordinary steps to prevent independent black business from gaining capacity and influence. Instead, crony capitalism thrived as politically favoured individuals – party elites, Mugabe's relatives, and military commanders – were awarded government tenders and contracts. Whereas white capital was not viewed as a political threat, a notionally socialist ZANU-PF was hostile to the development of black capitalist enterprise beyond its ambit.[51] But this was to change somewhat from the mid-1990s.

As the state's dealings with the established business associations withered, black business groupings (the Indigenous Business Development Centre (IBDC), the Affirmative Action Group (AAG), and the Indigenous Commercial Farmers' Union and the Zimbabwe Farmers' Union, ZFU) sought to foster relations with politically connected economic actors (the crony capitalists aligned to ZANU-PF). Taylor points to the emergence of a distributional coalition between the ruling party and indigenous business groupings from the time of the 1996 presidential election, when the latter sought to hitch their fortunes to Mugabe's re-election, invoking racial solidarity and blaming Zimbabwe's economic woes upon the white business and farming community. For its part, having long marginalized these groupings, ZANU-PF proved eager to align with them when faced with mounting political threats, and to burnish its image as black African and nationalist.

This was no 'reform coalition'. BSRs increasingly assumed mafia-like qualities in which 'the prerequisite for policies favorable to a company or association [was] not developmental potential or institutional strength but connectedness to the regime'.[52] The AAG's mode of operation is illustrative. Formed in 1993, the AAG bullied local and foreign companies by refusing to certify them as 'affirmative action compliant' unless they conceded part ownership or contracting arrangements to indigenous partners. Certainly, the rewards of such activities for the leaders of indigenous business associations' leaders could be tangible. One leader of the AAG, Philip Chiyangwa, (a local music producer), parlayed his proximity to ZANU-PF into a business empire and became an MP. Similarly, Enock Kamushinda, Secretary-General of the IBDC, helped steer Mugabe's 1996 presidential campaign, and thereafter expanded his business holdings until in 2001 he became Chairman of the Grain Marketing Board. In contrast, the rewards for the ordinary members of the indigenous business associations were hard to discern, while even those leaders who inserted themselves into ZANU-PF's good books always ran the risk of falling out of political favour.[53] In any case, by the late 1990s, ZANU-PF's need for coalition partners was mitigated as it increasingly transformed itself into a business actor in its own right, notably through the opportunities presented by Mugabe's decision to send

---

[51] Taylor, op. cit., 122.
[52] Ibid., 133.
[53] Chiyangwa was imprisoned in 2004 on charges of fraud (Taylor, op. cit., 150, n.188).

troops to assist DRC President Laurent Kabila. In return for Zimbabwean assistance, Kabila offered numerous business concessions, most of which went to companies and politicians linked to ZANU-PF as well senior military officers and connected business people (foreign as well as Zimbabwean) through a web of interlinked holding companies (see Chapter 10). The looting of the DRC became a major source of rents at a time when resources for patronage at home were collapsing, and also provided a means for placating an increasingly restive military.[54]

The contradictions of empowerment, Zimbabwe-style, are further demonstrated by the mining sector, where the collapse of production during the mining boom of the 1990s and early 2000s was prevented only by a small number of new and important platinum and diamond operations which were extensively foreign-owned (notably by South African interests). Paradoxically, while mineral production declined sharply, foreign investment actually increased during the early years of the new century, involving the entry of various new market players. Yet while ZANU-PF claimed its policies were enabling greater black participation, 'empowerment' tended to feature non-Zimbabweans and especially South African-backed players.[55]

By the late 1990s, ZANU-PF was replacing consultation with the established mining companies with nationalist posturing, stressing the need for government to assert sovereign rights over strategic resources. The mining sector, which had thrived during the 1980s, was a major casualty of the economic crisis and numerous mines were placed on care and maintenance. However, for those mining companies that considered disinvesting, the option of selling up to Zimbabweans was complicated not merely by their lack of capital but by the Western powers' imposition of 'targeted sanctions', involving the blacklisting of individuals or entities close to the regime. At the same time, the dilemmas posed by sanctions for Western companies increased the opportunities for new foreign players: less politically constrained, they had the political and financial resources to ensure investment security. In effect, this opened the door to an array of regionally based interests, most of them in South Africa and operating in neighbouring countries, with Chinese players entering the arena from the mid-2000s. Even so, new players in sectors such as platinum and gold undertook little renovation of their acquisitions, apparently viewing them primarily as prospects to be exploited in the future.

During the 1990s, unsystematic efforts pursued by the government at 'indigenizing' the mining sector had done little to alter patterns of ownership. As in other arenas, ZANU-PF favoured only its own, although ventures promoted even by these were subject to the vicissitudes of political currents. Illustrative is the fate of Mutumwa Mawere, a local mining magnate with close ties to ZANU-PF. His acquisition of a controlling share of Shabanie Mashaba asbestos mine in the late 1990s was enthusiastically celebrated by ZANU-PF but within a few years he was recast as a suspect businessman, his assets were seized, and he fled to South Africa. While other smaller-scale efforts at indigenization involving

---

[54] Taylor, op. cit., 135–36.
[55] Richard Saunders (2008), 'Crisis, capital, compromise: Mining and empowerment in Zimbabwe', *African Sociological Review*, 12: 1, 67–87. The following paragraphs are drawn from this invaluable source. The three largest platinum producers (notably Impala Platinum) and the largest gold producer (Metallon Gold) are all South African owned.

artisanal works were sometimes successful, too great success often saw them harassed by government officials.

In an environment characterized by nationalist claims to assets, the junior role assumed by Zimbabwean business people in new mining investments in the 2000s has been notable. Key investors have primarily included South African black empowerment figures working with white South African interests; international financial support; and, in one important case (Mwana Africa), a consortium put together by politically connected businessmen from the DRC, Kenya, Ghana, and South Africa as well as from Zimbabwe itself. The South African players include Mzi Kumalo, whose Metallon mining group bought Independence Gold Mines in 2002; Bridget Radebe, wife of the then South African Transport Minister Jeff Radebe, who took over the Eureka gold mine from Placer Dome SA in 2005; and African Rainbow Minerals, controlled by Patrice Motsepe (Bridget Radebe's brother) and South Africa's first black billionaire. Where black business groups have been involved, they have invariably been connected with powerful political factions within ZANU-PF and have accordingly been crucially affected for good or ill by intra-elite struggles. Yet ironically, as the government's desperation for foreign exchange-yielding mineral exports has increased, the state's empowerment demands have regularly stalled.

This is illustrated by the chaotic diamond rush from 2006 in eastern Zimbabwe, primarily within the Marange district, and the Ranch River mine near the border with South Africa. A rise in unregulated diamond sales fed into the emerging 'blood diamonds' trade, while allegations flowed that River Ranch was being used by the Zimbabwean and Congolese military elites as a conduit for DRC diamonds through to international traders in South Africa. While the government insisted that the mass of informal diamond diggers who had descended upon the fields were selling their diamonds to the Minerals Marketing Corporation of Zimbabwe (MMCZ), which was the state institution entrusted with overseeing most minerals sales, the World Diamond Council called for an investigation of the Zimbabwean industry, citing allegations of smuggling and unclear certification procedures. In response, the Kimberley Process (KP), which is the global industry body established to prevent the entry into global circuits of 'blood diamonds', announced that some diamond exporters were under investigation and that the Zimbabwean government was cooperating with their efforts. Even so, because the legal sole buyer MMCZ lacked financial resources and offered low prices, there was a continuing flood of sales onto the black market, denying the state much-needed revenue. Predictably, after the military was dispatched in December 2006 to put a stop to the illegal outflow of resources, there were multiple reports that senior government and military figures were joining in the thievery. A 2007 parliamentary investigation and a visit by a KP review team subsequently cleared government agencies of improper documentation of diamond sales, yet failed to address the role of government-linked individuals and security agencies in illegal mining practices.

The passage of an Indigenization and Economic Empowerment Bill into law in March 2008 sealed prior announcements that the government would move to acquire a 51 per cent stake in foreign-owned mining assets, this inclusive of an uncompensated and expropriated stake of 25 per cent. Unnamed Zimbabwean investors would benefit from the government's newly acquired shareholdings, and future new investments would be required to include state or indigenous participation from the outset. The initiative disrupted ongoing discussions with South Africa about a potential empowerment exchange programme and formulation of a mining charter.[56] Subsequently, the MDC's victory in the March 2008 parliamentary election and the September 2008 formation of the coalition government threatened ZANU-PF's capacity to extract rent from foreign capital. It precipitated a desperate attempt by the party to ratchet up the scope of empowerment deals, thereby circumventing the risk for the party elite of its losing political power. In consequence (and despite substantial differences with the MDC) pressure was increased massively upon foreign-owned mining companies, with foreign-owned banks likewise drawn into the ambit of indigenization.

In March 2011, foreign-owned companies were given 45 days to demonstrate how they would grant a 51 per cent shareholding to Zimbabweans within 5 years. Saviour Kasukuwere, the Minister for Youth Development, Indigenization, and Empowerment, proceeded to cancel the operating licence of the country's leading gold mine (the Canadian-owned Blanket Mine), and threaten the licences of major players such as Zimplats, Ango Platinum, and Aquarius Platinum. By August, Kasukuwere was reporting that the government had rejected the empowerment plans of some 175 mining companies, most of which were centred around the sale of 25 per cent stakes, with 26 per cent being made up of credits awarded for social investment made in infrastructure, health, and education facilities. At the forefront of the battle was Zimplats, owned by the South African Impala Platinum (Implats) and the biggest platinum producer in Zimbabwe which was under pressure to cede an immediate 29.5 per cent holding to the National Indigenization and Empowerment Fund (NIEF) as well as selling its holding in the Mimosa mine. The latter was a joint venture with Aquarius, another South African-owned company and the second-largest producer. Amidst the ensuing commotion, Kasukuwere announced that after mining, the government would shift its focus to the banking sector. British-owned banks Standard Chartered and Barclays, as well as the South African-owned Stanbic, Nedbank, and Old Mutual, were immediately targeted, Kasukwere requiring an equity participation of 40 per cent by Zimbabweans. He followed this up with the insistence that mining companies would have to bank locally in order to increase the liquidity of the banking sector.[57]

If they wanted to continue to extract minerals from Zimbabwean soil, mining companies were under particular pressure to comply. The major problem was that while share concessions were usually linked to future payments to be drawn from profits, there was considerable uncertainty as to whether in practice they would ever receive compensation from the Zimbabwean government. This was recognized by the South African Department of Trade and Industry, which – prompted by the Implats affair – entered into negotiations with the Zimbabwean government to ensure that a 2009 bilateral trade and investment agreement between the two countries would be honoured, and that South African firms complying with the indigenization requirements would not lose their assets or investments. (Ratified in 2011, the agreement gave South African companies

---

[56]   Ibid., 82.
[57]   *Sunday Times*, 21 August 2011; *Mail & Guardian*, 26 August–1 September 2011.

recourse if their assets were seized without compensation.) It was only after this, in March 2012, that Zimplats announced an empowerment deal which involved transferring 10 per cent of its shares to communities, 10 per cent to employees, and 31 per cent to the NIEF. Other companies soon began to follow suit.

Nonetheless, the indigenization demands caused major conflicts, not only within the coalition, but within ZANU-PF itself. Certainly, the domination of the mining, finance, and retail sectors by foreign (especially South African) capital meant that the call for indigenization resonated widely. However, the MDC was concerned that the ratcheting up of empowerment rhetoric would turn away investment, and portrayed the indigenization wave as cover for a feeding frenzy by ruling party cronies. On the other hand, ZANU-PF used indigenization to reposition itself as the party of African revolution, with the call upon Africans to 'reclaim their resources' linked to an urgent need for an early election, with or without a constitutional settlement. The strategy was not ineffective and the indigenization campaign allowed ZANU-PF to make inroads into MDC's constituency, and for Mugabe to recover considerable popularity.[58] Against this, it failed to obscure differences among the ZANU-PF elite, with even reserve bank governor Gideon Gono, a Mugabe stalwart, warning against the prospect of companies being grabbed by the same elite that had seized farms.[59] Indeed, in May 2012, ZANU-PF Mining Minister Obert Mpofu placed a rescue package for the iron and steel industry financed by Indian firm Essar (which had secured a majority holding in the previously state-owned Zisco) on ice, apparently lobbying in favour of Chinese bidders promoted by a clique of party loyalists.[60] For all the MDC's warnings that irresponsible indigenization would wreck prospects for recovery, its ability to confront the narrow class interests of the politico-military elite was always going to be in doubt.

Land reform

Liberation movement ideology proposes that the seizure of African land by white settlers was a motivating force driving the liberation struggle. The massive inequalities in land ownership which existed under colonialism and apartheid gave the land issue huge symbolic status. However, whilst land may have been vital to nationalist mythology, controversy attends the extent to which there is a popular demand for a radical reversal of ownership patterns. According to an Afrobarometer survey of the late 1990s, only 1.1 per cent of Zimbabwean respondents listed land among the top three problems with which the government should concern itself.[61] Another source, noting the low priority granted to land reform by the ANC government, ascribed the modest role it played in South African politics to the relatively high level of urbanization,[62] while yet

---

[58] *Sunday Independent*, 18 March 2012.
[59] *Mail & Guardian*, 5–11 August 2011.
[60] *Sunday Independent*, 20 May 2012.
[61] Robert Mattes, Yul Derek Davids and Cherrel Africa (2000), 'Views of democracy in South Africa and the region: Trends and comparisons', *Afrobarometer*, Paper No. 8.
[62] Reg Rumney, 'Who owns South Africa? An analysis of state and private ownership patterns', in John Daniel, Roger Southall and Jessica Lutchman (eds) (2005), *State of the Nation: South Africa 2004–05*, Cape Town: HSRC Press, 401–22.

another asserted that there is little demand for agricultural land even among the rural poor.[63] Against this, other commentators point to a serious underestimation of the demand for land reform in former settler territories which, together with official emphases upon market-led discourses which assume the inefficiency of peasant production, 'raise the spectre of increased land conflicts resulting from the demands of a growing but blocked peasantry, rising urban poverty, as well as a nascent African bourgeoisie, poised against minority white landlords'.[64] Nonetheless, despite such varying perspectives, there is wide agreement that the political salience of land reform has increased by leaps and bounds after the land issue leapt to prominence following the farm seizures in Zimbabwe.

The inequality in landholding as a result of colonial dispossession was dramatic. In Zimbabwe, the Land Tenure Act of 1969 had reserved 15.5 million hectares, largely in the most productive areas, to some 6,000 farms, owned by both individual white farmers and large estates; 16.4 million hectares to 700,000 black families; and 1.4 million hectares to 8,500 black small-scale farmers. By 1980, 42 per cent of the country was owned by white farmers, and inequality had been exacerbated by the bush war, when thousands of Africans left the land to escape the fighting or had been forcibly relocated into 'protected villages'.[65] Namibia's independence saw around 4,500 white farmers (and estates) owning the overwhelming proportion (95 per cent) of the 44 per cent of the land area devoted to commercial agriculture. The bulk of the population that lived in rural areas (988,000) occupied some 26 per cent of the land mass (the rest divided between national parks and the restricted diamond area).[66] In South Africa, in 1994, around 60,000 white-owned, commercial farms occupied 86 million hectares, including most of the limited high potential arable land. In contrast, more than 12 million people located in the former homelands occupied only 17 million hectares of land (of which only 15 per cent was potentially arable).[67] In all three countries, a deeply rooted agrarian structure pitted a commercial sector dominated by large-scale landholdings against a peasant or communal sector comprising smallholdings and common areas. In all three countries, inequality in landholding was indissolubly defined by colonial dispossession and race.

The settlements in all three countries entrenched property rights and espoused a liberal, market-driven approach to land reform, thereby pitting universal citizenship against historic relations of property, production, and power.[68] In legal terms, there was provision for compulsory purchase of property (with particular reference to the historic inequalities in landholding), this

[63] Centre for Development Enterprise (2005), *Land Reform in South Africa: A 21st Century Perspective*, Johannesburg: CDE.
[64] Sam Moyo (2007), 'The land question in southern Africa: A comparative review', in Ruth Hall and Lungisile Ntsebeza (eds), *The Land Question in South Africa: The Challenge of Transformation and Redistribution*, Cape Town: HSRC Press, 60–84.
[65] Bertus de Villiers (2003), *Land Reform: Issues and Challenges – A Comparative Review of Experiences in Zimbabwe, Namibia, South Africa and Australia*, Johannesburg: Konrad Adenauer Foundation, 6.
[66] Ibid., 33; Sherbourne, op. cit., 81–83.
[67] Rumney, op. cit., 411–12.
[68] Alison Goebel (2005), 'Is Zimbabwe the future for South Africa? The implications for land reform in southern Africa', *Journal of Contemporary African Studies*, 23: 3, 345–70.

subject to what the Zimbabwean constitution (Section V.1) termed 'adequate', the Namibian constitution (Ch. 3, Article 16) termed 'just' and the South African (1996) constitution (Section 25.1) termed 'just and equitable' compensation (with disputes about whether compulsory state purchase met these criteria to be subject to the decisions of the courts). It was therefore only in political terms that this was translated into the much-celebrated principle of 'willing buyer, willing seller' (WBWS), largely to placate donors and 'the market'. From this perspective, the prospects for land reform were dictated not only by the willingness of farmers to sell, but also the financial capacity of the state to buy, and certainly a lack of finance was always to operate as a serious constraint, notably in Zimbabwe. Meanwhile, whereas Zimbabwe and Namibia adopted reform strategies whereby land was to be acquired by the state which then assumed responsibility for redistribution, South Africa followed World Bank guidance by adopting a policy in which a lesser role was envisaged for the state whereby it would provide grants to prospective beneficiaries of land distribution who would buy land from sellers directly.[69]

In Zimbabwe, the government adhered to WBWS from 1980 through to the late 1990s, and made some reasonable progress (some 20 per cent of white commercial farmland having been transferred into black hands during the first decade and a half of independence). It was only from the mid-1990s that the government was to abandon WBWS, when, with the economy approaching crisis, it became political advantageous to do so. In contrast, despite very limited progress in land reform under WBWS, the SWAPO and ANC governments came to fear that any emulation of the Zimbabwean example would have a disastrous impact upon investor confidence and international reputation.

Radical land reform in Zimbabwe

The acceptance by the PF of WBWS at Lancaster House was extremely grudging, and given only under pressure from the other FLS to reach a deal. The conference was saved from collapse only by assurances granted by Britain and the US that they would provide funding to finance land reform, Britain promising £75 million and the US$500 million, with other donors also chipping in. However, the promises were not backed up by written guarantees.[70] By the year 2000, Zimbabwe had received less than £50 million, in contrast to Kenya where £500 million was provided for its postcolonial land and for its resettlement process, £500 million.[71] There were to be major disagreements between the Zimbabwean and British governments as to where the responsibility lay for this ultimately miserly provision, each blaming the other for broken promises. Yet, notoriously, following the accession to office of the Labour government in 1997, Claire Short, the Secretary of State for International Development, rejected the idea that Britain had to meet the costs of land purchase in Zimbabwe: 'We are a new government...without links to former colonial interests', prompting Sir Shridath Ramphal, the former Secretary-

---

[69] Moyo, op. cit., 73.
[70] De Villiers, op. cit., 7.
[71] De Villiers claims the amount was just £30 million. In contrast, Mamdani states that Britain paid out £44 million before 1992. See Mahmood Mamdani (2008), 'Lessons of Zimbabwe', *London Review of Books*, 30: 23, 4, (December) 17–21.

General of the Commonwealth, to reflect on the BBC in 2002 that Britain had let Zimbabwe down.[72] British culpability and stinginess were to provide Mugabe with a totally predictable weapon to attack 'imperialism' before the court of African opinion in the years ahead.

At independence, commercial farmers were providing 90 per cent of the country's marketed food requirements. Clearly, they needed to be offered some form of security, yet at the same time the government was faced by the urgent need for land reform in order to provide opportunities for the landless and war veterans, to relieve population pressures, and to address poverty in the communal areas as well as expanding production. Accordingly, a National Land Policy envisaged land redistribution according to two models: Model A, whereby individual households would be given a 5–6 hectare plot plus a share in a communal grazing area; and Model B, which provided for farming of commercial farms on a cooperative and mechanized basis. Land was not to be granted freehold but owned by the state; land could not be subdivided or leased, nor used for non-agricultural purposes. By 1982, the government had proposed that some 162,000 households would be resettled within two years. In practice, this proved wildly optimistic. By 1990, some 3.39 million hectares had been acquired, constituting some 20 per cent of white commercial farmland.[73] However, while 80 per cent of the beneficiaries of this period were resettled under Model A, the major emphasis of reform was upon the promotion of black large-scale farmers, who by 1999 owned some 11 per cent of commercial farmland. In other words, land reallocation was directed at racial rather than class imbalances, and did little to address overall patterns of inequality, landlessness, and rural poverty.[74]

In spite of this limitation, the first phase of land reform attracted favourable attention from foreign governments, international organizations, and NGOs (although they remained strangely reluctant to provide aid for the purchase of land). Nonetheless, the achievements fell far short of meeting official targets. Reasons given by the government were: the constraints of the constitution; lack of finance to purchase farms; a post-independence rise in land prices; the tendency of white farmers to offer only marginal land for sale; the drought of 1982–84; and the limited capacity and financial resources of the responsible agencies to successfully implement and support resettlement. Certainly, the government was scrupulous in adhering to the constitution, and backed this up with severe actions against squatters who encroached on white land. However, there were more fundamental reasons for the failures of the first period. A huge rise in communal agricultural production during 1981–87 may have contributed to government complacency. Certainly, official allocations for resettlement during these times consistently fell well below 1 per cent of the national budget. Second, socialist rhetoric gave way to capitalist principles as the emergent black elite jostled its way ahead of landless peasants in the queue for land, with some 300 black farmers (including 10 cabinet ministers) joining the CFU. Third, apart from problems associated with the lack of security of

---

[72] Cited in 'Background to land reform in Zimbabwe', http://www.zimembassy.se/land_reform_document.html

[73] The figures are taken from official government documentation. See Institute of Development Studies, University of Zimbabwe (2004), *Land Reform Programme in Zimbabwe: Disparity between Policy Design and Implementation*, May, 3–4.

[74] Moyo, op. cit., 75.

tenure granted to resettled farmers, the process whereby land was allocated was top down and ignored local stakeholders. The key players were, rather, central government and ZANU-PF, with the national committee overseeing the entire process chaired by the ZANU-PF national chairman.[75]

If land redistribution had taken a back seat as a policy issue during these early years, it was brought back with a vengeance from the mid-1990s. The slow pace of reform had failed to address the urgent needs of the rural population, with ESAPs being associated with strongly declining peasant production and intensified local struggles around land. Meanwhile, in urban areas, the hardships caused by ESAPs fuelled increasing political discontent and growing opposition to ZANU-PF, as indicated by the formation of the Zimbabwe Unity Movement by Edgar Tekere in 1989. With the need to regain political ground in rural areas, Mugabe declared that 'The biggest single issue yet to be resolved is that of land distribution.'[76] Thereafter, land became the core rallying point for constitutional and political change, with Tekere attempting to match Mugabe's increasingly strident commitment to a 'revolutionary land reform programme'[77] and the association of the struggle for land with the renewal of the Chimurenga. A growing demand for land reform came from 'two powerful groups at extreme ends of the social spectrum yet both firmly in Mugabe's camp: the veterans of the liberation war and the small but growing number of indigenous businesses'. At independence 20,000 veterans had been incorporated into the army, but 45,000 had not, and had been left to fend for themselves, which was why 'land occupations began in the countryside soon after independence'.[78]

With the land issue shooting up the national agenda, the government carried through one amendment to the constitution (No. 11 in 1990) and two in 1993 (Nos 12 and 13) whose various provisions were to render all land, not just that which was underutilized, liable to compulsory acquisition, with the state being required to pay 'fair compensation' within a 'reasonable time' as opposed to the 'prompt and adequate compensation' required under Lancaster House. The new constitutional framework was then carried through via the Land Acquisition Act of 1992, whose essence was to be preserved following a legal challenge in the courts in 1994. A further Land Acquisition Act in 1996 then enabled the government to designate land in large tracts for resettlement, following which a National Land Acquisition Committee accelerated the rate of identification of land for acquisition. Thus by November 1997, some 1,488 farms totalling 3.8 million hectares, had been identified for purchase, with a proposed budget of US$1.9 billion being drawn up for the exercise of land acquisition and settlement of some 150,000 families by 2004. In the interim, during the late 1990s, the government identified some 850 farms for expropriation under a fast-track system whereby farmers would have to vacate their properties with 30 rather than the previously prescribed 60 days' notice.[79]

Despite the radicalized agenda, the pace of reform carried out during this second phase actually declined. By 2000, a total of only 75,000 families had been settled, far short of the target prescribed in 1982. Meanwhile, the legisla-

---

[75] Institute of Development Studies, op. cit., 2–7; De Villiers, op. cit., 11–15.
[76] *The Herald*, 20 December 1989.
[77] *Financial Times*, 21 August 1989.
[78] Mamdani, op. cit., 17.
[79] Institute of Development Studies, op. cit., 5–10; De Villiers, op. cit., 9–16.

tive changes had sparked a scramble for land amongst the political elite, with some 400 farms acquired allegedly going to senior ZANU-PF officials. In turn, the landless peasants in whose name the reform process had been accelerated increasingly took matters into their own hands, short-circuiting the corruption which had shaped the allocation process by invading white land. According to the CFU, some 1,700 farm invasions took place during the late 1990s, and although court orders were regularly obtained to evict squatters, these were equally regularly ignored by the police, as ZANU-PF scampered to recover its support in rural areas. The toxic combination of high aims, increasing corruption, growing lawlessness and the failure of the government to oversee an orderly process of reform provided the context for a Donors Conference in September 1998, which resulted in donors pledging just Z$7.3 million of the $Z42 million requested. Indeed, by this time, growing unhappiness amongst donors (especially the UK) about the weakening commitment to WSWB had transformed itself into outright reluctance to provide aid. While donors emphasized macro-economic stability and democratic governance as conditions for increased support, the government argued that stability could only come as a result of more radicalized reform.[80]

Under increasing pressure, the government convened a Constitutional Commission charged with drawing up a proposal for a new constitution. The resultant draft proposed making the British government responsible for the cost of compulsory acquisition of land for resettlement. If it refused to do so, the Zimbabwean government itself would be relieved of any such obligation. Further, where compensation was payable, there was no requirement for it to be 'fair', but rather it was to be calculated according to a rather vague set of criteria such as history of ownership and the cost or value of improvements made on the land. However, when the draft was put to the constitutional referendum in February 2000, it was summarily rejected – to the government's shock and dismay.

Thereafter began the complex crisis that defines contemporary Zimbabwe. Spearheaded by the war veterans, land invasions gathered pace throughout the country as the government, in turn, without any legal basis, launched its fast track resettlement programme on 1 July 2000. The initial targets set were to acquire 1 million hectares and resettle 30,000 families, to be followed rapidly by an additional acquisition of 4 million hectares on which a further 120,000 families would be settled over three years. ZANU-PF thereafter contested the 2000 parliamentary election under the slogan 'Land is the economy, the economy is the land', yet only narrowly missed defeat to the newly formed MDC. Then, in November 2000, despite the proposed constitution having been rejected, a further Land Acquisition Act laid down that if Britain did not establish a compensation fund, compensation by the Zimbabwean government would only be payable for improvements to the land, with other provisions generally easing the measures whereby land could be acquired. In July 2002, notices were served on 2,900 white farmers out of the 4,500 remaining to stop all farming activities by 8 August, after which they had to vacate their land without any compensation. Further measures followed, as in turn the pace of land invasions stepped up, with the obstacles that were put in the path of the fast track resettle-

---

[80]   Institute of Development Studies, op. cit., 8–14; De Villiers, op. cit., 16–20.

ment programme by the courts being brushed aside by an executive assault upon the independent judiciary. Uncooperative judges were sacked. Within a space of four years, just a small number of individual white farmers remained although some 250 large farms and estates were unaffected. These were largely owned by South African-based companies (notably Triangle Sugar Corporation and Hippo Valley (Sugar) Estate) along with European and domestic white capital (with the state itself also a significant owner). Although further land redistribution thereafter whittled down the large-scale estates, the government sought to retain the considerable agro-industrial estates (notably, sugar, tea, and timber holdings) as critical to export growth, employment promotion, and agro-industrial production.[81]

Mamdani has referred to the 'greatest transfer of property in southern Africa since colonization' as a 'democratic revolution', in 'social and economic – if not political – terms'.[82] Yet as he also notes there was a heavy price to pay. The rule of law and the independence of the judiciary were swept away, alongside repression of the media and opposition forces; around 150,000 farm labourers, traditionally drawn from migrant labour, were displaced and – when they rallied behind the MDC – brutally hounded. However, about the same number threw in their lot with the land invaders or retained their jobs on the large sugar and tea estates. The urban poor, hoping to benefit via invasions of urban land and properties, proved too threatening politically to the government, resulting in massive repression, including Operation Murambatsvina. Not least, food production plummeted. Zimbabwe, formerly a food surplus country, was by 2003 lacking both food and foreign exchange to buy imports, and half the population was dependent upon food aid. Yet, as Mamdani also notes, what the overall outcome of radical land reform will be for Zimbabwe remains difficult to determine.

Mamdani challenges the conventional wisdom that the land reform process has been almost wholly destructive, involving coercion; corruption and incompetence; cronyism in the redistribution of land; lack of funds, and an absence of agricultural activity. He has aroused particular criticism for arguing that, while there is no denying Mugabe's authoritarianism and his willingness to tolerate his supporters' violence, 'he has not ruled only by coercion but by consent', his land reform measures having won him considerable popularity not just in Zimbabwe but throughout southern Africa.[83] He argues that the liberation war was centred on land, and thus it should come as no surprise that radical reform should attract broad-based support. When the draft constitution was put to the electorate in February 2000, it was defeated, with only 45 per cent of voters in favour – yet only just over 20 per cent of the electorate had voted, coming largely from the urban areas, while voting in the countryside was marked by large-scale abstentions. The War Veterans' Association, formed in 1988, claimed membership from across the country, in contrast to the ZCTU. ZANU-PF had little option but to side with the former against the urban-based trade union federation in the power struggle that has ripped Zimbabwe apart. In the years that have followed, whereas civil society activists have character-

---

[81] Sam Moyo (2011), 'Land concentration and accumulation after redistributive reform in post-settler Zimbabwe', *Review of African Political Economy*, 38: 128, 257–76.

[82] Mamdani, op. cit., 18.

[83] Ibid., 17.

ized ZANU-PF as promoting an 'exhausted nationalism', ZANU-PF nationalism has been able to withstand civil-society based opposition because it is 'supported by large numbers of peasants',[84]

Mamdani's critics have vigorously challenged his argument that ZANU-PF has ruled by consent. In responses to his article in the *London Review of Books*, prominent academics have argued that he systematically underplays the level of violence deployed by ZANU-PF and the military against its opponents, notably in the rural areas; that the land invasions were orchestrated by the military and the security services rather than having been a popular uprising; and that the collapse of food production and the effect of violence has seen 4 million people flee the country, with 5 million facing starvation.[85] Yet whilst this may be true, Mamdani is making the argument that for all the violent nature of the land reform process, it has enjoyed considerable popularity amongst the landless and a continuing body of rural support for Mugabe and ZANU-PF. For a start, there have been a significant number of beneficiaries of the reforms (some 130,000 families were resettled upon about 10 million hectares under the fast track resettlement programme between 2000 and 2004),[86] one good reason why the MDC has been wary of any suggestion of reversing them (even though it has called for their 'rationalization').[87] In addition, there is a growing body of scholarship which, whilst accepting that the land reform process has been heavily driven by political considerations, challenges the notion that it has benefited only supporters of ZANU-PF.

While recognizing that many farms have gone to the politically connected, there is no one story of how land reform occurred. The involvement of veterans, local chiefs, national politicians, and security personnel varied from place to place, as did the occurrence of violence or due process. One of the most engaged scholars of the reforms, Sam Moyo, notes that over 70 per cent of the agricultural land is now held by 1.3 million peasant families within the Communal Areas and by fast track resettlement programme beneficiaries, while about 20 per cent of farming land is now held by some 30,000 middle-scale black farmers, with land sizes ranging from 50 to 200 hectares. (Against this, he also acknowledges that rural women, whose skills and labour tend to be critical to food production and rural livelihoods, have been systematically disadvantaged.) Finally, alongside the remaining large estates, there are some 3,000 individual farmers operating on one-third of pre-2000 average larger-scale landholding sizes. Eighty per cent of these are blacks, 'including urban and rural-based professionals, public and private sector executives, other petty bourgeoisie elements and black capitalists' (who may, he says, be labelled 'land grabbers').[88] While such differentiation within and between peasants and between middle- and larger-scale farmers suggests the likelihood of considerable political contestation, it may also imply levels of support for ZANU-PF which extend beyond any politically beholden 'national bourgeoisie'. Against this, as critics of Mamdani

---

[84] Ibid., passim.

[85] Commentary by Terence Ranger on Mamdani's article, at http://www.lrb.co.uk/v30/n24/letters#letter2

[86] Moyo (2011), op. cit., 75.

[87] Movement for Democratic Change (2004), *RESTART: Our Path to Social Justice. The MDC's Economic Programme for Reconstruction, Stabilization, Recovery and Transformation*, Harare: Movement for Democratic Change.

[88] Moyo (2011), op. cit., 261.

have pointed out, in the 2008 elections ZANU-PF lost virtually all its seats in Manicaland and there were solid votes for the MDC in Mashonaland (areas which ZANU-PF had previously taken for granted) despite land redistribution.

The work of Ian Scoones of Sussex University and his associates in Masvingo province over a ten-year period has, as Mamdani points out, challenged what they have termed the myths around the land reform process: that it has been a total failure, that beneficiaries have been exclusively ZANU-PF political cronies, that there has been no investment in rural areas, and that the rural economy has collapsed. Household survey data in Masvingo demonstrates that benefici-aries were mostly local, poor households, who have invested in their new land and derived substantial livelihood benefits. Along with Moyo, they recognize that there have been distinctly mixed outcomes to the reforms, and amongst the beneficiaries there are three broad categories (of more or less equal size) composed of those who are 'doing well, improving'; those who were 'getting on, but with potential'; and the 'asset poor, often struggling'.[89] While it is dangerous to generalize from the study of just one area, findings from other provinces that are beginning to emerge are broadly consistent. Perhaps the long-term outcomes, in the spirit of Chairman Mao's assessment of the French Revolu-tion,[90] will be beneficial and productive. Nonetheless, in the short term, there is little doubt that the assault on property rights implemented by the Mugabe land reforms not only collapsed political democracy but accelerated the meltdown of the economy, and so undermined food security that, as late as 2009, nearly 3 million Zimbabweans were still critically dependent upon food aid.[91] From this perspective, the chaotic and brutal manner in which land reform was imple-mented has posted a 'warning of how not to go about it'.[92]

Land reform in Namibia and South Africa

The Zimbabwean land reforms have radically changed the debate about this process in neighbouring Namibia and South Africa.[93] Without doubt, Mugabe has played to the African gallery to dramatic effect in countries where the legacy of the settler land pattern remains and where, as both governments admit, land reform has been slow and faulty. Indeed, Mugabe has been lionized amongst elements of both SWAPO and the ANC, one reason why the leaderships have been reluctant to criticize him.

In 2001, Pintile Davies, the President of the Namibia National Farmers Union, proclaimed to President Nujoma that communal farmers were frustrated by the slow pace of WBWS land reform, and warned of a Zimbabwe-style popular land takeover.[94] Hitherto, there had been no land invasions, but in

---

89   Ian Scoones, Nelson Marongwe, Blasio Mavedzenge, Jacob Mahenehene, Felix Murimbarimba and Chrispen Sukume (2010), *Zimbabwe's Land Reforms: Myths and Realities*, Woodbridge: James Currey.

90   On being asked what he thought of the French Revolution, Mao is reputed to have said that 'it is too early to tell'.

91   Amin Kamete (2009), 'Zimbabwe', in Andreas Mehler, Henning Melber and Klaas van Walraven (eds), *Africa Yearbook 2009*, Leiden: Brill, 547.

92   Ranger, responding to Mamdani, op. cit.

93   Samuel Kariuki (2007), 'Political compromise on land reform: A study of South Africa and Namibia', *South African Journal of International Affairs*, 14: 1, 99–114.

94   *New York Times*, 8 August 2001.

2002, a first instance occurred on a farm outside Windhoek. Rather than condemning it, Nujoma attacked Western criticism of Zimbawe's land reforms as interference in African affairs.[95] In 2006, on a trip to Harare, Isak Katalie, the Deputy Minister of Agriculture, proclaimed that the speed with which Zimbabweans had taken back their land from white farmers was 'commendable', and 'if Zimbabwe did this, we can do it in the same manner'.[96] By March 2010, Henock ya Kasita, Deputy Minister of Lands and Resettlement, was complaining that WBWS was not working, and that Namibia might have to follow the Zimbabwean example.[97]

In South Africa, a National Land Summit in 2005 called for a rural charter which embodied radical demands. These were ignored by government but many were subsequently taken up by the Landless People's Movement which openly advocated land seizures. Thereafter, the demand for Zimbabwe-style reform was spearheaded by Julius Malema, President of the ANC Youth League, who by early 2011 was campaigning vigorously for expropriation of farmland without compensation. 'When the colonizers and those who have the land took it away from us, they did not compensate, so why should they demand anything from us?' Even so, he argued, expropriation would have to be done within the constitutional framework, 'because we respect the law'.[98] His arguments, which in effect embraced the land policies advocated by the PAC at its breakaway from the ANC in 1959, were endorsed by the ANCYL conference in June 2011, and Malema predicted that they would soon become ANC policy. While the ANC itself responded by stating 'unequivocally' that the ANCYL's resolutions did not alter its own policies, the indications were that, as in Namibia, the slow pace of land reform was edging the party closer to a reconsideration of WBWS.

In Namibia, the approach to land reform was laid down by a National Land Conference held in 1991. While rejecting restitution of ancestral claims to land in full, notably by Herero, Nama, and Damara which other political groupings recognized would be incompatible with competing claims, this endorsed a reform programme which would see foreigners barred from owning farmland but enabled to lease it; a reallocation of underutilized commercial land to bring it into productive use; and a ban on multiple ownership of farms. It rapidly extended to the introduction of an Affirmative Action Loan Scheme (AALS) in 1992 (designed to extend loans to communal farmers with sufficient stock to operate commercially). Thereafter, two major pieces of legislation followed : the Land Reform Act of 1995 and the Communal Land Reform Act of 2002, the latter complementing a National Resettlement Policy (NRP) introduced in 2001. The last mentioned elaborated procedures whereby commercial farmers wishing to sell their lands had to provide the government with the first option to purchase them at the price being offered. Between 1992 and October 2003, some 3.1 million hectares of land were purchased under the AALS through some 528 loans, at a cost between 1996–97 and 2003–04 of N$104 million, the overall objective being to help create a class of black commercial farmers and free up land in communal areas for smaller communal farmers. Meanwhile,

[95]   BBC News, 'Namibia: The next Zimbabwe?' 5 December 2002.
[96]   South African Press Agency, 29 June 2006.
[97]   *The Namibian*, 10 March 2010.
[98]   *Star*, 6 May 2011.

from 1996–97, government started allocating N$20 million a year for purchase of commercial land for resettlement which increased to some N$50 million from 2003–04. This followed the passage of resolutions at the 2002 SWAPO Congress demanding an increase of expenditure on land purchase to N$100 per annum, along with the expropriation of some 192 farms (deemed under-utilized or farmed by absentee owners).

While the government was rhetorically supportive of the Zimbabwean reform programme, its own actions were far more cautious, despite numerous statements that the land reform process was proceeding too slowly and that expropriations would be stepped up. In practice, expropriations were few – just three by 2006. Then, in 2007, an attempt to expropriate four more farms was slowed down by a challenge in the High Court made by the two German owners, the court ruling that the government had not followed proper procedures. In total, some 99 farms had been purchased by the government by 2008–09, resulting in a redistribution of land to black Namibians of some 11 per cent of available commercial farmland.[99] At present, with government complaining that insufficient commercial farms are offered for sale, it will take another 40 years for half of all commercial farmlands to be owned by black Namibians.

By 2002, Nujoma was warning that Namibia could not continue with a situation where white farmers owned 30.4 million hectares of commercial farms and blacks lived on 2.2 million. He did not signal a move away from WBWS, but called on donors to contribute N$900 million over five years to acquire an estimated 360,000 hectares for distribution.[100]

Despite fears that the continuing imbalance in ownership is politically volatile, the SWAPO government has continued to prefer radical rhetoric to radical action. One reason, apart from the government's *de facto* alliance with white farmers, is that as a small country, it is unwilling to risk a breach with foreign donors, notably Germany, with which it has a bilateral Protection of Investment Agreement (1993) under which Namibia would have to compensate Germans whose lands might be confiscated at market value in foreign currency. Another is the awareness of its own incapacity to use its own budget to purchase farms offered for sale. Further, government strategies to assist emergent farmers have enjoyed very limited agricultural success, with a tendency, for instance, for farmers settled under the NRP to rent out their leases to city-dwelling civil servants, thereby promoting 'hobby farming'. Then there is recognition of the dangers to food security. Although the contribution of agriculture to GDP has declined from 9.4 per cent in 1990 to 5.4 per cent in 2008, the dynamism that exists in the sector, notably in grape production and dairy farming, continues to come from the commercial agricultural sector. In contrast, subsistence agriculture is largely languishing, growing at just 0.4 per cent per annum. Sherbourne argues that the relatively poor performance of agriculture is a reflection of uncertainty about land ownership (although it is as likely to be due to challenges presented by the government's lowering of tariffs and exposure of commercial agriculture to increased South African competition).[101] Nonetheless, while it may well be that the Namibian government is

[99]   Sherbourne, op. cit., 344–50.
[100] De Villiers, op. cit., 39.
[101] Ibid., 79–103; 339–51.

aware of the costs of Zimbabwe-style reform, the slow pace of existing land reform is always likely to render expropriations more attractive, were SWAPO to come under radical pressure from below or to face serious challenges by opposition political parties.

Mixed results have similarly attended land issues in South Africa, where the post-1994 land reform policy distinguished between land restitution (involving the restoration of land or cash compensation to victims of forced removals since the 1913 Land Act), and land redistribution (through which citizens could apply for grants with which to buy land for farming and/or settlement).[102] By March 2009, some 2.48 million hectares of productive agricultural land had been transferred under the former programme, with some 315,000 beneficiary households comprising around 1.6 million people. By this time, just 5.4 per cent of valid claims for restitution were left outstanding, with settlement of claims having cost more than R20 billion (of which some 27 per cent had been spent as financial compensation).[103] Although this progress was described as slow (due to disputes with land owners and between land claimants, as well as high land prices and bureaucratic delays), in retrospect the achievement is not unimpressive.

In contrast, land redistribution has been far more troubled, with very questionable outcomes for agricultural production. The process has gone through four phases. The first, 1995–97, under which some 372 projects were approved, was decidedly experimental, enabling the Department of Land Affairs to refine policies. The second, 1998–2000, was a period of more extensive roll-out of land reform via the Settlement/Land Acquisition Grant, whereby government distributed small grants (around R16,000 per person) to poor households with an income not exceeding R1,500 per month. Both phases are retrospectively deemed to have failed, with the need of the government to be seen as moving forward held back by the incapacity of the Department of Agriculture to provide adequate technical and other support. In addition, this was not only a period when land became increasingly expensive because of a property boom, but one when the government was removing virtually all agricultural marketing supports, including agricultural price stabilization, tariff protection, and subsidies, while simultaneously slashing the value of the agricultural budget by as much as 50 per cent. Emergent farmers were therefore 'caught in a squeeze between rising land prices and declining farm gate prices, and faced increasingly stiff competition with foreign imports'.[104] Many were therefore forced to pool their subsidies in collective enterprises, causing many of them to fail because of complex management and social cohesion problems.

The third phase, launched in 2000, featured a more commercial approach under a Land Reform for Agricultural Development programme. Beneficiaries could access up to R100,000 per adult household member, according to capital contributions made by the beneficiary. The objective was to enable a greater

[102] Michael Aliber and Reuben Mokoena (2004), 'The land question in contemporary South Africa', in John Daniel, Adam Habib and Roger Southall (eds), *State of the Nation 2003–2004*, Cape Town: HSRC Press, 330–46.

[103] SAIRR (2010), *South Africa Survey 2009–10*, Johannesburg: SAIRR, 534–35.

[104] Doreen Atkinson (2010), 'Breaking down barriers: Policy gaps and new options in South African land reform', in John Daniel, Prishani Naidoo, Devan Pillay and Roger Southall (eds), *New South African Review 2010: Development or Decline?* Johannesburg: Wits University Press, 366.

degree of family farming, alongside the transfer of 30 per cent of commercial farmland to black farmers by 2014 (a target of 25.9 million hectares). Over time, agricultural budgets increased markedly, from the R650 million of 1996–97 to R3.4 billion in 2005–06, while land reform budgets stabilized at about R4 billion. Subsequently, a Comprehensive Agricultural Support Programme was launched, aimed at accelerating service delivery in the areas of restitution, redistribution, security, AgriBEE, and family farming. This involved the creation of post-settlement support services, aimed at improving sustainability and reducing poverty and unemployment.

Finally, a fourth phase was inaugurated by a renamed Department of Rural Development and Land Reform in 2009, aimed at combining sustainable land reform with food security, rural development, and job creation linked to skills training.[105] This was an outcome of a major assessment of land reform which reflected critically on the poor ability of government departments to provide support to land reform beneficiaries due to lack of interdepartmental coordination, unenthusiastic municipal involvement in land reform, deficient integration of land reform with other social services, and weak agricultural extension service.[106] Indeed, at the end of 2010, the government admitted that some 222 black farmers had been bailed out to the tune of R232 million after they had failed to pay back their start-up loans to the Land Bank.[107]

For the official target of redistribution (originally drawn up by the World Bank) of 30 per cent of commercial agricultural land by 2014 to be realized, some 25.86 million hectares will have to have been redistributed. However, by 2008–09, the total of land redistributed amounted to a dismal 2.88 million hectares (or just 11 per cent of the target).[108] Not surprisingly, the entire process has become increasingly controversial. Many blame the alleged recalcitrance of white farmers to sell at reasonable prices, while the commercial farming lobby blames the ineptitude of official bureaucracy, reflecting that there is more land available on the market than the government can reasonably buy or manage.[109] There are numerous conflicting perspectives, ranging from one admission from the government that the '30 per cent by 2014' target is too steep for it to manage, to indications that there is a lack of coordination between the two ministries responsible for land reform and agriculture. There is also confusion about whether land reform is primarily about poverty alleviation, the transformation of large-scale agriculture into smaller-scale farms, or contesting the power of white agricultural capital. The issue is complicated by the removal of virtually all kinds of market protection for commercial agriculture, with a resultant major decline in the number of commercial farm units from 57,987 in 1993 to 39,982 in 2007, and an associated casualization and decline of the level of farm employment. Commercial farmers going out of business usually sell to larger operations which, in turn, are more capital intensive – a process

---

[105] Samuel Kariuki (2010), 'The Comprehensive Rural Development Programme (CRDP): A beacon of growth for rural South Africa?' in Daniel et al. (2010), op. cit., 345–63.

[106] Atkinson, op. cit., 369.

[107] *Business Report*, 15 May 2011.

[108] SAIRR, op. cit., 537.

[109] If a recent calculation (from official data) by the SAIRR is correct (*Business Day*, 5 July 2012) that over 40 per cent of *privately owned* land is now in black hands, it would seem that white farmers are not reluctant to sell at an agreed price.

which the government has done nothing to prevent. Overall, a lack of engagement by government with commercial agriculture has meant that 'land transfer' has become the only key deliverable, with the result that 'land reform has generally failed as a contribution to rural development, because of its poor links to the agricultural, agro-processing and non-farm sectors'.[110] However, while there is increasing evidence that rural development and agricultural empowerment policies will only work if they establish linkages to commercial agriculture, the latter is increasingly exposed politically by the slow pace of land reform. Meanwhile, evidence indicates that while nearly half of South Africa's population and some 70 per cent of the poor live in the rural areas, the latter have benefited less from policy changes than urban areas since 1994, and the impoverishment of the rural population is worsening in absolute as well as relative terms.[111]

In mid-2011, then Minister of Rural Development and Land Reform, Gugile Nkwinti, put forward a Green Paper which promised a radical change in land ownership. It was constructed around the three pillars of sustainable growth, equitable and democratic land redistribution, and 'production discipline for sustainable food security'. Yet key to Nkwinti's strategy was a plea for partnership between all stakeholders in agriculture, as well as indications of his realization of the difficulties of managing land reform successfully, having recently issued a call for 'strategic partners' to assist in staving off the collapse of some 852 farms. Nonetheless, the prospect of a review of WBWS is continuously inviting. A senior official conceded that amendment of the policy to step up expropriations would be a long process, but the government was keen to do it. 'We have a black government and they welcome it. The government serves the people, and the people want land.'[112] However, given the weight of large-scale agricultural capital, Julius Malema's prediction that expropriation without compensation will soon become ANC policy is unlikely to occur in the near future. Nonetheless, its popular appeal seems destined to grow rapidly unless more radical action is taken to confront the dismal failures of government policy.

Political stalemate and economic crisis

Beyond its disastrous impact upon most Zimbabweans, the economic meltdown in Zimbabwe has also had profoundly negative consequences for the wider region in terms of reputation, alongside downturn in trade volumes and outflows of population to neighbouring countries (notably South Africa). Meanwhile, Namibia and South Africa are both confronting the major structural problems of massive unemployment, poverty, inequality, low productivity, and declining international competitiveness (let alone ecological issues which have not been touched upon here). In Zimbabwe, a radical assault upon the settler legacy was driven by the immediate political interests of ZANU-PF with

---

[110] Atkinson, op. cit., 367–80.
[111] Roger van den Brink, Glen Sowabo Thomas and Hans Binswanger (2007), 'Agricultural land redistribution in South Africa: Towards accelerated implementation', in Hall and Ntsebeza (eds), op. cit., 152–201.
[112] Ayanda Mduli (2011), 'Land grabs not the answer', *Business Report*, 15 May.

massive disregard for the productive capacity which that same legacy embodied. In Namibia and South Africa, the political elites have adopted gradualist policies to address racial inequalities. Even so, there are solid reasons for arguing that their transformation policies are leading to a decline in the productive capacities of their private sectors, and their economies are set on a downward spiral. The revival of the Zimbabwean economy demands a resolution of the continuing political crisis and the restoration of democracy. The relative descent of the Namibian and South African economies reflects the limits of liberation politics, as the NLMs' 'capture' of 'state power' steadily encroaches upon productive capacities whilst hollowing out democracy.

Market critics of the NLMs' economic management blame an excess of political intervention for declining performance. There is considerable strength to their arguments if, for instance, we take into account the effect in South Africa of aspects of rights-based labour laws upon the capacity of small businesses to survive in an era where jobs across many economic sectors are moving to China and India. They are similarly correct to question extensions of state control over the economy when, as is easily demonstrated, the state machineries themselves have a limited (if not declining) capacity to do their existing jobs efficiently. However, market critics regularly ignore the baleful results of free market ideology: its tendency to promote the financialization of economies, de-industrialization, and widening inequality, while simultaneously undermining social solidarity through payments of huge remuneration packages to senior executives in the name of 'global competitiveness'.

Radical critics blame 'neo-liberalism' and the willingness of the political elites to adjust to it, ally with large-scale capital, and to implement it. Again, there is much strength to their arguments. Structural adjustment in Zimbabwe reversed many of the social achievements of the first decade of independence and played a major role in stoking the political crisis. Likewise, the conservative macroeconomics pursued in both Namibia and South Africa failed miserably to attract the investment gains that were promised, and have overseen an alarming decline of manufacturing. Yet while criticism of the NLMs is easy, the solutions often put forward – notably pursuit of a 'developmental state' and forms of 'alternative economics' – too often ignore the obvious: that a 'developmental state' presumes a level of state capacity which the post-settler states manifestly do not have, and that for all their sins, the large corporates and smaller companies embody a productive capacity (capital, technology, skills and know-how) which is necessary for any country to compete in the modern global capitalist economy. Likewise, collective alternatives such as cooperatives should clearly have a major role to play in harnessing the productive capacities of people sidelined by the market, yet it is unlikely that they can succeed unless inserted into a wider economy underpinned by the private sector.

This chapter has reviewed three key dimensions of post-liberation economy. Regarding BSRs, it has argued that while ZANU-PF first promoted but then collapsed a 'reform coalition', more collaborative relationships between the state and business in Namibia and South Africa were strongly contributory to the promotion of higher levels of growth than had been achieved under the later years of apartheid. However, these have recently come under increasing strain.

The gap between business and the state could have been narrowed by BEE. In Zimbabwe, the initial 'reform coalition' was undermined not only by ZANU-PF's growing domination of the state but by its sidelining of black business. Currently, the pursuit of indigenization is more akin to the blackmailing of corporate capital than a serious promotion of a national capitalism. In Namibia, the late formalization of BEE has only reinforced the critique of those who identify 'empowerment' as promoting the interests of a comprador SWAPO elite. In South Africa, the shift from narrowly focused to 'broad-based' BEE sought to overcome the fundamental difficulty of blacks' lack of capital by shifting emphasis to the promotion of a black middle class and generally, a more skilled workforce. However, increasingly, the functionality of BEE has been undermined not merely by corporate 'box-ticking' to achieve 'BEE compliance', but massive abuse by state operatives in league with 'tenderpreneurs' in the allocation of state contracts.

Finally, the radical land reforms carried out in Zimbabwe were illustrative of the unrealistic economic foundations of all three political transitions. WBWS was put in place to confirm adherence to property rights and market-based reform. In Zimbabwe this wholly ignored the lack of financial capacity of the postcolonial state to address one of the most fundamental causes of racial inequality. Failure of Britain and the US to honour promises to provide the financial wherewithal of the state to uphold property rights was to undermine not only the viability of democracy, but wider African respect for Western political and moral critiques of ZANU-PF's assault on human rights. In Namibia and South Africa, the general hysteria in the media and business circles which attends any mention of 'expropriation' plays into the hands of nationalist populists such as Malema, rather than looking to the serious engagement between agro-capital and the state which is needed if the politically volatile land question is to be seriously addressed. As matters stand, pressures for radical land redistribution are steadily mounting: both the ANC's Polokwane Conference and its National Policy Conference in June 2012 called for a shift to state expropriation of land (albeit subject to 'just and equitable' compensation). Even though, with good reason, we may argue that the slow pace of land reform is far more due to state incapacity to manage it than to a lack of potential sellers, it is nonetheless becoming increasingly possible to envisage a Zimbabwean-style situation whereby invasions of farms by landless people and political entrepreneurs prompt a populist shift in ANC policy towards seizure of lands without compensation.

All such developments are indicative of the acute crisis of the post-liberation state for which there are no easy answers. Yet there are some pointers to a more constructive way forward. For a start, there is manifest growing regional impatience with ZANU-PF and the obstacles it is placing in the way of a constitutional settlement which could provide for a durable path to economic recovery. In South Africa, belated appreciation by both corporate and state elites of the political dangers of economic polarization (across racial as well as private-public sector lines) has been fired by Malema's populist campaign for nationalization. Loud critiques of the causes and consequences of perceived declining state capacity are beginning to be matched by an increasingly insistent call for a concerted dialogue of capital, government, labour, and civil society to address the need for a more socially inclusive growth path. All recognize the need for a major change in economic direction to address the needs of the region's impoverished black majority, if social disintegration and attendant political meltdown are to be avoided.

9.
The Party State, Class Formation, and the Decline of Ideology

NLMs in southern Africa provided for the political aspiration of frustrated nationalists, intellectuals, and revolutionaries to confront settler rule and colonial capitalism. The nature of their struggle took them into espousal of alliances between the petty bourgeoisie, working class, and peasantries, although the political weight of these different classes varied between the movements. As such, they became the locus of progressive tendencies aiming at the realization of democracy, human rights, and socialism, these ideas borrowed from liberating Western traditions (liberalism, Christianity, and nationalism) which, paradoxically, were imported as ideological dimensions of the oppressive practices of settler colonial rule. At the same time, the radicalization of the struggle caused by the rigidity of the settler state was to prompt liberation movements to adopt strategies guided by Marxism-Leninism, which from 1927 had argued for the simultaneity of nationalist and socialist struggle. This did not mean that liberation movements were 'communist', as were regularly accused of being by their Cold Warrior detractors. Rather, it meant that NLM ideologies constituted an uneasy mix of liberalism, nationalism, and Marxism-Leninism. However, once NLMs assumed power, the nationalist and Marxist-Leninist aspects of their ideologies tended to overwhelm (although never entirely extinguish) their liberalism.

The Marxist-Leninist tradition provided a coherent framework for understanding settler societies as simultaneously embodying racial, national, and class oppression. It also brought with it two particular conceptions which were to profoundly influence the post-liberation state: the ideas of the party as the vanguard of historical advance and of the need for the capture of state power. The outcome was the blurring of the personnel and roles of party and state, and the rise of the 'party state'.

The party state was simultaneously a 'party machine', a vehicle for the upward mobility of party elites and for material accumulation justified ideologically by reference to the historical rightness of transformation. Strategies of Africanization, affirmative action, BEE, and/or indigenization were central to this historical tendency. According to the theory of the NDR, a removal of racial shackles from the stunted class of capitalists whose development was held back by settler colonialism would enable the growth of a class of 'patriotic capitalists' able to challenge the prior dominance of white and international capital. However, the danger was that emergent black capitalists might acquire a material independence from the party state and come to challenge it. On the other hand, the primacy of the party state implied that the 'patriotic bourgeoisie' would become wedded to 'political connectivity'. Although enhanced educational opportunity and affirmative action would provide greater possibilities for formerly racially oppressed individuals to rise through the ranks of state and business to constitute a significant black middle class, they might simultaneously tie the fate of such elements to political favour.

It follows that the accumulation strategies of proto-capitalist and black middle-class elements were to become heavily centred on access to the party machine and its power to allocate resources. Simultaneously, because such resources were limited, the party machine became prone to internal strife between factions and networks (based around region, ethnicity, opportunity, industry, etc). Meanwhile, the centrality of the party machine to the accumulation process led to the party becoming ideologically hollowed out: ideologies which had become radicalized as the liberation struggles had intensified were to record substantial changes in their form and content as a party-state bourgeoisie consolidated. Two changes can be highlighted: first, a shift from socialism to 'transformation'; and second, the instrumentalization of ideology as a weapon in intra-party combat. A substantive outcome has been the replacement of social equality as an ideal by a stress on postcolonial racial equality.

Party predation, primitive accumulation, and class formation in Zimbabwe

Daniel Compagnon argues that whether or not it claimed Marxism as a creed, the incoming nationalist elite in Zimbabwe was primarily motivated by the prospects of upward mobility and accumulation offered by the capture of the settler state.[1] Similarly, David Moore has characterized a Zimbabwean 'party-state bourgeoisie' as having embraced a process of 'primitive accumulation'. Rather than diverting resources into productive investment, this kleptocratic bourgeoisie engaged in parasitic and mercantile activities which by the mid-2000s had totally bankrupted the state.[2] For this bourgeoisie, membership of the party-state machinery and the access it gives to position, privilege, power, and opportunity has become vital.

The majority of the nationalist leadership in Zimbabwe was part of an emerging African petty bourgeoisie in the 1950s and 1960s. The strongest components were former mission-school teachers (like Mugabe himself), nurses, and low-ranking civil servants who were frustrated by their lack of opportunity in segregationist Rhodesia. Entering nationalist politics was perceived as the fastest route to an improved status. 'Subsequent accumulation strategies were rooted in these early – largely legitimate – grievances', with one of the effects of the 1970s' armed struggle being to harden the determination of the nationalists to acquire wealth through the conquest of the state. Because government had played such a strong role in settler society, ZANU-PF's official socialist ideology 'conveniently justified a stronger direct and indirect control of the national economy of the 1980s'.[3] However, in spite of struggle rhetoric citing

[1] Daniel Compagnon (2010), *A Predictable Tragedy: Robert Mugabe and the Collapse of Zimbabwe*, Pennsylvania: University of Pennsylvania Press.
[2] David Moore (2003), 'Zimbabwe's triple crisis: Primitive accumulation, nation-state formation and democratisation in the age of neo-liberal globalisation', *African Studies Quarterly*, 7: 2 and 3, 35–47. See also http://web.africa.ufl.edu/asq/v7/v7i2a2.htm
[3] Compagnon, op. cit., 193.

the necessity of control of the means of production, Mugabe's government – constrained by Lancaster House, the advice of fellow African leaders, and the promises and reality of foreign aid – did not significantly alter the capitalist structure of the economy. The preservation of a large, white-controlled, private sector within Zimbabwe's mixed economy would mean that opportunities could be generated for the emerging black elites, while the expansion of the public sector provided a valuable resource for Mugabe's political patronage, lucrative positions for party cadres, political cronies, and family members. Through state interventions (expansion of the number and reach of parastatals, launch of party-related enterprises, pricing policies, and pressures on companies to sell to the state or to provide 'rents' to party connected elites) new opportunities were created for members of the new ruling class to enrich themselves.

Meredith has noted how rapidly the new elite of politicians, civil servants, and military and police chiefs adapted to the lifestyle once reserved for whites: 'moving into spacious houses; driving expensive cars; dining in fashionable restaurants; and buying farms, hotels and businesses,' as well as enrolling their children in private schools and staging sumptuous weddings, lavish funerals, and grand weekend parties.[4] Corruption within the civil service and amongst politicians became rapidly entrenched. One instance that hit the headlines in 1997 involved revelations that a long-term housing scheme administered by the Ministry of Local Government and National Housing had dished out loans to cabinet ministers and senior civil servants to build houses while denying loans to qualified people who had made required monthly payments. By January 1988, some 177 civil servants had been convicted since independence on corruption-related charges, while some 758 cases were outstanding.[5]

From early days, Mugabe lamented the corrupting influence of office amongst his senior party colleagues and the loss of a spirit of dedicated service amongst the party rank and file. He lashed out at ministers and other politicians on the eve of the anniversary independence in 1983:

> Even if the present White owners of property and natural resources were to be replaced by Black owners of property and natural resources, the need for a socialist revolution would still remain urgent. A bourgeoisie does not cease to be exploitative merely because its colour has turned Black or because it is now national rather than foreign...I wish to express my utter dismay at the bourgeois tendencies that are affecting our leadership at various levels of government.[6]

Local government councillors and mayors were using their positions to assign themselves money-making contracts, misappropriating public funds, and misusing public property, while:

> Even Cabinet Ministers...have proceeded to acquire huge properties by way of commercial farms and other business concerns...those who should mete out social justice to the people and society turn into a class of avaricious exploiters of the masses, and so traitors to their cause.[7]

---

[4]   Martin Meredith (2002), *Robert Mugabe: Power, Plunder and Tyranny in Zimbabwe*, Johannesburg and Cape Town: Jonathan Ball Publishers, 81.
[5]   *ACR 1987–88*, B847.
[6]   *ACR 1982–83*, B883.
[7]   Ibid.

At this stage, while pragmatic with regard to the need to abide by the terms of Lancaster House, Mugabe remained explicitly committed to building a socialist society (even if he was beginning to speak less of Marxism-Leninism). Denunciations of officials and leaders who used their positions to accumulate wealth were a regular theme of his speeches. Such behaviour was nothing less than 'daylight robbery', and 'socialist deviants' had to choose between their individual interests or 'walking the road to Socialism'.[8] By 1984, a party Leadership Code required that all party officials and senior civil servants owning more than 50 acres of land, more than one house, engaged in business, or raised loans except against the security of their earnings should declare their earnings and disclose how they acquired them.[9] Subsequently, a list of those failing to declare their assets was drawn up by the Central Intelligence Organization (CIO) but although they were given a warning, no action was taken against them. As Meredith observed of the code, 'no one paid much attention to it'.[10]

One reason was the shallow basis for socialism. Despite early post-independence declarations by Mugabe that ZANU-PF would declare formally for Marxism-Leninism, no grounding had been laid by the party. As observed by Maurice Nyagumbo, the party's national organizing secretary prior to ZANU-PF's first national congress since independence in 1984, there had been no political training of workers and peasants, and as a result, there was no ideological consciousness amongst them.[11] Indeed, in 1987, Mugabe openly castigated workers as irresponsible, lazy, and ill-disciplined and reminded them that Lenin had warned that 'those who don't work, neither shall they eat'.[12] However, it was the blatantly unsocialist behaviour of the party elite which more regularly aroused his ire.

Although he regularly threatened to choose a new party leadership that adhered to Marxist-Leninist thinking, Mugabe lacked the inclination to tackle the internal opposition this would arouse. In practice, it was far more important to keep the support of that same leadership which he was criticizing. Thus in 1985, the President gave his permission for General Solomon Mujuru, a key figure who had quelled the internal party revolt aimed at toppling him in 1978, to expand his business interests. Mujuru proceeded to acquire a supermarket chain as well as two farms, a hotel, and other properties in the Bindura area so that by 1992, when he resigned from the army, he had allegedly become one of the country's wealthiest individuals. Further, within a few years, he was to become the country's biggest landowner (although his business empire in Bindura was to collapse as a result of bad management).[13] However, the defining case of the era was the Willowgate scandal, when allegations were made by the *Bulawayo Chronicle* that a number of ministers had obtained new cars from the Willowgate assembly plant and sold them on at greatly inflated prices. Mugabe responded by establishing a Commission of Inquiry under Judge President Wilson Sandura in January 1989 whose proceedings led to the resignation of three ministers and a junior minister, Frederick Shava, along with

[8] *ACR 1986–87*, B892.
[9] *ACR 1983–84*, B879–880.
[10] Meredith, op. cit., 81.
[11] *ACR 1984–85*, B872–873.
[12] *ACR 1986–87*, B891–892.
[13] Meredith, op. cit., 82; Compagnon, op. cit., 203.

that of Maurice Nyagumbo (who then committed suicide). However, rather than prosecuting the offenders, Mugabe initiated (or at least condoned) the removal of the editor of the *Chronicle*, after which he used his presidential prerogative to pardon Shava after he had been convicted, thus precipitating the collapse of the Sandura Commission. Principle was trumped by party unity (especially at a time when the latter was reeling from the defection of Edgar Tekere to form ZUM).[14]

Reference to socialism might be used by Mugabe to constrain the behaviour of the nationalist elite, but more particularly Marxist-Leninist jargon was used to castigate the small pre-independence grouping of African entrepreneurs which had developed within the settler economy as a 'petty bourgeoisie'. ZANU-PF had little sympathy for blacks who had run successful businesses during the war. Whereas such African businessmen favoured market-oriented policies, the government favoured statist policies and a regulated economy. The populist-oriented labour policies of ZANU-PF in the first half of the 1980s, when wages were raised and the ZCTU established, 'made that ideological conflict more apparent'.[15] Little was done to promote the cause of African entrepreneurs, and those with an independent power base were regarded as a potential political threat to ZANU-PF leaders whose power was built on patronage. An illustrative case is that of Strive Masiyiwa, a particularly successful businessman. Although not a member of ZANU-PF, he was a member of the wider elite, and indeed, was part of Mugabe's extended family. After working for the government-owned Posts and Telecommunications Company (PTC), he formed his own electrical construction company, Retrofit, and soon secured several contracts from government (including the installation of the electrical system in Mugabe's rural mansion in Zvimba). However, when in 1994 he decided to enter the cellular telephone market in Zimbabwe and obtained a December 1995 Supreme Court judgement declaring the PTC monopoly on telecommunications to be contrary to the Bill of Rights, he infuriated his kinsman. Thereafter, his contracts with government were cancelled, and he was subject to vicious attacks from ministers and civil servants. After receiving death threats, he moved to South Africa for a period to ensure his safety. Masiyiwa's mistake was that he had openly criticized government economic policies, and through his leadership of the moderate IBDC had sought to mobilize an urban petty bourgeoisie in favour of an indigenization process which would have been independent of the party.[16]

Such incidents did not mean that the nationalist elite were hostile to business *per se*. On the contrary, key members of the ZANU-PF were soon heavily involved in business ventures. 'Through the years, names of ministers, MPs, Central Committee members, and high ranking civil servants would appear on lists of board members of private companies', some just 'eating', some using their positions for the more vigorous pursuit of wealth.[17] Indeed, throughout

[14] *ACR 1988–89*, B771.
[15] Compagnon, op. cit., 195.
[16] Ibid. Masiyiwa is nothing if not persistent. In 1998, he managed to launch his cell phone company, Econet Wireless, on the Zimbabwe Stock Exchange. It rapidly became the largest cell phone network in Zimbabwe, expanded into other African countries, and was subsequently launched on the London Stock Exchange.
[17] Ibid.

the 1980s, retired civil servants and ZANU-PF politicians were used as middlemen for white-owned corporations as political connections became increasingly vital to operate businesses in an economy ridden with all types of regulations and state interventions, so much so that by the end of the decade, there was the prospect of an unlikely, but real 'alliance between white settlers and the state'. By the early 1990s 'a merger between white and black elites appeared as a plausible scenario for the development of a post-independence ruling class'.[18]

Compagnon identifies the Willowgate scandal as a turning point which provided graphic evidence of a state-controlled economy which had limited bene-fits for established business.[19] A 'command economy' under the control of the ZANU-PF elite had become largely paralyzed by its own weaknesses: an oversize state bureaucracy, bloated parastatals, a ballooning budget deficit, and white-dominated, export-led commercial agriculture and mining sectors which were increasingly being squeezed by a shortage of foreign exchange to buy spare parts or invest, alongside a complex of regulations on prices, wages, repatriation of profits, and foreign exchange allocation, and so on which increasingly affected the competitiveness of the manufacturing sector. Capital goods installed in the 1950s and 1960s badly needed replacement, and the state was not in a position to sustain public investment at the level of the early 1980s, despite a significant inflow of foreign aid and high levels of corporate and personal income tax. By the late 1980s, the state's high level of spending on education and health for the poor was becoming unsustainable without a higher level of growth and increased private sector investment. The outcome was the adoption of ESAP: a shift to market-based reforms away from the command economy, the liberaliza-tion of foreign exchange and the import of various commodities, together with a reduction in public spending and the privatization of some parastatals.

Hevina Dashwood argues that the imposition of ESAP was a product of 'the emergence of a consensus among senior decision-makers that market-based reforms were desirable; the strong support of the entrepreneurial and agrarian elites for market-based reforms; and the embourgeoisement of the ruling elite'.[20] Compagnon is more doubtful, arguing that there was no conversion to neo-liberal economics on the part of the ZANU-PF leadership (with Mugabe being particularly hostile) and that they were no more committed to neo-liberalism than they had been to socialism. Instead, economic liberalization and privati-zation were embraced only to the extent that they provided the opportunity to manipulate economic policy to favour their own interests. They proceeded to slash expenditure on health, education, and social services, yet maintained high levels of spending on defence, redundant ministries such as National Affairs (which served as an unofficial channel for funding ZANU-PF), and maintained a bloated government structure which continued to provide extensive perks to ministers and senior civil servants. Indeed, it was the World Bank rather than the government which insisted on the creation of a Social Development Fund to cushion the poor against the worst effects of ESAP. In contrast, the elite showed marked caution when it came to privatization of loss-making parastatals, for

[18]   Ibid., 96.
[19]   Ibid., 198–99.
[20]   Hevina Dashwood (2000), *Zimbabwe: The Political Economy of Transformation*, Toronto: Univer-sity of Toronto Press, 191.

control of these was directly in its interests. By the end of the 1990s, only three out of fifty-odd parastatals – the Cotton Marketing Board, the Cold Storage Commission, and the Dairy Marketing Board – had been commercialized, with the state continuing to retain a controlling shareholding so that it was able to influence the appointment of directors and company policies. Nonetheless, after continuing negotiations with the Bretton Woods institutions, the government adopted the second phase of ESAP in 1998, listing 52 companies to be commercialized and then privatized. This facilitated the approval of a standby facility of US$193 million by the IMF in August 1999.[21] However, it was too late to rescue the incipient class alliance between the ZANU-PF elite and white business.

By this time collaborative relations between the government and business were becoming increasingly fraught, as the political elite embarked upon strategies of shameless predation in the name of 'indigenization'. Socialist discourse and the Leadership Code had become obsolete as a legitimizing ideology, and 'a new political rhetoric was needed to allow ZANU-PF big men to take full advantage of economic liberalization and to provide a smokescreen for accumulation strategies'.[22] 'Indigenization' became the slogan of the 1990s, and was used to legitimize the shameless seizure of private assets by the party-state elite, in many cases at the expense of genuine African entrepreneurs. The primary target soon became the white business sector and, after 2000, commercial farming, as continued white control of the most lucrative sectors of the economy was portrayed as the major obstacle to the empowerment of black Zimbabweans. Propaganda by individuals attached to the AAG was laced with racially charged undertones urging Mugabe to confiscate white land without compensation and to force established international companies to sell their assets. Yet the triggering event which ensured that indigenization became the backbone of Mugabe's economic policy was his encounter with the war veterans.

In 1997, enraged by the suspension of payments made to former combatants in the bush war by the War Veterans' Compensation Fund, veterans had jeered Mugabe at a Heroes' Day rally, following which the President appointed a judicial Commission of Inquiry. This confirmed allegations that the fund had been looted by top officials and civil servants who had received payouts on grounds of various degrees of disability (prompting Independent MP Margaret Dongo to remark caustically that she was surprised that the government could still function, administered as it was by so many ailing people).[23] However, it was the veterans' fury at the pillaging of their funds that catapulted Chenjerai 'Hitler' Hunzvi to political prominence and was ultimately to prompt Mugabe into backing the seizure of white farms.

By the late 1990s, mounting economic difficulties were translating into a reduced level of sources for appropriation, so it is no coincidence that the political elite plunged Zimbabwe into the war in the DRC. Horace Campbell stresses how ZANU-PF and military leaders saw the war as a route to easy riches and as an opportunity to outsmart South African mining capital. Lacking the requisite capital to compete with such major entities such as De Beers and Anglo-American, they moved swiftly to ingratiate themselves with Laurent Kabila, exchanging military support for the right to plunder under such auspices as Zimbabwe

---

21 Compagnon, op. cit., 200–02.
22 Ibid., 202.
23 *ACR 1996–98*, B782–83.

Defence Industries (ZDI), an entity which had been established in 1984 as the business arm of the Defence Forces. Even before the overthrow of President Mobutu, ZDI had signed a Z$53 million deal to sell food, bullets, bombs, and uniforms to Kabila's rebel forces; after Kabila was in power, his government allocated hugely lucrative mining, forestry, and agricultural concessions to several private Zimbabwean companies in which government ministers and military officers had either a controlling or major interest.[24] Its board stuffed with active and former military officers and senior civil servants, ZDI then entered a joint venture which flooded the Congolese market with goods not available locally. As Horace Campbell relates, 'Following the generals' example, many ZDF officers operating in the DRC got involved in diamond and gold smuggling and various forms of trafficking, if only by extending their protection to the smugglers for a commission.' Likewise Zimbabwean parastatals were encouraged to enter the Congolese market, initiatives including the proposed renovation of Congolese power plants by the Zimbabwe Electricity Supply Authority, the cultivation of land by the Zimbabwean Agriculture and Rural Development Authority, and the development of exports via the Zimbabwean railway.[25]

Ironically, realizing that they had neither the finance nor technical skills to exploit the deals being offered, members of the ZANU-PF elite struck up alliances with dubious individuals such as Billy Rautenbach and John Bredenkamp (both of whom had built major business empires under UDI and had worked with Smith to break sanctions) and with equally shady foreign partners. Rautenbach, a white Zimbabwean, had been granted a 38 per cent equity in the Congolese mining parastatal Gecamines, which exploited cobalt and copper, in November 1998. Appointed Chief Executive, he promised to make it profitable. Four-fifths of the cobalt-mining rights were to be transferred to a joint venture between Rautenbach's Virgin Island-registered Ridgepoint Overseas Development Ltd, and a company controlled by close advisers to Kabila and his Finance Minister, Pierre-Victor Mpoyo. Then in January 1998 Kabila granted Rautenbach and his associates (who included a string of Zimbabwean military and ZANU-PF officials) a cobalt mine near Likasi, provided it repaired a road between Matadi and Kinshasha. However, in 2000, Kabila cancelled all contracts with Rautenbach after he had failed to restore Gecamines to profitability, although in compensation – and along with Bredenkamp and ZANU-PF cronies – his company, Tremalt Ltd, received an 80 per cent share in Gecamines' concessions of copper and cobalt (being exploited by the Kababankola Mining Company) that were worth more than US$1 billion. The ultimate owners and beneficiaries of Tremalt were hidden by a web of trusts and private holding companies registered in the Virgin Islands and the Isle of Man, but it is known that Tremalt remitted 34 per cent of its profits to ZANU-PF big men under a profit-sharing agreement supervised by George Sekeramayi, a party official close to Mugabe.[26]

---

[24] Horace Campbell (2003), *Reclaiming Zimbabwe: The Exhaustion of the Patriarchal Model of Liberation*, Cape Town: David Philip, 230–46.

[25] Compagnon, op. cit., 214.

[26] Compagnon, op. cit., 216, drawing from the report of the UN Panel of Experts on the *Illegal Exploitation of Natural Resources and Other Forms of Wealth of the Democratic Republic of Congo*, appointed by the Security Council in 2000, notably paras.156–70. http://www.un.org/News/dh/latest,drcongo.htm

Mugabe's then General Chief of Staff Vitalis Zvinashe (whose transport company had already cleaned up a contract for carrying military supplies from Harare to the DRC) together with four high-ranking civil servants, formed a company called Osleg (short for the military codename for the intervention in the DRC, 'Operation Sovereign Legitimacy') to exploit diamonds in the ZDF-held zones of the war-torn country. Presented officially as the financial arm of the ZDF, Osleg was in fact a private company with no institutional link to the military, and thus straightforwardly allowed for the privatization of profit on the back of public office. Subsequently, in July 1999, Osleg formed a joint venture called Cosleg with a company in which Kabila was a majority stakeholder. Cosleg was granted exclusive rights to exploit diamonds and other minerals for 25 years in two of the DRC's richest diamond concession areas near Mbuji Mayi that were previously mined by a Congolese parastatal. In turn, Cosleg then formed another joint venture called Sengamines with Oryx-Zimcon, a subsidiary of a firm majority owned by Omanese businessman Thamer al-Shanfari (with Zidco and Congolese interests having minority holdings). Sengamines involved itself in mining operations while Cosleg engaged in timber and manganese processing.[27]

Overall, the war gave a new lease of life to Zimbabwean party-state entrepreneurs involved in transportation, railway, mining, armaments production, and timber. But the beauty of it all was that whereas Kabila had promised that the Congolese would cover the costs of the deployment of Zimbabwean troops, the major part of the burden was actually shouldered by the Zimbabwean taxpayer. In 1999, the Zimbabwean government had admitted to only US$3 million a month being spent on the war, and thereby duped the IMF into agreeing a line of standby credit in August of that year. When in September 2000 Finance Minister Simbi Makoni revealed that Zimbabwe had spent US$263 million on the war, the IMF pulled the plug. Subsequently, as the war was brought to a conclusion through South African and other negotiation, Mugabe maintained a peculiarly close relationship with Kabila, and Compagnon deems this to have been crucial for the perpetuation of Zimbabwean business interests in the DRC. Indeed, six new trade and service agreements were signed between the DRC and Zimbabwe prior to the announcement of the withdrawal of ZDF troops from the diamond centre of Mbuji Mayi late in August 2002.[28] From then on, the appropriation of settler farms under the fast track land reform was virtually child's play.

As indicated above, the land reform process was to see significant allocation of land to peasants and small farmers. Nonetheless, an investigation published in late 2010 which drew information from government documents and audit reports, and is compatible with Moyo's analysis, suggests that a 2,200 strong politically connected elite controls close to half the land seized from white farmers, with President Mugabe, his wife, ZANU-PF cabinet ministers, senior military officers, provincial governors, senior party officials, chiefs, and judges owning nearly 5 million hectares of agricultural land, including wildlife conservancies and plantations. At the top of the pile, according to the report, were Mugabe and his wife, who owned some 14 farms (extending to 16,000

---

[27] Ibid., 216–17.
[28] Ibid.; and Campbell, op. cit., 230–46.

hectares); his deputy, Joyce Mujuru, together with her late husband, former army General Solomon Mujuru and their close relatives, who owned at least 25 farms; and Constantine Chiwenga, the Defence Forces Commander, who had two farms near Harare, including the 1,200 hectare Chakoma Estates, which his wife allegedly seized from its former owners at gunpoint.

Overall, 90 per cent of the nearly 200 army officers from the rank of Major to Lieutenant-General owned farms, this pattern replicated throughout the air force, police, and prisons service, and the CIO, so that there are in total some 400 officers from the security forces who are alleged to have received farms above 250 hectares, while many lower-ranking officers and war veterans had smaller holdings. Similarly, all ZANU-PF cabinet ministers, 56 politburo members, 98 Members of Parliament, and 35 elected and unelected Senators had been allocated former white farms, with many owning more than one; all 10 provincial governors had seized farms, with 4 being multiple owners; and 65 per cent of the more than 200 mostly partisan traditional chiefs had also benefited from the land reforms. Likewise, 16 Supreme Court and High Court Judges, including Chief Justice Chidyausika, owned large farms ranging between 540 to 1,380 hectares; and 40 serving and former ambassadors, and over two-thirds of parastatals bosses also owned large tracts of land. Surprisingly, the Reserve Bank of Zimbabwe Governor Gideon Gono had missed out, but allegedly managed to buy four farms at knockdown prices from farmers who were under pressure from invaders to leave their properties. Meanwhile, no high-profile civil society or MDC officials had benefited, with the sole exception of Welshman Ncube, the Secretary-General of the splinter MDC.[29]

The skewed nature of the land allocation process has, unsurprisingly, failed to translate into productive commercial farming. Many former white farms have been allowed to run down or lie fallow, with beneficiaries having hopped from one farm to another. In other cases such as that of Perence Shiri, who commanded the Fifth Brigade's crackdown on Matabeleland in the early 1980s, seizure of farms has led to the eviction of numerous landless families. Many of the elite have become what Mugabe himself has termed 'mobile phone farmers', using their farms for recreation, leaving it to peasant and smaller farmers to engage in productive farming. Legal restrictions on the ownership of more than one farm are totally ignored, for politically accessed land ownership has become central to the alliance that holds ZANU-PF, the senior ranks of the public service, and the military together.

Yet after land, it is diamonds that remain ZANU-PF's best friend, even after the military pull-out from the DRC. Before 2004, diamond production in Zimbabwe was mainly limited to accidental finds in alluvial gold diggings, with the exception of the River Ranch kimberlite mine near the South African border. However, during the late 1990s, Rio Tinto Zimbabwe discovered a kimberlite cluster at Murowa, in central Zimbabwe, and began mining in 2004, producing diamonds, with an average value of US$65/ct. Then came the Marange strike of 2006 in Manicaland, close to the Mozambique border. The large proportion of diamonds from Marange are coarse and of low quality, worth at the time between US$6–10/ct; but around 10 per cent were of far higher quality, with a value of up to $150/ct. Legal control of the Marange diamond field had been

---

[29]   The authors remain anonymous for reasons of personal safety.

gained by African Consolidated Resources (ACR) after De Beers had relinquished its claim in April 2006. In June, the company went public with news of a big discovery of alluvial diamonds; in December, it was thrown off its concession by the military. By now a frenzied diamond rush had developed, with some 15,000 informal diggers scrabbling for diamonds for sale to a thriving black market. However, because Zimbabwe did not move to a US-dollarized economy until March 2009, only foreigners and ZANU-PF connected elites possessed the hard currency needed to buy and sell the diamonds, with most sales made to Lebanese buyers operating on the Mozambican side of the border. Inevitably the lion's share of the smuggling was controlled by elements within the military.[30]

At the same time as it had expelled ACR, the government had sent in the police to drive out the informal diggers with sjamboks, guns, and dogs but over subsequent months they quietly returned. This prompted the security forces to strike back in October 2008 with armed helicopters accompanied by police support units on the ground. There were reports that they mowed down up to 200 people. By January 2009, the vast Chiadzwa diamond fields resembled a military garrison. The miners had gone, but mining continued, this time by soldiers and by residents of Marange village (including children) in forced labour under military supervision.[31]

By this time, the government had appointed the MMCZ to act as the sole buying and selling agent, and had handed out licences to three mining companies, reputedly financed by South Africans but fronted by Zimbabweans who all had close links to ZANU-PF. One, Mbada Mining, backed by Johannesburg-based New Reclamation Ltd, was the best resourced and infamous for having had to pay huge fines after entering into plea bargains with the South African NPA to avoid prosecution for illegal bargaining practices. Another, Canadile, was a joint venture of the South African-registered Core Mining and the Zimbabwe Mining Development Corporation (ZMDC). A further sinister development was the alleged receipt of off-budget financing (perhaps as much as US$100 million) by the CIO from Sam Pa, a businessman who held leadership positions in an obscure network of companies known as the Queensway syndicate (largely owned by private Hong Kong business interests) and with a track record of opaque 'resources for infrastructure' deals across sub-Saharan Africa. In return, Sam Pa received diamonds and accessed business opportunities in the cotton and property development sectors.[32]

By 2009, international outrage at the human rights abuses occurring in Marange had forced the Kimberley Process, to which Zimbabwe was a signatory, to call a halt to the sale of Zimbabwean diamonds until conditions improved. The ZMDC responded with a security strategy for the Marange area which would see a total demilitarization of the 400-square-kilometre zone. An outer perimeter would be secured by the army and the police, while security inside the diamond fields would be handled by civilian operators, recruited and trained by the mining companies, which in turn committed to provision of extensive social facilities, such as schools and clinics, for the local population.

[30] Partnership Africa Canada (2009), *Zimbabwe, Diamonds and the Wrong Side of History*, March.
[31] *Sunday Independent*, 12 December 2010.
[32] Global Witness (2012), *Financing a Parallel Government? The Involvement of the Secret Police and Military in Zimbabwe's Diamond, Cotton and Property Sectors*, June.

In addition, the Zimbabwean government agreed to take action on smuggling and the legalization of small-scale mining. However, within two weeks of the KP go-ahead for the resumption of sales, it was business as usual for the Defence Force. By December 2009 it had brought in machinery and workers to plunder workings already excavated by Candile's operations, with military transports flying diamond-bearing ore to the army base in Mutare. When complaints were made to the government, a retired General was brought in to coordinate security, civilian security operators were forced out and replaced by police and military, following which scores of locals, including children, were reportedly forced to work, being kept in barbed-wire enclosures within the military base, inside the concession area. By the end of 2010, military control of the Marange diamond fields had been reimposed. Indeed, by now, Canadile's stockpile of diamonds had been seized and six of its directors arrested. Mining continued without the involvement of Core Mining, which resorted to action in the Zimbabwean courts.[33]

The formation of the coalition government had radically transformed ZANU-PF's agenda, and tightening its grip over the Marange diamond fields, with their potentially massive riches, became a major priority. This allowed both for rapid accumulation by the politico-military elite and for the massive financing of party operations, with a view to the holding of early elections.

After the resumption of sales under the KP, a first round of diamond sales to international markets had generated US$56 million, but a second round of sales was held behind closed doors. In November 2010, a third consignment of diamonds was certified for sale by Abbey Chikane, the monitor of the now thoroughly ineffective KP. Chikane was a former MK veteran and former member of the ANC's intelligence service, as was George Nene, Director-General of the South African International Cooperation Department. Both were close to ZANU-PF, with Chikane reportedly feeding a report of human rights abuses at Marange to the CIO.[34] Meanwhile, ZANU-PF kept control over the Ministry of Mines and Mining Development within the coalition government, as well as over both the Minerals Marketing and Development Corporations.

Finally, in November 2011, the bankruptcy of the KP was totally exposed when at its annual plenary meeting in Kinshasha, a deal was done which undercut the role of civil society in monitoring activity on the Marange mines. Whereas, under the 2009 agreement, local civil society activists had been granted the official status of being a 'Local Focal Point' allowing them to report back to the KP, this was taken away at meeting which the Kimberley Process Civil Society Coalition had boycotted over fears that substantive concerns about Zimbabwe's compliance would be ignored. Effectively, the KP had thrown away its key point of leverage over the Zimbabwean government by allowing it to export diamonds from the Marange region without first fulfilling its commitments to the diamond trade.[35]

Thus the frenzied looting continued, with reports of massive irregular sales to buyers in the United Arab Emirates, Lebanon, Pakistan, India, and elsewhere. Not

---

[33] *Sunday Independent*, 12 December 2010.
[34] 'Zimbabwe blood diamonds: The sensational Mr Abbey Chikane', http://cryptome.org. kimberley/kimberly-process.zip
[35] 'Kimberley Process lets Zimbabwe off the hook (again)', http://www.fataltransactions.org/ content/download/909/6227/file/111102_KP%20Statement.pdf

surprisingly, MDC Minister of Finance Tendai Biti claimed bitterly that few revenues were flowing into the Treasury. When Mugabe announced plans to apply the provisions of the 2008 Indigenization and Economic Act to foreign companies and banks in 2011, Tsvangirai denounced them as 'looting and plunder'.[36] However, Prime Minister though he was, he lacked the authority to halt the frantic looting of assets by an arrogant and parasitic politico-military elite determined to cling on to state power and the access to wealth that it granted.

Class formation and constrained opportunities in Namibia

As in Zimbabwe, socialist ideals were rapidly abandoned by a nascent party-state bourgeoisie in Namibia in favour of pragmatic accommodation to the settler-dominated economy. As argued by Tapscott, SWAPO was 'first and foremost a nationalist movement, composed of a broad spectrum of social strata, mobilized towards national liberation' which packaged its populism in the rhetoric of socialism. The cadre of party and military leaders which had emerged in exile formed the core of a new elite. It merged into an expanded organizational elite of senior black administrators, politicians, and business people, which in *de facto* alliance with the established white elite in business and politics, came to inhabit an 'economic and social world largely divorced from that of the majority of the urban and rural poor'.[37] Senior black civil servants purchased homes in the affluent and formerly exclusively white suburbs of Windhoek. By 1993, not a single cabinet minister lived in Katatura, the former bastion of political activism in Namibia, while the elite self-consciously sent their children to formerly exclusively white schools.[38]

Few would disagree with the summary statement that 'a new black middle class' has joined a 'predominantly white elite' in enjoying 'a virtually European standard of living, while broad sections of the predominantly black population live in extreme poverty.'[39] According the African Development Bank, by 2010, only 9 per cent of Namibians could be categorized as 'middle class' defined as living on the equivalent of between N$27 and N$134 in 2005 a day. This middle class was split into a 'lower middle-class', surviving on between N$27 and N$67 a day (3.8 per cent of the population), and an 'upper middle class', earning between N$67 and N$134 daily (5.3 per cent of the population). If it is assumed that the large number of 140,000-odd whites living in Namibia fall into the more elevated segment of this middle class, then the number of black middle-class Namibians has remained remarkably small (especially when compared to South Africa and Botswana, where 19.8 per cent and 29.3 per cent of the populations rank as middle class according to the Bank's very modest definition).[40] It is easy to surmise that the pressure for upward mobility

---

[36] *Business Day*, 19 April 2011.
[37] Christopher Tapscott (1993), 'National reconciliation, social equity and class formation in independent Namibia', *Journal of Southern African Studies*, 19: 1, 29–39, citation 31.
[38] Ibid., 35.
[39] BMZ (Federal Ministry for Economic Cooperation and Development), Namibia (2010). http://www.bmz.de/en/what_we_do?.../Namibia/zusammenarbeit.html
[40] African Development Bank (2011), *The Middle of the Pyramid: Dynamics of the Middle Class in Africa*.

amongst black Namibians must be enormous and provides the driving force behind SWAPO-led campaigns for BEE and land reform, even if hitherto these processes have seriously enriched a tiny politically connected elite. In turn, given the racial dynamics of income distribution, it is more than a little likely that black aspirations for upward class mobility and personal enrichment will be expressed in racial terms.

Unlike its ZANU-PF counterpart, the Namibian party-state bourgeoisie is hugely constrained by the overwhelmingly dominant white control of the South African-dependent economy. Unlike its counterpart, it has not been able to establish a command economy. Accordingly, its opportunities for using its control of the government to fashion state-centred patterns of patronage have been severely limited, and it has remained more acutely aware of its heavy reliance on revenues drawn from foreign and domestic corporations and interests which it does not, and is unlikely, to own.

As late as 2002, Namibia was ranked 28th out of 90 countries by Transparency International in terms of perception of corruption – second only to Botswana (24th) in Africa. However, since that date Namibia's ratings have plummeted, down to 56th out of 178 countries, and 6th in Africa.[41] Looking on at developments in Zimbabwe and (as we shall see) South Africa, elements among Namibia's elite seem increasingly eager to consolidate the underpinnings of the still very small party-state bourgeoisie within a context where growing class stratification is beginning to transcend previous racial and ethnic boundaries.[42] This development has seen the increasing embrace by the party-connected elite of corrupt practices.

One such instance involved the disappearance over a number of years of N$100 million via a shady investment transaction by top officials of the Overseas Development Corporation, the money supposedly having been used to enhance foreign investment through an export processing scheme. In 2003 another N$30 million went missing.[43] Subsequent was the loss of N$650 million made by the GIPF in doubtful BEE projects, the transfer of N$30 million by the Social Security Commission to a politically connected firm, and the general tendency for BEE projects to funnel public assets into private hands.[44] For some of the politically connected elite, complains one observer:

> ...anything that is not bolted to the floor is a good candidate for theft...the litany of either theft or corruption cases is now getting out of hand...some of these schemes take the form of facilitation fees, commissions or kick-backs sometimes running into millions, while others are simply theft. For example, how does one explain the N$100 million that was apparently 'invested' in Botswana which has disappeared without trace? Then you have the 'loan' given to former President Laurent Kabila of the DRC amounting to approximately N$50 million, the N$30 million at the Social Security Commission, N$3 million to buy arms from a bogus arms dealer, 42 brand new laptops at the ECN gone without any trace, missing diamonds running into millions of dollars at a polishing factory in Okahandja; not to mention the thousands of

---

[41] *New Era*, 20 May 2011.
[42] Tapscott, op. cit., 31.
[43] Henning Melber, 'Poverty, politics, power and privilege: Namibia's black elite formation' in Henning Melber (2007) *Transitions in Namibia: Which Changes for Whom?*, Uppsala: Nordic Africa Institute, 118.
[44] Ibid.

dollars that usually go missing at our magistrates courts, government ministries, parastatals, including also Unam (the University) which is supposed to be a beacon of good governance?[45]

The growth of parasitic behaviour is occurring despite proclaimed attempts by President Hifikepunye Pohamba to stamp out graft and corruption. However, such measures have proved highly uneven. In 2005, the Deputy Director in the Auditor-General's office lamented the leniency of checks and balances in public accounting and complained that instructions regarding transparency were 'totally ignored' by senior civil servants. Yet in 2010, anti-corruption enforcers laid charges against two senior Nambian officials, alongside a Chinese executive of a company, Nuctech, run by the son of Chinese President Hu Jintao, in connection with a N$12.8 million kickback for the sale of twelve X-ray scanners to the Namibian government.[46] This was despite the embarrassment this caused to the Chinese government, for allegedly this was but one example of an increasingly cosy arrangement between the politically connected and Chinese investors:

> The Chinese...were brought here by the Namibian regime for a purpose. They are always first in line to receive most of the multi-million government tenders...In the building industry they have now virtually replaced Namibians. And it doesn't end there; local corrupt officials are also selling communal land to the Chinese to rake in a quick buck. The same goes on in the fishing, tourism and the mining sectors where the elite are given quotas, licenses and EPLs (Exclusive Prospective Licences) which they then just sell to foreigners who end up controlling and thereby owning the country['s] natural resources. Thus the field for all sorts of corrupt activities is quite open and is widening further. The problem is that there are simply too many bribe-takers in the country. So in this sea of corruption, I don't see how we are going to arrest this growing national endemic within the current political set-up with its weak political institutions, including the justice system and also lack of political will on the part of leadership despite all the talk especially from President Pohamba who when he became President said 'there will be zero tolerance for waste and corruption in public life.'[47]

Against this, the Anti-Corruption Commission (ACC) pulled back from investigations into the award of a major contract by Namcor, the country's state oil corporation, to Namibia Liquid Fuel, a joint venture established by Philco Twenty. The latter is a BEE company, owned by former State House officials and other persons politically connected to former President Sam Nujoma, and the South African-owned Sasol. Indeed NLF had been set up only in 2004 on the initiative of Sasol in response to an advertised tender calling for a joint venture with a local company. ACC Director Paulus Noa indicated that as far as his agency was concerned, nothing prosecutable could be found in terms of the Anti-Corruption Act when the ACC investigated the three-year US$330 dollar deal to import 450,000 tonnes of fuel per year from South Africa. (The deal was reportedly later extended to five years.) Noa said that former Prime Minister Theo-Ben Gurirab had approved the NLF deal, through which the company reaped a US$55 million profit, even though examination of the transaction revealed that from the purchasing of the fuel in Durban to its transport to

---

[45] *The Namibian*, 9 August 2011.
[46] *New York Times*, 8 April 2010.
[47] *The Namibian*, 2 November 2011.

Namibia, the Namibian company was involved on paper only. According to a former trade unionist holding 14 per cent of the shares in NLF, the shareholders were 'just black entrepreneurs who needed the money'. The Namibian National Society for Human Rights stated that it was 'deeply dismayed, but not surprised' by the decision, for political patronage had become increasingly institutionalized since independence.[48]

For all that high SWAPO officials and politics decry such deals, warn about the spread of greed and corruption, and admit that get-rich-schemes masquerading as BEE widen the gap between rich and poor, they appear reluctant to do much about it. In Namibia, the party-state bourgeoisie has little choice but to maintain its class alliance with white capital, even while its abandonment of socialism in favour of black empowerment indicates its increasing impatience with the limits to accumulation set by the contours of the branch-plant economy.

Transformation, class formation, and party predation in South Africa

It is in South Africa that the processes of 'transformation' and class formation have become most programmatic. One overview concludes that a fairly rapidly growing black middle class has been the prime beneficiary of ANC rule.[49] The years of the ANC in power, it argues, have registered a remarkable transition away from white minority rule in that today, high political and state office is broadly reflective of the demographic composition of the population, whilst the public sector as a whole has made massive steps towards representivity. This transformation is the single most important factor accounting for the expansion of the black middle class, and is instrumental in consolidating the growth in the distribution of national income accruing to blacks: the African and black shares of total disposable income nationally increased from 35.7 per cent and 48.1 per cent in 1996 to 46.5 per cent and 59.6 per cent in 2007.[50] Thus, blacks now constitute an ever-increasing proportion of the middle class as a whole. According to another study, by 2007 'the burgeoning middle class' was 58 per cent African, 13 per cent Coloured, 6 per cent Indian, and just 23 per cent white, with the self-described upper-middle class being 41 per cent African, 42 per cent white, 8 per cent Indian, and 9 per cent Coloured.[51]

Even so, various fractions of the black middle class have shared these benefits differentially. It is the 'state managers' (senior political officeholders and top managers in parastatals and other state organs), along with the more advantaged members of the 'corporate black bourgeoisie' promoted by BEE, who have benefited the most and joined the majority of whites on higher income levels. In contrast, a considerably larger 'civil petty bourgeoise' (composed of middle- to lower-level public sector workers, along with independent professionals, many

---

[48] *Afrol News*, 9 August 2011; Melber, op. cit., 122.
[49] Roger Southall (2005), 'Political change and the black middle class in democratic South Africa', *Canadian Journal of African Studies*, 38: 3, 521–42.
[50] SAIRR, *South Africa Survey 2000/1*, 376; *2009/10*, 254.
[51] *Sunday Times*, 28 January 2007 (reporting on a survey by the International Marketing Council).

of whom hire themselves out to the state via consultancies and so on), is growing steadily, even while many are only modestly paid. This element has benefited from affirmative action and equity legislation which have brought about increased incomes, secure employment, and improved working conditions, all of these backed up by a high rate of unionization, even if – especially in the private sector – its upward movement is constrained by an invisible floating colour bar. Finally, there is a class fraction of black traders and business people. The majority still own or run small or medium size businesses, yet given a highly competitive business environment which whites continue to dominate, many are highly dependent upon state support (via supplier, procurement or direct assistance programmes offered by government under the rubric of broad-based BEE). Overall, the political weight of the trading bourgeoisie is minimal (if growing). It has an ambivalent relationship to the black corporate bourgeoisie, against which it is in constant competition, whilst simultaneously looking to it for leadership in battles against established white business. It is precisely its lack of independence which necessitates its connections with politicians at all levels of government, and has given rise to the phenomenon of 'tenderpreneurship'.[52]

Under the presidency of Thabo Mbeki, the increasing social differentiation amongst blacks, especially the character and lifestyle of the black elite, began to attract major attention. First, there was the rise to massive wealth, corporate power, and social visibility of the relatively few individuals who cropped up in the major empowerment deals of those years forged by large-scale capital, with Saki Macozoma, Cyril Ramaphosa, Tokyo Sexwale, and Patrice Motsepe at their head. They rapidly penetrated the top ranks of corporate power, so that by 2003, these four, alongside Lazarus Zim (then Deputy CEO of Anglo-American) and four leading 'state managers', could be nominated as members of South Africa's top twenty businesspeople (none had made the same list in 1993).[53] By that year, it was calculated that the top ten black Chief Executives presided over companies with a market capitalization of R41. 634 million. In 2005, the *Sunday Times* was able to report the movement into its otherwise white-dominated wealth 'rich list' of Motsepe (worth R2.8 billion), Sexwale (R260 million), and Marcel Golding (R135 million), (the last being Chairman of Hosken Consolidated Investments, the investment company of COSATU's clothing union). Other individuals who had entered the list included Andile Ngcaba, Gloria Serobe, and Smuts Ngonyama (because of their Elephant consortium's acquisition of a stake in Telkom), and Gary Morolo, Reuel Khoza, and Sam Nematswerani, (whose AKA capital was worth R243 million).[54] By 2007, the authoritative McGregor's *Who Owns Whom in Southern Africa*, ranked Motsepe, with a fortune of R7.94 billion, fourth out of the top 50 richest South Africans, followed some way behind by Sexwale (R979 million), Macozoma (R519.64 million); Ramaphosa (R490.53 million) and Golding (R360.87 million).[55] By 2011, Motsepe was listed as first, with JSE-listed investments of R22.9 billion, with Ramaphosa coming thirteenth with R2.22 billion.[56] Few doubted that this startling level of accumulation over

[52] Southall, op. cit.
[53] *Financial Mail*, 19 December 2003.
[54] *Sunday Times*, 21 September 2005.
[55] *Sunday Times*, 11 March 2007.
[56] *Sunday Times*, 4 September 2011.

the short period since 1994 was an outcome both of the corporate sector's drive to strike up collaborative relations with the ANC and the Mbeki government's own determination to legitimize and 'blacken' capitalism.

With such enormous rewards on offer, it was not surprising that senior public office was seen by many within the new elite as a take-off point for entry into the high ranks of the corporate sector. Comparatively, senior political positions were already well paid: reportedly, in 2010, President Zuma was in relative terms the fourth highest paid head of state in the world, so presumably his ministers and their deputies were similarly located.[57] Meanwhile, because of a lapse in the law which allowed local councils to determine the salaries of their office holders, many mayors earned higher salaries than the President. But the big public money was to be earned at the top of the parastatals, so that in 2007, for instance, whereas Thabo Mbeki as President earned R1.27 million, parastatal CEOs consistently earned considerable more than that, ranging from the paltry R1.5 million earned by Dali Mopfu at the SABC up to R7.9 million earned by Maria Ramos at Transnet. Shaun Liebenberg, at the perennially loss-making Denel, earned R7.4 million and Khaya Ngqula at South African Airways made R5 million, despite SAA having made a loss the previous year of R883 million.[58] Often generous honoraria to parastatal board members could provide a valuable supplement to other income, especially as appointment to one often led to another across both the public and private sectors: in 2007, for instance, SAA's eleven board members held 136 directorships, ESCOM's fourteen board members held 128, and Denel's board members held 111.[59] Even so, despite relatively handsome pickings in the public sector, it was widely recognized that yet more serious money was to made elsewhere, with the result that years in party or public service were often deemed preparatory to movement into the private sector, where the imperative to gain healthy BEE credentials had opened up impressive avenues. Former ministers, director-generals and parastatal bosses regularly abandoned state office for private business, often taking up top corporate positions or forging lucrative BEE deals.

Finally there was the tendency for the black elite to flaunt its prosperity in contrast to the behaviour of the white business elite which, perhaps wisely, sought largely to hide its wealth behind the high walls of suburbia or its golf clubs (although they were never shy in showing off their expensive cars). Examples were many and varied, captured in a notorious statement by Smuts Ngonyama, the ANC's spokesperson under Mbeki, when he declared that he 'did not join the struggle to be poor', this in response to criticism of a BEE consortium he had formed with Andile Ngcaba, a former Director-General of the Department of Communications, and Gloria Serobe of the ANC Women's League, to purchase 15 per cent in Telkom in 2004.[60] By the time of the Zuma ascendancy, it was well established that the political elite was prepared to take quite shameless advantage of their generous perks of office. Large amounts were spent on official luxury vehicles[61] and improvements to official resi-

---

[57] *Sunday Independent*, 24 April 2011.
[58] *Financial Mail*, 18 July 2008.
[59] *Business Day*, 4 June 2007.
[60] *Business Day*, 16 December 2004.
[61] Between January and September 2009, ministers and premiers ran up a bill of R30 million on the purchase of official luxury vehicles, with among them Blade Nzimande – Secretary-General

dences,[62] such expenditure justified by reference to what was allowed according to an Official Ministerial Handbook (which was declared confidential) as well as to the needs and expectations of office.[63] Meanwhile, calculations by the DA claimed that nineteen national government departments ran up bills of more than R3 billion on luxury travel, restaurants, and accommodation over the first nineteen months of the Zuma presidency.[64] Much was spent on 'bling', from lavish weddings[65] and anniversary celebrations[66] through to conspicuously extravagant behaviour such as the 'sushi parties' thrown by Kenny Kunene, an ANC-connected businessman, at which sushi was served off the bodies of semi-naked women.[67]

Kunene was openly criticized for his extravagance and for behaviour degrading of women by COSATU's Zwelinzima Vavi, yet just two years previously, the latter had himself staged a lavish wedding, featuring two horse-drawn carriages. The reception – funded by businessmen backing Jacob Zuma for the presidency – itself involved a blend of sexual and racial innuendo: 'We [are] here' stated a young waitress, 'because the BEE types like being served by young white girls.'[68]

Wealth, for many of the black elite, was for show, for demonstrating equality with whites. One black commentator declared that the very few black people who had acquired wealth should be allowed to enjoy it in the manner they deemed fit. It was good for blacks to display their wealth, for they were the 'visible proof to many destitute and discouraged children and adults that it is possible for one of their own...to make it':

of the SACP and Minister of Higher Education – unable to resist the temptations of a BMW750L at a cost of R1.1 million (see *Sunday Times*, 13 September 2009, reporting on findings of the Independent Commission for the Remuneration of Public Office-Bearers).

[62] The cost of purchasing and renovating residences and offices for ministers following the appointment of the Zuma cabinet had come to R108,035,340 by March 2011 (*Mail & Guardian*, 11–17 March 2011).

[63] 'If the head of Interpol visits me I don't want him to find me living in a shack or a house with one pot', declared Police Commissioner Cele Bheki after purchasing a plush home in Pretoria (*Sunday Times*, 12 September 2010).

[64] *Business Day*, 19 February 2010.

[65] For instance, in October 2005, South African Airways CEO Khaya Ngqula treated guests to one of the most extravagant traditional wedding ceremonies the Eastern Cape had ever seen, having already sealed his marriage to former beauty queen Mbali Gasa, nineteen years his junior, in a R1 million western ceremony at the exclusive Zimbali Lodge on the KwaZulu-Natal north coast. The bride had been 'draped in a glamorous dress created by Indian designer, Neeta Lulla', who had dressed a number of top Bollywood film stars. 'The straight-cut garment was encrusted with Swarovski crystals [and had] a three metre long train.' In preparation for the traditional ceremony, he had managed to persuade the local authority to upgrade the local road leading up to his 'peach coloured double-storey home' at a village outside Kingwilliamstown (*Sunday Times*, 16 October 2005).

[66] Commenting upon their plan for a five-day bash to celebrate their eighth wedding anniversary at the five-star Fairmont Hotel and Resort in Zimbali, Sibusiso Mpisane announced plans for an Egyptian royalty-theme party where they would be wearing identical outfits to those worn by pharaohs. 'We are a couple who like class', commented Mipisane, a former police constable in eThekwini (Durban) who drove a Lamborghini (*Sunday Times*, 20 March 2011).

[67] Kunene repudiated Vavi's criticism that his wedding had cost R700,000: 'It cost more than that', (*Sunday Times*, 29 October 2010).

[68] *Mail & Guardian*, 7–13 September 2007.

If you live in the townships or rural areas, please do not hide your success from us. We have seen enough battered cars and cheap suits in our lives. Please wear your latest suit when you come to our functions. Don't patronize us by dressing cheaply or by rocking up in an old Datsun, Mazda or Valiant.[69]

Julius Malema, President of the ANC Youth League agreed. When criticized for building a R16 million mansion in Sandhurst, Johannesburg's most exclusive suburb, he repudiated such criticism as the response of whites 'who always think Africans cannot and should not build houses of their own'. In his political life, he stated, he had learned 'the ability to live in the conditions of capitalism while fighting it and defeating it'. He did not exploit people and shared his money with the poor.[70]

The ambivalence about black wealth remains profound. On the one hand, the project of 'transformation' with its gospel of black empowerment and redistribution of wealth remains at the heart of the ANC's programme, connected to which is a strong desire for blacks to be seen as reaping 'white' success. On the other, there is growing appreciation of the perils of the blatant display of wealth. At a conference organized by the Black Management Forum in 2005, repeated criticisms were made that the black middle class was greedy, arrogant, and parasitic. Few of those attending were keen to own up to their own class identity, this ascribed by a black observer to the sense of guilt they felt about being members of a small privileged class living amidst a sea of black poverty.[71] Just months previously, Kgalema Motlanthe, then Secretary-General of the ANC, had blasted the black elite, complaining that BEE had become the preserve of the few, with key individuals benefiting from 'repeated bouts of re-empowerment'. BEE as it stood was about 'transfer' of wealth, not 'transformation', and needed to become more broadly-based.[72] He was soon joined by Finance Minister Trevor Manuel, who lamented the elite's get-rich-quick mentality, and Zwelinzima Vavi, who asked: '…How can we stop politics becoming discredited in the eyes of ordinary people if political office translates into a style of living way beyond the people who put us in office in the first place?'[73]

Criticism of the empowerment elite gave substantial impetus to Zuma's campaign for the presidency, even while Zuma himself received substantial backing from black business figures who either felt they had been left out in the cold under Mbeki or who looked to do better under his putative successor. Yet if the critics within the Alliance thought that the configurations of power and wealth would change under Zuma they were to be disappointed. By the time of the 2011 local government elections, continuous criticisms were being made by Vavi that the ANC under Zuma had become characterized by high levels of individualism and greed. The immediate problem for the ANC was that such a critique from inside its own camp could damage its hopes in the election, and Secretary-General Gwede Mantashe let Vavi know this in an abrupt manner. The more fundamental issue was that greed and corruption had become inherent in the way the ANC now operated.

---

[69] *Sunday Times*, 8 April 2007.
[70] *The Times* (Johannesburg), 21 July 2011.
[71] *Sowetan*, 20 October 2010.
[72] *Business Day*, 1 October 2004; 4 October 2004.
[73] *Mail & Guardian*, 15–21 October 2004.

Politics and plunder in South Africa

Jonathan Hyslop has pointed out that the discussion around corruption in South Africa is fraught with conflicting historical claims and conceptual difficulties. He comments that corruption in South Africa is nothing new, and makes a valuable distinction between 'rent-seeking', where a rent is characterized as 'an income which is higher than the minimum which a firm or an individual would have accepted given alternative opportunities', ranging through monopoly profits through to subsidies and transfers, legal and illegal, organized through political mechanisms, and patron-client relationships, 'repeated relationships of exchange between specific patrons and clients'. Again, these may be legal or illegal, although it is unlikely that patrons unwilling to break the law will be able to retain their client base. Both have obtained in different eras in South Africa. For instance, NP governments favoured Afrikaner enterprises, while the expansion of Afrikaner-dominated parastatals favoured the rent-seeking of party supporters, with the Broederbond coordinating the patronage activities that lay behind this process. Suffice it to say here that he identifies an 'efflorescence of corruption' from 1972 (linked to the decline of the Verwoerdian mission and the expansion of the Afrikaner middle and capitalist classes) and an era of 'looting of the state' between 1984 and 1994 (associated with a grab for resources by state elites as the end of white rule loomed and as Bantustan bureaucracies consolidated).[74] His fundamental points are first, that both rent-seeking and patron-client relationships have continued into the new order, and second, that to ask whether corruption has become 'better or worse' since 1994 is very possibly the wrong question, not least because any answer is going to incorporate all sorts of ideological assumptions. He suggests that it is of greater interest is to explore how the culture and mechanics of the ANC and its commitment to transformation have framed predatory behaviour by party elites at different levels since 1994.

There is a widespread perception, fuelled by constant media reports, that corruption has become pervasive at all levels of government under the ANC. Very often this is promoted by liberal or conservative commentators, but it is also a view shared by elements within the ruling Tripartite Alliance itself. Interestingly, both discourses tend to combine critiques of rent-seeking (with the focus upon BEE) with those of patron-client relationships (with a focus upon illegal award of state contracts). Both claim a commitment to constitutionalism and legality, and deplore the morally and functionally enervating effects of corruption. However, the Alliance critique then becomes hobbled by the political consequences of both the acknowledgement and prosecution of corruption as well as the institutionalization of rent-seeking by the ANC as an organization in its bid to secure a massive flow of party funding (see Chapter 10).

In 2007, Kgalema Motlanthe, then Secretary-General of the ANC, conceded that the extent of the corruption within the organization was 'far worse than

---

[74] Jonathan Hyslop (2005), 'Political corruption: Before and after apartheid', *Journal of Southern African Studies*, 31: 4, 773–89.

anyone imagines': 'This rot is across the board. It's not confined to any level or any area of the country. Almost every project is conceived because it offers opportunities for certain people to make money.'[75] He was confirming what was already being admitted openly by the ANC in a discussion document prepared for the party's July 2007 Policy Conference. The underlying premise of its analysis was that the challenge of transforming a racially polarized capitalist economy was providing opportunities for 'careerism, personal enrichment and corruption'. There were concerns that the ANC had opened itself up to the peddling of influence by donors; there was a lack of discipline which was 'symptomatic of a breakdown in our political culture'; entrepreneurship had become confused with 'adventurism of the pillaging sort'; the party had become attractive to morally dubious elements; and the ANC had failed to act swiftly and appropriately in cases of corruption even when comrades had admitted their guilt. In consequence, the name of the organization was often 'dragged through the mud' and cadres had learnt to make 'creative use' of the concept 'innocent until proved guilty'.[76]

Later in 2007, in the movement's annual report, Motlanthe lamented practices of gate-keeping, ghost members, commercialization of membership, rent-a-member, and other forms of fraudulent and manipulative practice, and recalled Lenin's warnings that a ruling party would always attract careerists. It was therefore imperative to ensure that the 'noble values and norms of the African National Congress' remained dominant.[77] Thereafter, admissions from within the Alliance that corruption was mounting became increasingly commonplace. In March 2010, for instance, SACP Deputy Secretary-General Jeremy Cronin warned that the 'honeymoon was over', and that the ANC risked losing support in much the way that ZANU-PF had done if the perception gained hold that a new elite was accumulating wealth on its own behalf. Debates about capitalism and socialism would become irrelevant 'if billions of rands get siphoned off through rent seeking'.[78] In 2011, Vavi submitted a report to COSATU's central committee in which he denounced a rising tendency within the ANC which was hell-bent on material gain, corruption, and looting, and referred to the 'prominence of a predator class, which relies on access to state levers for accumulation', a reflection of views he was regularly punting in the public arena at that time.[79]

Such openly expressed views within the Alliance mirrored analyses within wider society. Respected journalist Carol Paton could therefore comment with little fear of contradiction that there was 'unanimity in the Union Buildings and parliament, in the ranks of business and trade unions, that corruption is the biggest obstacle to achieving SA's social and economic goals'. She proceeded by citing an unofficial estimate 'doing the rounds in government' that the country was losing 20 per cent of its procurement budget each year through corrupt practices: 'rip-offs, overpricing and the failure of contractors to deliver what is

[75] *Financial Mail*, 19 January 2007.
[76] African National Congress (2007), 'Revolutionary morality: The ANC and business', discussion document, February.
[77] Kgalema Motlanthe (2007), '52nd National Conference: Organisational report', 17 December, paras. 45 and 63.
[78] *Business Report*, 17 March 2010.
[79] *Business Day*, 26 January 2011.

promised'. If procurement at all levels of government amounted to around R150 billion, then the black hole left by corruption was probably around R30 billion a year.[80]

The consequences of the drift towards the predatory state are increasingly evident. First has been the exploitation of the ambiguities of BEE and affirmative action. White domination of the upper reaches of the economy continues to present very real dilemmas around the creation of black capitalist and managerial strata. The price of continuing white corporate failure to promote blacks internally within corporate structures has been the wholesale diversion of BEE into rent-seeking and cynical appropriation of resources in the name of 'transformation'. The cross-over between BEE and rent-seeking remains difficult to negotiate. The corporate embrace of the likes of Cyril Ramaphosa, Tokyo Sexwale, and Saki Macozoma through the advance of share deals and appointments in the early 1990s made total sense to white capital. Such individuals were manifestly talented, and within a short period were to become respectable corporate magnates in their own right even while remaining closely connected to the ANC. Yet their involvement and that of others who held party or state office in one deal after another, was to legitimate corporate and personal strategies of rent-seeking and to reduce 'transformation' to cynical exercises of corporate promotion and individual enrichment. Similarly, affirmative action at all levels of the state has displayed an alarming tendency towards patronage which, in prioritizing the importance of race and loyalty over qualifications and competence, has severely compromised the functionality of state and parastatal operations.[81]

Crony-style BEE also fertilizes close links between political influence and state procurement. These have grown exponentially as a result of three interlocking developments: first, ANC deployment of party loyalists to bureaucratic positions at national, provincial, and local institutions; second, ironically, the implementation of the Public Finance Management Act of 1999 which, although highly stringent, has decentralized procurement to provinces and individual government departments; and third, the demand for BEE, which has encouraged companies doing business with the state to form partnerships or fronts with black-owned businesses, frequently connected to politicians. 'All three developments opened the floodgates to extensive corruption of the supply chain at all three levels of government.'[82] Hence the rise of the phenomenon of 'tenderpreneurship', the allocation of state tenders by political appointees to politically connected entities and individuals.

The arms deal of 1998 remains the most celebrated case of tenderpreneurship, and probably the most damaging, not just because of its misdirection of massive resources, but because of the determination of powerful forces within the ANC to block its full and proper investigation by state entities. However, as already discussed, President Zuma was prompted into appointing a Commission of Inquiry into the Arms Deal in November 2011 to pre-empt a likely order to do so by the Constitutional Court, after new revelations had continued to make their way into the local and international media. In May 2011, for

---

[80] *Financial Mail*, 21 May 2010.
[81] Louis Picard (2005), *The State of the State in South Africa*, Johannesburg: Wits University Press.
[82] *Financial Mail*, 21 May 2010.

instance, following investigations by Swedish authorities, the Swedish aerospace manufacturer Saab was forced into an admission that the account of its subsidiary, Sanip, had been used to pay the arms deal consultant, Fana Hlongwane R24 million in 'commission'. A former ranking commander in MK, Hlongwane had been special adviser to Joe Modise when he became Defence Minister. This was in return for his influence in ensuring that the South African government opted to purchase Gripen jet fighters to be supplied by Saab working in partnership with BAE. Subsequently, the DA's David Maynier released papers suggesting that BAE had paid a total of R98 million to Hlongwane via a front company, South African National Industrial Participation.[83]

Largesse from Hlongwane was extended to General Siphiwe Nyanda, formerly Chief of Staff of MK and from 1989 head of the SANDF. This took the form of a loan of R4 million when Nyanda resigned from the army in 2005, after which he became Chief Executive of Hlongwane's Ngwane Defence company. The loan was repaid in full on 11 May 2005, the day he was sworn in as Minister of Communications in the Zuma government. This event conveniently released Nyanda from the obligation as a minister and parliamentarian of having to declare a financial benefit that might have pointed back to the arms deal.[84] Thereafter, although he claimed to have withdrawn fully from the day-to-day operations of the company, General Nyanda Security Risk Advisory Services (GNS), in which his family trust owned a 45 per cent stake, Nyanda was revealed as having at least five contracts with government agencies. For one, Transnet Freight Rail had awarded GNS a tender for R55 million without proper tender processes having been followed. Likewise, tenders for R67.8 million and R19 million were awarded to GNS (by now known as Abalozi Security Services) by the Gauteng government without the tenders having been advertised. Exposure of the former deal led to the suspension by Transnet Freight Rail of its CEO, Siyabonga Gama (a known supporter, along with Nyanda himself, of Jacob Zuma). The government's disciplinary chairperson Nazeer Cassim pointed out that GNS had received the contract without any previous track record, with no employees, and had subcontracted the work involved to another company.[85] Although Nyanda hit back with court action to have the name of GNS/Abalozi cleared, Zuma felt obliged by the adverse publicity to redeploy him out of the cabinet in October 2010, subsequently appointing him to an advisory position in the presidency. However, before he lost his job, Nyanda had axed his Director-General, Mamapodu Mohlala, who had referred reports to the police and the Auditor-General, about how procedures for the award of tenders worth R70 million by the Communications Department had been flouted.[86]

Numerous other examples of apparent tenderpreneurship have hit the headlines at all three levels of government. At national level, a probe by the Special Investigating Unit into tenders awarded by the Department of Correctional Services was authorized by President Mbeki in March 2008 following allegations that the Minister, Ngconde Balfour, had received funding from undisclosed sources to

[83] *Sunday Independent*, 19 May 2011; *Business Day*, 24 June 2011.
[84] *Mail & Guardian*, 3–9 December 2010.
[85] *Mail & Guardian*, 29 January–4 February 2010; 1–8 April 2010; *Sunday Independent*, 4 April 2010.
[86] *Sunday Times*, 17 October 2010.

settle outstanding amounts remaining on the purchase of one or more luxury cars.[87] One enterprising official in the agricultural department of North West province was suspended after allegations of having provided contracts to his own companies.[88] In Limpopo, a cluster of ANC politicians were accused in 2008 of having used political influence with Premier Sello Moloto to ensure that hugely valuable rights to mine platinum were awarded to their empowerment companies;[89] in the Eastern Cape, Nelson Mandela District ANC Chairman Nceba Faku encouraged his supporters to burn down the offices of the *Eastern Province Herald* after it had exposed a scam he had been involved in. When he was Mayor of Port Elizabeth, he had allegedly leased the eight-storey Kwantu Towers in the central business district for the municipality at inflated rates from a local entrepreneur, Yossuf Jeeva, with whom he had previously been in business. As the newspaper had noted, such deals were ultimately facilitated by banks (in this case Investec) which put up the money for black business persons to buy buildings on the understanding that they would use their political connections to lease them to government.[90] In May 2008, Minister of Local Government Lindiwe Sisulu admitted that corruption in the award of tenders, contracts relating to construction, and sale of land at local level was so rife, and leading to so many disputes, that the delivery of new housing in some parts of the country had 'ground to a halt'.[91] By mid-2011, there were official probes into the award of 433 tenders by the eThekwini metropolitan council during the 2009–10 financial year alone.[92]

So it went on, with multiple revelations of tender-rigging that taxed newspaper headline writers in their competition to come up with the most arresting puns, from the somewhat obvious 'Toilet tenders stink' to the more nuanced 'Water-tender dispute dries up delivery'.[93] The growing embarrassment to the ANC was matched by the escalating financial cost to government. In August 2009, Finance Minister Pravin Gordhan launched a project which combined agencies that reported to him (the Financial Intelligence Centre, the Auditor-General's office, the Accountant-General, and the SA Revenue Service) to tackle corruption in the government's supply chain. This led immediately to the cancellation of contracts to the value of R500 million. (Just a month previously, the government had cancelled a R4.4 billion contract secured by a technology firm, Gijima AST, to modernize the Department of Home Affairs' identity-verification technology.) Gordhan also started using hitherto unused powers provided to the National Treasury to inspect public finances in the provinces, and in June 2011 instructed government departments to stop doing business with some 120 blacklisted companies for ten years.[94] Despite passage of a Prevention and Combating of Corrupt Activities Act in 2004 which had empowered the authorities to black list tender fraudsters, this was the first time that any had been banned from future dealings with government.

In 2011, the cabinet was shocked by a report from the Auditor-General's

[87] *Sunday Times*, 9 October 2009.
[88] *Mail & Guardian*, 28 November 2008, http://www.mg.co.za/article/2008
[89] *The Weekender*, 8–9 November 2008.
[90] *Mail & Guardian*, 27 May–2 June 2011.
[91] *Sunday Times*, 11 May 2008.
[92] *The Mercury*, 13 July 2011.
[93] *Mail & Guardian*, 13–19 May and 8–14 July 2011 respectively.
[94] *Financial Mail*, 21 May 2010.

office which recommended that the only way to put a stop to billions of rands of wasteful expenditure would be for the central government to take over the administration of more than a third of the country's 237 municipalities.[95] To observers' surprise, Gordhan was backed by Zuma, who proceeded to approve a Municipal Systems Amendment Bill, which banned local municipal officials from holding positions in political parties. Case studies indicate unambiguously that the merging of party with state is seen as the prerequisite by party elites for access to resources at local government level, with ANC branches being largely reduced to machines of patronage (save when they are revived to mobilize popular support at election times).[96] The Bill was an attempt to end the practice of deployment of petty politicians to positions in local government which required managerial, financial, and technical qualification. Yet however admirable the initiatives taken by government, they were largely confounded by a lack of capacity to implement them, or by politicians' and officials' active subversion. Thus a damning report by the Public Service Commission tabled in parliament in September 2010 had shown that while 251 officials had been found guilty of misconduct and 30 arrested since the launch of an official anti-corruption hotline in 2004, the number of cases reported had been 7,529.[97] Indeed there had been a recent decline in the government's responsiveness to corruption cases, and wasteful expenditure had rocketed. Corruption, claimed a respected academic, was so endemic that it was reaching a point of no return.[98] His argument was underlined by significant opposition to Zuma's move to ban the practice of deployment to local government, and it was denounced by the South African Municipal Workers' Union as an infringement of the right of local officials to belong to political parties.

The fundamental problem facing anti-corruption initiatives was the vested interests of politicians, officials, and 'tenderpreneurs' who blocked or sought to delegitimize investigations and prosecutions. As indicated, investigations of the arms deal had been regularly kicked into touch, apparently at the behest of the highest rank of politicians, until Zuma's hand was forced by the Constitutional Court. Prosecutions of a handful of figures implicated in the deal had proceeded, with Schabir Shaik being sentenced to a jail term of fifteen years.[99] In contrast, the prosecution of Jacob Zuma had been vigorously opposed by his supporters within the Tripartite Alliance, who denounced it as politically driven by Thabo Mbeki. Ultimately political pressure upon the then Public Protector forced him to drop the case. Other examples abound. In the Northern Cape, John Block, a powerful figure who rose politically through the ranks of the ANCYL and built a lucrative property empire faced numerous allegations of corruption. Nevertheless he was re-elected chair of the party's provincial executive in August 2008, and was beneficiary of debt write-offs by the //Khara Hais municipality. He was subsequently

---

[95] *Business Day*, 13 May 2011.
[96] Musawenkosi Malabela (2011), *The African National Congress and Local Democracy: The Role of the ANC Branch in Manzini-Mbombela*, MA research report, Department of Sociology, University of the Witwatersrand. .
[97] *Mail & Guardian*, 29 October–4 November 2010.
[98] Wits academic Ivor Sarakinsky, at an anti-corruption seminar staged by the SACP (*Business Day*, 30 March 2010).
[99] He was soon released from jail, serving the remainder of his sentence at his home on grounds of terminal illness. Once home he displayed a remarkable capacity to defy death, his health significantly improved by highly publicized rounds of golf.

appointed provincial MEC for Finance and Economic Affairs, even after he was arraigned by the Hawks, and charged with corruption and fraud in November 2011.[100] In KwaZulu-Natal, the NPA and the Hawks also charged the provincial legislature's speaker, Peggy Nkonyeni, and the MEC for Economic Affairs and Tourism, Mike Mabuyakhulu, with receiving a donation of R1 million to the party from South American businessman, Gaston Savoi, in exchange for a R45 million tender to supply water purifiers to state hospitals at inflated prices. Known as the Intaka case, this action was denounced by the provincial organizations of the ANC, COSATU, and the SACP as 'an internally hatched plot'.[101] However the charges were later controversially withdrawn against Nkonyeni and Mabuyakhulu, the opposition DA querying the statement of the KwaZulu-Natal NPA that there was no prospect of a successful prosecution.

Efforts to challenge corruption brokers can prove extremely dangerous. In March 2009, a local councillor, Moss Phakoe, who had handed over a dossier of tender allegations about office bearers and officials in the Bojanala District Municipality in North West province was gunned down. Phakoe's allegations appeared to contribute to the removal of Mathew Wolmarans as Mayor, but within months the latter was elected to the ANC provincial executive and returned to the council as speaker.[102] Solly Phetoe, the COSATU provincial secretary who had mobilized for more robust action by the police was thereafter reported as living in fear of his life. In Mpumalanga, in May 2010, Bomber Ntshangase, an SACP activist in the town of Bethel who had asked questions about the award of a contract to upgrade the hostel in which he lived was also assassinated. At the time of writing it is just the latest in a string of at least eleven murders in the province apparently linked to corruption.[103] In April 2010, the Mayor of Sabata Dalindyebo Municipality and his bodyguard were charged by police with having paid R10,000 to a hitman to assassinate five prominent provincial leaders of the ANC, their lawyer responding that the plot was a spin-off from internal party factionalism.[104] Early in July 2011, KwaZulu-Natal provincial politics were thrown into turmoil by the gunning down of ANC eThekwini's regional secretary Sibusiso Sibiya. Speculation linked his death to his having crossed an opposing faction within a metropolitan council whose budget exceeded R28 billion.[105] This was followed in May 2012 by the assassination of Owen Camagu, a prominent ANC/SACP member in the Nelson Mandela Metropolitan Municipality, and only a month later by the killing of Wandile Mkhize, ANC chief whip in the Hibiscus Municipality and a key player in provincial politics.[106] As R.W. Johnson has indicated, the elimination of rivals within the party is a longstanding tradition within the ANC.[107]

---

[100] *Mail & Guardian*, 10–16 December 2010.
[101] *Business Day*, 2 August 2011; *Natal Witness*, 2 October 2012.
[102] *Mail & Guardian*, 10–16 June 2011.
[103] *Financial Mail*, 21 May 2010.
[104] *Mail & Guardian*, 8–14 April 2010.
[105] *The Mercury*, 13 July 2011.
[106] *Business Day*, 2 July 2012.
[107] Johnson relates the tradition to Joe Modise's alleged culpability in the assassination of Chris Hani, but his text is littered with numerous unresolved killings of ANC activists involved in inter-party battles, these quite separate from ANC-driven killings of political opponents in local communities. See R.W. Johnson (2009), *South Africa's Brave New World: The Beloved Country since the End of Apartheid*, London: Allen Lane.

Party, class, and ideology

Fanon's analysis of the native middle class in postcolonial underdeveloped countries argues that having practically no economic power, it hopes merely to replace the departing middle class of the former colonial rulers. Without economic means, it is not engaged in production: rather 'it is completely canalized into activities of the intermediary type'. Lacking material and intellectual resources, this national bourgeoisie aspires to step into the shoes of the former European settlement: 'doctors, barristers, traders, commercial travellers, general agents and transport agents'. Its mission has nothing to do with transforming the nation; rather it consists in becoming the transmission line between the nation and a capitalism which puts on the mask of neo-colonialism. This 'same lucrative role, this cheap-jack's function, this meanness of outlook and this absence of all ambition symbolize the incapability of the national middle class to fulfil its historic role of the bourgeoisie'.[108]

The NLMs of southern Africa all expressed the intention to escape the fate reserved for the postcolonial national bourgeoisie of Fanon's unflattering description. While agreeing that the racially oppressed middle classes were small, lacked capital, and occupied 'intermediary' positions, they saw the role of the party as being to ensure that the emergent national bourgeoisie would 'repudiate its own nature in so far as it is bourgeois', and rather 'make itself the willing slave of the revolutionary capital which is the people'.[109] Yet how realistic was such a prospect in southern Africa?

The transitional settlements imposed obstacles to 'transformation'. As the idea of the 'racial bargain' implies, it was generally understood that whites would be steadily replaced in the public service by incoming blacks and should expect to withdraw to the private sector and professions, albeit with provision being made for retention of those with key skills. However, while priority was given to the 'transformation' of the state, subsequent demands that the private sector and professions adopt far-reaching programmes of BEE and indigenization indicated that the racial bargain was to be a continuously developing process. As it happened, it collapsed quite swiftly in Zimbabwe not only because of the precipitous economic decline and the seizure of white farms but also because of the lack of deep roots of many settlers, which predisposed them to emigrate rather than to face up to the consequences of black rule. In contrast, while the public services of both Namibia and South Africa were facing rapid change, the deeper roots of the white communities in both these countries were to render the racial bargain more viable and more lasting, even though as time wore on, demands for the racial transformation of the private sectors and professions became increasingly pressing.

Notwithstanding their variance, the racial bargains were crucial to the deracialization of social inequality. The extensive history of racial preference under settler colonialism and apartheid had long guaranteed white pay, pensions, and job security in the public services, not least by creating artificial shortages of

---

[108] Frantz Fanon (1974), *The Wretched of the Earth*, London: Penguin, 119–24.
[109] Ibid.

skilled and qualified labour in the middle to upper reaches of the civil service. In free market terms, whites had quite simply been paid too much – yet the transitional settlements sought to allay white fears and to stabilize new democracies by shoring up their positions, if only for an introductory period. Thus the social effects of racial transformation were double edged. On the one hand, 'transformation' as the pursuit of racial equality was interpreted as the upward advance of the formerly racially oppressed to equal pay scales, perks, and privileges with whites, for to do otherwise would be viewed as racially discriminatory. On the other hand, concerted black upward movement into artificially well-paid, middle to higher public service jobs confirmed existing income inequalities in wider society rather than seeking to narrow them.

When combined with deployment, the racial bargains provided not merely for the development of party-state bourgeoisies but for emergent alliances with established white capital. The political settlements were designed to provide the stability that white capital required, not least by blunting the liberation movements' more radical demands with the incorporation of their elites into the economic structures of settler colonialism. In so doing, they opened themselves up to rent-seeking by the new nationalist elites whose demands for transformation were to become formalized into BEE programmes or a campaign for indigenization. These came at the expense of any lingering hopes for 'socialism', but not to the notion of the NLM as the 'vanguard' – for this remained central to the project of accumulation by the emergent party-state bourgeoisies.

The ZANU-PF elite underpinned its rent-seeking activities with elaboration of a 'command economy'. The party's official socialist ideology provided a convenient justification for stronger and direct control of the economy during the 1980s, using the private sector as a milch cow. Meanwhile, the public sector became a valuable resource for political patronage, with party loyalists being deployed to positions across an increasingly bloated state and parastatal sector. Inevitably, this model of accumulation had its limits, for the command economy imposed severe constraints upon the capacity of the capitalist sector (notably in manufacturing) to modernize. When the economic crisis arrived in the 1990s, any prospects an alliance between the ZANU-PF elite and white capital were dashed. Economic liberalization required a change in tactics towards 'indigenization', while the populist demands of the war veterans prompted the party-state bourgeoisie to lurch more aggressively into 'primitive accumulation'. Thereafter, the productivity of the private sector declined, while the party-state bourgeoisie, increasingly intertwined with the military, adopted Mafia-like behaviour, resulting in the effective criminalization of the Zimbabwean state.[110]

The fundamental difference in Namibia and South Africa is that while both SWAPO and the ANC continue to adhere to the notion of the party as the revolutionary vanguard of transformation, the private sector has always been more powerful than in Zimbabwe, more industrially advanced, and far more robust. In short, it has had a greater ability to absorb the rent-seeking behaviour of the incoming political elites whilst simultaneously providing the surplus necessary to provide for programmes of limited redistribution. Broadly speaking, the racial bargains have been maintained, resting significantly upon a class alliance between the party elite's implementation of market-oriented policies, and

[110] Compagnon, op. cit., 92.

corporate capital's offering of position, privilege, and profit to such political figures, based upon the latter's 'political connectivity'. Yet this model of accumulation is increasingly bringing its own strains, primarily due to its limited effect on patterns of social inequality and economic inclusion. While both countries, most notably South Africa, have seen the emergence of a significant (albeit still small) black middle class, whites remain economically predominant, and on the whole, have fared relatively well since the end of apartheid. Meanwhile, the financialization of the South African economy, the continuing trends towards capital-intensity within the MEC, and the levels of de-industrialization experienced in key manufacturing sectors, have ensured that levels of unemployment have remained brutally high. The wider trend towards the informalization and casualization of employment within the private sector reinforces the problem.

The outcomes of the pattern of accumulation have been twofold. First, they have led to increasing assertions by the party-state bourgeoisie in each country that the market must give way to the 'developmental state'. Such a demand is not in itself unconvincing for there is evidence aplenty that unbridled market capitalism is unlikely, if not unable, to provide for the needs of the poorest of the global poor. Yet while the ANC, in particular, continues to call for the creation of a 'patriotic bourgeoisie', the character of the latter is seen as umbilically linked to its acceptance of the leadership of the state. Second, given the power of established capital and the centrality of state contracts to the development of such a patriotic bourgeoisie, the tendency towards not only rent-seeking but tender-fraud and outright looting of the public purse is reinforced. This in turn leads to the factionalization of the ruling party, centred on the scramble for state resources, and the extension of political protection from prosecution to some but not to others. As in Zimbabwe, there is an inherent tendency for the liberation movement to become a mafia. While this revolves around factional networks, it also assumes an institutional form as the party itself comes to feed directly off the state.

10.
Fuelling the Party Machines

Running political parties is expensive. Parties are complex organizations that need resources to pay staff salaries, run headquarters and regional offices, hold congresses, communicate with citizens, undertake research, develop policies, and stage electoral campaigns. Yet as Anthony Butler reminds us, money may be essential but it is also dangerous.[1] Parties that gain disproportionate access to financial resources can buy votes, monopolize airtime during campaigns, dispense jobs and patronage to supporters, and outpace competitors. Within parties, factions can build war chests to distort internal democratic outcomes. Even more troubling is the intersection between money, corruption, and interest, for those who donate money to parties require a return, usually implicit or covert, in terms of policies which suit them or the grant of concessions, tenders or contracts. The power of money therefore often serves to crowd out the voices of ordinary members of parties and to marginalize the poor.

ZANU-PF, SWAPO, and the ANC have followed broadly similar trajectories with regard to party funding, having moved from a heavy dependence upon foreign sources during the pre-liberation era towards mixed funding regimes. These regimes – which reflect a worldwide trend away from reliance on subscriptions paid by ordinary party members – revolve around four basic elements. First, incumbency enables the NLMs to use the administrative and financial resources of the state – official cars, fares, office supplies, and state personnel – to underpin party capacities, particularly during electoral campaigns. This can extend to the illegal diversion of state funds into party coffers. Second, ruling NLMs have benefited disproportionately from the public funding of political parties. Third, they have used their political dominance to access disproportionate funding from private capital, inducing donations through threats or promises of favour. Finally, they have created party business empires whose purpose is to feed off the state, notably via their accessing of tenders from parastatals. Thus tenderpreneurship is writ large via the incestuous relationship between party and state.

In what follows, an elaboration of the arrangements shaping party funding will be complemented by a review of the parties' business empires. However, three caveats are necessary. First, to avoid repetition of issues dealt with in Chapter 5 with regard to the use by the NLMs of state resources (including military power) during elections, the focus will be on the provisions for the public funding of parties and the formal regulation of private funding. Second, given that it is only since the late 1990s that there has been any concerted interest in the study of party funding in southern Africa, our knowledge of what went on

---

[1]   Anthony Butler (2010), 'Introduction: Money and politics', in Butler (ed.), *Paying for Politics: Party Funding and Political Change in South Africa and the Global South*, Auckland Park: Jacana, 1–19.

before is fragmentary and conjectural. Third, the discussion will be limited by the difficulties of penetrating obscurity, for as Butler observes, key actors in money politics – party and government officials, candidates, private business, and wealthy individual donors – tend to shun publicity, and most of what we learn about their actions comes as the result of the efforts of investigative journalists.[2]

The party-funding regimes

Their having to fight transitional elections meant the loss of financial support for the NLMs from established Western donors, notably Scandinavian governments and, in SWAPO's case, the UN. Donors were reluctant to be seen as backing individual political parties. In Namibia, many donors withdrew financial assistance to SWAPO because the Peace Agreement of 1987 included an impartiality clause. Yet the need for money did not disappear and these elections were fought with a mix of funding from Western support networks and sympathetic governments in the South, as well as business interests keen to get on the right side of future rulers. Details are shady, but it is likely that both ZANU-PF and SWAPO received financial support from their various backers in the then formally socialist world, and probably from the governments of the FLS. For its part, the ANC received money from the Indonesian, Malaysian, and Taiwanese governments (the last mentioned desperate to prevent a democratic South Africa severing its ties in favour of exclusive diplomatic links with the People's Republic of China); from social democratic parties in Europe and their related foundations; and not least, COSATU. More controversially, alongside modest donations from established and black business, the ANC also received R2 million from Sol Kerzner, the casino magnate who had made a fortune by investing in the homelands under apartheid.[3] Quite how the different parties raised money in the early post-transitional elections is still unclear, although ZANU-PF's politicization of the civil service and the media led to effective state support for the party in the elections of 1985 and 1990;[4] and in late 2000, a member of the ANC's NEC sought to persuade fellow MP Andrew Feinstein to drop his investigations into arms deal (covered in Chapter 6) because funding from companies which had won contracts had bankrolled the party's 1999 election campaign.[5] Indeed, a UK specialist risk company was later to record that the German shipping company, MAN Ferrostaal, paid Thabo Mbeki R30 million to guarantee it winning the contract to supply submarines to South Africa. When this was reported in the *Sunday Times* in 2007, Mbeki threatened to sue, but the threatened legal action never materi-

2 Ibid., 2.
3 Roger Southall and Geoffrey Wood (1988), 'Political party funding in southern Africa', in Peter Burnell and Alan Ware (eds), *Funding Democratization*, Manchester: Manchester University Press, 202–28.
4 Jonathan Moyo paid no attention at all to party funding in his valuable (1992) study, *Voting for Democracy: Electoral Politics in Zimbawe*, Harare: University of Zimbabwe Press, but mentioned in passing the effective politicization of the Zimbabwe Electoral Commission and the Zimbabwe Broadcasting Commission.
5 Andrew Feinstein (2007), *After the Party: A Personal and Political Journey inside the ANC*, Johannesburg and Cape Town: Jonathan Ball Publishers, 177.

alized.[6] However, despite the advantages of state power, the demise of the one party state debate in Zimbabwe and the financial challenges which all three parties faced in fighting competitive elections prompted legislation providing for the state funding of political parties.

Party funding and regulation

The first step was the Political Parties (Finance) Act of 1992 in Zimbabwe. This provided for state funding of political parties which held fifteen or more seats in parliament. The number of seats was carefully calculated, for at the time only ZANU-PF qualified for funding, holding a massive 117 seats in the 120 seats in the House of Assembly. Subsequently, this was challenged in the Supreme Court, which in 1997 ruled that the threshold for receiving state funding should be reduced to 5 per cent of the votes cast in the last general election, effect being given to this by an amending act later in the year. The amounts allocated to parties were to be determined by this formula from an annual budget presented to parliament. Meanwhile, the Act also prohibited parties and candidates from receiving funds from foreign donors, with contravention of this provision being punishable by a fine equal to any donation and its forfeiture to the state.[7]

A similar Act passed in Namibia in 1997 provided for parties represented in the National Assembly to receive public funds on an annual basis, in proportion to the votes they garnered in the previous election, with such funding being restricted to 0.2 per cent of the state budget of the previous year. There were no restrictions on the receipt of foreign funding, although the Electoral Act of 1992 had required disclosure of receipt of such funds.[8]

In South Africa, state funding was instituted via the Public Funding of Represented Political Parties Act of 1997. This prescribed that any party which was represented in the National Assembly or any provincial legislature was entitled to allocations of funding distributed by the IEC. Allocated funds might be used for party organization, promoting democracy, and voter education, but there were prohibitions upon parties expending official monies on direct or indirect remuneration to elected representatives or public officials, starting or participating in businesses, or engaging in unethical activities. The Act empowered the President, acting upon recommendations from parliament, to proclaim regulations not directly prescribed by the Act. This meant that it was parliament, controlled by the ANC, which assumed ultimate responsibility for deciding on the funding which would be provided by the state, and which was to insist that such money be distributed upon a basis which was strictly proportional to parties' representation in legislatures.[9] During the financial year of 2006–07, for instance, the ANC received R49.3 million of the R74.1 million administered by the Political Parties Fund.[10]

6   *Sunday Times*, 15 August 2010.
7   Electoral Institute of Southern Africa (undated), 'Zimbabwe: Party regulation and funding', http://www.eisa.org.za/WEP/zimpartiesc.html
8   Electoral Institute of Southern Africa (undated), 'Namibia: Party funding', http://www.eisa.org.za/WEP/namparties4.htm
9   Roger Southall (2008), 'The ANC for sale? Money, morality and business in South Africa', *Review of African Political Economy*, 35: 116, 281–99.
10 Vicki Robinson and Stefaans Brummer (2006), *Corporate Fronts and Political Party Funding*, Institute for Security Studies, Paper 129, November, 1–40.

While there is a reasonable basis for the distribution of state funding to parties on a basis of their proportional representation in legislatures, it has had the obvious outcome of reinforcing ruling party political dominance. In 2007, for instance, SWAPO received 11 times as much official funding as any other party represented in parliament, and 3.2 times as much as all the other opposition parties put together.[11]

In all three countries, opposition parties have complained that they are systematically disadvantaged by the proportionality ruling. Equally, in all three countries, the ruling parties have shown a disinclination to alter the status quo. However, the rise of the MDC prompted a change in the funding situation with the passage by the then still ZANU-PF-controlled parliament of the Political Parties (Finance) Act of 2001. This reinforced the ban on parties receiving funds from foreign donors, whether channelled directly or indirectly. This was followed up by a Bill in 2004 which similarly aimed to ban foreign funding for NGOs. The motivation behind the Act was to highlight (and cut off) the MDC's alleged support from Western 'imperialism', but more particularly, perhaps, to stem financial support to the opposition from the Zimbabwean diaspora. Both moves were designed to curtail the democratic space within which opposition forces could operate, yet conveniently overlooked the extent to which ZANU-PF itself had benefited from a patchwork quilt of financial and other support from the West in the past.[12] Nor did it prevent ZANU-PF continuing to receive gifts from afar. For instance, complaints that ZANU-PF was fuelled by Colonel Muammar Gaddafi's regime in Libya found a specific instance in the MDC's protest in January 2011 about ZANU-PF politburo member Webster Shamu receiving nine tractors from Libya on behalf of the party to improve his declining fortunes in Chegutu East constituency.[13] ZANU-PF spokesman Rugare Gumbo responded that ZANU-PF had received funding from Russia and China as well as Libya and would continue so, while branding MDC receipt of foreign finance as intolerable. 'You cannot compare the Libyans to the Americans and British who have imposed sanctions on us.'[14]

Nonetheless, for all its importance, state funding has proved inadequate in meeting parties' needs. In South Africa, in the run-up to the 1999 elections, represented parties had access to some R53 million in public funding, yet they reportedly spent between R300 and R500 million.[15] This has compelled all parties to look for alternative sources of funding.

Misappropriation of state resources

One alternative for the ruling NLMs has been the blatant misappropriation of state resources. Media revelations in South Africa uncovered how the state oil

[11] EISA (2009), *Namibia: Presidential and National Assembly Elections 27 and 28 November 2009*, Johannesburg: EISA, 15.

[12] David Moore (2005), 'ZANU-PF and the ghosts of foreign funding', *Review of African Political Economy*, 32: 103, 156–62.

[13] 'MDC warns foreign embassies to stop funding ZANU-PF', http://www.swradioafrica.com/pages/mdcwarns060111.htm

[14] 'ZANU-PF and MDC clash over foreign funding', *Zimbabwe Online*, 7 January 2011, http://zimbabweonlinepress.com/index.php?news=3180

[15] Andile Sokomani (2010), 'Party financing in democratic South Africa: Harbinger of doom?' in Butler (ed.), op. cit., 170–86.

company, PetroSA, irregularly made an advance payment of R15 million to Imvume Management for the supply of oil condensate sourced from a Swiss company, Glencore. Imvume was headed by Sandi Majali, an 'economic adviser' to Kgalema Motlanthe, then ANC Secretary-General, with empowerment magnate Tokyo Sexwale holding a clutch of shares. However, when Imvume diverted R11 million of this sum to the ANC ahead of the 2004 general elections, Glencore turned to PetroSA for direct payment of the R15 million, and another R3 million owing to it from Imvume. The latter thereupon paid Glencore the R18 million for fear that its Mossel Bay gas-to-liquid fuel point would have to close down. That senior members of the ANC knew of the transaction is suggested by the fact that Motlanthe, party treasurer Msimang and the ANC's head of the presidency, Smuts Ngonyama, had travelled with Majali to Iraq in December 2000 in support of the latter's bid to negotiate an allocation of oil to Imvume by Saddam Hussein under the UN's Oil-for-Food programme (the Security Council having imposed sanctions upon Iraq following the latter's invasion of Kuwait in 1990). Furthermore, PetroSA had allegedly been pressured to make the advance payment to Imvume by Phumzili Mlambo-Ngcuka, then Minister of the Department of Minerals and Energy, at a time when the ANC was in dire financial straits, with a bank overdraft of more than R100 million.[16]

The ANC's response to the exposé was that there was nothing wrong with a private company making a donation and it tried to gag leading newspapers from exploring its relationship with Imvume. When DA leader Tony Leon referred the allegations to Public Protector Lawrence Mushwana, the latter simply cleared PetroSA of wrongdoing. A subsequent report of an inquiry by Judge Michael Donen stated that no South African laws had been breached, although Mbeki declined to make his findings public. However, the ANC opted to return the money to avoid further embarrassment, although Mushwana declined to investigate Imvume's conduct, stating that his mandate did not allow him to inquire about the R11 million payment once it was held by a private company.[17]

In June 2011, allegations were made that South Africa was shielding Zimbabwe's breach of the Kimberley Process when there was growing evidence that smuggling from the Marange diamond field was funding ZANU-PF. Linda Makatini, Chairperson of South Africa's State Diamond Trader, created in 2008 to buy diamonds mined in South Africa to sell to local cutting and polishing companies, was accused of importing rough diamonds worth US$1 million from Marange in contravention of the KP, and then offering them for sale on the Diamond Market Exchange. Whether this was on behalf of the State Diamond Trader or private diamond companies for which, remarkably, she simultaneously served as Director, is unknown, but demands for an investigation made by the DA were brushed aside by Mining Minister Susan Shabangu, on the grounds that Zimbabwe was KP compliant. Thus an opportunity to expose how profits from Marange were being diverted into ZANU-PF party coffers at the expense of the Zimbabwean treasury was avoided.[18]

It is not always easy to identify where legitimate relationships between ruling party and government begin and end. How to classify, for instance, the sale by

[16] Southall, op. cit., 290–91.
[17] Sokomani, op. cit., 179–80.
[18] *Mail & Guardian*, 10–16 June 2011.

SWAPO of its initial headquarters in the centre of Windhoek to government after the transition?[19] How, at the present time, can we differentiate the finances of the CIO (estimated as rising from US$121 million in 2011 to US$206 million in 2014) which fall directly under the President's Office and are not subject to audit by the Comptroller General or parliamentary oversight from those of ZANU-PF?[20] However, what is clear is that outright misappropriation of state funding holds ruling parties hostage to fortune, for details usually leak out into the public domain, causing embarrassment. It is therefore not surprising that the NLMs have looked to secure funding from business.

Donations from private sources

None of the original acts governing party financing imposed serious restrictions on the receipt of private funding. Nor indeed was there any obligation made to disclose such funding (except in the Namibian case, via the Electoral Act of 1992, foreign funding). Overall, ZANU-PF, SWAPO, and the ANC have been strongly resistant to revealing the sources and amounts of the bulk of their funding, as have the opposition parties. Whereas the former are reluctant to encourage any *post hoc* matching of benefits granted to donations, the latter fear that disclosure will lead to penalties being inflicted upon their benefactors. Nonetheless, it is clear that major funding is now drawn by all three ruling parties from business. Initially, businesses made donations of value (if not money, then free use of offices, vehicles, and other equipment) during the political transitions to establish productive relations in the future and to distance themselves from the past. Subsequently, relationships with business around funding have become increasingly formalized.

It is the ANC which has been the most creative in tapping into corporate largesse. The above-ground opening of its efforts was the launch of its 'Network Lounge'. This was introduced at its 2002 National Conference, where eighteen corporations and eleven parastatals and government departments paid substantial sums to associate with the ANC elite. After the 2007 Conference at Polokwane, the opposition DA complained that participation in the Network Lounge by public entities, each of which would have been required to pay R5 million, may have resulted in up to R40 million of taxpayers' money having been channelled to ANC coffers. Meanwhile, in 2006, the ANC had also established a Progressive Business Forum, whereby small businesses are offered silver, gold or platinum memberships (for prices between R3,000 and R7,000) with large corporations being charged between R12,500 and R60,000 to enable businesspeople 'to network with ANC policymakers'.[21] Whilst critics objected that the Forum trampled upon ethical concerns, the ANC insisted it was a legitimate platform for encouraging dialogue between business and the party.[22] ZANU-PF subsequently borrowed

---

[19]   Ilina Soiri (2003), 'SWAPO wins, apathy rules: The Namibian 1998 local authority elections', in Michael Cowen and Liisa Laakso (eds), *Multi-Party Elections in Africa*, London: Palgrave Macmillan, 196.

[20]   Global Witness (2012), *Financing a Parallel Government? The Involvement of the Secret Police and Military in Zimbabwe's Diamond, Cotton and Property Sectors*, June.

[21]   Southall, op. cit., 287

[22]   Ibid.

the idea, and by late 2010, Mugabe was eating sandwiches and drinking tea with representatives of the country's largest banks, mines, and industries, who 'exchanged laughter and light banter with top members of the ZANU-PF politburo'. The gathering was dubbed 'business talks to ZANU-PF', but its real intent was to raise money for ZANU-PF's forthcoming Conference, where companies would pay to exhibit.[23]

Sometimes, the returns to those making gifts to power-holders seem explicit. It was reported that the financial backing given by prominent businessman Robert Gumede to the ANC was profitably followed by his companies receiving multi-million contracts with variously, the police, departments of Justice and Correctional Services, Home Affairs, and Telkom.[24] On other occasions, the returns can only be speculated upon. Publicized donations to ZANU-PF by Phillip Chiyanga, Mugabe's nephew (and ironically, a former Selous Scout who served the Smith regime) were surely intended to protect the family interest.[25] Similarly, those who seek to benefit from BEE or indigenization policies are wise to maintain a cosy relationship with powers that be if they wish their tenders to win out. Or perhaps, as observed on the donation of N$2.5 million-worth of party paraphernalia (T-shirts, bill boards, etc) by the Pakistan Oshikango Welfare Association in the lead-up to SWAPO's 2009 election campaign, donors seek political protection as much as favour.[26] Thus in 2011, it was reported that ZANU-PF was effectively blackmailing firms to make hefty donations to fund a dinner and concert involving popular artists as part of its anti-sanctions campaign.[27]

In passing, it is worth noting the crossover between business interests and income raised from individual party memberships. During the lead-up to party congresses (where positions are at stake) and to election campaigns, parties drive for membership. Sale of membership cards, as well as whipping up popular enthusiasm, can generate revenue. However, it is also subject to considerable abuse. In Zimbabwe, the militarization of ZANU-PF's election campaigns has rendered non-possession of a party card dangerous. In all three countries, party membership is viewed as a prerequisite for deployment and eligibility for tenders or employment. Likewise, it is likely that the phenomenon of businesspersons-cum-political-entrepreneurs paying for memberships to secure backing within party structures is widespread. Malabela, in his study of the ANC in Manzini-Mbombela, demonstrated that the local branch of the party was significantly composed of 'members of members'.[28]

Nonetheless, reciprocal relationships between parties and businesses are usually difficult to prove. It is possible that the donations made to the ANC by the major mining companies prior to the 2004 election were designed to get the ANC to reconsider the draft of its mining charter for BEE. The leak of this

---

23 'ZANU-PF courts big businesses ahead of elections', http://newsdzezimbabwe.wordpress.com/2010/12/10/zanu-pf-courts

24 *Mail & Guardian*, 5–11 November 2010.

25 'Philip Chiyangwa to fund ZANU-PF election campaign', http://www.zimeye.org/?p=23655

26 *The Namibian*, 30 September 2009.

27 'ZANU-PF accused of forcing local firms to sponsor party's anti-sanctions campaign', http://www.voanews.com/Zimbabwe/news/Zanu-PF-Accused-of-Forcing-Companies-to-Sp

28 Musawenkosi Malabela (2011), *The ANC and Local Democracy: The Role of the ANC Branch in Manzini-Mbombela*, MA Research Report, Department of Sociology, University of the Witwatersrand.

document in 2003 wiped millions of rands off the stock exchange.[29] In 2010, Agriculture Minister Tina Joemat Pettersson and, allegedly, the ANC-inclined officials of Marine and Coastal Management were accused by the DA of exchanging the allocation of fishing deals for contributions to the party's election account.[30] However, at the end of the day, it is largely speculation that attends the benefits resulting from donations. By their nature, the details of party-business relationships tend to emerge only when things go wrong and are leaked by offended interests or in court proceedings.

One such example is provided by the dealings between the ANC and Brett Kebble, the mining magnate who plundered more than R2 billion from his companies, Johannesburg Consolidated Investments (JCI) and Randgold Exploration (R&E). Kebble funnelled more than R25 million to the ANC, the ANCYL, and their investment arms during 2002 and 2005 in a series of operations which were designed to drain money from the shareholders of his own companies. The eventual outcome was the collapse of his empire, his apparent involvement in drug-dealing and his eventual violent death in mid-2006. Ironically, much of the money given to the ANC had to be returned when it emerged later from legal proceedings that it had been stolen from JCI and R&E. However, in June 2007, the ANC argued in court that all such monies should not be returned as Kebble's companies had received equivalent value in the 'indirect benefit' they had obtained. Intriguingly, Kebble's principal cronies within the ANC were those who lined up with Zuma against Mbeki, and it may well be that he was looking to a Zuma presidency to get himself out of trouble.[31]

Finally, it is worth stressing that the opaque nature of party-business relationships obscures what are if not actually criminal then grossly unethical practices. Attention has already been directed to how the plundering of the diamond fields by the ZANU-PF political-military elite is directing funding into party coffers. As noted already, the incestuous relationship between Sam Pa and the Queensway Syndicate and the CIO has led to massive funding (US$100 million) of the latter and its steadily increasing capacity to deploy violence against the MDC. The CIO only achieved off-budget funding after the MDC took control of the Ministry of Finance.[32] Today it operates as a rogue force well beyond control of the coalition government, its mandate under Mugabe being to secure a victory for ZANU-PF at the next election.

The party-business empires

Over and above their links with established capital and black business, the NLMs have created their own companies and made investments designed to ensure a constant flow of income. Such operations are not designed to promote entrepreneurial ventures but to secure financial returns from the merging of party and state. A great deal of such investment has been covert and some of it has bordered on the criminal – both good reasons why ruling parties prefer not to

[29] Ivor Sarakinsky (2007), 'Political party finance in South Africa: Disclosure versus secrecy', *Democratization*, 14: 1, 111–28.
[30] *Business Day*, 2 July 2010.
[31] Barry Sergeant (2006), *Brett Kebble: The Inside Story*, Cape Town: Zebra Press.
[32] Global Witness, op. cit., 6.

make private funding for parties subject to public audits and for party-created companies to remain private. Equally, the often shady deals which accompany such investment activity can be a recipe for loss-making, for the parties have been no more able to shield themselves from self-serving behaviour by their cadres than the governments which they run.

Private interest and party business in Zimbabwe and Namibia

ZANU-PF launched its business interests in 1980, taking over a company, M&S, which had been established the previous year as an investment vehicle for the Muzenda and Sumbureru families. By the early 1990s, M&S had acquired a $13 million interest in Treger Holdings, previously a family concern, and also owned Jongwe Printing and Publishing Company, and half of Woolworth Trading and F.W. Woolworth & Co (Zimbabwe). However, ZANU-PF's main operation was Zidco Holdings, established in 1981, which focused on an import and export business, and extended into textbook production, vehicle manufacture and distribution, property investment, and farm management. Both M&S and Zidco were partly owned and controlled by the Joshi brothers – local Asian businessmen. In 1987 they acquired a 50 per cent holding in a leading blanket-manufacturing company, this supplementing other investments which both M&S and Zidco had in companies listed on the Zimbabwe Stock Exchange. By the early 1990s, Zidco's companies employed some 10,000 people and was generating an annual turnover of Z$350 million.[33]

The origins of SWAPO's business interests lie in buses, originally donated to its refugee camps, that formed the nucleus of a bus and haulage company, Namib Contract Haulage. It is reported that by 2010, SWAPO's principal investment vehicle, Kalahari Holdings, presided over a clutch of other subsidiaries, notably Namprint, Kudu Investment, Klondike Properties, New Dawn Video Production, the farm De Rust, and Ndilimani Cultural Troupe. It also had joint ventures, in which it normally owned 51 per cent, in Multichoice Namibia (with Multichoice Africa, a subsidiary of the major South African satellite television operator); Springbok Patrols Namibia, co-owned with Bartmann (South Africa); Radio Energy, a commercial radio station, co-owned with Zebra Holdings; and a minority interest in MWeb, an internet service provider, with TelkomSA. In addition, it had a 17 per cent interest in NamHealth Holdings, in which the SWAPO Youth League and trade unions affiliated to the party also had substantial shareholdings.[34]

The basic mode of operation of such party operations was threefold. First, they relied on a regular supply of contracts from government or the party itself. Thus Jongwe Printing supplied textbooks for Zimbabwean state schools and New Dawn Video Production made a documentary of SWAPO's fourth congress. Second, they could sometimes rely on loans from government institutions, with Kudu Investment, for instance, operating a major business complex in Windhoek via funding provided by the Government Institutions Pension Fund. Third, they were often facilitated by the state's legal power to issue licences for businesses in restricted areas, such as broadcasting, with the

---

[33]   *ACR 1992–94*, B728; Martin Dawson and Tim Kelsall (2012), 'Anti-developmental patrimonialism in Zimbabwe', *Journal of Contemporary African Studies*, 30: 1, 49–66.

[34]   *The Namibian*, 10 February 2010.

party essentially trading the permission to operate for a majority shareholding with an established company, which then supplied the necessary professional and managerial services.

However, a fundamental problem besetting such party business empires was their lack of transparency. With many operations listed as private companies, there was no need to make their accounts public, which resulted in few people even within ZANU-PF and SWAPO themselves knowing the state of affairs, and arousing deep suspicion whether such profits as the operations were making were being returned to the party.

In Namibia, Festus Naholo, who became responsible for running SWAPO's business interest in the early 1990s, was accused by the party leadership of enriching himself. Nujoma informed the party Central Committee in 2002 that Naholo had sold the party's mobile radio equipment, worth 25 million UK pounds, to the DRC. Denying that he had run Kalahari Investments into the ground leaving it with a debt of N\$30 million, Naholo responded that it was 'swimming in a huge ocean of money from dividends', that Nujoma had orchestrated the sale to the DRC, and that assets had been diverted into the pockets of the President and other party high-ups. Overall, his assertions that the party's joint ventures with major companies are profitable are highly credible (with MultiChoice Namibia, for instance, having by 2010 reportedly paid dividends of N\$20 million).[35]

The fate of ZANU-PF's businesses has been even more obscure, but it would seem that after some reasonable profitability in the 1980s and early 1990s, they have been reduced to penury. A committee to investigate the state of the companies was set up in early 2004, apparently as a result of factional struggles between General Mujuru and Emmerson Mnangagwa, Speaker of Parliament and a key player in the party's business empire. Its report was never publicly released, but details found their way into the independent media. The thrust of the revelations was that funds had been moved from the party firms to shelf companies in order to evade the sanctions that had been imposed by the West upon companies and banks connected to ZANU-PF. These included Segmented Investments, Sovereign, Hustonville, Tescrom, Amelia, Ryobi, Prinfit, and M&S Investments, some of which listed a prominent lawyer, Edwin Manikai, as Director. Manikai had emerged as the key figure behind the companies' sanctions-busting activities, and was a key adviser to Reserve Bank governor Gideon Gono.[36]

Seven of the shelf companies, notably Segmented Investments, had a 32.05 per cent holding in First Banking Corporation Holdings which controlled First Bank, Southern African Reinsurance, and National Discount House. Although the latter was financially troubled, Gono did not pounce on it as he had done with other banks facing financial difficulties, and it emerged as the principal channel for the party's money laundering activities. In turn, the Reserve Bank of Zimbabwe was operating with a total lack of transparency, being used to extend largely unsupervised loans to ZANU-PF shelf companies. It is claimed that the money was often used to purchase commodities such as fuel but in at

[35] *The Namibian*, 10 February 2010.
[36] Dawson and Kelsall, op. cit., and Mduduzi Mathuthu, 'Busting Zimbabwe's sanctions busters', http://www.newzimbabwe.com/pages/sanctions.13734.html

least one instance to purchase interests in UK companies, as well as being used by Mugabe for his personal transactions. However, while the Reserve Bank had in effect been transformed into 'a patronage dispensing machine under the cover of busting sanctions',[37] its benefits flowed to highly placed individuals rather more than to the party itself.

In April 2009, ZANU-PF's politburo established yet another probe into the state of affairs of the party's businesses, which was to be undertaken by a committee which included Emmerson Mnangagwa, Solomon Mujuru, Simbi Mukoni (the former Finance Minister), Matabeleland North's Governor, Obert Mpofu, and Thoko Mathuthu, the party's Deputy Secretary for Transport and Welfare. It was subsequently widely stated that Mnangagwa and other highly placed figures had been found guilty of 'improper conduct', but that the findings could well split the party. Yet again, the report was never published.[38]

By 2011, ZANU-PF's finance department was reporting that the party was broke and was surviving on bank overdrafts with no returns coming from its investments in over 30 companies.[39] In part, this was because the party's salary bill had surged by more than 100 per cent to US$1.2 million, with further costs incurred by legal fees arising from the 2008 general elections.[40] At about this time, arrangements were being put in place to bail out Lobels Bread, a party-owned firm which had gone into liquidation. The funds were to come from the state-majority-owned CBZ Bank Ltd, despite the allegation that Lobels had been a recipient of a large advance from the National Social Security Authority which had subsequently gone missing. Meanwhile, a similar bailout had just been denied to Renaissance Merchant Bank, whose officials were said to be linked to the MDC.[41] Despite the coalition government, the Zanuification of much of the financial machinery of the state continues.

The ANC as tenderpreneur: public money for party profit

The ANC launched its first business in 1992 when Nelson Mandela, Walter Sisulu, and Tokyo Sexwale founded the Batho Batho Trust. Its official mandate was to benefit 'the broader South African community, especially historically disadvantaged communities', but its unofficial purpose was allegedly to finance the ANC. The trust established Thebe Investments, whose early business was obtained through its being viewed as the ANC's investment arm and as a potential line of communication to the new government.[42] It was to acquire significant shareholdings in private health provision, finance, and insurance, with an annual revenue of around R650 million. However, as time wore on, the relationship between the Batho Batho Trust/Thebe and the ANC was to become more distant. In the late 1990s, Batho Batho diluted its stake in Thebe to 74 per cent, selling 26 per cent to Sanlam and Investec. Then, in 2006, it sold

[37] Mathuthu, op. cit.
[38] 'ZANU-PF companies probe report kept secret', http://www.newzimbabwe.com/pages/mnanga5.11372.html
[39] *Zimbabwe Independent*, 23 December 2010; *Financial Gazette*, 8 June 2012.
[40] 'We are broke – ZANU (PF) finance boss', http://newsdzezimbabwe.wordpress.com/2011/01/14/we-are-broke-zanu-pf-finance-boss/
[41] *The Zimbabwean*, 23 July 2011.
[42] Duncan Randall (1996), 'Prospects for the development of a black business class in South Africa', *Journal of Modern African Studies*, 34: 4, 661–86.

another 22 per cent to company management for around R100 million. Furthermore, in contrast to the demand by then party Treasurer, Selby Msimang, that the proceeds of this sale should be used to pay off the ANC's debts (R100 million at the time), the trustees insisted that they had a fiduciary duty to respect Batho Batho's official mandate, and that the ANC's request for funding would be adjudicated like that of any other applicant.[43]

As far as the ANC was concerned, it would seem that an arms-length relationship with a company operating largely in the private market was not the way forward. Nor indeed (as indicated in records that have surfaced from the ANC's archives donated to the University of Fort Hare) was reliance upon private companies owned by ANC luminaries attractive, for these provided fertile ground for the party itself to become a victim of fraud and brazen looting. One such experience allegedly resulted in the party being defrauded of R400,000 earmarked for investment in property. (Suffice it to say that the luminaries identified in an internal party investigation, Mzi Khumalo and Mike Sutcliffe, later to become city manager in Durban, strongly denied the allegations which were left hanging in the air because of the ANC's reluctance to have such matters investigated.)[44] What the Fort Hare documents did illustrate (even if they were rapidly withdrawn from public gaze) was how quickly the party turned to the idea of launching vehicles that would have an intimate relationship with the state.

According to a document entitled 'President's report' submitted to Mandela in 1995, Thabo Mbeki played a key role in advising Schabir Shaik to create a company (Nkobi Holdings) that would fund the ANC through 'patriotic' dividends paid for by major government contracts. He told him to 'dislodge from party control' and 'to develop (Nkobi) into another structure like that of Thebe Investment'. At a meeting also attended by Joe Modise, Minister of Defence, and Joe Nhlanhla, Minister of Intelligence, Mbeki proposed that the fact that Shaik knew several ministers as members of the ANC and as friends did not disqualify him from meeting them. Subsequently, Shaik entered secret negotiations with arms deal beneficiaries Advanced Technology and Engineering and Plessey Tellumat for a joint venture, four years before the contracts were actually awarded. He also had regular meetings with Ronnie Kasrils, then Deputy Minister of Defence, on potential contracts, as well as with senior ministers such as Trevor Manuel, Alec Erwin, and Jeff Radebe. According to the document, he also introduced Malaysian investors to Manuel, then Minister of Trade and Industry. By June 1995 they had acquired major interests in their respective fields in South Africa worth R500 million.

Subsequently, Nkobi became involved in private and government contracts worth more than R8 billion and was to pass on millions to the ANC. Asked why Shaik had never disclosed in his court case that Mbeki had urged him to create Nkobi Holdings, a senior member of the ANC stated: 'It was either the entire party being deemed corrupt or just one person taking the fall...[Shaik] felt almost duty-bound to take the blame.'[45]

Further, when Judge Chris Nicholson threw out the corruption charges

---

[43] *Mail & Guardian Online*, 1 March 2007.
[44] *Sunday Times*, 22 August 2010.
[45] *Sunday Times*, 15 August 2010.

against Zuma in September 2008, he observed: 'The court can hardly be unaware of the other dark mutterings emanating from [Zuma] that if he goes down others will follow him. Like a blinded Samson he threatens to make sure the temple collapses with him.'[46] If the temple collapsed upon Nkobi Holdings, it has hitherto spared Chancellor House, although this ANC funding vehicle has become embroiled in massive controversy.

Chancellor House Trust was established at about the same time as Nkobi. Chaired by ANC historian-activist Ben Magubane, it was listed as a charitable foundation whose principal purpose would be to 'facilitate the participation and involvement in all economic and political sectors of South African persons and entities which [had] been historically disadvantaged'. However, as with Batho Batho/Thebe and Nkobi, the intention was for the proceeds of the Trust to fund the ANC. In March 2003, the Trust launched Chancellor House Holdings (CHH).[47] The board of CHH was chaired by Professor Taole Mokoena (close friend of Manto Tshabala-Msimang, ANC's Treasurer Selby Msimang's wife), and included Sivi Gounden (former Director-General in the Department of Public Enterprise) and Irene Charnley (Director of cellular telephony company MTN).

By 2006, when Chancellor's role as an ANC funding front came to light, it had significant holdings, notably in mining, energy, engineering, and IT companies with BEE credentials, almost all of which were locked into contracts with government departments or parastatals. These included an interest in Continental Africa Gold Resources, which held a 23 per cent share in Wits Gold, the latter having been granted 'new-order' gold prospecting rights by the Department of Minerals and Energy for six of the nine areas it had applied for in 2006; and a 10 per cent holding in Bateman Africa, an empowerment venture in engineering whose CEO was Sivi Gounden, and whose focus was in natural resources and power generation, an area heavily dependent upon parastatal contracts. In addition, it also became closely aligned with United Manganese of Kalahari (UMK).

UMK was a joint venture between Chancellor and Pitsa ya Setshaba Holdings which was awarded 'new order' prospecting rights to eight farm portions in the Kuruman district of the Kalahari. Under the Mineral and Petroleum Resources Development Act of 2002 (in force from 1 May 2004) the state owned – and still owns – all mineral rights. This required existing rights-holders to convert their 'old order' rights to 'new order' rights over time, meeting progressive empowerment targets. UMK shared these rights (51 per cent) with Renova Manganese Investments (RMI). The latter was a Bahamas-registered subsidiary of Renova, an investment group controlled by Viktor Vekselberg, a Russian oligarch with massive wealth accumulated through deals in metals and oil. UMK was funded by Renova to the tune of US$20 million, effectively gifting nearly half this sum to Chancellor and Pitsa as RMI's partners. However, with 80 per cent of the world's known commercially exploitable reserves of manganese located in the Kalahari, Renova was said to be confident that the value of the project would rocket to US$1 billion.

The grant of prospecting rights to UMK drew complaints from two other

---

[46] Ibid.
[47] What follows is drawn from the superb exposé by Vicki Robinson and Stefaans Brummer in the *Mail & Guardian*, 10–16 November 2006 and 8–14 February 2006.

ANC-related BEE entities, Kalahari Resources and Direleton Minerals & Energy, which protested that Pitsa ya Setshaba had been unduly favoured. If this were true, it may well have been because of Vekselberg's emergence as a key player in South African-Russian relations, having accompanied Russian President Putin on a visit to South Africa in September 2005, and having been appointed by Mbeki to his International Investment Council. Diplomatic expediency seems to have been underpinned by Renova's relationship with Chancellor House as a funding front for the ANC.

However, it was Chancellor's involvement in another entity that highlighted its 'role...as both referee...through its cadres deployed in government and state-owned enterprises – and player' when it allied with Babcock-Hitachi Europe to establish Hitachi Power Africa. The aim was to form a bid for the ESCOM programme to build new power stations to meet the country's growing energy demands. CHH took a 25 per cent holding in the joint venture, and in 2007 won a R38.5 billion tender from ESCOM to supply six giant boilers for the new Medupe and Kusile power stations (perhaps the single largest procurement in South Africa's history). Subsequently, it was revealed that the ESCOM Chairman, former ANC cabinet minister Valli Moosa, had presided over the board meetings while also serving on the ANC's fundraising committee. A subsequent investigation by the Public Protector, launched after the ANC's interest in ESCOM's programme came to light in 2010, confirmed that Moosa should have acknowledged a conflict of interest. By this time, it was also clear that the ANC itself had an acute conflict of interest, for although publicly opposing ESCOM's decision to impose massive tariff increases to fund its expansion programme, it stood to gain from it through CHH.[48]

The incestuous relationship between the ANC, CHH, and ESCOM aroused bitter controversy even within the party and amongst its allies. COSATU's Zwelinzima Vavi argued that the ANC stood to benefit at the expense of the poor. This prompted a response from ANC Secretary-General Gwede Mantashe that Vavi's reaction was 'populist' and that for CHH/Hitachi not to have bid for the contract would have left the investment opportunity to monopoly capital.[49] Then, in April 2010, Mathews Phosa, ANC Treasurer-General stated that he had advised CHH to exit from Hitachi and that Chancellor had agreed to do so within six weeks.[50] However, he was soon contradicted, with key players in CHH arguing that it was an independent entity, and that Phosa was entitled to speak for neither the ANC nor the company. Ultimately, Phosa was isolated, and CHH retained its shares in Hitachi.

Whatever the niceties, the ANC's investments through Chancellor House seem to have paid off rapidly, for at the Polokwane Conference Mendi Msimang reported that the ANC's portfolio of investments had enabled the party to achieve a sound financial position. He was understating his case. By the time of the Polokwane Conference in December 2007, the ANC's assets amounted to more than R1.75 billion.[51]

[48] Sam Sole (2010), 'Money politics in South Africa: From covert party funding to the problem of black economic empowerment', in Butler, op. cit., 187–200.
[49] Ibid.
[50] Cited in Zwelethu Jolobe (2010), 'Financing the ANC: Chancellor House, Eskom and the dilemmas of party finance reform', in Butler, op. cit., 201–17.
[51] *Sunday Independent*, 2 March 2008.

State power and party funding: the machine as monster?

Party funding poses major dilemmas even in established democracies. The massive funding by corporations of the competing oligarchies of the Republican and Democratic parties in the US has long been notorious. In Europe, the slow decline of the political party as a membership organization has involved even social democratic parties, which pride themselves on a higher level of morality than their conservative rivals, in embarrassing funding scandals. Politics, say the cynical, is overwhelmingly about power and profit, with principle lagging far behind.

Party funding issues are even more problematic in former settler Africa where at the transitions to democracy, there was a divide between new political power without money and old money which had just lost political power; yet each needed each other to advance their interests. How precisely were the incoming liberation movements to fund their activities when they themselves came from a background of dependency upon foreign governments and solidarity organizations, few of which required serious financial accountability? How reasonable was it to suppose that they would act as model democrats when the model of liberal democracy imported from the West was itself increasingly struggling with dilemmas around party funding – not to mention the huge interest which large international companies from that selfsame West had in ingratiating themselves with the new governments? In short, the situation was structurally set up to encourage corruption and an incestuous relationship between emergent party-states and international capital. Ultimately, the cost was huge.

First, the imbalance between money and political power corrupted the NLMs themselves, diverting them from their proclaimed progressive aims. The suggestion that this was inevitable is negated by the fact that, despite internal critiques and lamentations about class formation and the adoption by party elites of extravagant lifestyles, no corrective measures were every seriously attempted.

Second, party ideologies – notably the focus upon acquiring state power and the merging of party with state – legitimized the accumulation of unequal financial advantage and delegitimized opposition parties while justifying limits being placed upon their ability to secure funding that would allow them to compete effectively.

Third, ironically, the party funding regimes which have arisen around the conflation of party and state power have undermined the capacities of the parties themselves. Careless disregard for the law and accountability has created opportunities for party funding to be transformed into vehicles for personal and factional advantage. Just as party positions and connections provide for the diversion of state monies into personal pockets, so the monies supposedly due to the party spark bitter internal competition for financial advantage. Thus it has been suggested that the refusal of ZANU-PF to open the books of its aligned companies is matched by the replacement of directors favourable to Zuma on the board of CHH following the fall of Mbeki.[52]

---

[52] Sole, op. cit., 194.

In 2007, as the ANC grappled with the growing influence of money upon the behaviour of its cadres and its own incestuous financial relationship with parastatals, it produced a discussion document, entitled 'Revolutionary morality: The ANC and business', which had two broad thrusts. The first was the need for the building of a 'new political culture' around principles which would balance the right of all party members to earn a living and participate in business against the requirements of legal and ethical behaviour. Such principles would require the development of guidelines for ANC national officer bearers, national and provincial executive committee members, regional and branch executive members, as well as for ordinary members; for the ANC as an investor; and for the ANC as a fundraiser. The second was the need for a new set of party controls, modelled (somewhat curiously, but presumably coming via the SACP's fraternal relations) upon those of the Central Control and Auditing Commission of the Communist Party of the Russian Federation, which would supplement the work of the party's Disciplinary Committee and which would proactively monitor party programmes, finances, and policy implementation. New codes of conduct, it was acknowledged, would not make a difference if not accompanied by effective enforcement.

That the ANC could come up with such a document indicated that there was genuine unease within the party about the deleterious impact of money upon its moral standing and political commitments. The immediate irony was that the ANC was about to elect as its new leader a man who stood before the courts as mired in corrupt relationships flowing from the arms deal and who was so indebted to a raft of party factions that it was unlikely that he would embark upon a commitment to 'revolutionary morality'. As indicated above, numerous initiatives to tackle corruption are embarked upon by various organs of state, yet their reach and impact is limited, and acutely subject to political influence. Indeed, is not Jolobe correct to ask whether Chancellor House, by having become the source of party salaries, now controls the ANC at cost of internal party controls?[53] Has money become the monster that dictates party morality?

In all three countries, there is urgent need for public debate regarding the rules and practices of party funding, extending to discussion concerning the merits of increased public funding to counter private donations, the need for greater accountability and transparency, the possibilities of limits on party expenditure during election campaigns, and above all, the appropriateness of parties involving themselves in businesses that will enter into contracts with government. However, whilst there is currently much talk about the virtues of levelling the playing fields, the parties are reluctant to implement major reforms to funding regimes which systematically favour their interests, even though these undermine the values for which they fought during their struggles for liberation.

[53]   Jolobe, op. cit., 214.

11.
Reaching its Limits? The ANC under Jacob Zuma

The elevation of Jacob Zuma to the presidency was hailed by his supporters as inaugurating a new era for the ANC. Officially, Thabo Mbeki had been removed from the presidency for abusing power. However, the reality was that he had simply offended too many within the Tripartite Alliance, and they had seized the opportunities offered by Polokwane and the Nicholson judgement to remove him.

For COSATU and the SACP, it was strategic to present Mbeki as representing GEAR, the 'class of 1996', and capitalist growth patterns inimical to the working class; for the wider 'coalition of the aggrieved', Mbeki was simply portrayed as dictatorial. In contrast, Zuma was propelled to the presidency not only as one who had been unjustly persecuted, but as a leader who would put the party back in touch with the masses. The further implication was that whereas Mbeki's technocratic instincts had subordinated the ANC to the state, the ANC would now subordinate the state to the party, ensuring that government would implement policies adopted at Polokwane. From this perspective, it mattered little that Zuma carried with him a large amount of baggage, ranging from a questionable record as head of intelligence in exile through to his sexual peccadilloes and his alleged involvement in corruption around the arms deal. What did matter was that he was the antithesis of Mbeki and that those who felt excluded from power saw him as their vehicle for political inclusion. Whereas Mbeki was awkward and reserved, Zuma was warm and easy in company; whereas Mbeki was self-consciously cerebral, Zuma made much of his limited education; whereas Mbeki broke with Mandela's policy of reconciliation to stress Africanization and BEE, Zuma was a political chameleon who was as willing to charm whites as to toyi-toyi with the masses, simultaneously playing to African traditionalist themes of patriarchy and male sexuality. Zuma, furthermore, seemed unthreatening because he presented himself as a humble servant of the people, seeking the presidency only because the ANC had called upon him to do so. Additionally, he declared that he would be only a one-term president, thereby swinging behind him aspirants to the top job who were looking to the future. Amidst all this, Zuma was personally motivated by the desire to stay out of jail, to thwart the state's will and capacity to prosecute him for corruption by exploiting anti-Mbeki sentiment through the mobilization of mass support. Subsequently, having apparently achieved this objective, he arrived at State House with no political agenda other than to protect his back and soon, to extend his stay in power.

Unburdened by policy commitments, his presidency swiftly became characterized by four elements. First, his abandonment of responsibility for stamping direction upon government; second, his use of office to access state-derived wealth for his family and associates; third, reneging on his earlier denial of personal ambition, his determination to secure himself a second term in office through the selective prosecution of his enemies and the negation of political challenge to his leadership at the ANC's 53rd National Conference in Mangaung (Bloemfontein) in December 2012; and fourth, the extension of the security powers of the state to buttress his personal position and that of the executive in general. Zuma, argued Moeletsi Mbeki in October 2011, had done nothing to address South Africa's looming problems:

> When they kicked out my brother, Zuma did not change anything in Thabo's policies. In fact, they were not even Thabo's policies, they were Mandela's. But Zuma added another economic policy which is called corruption.[1]

His statement highlighted wider perceptions that corruption had come to assume more startling proportions under Zuma's tenure. The ANC, so it was commonly said, had become increasingly characterized by parasitism, plunder, and patronage and a resulting paralyzing factionalism. Thus in the year (2012) that the ANC was celebrating its centenary amidst pomp and display, there were many (even within the party itself) who now suggested that it had reached its nadir – that it had lost its moral anchor, and stood in serious danger of forfeiting mass support, and even losing its hold on power in the near future. The ANC, it was regularly said, had failed to surmount the transition from liberation movement to governing party, and failing a political and moral renewal, would very possibly implode, with alarming consequences for democracy and development.

Clearly, if this was the case, then Zuma himself was more likely the product of underlying degenerative tendencies than their cause, an expression of the historical limitations of the ANC as a liberation movement rather than its nemesis. Yet in so far as he was that expression, it is important to understand how his presidency reflected the general malaise.

Zuma's style of governance

Mbeki's leadership style, argued Tom Lodge, was 'that of a political manager, not a charismatic populist'.[2] This led him to transform the small, decentralized office of Mandela into a much more powerful and centralized presidency as the node of policy formulation and coordination.[3] Similarly, he tightened the reins of the centre over the governments of the municipalities and provinces within the ANC, exerting presidential control over key appointments. Strategically, he found it necessary to appoint his ministers from the major constituencies that made up the Alliance.[4] Nonetheless, his rule was characterized by top-down control. By accounts of former ministers such as the late Kader Asmal, he exerted strong personal authority over the cabinet. Significant items (notably the arms deal) were well beyond the bounds of discussion, and dissent (as in the party) was not tolerated (a factor which accounts for the failure of ministers who should have known better to stand up to him on such issues such as HIV-

---

[1] Presentation by Moeletsi Mbeki to *The Herald*-NMMU* Community Dialogue, New Brighton, Port Elizabeth, 1 October 2011. [*Nelson Mandela Metropolitan University]
[2] Tom Lodge (2002), *Politics in South Africa: From Mandela to Mbeki*, Oxford: James Currey, 247.
[3] Mark Gevisser (2007), *The Dream Deferred: Thabo Mbeki*, Johannesburg and Cape Town, Jonathan Ball Publishers, 714.
[4] Lodge, op. cit., 251.

AIDS which, apart from anything else, were deeply damaging to his own reputation and that of his government). In essence, his imperial style was reminiscent of P.W. Botha, prompting SACP leader Blade Nzimande to hint at one point that the ANC under Mbeki was like ZANU-PF under Mugabe.[5] Like Botha, his style was ultimately his undoing, for it made him many enemies who eventually were to congregate behind Jacob Zuma.

Zuma had been chosen as his Deputy President in considerable measure because Mbeki regarded his clear imperfections as rendering him unlikely to represent a threat. Indeed, although he was subsequently to pose as a champion of the left, those who knew him well recognized him as lacking political conviction save in his loyalty to the ANC. Nonetheless, Zuma's pique at being sidelined, and Mbeki's own growing suspicion that Zuma was becoming a focal point of covert opposition was to be responsible for the two men's falling out.[6] Whether or not the legal pursuit of Zuma was politically motivated, Mbeki had used the judgement of the High Court in September 2005 that Zuma had been in a corrupt relationship with Schabir Shaik to dismiss him as Deputy President. Mbeki's objective was to undercut Zuma politically, but this of course was to prove a fatal miscalculation. The ANC NEC declined to dismiss Zuma from the deputy leadership of the party, freeing him to mobilize support as a victim of Mbeki's conspiracy. His subsequent arraignment for rape and the concerted efforts of the legal authorities to prosecute him were all thereafter taken as proof by his following that he was being persecuted.

Zuma was to play the victim skilfully, his followers lionizing him throughout his courtroom dramas in massive public displays of support. When, eventually, in September 2008, with the ruling by Judge Nicholson that the NPA's attempts to prosecute Zuma were politically motivated, Mbeki's emboldened enemies offered him no quarter, demanding that he leave the presidency. Subsequently, when the Supreme Court of Appeal unanimously overturned the Nicholson judgement (dismissing it with contempt and declaring that it had erred in declaring the charges against Zuma as unlawful),[7] the ANC offered no apology to the former President, and merely sulked in embarrassed silence. It was a fitting conclusion to the entire tawdry exercise when, following Zuma's eventual ascendance to the presidency, the continuing efforts of the legal authorities to prosecute him were brought to an end as a result of tapes provided to them by his defence team which themselves were probably illegally leaked (see Chapter 6).

Zuma's ascendance indebted him to many constituencies. The immediate result was that when he made his initial appointments, it was to an expanded government of 34 ministers (rather than Mbeki's 28), plus an additional 27 deputy-ministers, with a reconfiguration of ministries suggesting that much thought had been given to balancing various interests. Trevor Manuel, *bête noire* of the left, was sidelined to a new Ministry of Planning, while the markets were simultaneously calmed by the appointment of Pravin Gordhan, who had done an excellent job in running the Revenue Service, as his successor in Finance. Meanwhile, appointments of SACP loyalist Rob Davies to Trade and Industry,

5   Gevisser, op. cit., 714.
6   Richard Calland and Chris Oxtoby (2010), 'Machiavelli meets the Constitution', in Daryl Glaser (ed.), *Mbeki and After: Reflections on the Legacy of Thabo Mbeki*, Johannesburg: Wits University Press, 71–104.
7   NDPP v Zuma 573/08 (20009) ZASCA (12 January 2009).

former trade unionist Ebrahim Patel to a new Ministry of Economic Development, and SACP Secretary-General Blade Nzimande to Higher Education made
Zuma's cabinet as much a Tripartite Alliance as it was an ANC one, with other
appointments being made from amongst both the politically prominent and
politically obscure.

The new President left his ministers alone. This had the merit that competent
ministers were free to run their ministries without interference, although simultaneously it followed that economic strategy became a battleground between
left and right. Ultimately, this was to prove an unequal struggle, for whilst
Gordhan inherited the Treasury, Patel had not only to construct a new ministry
from scratch but to differentiate it from Planning. The result was that although
both Patel's and Manuel's responsibilities encouraged a new emphasis on long-
term economic thinking (resulting in the former devising of the New Growth
Path in 2011 and the latter coordinating the more weighty first report of a
National Planning Commission in 2012, both of which were widely recognized
as thoughtful documents with the former being more 'statist' in its approach
than the latter), macro-economic management jogged on much as before, to
the considerable disappointment of the organized left. Meanwhile, the latitude
that Zuma allowed them left free ministers who lacked ability, some of whom
had been appointed purely out of presidential indebtedness, this resulting in
areas of major inefficiency. Worse, while the relaxation of control from above
was less stifling, it allowed corruption and factionalism to flourish, with Zuma's
own actions guided far more by his concern to keep his patchwork coalition
together than to secure good government. The resulting paralysis meant that
Zuma rapidly disappointed many within his coalition. But what made matters
significantly worse was the apparent rise of tenderpreneurship and corruption
within the ANC, symbolized by the blatant manner in which political connection was put to advantage by the President's own family and close associates.

'Zuma Inc'

Before they were dropped, Zuma had been facing some 783 criminal charges
involving fraud, corruption, and racketeering. In the new President, powerful
elements within the ANC saw a man who would not be overly concerned with
ethical or legal concerns when it became time to cash in their cards for
supporting him. The evidence of this soon began to accumulate.

The evidence laid before the court in Schabir Shaik's trial of Zuma's heavy
reliance upon his friend for financial support suggest that his personal means
were not significant before his rise to the presidency. This makes the improvement in his fortunes after he became ANC President all the more remarkable. To
be sure, evidence was produced during Shaik's trial that alleged bribes from the
French arms firm Thales were used by Zuma to expand his family homestead at
Nkandla in rural KwaZulu-Natal, but within months after he became President
the bill for new building rose to R65 million. By late 2012 these costs had reportedly shot up to a massive R240 million (compared to the R23 million which
had been spent on Nelson Mandela's home in Qunu in the Eastern Cape).[8] The

---

[8] *Mail & Guardian*, 5–11 October 2012.

expansion was designed to turn the presidential homestead into a sprawling precinct that would include a police station, helicopter pad, military clinic, visitors' centre, and parking lot as well as the construction of a double-storey mansion, underground bunker and gymnasium, guesthouse and three smaller houses, as well as twenty houses for security personnel and homes outside the compound for families who had been relocated.

Initially, assurances were given that Zuma had funded the construction of his new home himself, and denials were made that expenditure had been largely funded by the public exchequer. Subsequently, however, as the full cost of the project emerged, the government resorted to Section 1 of the National Key Points Act of 1980 (a notorious piece of apartheid legislation allowing for the designation of 'national key points' if the Minister of Defence should deem it expedient or necessary for the safety of the Republic) to justify the expense, claiming that his role as President demanded it. In the furore that followed (Helen Zille leading a DA march on Nkandla to 'inspect' the works, only to be blocked from going nearer by local cohorts of the ANC), Zuma declared the unreasonableness of demands that he should have tracked the expense.[9] However, he made no response when, two weeks before Mangaung, the *Mail & Guardian* published the contents of the 500-page forensic report prepared by KPMG for the NPA as its basis for taking Zuma to trial. This made the case that the President's expensive lifestyle had been funded not only by Shaik, who personally and via his Nkobi Holdings had made payments to Zuma amounting to R4,072,500 (well beyond the figure of around R1.25 million known at the time of Shaik's trial) but by a host of other willing benefactors (including Nelson Mandela) to the tune, up to mid-2006, of R7 million. Additionally, the Report suggested that Zuma had been treated exceptionally leniently by the banks (ABSA explicitly justifying this on grounds that links with him were 'politically' and 'strategically' valuable), with the Standard Bank having written off an overdraft of R123 000 debt in 2002 and a bond of nearly R200 000 which he owed in 2005![10] Unsurprisingly, Zuma had proved reluctant to declare his assets and business interests within 60 days of his becoming President as was required by the law, only doing so after his failure to do so was exposed by the press.[11] In the wake of the publication of the KPMG report, the DA demanded to know whether Zuma had paid tax on the gifts made to him in accordance with the law.

The law requires that politicians serving in executive positions in government withdraw from active involvement in business. Consequently, it is to those around the President that it is necessary to look to explain the improving fortunes of what the media were soon referring to 'Zuma Inc'. In 2010, this

---

[9] *Mail & Guardian Online*, 17 August 2011; *Mail & Guardian*, 3–9 August 2012.

[10] Other benefactors included Jurgen Kogl (R1,075,091), a broker, investor, and 'financial adviser' to Zuma; Vivian Reddy (R324,110) a prominent Durban businessperson well known for his ties to Zuma, who assisted him in obtaining a R900,000 bond from First National Bank for Nkandla, and serviced it until 25 May, 2005; Khulubuse Zuma (R180,000) Zuma's nephew and businessperson; and Nora Fakude-Nkuna (R174, 200), an Mpumalanga businessperson, who paid architects' fees on the Nkandla estate. See *Mail & Guardian*, 7–13 December 2012; and for the full report, 'The State versus Jacob G Zuma and others', Forensic Investigation, Draft Report on factual findings, http://www.mg.co.za/kpmg. Although it was labelled a draft report, the *Mail & Guardian* understood it to be the final version.

[11] *Sunday Times*, 22 March 2010.

was reported as involving Zuma himself, along with fifteen adult members of his family who then held some 134 company directorships or memberships of close corporations, at least 83 of which had been registered in the post-Polokwane period, and were linked to industries in which the state played a key role.[12] Most prominent was Zuma's nephew, Khulubuse Zuma, who by 2012 had 26 directorships and extensive interests across an array of business sectors (including the transport of crude oil) and was reportedly worth R100 billion. Nor did the wives do too badly. In January 2008, Nompumelo Ntuli had become Zuma's second wife, and rapidly acquired business interests, joining ten private companies with interests in logistics, construction, and trade.[13] Two years later, Zuma took Tobeka Madiba, a 37-year-old cell phone company executive from Durban, as his third wife. Within a couple of months, she had added to her existing portfolio of investments in five private companies by investing in four more, three of them companies co-owned by Dr Mandisa Mokwena, a former South African Revenue Service commissioner on trial for fraud, money laundering, and racketeering.[14]

Less impressive, although suggestive of the improvement in Zuma Inc's collective well-being, was the deal whereby in 2009 a company linked to Zuma's nephew, Mandla Gcaba, was awarded a contract to run Durban's bus fleet, allegedly without a tender. In another deal, a R3.5 million catering contract had been awarded, again allegedly without tender, by the KwaZulu-Natal legislature to Bucebo General Trading, a company owned by Nonkulelo Mhlong, mother of two of his children.[15] In another instance, an events management company, Ikhono Communications, owned by Don Mkhwanazi, who had established the Friends of Jacob Zuma Trust in 2005 to raise money for Zuma's defence, managed to win a series of tenders from the eThekwini municipality in Durban.[16] If 'political connectivity' behind such deals was not explicit, it certainly appeared that a close relationship to the President did no harm to those engaging in business with the different levels of government. However, the dealings that attracted the most notoriety to Zuma Inc involved Zuma family linkages with an Indian family, the Guptas, and Khulubuse Zuma's centrality to a mining scandal.

Family ties with dubious deals

The Gupta family, originally from Saharanpur in India, has focused on building its empire in South Africa rather than in its home country. Its business is divided into two main groups. The first is Sahara Holdings, which houses the family's IT interests. It was set up in 1997, and by 2010 had a turnover of about R1 billion, with R500–R600 million of this coming from Sahara Computers, a subsidiary which assembles laptops and PCs. The second is Oakbay Investments, which owns businesses related to mining. While the details of the Guptas' corporate expansion are obscure, it is clear that they have gone out of their way

---

[12] 'DA's plan to address the rise of Zuma Inc', *Politicsweb*, 29 August 2011.
[13] Adrian Basson (2012), *Zuma Exposed*, Cape Town and Johannesburg: Jonathan Ball Publishers, 139. Zuma divorced his first second wife Nkosana Dlamini-Zuma in 1998.
[14] Ibid., 139–40. For a graphic of Zuma Inc, itemizing the family investments and involvements, see Basson op. cit., 140–41.
[15] Ibid.
[16] *Sunday Times*, 17 June 2012.

to cultivate strong links with the ANC and empowerment moguls, although it is with Zuma and his associates that they have cultivated their strongest connections. These have included a particularly close relationship with Duduzane Zuma, one of the President's sons, who at some point became a Director of Sahara Computers, while his own company, Mabalenga Investments, formed in mid-2008, was 40 per cent owned by Oakbay. Together with Oakbay, Zim Holdings (owned by Lazarus Zim, a prominent empowerment figure) and smaller investors including the MK Veterans' Association (2.5 per cent) and the MK Veterans' Association Women's Group (2.5 per cent), Mabalenga owned Islandsite Investments 255. The latter, in turn, was partner with Oakbay Resources in owning Shiva Uranium (purchased in 2010 for $38 million and backed by the Industrial Development Corporation and the Development Bank of South Africa, after alleged lobbying by the President), whose main asset was the closed-down Dominion mine in Klerksdorp.[17] Having moved into close proximity with the political elite in 2006 after both Zim and Tokyo Sexwale's Mvelaphanda had bought a large stake in Sahara Computers, the Guptas sought to consolidate their influence when in 2010 they bankrolled a new newspaper, *New Age*, whose rationale was to offer more balanced coverage to the ANC than was provided by the established private media.

However, not all their deals were to go smoothly. In early 2011, Afripalm Resources, co-owned (via a paper trail) by the Guptas, Duduzane Zuma, and Lazarus Zim, signed a memorandum of understanding with the Steel Authority of India (Sail), an Indian parastatal, to investigate building a R21 billion steel mill in South Africa. The outcome, it was said, would be to force down prices in a domestic steel market dominated by near-monopoly producer ArcelorMittal SA.[18] However, in August 2011, Afripalm announced a deal with the China Railway Construction Corporation whereby they would be in pole position to cash in on the government's planned R550-billion rail infrastructure programme. This followed Zim's accompanying President Zuma on a state visit to China.

If the deal between Afripalm and Sail were to go through, Sail would need access to cheap iron ore and coking coal. This appeared to be addressed in April 2009. Kumba, an Anglo-American subsidiary, had failed to convert its mining rights, held via a 21 per cent holding in the Sishen Iron Ore Company, to 'new order' rights under the new mining Act. These were now awarded by the Department of Mineral Resources to Imperial Crown Trading (ICT). ICT had been founded by, amongst others, Prudence Gugu Mtshali (Kgalema Motlanthe's partner), and was co-owned by Pragat Investments, a part of the Gupta empire. However, its lack of a track record raised immediate suspicions that it had gained favour through political influence. Meanwhile, the transfer of the rights from Kumba to Sishen had major implications for ArcelorMittal, which had previously sourced ore and coal from the former at cost plus 3 per cent.

ArcelorMittal sought to assure its supply chain by announcing in August 2010 that it would buy ICT for R800 million and do a parallel transaction in

---

[17] *Business Day*, 4 March 2011. Zuma is alleged to have contacted Deputy Finance Minister Nhlanhla Nene, who also served as Chairperson of the IDC, to extend the tenure of 'controversial PIC boss Brian Molefe, who the Gupta's were expecting to facilitate PIC funding for the purchase of Dominion'. http://www.mg.co.za/article/2010–05–14–Zuma-meddled-in-mine-buyout

[18] *Mail & Guardian*, 25 February–3 March 2011.

which ICT's shareholders (inclusive of the Gupta family and Duduzane Zuma) would obtain ArcelorMittal shares with a face value of more than R7 billion. ArcelorMittal would also take on Ayigobi Consortium, an investment vehicle led by Duduzane Zuma in association with Gupta executive, Jagdish Parekh, and Gugu Mtshali, as a BEE partner. Zuma would gain shares with a face value approaching R1 billion, with Mtshali creaming shares with a face value of about a third of that amount.[19]

Unsurprisingly, the projected deal provoked a major corporate battle (and strains between the Guptas and Lazarus Zim). Kumba went to court to have the loss of its mining rights in Sishen set aside, with the situation rendered yet more confusing by ArcelorMittal effectively switching sides, choosing to back Kumba, and announcing in September 2011 that it was pulling the plug on the deal with ICT and Ayigobi.[20] Zim thereafter severed his ties to the Guptas, whose alleged influence was now stirring major controversy within the Alliance. Major figures within the party were joined by the Youth League in openly criticizing the Guptas, while COSATU announced that it would investigate allegations that they were plundering the country.[21] In contrast, the MK Veterans' Association leapt to their defence, as did the Women's League, whose spokesperson stated that she saw nothing wrong with the Zuma family benefiting from deals facilitated by government. The SACP stated that those attacking the Guptas were attacking President Zuma.[22]

The Guptas countered by choosing to withdraw from political view, although their appointment of Gloria Bongi Ngema – about to become Zuma's next wife – as head of the marketing department at Oakbay's subsidiary, JIC Mining Services, suggested a determination to maintain influence behind the throne.[23] They were later alleged to have been assisting her to pay off her bond on a R5.2 million house in the exclusive Pretoria suburb of Waterkloof Ridge.[24] Further, according to one source, Zuma was in the habit of consulting the Guptas on all cabinet reshuffles and appointments.[25]

Meanwhile, Khulubuse Zuma's involvement in Aurora Empowerment Systems had an even more unhappy ending. In October 2009, the company, which he headed alongside Zondwa Mandela (Nelson's grandson), and Michael Hulley (the lawyer who had defended Zuma against charges of corruption) took over Pamodzi Gold, which had gone into liquidation. The takeover was controversial, for Aurora was totally inexperienced in this field.

Seven shafts at Pamodzi's Grootvlei mines and six at Orkney were still operational, but thereafter followed a tale which unions described as blatant asset stripping, with Aurora selling gold, machinery and scrap for unknown millions, and misappropriating unemployment and pension funds. Within months, some 5,000 mineworkers were being left unpaid; water and electricity was cut off to their hostels because of unpaid bills; and water pumps stopped operating, threatening the mines with flooding.

---

[19] *Mail & Guardian*, 13–29 August 2010.
[20] *Business Day*, 28 September 2011.
[21] *Sunday Times*, 27 February 2011.
[22] *Business Day*, 7 March 2011.
[23] *Mail & Guardian*, 18–24 March 2011.
[24] *Mail & Guardian*, 30 November–6 December 2012.
[25] Basson, op. cit., 153.

Aurora denied asset stripping, blaming thefts upon illegal miners, and gained successive stays of execution from government liquidators by promising that they were bringing in major investors to reopen the mines. Amidst the controversy, Khulubuse Zuma donated R1 million to the ANC, despite owing far in excess of that in wages to the unpaid miners. However, in early 2011 Aurora was finally expelled from its mines after Enver Motala, a government liquidator who had been accused by the unions of protecting the company, was fired. New liquidators were brought in, and the assets sold to China African Precious Metals for a mere R150 million. By mid-2012, the Aurora directors were facing a suit for R1.7 billion filed by Pamodzi's liquidators. Zuma chose to defend himself separately, claiming that he had not been involved in the company's day-to-day affairs. Were the defendants to lose the case (which was still proceeding at the time of writing), the consequences for his fellow directors would be far more serious than for Zuma himself, who with his considerable fortune was in no danger of being bankrupted. (However, by late 2012 he was strapped for ready cash to repay R700 million to the liquidators, and was having to sell a number of his fifteen luxury cars.) It remained a moot point whether the workers would ever be properly paid.[26]

Jacob Zuma himself had had no direct involvement in either of the deals which had gone wrong. Nonetheless, he appeared to have had no compunction in associating with business interests which had traded on their political connections and were prepared to sail very close to the law.

Private interest and public property: friends as tenderpreneurs

In early 2011, South Africans were reading about a property scam involving Roux Shabangu, a BEE businessman said to be close to Jacob Zuma, and Bheki Cele, Zuma's appointee as Commissioner of Police. While Zuma was to refute a close connection with Shabangu, it was impossible for him to deny a long involvement with Cele, with whom he had had a strong connection going back to shared days in MK. Cele was known as a significant power-broker in KwaZulu-Natal, who had strongly backed Zuma for the presidency.

Media investigations were to uncover the leasing from Shabangu of one building for R500 million over ten years as new headquarters for the South African Police Service in Pretoria, and of another, for R137 million, to be the headquarters for the police department's Independent Complaints Directorate. The sums involved in both deals were highly inflated. Geoff Doidge, Minister of Public Works, suspended the lease after he had been informed of 'inconsistencies' by his Director-General, Siviwe Dongwana, but was then 'redeployed' out of the cabinet in November 2010. Subsequently, both deals were authorized under his successor, Gwen Mahlangu-Nkabinde, despite two legal opinions offered to her which indicated that their approval would be illegal.[27]

The publicity scuppered two other deals: one whereby Shabangu would have leased yet another building in Durban for a new police headquarters for R100 million,[28] and another whereby the Billion Group, a property company with which Lonwabo Sambudla (the husband of the President's daughter, Duduzile)

---

[26] *Sunday Independent*, 1 July 2011; 29 April 2012. See also Basson, op. cit., 150–52.
[27] *Mail & Guardian*, 3–9 June 2011.
[28] *Sunday Times*, 8 May 2011.

was closely associated, would have won a tender for the construction of a new headquarters for the Department of Public Service.[29] Billion was later revealed as having already leased a building to the Department of Public Works which, even after payment of some R68 million, remained empty. This seemed a valuable return upon a donation of R1 million which Billion was said to have made to the ANC.[30]

The media attention prompted a formal investigation by Thuli Madonsela, recently appointed as Public Protector. Despite having been raided by two police intelligence officers demanding documents related to the lease and her office having its computers hacked, she forwarded provisional findings to Zuma, Mahlangu-Nkabinde, Cele, Shabangu, Police Minister Nathi Mthetwa, and Finance Minister Pravin Gordhan in June 2011. These were leaked to the press, leading to lurid headlines. Madonsela had reported that Siviwe Dongwana (by now suspended as DG of Public Works) had been pressured into approving the deals by Mahlangu-Nkabinde and that he now lived in fear for his life. Madonsela submitted that Mahlangu-Nkabinde had been guilty of improper conduct; that Cele was guilty of unlawful conduct for driving the R1.1 billion Durban deal; that the tender for the latter had been rigged to favour Shabangu; and that the Treasury should blacklist Shabangu's company, Roux Property Fund, for its involvement in 'unlawful and irregular procurement'.[31]

The political fallout was immediate. Madonsela found herself confronting reports that she was to be charged with corruption for irregular business dealings with the South African Law Reform Commission when she had worked there as a Commissioner, and announced that she feared for her safety. However, the public outrage against any idea of her being charged was such that Justice Minister Jeff Radebe swiftly announced that there was no intention to institute proceedings against her. Subsequently, in July 2011, she submitted her updated report, arguing that the lease agreements were invalid and calling upon President Zuma to take action against Mahlangu-Nkabinde, Cele, and senior officials in the Department of Public Works and the South African Police.[32]

Mahlangu-Nkabinde eventually referred the Pretoria and Durban leases to the courts to have them declared invalid, complaining that she had been obstructed in her investigations by senior officials within her department. Meanwhile, Zuma had at last opted to call Cele to account, asking him to give reason why he should not be suspended. However, speculation was rife that the principal motivation behind Zuma's action was an intelligence report handed to him in October 2010 which suggested that, apart from being deeply implicated in organized crime in KwaZulu-Natal, Cele had flirted with an anti-Zuma faction which included Human Settlements' Minister Tokyo Sexwale, Sports Minister Fikile Mbalula, and Arts Minister Paul Matshatile.[33]

That Zuma's actions were guided by political interest were also suggested by

29 *Mail & Guardian*, 21–18 August 2011. Sambudla represented the interests of Billion at one or more meetings with Public Works officials regarding the deal, accompanying Sisa Ngelubana, Chairman and founder of the company.
30 *Mail & Guardian*, 5–11 August 2011.
31 *Sunday Times*, 19 June 2011.
32 *Business Day*, 7 July 2011; *Mail & Guardian*, 8–14 July 2011.
33 *Mail & Guardian*, 23–29 September 2011.

a related move in which National Director of Public Prosecutions, Menzi Simelane, laid charges against renowned corruption-buster, Willie Hofmeyr, who
headed the Asset Forfeiture Unit and the Special Investigating Unit. This was in
relation to various actions he had taken, notably in regard to the Intaka case
whereby senior ANC figures had allegedly received a donation of R1 million for
the party from South American businessman, Gaston Savoi, in exchange for a
R45 million tender to supply water purifiers to state hospitals at inflated prices.
His actions had aroused the ire of high-level politicians, including KZN Premier
Zweli Mkhize, whose support for Zuma in any forthcoming leadership battle
within the ANC would be vital.[34] 'We're fucked, just like the Scorpions',
concluded one SIU official.[35] As noted in Chapter 9, the charges regarding
Intaka were later dropped.

Patronage, philanthropy, and power: Zumaville and Zuma.Org

Zuma's political persona is strongly connected to his identification with Zulu
culture and his home province, where he has played a crucial role in realigning
popular sentiment away from the IFP to the ANC. Never is he happier, claimed
one his erstwhile journalistic supporters, than when he 'wanders about freely
in the serenity of the rolling hills and valleys in a wholly relaxed state', the only
place he appears to be 'completely comfortable and at peace with the world,
always mindful of the tranquillity of rural KwaZulu-Natal'.[36] However, the
prospect of Zuma enjoying the peace of his rural idyll either during or after his
presidency seemed at odds with his transformation of his home area into a
building site – not merely the garish monstrosity he is having built at Nkandla,
but the selection of an area just over three kilometres away as the location of
South Africa's first new town since the inauguration of democracy.

Officially, 'Zumaville' as the new town was dubbed by the media, was the
vision of the Masibambisane Rural Development Initiative, which Zuma himself
chairs. By late 2012, it was reported as entailing an expenditure of R2 billion,
except that by this time Masibambisane was claiming that it was bankrupt, and
various of the big business 'partners' who had been named as involved in the
project were denying any association with it.[37] Yet work continued, and despite
various denials that R800 million of official money had been allocated to fund
it, it soon emerged that the larger portion of the finance required to build the
new town was being provided both by the provincial and national governments,
the latter claiming it as part of its comprehensive agricultural support
programme.[38] However, no explanation was forthcoming on the sheer coincidence of the new town being built so close to Nkandla, and no convincing effort
made to dispel the appearance of favourable treatment being offered to the President's home area (nor indeed, for the waiving of the requirement for a full environmental impact assessment). While there was no doubt that, given past

---

[34] *Business Day*, 2 August 2011
[35] *Sunday Times*, 17 July 2011.
[36] Ranjeni Munsamy, 'Allowing Zuma to play victim', *The Star*, 7 November 2012. Munsamy had
been a controversial supporter of Zuma before Polokwane, but subsequently became critical of
his performance as President.
[37] Although Old Mutual acknowledged its allocation of R600,000 to Masibambisane from its
annual corporate social investment budget.
[38] *Mail & Guardian*, 3–9 August 2012; 10–16 August 2012.

neglect, building a major project in an impoverished rural area would likely be far more expensive than its equivalent in an already urbanized location, fears were expressed that Zumaville was draining funding from other rural initiatives (notably the Department of Agriculture's Zero Hunger Programme, designed to support food security in rural areas), whilst simultaneously serving as an expression of Zuma's patronage.

Zuma, it seemed, was intent upon becoming a typical 'big man' in the style of numerous other presidents in Africa. By 2012, this impression was reinforced by the existence of a series of family foundations, soon nicknamed 'Zuma Org.': the Jacob Zuma RDP Education Trust, the Jacob Zuma Foundation, the Thobeka Madiba-Zuma Foundation, the Ma-Ntuli Foundation, the Bongi Ngema-Zuma Foundation and the Zodwa Khoza Foundation, all with philanthropic aims.[39] Between them, they had received significant funding from private donors. These included major companies such as Patrice Motsepe's African Rainbow Minerals, De Beers, and Harmony Gold, as well as companies (such as Edusolutions) which had received major contracts from government. A further donor was Kase Lawal, a controversial Nigerian-American businessman, and Chief Executive of Camac International, an energy company involved in exploration, development, and operation of oil companies in Africa and South America.[40] By 2012, only the Jacob Zuma Education RDP Trust had lodged annual reports with the Department of Social Development (as was required by registered non-profit organizations) and the suspicion was that, alongside pursuit of their philanthropic aims, the trusts and foundations had been established to elicit financial support from the private sector to maintain the lifestyles of the Zuma family, and to provide the wherewithal for Zuma's patronage, notably in provinces where in the lead-up to Mangaung his support was shaky.[41]

Re-establishing control: from paralysis to pre-emption

In October 2011, Zuma responded to criticism of his indecision with moves whose effect was to challenge those who were campaigning overtly or covertly to replace him as party leader at the forthcoming ANC National Conference in Mangaung in December 2012.

First, he announced a cabinet reshuffle in October 2011 which removed ministers who had become an embarrassment. The changes included the

---

[39] Zodwa Khoza, the daughter of Irvin Khoza, a major backer of the ANC, was a lover of Zuma and gave birth to his child in October 2009, much to the disgust of the mother's parents. Basson, op. cit., 157–63.

[40] Lawal and Camac, backed by Thabo Mbeki, had established a South African Oil Company in 2003 which negotiated a long-term crude oil contract for South Africa from the Nigerian government, but mysteriously neither the oil nor the profit reached South Africa, although Lawal's lawyers denied all impropriety. Subsequently, a UN expert group monitoring compliance with arms sanctions in the DRC identified Lawal as having paid R50 million to a wanted Congolese warlord in an illegal gold deal (Stefaans Brummer, 'Texas oilman is at it again – now with Zuma', www.amabhungane.co.za/article/2012–02–17–texas-oilman-is-at-it again-now–its-with-Zuma). Owner of the second-largest black-owned business in the US, Lawal had served as an adviser to both the Bush and Clinton administrations before being appointed by President Obama to his Advisory Policy for Trade Negotiations.

[41] *Mail & Guardian*, 10–16 August 2012.

dismissal of Mahlangu-Nkabinde and the Cooperative and Traditional Affairs Minister Sicelo Shiceka, whom Zuma had protected for well over a year, despite his being on sick leave and in face of findings that he had misused taxpayers' money. They were replaced respectively by Thulas Nxesi, formerly Deputy Minister of Rural Development and Land Reform, and Richard Baloyi, who had been nursing Shiceka's post even while he had served as Minister of Public Service and Administration. These appointments were not without their political advantages. Nxesi was a former Secretary-General of the South African Democratic Teachers' Union, where he remained popular, while Baloyi was still a significant figure on the ANC's provincial committee in Limpopo, where Zuma needed support to counter the increasingly dangerous influence of Youth League leader Julius Malema.

Second, Zuma simultaneously suspended Bheki Cele on full pay, although earning criticism for appointing Major General Nhlanhla Mkhwanazi as his acting replacement because the latter was ranked below some 26 senior officers.[42] It did not go without comment that Mkhwanazi's appointment consolidated Zuma's wider 'Zulu-ification' of the senior positions in the security apparatus.

Third, he made two moves calculated to stem criticism that he was soft on corruption, but which had the considerable advantage that they could compromise those who might dare to oppose him at Mangaung. The first was his announcement that he would release the Donen report on the 'oilgate' scandal relating to diplomatic favours which were traded for oil under the UN's Oil-for-Food programme for Saddam Hussein's Iraq and which had resulted in money flowing into the ANC's coffers. The report had been kept under wraps by the presidency long before Zuma took office, and was probably released now only because it was likely that the government was going to be ordered to do so by the courts, following applications made under the Promotion of Access to Information Act by the *Cape Argus* newspaper. The Report had cleared Motlanthe and other ANC figures of any violation of the law, but it was nonetheless an embarrassment to the former (now being touted by the Youth League as a possible challenger to Zuma). The Report implicated his partner, Gugu Mtshali, in attempts to solicit a R104 million bribe to obtain government support for South African companies in their attempts to clinch a R2 billion sanctions-busting deal with Iran.[43] The second move was his bid to pre-empt a likely order by the Constitutional Court that he appoint a Commission of Inquiry into the arms deal by appointing one himself under Supreme Court of Appeal Judge Willie Seriti. This was in itself a triumph for the Constitution, for it is clear that Zuma only made his move under judicial duress, and it exposed him to the danger that he might be subpoenaed to give evidence under oath. Arguably, however, the risks were higher for other major figures within the ANC, including Mbeki. They might well lead to indications that Zuma had indeed been but a

---

[42] Mkhwanazi was immediately promoted from Major-General to Lieutenant-General.

[43] Motlanthe immediately responded by asking the Public Protector to investigate the alleged improper involvement of Mtshali in the Iranian deal. There are considerable grounds for arguing that the investigations and findings of the Donen Report were flawed. This may have contributed to the Public Protector's issuing a finding in September 2012 that neither Motlanthe nor Mtshali were implicated in soliciting a R104 million bribe to obtain a sanctions-busting deal with Iran.

minor player in the drama, and endorse Judge Nicholson's view that he had been selectively prosecuted. However, apart from the advantage to Zuma that it was reckoned that the Commission would have to sit for at least two years, ensuring that no findings could be made before Mangaung, there were also suggestions that over the course of time, Zuma might be able to circumscribe its operation.[44]

These moves came against the background of related actions to consolidate his support in strategic provinces (notably North West, Free State, Limpopo, Eastern Cape and KwaZulu-Natal) ahead of Mangaung. Most notably, these involved his decision to take on Julius Malema, who by this time had moved into open opposition to his continued stay in the presidency.

Street-fighting on the road to Mangaung: Zuma versus Malema

The ANCYL had gained in importance after the mother body had decided in 2001 to grant it a portion of the block vote at its National Conferences, allowing it to have a say in the election of leadership positions. Under the presidency of Fikile Mbalula (2004–08), the League had become increasingly active, but it was under Malema that it assumed a major role in the national consciousness. The son of a domestic worker and single parent in Seshogo (Limpopo) Malema struggled to complete secondary school, later achieving a two-year diploma in youth development through UNISA in 2010. Despite his limited attention to books, he became chairman of the Congress of South African Students in Limpopo (COSAS) in 1997, before being elected to the organization's national presidency in 2001. He had joined the ANC as a child from the moment of its unbanning, attracted by the militancy of Chris Hani. As he grew up, he was taken under the wing of, amongst others, Winnie Madikizela-Mandela, 'who began to groom him in the art of politics and rebellion'.[45] When his tenure as President of COSAS ended, he returned home to Limpopo to revive a flagging provincial wing of the Youth League. From there he rose through the ranks under Mbalula's stewardship until he clambered to the presidency (facing down accusations of vote-rigging) in April 2008, having used the intervening years to become a major force within the provincial ANC in Limpopo. Here, Premier Sello Moloto soon found himself in a power struggle with Malema and his ally Cassel Mathale, the ANC's Provincial Secretary, who between them controlled many of the party's provincial branches.

Upon assuming presidency of the Youth League, Malema announced his arrival with a statement that he would 'kill for Zuma' if the legal charges hanging over him were not dropped. Forde, Malema's biographer, interprets Malema's ideological position as akin to the anti-communist Africanism of the original Youth League of the late 1940s, and deeply hostile to the ANC's official position of non-racialism. As such, Mbeki's own inclinations towards Africanism might have appealed to him, yet the then President's elitism and his perceived collaboration with the corporate establishment did not. In contrast,

---

[44] *Sunday Independent*, 30 September 2011.
[45] Fiona Forde (2011), *An Inconvenient Youth: Julius Malema and the 'New' ANC*, Johannesburg: Picador Africa, 62.

Zuma's positioning as the victim of a conspiracy and as the standard-bearer of the poor against that same establishment provided the ideal focal point for Malema to mobilize a personal constituency amongst both anti-Mbeki elements and party foot-soldiers who felt that their interests had been ignored. Equally, Malema positioned himself as the leader of a generational revolt against a party leadership which had become fat and comfortable while the black youth of the country confronted unemployment and a life without hope. Zuma himself was simultaneously grateful to and dependent upon the Youth League, many of whose activists served as his shock troops in the lead-up to Polokwane, and once he had become President, was initially to become dangerously indulgent of Malema's increasingly controversial statements. In 2009, Zuma praised him as 'a leader in the making'.[46]

Malema soon became notorious for espousing a lumpen radicalism which was anti-elitist, anti-white, anti-communist, and anti-imperialist, wrapping this up in a claim that his Youth League was the lineal successor to the 1948 Youth League rebels against the ANC's then conservative establishment. He was uninhibited in his disrespect for authority and political correctness and was always eager to embrace the outrageous in the desire to shock, as when in 2009 he had declared that the woman who had accused Jacob Zuma of rape had had a 'nice time' (a statement which doubtless appealed to many of the unemployed male youths who formed the bulk of his supporters). From early on in Zuma's presidency, he began to voice increasingly radical nationalist positions that worried the party's hierarchy whilst playing to the hopes and fears of many amongst its poorer membership. He ran into a barrage of complaints for singing a struggle song *Dubul'ibhunu* ('Shoot the Boer'), confronting claims and (later) Court rulings that he was guilty of using hate speech, although he earned the support of senior ANC figures for his right to sing it on the grounds that it was integral to the movement's history. However, when in April 2010 Malema defied ANC instructions that he obey court orders to desist from singing the song, Zuma slapped him down as out of order. In response, Malema declared that the judiciary was racist, untransformed, and protective of minorities.

By this time, Zuma had become unnerved by statements from Malema that contradicted the ANC's official policy positions. It signalled that his former supporter had moved into open opposition ahead of Mangaung. In particular, Zuma was infuriated by Malema's suggestion that he had become worse than Thabo Mbeki. Malema was hauled before an ANC disciplinary committee, slapped with a number of charges, and warned that further breaches of the ANC constitution could result in his being expelled.

This did little to subdue him. While it remained uncertain who Malema would like as a replacement for Zuma, it was soon clear that he was propelling his Youth League predecessor, Fikile Mbalula into the key position of ANC Secretary-General in place of the current incumbent, Gwede Mantashe. The objective was to combine a major generational shift at the head of the ANC, the displacement of the organized left, and the extension of state ownership in place of private capital. In all this, the role of Julius Malema was doubtless envisaged as pivotal.[47]

[46] Ibid., 179.
[47] *Business Day*, 5 November 2011.

Malema was aggressively cultivating his iconic image as the standard-bearer of a still-downtrodden African majority by calling for the nationalization of mines and the expropriation of white-owned land without compensation on the grounds that it had been stolen. Further, he called for a fairer sharing of the nation's wealth, claiming that such policies were legitimized by the Freedom Charter, and asserting that whatever the Youth League hierarchy ordained, they would inevitably be endorsed at Mangaung.[48] In April 2010, on a trip to Zimbabwe to learn about ZANU-PF's land reforms and indigenization plans, he was feted by Mugabe. In addressing ZANU-PF Youth, he warned them against using violence, but urged them to arm themselves for the struggle for economic emancipation. This earned praise from Indigenization and Empowerment Minister, Saviour Kasukwere who claimed that Malema had delivered a speech whose message would forever ring in ZANU-PF ears. On his return to South Africa, Malema declared to a news conference at Luthuli House that 'We want ZANU-PF to be retained in power'. He described the MDC as 'Mickey Mouse' and jeered at its headquarters' location in Sandton (the upmarket financial and business centre to the north of Johannesburg). It was a moment when he burnished his international notoriety, for when a BBC journalist, Jonah Fisher, pointed out that Malema himself had a house in Sandton, he lost his temper. He accused Fisher of racist condescension, and ordered his expulsion from the conference in the full glare of the cameras.[49]

By this time, Malema had begun to make numerous enemies beyond and within the Alliance. His calls for nationalization and land seizure prompted siren wails of distress from large-scale capital, which lamented the damage to South Africa's reputation as an investment destination. Equally, he had alienated the ANC's economic hierarchy, which rushed forward to calm the markets by insisting that nationalization would not become the policy of the government. In addition, he found himself in outright confrontation with the SACP, which alleged repeatedly that Malema was being used by empowerment figures with mining interests who wanted the state to buy them out, as well as by aspirants to the leadership who wanted to use him as a stalking horse to unseat Zuma. Meanwhile, Malema found himself confronting the particular opposition of the National Union of Mineworkers, which was strongly opposed to the nationalization of the mines, and COSATU. Indeed, divided though they increasingly were about the economic policies of Zuma (the SACP identifying closely with them, COSATU highly critical), they were united in their rejection of Malema's claim that the ANCYL was usurping their role as 'vanguard of the working class'.[50] Yet Malema had made life easy for his critics by his high-rolling life style.

In asking pointed questions about living in Sandton, Jonah Fisher was referring to reports that Malema had bought a house in South Africa's most expensive suburb for R3.5 million, had proceeded to knock it down and to build a new mansion for R16 million. Malema was combining this with displays of extravagant living for which he was unapologetic, dismissing criticism as the racist attacks of those who resented him for emulating the lifestyle of whites. Yet the

[48] *Sunday Independent*, 11 September 2011.
[49] Forde, op. cit., 171–96.
[50] *City Press*, 26 June 2011; *New Age*, 27 June 2011.

obvious questions were posed about where a still young man, whose official salary from the Youth League was little more than R20,000 per month, had found the money. His answers (when sufficiently polite to cite) were essentially that they flowed from his legitimate business interests, which, because he held no public office, were a private matter. However, this stance became increasingly difficult for him to maintain as revelations leaked out about his extensive involvements in property deals and his directorships and shareholdings in companies which had acquired tenders from Polokwane Municipality and the Limpopo provincial government.

Malema's interests were obscured by his having established a trust named after his son, Ratanang, which he claimed to have charitable purposes, a claim that was to wear increasingly thin. In particular, attention focused upon a particular company, On-Point Engineers, co-owned by his family trust and which had become influential in the allocation of multi-billion rand contracts issued by the Limpopo Department of Roads and Transport. Insiders as well as company contractors broke ranks to accuse On-Point not merely of receiving kickbacks, but of insisting on being written into contracts once they were awarded – this to the extent that they would sometimes reap as much as 70 per cent of the profits.[51] An initial non-committal investigation by the Public Protector did little to stem further complaints from a Forum of Limpopo Entrepreneurs who claimed that from 2009, they had been unable to secure contracts from the Limpopo government. They ascribed this outcome to On-Point's having secured the tender to run Programme Management Units, notably for the provincial Department of Roads and Transport, placing it in a position of huge influence in decisions on which companies received contracts to spend sizeable portions of Limpopo's R43 billion annual budget.[52]

Malema's fight-back strategy against corruption allegations was to consolidate his position within the ANCYL by securing a second term as President in early 2011 while continuing to mobilize his troops with calls that sought to place himself at the head of the poor against the ANC elite. Zuma, meanwhile, was awaiting his moment to attack, and Malema offered it to him by an unsolicited excursion into foreign policy. Having earlier embarrassed the government by his open embrace of Mugabe, he called for 'regime change' in Botswana, stating that the ANCYL would offer assistance to opposition parties in that country to overthrow the government of Ian Khama, which he accused of being in discussions to open a military base for 'the imperialists' (the US).[53] He had broken the golden rule whereby countries within SADC did not criticize each other openly, and endangered relations with a government with which South Africa was in close accord. Zuma pounced, and on 19 August 2011, Malema and his four chief henchmen within the Youth League were charged with bringing the ANC into disrepute.

Zuma and Malema now entered into a trial of strength. When the disciplinary committee first met at Luthuli House in downtown Johannesburg at the end of August, 5,000 of Malema's supporters massed to provide him with their open backing. Yes this misfired badly, for the demonstration lapsed into open

---

[51] *Mail & Guardian*, 19–25 August 2011.
[52] Forde, op. cit., 144–77.
[53] *Botswana Gazette*, 3 August 2011.

hooliganism, confirming the Malema Youth League's reputation for indiscipline. Worse, they burnt the ANC flag and T-shirts bearing the face of Jacob Zuma.[54] The hearings were postponed and moved to an out-of-town venue, where they dragged on. During a break, Malema celebrated the League's 67th anniversary by promising that

> The ANC will correct itself. Those who have wronged the ANC in the last five years, they will see the ANC cleaning itself in December 2012...We have not done anything wrong...the poor continue to suffer. Let us liberate them economically...The crime we have committed is to remind them not to forget the Freedom Charter because the Freedom Charter is the bible of our revolution.[55]

Key to Malema's strategy was that his defence was led by Tokyo Sexwale, and had the open support of Winnie Madikizela-Mandela and others who argued that he had said little which was contrary to ANC policy, and that the charges had been laid without proper procedures having been followed. Meanwhile, Zuma acted to undermine Malema's position within the Youth League. In particular, the League's KwaZulu-Natal region went into open rebellion against the executive. Elsewhere, too, significant fragments of Malema's support base peeled away. Although they were unable to dislodge Malema's backers from their control over the organization, their revolt transformed the Youth League into a battleground.[56] Although Malema supporters regrouped behind an 'Economic Freedom' march from Johannesburg to Pretoria which drew not unfavourable headlines, its impact was immediately weakened by Malema's leaving its closing rally early to jet off to an over-the-top R10-million wedding in Mauritius.[57] Thereafter, the country was treated to an extended ANC disciplinary process. This lasted from August 2011 to April 2012, involving trial and appeals culminating in the decision of the National Disciplinary Committee (chaired by Cyril Ramaphosa) confirming that Malema, originally suspended from the party for five years, would be dismissed from the organization. His senior allies, Youth League spokesman, Floyd Shivambu, and Secretary-General, Sindiso Magaqa, were suspended for three years and one year respectively. Although, constitutionally, Malema could have had these sentences quashed by the party's NEC, he lacked the necessary support on that body, and his last hope was to appeal for the overturning of his expulsion by the National Congress in Mangaung.[58]

Malema's prospects for success at Mangaung were meanwhile considerably undercut by the decision of the Treasury to invoke constitutional powers to place the Limpopo Treasury and four other provincial departments under central government control. Evidence had come to light of massive financial management, dubious tendering practices, and a dismal record in service delivery, this reining in Malema's key ally, Cassel Mathale, who was now the province's Premier. Additionally, the Treasury leaked a damning report of an audit into Malema's financial affairs which provided further detail of how Limpopo cash

---

[54] *ANC Media Statement*, 30 August 2011.
[55] *Sunday Independent*, 11 September 2011.
[56] *Sunday Times*, 25 September 2011.
[57] *Sunday Times*, 30 October 2011.
[58] *Mail & Guardian Online*, 24 April 2012. Malema subsequently appealed to the party hierarchy at Mangaung to restore his membership and responsibilities in the ANC, promising to be subject to its discipline, to no avail.

had found its way into the bank accounts of On-Point Engineers, the Ratanang Family Trust, and various of his cronies.[59] By September 2012, the Limpopo Roads and Transport Department had been instructed by the Public Protector to blacklist On-Point Engineering. Malema himself was charged with money-laundering, an offence for which if found guilty he could be jailed for up to fifteen years. In addition, the South African Revenue Service was claiming R16 million from him in outstanding taxes, penalties, and interest; and in December, the NPA had indicated that it would add another 50 new charges relating to corruption and fraud when he was brought to trial in 2013.[60]

Zuma's affability, his early condonation of Malema's wayward statements, the involvement of his own family in dubious dealings, and his lack of assertive-ness during the early years of his presidency, may have induced the Youth League leader into thinking that he was an easy target. Malema clearly over-estimated the role of the Youth League in propelling Zuma into power and appeared to assume that it could repeat the exercise in Mangaung, even in the face of the open enmity of COSATU and the SACP. He also miscalculated the extent to which the ANC places boundaries on dissent, and how seriously charges of 'sowing division' within the party are regarded by the party hier-archy.[61] But above all, Malema had underestimated the history of Zuma as an experienced street-fighter, hugely experienced in fighting dirty when pressed, from his days in MK through to his titanic struggle with Mbeki in his battle for the presidency. Now that he was armed with the powers of state, he could use his official might to consolidate his position within the party, and his confronta-tion with Malema would serve as powerful lesson to all those who might dare to oppose him on the road to Mangaung.

The struggle for the presidency

Following his expulsion from the ANC, Malema publicly apologized for having helped Zuma into power. This was consistent with a wider discontent. Certainly, there were those who thought that Malema was being used by powerful figures within the party to prepare the ground for the emergence of alternative candi-dates for the party leadership. Tokyo Sexwale – who had made a R100,000 dona-tion to the Ratanang Trust – was the most widely cited in this regard. Others simply argued that while the Youth League had needed to be reined in, it had highlighted the urgent need for a change at the top to overcome the deficits of the Zuma presidency, the most widely canvassed name as a possible 'Anyone but Zuma' (ABZ) successor being that of Deputy President Motlanthe. However, that Zuma was determined to stand for a second term and to make a fight of it with any would-be challenger was brutally evident. Febrile speculation now attended his every move, interpreted in the light of his efforts to cling on to power, espe-cially after the Supreme Court of Appeal responded positively in early 2012 to a plea by the DA that it had the legal standing to ask for a review of NPA's 2009

---

[59] *Business Day*, 5 June 2012; *Sunday Times*, 20 May 2012; *Sunday Independent*, 17 June 2012.
[60] *Sunday Independent*, 23 September 2012; *Star*, 26 September; *City Press*, 2 December 2012.
[61] On this as major factor in Malema's case, see Clive Glaser (2012), *The ANC Youth League*, Auck-land Park: Jacana, 145–47.

decision to withdraw corruption charges against him. It reopened the possibility that Zuma might at some point in the future find himself in the dock.[62] Yet while many spoke of the prospect of Mangaung becoming another Polokwane, the obstacles to its becoming so were being put in place.

The problem for the ABZ camp (later to be depicted as the 'Movement for Change') was that the ANC had no tradition of open elections for leadership positions, and in effect, the party's practices were very much in favour of Zuma as the presidential incumbent. According to ANC mythology, leaders emerge only after having been nominated as candidates for high office via the party's internally constituted democratic processes. Since the early 1990s, this has meant that candidates for leadership positions have to be put forward by one or more of the party's nine provinces, who in theory respond in making their choice to the expressed views of the party's branches, which constitute the organization's ground floor. Supposedly, therefore, with candidates eschewing personal ambition and only responding to calls from below to stand for election in terms of their selfless devotion to duty, open campaigning for office is officially frowned upon. In the case of Mangaung, the ANC had prescribed that candidates for leadership positions could not be nominated by branches and structures (such as the Leagues) before the first of October, just three months before the National Conference. This meant, in practice, that any aspirant hoping to replace Zuma as party President was severely limited before that time, although the reality was that the Zuma himself had unofficially rewritten the rules in the lead-up to Polokwane.

While ANC tradition claimed that leaders served by democratic writ, the transitions in power from Tambo to Mandela, and from Mandela to Mbeki, had been managed by the party elites, and endorsed by party delegates at national conferences. In contrast, Zuma's challenge to Mbeki at Polokwane had provoked a genuine contest which was complicated by the different conditions and timing which attached to the two positions of the party President and the state President.

On the one hand, while Mandela had established the precedent of stepping down from the party presidency after two terms, there were no party rules demanding it, rendering Thabo Mbeki eligible as a candidate for a third term. Fatefully, and unwisely, he chose to pursue that option rather than making political space for another candidate to step up to challenge Zuma.

On the other hand, the constitution restricted a state President to two terms in office. The consequence would have been that if Mbeki had been re-elected at Polokwane, the two presidencies would have been split following the April 2009 election, at least until the convening of the 53rd Conference at Mangaung in 2012, with the ANC being required to put forth another candidate for the post of

---

[62]   The Supreme Court ordered that the record (i.e., the tape recordings of discussions between Scorpions boss Leonard McCarthy and the then NDPP, Bulelani Ngcuka which the Acting NDPP Mokotedi Mpshe used to justify the withdrawal of the charges against Zuma on the grounds that they indicated political interference in the decision to charge him) be made available to the DA, in its capacity as applicant for their release, by April 2012, preparatory to a review of the decision in the North Gauteng High Court. However, the NPA had failed to comply with the order of the Court by November, at which point the *Sunday Times* (18 November 2012) summarized the 300 pages of leaked material, as well as extracts from the tape recordings, which suggested that the conversations were anodyne, and that Mpshe's judgement that they indicated political interference could not be reasonably sustained.

state President. Meanwhile, with the ANC conference cycle geared to a party leader's election some sixteen months or so before a general election is likely to take place (after which parliament elects a state President), there is always likely to be a gap between the time a new party president assumes the state presidency.[63]

In the case of Mbeki, the Zuma camp found reason to 'recall' him from the state presidency in September 2008, replacing him with Motlanthe as a stand-in until after the 2009 general election. However, the broader point is that, in the build-up to Polokwane, Zuma had used his unique circumstances to campaign vigorously for the party presidency without declaring that he was doing so. The strength of anti-Mbeki feeling was sufficient for him to mobilize the support of a 'coalition of the aggrieved' behind him. This enabled him, in defiance of Mbeki, to retain the deputy leadership of the party after having been ousted as Deputy President and thereby to mobilize financial and organizational resources for well over a year. During this period, he had no distracting state responsibilities. Furthermore, of course, he managed to merge his desperate need to fend off prosecution for corruption with his campaign for the presidency, presenting himself as a victim of political persecution. In essence, therefore, Zuma had ridden roughshod over established ANC practice, setting the precedent that an incumbent party President was there to be challenged. However, in 2012, the problem for the ABZ camp was that they had no one candidate behind whom to congregate.

Without explicit declarations by potential candidates, both the party and the media were condemned to indulge in wearying speculation about who might challenge Zuma for the party presidency. There were to two major prospective alternatives, Tokyo Sexwale and Kgalema Motlanthe, the former having given clear indications of his desire to lead. Broadly, opinion was that the former had both the ambition and financial resources but lacked crucial support in the branches, whilst the latter's desire for higher office and drive to win was questionable. Nonetheless, Motlanthe became increasingly viewed as the popular alternative. The problem for his supporters was not merely that he steadfastly declined to declare himself as a candidate, but that he refused to engage in unofficial campaigning, let alone in mobilizing support behind him. By default, therefore, his tilt at the presidency – if that is what it was – was left to be organized by others. However, the Zuma camp was determined that Mangaung was not going to be a repeat of Polokwane, and considerable obstacles were placed in the path of any 'Movement for Change'.

Zuma's extension of control over the party machinery

The ANC's constitution (Section 10.1.1) lays down that the National Conference, where the vote for the election of senior office bearers takes place, is to be 90 per cent composed of delegates elected from branches (drawn from provinces in proportion to the paid up membership of each province), together with the members of the NEC (80 since Polokwane), and the 10 per cent remainder to be drawn from the Provincial Executive Committees and the Youth, Women's, and

---

[63] Post-Polokwane, this unintended outcome of the transition to democracy appears likely to be a constant source of political instability, the obvious solution being for a party President defeated for the leadership at a party conference to resign as State President, with parliament proceeding to elect his successor as State President, thus bringing the two positions into alignment.

Veterans' Leagues. This overwhelming representation of the branches (new ones of which can be formed by groupings of twelve paid-up members or more subject to approval from above) made them the clear focus of campaigning attention in the lead-up to Mangaung.

Zuma had won his battle with Mbeki because his supporters had taken control of the majority of ANC branches around the country, ensuring that the majority of the delegates who attended Polokwane were mandated to support him (and did). Mbeki had lost because he had neglected to build up his defences at branch level before it was too late. Zuma was determined not to make the same mistake. Apart from the fact that after Polokwane, his supporters had wrested control from pro-Mbeki forces at many branches and most provinces countrywide, Zuma had been particularly active in expanding his organizational base in KwaZulu-Natal. The table below is illustrative:

Table 11.1 Provincial Composition of ANC Membership December 2007, January 2012, and September 2012

Province	Members December 2007	%	Members January 2012	%	Members September 2012	%
Eastern Cape	153,164	24.7	225,597	22.0	187,585	15.4
KwaZulu-Natal	102,742	16.6	244,900	23.8	331,820	27.2
Western Cape	36,497	5.9	43,397	4.2	38,499	3.2
Gauteng	59,909	9.7	121,223	11.8	134,909	11.1
Free State	61,310	9.9	76,334	7.4	121,074	9.9
Mpumalanga	54,913	8.8	98,892	9.6	132,729	10.9
Limpopo	67,632	10.9	114,385	11.1	161,868	13.3
North West	47,353	7.6	60,319	5.9	75,145	6.2
Northern Cape	37,262	6.0	42,342	4.1	36,428	3.0
Total	620,782	100	1,027,389	100	1,220,057	100

Sources: Organisational Report to the ANC National General Council, 20 September 2010 and ANC NEC's 8 January 2012 Statement; Sunday World, *1 October 2012.*

What can be immediately seen, in the context of the ANC's recruitment drive in order to achieve 1 million members in the lead-up to its centenary, is that since Polokwane the increase in membership in KwaZulu-Natal had far outstripped that in any other single province. Whereas by January 2012, KwaZulu-Natal membership had increased by 138 per cent since 2007, in the other provinces combined it had risen by only 51 per cent. Consequently, on the not unrealistic assumption that the KwaZulu-Natal delegates would vote overwhelmingly for Zuma, any challenger would have to secure two-thirds of the votes of the delegates from the other eight provinces – yet by early 2012, the majority of them were divided (in different proportions). Although, given the fluidity of the situation, unseating Zuma would be by no means impossible, the arithmetical cards were stacked in his favour.[64]

Meanwhile, although not openly declaring himself as a candidate, Zuma was transparently campaigning for his re-election across the country: once again

[64] 'The ANC: The arithmetic of Mangaung', *Politicsweb*, 9 January 2012.

tapping into support amongst African and Pentecostal churches; securing declarations that he should serve another term from high officer bearers within the party and the Alliance; aligning traditional leaders and rural constituencies behind him; and even hosting a huge birthday celebration for himself at the Durban International Convention Centre which thousands attended. Nor was the opportunity missed to again depict himself as a martyred victim when in May 2012, Johannesburg's Goodman Gallery displayed a painting by the provocative artist, Brett Murray, which depicted him in Leninist pose but with his genitals showing. After, curiously, waiting two weeks before it reacted, the ANC organized demonstrations in protest, backing Zuma's plea to the High Court in Gauteng to have the portrait removed on the grounds that it played up to crude stereotypes of African sexuality, that it was racist, that it impugned his dignity, and – ingenuously – that it depicted him as a philanderer and womanizer.[65]

By the end of September 2012, when the process of nomination of favoured candidates for top party positions by branches was brought to an official close, the membership of the ANC, as announced by Secretary-General Gwede Mantashe, had increased a further 19 per cent to a total of over 1.2 million. Curiously, however, whereas KwaZulu-Natal had increased from 23.8 per cent of the total to 27.2 per cent since January, the Eastern Cape (the second-largest province, where the party membership was known to be highly divided, with probably a majority in favour of Motlanthe) had shrunk from 22.0 per cent to 15.4 per cent. The outcome was that the composition of the 4,413 delegates attending Mangaung would be as follows:

Table 11.2 Composition of Delegates to ANC Mangaung Conference, December 2012

KwaZulu-Natal	974
Eastern Cape	676
Free State	324
Gauteng	500
Limpopo	574
Mpumalanga	467
Northern Cape	176
North West	234
Western Cape	178
Women's, Veterans' and Youth Leagues	45
National Executive Committee	82
Provincial Executive Committees	180

---

[65] In the event, the painting was removed by the gallery after it had been damaged, in separate incidents, by a white Christian fundamentalist and a Zuma supporter, with the court case being withdrawn after negotiations between the gallery and the ANC. Thus the issue of whether it offended the constitutional provision against hate speech was never judicially tested, perhaps fortunately for the judge who might have had to give his opinion as to whether its alleged depiction of Zuma as a womanizer was fair comment.

Unsurprisingly, questions were raised about the neutrality of the process whereby the membership of branches was approved and audited by the party hierarchy, with suggestions emerging from those opposed to Zuma that membership figures were being skewed in his favour. Certainly, the tales about how the party's membership had been manipulated were many and lurid. Massive amounts of money were rumoured to have been spent to consolidate the Zuma alliance; meetings were said to have been packed by factions, with their opponents physically excluded; numerous branches had failed to achieve the quorum of 50 per cent of members required by their nomination meetings, with resultant abuses of procedure; factional killings had occurred in some provinces; and at least one provincial congress descended into violence between supporters of Zuma and Motlanthe.

Generally, the complaint of the ABZ camp was that a pro-Zuma majority was being artificially inflated, with fees being paid for thousands of ghost members; and in both the Free State and North West, defeated Motlanthe supporters turned to the High Court to protest against the manner in which the elective processes had been conducted. The former claimed that the provincial nomination conference had been conducted in defiance of ANC rules, while the latter insisted that the majority of nominated delegates to the National Conference were not from legitimate branches or that pro-Zuma delegates had been illegitimately substituted for pro-Motlanthe candidates.

Whatever the truth of the huge numbers of complaints (and there was recognition by the party hierarchy that the electoral process had been severely compromised by what it termed factionalism and ill-discipline) there can be little doubt that Zuma had managed to put in place a strong network of backers at provincial level across the country, so that even in provinces where his support was in a minority, they were able to put in a strong bid to counter challenges from those favouring a change in leadership. Accordingly, by the time that the nominations in favour of candidates by branch delegates had been counted, it was reported that 2,593 had declared in favour of Zuma and just 877 in favour of Motlanthe. In addition, while the disgruntled Youth League had formed the backbone of the anti-Zuma campaign, the Women's and Veterans' Leagues were strongly behind him, as were a majority on national and provincial executives.

Motlanthe supporters were left with the rather desperate hope that when it came to the crunch and delegates were given the opportunity to vote at the Conference, the Zuma support base would drain away.[66] However, given the President's clear control over the party machinery and the patronage that went with it, this was always highly unlikely.

Institutionalized divisions among ABZ ranks

Prior to Polokwane, SACP, COSATU, and the Youth League had been united in their determination to oust Mbeki. Neither the SACP nor COSATU had the right to nominate delegates to the National Conference directly; in contrast, while the Youth League as a wing of the ANC did, its mere handful of votes rendered it a minor player come the final reckoning. Consequently, the influence of these

[66] According to rumour, delegates offered financial inducements to vote one way or another would only receive their reward if able to produce photographs on their cell phones of their marked ballot slips to their patrons.

organizations at Polokwane had been indirect, owing to the fact that the majority of their individual members were also members of the ANC, and could therefore be mobilized to participate in branch elections and dominate the party electoral process. Together, their campaigning against Mbeki was complementary. However, in the lead-up to Mangaung, there was no possibility that an anti-Zuma candidate would enjoy a similar advantage.

The SACP under Blade Nzimande remained unambiguously behind Zuma. In contrast, the leadership of COSATU was divided. SACP influence within the trade union federation was reflected in the pro-Zuma camp including COSATU's President and the leadership of three of the largest affiliates: the National Union of Mineworkers (NUM), the National Education, Health and Allied Workers' Union, and the South African Democratic Teachers' Union. Opposing them (although never stating explicitly that he was opposed to Zuma's re-election) was the Secretary-General, Zwelinzima Vavi, who was deeply critical of corruption within government, and hugely popular on the shop-floor. Alongside stood the National Union of Metalworkers of South Africa, second only in size to the NUM, which demanded a swing to the left in government policy and the removal of the ANC's current leadership.

Given the need to preserve unity, COSATU had initially pledged to uphold a May 2008 agreement with the ANC that it would not openly pronounce a preference for ANC leadership, and that it would not be going to Mangaung with a 'slate' of candidates for the top ANC positions. At most, it was said, it might publish criteria for leadership as a recommendation to delegates.[67] However, at a later meeting of its Central Executive Committee, COSATU changed its mind and decided to endorse Zuma for a second term, a move which controversially ignored manifest divisions among its membership. Confusion followed when a few days before Mangaung, a press statement was issued on behalf of the Forum for Public Dialogue (which had been commissioned by COSATU to survey attitudes of 2,000 shop stewards). This purported to indicate that its findings demonstrated that the majority of those interviewed had no faith in the SACP, wanted COSATU to form a labour party, and did not support Zuma for re-election as President of the ANC. However, the report was immediately refuted by the Forum's board, the CEO Prince Mashele who had released it, dismissed, and it was subsequently claimed that the survey indicated stronger support for Zuma than Motlanthe. Whatever the truth of the matter,[68] the 'Movement for Change' could take heart from these shenanigans, although it was by no means clear that shop-floor anti-Zuma sentiment would be translated into a pro-Motlanthe majority amongst union members serving as ANC delegates. COSATU, in short, was deeply divided in contrast to its show of unity at Polokwane. However, it sought to paper over the cracks by releasing a booklet to delegates at Mangaung advising them to concentrate on policies rather than personalities.

Meanwhile, although the national machinery of the Youth League remained firmly in pro-Malema hands (indeed, the League had refused to replace him as

---

[67]   *Business Day*, 16 May 2012. COSATU unions were also divided over issues, with in particular NUMSA supporting nationalization of the mines, and the NUM opposed.

[68]   Terry Bell, veteran labour analyst and a member of the Forum's board, subsequently claimed that Mashele's action had impugned the integrity of the research, and that his statement had been 'entirely contrary to the data', *Mail & Guardian*, 8–14 February 2013. At time of writing, the research had not yet been fully analysed, and its results remained unpublished.

President), there were many within the structure who had welcomed his ejection. They congregated around two figures, Pule Mabe, whose ousting as the League's Treasurer by the pro-Malema forces in May 2012 the mother body had refused to recognize, and Mduduzi Manana, a member of the Youth League executive, touted as the Zuma camp's eventual replacement for Malema after Mangaung. Nonetheless, the machinery of the Youth League remained in pro-Malema hands and served a key role in mobilizing for Motlanthe, whilst remaining hugely frustrated by his refusal to declare his candidacy and campaign.

In short, by the time of Mangaung, the pre-Polokwane alliance of convenience between the SACP, COSATU, and Youth League had long fallen apart, with the SACP and the Youth League regularly exchanging insults, and the relationship between the SACP and elements within COSATU under severe strain.

Zuma's control over the security services

The final difficulty facing Zuma's opponents was that the merging of party and state under the ANC had resulted in the politicization of the security services. Formally, government operates according to the constitution, and responsibility for governance lies with the President, cabinet, civil service, and the institutions charged with legal and political authority at provincial and local government levels. Decision-making by such bodies is subject to political bargaining and negotiation, with policy outcomes the result of diverse pressures, and implemented according to bureaucratic, political and legal constraints, with departures from legality investigated and prosecuted by authorities constitutionally independent of the political executive. Increasingly, however, the formal operations of government are being eroded by the interests of factions within the ANC, a development driven by the struggle for state resources.

These tendencies, already pronounced under Mbeki, had gained serious momentum under Zuma who ascended to the presidency determined to reinforce his political authority with control over the intelligence, police, and prosecution services. Zuma built upon his existing support within the intelligence services, where key operatives (including the Shaik brothers) from Operation Vula (an underground operation established by the ANC in the late 1980s to prepare for revolution had the negotiation process failed) had already established a firm presence and had allegedly used arms deal cash to fight the factional battle against Mbeki. Key appointments and decisions followed. Siyabonga Cwele, who had served under Zuma in exile, was appointed Minister of State Security; Bheki Cele, who had spearheaded support for Zuma in KwaZulu-Natal before Polokwane, was appointed National Police Commissioner; and Menzi Simelane, who openly proclaimed himself a deployee of the ANC, replaced Vusi Pikoli (who been central to the drive to prosecute Zuma for corruption) as NDPP. They were later to be joined by Mac Maharaj, another former Vula operative who had been fired as Minister of Transport by Mbeki, to the role of presidential spokesperson.

Alas for Zuma, this clutch of appointments ran into copious problems. Initially, Zuma had publicly declared the imperative of restoring the independence of the intelligence services, but by late 2011, Gibson Njenje, the head of the National Intelligence Agency (responsible for domestic concerns), his counterpart at the Secret Service (foreign affairs), Moe Shaik, and the Director-General of the Security ministry, Jeff Maqetuka, were clashing with Cwele, allegedly for his attempting to involve them in political investigations ahead of Mangaung. By this time, Shaik family's relations with Zuma had soured following the latter's distancing himself from Schabir. In the event, Zuma backed Cwele, while Njenje, Maqetuka and (eventually) Shaik all resigned. Meanwhile, as noted above, Cele had by late 2011 fallen victim to corruption allegations and his flirtation with anti-Zuma forces. Further, in early December 2011, the Supreme Court of Appeal had ruled that Zuma's appointment of Menzi Simelane had been irrational, invalid, and unconstitutional (given the comments about his lack of integrity made by the Ginwala Commission). Nor were Zuma's replacements uniformly successful. As indicated, Nhanhla Mkhanawazi's appointment as acting National Commissioner of Police had been strongly criticized for his preferment above more senior officers, a controversy enhanced by his subsequent purge of five top police generals. Allegedly, this followed from a Hawks investigation into their abuse of the intelligence services' secret account (reputed to be between R200 and R400 million a year) but according to some sources, it was actually driven by the urgency of securing political control of those funds ahead of Mangaung.[69] However, the appointment that gained most notoriety was that of Lieutenant-General Richard Mdluli to head the Crime Intelligence Service (CIS).

Mdluli had been appointed to head the CIS in November 2009 in a process later described as 'political' and 'irregular', normal procedures having been hijacked by a cabal of four ministers under the leadership of Cwele. Mdluli, who had joined the police before 1994, appears to have gained Zuma's favour when, as deputy to the Gauteng Police Commissioner, he supposedly assisted with securing the former's acquittal in the 2006 rape case, and subsequently by playing a key role in the campaign against the Scorpions. Nonetheless, in early 2011, following media investigations (possibly prompted by anti-Zuma forces within the ANC), he was arrested for the 1999 murder of Oupa Ramogibe, who had married Mdluli's former lover. However, in early 2012 the charges against him were withdrawn, supposedly for lack of evidence and apparently at Zuma's direct intervention. His suspension from office was lifted, although this was a step too far, even by Zuma's own diminished standards. Mdluli had by now aroused considerable antagonism within both the police and the ANC, and following the leak of the Hawks' report into the misuse of police slush funds to the media, Mkhanawazi was forced to move him sideways to another portfolio before again suspending him.[70]

Nonetheless, despite all these complications, there were extensive indications that Zuma successfully extended greater presidential control over the security services. Not least was the promotion of an Intelligence General Laws Amendment Bill which would amalgamate the hitherto separate intelligence agencies under a single body (the State Security Agency), and reduce liability of the National Communications Centre, which had the capacity for bulk interception of communications, to legal restraint.[71] Meanwhile, for all their divisions, the

[69] Sam Sole (2012), 'Claims of SAPS plot against minister', M&G Centre for Investigative Journalism, 20 July, www.amaBhungane.co.za.
[70] *Business Day*, 13 April 2012.
[71] Drew Forrest and Stefaans Brummer (2012), 'Spies bid for new powers', *Mail & Guardian*, 3–9 February.

intelligence services remained overwhelmingly united behind the expansive definition of state security put forward by the 'Secrecy' Bill, which by late 2012 was being driven through parliament by the ANC majority over the head of strong objections from the opposition and civil society.[72]

By its nature, it is difficult to verify the widespread claims (for instance as editorialized by *Business Day*)[73] that Zuma was using the security forces in his battle to secure re-election at Mangaung. However, what cannot be doubted is the rise of fear within ANC ranks of running foul of a nascent security state. Suspicion before the Conference was rife even amongst Zuma loyalists that phones were liable to be tapped and emails hacked; laptop computers were stolen from prominent individuals in mysterious circumstances; and there was a widespread assumption that leaks to the media regarding alleged corruption, dubious business involvements or factional alignments often originated from within the security services. Further, it was widely believed that, while revelations of corruption constantly battered the South African public, prosecution of those accused was often politically selective. Finally, it was openly admitted that Mangaung would see the mounting of an unprecedented security and intelligence operation. Supposedly, this was to ensure that the Conference would not be marred by violence, but one Central Intelligence Service operative admitted to a journalist that in the weeks leading up to the conference, 'every resource, every effort [had] been channelled into getting the president successfully re-elected for another term'.[74]

Zuma triumphant

Speculation about whether Motlanthe would challenge Zuma reached its zenith when in June 2012 the former used a lecture to a small conference on ANC history to air strongly worded criticisms of a discussion document which broached the idea of a 'second transition'. The document had been prepared for the party's National Policy Conference, a five-yearly event charged with drawing up recommendations for the National Conference, which was about to take place. Motlanthe's critique was of particular significance, for as was to be made clear when Zuma opened the conference a few days later, he had adopted the notion of 'the second transition' as his own, promoting it as vehicle for demanding radical change, although it was more likely that he was seeking to promote it in place of Malema's populist demands for 'economic freedom' and nationalization.

---

[72] In response to criticism, the government had made significant concessions regarding the thrust of the Protection of Public Information Bill, but major concerns still remained, notably (i) state departments other than security services would be able to classify information, opening the potential for abuse; (ii) the mere possession of classified information could still lead to up to five years' imprisonment; and (iii) while the Bill would now protect those who possess or disclose classified information, if disclosure reveals criminal activity, it would not cover offences of 'espionage', 'receiving state information unlawfully', and 'hostile activity', rendering liable journalists and whistleblowers even when they believed themselves to be covered by the defence of public interest. See 'Corruption watch', *Sunday Times*, 16 December 2012.

[73] 23 April 2012.

[74] Sally Evans, 'Why spies are flocking to Mangaung', *Mail & Guardian*, 14–20 December 2012.

The document's central idea was that the 'implicit bargain, involving the ANC committing to macroeconomic stability and international openness, and white business agreeing to participate in capital reform to modify the racial structure of asset ownership and to invest in national priorities', had failed to address the apartheid legacies of 'unemployment, poverty and inequality' (para. 33). Further, while the government had achieved macro-economic stability, 'the structure of the apartheid colonial economy has remained the same, and...in this form...is incapable of fostering either higher or inclusive growth' (para. 167). There was therefore a need for a new social national consensus to 'lay the basis for a second transition of social and economic transformation' (para. 165). Although the way to achieve this would continue to be a 'mixed economy with state, cooperative and other forms of social ownership co-existing with a vibrant private sector', the document clearly leaned towards a greater degree of state intervention, entailing the government's rolling out a massive infrastructure investment programme.[75] Meanwhile, although wholesale nationalization was dismissed, 'strategic nationalization' of the mining sector was envisaged, with fiscal interventions to secure the state greater returns from mineral resources, the consolidation of state mining assets into a single company, and the latter's partnering with private sector ventures. However, whether or not he agreed with these thrusts, Motlanthe had subjected the document's central premise to withering criticism: 'This transition...From what or from where to where? What constituted the first transition? What were the tasks of that phase? Have all of those tasks been accomplished or not?'

The notion of the second transition, he implied, was empty. Wrapped up in a 'smattering of Marxist jargon', it was expressive of the ANC's continuing adherence to a world view which was now outdated. The party had to engage in serious self-examination, for it was itself becoming a very different body from that which had drawn selfless commitment to the struggle against apartheid. Today the quality of cadres was declining and the party was becoming viewed by members as 'a legitimate stepping stone to opportunities of self-enrichment'. Unless the ANC made a serious commitment to renewal, it would soon face 'a realignment of forces'. In this regard, interestingly, he made glowing references first, to the manner in which 'co-determination where government, organized labour, business, etc.' had worked together to reconstruct the post-Second World War German economy; and second, to how the Chinese Communist Party had acknowledged that it had committed a 'fundamental mistake' by assuming that they could 'jump out of capitalism into socialism', and had now adopted a 100-years' development path based upon raising the education level of the entire nation; modernizing the forces of production, notably by attracting foreign investment; and closing the gap between urban and rural.[76]

In the event, the policy conference rejected the idea of a 'second transition' as having no serious basis in previous ANC theorizing, and adopted a compromise wording calling for 'a *second phase* of transition' to a 'national democratic society'. Prior to the conference, there had been much suggestion that the

---

[75] ANC (2012), 'The Second Transition? Building a national democratic society and the balance of forces in 2012', a discussion document towards the National Policy Conference, Version 7.0 as amended by the Special NEC, 27 February.

[76] Address by Deputy President Kgalema Motlanthe at the Liliesleaf Trust's Commemorative Gala Dinner in honour of the Harold Wolpe Trust, 14 June 2012.

'second transition' would serve as a proxy for a battle between those who supported Zuma and those who did not. From this perspective, its defeat registered a defeat for Zuma and a victory for Motlanthe. However, such an interpretation was empty, for Zuma swiftly distanced himself from the 'second transition' and embraced 'the second phase'. More significantly, while rejecting the terminology, the conference had embraced the idea of 'radical change', with much being made of its abandonment of the WBWS approach to land reform and its commitment to a strong state role in mining. Meanwhile, a further document on 'organisational renewal' lamented that the political life of the ANC had come to revolve around 'permanent internal strife and factional battles for power' (para. 29.2) and threats to unity that any governing party had to contend with. These 'subjective weaknesses' had undermined 'the ANC's progressive outlook and the capacity of the developmental state to carry out a thorough-going transformation agenda' (para. 22). While these deficiencies should be addressed by appropriate measures (these largely a repeat of exhortatory recommendations made at earlier conferences with the addition that the party should not 'deploy' candidates facing legal charges of fraud), the document recommitted the party to pursuing transformational politics at the 'strategic centres of power' with ANC headquarters at the 'apex' (para. 100).[77]

Motlanthe's ruminations confirmed that, in some quarters, serious thinking was afoot. However, for all that the party was open in analysing its having fallen victim to what Mbeki-loyalist Joel Netshitenzhe had recently termed 'the sins of incumbency',[78] it gave no serious indication that it was preparing to move beyond radical rhetoric. As Fiona Forde noted, after the conference, the party bosses simply climbed back into their luxury cars, and drove off 'shameless in their hypocrisy'.[79] Although Zuma may have been embarrassed, those who wanted to replace him continued to lack a convincing and determined champion, Motlanthe adhering to the view right up to the verge of the National Conference that leaders of the party should emerge as result of the expressed wishes of the party's membership in branches, rather than campaigning actively among them.[80] In particular, he publicly railed against the Polokwane-style practice of leadership candidates competing at the head of 'slates', that is, an informally pronounced list of top supporters for the party's six most senior positions, maintaining instead that delegates should vote according to their judgements of the qualities of individuals.

It was only on the very eve of the conference that Motlanthe indicated that he would accept nominations from below to contest for the presidency, further complicating the situation by also initially accepting nominations to contest for the deputy presidency and for membership of the NEC. In so doing, he finally closed the door upon the making of any deal whereby, in a move to present the party as united, he would have withdrawn from the presidential race and agreed

---

[77] ANC (2012), 'Organisational renewal: Building the ANC as a movement for transformation and a strategic centre of power', a discussion document towards the National Policy Conference, Version 9, released on 10 April.

[78] Joel Netshitenzhe (2012), 'Competing identities of a national liberation movement and the challenges of incumbency', *ANC Today*, 15–21 June.

[79] *Sunday Independent*, 1 July 2012.

[80] For profoundly sympathetic (if at times hagiographic) treatment of Motlanthe's views, see Ebrahim Harvey (2012), *Kgalema Motlanthe: A Political Biography*, Auckland Park: Jacana Media.

to continue as Zuma's deputy. In any case, by this time, sensing that Motlanthe's position was immovable, the Zuma camp had already opened negotiations with Cyril Ramaphosa (whose heading of the Malema disciplinary committee had signalled a willingness to return from business to politics) with a view to his replacing Motlanthe as Deputy President. The reasoning, apparently, was that not only had Ramaphosa quietly backed Zuma against Mbeki, but that he was an alternative candidate of genuine substance with the potential ability to bridge the gaps between the government, business, and labour. However, the immediate problem was that Ramaphosa proved unwilling to contest the deputy presidency with Motlanthe, who had replaced him as Secretary-General of the NUM, and for whom he continued to have deep respect. The upshot, ironically, was the sort of deal that Motlanthe had hitherto eschewed. He agreed to withdraw from the contest for the deputy presidency, leaving the way clear for Ramaphosa to compete against Tokyo Sexwale and Matthews Phosa (who were splitting the opposition vote). With the Zuma slate finalized, it proceeded to sweep the board, Zuma defeating Motlanthe by 2,983 votes to 991.[81]

Motlanthe had formally accepted his nomination despite it being clear that, come the election, he would go down to defeat. Yet more than simply tilting at windmills, he was signalling his continued adherence to his principled notions of the ANC constituting a movement of selfless cadres committed to democracy and development. By implication, too, not least because he proceeded to decline his nomination to serve on the NEC, thus indicating his withdrawal from the party's top leadership structures, he was signalling his disillusion with the ANC as it had continued to evolve under Jacob Zuma. He may have been, as one commentator declared, a rare being who had given his life to the ANC and asked for nothing in return.[82] A less flattering judgement may be that, in adhering to a political culture of liberation whose time had long since passed, he had failed to rise to the challenge of seek to modernize the ANC.

Continuity or change after Manguang?

The battle for Mangaung received almost obsessive attention from the media because there was a sense that under Zuma, the ANC had become more powerful, or in other words, that there had been in a shift in weight after Polokwane from the state to the party. Yet there were also other concerns. Despite Gwede Mantashe's assurance to the National Conference that after Polokwane

---

[81] The results of the other contests for the top six were as follows: (Deputy-President), Cyril Ramaphosa, 3,018; Matthews Phosa, 470; Tokyo Sexwale, 463; (Secretary-General), Gwede Mantashe, 3,058; Fikile Mbalula, 901; (National Chairperson), Bakela Mbeta, 3,010; Thandi Modise, 939; (Treasurer-General), Zweli Mkhize 2,988; Paul Mashatile, 961; (Deputy Secretary General), Jesse Duarte (unopposed). Ultimately, there were only 4,076 delegates accredited to the conference, one reason for the reduction in numbers being the ANC's dissolution of its Free State provincial executive. This followed the judgement of the Constitutional Court, in response to the bid by dissentient members from the province seeking to have the Free State delegation excluded, that the provincial conference had been illegally constituted. However, the ANC interpreted this as meaning that while the members of the provincial executive should be excluded from the conference, the delegates from the province's branches should be enabled to attend and vote.

[82] Peter Bruce, *Business Day*, 19 December 2012.

the ANC had become more stable and its structures more operational,[83] there were dire warnings the party had drifted into a morass of corruption, [84] and that it was characterized by little more than an endemic factionalism related to vicious struggles for resources, with provincial and branch structures transformed into nodes of patronage. Nor indeed, had the wounds of Polokwane died away, with Mbeki loyalists becoming increasingly assertive in defending his record, deploring his dismissal from the presidency,[85] and with multiple predictions being made that after Mangaung, those who had supported Motlanthe would be subject to a purge.[86] Additionally, various views were expressed that Zuma was manifestly unsuited to office, that he had a 'disastrous track record', that the country was 'going backwards', and that it was doubtful whether South Africa could 'survive another effective seven years of a Zuma presidency as a constitutional democracy'.[87]

While such damning judgements might be those of both business and liberal elites, often vocally backed by pro-Mbeki and pro-Motlanthe protagonists, they recorded the deep uneasiness felt by many about the state of South Africa after twenty years of democracy. Indeed, the battle for Mangaung had been fought against the background of an economy in apparent decline, increasingly unable to realize the ANC's promises of 'a better life for all'. During 2012, the economy had begun to buckle under the full weight of the global depression, with growth falling to a pitiful 2 per cent, export markets shrinking (despite a falling rand) and business confidence at its lowest ebb for two decades. In particular, South Africa's economic prospects and reputation had been severely damaged by the shocking events in August 2012 at the Marikana mine of Lonmin on the platinum belt, when a violent response to an unofficial strike by migrant workers, police shootings resulted in the death of 34 miners and the wounding of many others. Amidst all the confusion and recrimination that followed, with blame spread around more or less equally to the company, the police, the government (for a totally inadequate response to an emergency) and to the NUM (for its losing the confidence of its members), sage conclusions were drawn that the tragedy pointed to the growing impatience of the poor, their increasing anger with both political and business elites, and hence their greater receptivity to

---

[83] NEC Organisational Report to the 53rd ANC National Conference, by Secretary General, Gwede Mantashe.

[84] A fear expressed by former Reserve Bank Governor, Tito Mboweni, during the ANC's centenary lecture in honour of Thabo Mbeki as a former leader at the University of Johannesburg, *Sunday Independent*, 25 November 2012.

[85] For an extended treatment of post-Polokwane pain which received much favourable attention, see Frank Chikane (2012), *Eight Days in September: The Removal of Thabo Mbeki*, Johannesburg: Picador Africa. Also notable was the vigorous defence of Mbeki's economic record delivered by Tito Mboweni during an ANC centenary lecture at the University of Johannesburg, 2012. He dismissed as 'an insult' the notion, promoted by notably Blade Nzimande, of the Mbeki government as 'the 1996 Class Project': 'Had we not done (what we did, in 1997), that burden of the economy would have worsened.' See Tito Mboweni, 'The Cruel Challenges of Politics and "Politics within Politics"', http://www.ujoh,co.za/opinions/mboweni-full-text-on-mbeki-lecture

[86] Although Zuma made a plea for unity after his re-election, those who had backed Motlanthe were largely voted off the 80-strong NEC. Similarly, Malema's written plea to be readmitted as a member of the party, enabling him to resume his position as president of the Youth League, was excluded from the conference programme.

[87] The citations, from a *Business Day* editorial (3 December 2012), were by no means unrepresentative of wider opinion.

allegedly destabilising manifestos.[88] A post-Marikana wave of industrial unrest that spread across the country prompted fears of a collapse of foreign investment, the further decline of the already troubled mining industry, and most immediately, the downgrading of the economy by international ratings agencies. With Gill Marcus, Governor of the Reserve Bank, warning that the global downturn looked set to continue for several years, business lobbied the ANC in the lead-up to Mangaung to stick to market-friendly policies in order to arrest the decline in confidence in South Africa's future. Government debt, warned the business press, was increasing rapidly as unemployment increased and tax revenue declined, with the result that the cupboard was bare and that the ANC would have to find 'another path to growth'.[89]

It was often stated, in this context, that the policy decisions which the ANC would make at Mangaung were more important than the leadership contest. From this perspective, the business community worried that ANC policy positions would move to the left, whilst COSATU, in contrast, was determined to achieve precisely that. In the event, Mangaung largely endorsed the measures proposed by its policy conference which, while supporting the idea of a more state-led economy, in practice presaged little change from the status quo. As remarked by Steven Friedman, it was important in a country with massive social inequalities for the ANC to dress up whatever it did with a radical rhetoric. The reality was that the party was increasingly dominated by business lobbies who wanted greater state intervention because they could get more of the action.[90] (Tito Mboweni had earlier put it more explicitly when he stated that they wanted to 'loot').[91] In any case, as noted by Aubrey Matshiqi, there was a direct link between ANC internal dynamics and state capacity, so Manguang needed to be more concerned to stabilize and modernize the party rather than to elaborate its policies.[92]

Enter Cyril Ramaphosa. On his election as ANC Deputy President, and with the prospect that he would now play a major role in government (many predicting him becoming a *de facto* Prime Minister as Mbeki had been to Mandela from 1996), the business sector and the financial markets rejoiced.[93] Indeed, there was excited speculation that Ramaphosa would play a major role in activating the National Development Plan, create the conditions for government, business, and labour to work together more productively, and hence bring about a decisive economic shift towards greater growth, employment, and

[88] While the weeks and months after the shootings indicated the growing influence of the Democratic Socialist Movement, a lineal successor to the Marxist Workers' Tendency which the ANC had expelled in 1979, the most alarming indication of popular alienation from the ANC was the massively warm welcome given to Julius Malema when they would listen to no other established politician.
[89] 'Mangaung must realize ground has been shifting', *Business Day* (editorial), 14 December 2012.
[90] Steven Friedman, 'Don't hold breath for a jump to the left', *Business Day*, 10 December 2012. As he observed, 'The ANC's national executive committee is dominated by shareholders, more than a few of who sit on company boards, which is why economic policy never really moves left.'
[91] Mboweni, op. cit.
[92] Aubrey Matshiqi, 'Put fixing the party top of the agenda', *Business Day*, 14 December 2012.
[93] Business was to be further rewarded when, in order to calm the markets, Zuma intervened to have the word 'nationalization' removed from ANC policy proposals and replaced by the term 'strategic state ownership'.

equality. Ramaphosa, remarked a veteran observer, was too clever a campaigner not to have driven a hard bargain with Zuma, who in any case probably recognized that he needed the former to render his second term an unexpected success.[94] However, only time would tell whether Ramaphosa would prove able to rise above the tarnished limitations of the Zuma presidency and to reform and modernize the ANC.

[94] Allister Sparks, 'Ramaphosa moves make sense if he is delegated wider powers', *Business Day*, 19 December 2012.

Conclusion.
The Slow Death of the Liberation Movements

We are reaching the end of an era in southern Africa. The NLMs which acceded to state power in Zimbabwe, Namibia, and South Africa embodied the hopes of new democracies. However, as more history of the struggle for democracy is uncovered, we have come to appreciate that these were flawed organizations. Whereas they had projected unity, they had been at times bitterly divided; they had proclaimed human rights, but had been guilty of terror and atrocities; they incorporated women, yet were overwhelmingly patriarchal; and while declaring themselves democratic, they were in many of their practices deeply authoritarian. However, the liberation movements were simultaneously recognized as the vehicles of freedom, and rightly so, because for all their faults, and at their best, they embraced liberal and democratic values; they ultimately proved willing to embrace those against whom they had been fighting; and they were genuinely supportive of racial inclusiveness and equality. Furthermore, because they combined socialist with democratic aspirations, they offered the promise that the racial inequalities of the past would be addressed by redistribution alongside the reconstruction of war-torn economies.

As we know now, ZANU-PF, SWAPO, and the ANC have not merely failed to live up to expectations, but have become an increasing threat to democracy. The promise that they once embodied is now dead. That they will survive organizationally, in one form or another, is not in doubt, but their essence as 'liberation movements', as harbingers of hope and freedom, is dying, even as they cling on to power against a future where their continuation as ruling parties is increasingly uncertain. ZANU-PF, SWAPO, and the ANC now seem destined to become 'ordinary' political parties amongst others, unless – and it seems an unlikely 'if' – they can reform themselves intellectually and morally as well as politically.

This text has sought to grapple with both why and how this has happened. In seeking to draw diverse arguments together, questions come crowding in. Were the hopes placed in the NLMs always too extravagant? Was their failure inevitable given the highly racialized and unequal capitalist political economies they inherited? Could they have done a better job, even against the difficult odds they faced? Why and how have they lost their moral compass? What can be rescued from the ruins? In the following pages, an attempt will be made to disentangle structure from agency, to both explain and blame, through a series of propositions.

1. *The liberation movements inherited highly unequal settler colonial economies which were relatively advanced industrial capitalist formations. Attempts to radically reform such formations would inevitably encounter massive resistance from local and international capitalist and capitalist-aligned forces, while posing massive challenges of economic management and transformation.*

Conclusion: The Slow Death of the Liberation Movements

White settlement in Africa brought about far more advanced levels of capitalist development than in non-settler territories. In southern Africa, this was driven by massive inflows of international capital attracted by the prospect of the exploitation of mineral wealth, which in turn spurred minerals-led industrialization and the expansion of commercialized white agricultural sectors which were heavily advantaged by preferential land deals and extensive state support. White settlement was the accompaniment of industrialization, with the political subordination of indigenous populations and the creation of an ample supply of cheap black labour for the mines. Capitalist development reached its apex in South Africa, where the MEC underpinned the highest level of industrialization on the continent, providing the political economy with a relatively high level of autonomy within both the British Empire, and more generally, the international capitalist order. South Africa served as the core of a regional economy which extended its tentacles across surrounding borders, effectively incorporating South West Africa from 1915 and establishing close links with Rhodesia from considerably before that.

In a way that Kenya Colony could hope for but never quite achieve, settler populations in South Africa, Rhodesia, and South West Africa defined their territories as 'White Man's countries' whose trajectories would be decided locally rather than by any metropolitan power. This was confirmed by Britain's ceding of effective sovereignty to South Africa in 1910 and autonomy from Whitehall to Rhodesia in 1923. However, for all that they acquired political autonomy, settler populations were confronted by the unavoidable contradiction that the capitalist development over which they were presiding summoned up relatively advanced class formations amongst subordinated populations. Land loss and political subjection encouraged the early growth of nationalist consciousness and nascent alliances between defeated traditional rulers and emergent African middle classes, the latter a product of mission education provided for the few. Minerals-led development depended upon migrant labour drawn from across the region, but migrancy and limits placed on urbanization could only inhibit but not stop proletarianization, nor, despite state repression, the steady growth of both political and trade union organization. Indeed, migrancy guaranteed the circulation of counter-hegemonic ideas across urban-rural divides, ethnic, religious and racial boundaries, and territorial borders. Southern Africa assumed a unity in the consciousness of the oppressed from an early period just as it promoted a unity of purpose among the board members of mining and industrial enterprises. However, the uneven development of capitalism and urbanization encouraged different political trajectories amongst and between the populations in South Africa, Rhodesia, and South West Africa, leading to the formation of territorially differentiated nationalist movements. Nonetheless, this widespread nationalist consciousness was intertwined, stimulated by trans-territorial organizations such as the IWW and ICU, as well as by Christian and liberal sentiments citing human equality.

The discovery of diamonds and gold on the Witwatersrand had prompted a bitter war to curb Boer nationalism and impose British hegemony upon what became the Union of South Africa. No wonder, then, that when the post-1945 wave of decolonization threatened to engulf southern Africa, Britain declined to follow the convictions of its liberal imperialism and to force a democratic settlement in Rhodesia, and used its still considerable influence to protect white rule in South Africa. British decolonization of its African territories to the north and east had provided for the emplacement of nationalist leaderships who, with a few exceptions (notably Nkrumah in Ghana), were not unduly radical, and did not threaten to disrupt economic linkages with the metropole. Few nationalist movements had been prepared to take up arms, and where they had (as in Kenya) they had been first defeated and then replaced by conservative successors. But in southern Africa, the odds were considerably higher. British and Western investments were far more significant than elsewhere. In Rhodesia, power was taken by a settler government which proved ready to defy any British move to construct a neo-colonial settlement with African nationalism that would favour metropolitan over settler interests. For its part, a Britain which had used military power to vanquish the Mau Mau had no appetite to use force to quell a white revolt, nor was there any desire in London or Washington to confront a robustly independent NP regime in Pretoria. However much apartheid represented an embarrassment, the will and capacity of the NP government to contain African nationalist protest indicated that it was a regime that was there to stay. Above all, the decision of African nationalist organizations to take up armed struggle against politically rigid regimes, to transform themselves into liberation movements, and in so doing to strengthen their linkages with communist sympathizers, both frightened and comforted Western powers. The merest threat of southern Africa's strategically vital mineral and industrial wealth falling prey to Soviet influence caused alarm amongst Western governments and investors; simultaneously, the opportunity to project the NLMs as communist provided the ideological rationale for associating politically with the apartheid regime in the cause of 'Western freedom'. Thus it was that the war for liberation in southern Africa got sucked into the Cold War and NATO into the defence of Portuguese colonialism, settler rule in Rhodesia, and apartheid in South Africa and South West Africa.

The assumption of power by FRELIMO in Mozambique and the MPLA in Angola, both of which proclaimed themselves Marxist, brought liberation war to Rhodesia and signalled the beginning of the end for the settler regime. As evidence grew that Rhodesia was losing its war, the US, Britain, and South Africa colluded to force a settlement for Zimbabwe. Whilst conceding to the liberation movements, these exterior powers sought simultaneously to contain the extent of the latter's victory by protecting white settler minority rights and economic interests. The time had now come for the battle against communism to hunker down behind the protective wall offered by apartheid, and to rely on the considerable armed might that Pretoria offered for confronting the Soviet-backed forces supporting the MPLA and FRELIMO in vicious civil wars against Western-fuelled rebel movements.

Ironically, it was the victory for the West in the Cold War which was to deprive Pretoria of its political utility. Just as the Soviet Union collapsed under the strains imposed by fighting the West, so the apartheid regime was fatally weakened by the military struggles against 'communism'. Critically, too, NP rule was undermined by outflows of international capital, differences with domestic capital, and internal divisions about how to respond to an increasingly vigorous domestic opposition which had morality on its side. The end of the Cold War tolled the death knell for apartheid. The regime conceded to a transition under UN auspices in Namibia, and President de Klerk had both the common sense and courage to take the regime into negotiations with its adversaries. Likewise, the ANC/SACP alliance, deprived of the international support of the USSR, and in earnest to harness the energies of domestic resistance, resolved to find an accommodation with both Pretoria and international capital.

There was no automatic outcome to the negotiation processes in either Namibia or South Africa. In both cases the South African regime fought hard to delay change, exploit divisions amongst its foes, and entrench white minority interests. For their part, SWAPO and the ANC had to establish themselves on the ground, forge alliances with other democratic forces, and debate major internal differences as well as engaging in hard-fought negotiations. The democracy that they won politically was counterbalanced by their acceptance of the continuing capitalist framework of national economies which were overwhelmingly owned and dominated by South African capital – the colour of which, of course, was white.

2. *Although they acceded to political settlements which embraced liberal democracy, the liberation movements espoused ideologies prioritizing 'the capture of state power' as the means to transform societies structurally skewed by settler colonialism in favour of white privilege, power, and wealth. Tension between the values of liberal democracy and 'transformation' were inevitable.*

Demands for human rights and the realization of political equality had been central to the liberation struggles against regimes which had enforced racial inequality by massive abuses of individual rights. At the same time, national liberation struggle constituted struggle for the equal rights of oppressed peoples as (incipient) nations, thereby setting up a tension between individual rights and the rights of nations (that is, racially defined national groups) which even the ANC's doctrine of 'non-racialism' was unable to wholly resolve. This tension was to be captured in the elaboration by the SACP of the theory of South Africa as the victim of 'colonialism of a special type' in which the majority nation, black South Africans, was subject to the 'internal colonialism' of a minority white 'nation'. The realization of true democracy would therefore entail pursuit of transformative policies which, whilst recognizing the rights of whites as individuals, would abolish the privileges and powers which they enjoyed structurally within society as a group. Thus the Freedom Charter adopted at Kliptown in 1956 averred both that 'The People shall Govern!' and that 'All National Groups shall have Equal Rights!' In essence this translated into the equation that, as the true representative of 'the people', the victorious liberation movement would use state power to realize equality between 'nations'.

The tension between individual and collective rights was inherent in the dilemmas posed by the recognition of whites as citizens in new democracies in which the majority of people were black. While liberal constitutions seek to protect the rights of the individual against unjustifiable intrusions by the state, the demand for 'transformation' implied that the liberation movements had an obligation to realize the rights of the majority through their acquisition and implementation of state power to overcome the structural imbalances of the past. Within the theory of the NDR, the party is envisaged as the leading force of the revolution, tasked variously with realizing equality for all, building productive forces and challenging the continued domination of private capital.

Such a perspective sits uneasily with any form of liberal constitutionalism which seeks to protect the rights of forces that national revolutionary movements deem hostile to 'transformation'. In Zimbabwe, ZANU-PF's assertion of its domination over the state was to be facilitated by the adoption at independence of a system of parliamentary democracy which was formally subject to the constitution but which in practice was subject to the expressed will of a parliament controlled by the ruling party. In both Namibia and South Africa, the supremacy of the constitutions over the will of parliament has proved a much stronger constraint upon the capacity of the liberation movements to implement arbitrary laws and have served to protect a democracy that simultaneously balances 'rights' against 'redress'. Nonetheless, the very real tension between the ruling movements' quest for transformation and constitutional democracy has remained.

3. *Notwithstanding the liberation movements' capture of state power and their commitment to transformation, the transitional settlements combined with the global shift to neo-liberalism to induce them to implement economic strategies which, whilst facilitative of capitalist growth, placed severe limitations upon the ability of governments to overcome the structural inequalities of the past and planted the seeds for subsequent social and political crisis.*

The transitional settlements were underwritten by the liberation movements' recognition that they would have to run capitalist economies whose structural inequalities had been determined by colonialism and apartheid and that addressing them presented enormous challenges. Whatever their rhetoric, ZANU-PF, SWAPO, and the ANC all effectively withdrew from previously announced commitments to socialism, and took shelter under languages of 'reconstruction and development' which sought to combine acceptance of capitalism with the realization of popular aims. The ambiguity of their language reflected both their internal soul-searching and the need to placate internal opposition. It was no accident that while COSATU and the SACP denounced GEAR as the enthronement of neo-liberalism, the ANC government, paradoxically, pronounced it the implementation of the RDP.

Fundamentally, the liberation movements accepted capitalist economics for three reasons. First, they had little option if they wanted to accede to state power. They were confronting regimes which, while prepared to concede state power in return for minority protections, were not prepared to concede economic power. Backed by the forces of national and international capital, as well as by the West, they would have been prepared to continue military and political struggle if the NLMs had maintained their commitments to socialism. In turn, the liberation movements were pragmatic enough to recognize that the continuation of the liberation struggle would lead to their inheriting ruined economies, with the advantages of productive capacity which had been built up under settler capitalism being lost. ZANU-PF faced the additional reality that it faced the implacable hostility to socialism of a still overwhelmingly powerful apartheid regime which had the power to launch military strikes by air or land and to starve the Zimbabwean economy of oil, money, supplies, and opportunity by closing the borders. SWAPO had little option but to recognize the limitations imposed by the peripheral nature of the economy it was inheriting, and to hope for early political change next door. The ANC recognized the enormous class power which ran the massive corporate structures that controlled the most advanced capitalist economy upon the continent.

Second, the NLMs came to power in an era when the tide was turning against socialism globally. The collapse of the Bretton Woods system, the economic crises of the early 1970s, the associated defeats handed out to social democratic parties in Western Europe, and the rise of neo-liberal ideology meant that the liberation movements were subject to massive pressures to accept that the world had changed and that socialist alternatives, such as nationalization, were no longer viable. This was a gospel reinforced by the increasing difficulties confronting the centralized economy of the Soviet Union, leading up to its implosion. By the late 1980s, this led to Soviet reluctance to continue its support for the liberation struggle in southern Africa. Meanwhile, the NLMs were told that economic growth depended upon their capacity to increase exports and to adopt policies which would attract a constant flow of investment capital.

Third, the nearer they moved towards power, the more the NLMs recognized the desirability of partnering with capital if they were to make their national economies work. Whilst having developed enormous political and diplomatic capacities, they had few adherents who had gained the skills needed to run advanced economies. Applied economics would have to be learnt on the job while, for the moment at least, new governments depended heavily upon white managers in both the private and public sectors. On the other hand, the political transitions brought to the fore the class differences which had always existed within the nationalist alliances. Black middle classes, small in number and economically weak though they might be, were disproportionately influential within the NLMs, notwithstanding the latter's self image as the vanguard of the masses. Despite the ideological commitments of progressive intellectuals, middle-class cadres often envisaged liberation in nationalist rather than socialist terms. Further, the background of most predisposed them to becoming state managers, for only preferential access to the state could enable them to become a 'proper' bourgeoisie. However, as the theory of the NDR suggested, a small capitalist stratum would need assistance from the state if it were to transform into autonomous 'patriotic capital', yet it was far more obtuse about the potential for aspirant black capitalists being sought out as allies by large-scale (white) capital, and the implications this would have for newly democratic governments.

The business sectors in all three countries recognized the need to establish collaborative working relations with the incoming governments. Beyond the confidence that a return to peace and political stability would bring, they wanted security of property; guarantees against nationalization; market freedoms to access and move capital; and the creation of investment-friendly conditions. For their part, the liberation movement governments needed to partner with business to achieve the high rates of growth necessary to facilitate 'development'. This required a restructuring of highly unequal economies hitherto directed towards the satisfaction of minority needs in order to achieve improved levels of social equity and provision of social goods (education, health care, housing, access to water, and so on) to the impoverished masses of the population. These two sets of needs were neither necessarily mutually complementary nor mutually incompatible. In short, they needed to be negotiated, in both formal arenas and through day-to-day relationships between business and government. To establish what Taylor has termed 'reform coalitions', recognition of mutual interest would require concessions from both sides in order to realize mutual advantage, and the maintenance of balance between government and business.

Critics have argued that the embrace of neo-liberalism (albeit by ZANU-PF in the guise of structural adjustment) ensured that growth would be skewed in the interests of large-scale capital at the expense of the working classes and the poor. They are right, as the Namibian and South African examples illustrate, in so far as the trajectories pursued under democratic governments have had limited success in effecting pro-poor social change. Indeed the pursuit of pro-market policies has led to de-industrialization and a failure to provide the necessary jobs to make a significant dent in appallingly high levels of unemployment. They are equally right because implementation of neo-liberal policies in southern Africa, as elsewhere, delegitimizes government intervention in the economy, privileges the powerful, and widens rather than narrows the boundaries of social inequality. However, while such sweeping criticisms are valid, they are not particularly helpful unless they proffer realistic alternative strategies which liberation governments might have been able to follow in conditions of constrained choice.

As Marais has so cogently argued, suggestions by the ANC's economic policy managers that there was no alternative to the adoption of GEAR are nonsense. 'For the ANC's top leadership, the choices had become stark and binary: either they yield to the injunctions of corporate capital or expose the economy to the wrath of the markets (and put the democratic transition at risk).'[1] However, it was rather the case that the 'capitulation to neoliberal orthodoxy' reflected not only the movement's lack of previous investment in economic capability, but also the interests of conservative elements within the ANC which had increasingly been brought into the orbit of large-scale capital and which drew heavily on the views put forward by business. The outcome was a *de facto* alliance between the large conglomerates, the government, and developing pro-business interests within the ANC.

Other choices had been available. The RDP had envisaged Keynesian-like policies which proposed a more assertive role for the state in regulating large-scale corporations and investing heavily in social sectors such as housing and infrastructure in order to stimulate demand. It was by no means a given that the neo-liberal agenda had to be accepted lock, stock, and barrel. As Marais also stresses, while neo-liberalism has a solid core of principles, its practice has varied considerably from time to time and place to place. 'The idea of neo-liberalism as a pristine, ironclad blueprint is a fiction', even while neo-liberalism has become the primary mode of capital accumulation in the present era.[2] That choice was available is also implied by the successive variations on the theme of GEAR which the ANC government has introduced to tackle successive problems. Furthermore, as critics also propose, government policies have systematically favoured the interests of the conglomerates and large corporations at considerable cost to the interests of small business, widely viewed as the most likely vehicle to promote employment creation.

---

[1]   Hein Marais (2010), *South Africa Pushed to the Limit: The Political Economy of Change*, Cape Town: University of Cape Town Press, 106.
[2]   Ibid., 135.

Whatever the perspective adopted regarding what many view as the lamentable outcomes of the unholy alliance between business and government in both Namibia and South Africa, the contrast with what has occurred in Zimbabwe is stark. Rates of economic growth in both Namibia and South Africa may have been consistently disappointing. Nonetheless, low though it may have been, growth has been consistently positive, and importantly, has provided for the emplacement of social welfare regimes which have mitigated poverty. In Zimbabwe, the consequences of the collapse of the initial partnership between business and government have been extreme.

There is little need here to review once again the deterioration in relations between ZANU-PF and the private sector. What is more interesting is to turn to the views of the Zimbabwean crisis from the perspective of the theory of the NDR, as depicted by Thabo Mbeki in a treatise distributed to members of the ANC in July 2001. Although interesting for helping us to understand why Mbeki consistently favoured ZANU-PF during the years of his 'quiet diplomacy', it is also extremely valuable as a guide to what he conceived as appropriate relations with business.[3]

Mbeki's starting point was to congratulate ZANU-PF on the 'successful conclusion' of the first phase of the NDR, that being 'the struggle for liberation from foreign and white minority rule', even though the issues of 'white property rights and the relative autonomy of the state administration' might not have been fully resolved.[4] Thereafter, the tasks of the second stage were economic and political. In contrast to earlier decades when it might have been possible 'to mobilize the disciplined socialist and anti-imperialist forces...to act as a counterweight to the developed capitalist countries',[5] ZANU-PF was constrained by highly adverse 'objective circumstances brought about by the processes of globalization'.[6] Even so, it had been charged with bridging the disparities between the formerly colonized and the former colonizers in terms of wealth, income, and opportunity and deracializing the patterns of ownership of productive property. In practice, however, it had failed dismally. Poverty had worsened, there had been no significant narrowing of the gap between black and white, and the economy had contracted. Meanwhile, corruption within the civil service had contributed to ZANU-PF's alienation from the masses, leading to the emergence of the MDC, which Mbeki projected as a multi-class and multi-sector protest movement.

Mbeki identified an excessive reliance on the public sector as the primary cause of the crisis enveloping Zimbabwe. The private sector had contributed to the battle against poverty in so far as it had provided jobs during years of economic expansion, yet on the whole it had failed to improve real wages and salaries. Meanwhile, the 'sunset clauses' in the constitution had imposed 'a virtual freeze on any land redistribution, to keep the most productive land in the hands of white landowners', and to ensure the provision of job security, protected benefits and pensions schemes for Rhodesia's civil servants. Thus it was that the state (assisted by donors) had taken upon itself the leading role in

[3]   Thabo Mbeki (2001),'How will Zimbabwe defeat its enemies? A discussion document', circulated to members of the ANC as part of a larger document.
[4]   Ibid., 370.
[5]   Ibid., 388.
[6]   Ibid., 371.

narrowing the gap between black and white, and in promoting development via heavy expenditure on education, health, and social services combined with price controls on basic necessities and the subsidization of public enterprises. As a result of sluggish growth, the state maintained a complex system of controls 'which increased the cost of doing business in Zimbabwe and acted as a disincentive to investors'. Ultimately, this project proved unaffordable. The state ran up a high deficit, it was forced to cut back on social services even while employment declined, and the downward spiral forced Zimbabwe to turn for assistance to the IMF. Overall, the 'party of the revolution' had misunderstood the laws of supply and demand, and had not moved beyond the idea that 'the major and sole economic task of the national democratic state is the redistribution of wealth'. The Zimbabwean state should rather be committed to building a growing economy to provide the material base necessary for meeting the needs of the people.[7]

It was here that Mbeki turned to the relationship with white settler capital. Zimbabwe's remained a capitalist economy largely owned and dominated by a white minority, yet ZANU-PF should not have treated 'white capitalists as enemies of the national democratic revolution and state'. It was not the role of the national democratic state to 'punish these white capitalists by stripping them of their wealth, as much as possible, and to distribute this wealth among the formerly colonized', for this would lead to economic collapse. Rather, there was need for pragmatism.

The reality that the party of revolution has to contend with is that capital in general (including 'white capital' in Zimbabwe) is central to economic growth and development. Accordingly, the national democratic state has to treat capital as a social partner in the reconstruction and development of Zimbabwe, while recognizing the fact that the relationship between state and capital will, to some extent, be characterized by the existence of contradictions between them.[8]

The Zimbabwean state – which had just dispossessed farmers under its fast track land reform and alienated industrialists as social partners – should therefore re-examine its approach in order to take the correct decisions that would lead to economic recovery. This meant the adoption of 'correct positions' regarding growth, or, as Moore puts it, 'neo-liberal economic policies'.[9]

Mbeki proceeded to make it clear that while ZANU-PF may have lost popular support and alienated whites, it remained the vehicle of revolution. The MDC, he implied, was backed by those with less than noble motives and was in essence a product of reaction, and thus could not be trusted to take the NDR forward. It was therefore ZANU-PF's historic task to correct its errors and not only to win back the support of the masses but to convince those whites not hopelessly lost to the legacy of colonialism that, objectively, 'it was only the national democratic revolution than can serve their interests'.[10]

What is fascinating is how Mbeki attributed the decline in the fortunes of ZANU-PF to the atrophy of its structures as it had gained access to positions of 'employment, resources and authority', and its dispensation of patronage.

---

[7] Ibid., 375–80.
[8] Ibid., 380.
[9] David Moore (2010), 'A decade of disquieting diplomacy: South Africa, Zimbabwe and the ideology of the National Democratic Revolution, 1999–2009', *History Compass*, 8: 8, 752–67.
[10] Mbeki, op. cit., 393.

ZANU-PF had come to rely on the state machinery to guarantee the support of the masses of the people. Put crudely, the party of revolution sought to use the fact of its being the ruling party to use public resources to buy the allegiance of the masses of the people. It sought to use these resources to bribe the people to support its cause. This occurred in a situation in which objectively these bribes were unaffordable.[11]

This had resulted in the party's resort to violence and its assaults upon the rule of law. ZANU-PF had abandoned one of its most fundamental tasks: the construction of a genuinely popular democracy. It therefore had no choice but to engage in new thinking to produce new solutions, and to launch a recovery programme which would bring 'social partners together, encompassing government, business, labour and civil society'.[12]

Mbeki was proposing the 'objective' need for NLM governments to partner with business to achieve growth under capitalist conditions. However, what he did not explore was whether there was any inherent connection between a failure of post-liberation governments to maintain partnership with business and their decline into patronage and repression.

4. *As extension of liberation movements' control over the state machinery grew, and as party activities extended into the economy via parastatals and party-aligned companies, approaching limits to growth were allied to an erosion of party commitments to constitutionalism and democracy.*

Taylor's notion of 'reform coalitions' is in essence that of liberal pluralism, with 'balance' between diverse interests in society, in this case business and the state, being productive of virtuous outcomes. In this it differs from 'developmental state theory' in that the latter prioritizes the role of a suitably capable state in 'disciplining' capital in order to promote and shape growth. Inevitably, liberation movements were to be more attracted to the latter than to a strategy which allowed capital unfettered freedom. Indeed, notions of the 'developmental state' flowed easily from the vanguard role envisaged by the party-controlled state of the NDR. However, there was always likely to be a potential contradiction between the 'party state' and the 'developmental state'.

Incoming liberation movement governments were understandably concerned to secure control of states hitherto run by white minorities. The new state machineries they envisaged would be both demographically representative and capable of internal restructuring to ensure that they served the needs of marginalized black majorities. Such states would also be democratic and accountable, although the liberation movements also envisaged that these states would be answerable to the party. However, the outcome was to prove an unhappy mix. First, emphasis upon political loyalty and transformation served to undermine state capability; second, the party state was to become a significant vehicle of class interests; third, the party state constituted a threat to constitutionalism and democracy; and fourth, the party state compromised capacity for economic management.

Under late settler colonialism, the state had been subordinated to party. Respect for the Westminster heritage provided considerable protection for the

---

[11] Ibid., 383.
[12] Ibid., 395.

notion of a civil service independent of the ruling party in Rhodesia, yet from the moment that the bureaucracy accepted unilateral independence and revolt against the British Crown, it *de facto* threw in its lot with Smith and the RF. In South Africa and Namibia, the relative independence of the state machinery under the United Party was systematically eroded by NP discrimination in favour of Afrikaners and party loyalists after 1948. These were the states which the successor liberation movements were charged to renew and reform, both by historical circumstance and by their ideologies of transformation, notwithstanding their commitments to racial reconciliation and their recognition of continuing reliance upon white expertise for at least an initial period. But could old-order white civil servants be trusted to obey the new black governments?

Caution, if not outright distrust of inherited state machineries prompted deployment of those deemed loyal to the new ruling parties to high positions within the civil service, a policy which steadily percolated down through state structures. Cadre deployment, whether explicit as under the ANC or implicit under ZANU-PF and SWAPO, overlapped significantly with positive discrimination in favour of appointments guided by race and ethnicity. Commonly, the ceaseless search for trust and loyalty trumped the virtues of skill and experience, despite the lack of appropriately educated and trained recruits amongst black populations which had been systematically disadvantaged by racially skewed educational systems. To be sure, the outcome was uneven. A concentration of skills in key areas, such as the Treasuries and tax collection services in South Africa and Namibia, have allowed for the consolidation of islands of high competence amongst a wider sea of lower levels of efficiency. Yet overall, as Karl von Holdt has illustrated with regard to the downward spiral of the South African public hospital system since 1994, the combination of emphasis upon trust, affirmative action, and ambivalence towards skills translates into not only dysfunction but a culture of defensiveness about performance and deference to superiors, as well as an orientation towards administrative (and budgetary) procedures more concerned with formal appearance than with substance.[13] Yet it was not only in the civil sphere that emphasis upon political loyalty became paramount. In Zimbabwe, particularly, the military was to become deeply politicized as ZANU-PF searched for security in the face of external threat from apartheid South Africa and ZAPU's hold on political loyalties in Matabeleland.

Transformation policies easily lent themselves to an elision of race and class, with the 'general' interests of blacks translating themselves into the more particular interests of the emergent black middle classes. Affirmative action in the civil service, parastatals, and public institutions provided for expansion of hitherto small middle classes amongst blacks. Black empowerment and indigenization policies applied to private sectors, justified by reference to inequities of ownership patterns and the past impermeability of hostile managerial cultures to black entry, prompted defensive strategies from private capital which combined the search for alliances with party-connected elites with a blackening of middle management. Likewise, continuing white

---

[13] Karl von Holdt (2010), 'The South African post-apartheid bureaucratic state: Inner workings, contradictory rationales and the developmental state', in O. Edigheji (ed.), *Constructing a Democratic Developmental State in South Africa: Potential and Challenges*, Cape Town: HSRC Press, 241–60.

domination of agriculture and highly unequal land ownership patterns provided a resource which spoke readily to African nationalist settlement, and which could be kept in reserve or employed for popular mobilization according to political need. However, as the land seizures in Zimbabwe illustrate, the benefits of race-justified policies were likely to flow disproportionately to party-connected elites. The gospel of the NDR, formally (and formerly) committed to providing a foundation for socialism, readily appropriates black embourgeoisement as the embodiment of its historical mission under conditions of late capitalism.

The primacy of party and its symbiotic interaction with the interests of party elites easily translates into an assault upon constitutionalism and democracy. Paul Hoffman stresses that a society which has the necessary political will and capacity to exact accountability from those in charge is one in which constitutional rule obtains. Constitutionalism allows 'people power' and democracy to flourish, for societies in which elites manage to obscure their actions is one in which private interest becomes the proxy for the public good. However, in southern Africa, the commitment of liberation movements to 'transformation' predisposes them to deliberate avoidance of accountability. The role of the party as the vehicle of liberation serves as justification for their defiance or distortion of the constitution in the supposed interests of the NDR, with the constitution often being depicted as unduly protective of minority rights. What started off as the people's liberation struggle for freedom transmogrifies into party elites' struggle for power, privilege, and resources, at the cost of democracy and human rights.[14]

Their legacy as liberators predisposes NLMs to disavow the contribution of other popular forces to the struggle for democracy, to render them subordinate to the party, and to identify dissent and opposition as illegitimate and disloyal. In Zimbabwe, the white settlers, embraced as citizens at independence, were soon dismissed as aliens and 'Rhodesians' who had rejected the hand of friendship offered to them. Regrettably, of course, too many of them fulfilled the stereotype, although this should have had no implications for their rights as citizens; yet in turn, the MDC was regularly denounced as un-Zimbabwean, as traitorous, as the tool of the white farmers, and as in league with the British and the West. In a chilling echo of the Khmer Rouge, Didymus Mutasa, ZANU-PF's then organizational Secretary, once declared in regard to a country of twelve million people, 'We would be better off with only six million people, with our own people who support the liberation struggle'.[15] It was a small step to the militarization of power in the name of liberation.

In Namibia, SWAPO's reluctance to 'break down the wall of silence' with regard to its past treatment (and torture) of internal dissidents has continued, in defiance of the latter's wish for their maltreatment to be recognized. Not surprisingly, Sam Nujoma was to echo Mugabe's rejection of NEPAD's 'good governance' provisions as colonially inspired.[16] In South Africa, the ANC's

14 Paul Hoffman (2011), 'Democracy and accountability: Quo vadis South Africa?' in John Daniel, Prishani Naidoo, Devan Pillay and Roger Southall (eds), *New South African Review 2: New Paths, Old Compromises?* Johannesburg: Wits University Press, 83–99.
15 *Sunday Times*, 1 September 2002.
16 Roger Southall (2003), 'Democracy in southern Africa: Moving beyond a difficult legacy', *Review of African Political Economy*, 30: 96, 255–72.

efforts to block investigation of the 1998 arms deals undermined the independence of parliamentary committees, eroded the integrity of state institutions charged with rendering government accountable, collapsed the Scorpions and, by a tortuous route, led to the election of a President whose prosecution for corruption could well have seen him jailed.

Challenges to constitutionalism also represent a threat to growth and development. The rule of law provides predictability and security for domestic investment and helps attract foreign capital. Given the limited capacity of governments for the constructive investment of public funds, the encouragement of private investment harnessed to official objectives appears necessary for the creation of jobs and provision of expanded social services. In turn, the protection of property rights (according to constitutional constraints) is central to the maintenance of the rule of law. Of course, the sanctity of property rights as first-order rights is often disputed, yet none of the three constitutions at issue here regarded property rights as absolute. All were bound by public interest provisions, subject to compulsory acquisition being in accord with due process and payment of appropriate financial compensation. Nonetheless, it has proved easy enough for liberation movements to ignore constitutional niceties. In Zimbabwe, ZANU-PF collaborated happily with white commercial farmers and alienated donors who were offering (limited) funding to promote the redistribution of land during the 1980s and 1990s. But ZANU-PF resorted to arbitrary seizure of white farms when prompted by the war veterans' challenge to party authority. The safeguards offered to property rights in the constitution were identified as merely protections of unjust white interest. The right to 'adequate compensation' was eroded by changes to the law, delayed payment, inflation, and defiance of court judgements. Ultimately, when the SADC Tribunal declared the land seizures illegal, ZANU-PF prevailed upon fellow governments to dissolve it. In Namibia and South Africa, both countries where land reform policy has stalled due far more to policy implementation failures than to lack of money, land claims vie with populist assertions that whites have 'stolen' the land to promote insecurity and an accompanying lack of investment. Ironically, too, latent hostility to white farmers in policy circles has combined with neo-liberal reduction of protections of agriculture to bring about a reduction in their number and an increase in the average size of commercial farms. These in turn are more likely to be owned by large-scale financial interests and multi-national companies whose vast power may well increase their capacity to resist far-reaching land reform.

Finally, the party-state severely compromises the capacity for economic management. The more the party gains control over the state, the more party interests and concerns are likely to impinge upon relationships with business.

The irony has been noted in Zimbabwe, where there was initially convergence between the business sector (including commercial farming) and the government around the desirability of economic liberalization. However, political interests within ZANU-PF (favouring cheap imports of consumer goods) worked to overcome the concerns of local manufacturers when the latter found themselves too abruptly exposed to international competition. This led to disastrous results for the survival of firms and employment levels across a wide swathe of Zimbabwean industry. Their failure was merely the preliminary to the pursuit of a land reform strategy under which the interests of the established commercial sector were abruptly swamped by those of a ruling party in crisis.

In both Namibia and South Africa, the liberation governments emphasize the important role to be played by parastatals in promoting the integrated development of infrastructure, but the accompanying commitment to using them as vehicles for black empowerment and employment appears to compromise their efficiency, and to increase markedly the costs for private capital of doing business. The ANC's incestuous relationship with ESCOM, and the reliance of key factions within both the ANC and SWAPO on securing state tenders, serve simultaneously to impede delivery of services and to undermine faith in the notion of the 'developmental state'.

In all three countries, long-term productive relationships between business and state are eroded by the growth of corruption and tenderpreneurship. The resulting tendency towards the criminalization of the state leads not only towards a declining accountability of both the public and private sectors in economic affairs, but to the growth of crony capitalism. In Zimbabwe, ZANU-PF's control of state diamond market agencies and the military is diverting the public investment potential of profits from the Marange diamond fields into private pockets. An unintended result is that while governments and their allies espouse the need for the developmental state, corruption in business-state relationships lends greater credence to business ideologies which argue against any form of direct state intervention.

5. *The particular combinations of the party state and liberal economics against the inheritance of racially skewed inequalities and black marginalization has led to economic and political crisis, now greatly magnified by the crisis of international capitalist economy.*

The inheritances of profound inequality and the racialized distribution of economic power were always going to narrow the scope for economic choices. In these circumstances, balanced business-state relations, suitably leavened by the rights and interests of labour, were the best way forward for producing the necessary growth to ease resistance to deracialization, to provide leeway for redistribution, to build mutuality of interests, and to underpin the racial bargains upon which productive growth heavily depended in order to legitimize the state as the agent of development. But 'balanced' BSRs were undermined by the dual effects of the growth of the party state, which tends to aggrandize the latter, and pressures from big business for neo-liberalism, which seeks to privilege capital and shrink the state. The outcome has been mounting crisis. However, we need to distinguish, once again, between Zimbabwe, on the one hand, and Namibia and South Africa.

In Zimbabwe, the crisis is extreme. The divisions between the different sectors of business, exacerbated by their differential capacity to respond to the challenges of the opening up of the post-UDI economy to external competition, weakened collective leverage relative to a party state which grew in reach and confidence and which was ultimately indifferent to the interests of manufacturing. The drastic decline in levels of production, employment and, for the majority, livelihood opportunities during the 1990s was accompanied by the increasing authoritarianism of the state as it lost support. The political challenge to ZANU-PF hegemony in the 2000 election heralded a growing militarization of the party-state which has not only negated democracy but blocks resolution of the conjoined economic and political crisis. The outcome since 2008 has been an overwhelmingly dysfunctional coalition government followed by an election in 2013, which although supposedly conducted under reformed conditions, delivered a heavily skewed result in favour of ZANU-PF. This reflects the facts that:

- The MDC's limited capacity to facilitate necessary reforms was countered by ZANU-PF's retention of control of the security forces and key economic ministries;
- The ambiguities of its situation disempowered the MDC as its leading figures sought to contain popular discontents amongst supporters and resolve their own internal differences while ZANU-PF claimed credit for relative economic improvements and blamed its coalition partner for continuing economic woes; even while
- After the 2013 election, ZANU-PF itself has been deeply divided along factional lines around the succession to the ailing Mugabe regime and the uncertain prospects for the party's future and individuals' political survival.

The MDC had hoped that the 2013 election would strengthen its position, even if it was again compelled to operate within a coalition with ZANU-PF. In the event, a toxic combination of the MDC's naivety and ZANU-PF's flouting of electoral reforms led to the latter routing its opposition. ZANU-PF had retained the loyalties of the party-aligned individuals whom it had appointed to state and public positions. True, such loyalties may dissipate if, in the wake of Mugabe's death, ZANU-PF's unity finally dissolves. Yet how much benefit would accrue to a hopelessly divided MDC, or any successor opposition formation, from a ZANU-PF meltdown remains deeply uncertain. Indeed, whoever rules, potential economic recovery, let alone pro-poor oriented development, would appear to be held hostage to two conflicting tendencies:

- On the one hand, dependence of macro-economic stabilization of the economy upon international loans, donor funding and foreign investments;
- On the other, ZANU-PF's drive for further 'indigenization' of multi-national corporations, which is ideologically justified in terms of empowerment of Zimbabweans, but is more driven by a scramble by the party-state elite to grab resources whilst they maintain their hold on the state.

Both tendencies point to the mortgaging of the state and economy to external interests: foreign donors, the IMF and World Bank, Western and South African corporations, and not least, incoming Chinese capital. The irony and tragedy of ZANU-PF rule, forged in the anti-imperialist struggle, is that is has collapsed the Zimbabwean economy to a state of acute neo-colonial dependence, where the prospects for recovery are now far more reliant upon external interests than they were at even the fraught moment of independence.

Both the ANC and SWAPO claim credit for, and should receive political due for their far more judicious husbandry of their economies. The transitional settlements provided the basis for partnerships between business and the state which have not been unproductive, having provided for consistent (albeit limited) growth and, importantly, for the considerable extension of welfare provisions. Yet the transitional economic bargains:

- were essentially between big business and key elements within government, rendering structural change away from the constraints imposed by the legacy of the MEC unlikely, and favouring admission by new political elites to existing economic power structures over changing the status quo;
- were initially accommodating to the interests of organized labour through the democratization of industrial relations systems, but systematically underplayed the interests of smaller business, including emergent black business, seriously limiting scope for the creation of jobs;
- facilitated an uncritical embrace of neo-liberal mantras by government, curtailing alternative options for more extensive redistribution, thus lessening inequalities and incurring avoidable job losses in the private sector as it sought to adjust to the abrupt opening up of the economy;
- enabled the far-reaching financialization of the economy, rendering it acutely exposed to short-term movements of international capital;
- led to the relative growth of the state sector as the principal provider of jobs and resources to politically connected elites, with resultant rising economic costs, notably increasing tax and debt burdens, inhibiting public investment levels and questionable efficiencies.

The limitations of the model has led to increasing strains, massively so within the ANC. Adoption of GEAR eroded the basis for a tripartism which could have rounded out the business-state relationship, and provided the backdrop to growing tensions within the Alliance. These were to culminate in the ousting of Mbeki and the rise of Zuma, whose presidency has provided increased cover for the predatory instincts of party-aligned elements with the correct political connections, alongside growing threats to constitutionalism and the rule of law. As the battle for resources within the party state at all levels has intensified, the discontents of the politically excluded have fuelled a growing factionalism. Malema's messianic championship of nationalization was but one expression of an attempt by those amongst the party elite disappointed by the material returns of the Zuma presidency to restructure the alliance between the ANC and business in the former's favour, and to consolidate the returns of tenderpreneurship by providing more resources for the state.

The nationalization debate unsettles 'white' business and frightens foreign investors; black business complains about its exclusion from white-dominated counsels; Malema's Zanuification of the political debate threatens a racial bargain already challenged by continuities in racial inequality; exorbitant remuneration for executives in both the state and business provoke an angry response from organized labour; and the township poor, ambivalent about an ANC which has erected an extensive system of social grants but whose capacity for 'delivery' is deeply compromised by predatory officials, resort to violent protest against authority. The increasing contradictions of the ANC's situation result in increased dangers to constitutionalism and democracy.

Conclusion: The Slow Death of the Liberation Movements

What way forward, if any, for the liberation movements of southern Africa?

6. *Inherent in the slow death of the liberation movements as we know them are the struggles of a more democratic political economy waiting to be born, provided it can surmount the dangers posed by the present global crisis of capitalism and its accompanying politics of extremism and division.*

Ruling is more difficult than opposing; triumph over the enemy poses new dilemmas; and the realities of governing expose the limitations of previously held world views. ZANU-PF, SWAPO, and the ANC were all played difficult hands by history. As movements, their radicalization had been cultivated by the intractability of the regimes they faced, yet having boxed their opponents to stalemate, they inherited relatively advanced economies. Notwithstanding these hugely skewed legacies, the raising of productive forces under settler capitalism had offered a potential for growth which was considerably in excess of non-settler former African colonies (or at least, those who failed to find oil). Yet, as we have seen, the difficulties of nurturing the development of these economies were to be compounded by the transformation of the liberation movements into party machines. The meltdown in Zimbabwe alongside the increasing evidence of the limitations to equalizing growth in Namibia and South Africa poses fundamental challenges to the NLMs which they are unlikely to surmount.

The ideology of the NDR sits uneasily with democracy and constitutionalism because ultimately it espouses the monopoly power of the liberation movement as the vehicle of social progress: history without end! Or as Jacob Zuma put it in regard to the ANC in May 2008, 'Even God expects us to rule this country...It is even blessed in Heaven. That is why we will rule until Jesus comes back.'[17] However, by promoting the party state, such ideology negates the political diversity and economic innovation which is unleashed by democracy. Economic crisis, accentuated by the increasing exposure of previously protected economies to global markets, enhances statist thinking, to the potential or actual detriment of private profit and the capacity of key sectors (notably manufacturing) to produce; likewise, to the capacity of the economy to attract foreign capital. Emphasis on political monopoly seeks to delegitimize dissent and to shut down alternatives. In turn, these complexities and strains awaken ideological contradictions and factional currents which have always been inherent in the liberation movement condition.

National liberation ideology may foreground political monopoly and the primacy of 'nation', yet the nationalist movements have also drawn heavily on Christianity, liberalism, and democracy. Hence follows their ambiguity towards their transitional settlements, welcoming democracy whilst espousing, in much ideology and practice, its contradiction. As the costs of political monopoly rise, opposition to dominant party elites increases both inside and outside ruling parties, threatening their capacity for continued domination. Within ZANU-PF today, increasing struggles occur between hardliners and moderates, with the latter more reconciled to a genuine sharing of power with the MDC and more accommodating to multi-national capital. In Namibia and South Africa, internal tensions – inherent in the popular alliances which underpin both

[17] IOL News, 5 May 2008, http://www.iol.co.za/news/politics/any-to-rule-until-jesus-comes-back-1.398843

343

SWAPO and the ANC – are encouraged by struggles for resources, the search for economic alternatives, internal protest against elites' domination, and demands for greater internal democracy. Within the ANC, the political practices of monopoly, such as the maintenance of limits on internal discussion around presidential succession, are blown apart by reality, while political discipline is undermined by factionalism and policy differences. The resulting vacuum is filled by the rise of social movements, alongside civil society, the courts, and the non-state media as the defenders of the constitution.

Thus the present era is one of a rethinking of party ideologies and a looming realignment of forces, with little coherent political alternative on offer to Fukuyama's triumph of liberal democracy, albeit amplified by mounting pressures for 'democratic deepening' and a participatory democracy in constant debate with constitutionalism. Simultaneously, changes in thinking caused by the current global crisis offer the opportunity for changes in how the business-government relationship is conceived and how economies should be restructured to meet the needs of their populations. Yet global crisis offers the potential for reaction as well as renewal, and in southern Africa the strains of peripheralized development may reinforce divisions between rulers and ruled, elites and masses, races and ethnic groupings, and insiders and outsiders. Nonetheless, with the barrenness of neo-liberalism increasingly exposed, capitalism is being forced – if it does not want to be surpassed – to reinvent itself to allow for greater global justice as well as local equalities, for social inclusion and social solidarity, and for sustainable ecology.

There is no shortage of prescriptions for constructive change. In South Africa, Sampie Terreblanche has called for the governing elite to abandon the free market ideology of the Anglo-American capitalist world in favour of 'a well balanced, social democratic and humane system of democratic capitalism', this involving a trade-off between efficiency and equality.[18] Similarly, Seekings and Nattrass have argued for a social accord whereby the search of business for profit and organized labour for higher wages would be broadened to include the interests of 'outsiders', this requiring trade unions to agree to labour market reforms which would encourage the growth of labour-intensive firms and sectors.[19] Recently, the National Planning Commission has endorsed a developmental state which '...through careful alliances, clear purpose and by leveraging its resource and regulatory capacity, can align market outcomes with development needs'. The new growth path would envisage the state facilitating an extensive social dialogue,[20] a call now widely regarded amidst a global crisis which has seen the economy lose a million jobs. In short, there is growing appreciation that the prospects for better and more inclusive growth revolve around notions of social partnership and class compromise. But does the post-liberation ANC exhibit the capacity for embracing and implementing such a programme?

In their consideration of 'social democracy in the global periphery', Richard Sandbrook and his associates note how social democratic regimes can provide

---

[18] Sampie Terreblanche (2002), *A History of Inequality in South Africa 1652–2002*, Pietermaritzburg: University of Natal Press, 460–70.

[19] Jeremy Seekings and Nicoli Nattrass (2005), *Class, Race and Inequality in South Africa*, Pietermaritzburg: University of KwaZulu-Natal Press, 388–92.

[20] Republic of South Africa (2010), 'The new growth path: The framework', para. 34.

an antidote to the destructive social consequences of neo-liberalism. 'Not only can their inclusive and well-organized democratic institutions mediate distributional conflicts, but economic security, social cohesions, and equality are also enhanced through such redistributive mechanisms as land reform, job creation, progressive taxation, labour-market regulation, social insurance, and welfare provisions.'[21] However, they also note that the route to social democracy is not immediately evident. Even in Western Europe, where social democracy was originally exemplified, successive waves of economic crisis have forced social democratic parties to drop any theoretical commitment to socialism, and to accept that their role is essentially remedial of capitalism. They have become more market friendly; they have reinterpreted social equality as involving moves towards the equality of opportunity relative to equality of outcome through redistribution; and they have loosened their links to organized labour in an effort to appeal to middle-class voters.[22] Socio-economic reform, they argue, can be achieved without adverse economic repercussions, provided that a well organized party strongly based in the middle and working classes delineates the limits of reform.

Sandbrook and his associates argue that social democratic traditions are entrenched in quite a number of developing countries. However, they also observe that the difficulties of promoting social democracy in the global periphery are likely to be considerably greater than they have been in Europe.

First, if the essence of social democracy is class compromise, then social democratic regimes in the periphery are likely to face major obstacles in their attempts to promote growth and equity through industrial and social policies. These will include the heavy dependence of peripheral countries upon a handful of industrial economies for markets, investments, and imports, along with the global rules set by international financial institutions which work to the disadvantage of the South.[23]

Second, whereas in Europe social democracy built upon an historical sequencing of industrialization, democratization, and social citizenship, in the contemporary South these phases overlap. This requires social democratic regimes to pursue productive class compromises before a productive capitalism has generated a strong material base and to do so in the context of a heterogeneous and differentiated class structure. The latter is often inclusive of economic elites which prosper by extracting rents, and organized labour co-exists with a large pool of labour which is rurally based or working in the informal sector. Competing demands made by capital, organized workers, middle classes, and the poor will make for more fragile social pacts, meaning that often the least organized will remain marginalized. Meanwhile, globalization has systematically strengthened the position of capital, narrowing the margins wherein social democratic governments can secure class compromise.[24]

Consequently, third, 'a strong and capable state is necessary. *Social democracy in the periphery essentially involves a social-democratic developmental state*'

---

[21] Richard Sandbrook, Marc Edelman, Patrick Heller and Judith Teichman (2007), *Social Democracy in the Global Periphery: Origins, Challenges, Prospects*, Cambridge: Cambridge University Press, 6.

[22] Ibid., 14–15.

[23] Ibid., 18–19.

[24] Ibid., 19–22.

(their italics). Whilst admitting that traditionally developmental states have been authoritarian or semi-authoritarian, they quote Chalmers Johnson as arguing that 'there is no inherent reason why developmental states cannot be democratic – provided that the democracy in question is consolidated and not "underinstitutionalised".' Indeed, democracy and a developmental state may reinforce each other in a virtuous circle. Democratic demands can motivate elites to act developmentally; growth and equity may consolidate democratic institutions; and democratic institutions may enhance the autonomy of bureaucratic and political elites (although the latter will need to be 'inclusively embedded' in society).[25]

However, they also warn of the dangers of populism and corporatism which, often confused with social democracy, involve different modes of incorporating the masses into political life. Both types of regime are similar to social democracy in that they entail an interventionist state and leaders who champion the demands of at least some subordinate groups. Meanwhile, populism involves a personalistic relationship between leaders and masses (often versed in terms of the interests of 'the people' in opposition to elites); and populists depend heavily on clientelism, rather than policy appeals, for support among the urban poor, peasants and workers:

> Their parties therefore resemble political machines that service extensive patron-client networks. Social-democratic regimes, in contrast, typically involve political movements that mobilize class support on a programmatic basis, depending less than populists on clientelism, personalities, or charismatic leaders. Social-democratic policies are more policy-oriented and institutionalized than populism; equally, they are more genuinely democratic, rights-conscious, and open to autonomous self-organization of constituent groups than state corporatism. There is a danger, however, that social-democratic movements will degenerate into populist-corporatism.[26]

What are the prospects for progress towards a 'social-democratic developmental state' in conditions where the liberation movements have indeed become 'political machines'? What prospects for South Africa under the ANC, for Namibia under SWAPO, and for Zimbabwe under any governing arrangement where ZANU-PF retains significant power?

Any government would be pushed to maintain reasonable growth rates and even the lamentably low level of current employment amidst the current global crisis. Yet after nearly twenty years in power, the contemporary ANC, as core of a governing alliance, seems less and less capable of addressing South Africa's enormous challenges.

First, the ANC, which has always prided itself on being a broad church, is today increasingly divided along lines of interest and faction. The Zuma presidency has opened the door wide to massive levels of tenderpreneurship which the government shows only half-hearted commitment to tackle. Access to the party state is viewed as the primary route to wealth by an ANC constituency which has become hugely swelled by opportunistic elements, and by those who see party membership as the surest way out of poverty and disadvantage. The ousting of Mbeki via mobilization of support for Zuma within party structures

[25] Ibid., 23.
[26] Ibid., 28–29.

from bottom to top has provided a template for resource-driven factionalism by those excluded from current positions of party and power, as the ANC has become victim to constant battles around leadership succession. Branches, regions, provincial and national organs are torn apart by constant politicking between in-groups and out-groups; intra-party alliances cohere and dissolve according to short-term political interest; and under Zuma, the ANC has become increasingly subject to ethnically fissiparous tendencies.

Second, tensions within the Alliance are widening. COSATU and the SACP, marginalized under Mandela and Mbeki, aligned behind Zuma and triumphed at Polokwane, yet they are now deeply divided. The SACP, under Blade Nzimande, has suppressed internal dissent and remained firmly in the Zuma camp, its influence extending to senior levels amongst COSATU affiliates. Yet many within COSATU have become disillusioned with the limited gains offered by Zuma's presidency. Some bemoan the SACP's inability to provide ideological leadership; SACP bemoans COSATU's ideological limitations and deviations. Within COSATU, the weight of public sector unions progressively constrains government capacity to control and discipline public employees and to introduce much-needed reforms within the public service. COSATU, meanwhile, espouses policy positions which inhibit consideration of labour regime reforms which might encourage job creation, widening the gap between its own members and those of the informally employed. For its part, the ANC fears a rupture and the federation's deserting to form a South African version of the MDC. COSATU, complains former Mineworkers' Union leader Gwede Mantashe, now adopts many stances on major issues which are similar to those of the parties in opposition.[27]

Third, the growth of a black middle class has been incestuously tied to the party state. The early days of BEE facilitated an alliance between large-scale capital and leading elements within the ANC and for the partial deracialization of the apex of the class structure. Yet BEE simultaneously facilitated a rapid expansion of crony capitalism constructed around 'political connectivity'. Large-scale capital blurred the alliance with corruption, the arms deal the epitome of a connection which was significantly underpinned by direct funding to the ruling party. Ironically, much implementation of BEE left black business out of the picture through policies which favoured large-scale capital, although simultaneously managing to render black businesses heavily dependent upon allocation of government and parastatal contracts. Meanwhile, business complains of its distance from government while numerous doubts attend the capacity of the government to reassemble the 'reform coalition' that characterized the early years of ANC rule.

Fourth, the ANC continues to look wedded to policies which undermine the capacity of the state to function efficiently and effectively and to transform South Africa into a 'social democratic developmental state'. Two dimensions, in particular, systematically undermine state capacity. First, the continuing commitment to 'cadre deployment' prioritizes political loyalty over ability, while simultaneously eroding levels of accountability to constitutional authority, citizens, and communities. Second, the ANC presides over a public educational system that is simply not working and which is severely constraining the supply

---

[27] *Sunday Independent*, 25 September 2011.

of skills needed for the economy. Public expenditure remains remarkably high, but outcomes are declining. The pass rate for final year at high school dropped consecutively for five succeeding years, from 73 percent in 2003 to 61 percent in 2009, while the entry of underprepared students into higher educational institutions has led to a dismally low completion rate (only 15 per cent of students who entered education in 2002 graduated over the next five years). Although significant efforts have been made to address racial inequalities, educational achievement continues to reflect the apartheid racial hierarchy. Those members of the black elite who can afford it, now send their children to private schools; notoriously, members of the South African Democratic Teachers' Union (SADTU) who work in township schools scramble to send their children to the deracialized high schools in white suburbs; and the children of the black poor, urban and rural, experience a dismal educational experience which condemns them to a life of limited literacy and even lower opportunity. Part of the problem stems from policy mistakes (such as the closure of many teacher training colleges after 1994); and some from social issues (the relative decline in prestige and pay of the teaching profession). However, there is a growing consensus that the ANC is frightened to tackle the stranglehold on public schools wielded by SADTU, whose short-sighted trade union commitments have virtually extinguished any appropriate commitment to teacher professionalism.

Finally, the ANC has become increasingly distant from its constituency. The relationship between the ANC and the mass of poor South Africans remains a complex one. On the one hand, the ANC is presently assured of repeat electoral victories. On the other, recent years have been characterized by highly publicized protest actions at provincial and local levels, choreographed as protests against 'delivery'. The latter commonly involve violence against state officials, police and public property, and reflect feelings of relative deprivation within a highly unequal, consumerist society. Above all, however, they reflect resentment at political office bearers and public servants who are appointments or beneficiaries of the ANC. Thus voting and protest feature as alternative and complementary strategies of engagement with the ruling party. Meanwhile the attachment of ANC voters to their party grows weaker as liberation recedes and as the average age of voters gets younger.

According to Moeletsi Mbeki, the ANC is moving rapidly towards its nadir. Its economic policies are failing; the electorate increasingly recognizes that it cannot deliver; it is unable to cope with the massive demands being made upon it; and, above all, ANC politicians themselves (perhaps in anticipation of Jesus's second coming) are scrambling to line their pockets.[28] Far from constructing a developmental state, the ANC's South Africa is facing the prospect of long-term decline. Hence, Mbeki argues, the ANC is facing a crisis of survival which it can only surmount by abandoning an ideology of national liberation which is wholly unsuited to grappling with the profound complexities of a crisis-ridden capitalist world. Whether the party proves able to meet these challenges will depend upon its capacity to accommodate change rather than lapse into the populist authoritarianism already canvassed by Zuma in the lead up to Polokwane and by Malema in his own bid for influence.

---

[28] *Business Report*, 26 September 2011.

So what of the future for SWAPO and ZANU-PF? Of the former, there is little to be said, save that it appears to suffer from virtually all the same pathologies as does the ANC, although its survival prospects may well be better simply because it presides over a far less complex society, and is better able to maintain its political domination through the intertwined structures of party and government. Given the extent of its mineral wealth, perhaps to be supplemented by revenues deriving from recent discoveries of oil, the rents demanded by its political elite from large-scale capital are likely to be regarded as highly tolerable in return for guarantees of secure investment and political stability. Continued elite domination is also likely to be underwritten by the peculiar patterns of Namibia's demographic geography. Reflecting both historical patterns of black marginalization alongside those imposed by a harsh, dry, and unforgiving ecology, these render political coordination of social protest against SWAPO rule particularly difficult – and in any case, porous borders with South Africa and oil-rich Angola are likely to tempt away those whose entrepreneurial ambitions are thwarted by conditions at home while providing ample opportunities for escape for individuals fleeing political repression. Yet this is not to say that SWAPO will remain untouched by any meltdown within the ANC. The histories of the two parties are so closely intertwined that factionalism may find it easy to cross borders; the passing of the liberation generation will lead to challenges to leadership from impatient youth below; networking via modern communications will establish linkages with South African and global social movements, notably around threats posed to environmental security; and any breach between COSATU and ANC could well be replicated between NUNW and SWAPO.

Finally, it is fitting that a text so heavily burdened with the disasters inflicted upon Zimbabwe should end with consideration of the fate and deserts of ZANU-PF. It has been protected from its own people for well over a decade by South Africa and its liberation movement allies in SADC, yet even they are now wearying of a regime which has brought so many problems and disrepute to the region. The passing of Mugabe will be marked with due pomp and ceremony, yet underlying the lamentations will be immense relief that the history of Zimbabwe can start anew. Given the manner that ZANU-PF loyalists have entrenched themselves in positions of state and power, there will be regional concerns to contain turmoil and popular calls for revenge, with a premium placed on maintenance of some modicum of political stability. As argued above, this could well result in the emplacement of a further MDC-ZANU-PF coalition, albeit with the former now substantially strengthened by international support and far greater acceptance within the region. Divisions between moderates and hardliners within ZANU-PF might well see the former decamp into some viable relationship with the MDC, although any such connection will have to be founded upon a broad acceptance by the latter of many of the new patterns of class and privilege brought about by ZANU-PF hegemony. Above all, Zimbabwe will need the making of a new social contract between its ruling elite and its people as well as national healing respectful of popular concerns, interests, and bitter experiences. In this, it may well look to the valuable experience provided by South Africa during 1990–94, and the subsequent appointment of the Truth and Reconciliation Commission. Who knows, a concerted move back to constitutional democracy in Zimbabwe may provide a valuable corrective to ANC-inspired assaults upon constitutionalism and democracy in South Africa.

Construction of a 'developmental state' may well prove a step too far for a Zimbabwe reduced to neo-colonial penury and dependence upon inflows of international capital and aid for economic recovery. The MDC has been subject to much criticism for its alleged weaknesses and the compromises it has made since going into forced coalition with ZANU-PF. However, without them, writes Peta Thorneycroft, one of the country's foremost journalists, a country 'just hanging together...would have completely fallen apart'.[29]

Social democracies, it is said, are not born, but are made.[30] Last words then to MDC Secretary-General and Minister of Finance in the coalition government, Tendai Biti:

> I have learnt that the secret of good governance is not constitutions, it's not about the army or police, it is about love and caring.[31]

We may choose to reply that constitutionalism is fundamental to good government; but none will dispute that Zimbabwe needs a government constructed around the obligations of loving and caring. Sadly, notwithstanding the MDC's best intentions, the legacy it may inherit makes it difficult to see that happening.

[29] *Sunday Independent,* 25 September 2011.
[30] Sandbrook et al., op. cit., 22.
[31] *Sunday Independent,* 25 September 2011.

SELECT BIBLIOGRAPHY

Abrahamsen, Rita (2003), 'African studies and the postcolonial challenge', *African Affairs*, 102: 407, 189–210.

Adam, Heribert (1972), *Modernizing Racial Domination: The Dynamics of South African Politics*, Berkeley CA: University of California Press.

African Development Bank (2011), *The Middle of the Pyramid: Dynamics of the Middle Class in Africa*.

African National Congress (ANC) (1998), 'The state, property relations and social transformation', *Umrabulo*, 5: 3. http://amandlandawonye.wikispaces.com/1998.ANC

—— (2005), National General Council, 'Development and underdevelopment', NGC discussion document.

—— (2007), 'Revolutionary morality: The ANC and business', discussion document, February.

—— (2012) 'Organisational renewal: Building the ANC as a movement for transformation and a strategic centre of power', a discussion document towards the National Policy Conference, Version 9, released on 10 April.

—— (2012), 'The second transition? Building a national democratic society and the balance of forces in 2012', a discussion document towards the National Policy Conference, Version 7.0 as amended by the Special NEC, 27 February.

Alexander, Peter (2000), 'Zimbabwean workers, the MDC and the 2000 election', *Review of African Political Economy*, 85, 385–406.

Aliber, Michael and Reuben Mokoena (2004), 'The land question in contemporary South Africa', in John Daniel, Adam Habib and Roger Southall (eds), *State of the Nation 2003–2004*, Cape Town: HSRC Press, 330–46.

Amin, Samir (1990), 'The social movements in the periphery: An end to liberation?' in Samir Amin, Giovanni Arrighi, Andre Gunder Frank and Immanuel Wallerstein (eds), *Transforming the Revolution: Social Movements and the World System*, New York: Monthly Review Press, 96–138.

—— (1997) 'For a progressive and democratic new world order', conference paper, Afro-Asian Solidarity Conference, Cairo, April.

Amnesty International (2000), *Zimbabwe: Terror Tactics in the Run up to Parliamentary Elections, June 2000*, London: Amnesty International.

Anglin, Douglas (1991), 'Namibian relations with South Africa: Post-independence prospects', in Larry Swatuk and Timothy Shaw (eds), *Prospects for Peace and Development in Southern Africa in the 1990s: Canadian and Comparative Perspectives*, Lanham NY: University of America Press, 93–114.

Apter, David (1995), *The Gold Coast in Transition*, Princeton: Princeton University Press.

Arrighi, Giovanni (1973), 'Labour supplies in historical perspective: A study of the proletarianization of the African peasantry in Rhodesia', in Giovanni Arrighi and John Saul, *Essays on the Political Economy of Africa*, New York and London: Monthly Review Press, 180–234.

Astrow, Andre (1983), *Zimbabwe: A Revolution That Lost Its Way?* London: Zed Press.

Atkinson, Doreen (2010), 'Breaking down barriers: Policy gaps and new options in South African land reform', in John Daniel, Prishani Naidoo, Devan Pillay and Roger Southall (eds), *New South African Review 2010: Development or Decline?* Johannesburg: Wits University Press, 364–82.

Badela, Mono and David Niddrie (1989), 'Restrictions on the media', http://www.sahistory.org.za/archive/restrictions-media

Baker, Colin (1982), 'Conducting the elections in Zimbabwe 1980', *Public Administration and Development*, 2, 45–58.

Ballard, Richard, Adam Habib, and Elke Zuern (2006), 'Introduction: From anti-apartheid to post-apartheid social movements', in Richard Ballard, Adam Habib and Imraan Valodia (eds), *Voices of Protest: Social Movements in Post-Apartheid South Africa*, Pietermaritzburg: University of KwaZulu-Natal Press, 1–22.

Bank, Leslie (2011), 'Bring back Kaiser Matanzima? Communal land, traditional leaders and the politics of nostalgia', in John Daniel, Prishani Naidoo, Devan Pillay and Roger Southall (eds), *New South Africa Review 2: New Paths, Old Compromises?* Johannesburg: Wits University Press, 118–41.

Basson, Adrian (2012), *Zuma Exposed*, Cape Town and Johannesburg: Jonathan Ball Publishers.

Bond, Patrick (2000), *Elite Transition: From Apartheid to Neoliberalism in South Africa*, Pietermaritzburg: University of Natal Press.

Bond, Patrick and Masimba Manyana (2003), *Zimbabwe's Plunge: Exhausted Nationalism, Neoliberalism and the Search for Social Justice*, Pietermaritzburg: University of KwaZulu-Natal Press.

Bonner, Philip (2011), Plenary presentation to the conference 'One Hundred Years of the ANC: Debating Liberation Histories and Democracy Today', 20–24 September.

Booysen, Susan (2011), *The African National Congress and the Regeneration of Political Power*, Johannesburg: Wits University Press.

Booysen, Susan and Grant Masterson (2009), 'South Africa', in Denis Kadima and Susan Booysen (eds), *Compendium of Elections in Southern Africa 1989–2009: 20 Years of Multiparty Democracy*, Johannesburg, Electoral Institute of Southern Africa, 387–460.

Booysen, Susan and Lucient Toulou (2009), 'Zimbabwe', in Denis Kadima and Susan Booysen (eds), *Compendium of Elections in Southern Africa 1989–2009: 20 Years of Multiparty Democracy*, Johannesburg: Electoral Institute of Southern Africa, 629–58.

Brett, Edward A. (1973), *Colonialism and Underdevelopment in East Africa: The Politics of Economic Change 1919–1939*, London: Heinemann.

Brummer, Stefaans, 'Texas oilman is at it again – now with Zuma', http://www. amabhungane.co.za/article/2012-02-17-texas-oilman-is-at-it-again-now–its-with-Zuma

Buhlungu, Sakhela (2010), *A Paradox of Victory: COSATU and the Democratic Transformation in South Africa*, Pietermaritzburg: University of KwaZulu-Natal Press.

Buhlungu, Sakhela, Roger Southall, and Edward Webster (2006), 'Conclusion:

COSATU and the democratic transformation of South Africa', in Sakhela Buhlungu (ed.), *Trade Unions and Democracy: COSATU Workers' Political Attitudes in South Africa*, Cape Town: HSRC Press, 199–218.

Butler, Anthony (2009), 'The ANC's national campaign of 2009: *Siyanqoba!*' in Roger Southall and John Daniel (eds), *Zunami! The 2009 South African Elections*, Johannesburg: Jacana Media, 85–113.

—— (2009), 'Considerations on the erosion of one-party dominance', *Representation: Journal of Representative Democracy*, 45: 2, 159–72.

—— (2010), 'Introduction: Money and politics', in Anthony Butler (ed.), *Paying for Politics: Party Funding and Political Change in South Africa and the Global South*, Auckland Park: Jacana, 1–19.

—— (2011) 'Born frees set to repeat patterns of prejudice', *Business Day*, 14 October.

Calland, Richard (2006), *Anatomy of South Africa: Who Holds the Power?* Cape Town: Zebra Press.

Calland, Richard and Chris Oxtoby (2010), 'Machiavelli meets the Constitution', in Daryl Glaser (ed.), *Mbeki and After: Reflections on the Legacy of Thabo Mbeki*, Johannesburg: Wits University Press, 71–104.

Callinicos, Alex (1981), *Southern Africa after Zimbabwe*, London: Pluto Press.

Callinicos, Luli (2004), *Oliver Tambo: Beyond the Engeli Mountains*, Claremont: David Philip.

Campbell, Horace (2003), *Reclaiming Zimbabwe: The Exhaustion of the Patriarchal Model of Liberation*, Cape Town: David Philip.

Cargill, Jenny (2010), *Trick or Treat: Rethinking Black Economic Empowerment*, Johannesburg: Jacana.

Catholic Commission for Justice and Peace in Zimbabwe (CCJP) (2000), *Crisis of Governance: A Report on Political Violence in Zimbabwe: Volume 2*, Harare: CCJP.

Caute, David (1983), *Under the Skin: The Death of White Rhodesia*, Evanston, IL: Northwestern University Press; London: Allen Lane.

Centre for Development Enterprise (CDE) (2005), *Land Reform in South Africa: A 21st Century Perspective*, Johannesburg: CDE.

Cheater, Andrea (1991), 'The University of Zimbabwe: University, national university, state university or party university?' *African Affairs*, XC, 189–205.

Cheeseman, Nic and Tendi Blessing-Miles (2010), 'Power-sharing in comparative perspective: The dynamics of unity government in Kenya and Zimbabwe', *Journal of Modern African Studies*, 48: 2, 203–30.

Chennels, A.J. (1989), 'White Rhodesian nationalism: The mistaken years', in Canaan Banana (ed.), *Turmoil and Tenacity: Zimbabwe 1890–1990*, Harare: The College Press, 26–7.

Chikane, Frank (2012), *Eight Days in September: The Removal of Thabo Mbeki*, Johannesburg: Picador Africa.

Chimombe, Theresa (1986), 'Foreign capital', in Ibbo Mandaza (ed.), *Zimbabwe: The Political Economy of Transition 1980–1986*, Dakar: Codesria; Harare: Jongwe Press, 123–40.

Clarke, Duncan (1980), *Foreign Companies and International Investment in Zimbabwe*, Gweru: Mambo Press.

Cliffe, Lionel and John Saul (eds) (1972), *Socialism in Tanzania: An Interdisciplinary Reader. Vol. 1. Politics*, Nairobi: East African Publishing House.

Commonwealth Secretariat (2000), *The Parliamentary Elections in Zimbabwe 24–*

25 June 2000: The Report of the Commonwealth Observer Group, London: Commonwealth Secretariat.

—— (2002), *Zimbabwe Presidential Election 9–11 March 2002: Report of the Commonwealth Observer Group*, London: Commonwealth Secretariat.

Compagnon, Daniel (2010), *A Predictable Tragedy: Robert Mugabe and the Collapse of Zimbabwe*, Philadelphia: University of Pennsylvania Press.

Corder, Hugh (2011), 'Constitution reigns whether Zuma likes it or not', *Business Day*, 31 August.

Crawford-Browne, Terry (2004), 'The arms deal scandal', *Review of African Political Economy*, 100, 329–42.

Crisis in Zimbabwe Coalition (2005), *Things Fall Apart: The 2005 Parliamentary Election: Prospects of True Democracy in Zimbabwe*, Harare: Crisis in Zimbabwe Coalition.

Crotty, Ann and Renee Bonorchis (2006), *Executive Pay in South Africa: Who Gets What and Why?* Cape Town: Double Storey.

Dangerfield, George (1997), *The Strange Death of Liberal England*, Stanford CA: Stanford University Press.

Daniel, John (2006), 'Soldiering on: The post-presidential years of Nelson Mandela', in Roger Southall and Henning Melber (eds), *Legacies of Power: Leadership Change and Former Presidents in African Politics*, Cape Town: HSRC Press, 26–50.

Daniel, John and Roger Southall (2009), 'The national and provincial electoral outcome: Continuity with change', in Roger Southall and John Daniel (eds), *Zunami! The 2009 South African Elections*, Johannesburg: Jacana Media, 215–31.

Dashwood, Hevina (2000), *Zimbabwe: The Political Economy of Transformation*, Toronto: University of Toronto Press.

Day, John (1975), 'The creation of political myths: African nationalism in Southern Rhodesia', *Journal of Southern African Studies*, 2: 1, 52–65.

Davies, Rob (1988), 'The transition to socialism in Zimbabwe: Some areas for debate', in Colin Stoneman (ed.), *Zimbabwe's Prospects: Issues of Race, Class, State and Capital in Southern Africa*, Basingstoke: Macmillan, 18–31.

Davies, Robert, Dan O'Meara and Sipho Dlamini (1984), *The Struggle for South Africa: A Reference Guide to Movements, Organisations and Institutions*, London: Zed Books.

Davis, Gavin (2005), 'Media coverage in Election 2004: Were some parties more equal than others?' in Jessica Piombo and Lia Nijzink (eds), *Electoral Politics in South Africa: Assessing the First Democratic Decade*, Cape Town: HSRC Press, 231–49.

—— (2010), 'An independent cadre is a contradiction in terms amid party loyalty', *Mail & Guardian*, 19–25 November.

Dawson, Martin and Tim Kelsall (2012), 'Anti-developmental patrimonialism in Zimbabwe', *Journal of Contemporary African Studies*, 30: 1, 49–66.

De Klerk, Frederick (F.W.) (1998), *The Last Trek: A New Beginning*, London and Basingstoke: Macmillan.

Devenish, George (2010), 'Constitution vs "national democratic constitution"', *Mail & Guardian*, 14–20 May.

De Villiers, Bertus (2003), *Land Reform: Issues and Challenges – A Comparative Review of Experiences in Zimbabwe, Namibia, South Africa and Australia*, Johannesburg: Konrad Adenauer Foundation.

Diescho, Joseph (1996), 'Government and opposition in post-independence Namibia: Perceptions and performance', in *Building Democracy: Perceptions and Performance of Government and Opposition in Namibia*, Windhoek: Namibia Institute for Democracy and Konrad Adenauer Stiftung, 4–25.

Dobell, Lauren (1997), 'Silence in context: Truth and/or reconciliation in Namibia', *Journal of Southern African Studies*, 23: 2, 372–73.

—— (1998), *Swapo's Struggle for Namibia, 1960–1991: War by Other Means*, Basel: Basel Africa Bibliographien.

Dorman, Sarah (2003), 'NGOs and the constitutional debate in Zimbabwe: From inclusion to exclusion', *Journal of Southern African Studies*, 29: 4, 845–63.

Dubow, Saul (2000), *The African National Congress*, Johannesburg: Jonathan Ball Publishers.

Duncan, Jane (2009), 'Desperately seeking depth: The media and the 2009 elections', in Roger Southall and John Daniel (eds), *Zunami! The 2009 South African Elections*, Johannesburg: Jacana Media, 215–31.

—— (2011), 'The print media transformation dilemma', in John Daniel, Prishani Naidoo, Devan Pillay and Roger Southall (eds), *New South African Review 2: New Paths, Old Compromises?*, Johannesburg: Wits University Press, 345–68.

Du Pisani, Andre (2003), 'Liberation and tolerance', in Henning Melber (ed.), *Re-examining Liberation in Namibia: Political Culture since Independence*, Uppsala: Nordic Africa Institute, 129–36.

Economist Intelligence Unit (EIU) (1991), *Namibia Country Profile: Annual Survey of Political and Economic Background 1989–92*, London: EIU.

Electoral Institute of Southern Africa (EISA) (2008), *Zimbabwe: The Harmonised Elections of 29 March 2008*, EISA Election Observer Mission Report No. 28, Johannesburg: EISA.

—— (2009), *Namibia: Presidential and National Assembly Elections 27 and 28 November 2009*, Election Observer Mission Report No. 34. Johannesburg: EISA.

—— (undated), 'Zimbabwe: Party regulation and funding', http://www.eisa.org.za/WEP/zimpartiesc.htm

—— (undated), 'Namibia: Party funding', http://www.eisa.org.za/WEP/namparties4.htm

Ellis, Steven and Tsepo Sechaba (1992), *Comrades against Apartheid: The ANC and the South African Communist Party in Exile*, London: James Currey.

Fanon, Frantz (1974), *The Wretched of the Earth*, London: Penguin.

February, Judith (2009), 'The electoral system and electoral administration', in Roger Southall and John Daniel (eds), *Zunami! The 2009 South African Elections*, Johannesburg: Jacana Media, 47–64.

Feinstein, Andrew (2007), *After the Party: A Personal and Political Journey inside the ANC*, Johannesburg and Cape Town: Jonathan Ball Publishers.

Fine, Ben and Zavareh Rustomjee (1996), *The Political Economy of South Africa: From Minerals Energy Complex to Industrialisation*, London: Hurst.

Fleermuys, Floris, Florette Nakusera, Fenni Shangula and John Steytler (2007), 'Overview of broad-based empowerment in Namibia', in *Broad Based Economic Empowerment: Experience from Other Developing Countries*, Bank of

Namibia Annual Symposium, Windhoek.

Forde, Fiona (2011), *An Inconvenient Youth: Julius Malema and the 'New' ANC*, Johannesburg: Picador Africa.

Forrest, Drew and Stefaans Brummer (2012), 'Spies bid for new powers', *Mail & Guardian*, 3–9 February.

Friedman, Steven (2012), 'Don't hold breath for a jump to the left', *Business Day*, 10 December.

Gargallo, Eduard (2010), 'Land, restitution and traditional authorities in Namibia's agrarian reform', 7th Congress of African Studies, Lisbon.

Gevisser, Mark (2007), *The Dream Deferred: Thabo Mbeki*, Cape Town and Johannesburg: Jonathan Ball Publishers.

Gewald, Jan-Bart (2003), 'Herero genocide in the twentieth century: Politics and memory', in Jon Abbink, Mirjam de Bruijn and Klaas van Walraven (eds), *Rethinking Resistance: Revolt and Violence in African History*, Leiden and Boston: Brill, 279–304.

Gibbon, Peter (ed.) (1995), *Structural Adjustment and the Working Poor in Zimbabwe*, Uppsala: Nordic Africa Institute.

Gibson, Richard (1972), *African Liberation Movements: Contemporary Struggles against White Minority Rule*, London: Oxford University Press.

Giliomee, Hermann (1979), 'The Afrikaner economic advance', in Heribert Adam and Hermann Giliomee, *The Rise and Crisis of Afrikaner Power*, Cape Town: David Philip, 145–76.

Giliomee, Hermann, John Myburgh and Lawrence Schlemmer (2001), 'Dominant party rule, opposition politics and minorities in South Africa', in Roger Southall (ed.), *Opposition and Democracy in South Africa*. London: Frank Cass, 161–82.

Giliomee, Hermann and Charles Simkins (eds) (1999), *The Awkward Embrace: One Party Domination and Democracy*, Cape Town: Tafelberg.

Glaser, Clive (2012), *The ANC Youth League*, Auckland Park: Jacana.

Global Witness (2012), *Financing a Parallel Government? The Involvement of the Secret Police and Military in Zimbabwe's Diamond, Cotton and Property Sectors*, June.

Godwin, Peter and Ian Hancock (1993), *Rhodesians Never Die: The Impact of War and Political Change on White Rhodesia, c1970–1980*, London: Macmillan.

Goebel, Alison (2005), 'Is Zimbabwe the future for South Africa? The implications for land reform in Southern Africa', *Journal of Contemporary African Studies*, 23: 3, 345–70.

Good, Kenneth (1976), 'Settler colonialism: Economic development and class formation', *Journal of Modern African Studies*, 14: 4, 597–620.

Green, Reginald and Kimmo Kiljunen (1981), 'Unto what end? The crisis of colonialism in Namibia', in Reginald Green, Marija-Liisa Kiljunen and Kimmo Kiljunen (eds), *Namibia: The Last Colony*, Essex: Longman, 1–22.

Groth, Siegfried (1995), *Namibia: The Wall of Silence*, Wuppertal: Peter Hammer Verlag.

Gurirab, Tsudao (1998), 'Preliminary notes on the process of land theft and the genesis of capitalist relations of production in Namibia's agriculture (1884–1960)', in Brian Wood (ed.), *Namibia 1884–1984: Readings on Namibia's History and Society*, London and Lusaka: Namibia Support Committee and United Nations Institute for Namibia, 314–23.

Habib, Adam (2004), 'State-civil society relations in post-apartheid South Africa', in John Daniel, Adam Habib and Roger Southall (eds), *South Africa: State of the Nation 2003–2004*, Cape Town: HSRC Press, 227–41.

Hamill, James and John Hoffman (2011), 'The African National Congress and the Zanuification debate', in John Daniel, Prishani Naidoo, Devan Pillay and Roger Southall (eds), *New South African Review 2: New Paths, Old Compromises?* Johannesburg: Wits University Press, 50–67.

Handley, Antoinette (2005), 'Business, government and economic policy-making in the new South Africa, 1990–2000', *Journal of Modern African Studies*, 43: 2, 211–39.

Hanlon, Joseph (1986), *Beggar Your Neighbours: Apartheid Power in Southern Africa*, London: James Currey.

Harris, Peter (1975), 'Industrial workers in Rhodesia, 1946–1972', *Journal of Southern African Studies*, 1: 2, 139–61.

Harvey, Ebrahim (2012), *Kgalema Motlanthe: A Political Biography*, Auckland Park: Jacana Media.

Herbst, Jeffrey (1990), *State Politics in Zimbabwe*, Harare: University of Zimbabwe Publications.

Hinz, Manfred (2008), 'Traditional governance and African customary law: Comparative observations from a Namibian perspective', http://www.kas.de/upload/auslandshomepage/namibia/..../hinz.pdf

Hirsch, Alan (2004), *Season of Hope: Economic Reform under Mandela and Mbeki*, Pietermaritzburg: University of KwaZulu-Natal Press.

Hoffman, Paul (2011), 'Democracy and accountability: Quo vadis South Africa?' in John Daniel, Prishani Naidoo, Devan Pillay and Roger Southall (eds), *New South African Review 2: New Paths, Old Compromises?* Johannesburg: Wits University Press, 83–99.

Holden, Paul (2008), *The Arms Deal in Your Pocket*, Jeppestown: Jonathan Ball Publishers.

Holden, Paul and Hennie van Vuuren (2011), *The Devil in the Detail: How the Arms Deal Changed Everything*, Jeppestown: Jonathan Ball Publishers.

Hopwood, Graham (2007), *Guide to Namibian Politics*, Windhoek: Namibia Institute for Democracy.

Horowitz, Daniel (1991), *A Democratic South Africa? Constitutional Engineering in a Divided Society*, Berkeley CA: University of California Press.

Hyslop, Jonathan (2005), 'Political corruption: Before and after apartheid', *Journal of Southern African Studies*, 31: 4, 773–89.

Hunter, Justine (ed.) (2005) *Spot the Difference: Namibia's Political Parties Compared*, Windhoek: Namibia Institute for Democracy.

Institute of Development Studies, University of Zimbabwe (2004), *Land Reform Programme in Zimbabwe: Disparity between Policy Design and Implementation*, May.

Jauch, Herbert (1999), 'Human resource development and affirmative action in Namibia: A trade union perspective', Windhoek: Labour Resource and Research Institute (LaRRI).

—— (2010), 'Serving workers or serving the party? Trade unions and politics in Namibia', in Bjorn Beckman, Sakhela Buhlungu and Lloyd Sachikonye (eds), *Trade Unions and Party Politics: Labour Movements in Africa*, Cape Town: HSRC Press, 167–90.

—— (2010), 'Workers take back control: Congress of National Union of Namibian Workers', *South African Labour Bulletin*, 34: 5, 25–26.

Jeffrey, Anthea (2010), *Chasing the Rainbow: South Africa's Move from Mandela to Zuma*, Johannesburg: South African Institute of Race Relations.

Johnson, R.W. (2001) 'The final struggle is to stay in power', *Focus*, 25. Johannesburg: Helen Suzman Foundation.

—— (2009), *South Africa's Brave New World: The Beloved Country since the End of Apartheid*, London: Allen Lane.

Jolobe, Zwelethu (2009), 'The Democratic Alliance: Consolidating the official opposition', in Roger Southall and John Daniel (eds), *Zunami! The 2009 South African Elections*, Johannesburg: Jacana Media,131–46.

—— (2010), 'Financing the ANC: Chancellor House, Eskom and the dilemmas of party finance reform', in Anthony Butler (ed.), *Paying for Politics: Party Funding and Political Change in South Africa and the Global South*, Auckland Park: Jacana, 201–17.

Kaapama, Phanuel (2005), 'Pre-conditions for free and fair elections: A Namibian country study', in Jeanette Minnie (ed.), *Outside the Ballot Box: Preconditions for Elections in Southern Africa 2004/05*, Windhoek: Media Institute for Southern Africa.

Kabemba, Claude (2004), 'An assessment of Zimbabwe's electoral administration', in Wole Olaleye (ed.), *Negotiating the Impasse: Challenges and Prospects for Democratization in Zimbabwe*, Johannesburg: EISA Research Report No. 9, 9–27.

—— (2005), 'Electoral administration: Achievements and continuing challenges', in Jessica Piombo and Lia Nijzink (eds), *Electoral Politics in South Africa: Assessing the First Democratic Decade*, Cape Town: HSRC Press, 87–105.

Kadhani, Xavier (1986), 'The economy: Issues, problems and prospects', in Ibbo Mandoza (ed.), *Zimbabwe: The Political Economy of Transition 1980–1986*, Dakar: Codesria; Harare: Jongwe Press, 99–122.

Kagwanja, Peter (2005), *When the Locusts Ate: Zimbabwe's March 2005 Elections*, Electoral Institute for Southern Africa Occasional Paper No. 32.

Kamete, Amin (2004), 'Zimbabwe', in Andreas Mehler, Henning Melber and Klaas van Walraven (eds), *Africa Yearbook 2004*, Leiden: Brill, 480–92.

—— (2008), 'Zimbabwe' in Andreas Mehler, Henning Melber and Klaas van Walraven (eds), *Africa Yearbook 2008*, Leiden: Brill, 505–16.

—— (2009), 'Zimbabwe', in Andreas Mehler, Henning Melber and Klaas van Walraven (eds), *Africa Yearbook 2009*, Leiden: Brill,537–47.

Kariuki, Samuel (2007), 'Political compromise on land reform: A study of South Africa and Namibia', *South African Journal of International Affairs*, 14: 1, 99–114.

—— (2010), 'The Comprehensive Rural Development Programme (CRDP): A beacon of growth for rural South Africa?' in John Daniel, Prishani Naidoo, Devan Pillay and Roger Southall (eds), *New South African Review 2010: Development or Decline?* Johannesburg: Wits University Press, 345–63.

Karume, Shumbana (2004), 'An assessment of the impact of democratic assistance', in Wole Olaleye (ed.), *Negotiating the Impasse: Challenges and Prospects for Democratization in Zimbabwe*, Johannesburg: EISA Research Report No. 9, 28–45.

Katjavivi, Peter (1988), *A History of Resistance in Namibia*, London: James Currey.

Kempton, Donald and Roni du Preez (1997), 'Namibian-De Beers state-firm relations: Cooperation and conflict', *Journal of Southern African Studies*, 23: 4, 585–613.

Ketelo, Bandile, Amos Maxongo, Zamxola Tshona, Ronnie Masango and Luvo Mbengo (2009), 'A miscarriage of democracy: The ANC security department in the 1984 mutiny in Umkhonto weSizwe', in Paul Trewhela (ed.), *Inside Quatro: Uncovering the Exile History of the ANC and Swapo*, Johannesburg: Jacana Media, 8–45.

Kriger, Norma (1988), 'The Zimbabwean war of liberation: Struggles within the struggle', *Journal of Southern African Studies*, 14: 2, 304–22.

—— (1992), *Zimbabwe's Guerrilla War: Peasant Voices*, Cambridge: Cambridge University Press.

Kossler, Reinhardt (2010), 'Images of history and the nation: Namibia and Zimbabwe compared', *South African Historical Journal*, 62: 1, 29–53.

Lamb, Guy (2007), 'Militarising politics and development: The case of post-independence Namibia', in Lars Buur, Steffen Jensen and Finn Stepputat (eds), *The Security-Development Nexus: Expressions of Sovereignty and Securitization in Southern Africa*, Uppsala: Nordic Africa Institute.

Legassick, Martin (1974), 'South Africa: Capital accumulation and violence', *Economy and Society*, 3: 3, 253–91.

Leon, Tony (2008), *On the Contrary: Leading the Opposition in a Democratic South Africa*, Jeppestown: Jonathan Ball Publishers.

Leys, Colin and John Saul (eds) (1995), *Namibia's Liberation Struggle: The Two-Edged Sword*, London: James Currey.

Lindsay, Don (2011), 'BEE reform: The case for an institutional perspective', in John Daniel, Prishani Naidoo, Devan Pillay and Roger Southall (eds), *New South African Review 2: New Paths, Old Compromises?* Johannesburg: Wits University Press, 236–55.

Linington, Greg (2012), 'Reflections on the significance of constitutions and constitutionalism for Zimbabwe', in Eldred Masunungure and Jabusile Shumba (eds), *Zimbabwe: Mired in Transition*, Harare: Weaver Press, 63–98.

Lodge, Tom (1983), *Black Politics in South Africa since 1945*, Johannesburg: Ravan Press.

—— (2002), *Politics in South Africa: From Mandela to Mbeki*, Oxford: James Currey.

—— (2005), 'The African National Congress: There is no party like it; Ayikho Efana Nayo', in Jessica Piombo and Lia Nijzink (eds), *Electoral Politics in South Africa: Assessing the First Democratic Decade*, Cape Town: HSRC Press, 109–28.

Lodge, Tom, Denis Kadima and David Pottie (eds) (2002), *Compendium of Elections in Southern Africa*, Johannesburg: Electoral Institute of Southern Africa.

Logan, Carolyn, Telsuya Fujiwara and Virginia Parish (2006), *Citizens and the State in Africa: New Results from Afrobarometer Round 3*, Afrobarometer Working Paper 61, Cape Town: Institute for a Democratic Alternative in Southern Africa (IDASA).

Loney, Martin (1975), *Rhodesia: White Racism and Imperial Response*, Harmondsworth: Penguin.

359

Madlala-Routledge, Noziwe (2012), 'Scrap the "Bantustan" Traditional Courts Bill', Wolpe Dialogue, University of the Witwatersrand, 17 May 2012.

Magure, Booker (2009), 'Civil society's quest for democracy in Zimbabwe: Origins, barriers and prospects, 1900–2008', Ph.D. thesis, Rhodes University.

Makumbe, John (1998), 'Is there a civil society in Africa?', *International Affairs*, 74: 2, 305–17.

—— (2003), *Zimbabwe's Turmoil: Problems and Prospects*, Pretoria: Institute for Security Studies.

—— (2010), 'Local authorities and traditional leadership', in Jaap de Visser, Nico Steytler and Naison Machingauta (eds), *Local Government Reform in Zimbabwe*, Cape Town: Community Law Centre, University of the Western Cape, 87–100.

Malabela, Musawenkosi (2011), *The African National Congress and Local Democracy: The Role of the ANC Branch in Manzini-Mbombela*, MA research report, Department of Sociology, University of the Witwatersrand.

Mamdani, Mahmood (1996), *Citizen and Subject: Contemporary Africa and the Legacy of Late Colonialism*, London: James Currey.

—— (2008), 'Lessons of Zimbabwe', *London Review of Books*, 30: 23, 4 (December), 17–21.

Mandaza, Ibbo (1986), 'Introduction: The political economy of transition', in Ibbo Mandaza (ed.), *Zimbabwe: The Political Economy of Transition 1980–1986*, Dakar: Codesria; Harare: Jongwe Press.

—— (1986), 'The state and politics in the post-settler situation', in Ibbo Mandaza (ed.), *Zimbabwe: The Political Economy of Transition 1980–1986*, Dakar: Codesria; Harare: Jongwe Press, 21–74.

Mandaza, Ibbo and Lloyd Sachikonye (eds), (1991) *The One Party State and Democracy: The Zimbabwe Debate*, Harare: SAPES Trust.

Mandela, Nelson (1994), *Long Walk to Freedom*, London: Little, Brown and Co.

Marais, Hein (2010), *South Africa Pushed to the Limit: The Political Economy of Change*, Cape Town: University of Cape Town Press.

Martin, David and Phyllis Johnson (1984), *The Struggle for Zimbabwe: The Chimurenga War*, London and Boston: Faber & Faber.

Matombo, Lovemore and Lloyd Sachikonye (2010), 'The labour movement and democratization in Zimbabwe', in Bjorn Beckman, Sakhela Buhlungu and Lloyd Sachikonye (eds), *Trade Unions and Party Politics: Labour Movements in Africa*, Cape Town: HSRC Press, 109–130.

Matshiqi, Aubrey (2012), 'Put fixing the party top of the agenda', *Business Day*, 14 December.

Mattes, Robert, Yul Derek Davids and Cherrel Africa (2000), 'Views of democracy in South Africa and the region: Trends and comparisons', *Afrobarometer Paper No. 8*.

Mattes, Robert and Roger Southall (2004), 'Popular attitudes towards the South African electoral system', *Democratization*, 11: 1, 51–76.

Matyszak, Derek (2010), *Law, Politics and Zimbabwe's 'Unity' Government*, Harare: Konrad Adenauer Stiftung in association with the Research and Advocacy Unit.

Mbeki, Moeletsi (2009), *Architects of Policy: Why African Capitalism Needs Changing*, Johannesburg: Picador Africa.

Mbeki, Thabo (2001), 'How will Zimbabwe defeat its enemies? A discussion document', circulated to members of the ANC. An amended version was published as 'The Mbeki-Mugabe papers: How will Zimbabwe defeat its enemies?' *New Agenda*, 2008: 2, 56–75.

Mboweni, Tito, 'The cruel challenges of politics and "politics within politics"', http://www.ujoh.co.za/opinions/mboweni-full-text-on-mbeki-lecture

McGregor, Andrew, Robert Rose and Steven Cranston (2009), 'Power-shift', *Financial Mail*, 23 January.

McKinley, Dale (2010), 'The age of polipreneurship', http://www.sacsis.org.za/sote/article/592.1, 6 December.

—— (2011), 'The real history and contemporary character of "black economic empowerment" (Part 1)', http://www.sacsis.org.za/site/article/600.1, 10 January; Part 2: 9 February.

Melber, Henning (2002), 'From liberation movements to governments: On political culture in Southern Africa', *African Sociological Review*, 6: 1, 161–72.

—— (2003), 'Limits to liberation: An introduction to Namibia's postcolonial political culture', in Henning Melber (ed.), *Re-examining Liberation in Namibia: Political Culture since Independence*, Uppsala: Nordic Africa Institute, 9–25.

—— (2003), 'Namibia, land of the brave: Selective memories on war and violence within nation-building', in Jon Abbink, Mirjam de Bruijn and Klaas van Walraven (eds), *Rethinking Resistance: Revolt and Violence in African History*, Leiden and Boston: Brill, 305–27.

—— (2003), 'Of big fish and small fry: The fishing industry in Namibia', *Review of African Political Economy*, 30: 95, 142–49.

—— (2004), 'Namibia', in Andreas Mehler, Henning Melber and Klaas van Walraven (eds), *Africa Yearbook 2004*, Leiden: Brill, 443–50.

—— (2006), 'Namibia', in Andreas Mehler, Henning Melber and Klaas van Walraven (eds), *Africa Yearbook 2006*, Leiden: Brill, 458–67.

—— (2006) '"Presidential indispensibility" in Namibia', in Roger Southall and Henning Melber (eds), *Legacies of Power: Leadership Change and Former Presidents in African Politics*, Cape Town: HSRC Press; Uppsala: Nordic Africa Institute, 98–119.

—— (2007), 'Namibia', in Andreas Mehler, Henning Melber and Klaas van Walraven (eds), *Africa Yearbook: Politics, Economy and Society South of the Sahara in 2006*, Leiden; Boston: Brill, 459–68.

—— (2007), 'Poverty, politics, power and privilege: Namibia's black economic elite formation', in Henning Melber (ed.) *Transitions in Namibia: Which Changes for Whom?* Uppsala: Nordic Africa Institute, 120–29.

—— (2009), 'Governance, political culture and civil society under a civil liberation movement in power: The case of Namibia', in Nuno Vidal and Patrick Chabal (eds), *Southern Africa: Civil Society, Politics and Donor Strategies. Angola and Its Neighbours*, Luanda and Lisbon: Media XXI & Firmamento, 199–212.

—— (2009), 'One Namibia, one nation? The Caprivi as contested territory', *Journal of Contemporary African Studies*, 27: 4, 463–82.

—— (2010), 'Namibia's National Assembly and presidential elections 2009: Did democracy win?' *Journal of Contemporary African Studies*, 28: 2, 203–14.

—— (2011), 'SWAPO is the nation, and the nation is SWAPO: Government and opposition in a dominant party state – the case of Namibia', in Katharina Hulterström, Amin Kamete and Henning Melber, *Political Opposition in*

African Countries: The Cases of Kenya, Namibia, Zambia and Zimbabwe, Uppsala: Nordic Africa Institute, 61–83.

Melber, Henning (forthcoming), *Namibia, Africa Yearbook: Politics, Economy and Society South of the Sahara in 2012*, Leiden; Boston: Brill.

Meredith, Martin (2002), *Robert Mugabe: Power, Plunder and Tyranny in Zimbabwe*, Johannesburg and Cape Town: Jonathan Ball Publishers.

Metsola, Lalli (2007), 'Out of order? The margins of Namibian ex-combatant "reintegration"', in Henning Melber (ed.), *Transitions in Namibia: Which Changes for Whom?* Uppsala: Nordic Africa Institute, 130–52.

Michels, Robert (1959 [1912]), *Political Parties*, New York: Dover Books.

Milne, C. (2009), 'Affirmative action in South Africa: From targets to empowerment', *Journal of Public Administration*, 44: 4.1, 969–90.

Mohamed, Seeraj (2010), 'The state of the South African economy', in John Daniel, Prishani Naidoo, Devan Pillay and Roger Southall (eds), *New South African Review 2010: Development or Decline?* Johannesburg: Wits University Press, 39–64.

Moorcroft, Paul (2012), *Mugabe's War Machine*, Johannesburg and Cape Town: Jonathan Ball Publishers.

Moore, David (2001), 'Is the land the economy and the economy the land? Primitive accumulation in Zimbabwe', *Journal of Contemporary African Studies*, 19: 2, 253–66.

—— (2003), 'Zimbabwe's triple crisis: Primitive accumulation, nation-state formation and democratisation in the age of neo-liberal globalisation', *African Studies Quarterly*, 7: 2 and 3; http://web.africa.ufl.edu/asq/v7/v7i2a2.htm

—— (2005), 'ZANU-PF and the ghosts of foreign funding', *Review of African Political Economy*, 32: 103, 156–62.

—— (2010), 'A decade of disquieting diplomacy: South Africa, Zimbabwe and the ideology of the National Democratic Revolution, 1999–2009', *History Compass*, 8: 8, 752–67.

Moorsom, Richard (1980), 'Namibia in the frontline: The political economy of decolonization in South Africa's colony', *Review of African Political Economy*, 17: 71–82.

Motlanthe, Kgalema (2007), '52nd National Conference: Organisational report', African National Congress, 17 December.

—— (2011), 'A new world is possible!' *ANC Today*, 7–13 October.

Movement for Democratic Change (MDC) (2004), *RESTART: Our Path to Social Justice. The MDC's Economic Programme for Reconstruction, Stabilization, Recovery and Transformation*, Harare: Movement for Democratic Change.

Moyo, Gugulethu (2007), 'Corrupt judges and land rights in Zimbabwe', in Transparency International, *Global Corruption Report 2007*, Cambridge: Transparency International and Cambridge University Press, 35–39.

Moyo, Jason (1993), 'Civil society in Zimbabwe', *Zambezia*, 20: 1, 1–14.

Moyo, Jonathan (1992), *Voting for Democracy: Electoral Politics in Zimbabwe*, Harare: University of Zimbabwe Press.

Moyo, Sam (2007), 'The land question in southern Africa: A comparative review', in Ruth Hall and Lungisile Ntsebeza (eds), *The Land Question in South Africa: The Challenge of Transformation and Redistribution*, Cape Town: HSRC Press, 60–84.

—— (2011), 'Land concentration and accumulation after redistributive reform in post-settler Zimbabwe', *Review of African Political Economy*, 38: 128, 257–76.

Moyo, Sam and P. Yeros (2005), 'Land occupations and land reform in Zimbabwe: Towards the national democratic revolution', in Sam Moyo and P. Yeros (eds), *The Resurgence of Rural Movements in Africa, Asia and Latin America*, London: Zed Press, 44–77.

Mtisi, Joseph, Munyaradzi Nyakudye and Teresa Barnes (2009), 'War in Rhodesia, 1965–1980', in Brian Raftopoulos and Alois Mlambo (eds), *Becoming Zimbabwe: A History from the Pre-Colonial Period to 2008*, Harare: Weaver Press, 141–66.

Mugabe, Robert (1989), 'The Unity Accord: Its promise for the future', in Canaan Banana (ed.), *Turmoil and Tenacity: Zimbabwe 1890–1990*, Harare: The College Press, 336–59.

Mumbengegwi, Clever (1986), 'Continuity and change in agricultural policy', in Ibbo Mandaza (ed.), *Zimbabwe: The Political Economy of Transition 1980–1986*, Dakar: Codesria; Harare: Jongwe Press, 204–22.

Musarurwa, Albert (1990), 'A. Trade unionism and the state', conference on 'Zimbabwe's first decade of political independence: Lessons for Namibia and South Africa', Harare, 30 August – 2 September.

Musiyiwa, Ambrose (2005), 'Military dictatorship in Zimbabwe', http://www.worldpress.org/Africa/2200.cfm

Musuva, Catherine (2009), *Promoting the Effectiveness of Democracy Protection Institutions in South Africa: South Africa's Public Protector and Human Rights Commission*, Johannesburg: EISA Research Report 41.

Mutyanda, Nunurayi and Taurai Mereki (2012), 'ZCTU congress aftermath: Cracks deepen', *South African Labour Bulletin*, 36: 1, 54–7.

Muzondidye, James (2009), 'From buoyancy to crisis', in Brian Raftopoulos and Alois Mlambo (eds), *Becoming Zimbabwe: A History from the Pre-Colonial Period to 2008*, Harare: Weaver Press, 167–200.

Naidoo, Vino (2008), 'Assessing racial redress in the public service', in Kristina Bentley and Adam Habib (eds), *Racial Redress and Citizenship in South Africa*, Cape Town: HSRC Press, 99–128.

Namibia Institute of Democracy (2009), *Guide to Civil Society in Namibia*, Windhoek: Namibia Institute of Democracy.

Namibian Society for Human Rights (2004), 'Concern over judicial independence and integrity', http://www.nshr.org.na/index.php?module=News&func=display&sid=319

Nattrass, Jill (1981), *The South African Economy: Its Growth and Change*, Cape Town: Oxford University Press.

Ndletyana, Mcebesi (2008), 'Affirmative action in the public service', in Kristina Bentley and Adam Habib (eds), *Racial Redress and Citizenship in South Africa*, Cape Town: HSRC Press, 77–98.

Ndlovu-Gatsheni, Sabelo (2011), *Reconstructing the Implications of Liberation Struggle History on SADC Mediation in Zimbabwe*, Johannesburg: South African Institute of International Relations.

Netshitenzhe, Joel (2012), 'Competing identities of a national liberation movement and the challenges of incumbency', *ANC Today*, 15–21 June.

Ntsebeza, Lungisile (2006), 'Rural development in South Africa: Tensions between democracy and traditional authority', in Vishnu Padayachee (ed.), *The Development Decade: Economic and Social Change in South Africa, 1994–2004*, Cape Town: HSRC Press, 444–60.

Nujoma, Sam (2001), *Where Others Wavered: The Autobiography of Sam Nujoma*, London: Panaf.

Odendaal, Andre (1984), *Vukani Bantu! The Beginnings of Black Protest Politics in South Africa to 1912*, Claremont: David Philip.

Partnership Africa Canada (2009), *Zimbabwe, Diamonds and the Wrong Side of History*, March.

Pepetela [A.C.M. Pestana] (1996), *Mayombe*, London: Heinemann.

Picard, Louis (2005), *The State of the State in South Africa*, Johannesburg: Wits University Press.

Pillay, Devan (2010), 'South Africa and the eco-logic of the global capitalist crisis', in John Daniel, Prishani Naidoo, Devan Pillay and Roger Southall (eds), *New South African Review 2010: Development or Decline?* Johannesburg: Wits University Press, 24–38.

Plaatjies, Daniel (2010), 'Deployment of loyalists is crucial for the survival of ruling parties', *Sunday Independent*, 21 March.

Preston, Rosemary (1997), 'Integrating fighters after war: Reflections on the Namibian experience, 1989–1993', *Journal of Southern African Studies*, 23: 3, 453–72.

Pupkewitz, Harold (1996), 'Perceptions and performance of government and opposition in Namibia', in *Building Democracy: Perceptions and Performance of Government and Opposition in Namibia*, Windhoek: Namibia Institute for Democracy and Konrad Adenauer Stiftung.

Raftopoulos, Brian (2006), 'The Zimbabwean crisis and the challenges of the left', *Journal of Southern African Studies*, 32: 2, 203–19.

—— (2009), 'The crisis in Zimbabwe', in Brian Raftopoulos and Alois Mlambo (eds), *Becoming Zimbabwe: A History from the Pre-Colonial Period to 2008*, Harare: Weaver Press, 201–32.

—— (2010), 'The global political agreement as a "passive revolution": Notes on contemporary politics in Zimbabwe', *The Round Table*, 99: 411, 705–18.

Randall, Duncan (1996), 'Prospects for the development of a black business class in South Africa', *Journal of Modern African Studies*, 34: 4, 661–86.

Ranger, Terence (1985), *Peasant Consciousness and Guerrilla War in Zimbabwe: A Comparative Study*, London: James Currey.

—— (2003), 'Nationalist historiography, patriotic history, and the history of the nation: The struggle over the past in Zimbabwe', *Journal of Southern African Studies*, 30: 2, 215–34.

Reeler, Tony and Kuda Chitsike (2005), *Trick or Treat? The Effects of the Pre-Election Climate on the Poll in the 2005 Zimbabwe Parliamentary Elections*, Cape Town: Institute for Democracy in Southern Africa.

Republic of South Africa (2009), 'Development indicators', http://www.info.gov.za/other-docs 2009/developmentindicators2009

—— (2010), 'The new growth path: The framework', http://www.info.gov.za 20 December.

Rich-Dorman, Sarah (2001), 'Inclusion and exclusion: NGOs and politics in Zimbabwe', Ph.D. thesis, University of Oxford.

Riddell, Roger (1978), *The Land Question in Rhodesia*, Gwelo: Mambo Press.

Robinson, Vicki and Stefaans Brummer (2006), *Corporate Fronts and Political Party Funding*, Institute for Security Studies, Paper 129, November.

Roux, Theunis (2012), *The Politics of Principle: The First South African Constitutional Court*, Cambridge: Cambridge University Press.

Rumney, Reg (2005), 'Who owns South Africa? An analysis of state and private ownership patterns', in John Daniel, Roger Southall and Jessica Lutchman (eds), *State of the Nation: South Africa 2004–05*, Cape Town: HSRC Press, 401–22.

Sachikonye, Lloyd (2002), 'The state and the union movement in Zimbabwe: Cooptation, conflict and accommodation', in Bjorn Beckman and Lloyd Sachikonye (eds), *Labour Regimes and Liberalization: The Restructuring of State-Society Relations in Africa*, Harare: University of Zimbabwe Publications.

—— (2011), *When a State Turns on its Citizens: Institutionalised Violence and Political Culture*, Johannesburg: Jacana Media.

Saller, Karla (2004), *The Judicial Institution in Zimbabwe*, Cape Town: University of Cape Town Press.

Sampson, Anthony (1999), *Mandela: The Authorised Biography*, Cape Town: Jonathan Ball Publishers.

Sandbrook, Richard, Marc Edelman, Patrick Heller and Judith Teichman (2007), *Social Democracy in the Global Periphery: Origins, Challenges, Prospects*, Cambridge: Cambridge University Press.

Sarakinsky, Ivor (2001), 'Reflections on the politics of minorities, race and opposition in contemporary South Africa', in Roger Southall (ed.), *Opposition and Democracy in South Africa*, London, Portland: Frank Cass, 149–60.

—— (2007), 'Political party finance in South Africa: Disclosure versus secrecy', *Democratization*, 14: 1, 111–28.

Sarkin, Jeremy (2011), *Germany's Genocide of the Herero: Kaiser Wilhelm II, His General, His Settlers, His Soldiers*, Woodbridge, Suffolk: James Currey.

Saul, John (1994), 'The Southern African revolution', in John Saul (ed.), *Recolonization and Resistance: Southern Africa in the 1990s*, Trenton NJ: Africa World Press, 1–34.

—— (1997), 'Liberal democracy vs. popular democracy in sub-Saharan Africa', *Review of African Political Economy*, 24: 73, 339–52.

—— (2005), 'The post-apartheid denouement', in John Saul, *The Next Liberation Struggle*, Pietermaritzburg: University of KwaZulu-Natal Press, 195–228.

—— (2008), *Decolonization and Empire: Contesting the Rhetoric and Reality of Resubordination in Southern Africa and Beyond*, Johannesburg: Wits University Press.

—— (2011), 'The success and failure of the "thirty years war for southern African liberation" in South Africa and beyond', Conference on One Hundred Years of the ANC: Debating Liberation Histories and Democracy Today, Universities of Johannesburg and the Witwatersrand, 20–24 September.

Saul, John and Colin Leys (1995), 'The politics of exile', in Colin Leys and John Saul (eds), *Namibia's Liberation Struggle: The Two-Edged Sword*, London: James Currey, 40–62.

—— (2003), 'Lubango and after: "Forgotten history" as politics in contemporary Namibia', *Journal of Southern African Studies*, 29: 2, 333–53.

Saunders, Christopher (2003), 'History and the armed struggle: From anti-colonial propaganda to "patriotic history"?' in Henning Melber (ed.), *Re-examining Liberation in Namibia: Political Culture since Independence*, Uppsala: Nordic Africa Institute, 13–28.

—— (2003), 'Liberation and democracy: A critical reading of Sam Nujoma's "Autobiography"', in Henning Melber (ed.), *Re-examining Liberation in Namibia: Political Cultures since Independence*, Uppsala: Nordic Africa Institute, 87–98.

Saunders, Richard (2008), 'Crisis, capital, compromise: mining and empowerment in Zimbabwe', *African Sociological Review*, 12: 1, 67–87.

Schulz-Herzenberg, Colleen (2009), 'Trends in party support and voter behaviour, 1994–2009', in Roger Southall and John Daniel (eds), *Zunami! The 2009 South African Elections*, Johannesburg: Jacana, 23–46.

Scoones, Ian, Nelson Marongwe, Blasio Mavedzenge, Jacob Mahenehene, Felix Murimbarimba and Crispen Sukume (2010), *Zimbabwe's Land Reforms: Myths and Realities*, Woodbridge: James Currey.

Seekings, Jeremy (2001), *The UDF: A History of the United Democratic Front in South Africa 1983–1991*, Claremont: David Philip.

Seekings, Jeremy and Nicoli Nattrass (2005), *Class, Race and Inequality in South Africa*, Pietermaritzburg: University of KwaZulu-Natal Press.

Sefara, Makhuda (2011), 'The rise of unreason', *Sunday Independent*, 21 August.

Seidman, Ann and Neva Seidman Makgetla (1980), *Outposts of Monopoly Capitalism: Southern Africa in the Changing Global Economy*, Westport CT: Lawrence Hill & Company; London: Zed Press.

Sergeant, Barry (2006), *Brett Kebble: The Inside Story*, Cape Town: Zebra Press.

Sherbourne, Robin (2010), *Guide to the Namibian Economy 2010*, Windhoek: Institute for Public Policy Research.

Sibanda, Arnold (1988), 'The political situation', in Colin Stoneman (ed.), *Zimbabwe's Prospects: Issues of Race, Class, State and Capital in Southern Africa*, Basingstoke: Macmillan, 257–83.

Simons, Jack and Ray Simons (1969), *Class and Colour in South Africa*, Harmondsworth: Penguin.

Sithole, Masipula (1986), 'The general elections: 1979–1985', in Ibbo Mandaza (ed.), *Zimbabwe: The Political Economy of Transition 1980–1985*, Dakar, Codesria; Harare: Jongwe Press, 75–98.

Skinner, Kate (2011), 'The South African Broadcasting Corporation: The creation and loss of a citizenship vision and the possibilities for building a new one', in John Daniel, Prishani Naidoo, Devan Pillay and Roger Southall (eds), *New South African Review 2: New Paths, Old Compromises*, Johannesburg: Wits University Press, 369–86.

Smith, Janet and Beauregard Tromp (2009), *Hani: A Life Too Short*, Johannesburg and Cape Town: Jonathan Ball Publishers.

Soiri, Ilina (2003), 'SWAPO wins, apathy rules: The Namibian 1998 local authority elections', in Michael Cowen and Liisa Laakso (eds), *Multi-Party Elections in Africa*, London: Palgrave Macmillan, 187–216.

Sokomani, Andile (2010), 'Party financing in democratic South Africa: Harbinger of doom?' in Anthony Butler (ed.), *Paying for Politics: Party Funding and Political Change in South Africa and the Global South*, Auckland Park: Jacana, 170–86.

Sole, Sam (2010), 'Money politics in South Africa: From covert party funding to the problem of black economic empowerment', in Anthony Butler (ed.), *Paying for Politics: Party Funding and Political Change in South Africa and the Global South*, Auckland Park: Jacana, 187–200.

—— (2012), 'Claims of SAPS plot against minister', M&g Centre for Investigative Journalism, 20 July, http://www.amabhungane.co.za

Solidarity Peace Trust (2005), *The Role of the Judiciary in Denying the Will of the Zimbabwean Electorate since 2000*, Port Shepstone: Solidarity Peace Trust.

South African Institute of Race Relations (SAIRR), *South Africa Survey*, various years.

Southall, Roger (1983), *South Africa's Transkei: The Political Economy of an 'Independent' Bantustan*, London, Heinemann.

—— (1995), *Imperialism or Solidarity? International Labour and South African Trade Unions*, Cape Town: University of Cape Town Press.

—— (1998), 'The centralization and fragmentation of South Africa's dominant party system', *African Affairs*, 97, 443–69.

—— (1999), 'The struggle for a place called home: The ANC versus the UDM in the Eastern Cape', *Politikon*, 26: 2, 155–66.

—— (2001), 'Conclusion: Emergent perspectives on opposition in South Africa', in Roger Southall (ed.), *Opposition and Democracy in South Africa*, London: Frank Cass, 275–84.

—— (2003), 'Democracy in southern Africa: Moving beyond a difficult legacy', *Review of African Political Economy*, 30: 96, 255–72.

—— (2004), 'The ANC and black capitalism in South Africa', *Review of African Political Economy*, 31: 100, 313–28.

—— (2004), 'The state of party politics: Struggles within the Tripartite Alliance and the decline of the opposition', in John Daniel, Adam Habib and Roger Southall (eds), *State of the Nation: South Africa 2003–2004*, Cape Town: HSRC Press, 53–77.

—— (2005), 'Political change and the black middle class in democratic South Africa', *Canadian Journal of African Studies*, 38: 3, 521–42.

—— (2006), 'Ten propositions about black economic empowerment in South Africa', *Review of African Political Economy*, 34: 111, 67–84.

—— (2007), 'The ANC, black economic empowerment and state-owned enterprises: A recycling of history?' in John Daniel, Sakhela Buhlungu, Roger Southall and Jessica Lutchman (eds), *State of the Nation: South Africa 2007*, Cape Town: HSRC Press, 201–25.

—— (2007), 'Does South Africa have a racial bargain? A comparative perspective', *Transformation*, 64, 66–90.

—— (2008), 'The ANC for sale? Money, morality and business in South Africa', *Review of African Political Economy*, 35: 116, 281–99.

—— (2009),'Understanding the "Zuma tsunami"', *Review of African Political Economy*, 121, 317–33.

—— (2010) 'South Africa 2010: From short-term success to long-term decline?', in John Daniel, Prishani Naidoo, Devan Pillay and Roger Southall (eds), *New South African Review 1: Development or Decline?* Johannesburg: Wits University Press, 1–21.

Southall, Roger and Henning Melber (eds) (2008), *A New Scramble for Africa? Imperialism, Investment and Development*, Pietermaritzburg: University of

KwaZulu-Natal Press.

Southall, Roger and Edward Webster (2010), 'Unions and parties in South Africa: Cosatu and the ANC in the wake of Polokwane', in Bjorn Beckman, Sakhela Buhlungu and Lloyd Sachikonye (eds), *Trade Unions and Party Politics: Labour Movements in Africa*, Cape Town: HSRC Press, 131–66.

Southall, Roger and Geoffrey Wood (1988), 'Political party funding in southern Africa', in Peter Burnell and Alan Ware (eds), *Funding Democratization*, Manchester: Manchester University Press, 202–28.

South West African People's Organisation (SWAPO) (1981), *To Be Born a Nation: The Liberation Struggle for Namibia*, London: Zed Press.

Sparks, Allister (2012), 'Ramaphosa moves make sense if he is delegated wider powers', *Business Day*, 19 December.

Sparks, Donald and December Green (1992), *Namibia: The Nation after Independence*, Boulder CO: Westview Press.

Stoneman, Colin (1988), 'The economy: Recognizing the reality', in Colin Stoneman (ed.), *Zimbabwe's Prospects: Issues of Race, Class, State and Capital in Southern Africa*, Basingstoke: Macmillan, 43–62.

Stopford, John and Susan Strange (1991), *Rival States, Rival Firms: Competition for World Market Shares*, Cambridge: Cambridge University Press.

Strange, Susan (1992), 'States, firms and diplomacy', *International Affairs*, 68: 1, 1–16.

Suttner, Raymond (2009), *The ANC Underground in South Africa, 1950–1976*, Boulder CO: First Forum Press.

—— (2009),'The challenges to African National Congress dominance', *Representations: Journal of Representative Democracy*, 45: 2, 173–92.

Sycholt, Martin and Gilton Klerck (1997), 'The state and labour relations: Walking the tightrope between corporatism and neo-liberalism', in Gilton Klerck, Andrew Murray and Martin Sycholt (eds), *Continuity and Change: Labour Relations in Independent Namibia*, Windhoek: Gamsberg Macmillan, 79–115.

Tangri, Roger and Roger Southall (2008), 'The politics of black economic empowerment in South Africa', *Journal of Southern African Studies*, 34: 3, 699–716.

Tapscott, Christopher (1993), 'The autocratic temptation: Politics in Namibia now', *Southern Africa Report*, 12: 3.

—— (1993), 'National reconciliation, social equity and class formation in independent Namibia', *Journal of Southern African Studies*, 19: 1, 29–39.

Taylor, Scott (2007), *Business and the State in Southern Africa: The Politics of Economic Reform*, Boulder, London: Lynne Riener Publishers.

Terreblanche, Sampie (2002), *A History of Inequality in South Africa 1652–2002*, Pietermaritzburg: University of Natal Press.

Tonchi,Victor (2002), 'Civil society and democracy in Namibia', Development Policy Management Forum, Policy Brief Series 6, Addis Ababa.

Tordoff, William (2010), *Government and Politics in Africa*, London: Palgrave Macmillan.

Trapido, Stanley (1971), 'South Africa as a comparative study of industrialisation', *Journal of Development Studies*, 7: 3, 309–20.

Trewhela, Paul (2009), 'The ANC NWC on Thami Zulu', *Politicsweb*, 1 April.

—— (ed.) (2009), *Inside Quatro: Uncovering the Exile History of the ANC and*

Swapo, Johannesburg: Jacana Media.

Turner, Richard (1971), 'The relevance of contemporary radical thought', in Peter Randall (ed.), *Directions of Change in South African Politics*, Johannesburg: Spro-Cas, 72–85.

Turok, Ben (2009), *From the Freedom Charter to Polokwane: The Evolution of ANC Economic Policy*, Cape Town: New Agenda.

United Nations (2002), UN Panel of Experts, *Illegal Exploitation of Natural Resources and Other Forms of Wealth of the Democratic Republic of Congo, appointed by the Security Council in 2000*, http://www.un.org/News/dh/latest.drcongo.htm

Van Cranenburgh, Oda (2006), 'Namibia: Consensus institutions and majoritarian politics', *Democratization*, 13: 4, 584–604.

Van den Brink, Roger, Glen Sowabo Thomas and Hans Binswanger (2007), 'Agricultural land redistribution in South Africa: Towards accelerated implementation', in Ruth Hall and Lungisile Ntsebeza (eds), *The Land Question in South Africa: The Challenge of Transformation and Redistribution*, Cape Town: HSRC Press, 152–201.

Van der Walt, Lucien (2011), 'Black syndicalists and the radicalisation of the SA Native National Congress (SANNC), 1917–1920: The industrial workers of Africa, the International Socialist League and the left wing of Congress', presented to the conference 'One Hundred Years of the ANC: Debating Liberation Histories and Democracy Today', Universities of Johannesburg and the Witwatersrand, 20–24 September.

Van Doepp, P. (2006), 'Politics and judicial decision making in Namibia: Separated or connected realms?' IPPR Briefing Paper 39, October.

Van Zyl Slabbert, Frederick (1992), *The Quest for Democracy: South Africa in Transition*, London: Penguin.

Verhoef, G. (2003), '"The invisible hand": The roots of BEE, Sankorp and societal change in South Africa 1995–2000', *Journal for Contemporary African History*, 28: 1, 22–47.

Von Holdt, Karl (2010), 'The South African post-apartheid bureaucratic state: Inner workings, contradictory rationales and the developmental state', in O. Edigheji (ed.), *Constructing a Democratic Developmental State in South Africa: Potential and Challenges*, Cape Town: HSRC Press, 241–60.

Webster, Edward (2001), 'The Alliance under stress: Governing in a globalizing world', in Roger Southall (ed.), *Opposition and Democracy in South Africa*, London: Frank Cass, 255–74.

Webster, Edward and Dinga Sikwebu (2010), 'Tripartism and economic reforms in South Africa and Zimbabwe', in Lydia Fraile (ed.), *Blunting Neoliberalism: Tripartism and Economic Reforms in the Developing World*, London: Palgrave Macmillan, 177–222.

Welsh, David (1975), 'The growth of towns', in Monica Wilson and Leonard Thompson (eds), *The Oxford History of South Africa: Volume Two, South Africa 1870–1966*, Oxford: Clarendon Press, 172–243.

—— (2009), *The Rise and Fall of Apartheid*, Jeppestown: Jonathan Ball Publishers.

Zimbabwe African National Union (ZANU) (1973), 'Zimbabwe: From confrontation to armed liberation struggle', in Olav Stokke and Carl Widstrand (eds), *Southern Africa: The UN-OAU Conference, Oslo, 9–14 April*

1973, Papers and Documents, Uppsala: Scandinavian Institute of African Studies.

Zimbabwe Institute (2008), *The Security-Military Business Complex and the Transition in Zimbabwe*, Cape Town: Zimbabwe Institute.

Zolberg, Aristide (1966), *Creating Political Order: The Party-States of West Africa*, Chicago: Rand McNally Publishing Company.

Zuma, Jacob (2008), 'Letter from the President: A common history and a shared future', *ANC Today*, 8: 49, 8 December.

INDEX

www.ingramcontent.com/pod-product-compliance
Lightning Source LLC
Chambersburg PA
CBHW050624280326
41932CB00015B/2516